WORKING AMERICANS
1880–1999

Volume III: The Upper Class

WORKING AMERICANS
1880–1999

Volume III: The Upper Class

by Scott Derks

A UNIVERSAL REFERENCE Book

Grey House
Publishing

MILLERTON, NY 12546

PUBLISHER: Leslie Mackenzie
EDITORIAL DIRECTOR: Laura Mars-Proietti
EDITORIAL ASSISTANT: Pamela Michaud
MARKET RESEARCH: Jessica Moody

AUTHOR: Scott Derks
CONTRIBUTOR: Erika Watson DePaz
EDITORIAL ASSISTANTS to the author: Cheryl Quick, Linda Kelly

COPYEDITOR: Elaine Alibrandi
COMPOSITION & DESIGN: Stratford Publishing Services

A Universal Reference Book
Grey House Publishing, Inc.
185 Millerton Road
Millerton, NY 12546
518.789.8700
800.562.2139
FAX 518.789.0545
www.greyhouse.com

First edition published 2001

Printed in the USA

Library of Congress Cataloging in Publication Data available

ISBN 1-930956-38-X   hardcover

TABLE OF CONTENTS

INTRODUCTION

Working Americans 1880–1999 Volume III: The Upper Class is the third volume of a multi-volume set. Like its predecessors, *Volume I: The Working Class* and *Volume II: The Middle Class,* this volume looks, decade by decade, into the work, homes, and lifestyles that defined the Upper Class—from a wine merchant from California to a record producer from Tennessee. This volume also looks at the society and history that shaped the world of the Upper Class from 1880–1999.

> *"... The well organized books are designed to facilitate our understanding of the growth and development, as well as the lifestyle and economic life of the working and middle classes over a century .... these interesting, unique compilations of economic and social facts, figures, and graphs will support multiple research needs. They will engage and enlighten patrons in high-school, public, and academic library collections."*
>
> Booklist

> *"An interesting look at Americans, focusing on their lifestyles and economic life, by decade ... Period photographs, newspaper advertisements, cartoons and first person remembrances help to make this an excellent resource for study of American during this time period."*
>
> Pennsylvania School Librarians Association

As in the first two volumes, the chapters in Volume III have been carefully designed to enhance our understanding of the growth and development of the Upper Class over more than a century. This volume begins in the late 1800s at a time when the economy was shifting from the agrarian to the industrialized sector. Also, better record-keeping during this time, and the increase in gathering statistics, provided a wealth of archives from which to draw original material for this book.

From the many government surveys, social worker histories, economic data, family diaries and letters, newspaper and magazine features, this unique reference assembles a remarkably personal and realistic look at the lives of Upper Class Americans.

Family Profiles

Each chapter of *Working Americans 1880–1999 Volume III: The Upper Class* covers a decade, and opens with an overview of important events to anchor the decade in its time. The Upper Class is then explored by examining the lives of a number of Upper Class working families. These Family Profiles examine income, expenses, life at home, life at work, and life in the community. The information is presented in narrative form, but hard facts and real life situations back up each story.

The basis of every Family Profile is a study that either details the family's finances or lifestyle. In most cases, a governmental study identified the family statistically, and this data was used to form the base of the profile. Extensive research into the times, professions, and geographic locations pumped additional life into these families. To further identify each family with their community, we gave each a name. The Colorado silver miner from 1892 is John Gustin, heiress Susannah Wainwright depicts life in Hawaii in 1936, Nashville-based record producer in 1969 is Verne Cringely, and Liming Shao is the Chinese-born immigrant who makes his millions as an entrepreneur in New York City.

Economic Profiles

Each chapter also includes an Economic Profile. These are a series of statistical comparisons designed to put the family's individual lifestyles and decisions in perspective. These charts include the average wages of other professions during the year being profiled, a selection of typical pricing, and key events and inventions of the time. Enhancing some of the chapters are examinations of important issues faced by the family, such as how Americans coped with war and civil rights issues.

In addition to the detailed economic and social data for each family, each chapter is further enriched with Historical Snapshots, News Profiles, articles from local media, and illustrations derived from popular printed materials of the day, such as clippings from cereal boxes, campaign buttons, postcards, and posters. Each graphic was carefully selected to add depth to the understanding of the world that the families lived in. The material used in *Working Americans, Volume III* is a compilation drawn from many different sources, which are listed in detail at the back of the book.

In more than 550 pages, *Working Americans 1880–1999 Volume III: The Upper Class* offers 75 Profiles that cover more than 30 pursuits and dozens of ethnic groups. Geographically, the text travels the entire country, from Hawaii to New York, from sophisticated cities to quiet country homes.

The Table of Contents provides a clear guide through each chapter, outlining each section, from Life at Home to Selected Prices, and quickly illustrates the wealth of information for each decade. In addition, Volume III includes a comprehensive index, providing the reader with easy access to the thousands of specific topics in this volume.

Next in this series is *Working Americans 1880–1999 Volume IV: Their Children*. This volume will explore the lives of school age children from all economic levels.

PREFACE

This is the third volume in a series focused on the social and economic lives of working Americans, using everyday details to describe their lives. The first volume of Working Americans: 1880-1999 examined the struggles of the working class through the eyes and wallets of three dozen families. It studied the factors that shaped their jobs, wages, family life, expenditures and hobbies. The second volume captured the endeavors of the middle class in a similar but sometimes subtly different way, describing the emergence of two-income families, professional managers, increased disposable income, the move into suburbia and the establishment of regular paid vacations and insurance.

This volume focuses on the fascinating and often complex world of the upper class. Throughout the book, three dozen profiles carefully examine the lifestyles of business magnates, inventors, scientists, architects and investors, frequently pausing in this gallop through history to discuss the expansion of the telephone, the manufacture of the Olds automobile, the creation of frozen foods, the rebuilding of Britain, the popularity of Lionel Trains or the rise of Internet millionaires.

What emerges is the story of men and women who, through hard work, grit, good luck or inheritance, have been elevated to the highest pinnacle of economic prosperity. For many, this level of wealth provides luxuries such as world travel and multiple homes, even a life totally free of work responsibilities. For others, it is the opportunity to influence the development of cities, or fund the college education of those less affluent. Along the way, fortunes are lost and gradually rebuilt, as in the aftermath of San Francisco's earthquake and fire in 1906. Estates were sold through bankruptcy as a result of the Great Depression, and homes were built on the most exclusive spot in Hawaii.

Every generation endows a certain level of romance to the age gone by. The patina embellishing the upper class is even more alluring. The rich become richer, the cars bigger and the parties wilder. Using the public documents of the day, this book attempts to uncover the false veneer of memory in hopes of capturing single snapshots in time: the excitement of traveling out West by train, the love of a man for his recently departed wife, the shock of having a home robbed and vandalized, or the willingness to gamble your family fortune on the potential growth of cellular telephones.

In preparing this book, I found that all families—no matter their economic situation—experience loss, pain and insecurity, as well as immeasurable joy and freedom. For that reason, each profile is different, as each family is different. None of us is average and neither were our ancestors. Some profiles intimately study the family's personal life—how they coped with losing their home during the Depression, the indulgence in a luxurious lifestyle during the Gilded Age or the love of one man for African art. Others peer intently at professional pursuits such as the contributions of the unofficial mayor of Tulsa, Oklahoma or the decisions of a highly focused Mr. Corporate Fix-it who is often called upon to turn around failing companies.

Many of these people led very public lives. All of the profiles are modeled on real people and events, although, as in the previous books of the series, the families' actual names have not been used. Otherwise, every effort has been made to ensure that all other details about their business, the conditions within the community or the cost of goods and services reflect the knowledge and standard of that day. The newspaper and magazine stories strategically placed throughout the book remind us that many of yesterday's critical issues are still with us. Happily, some issues, such as a shortage of metal hairpins during the Second World War, seem less pressing today.

Ultimately this volume and its two predecessors together represent the history and ancestry of the vast majority of Americans. At the turn of the twentieth century, 10- and 12-hour workdays were standard by dictum; as we reached the end of the century, workdays of the same length were often adhered to by choice. The American economy is complex, made more so by people who insist on explaining the intricacies of money movement without mentioning the lives of the families whose investments, decisions and spending drive the economy. *Working Americans*, volumes I, II or III, is not the total answer; it is simply a clue to understanding whence we came and where we are headed.

Scott Derks

For Good Friends:

Kenol and Deloude, Carol and Austin, deRo and Felicity, Bobby,
Dee and Ed, Dee, Jim and Betsy, Bill, Louise and Mal, Grahame,
Sonny and Margaret, and Jim.

ACKNOWLEDGMENTS

The author wishes to thank Erika DePaz for her enthusiasm, research skills and, most of all, willingness to spend hours in the darkest corners of various libraries uncovering a plethora of exciting and valuable facts. Thanks also go to Linda Kelly for her editorial assistance, especially her fact-checking, well-timed questions and dedication to creating the best book possible. Once again, I also must provide a deep bow to Elaine Alibrandi for both her editorial skills and sense of humor. In addition, this book was created through the kindness of friends and temporary enemies whose advice, suggestions, pictures and critiques—both solicited and otherwise—improved the final product. Finally, this work was enriched by the research prowess and contributions of Robin Richburg, Townsend Zeigler, Marshall Derks, Carla Brown, Elizabeth Derks, Austin Watson, Jim McColl and, most of all, my wife, The Reverend Ellen J. Hanckel, for being Ellen.

1880–1899

The last two decades of the nineteenth century danced in the reflected glow of the Gilded Age, when the wealth of a tiny percentage of Americans knew no bounds. It was a time of vast, accumulated wealth and an abundance of emerging technology—all racing to keep up with the restless spirit of the American people. The rapid expansion of railroads opened up the nation to new industries, new markets and the formation of monopolistic trusts that catapulted a handful of corporations into positions of unprecedented power and wealth. This expanding technology also triggered the movement of workers from farm to factory, the rapid expansion of wage labor, and the explosive growth of cities. Farmers, merchants and small-town artisans found themselves increasingly dependent on regional and national market forces. The shift in the concentrations of power was unprecedented in American history. At the same time, professionally trained workers were reshaping America's economy alongside business managers or entrepreneurs eager to capture their piece of the American pie. It was an economy on a roll with few rudders or regulations.

Across America the economy—along with its work force—was running away from the land. Before the Civil War, the United States was overwhelmingly an agricultural nation. By the end of the century, non-agricultural occupations employed nearly two thirds of the workers. As important, two of every three Americans came to rely on wages instead of self-employment as farmers or artisans. At the same time, industrial growth began to center around cities, where wealth accumulated for a few who understood how to harness and use railroads, create new consumer markets, and manage a ready supply of cheap, trainable labor. Jobs, offering steady wages and the promise of a better life for workers' children, drew people from the farms into the cities, which grew at twice the rate of the nation as a whole. A modern, industrially-based work force emerged from the traditional farmlands, led by men skilled at managing others and the complicated flow of materials required to keep a factory operating. This led to an increasing demand for attorneys, bankers, and physicians to handle the complexity of the emerging urban economy. In 1890, newspaper editor Horace Greeley remarked, "We cannot all live in cities, yet nearly all seem determined to do so."

The new cities of America were home to great wealth and poverty—both produced by the massive migrations and influx of immigrants willing to work at any price. It was a time symbolized by Andrew Carnegie's steel mills, John D. Rockefeller's organization of the Standard Oil monopoly, and the manufacture of Alexander Graham Bell's wonderful invention, the telephone. By 1894, the United States had become the world's leading industrial power, producing more than England, France, and Germany—its three largest competitors—combined. For much of this period, the nation's industrial energy focused on the need for railroads requiring large quantities of labor, iron, steel, stone, and lumber. In 1883, nine tenths of the nation's entire production of steel went into rails. The most important invention of the period—in an era of tremendous change and innovation—may have been the Bessemer converter, which transformed pig iron into steel at a relatively low cost, increasing steel output 10 times from 1877 to 1892.

The greatest economic event during the last two decades of the nineteenth century was the great wave of immigration that swept America. It is believed to be the largest worldwide population movement in human history, bringing more than 10 million people to the United States to fill the expanding need for workers. In the 1880s alone, 5.25 million immigrants arrived, more than in the first six decades of the nineteenth century. This wave was dominated by Irish, German, and English workers. Scandinavia, Italy, and China sent scores of eager workers, normally men, to fill the expanding labor needs of the United States. To attract this much-needed labor force, railroad and steamship companies advertised throughout Europe and China the glories of American life. To an economically depressed world, it was a welcome call.

The national wealth in 1890 was $65 billion; nearly $40 billion was invested in land and buildings, $9 billion in railroads, and $4 billion in manufacturing and mining. By 1890, 25 percent of the world's output of coal was mined in the United States. Annual production of crude petroleum went from 500,000 barrels in 1860 to 63.6 million in 1900. This was more than the wealth of Great Britain, Russia, and Germany put together.

Despite all the signs of economic growth and prosperity, America's late-nineteenth-century economy was profoundly unstable. Industrial expansion was undercut by a depression from 1882 to 1885, followed in 1893 by a five-year-long economic collapse that devastated rural and urban communities across America. As a result, job security for workers just climbing onto the industrial stage was often fleeting. Few wage-earners found full-time work for the entire year. The unevenness in the economy was caused both by the level of change under way and irresponsible speculation, but more generally to the stubborn adherence of the federal government to a highly inflexible gold standard as the basis of value for currency.

Between the very wealthy and the very poor emerged a new middle stratum, whose appearance was one of the distinctive features of late-nineteenth-century America. The new middle class fueled the purchase of one million light bulbs a year by 1890, even though the first electric light was only 11 years old. It was the middle class also that flocked to buy Royal Baking Powder, (which was easier to use and faster than yeast) and supported the emergence and spread of department stores that were sprouting up across the nation.

1880 FAMILY PROFILE

Donald Rutherford, already rich and looking for a new challenge at 39, left a rapidly expanding investment business a year ago to join a group of wealthy Boston businessmen who are intrigued by the latest innovation—the telephone. He and his wife, Sybil, have six children, all boys, who enjoy horseback riding, sailing and touring the West by train.

Annual Income: More than $200,000; their total holdings exceed $1 million.

Life at Home

- Raised near Boston, Massachusetts, Donald is the son of a wealthy merchant, whose fortune was earned through trade with China.
- His father's business was so lucrative and the opportunities so great, he left his new wife of one month for nearly three years to complete a business deal; by the time he returned home his fortune had been made.
- For the past 20 years, Donald has been working for his father's import business and investing in railroad development in the West, as well as some local development.
- He believes it is part of his Scottish heritage to make money and pass it along to his children.
- He is 39, rich and looking for a new challenge; the development of the telephone looks like a good way to regain his energy and possibly make some money.
- During the past decade, his investments in western railroads have afforded the family more economic freedom and an excuse to travel by train throughout the West.

Donald Rutherford is well-known for his ability to make money.

His sons are fascinated by the sights and sounds of cowboys during railroad trips West.

- The family, especially his sons, are fascinated by the sight of Indians, cowboys and buffalo on the plains.
- Entertaining his children and making money both give him great pleasure.
- He also enjoys a very prominent place in society, which he inherited from his father, but has maintained through his own abilities.
- The Rutherfords recently attended a costume ball to celebrate the end of the Christian season of Lent; they agree with newspaper stories claiming that this evening event cost $250,000, with $11,000 spent on flowers, $155,730 for costumes and $62,270 for champagne.
- One story about the party reads, "The season brings the flowers again and Easter brings the new bonnets, but not the bonnets alone. It brings to that unemployed, pleasure-seeking society relaxation from the restraints of Lent and ushers in a round of entertainment all the more rapid in procession and delirious in excitement for the long season of fasting and self-denial which has gone before."
- Sybil has come to enjoy coaching, or riding through the woods in a perfectly appointed coach drawn by four horses and attended by three or four coachmen.

Their home on the family estate employs a Greek Revival style.

- Donald thinks the $20,000 cost of operating a coach for the season is excessive, but says little.
- He indulges in buying objects made of ivory, mostly from China, where he occasionally travels on business with his father; his constant companion is a silver walking cane topped with a highly carved ivory handle shaped like an elephant's head whose trunk is grasping the cane as though it were a log.
- He made sure that the cane was prominent in a recent painting done of his entire family. During a visit to New York, he learned that oil paintings of families—including grandparents—drawn against the background of an estate are very popular; he hired a family portrait painter for his wife's birthday.
- When away from work on his estate overlooking Boston, he loves to invent charades and organize costume parties.
- Currently, he and Sybil are members of a group of 20 friends known as the Game Club, whose evening meetings are scheduled for every fortnight during the winter and spring months at the homes of its members.
- Upon arrival, members are presented with a slip of paper on which subjects are written; each person has to write a poem on that topic, which is then read and discussed during dinner.
- Sybil recently wrote a poem entitled, "Few and Faint But Fearless Still," which began "Up on her tousled hair, with a lofty courage undaunted, / Lightly she balanced a structure, most marvelous and aesthetic, / Fuzzy and wide and reckless, and adorned with manifold colors; / Here lay a plume, soft and long, exactly the shade of a pickle, / When it emerges, fresh and green, from a wide-mouthed bottle. / Next to it nestled another, as red as a much-faded car seat."

- Born in 1840, Donald grew up on his father's estate and later attended Harvard; he was expelled when a fraternity prank resulted in the injury of a watchman.
- Donald's father, through his lawyers, purchased a building which Harvard had wanted to acquire; as a result, criminal charges were not filed, but expulsion could not be avoided.
- Donald fought in the Civil War, attaining the rank of colonel for his gallantry on behalf of the Union Army.
- In 1865, he married Sybil, the daughter of a well-known writer and philosopher.
- They set up housekeeping in a cottage adjoining his father's home; an arbor vitae hedge bordered their driveway, a wisteria vine swarmed up over the front porch, and an apple orchard could be seen in the distance.
- By 1876, Donald had built a large home on the family estate using a Greek Revival style of architecture.
- While it was being built, the couple's two oldest boys lived on the family yacht (along with two servants), which was anchored in the cove and brought ashore for meals.
- When the house was completed, it was capped with a weather vane designed and executed by a local artisan, and depicting Donald riding his prize horse.

The house is capped with a weather vane depicting Donald astride his favorite horse.

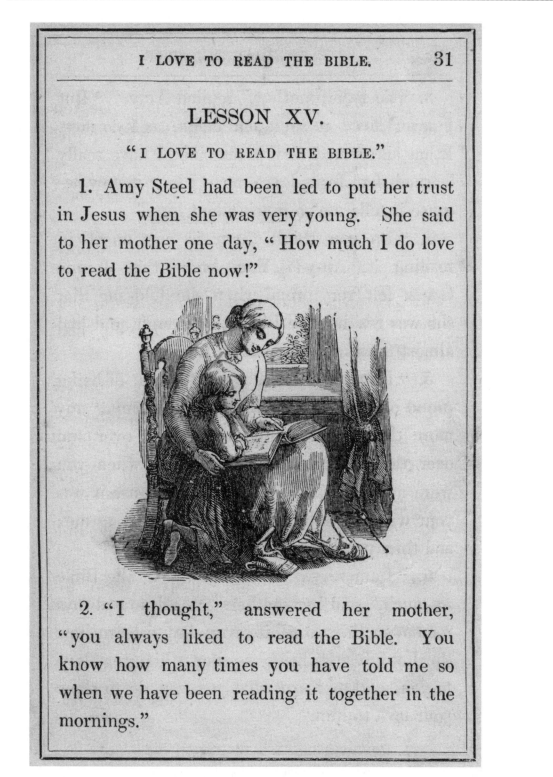

I LOVE TO READ THE BIBLE.   31

LESSON XV.

"I LOVE TO READ THE BIBLE."

1. Amy Steel had been led to put her trust in Jesus when she was very young. She said to her mother one day, "How much I do love to read the Bible now!"

2. "I thought," answered her mother, "you always liked to read the Bible. You know how many times you have told me so when we have been reading it together in the mornings."

Even though he rarely goes to church himself, Rutherford insists that his children attend Sunday school.

- With his brother-in-law, Donald is developing a Concord grape-growing venture on his property—as a sideline.
- He insists that his children attend church, although he rarely goes himself; his family donated the land and the money to have the chapel built several years ago.

Life at Work

- Donald Rutherford is well-known for his head for figures and taste for making money and social connections—the perfect combination to assist a young company struggling to survive.
- He has been on the job one year, during which the lawsuits with Western Union and others were settled and the company could begin focusing on cautious, deliberate expansion.
- The telephone, under Patent No. 174,465, entitled "Improvement in Telegraphy," had been approved four years earlier on March 7, 1876.
- The explanation of an unbroken electrical current, magnets and variable resistance in the design of the telephone makes this patent potentially one of the most valuable of the day.
- The hard work of creating a commercially successful telephone company is just beginning.
- The original telephone company, created by inventor Alexander Graham Bell and his father-in-law, ran out of money in 1879, drained of nearly $100,000 in patent legal battles.
- To survive, Bell and his backers turned National Bell Telephone over to a group of Boston investors, including Rutherford, to run.
- Within months of taking over the company in 1879, the Boston group ended the pitched battle with competitor Western Union in an agreement through which Western Union sold all its telephone properties; in return, Western Union is to receive 20 percent of National Bell Company's license fees—the fees from district exchanges.
- In addition, Bell Company agreed to keep out of the telegraph business and deliver to Western Union any telegraph messages it might receive for transmission.
- Bell stock, which was unsellable at $50 a share, zoomed to $1,000 a share in November after the settlement was announced.
- Donald's job is to make Bell Telephone profitable; he does not like to take chances, believing that slow, deliberate use of capital will result in survival, and the Board, composed of his friends in Boston, agrees.
- Currently, he is in conflict with Bell Telephone's general manager, who is pushing to invest in higher quality service to customers; this will simply drive up costs, Rutherford believes.
- Donald holds that when you own a monopoly and have no competitors, you don't have to provide the highest level of service to compete; his priority is to control costs so the company can return a large profit to its Boston investors—period.
- Recently, to control costs, the Board has agreed that inventor Alexander Graham Bell is no longer providing enough service to the company to warrant his $5,000 annual wage and should be terminated.
- Now that the patent lawsuits are no longer an issue, Bell is not needed for his testimony in court cases; besides, Bell is more interested in inventions for the deaf, and is not living up to his contract to advance the science of the telephone.
- Legal fees of the law firm that spent several years attempting to save Bell Telephone amounted to $50,000; the lawyers have agreed to accept $20,000.
- Donald's experience investing in western railroad expansion taught him that too much activity can cause jealousy and competing factions, so he understands that building a monopoly is dangerous, making it open to attack; however, he believes a monopoly is necessary if the telephone is to prosper and spread across the nation.
- This is why he has been so aggressive in defending Bell's ability to set rates and expand service.
- He has publicly stated that "the complaints as to rates are often made thoughtlessly, and in ignorance of the expenses and risks which attend the business."
- He also opposes all regulation, saying, "No state in fairness ought to destroy that which the patent system has created," and has warned those who wish to regulate the business

When they travel by rail, they enjoy all the comforts available.

that "the attack upon rates is one of the most direct methods of removing all inducement to extend telephone facilities."

- The cost of phone service varies nationally; in San Francisco, where the competing service just folded, Bell is preparing to raise its charges from $40 to $60 a year.
- The common practice is to allow unlimited calls, charging instead a flat rate for the service.
- The first phone subscribers have tended to be physicians concerned about emergencies; the New York and New Jersey Telephone Company serves 937 physicians and hospitals.
- Other major New York subscribers include 401 drugstores, 363 liquor stores, 315 livery stables, 162 metalworking plants, 146 lawyers, 126 contractors and 100 print shops.
- Currently, there are 132,692 telephones in the hands of American licensees, and only nine cities in the United States with populations of over 10,000 which do not yet have a telephone exchange.
- The rapid expansion of telephones, requiring thousands of wires strung between poles, is causing political conflicts; Donald believes that cities should stay out of the way of progress.
- Putting telephone lines underground is not economically or technically practical.
- Although various cities may prevent the expansion of telephones into residential areas, Donald believes that business phones are more profitable, and has little desire to use capital on residential expansion anyway.
- Bell Telephone, which opposes reduced rates for residential customers, declared, "Cheaper service will simply multiply the nuisance of wires and poles and excite political

The first telephone subscribers tended to be physicians.

pressure to put wires underground without materially improving profits or permanently improving relations with the public."

- Net earnings of the company are more than $200,000 this year, of which $178,500 will be paid in dividends to stockholders; earnings in 1881 are expected to be even better.
- The company has only 540 stockholders currently, so the average annual payout per stockholder this year is $330.
- It is the policy of the company's Boston investors to payout most of the profits to stockholders as dividends rather than to plow the proceeds back into the company for maintenance and expansion.

Life in the Community: Boston, Massachusetts

- Approximately 350,000 people live within the boundaries of Boston; another 350,000 live in the surrounding areas and suburbs of the city.
- Founded in 1630 by members of the Massachusetts Bay Colony, Boston is the capital of the state and its most populous city.
- The population is growing rapidly—about 20 percent per decade—driven by immigrants and farmers moving into the city for better-paying jobs.
- Social background exerts a profound influence upon jobs and where people live; the Boston Irish newspaper, *The Pilot*, says, "The race is not run with an equal chance; the poor man's son carries double weight."
- A center of learning and culture, Boston was visited by Charles Dickens for a reading of "A Christmas Carol," and the Old Corner Bookstore is the meeting place for Henry Wadsworth Longfellow, Ralph Waldo Emerson and Oliver Wendell Holmes, Sr.
- Only three years earlier, more than 100 clergymen, including Rector Phillip Brooks, walked in procession reciting Psalm 24 with the wardens of the new Trinity Church to dedicate the structure built on land created by the filling in of Back Bay.
- Christian Science began at the Mother Church in Boston, while King's Chapel is the birthplace of American Unitarianism.
- The city's elite still pride themselves, as the Duke of Newcastle once said about Boston, that everything about the city is "in better taste than the entertainment of the New Yorkers."
- Fashionable ladies are now sporting bustles, called the "improver," requiring three great pads of horsehair, over which a cascade of silk drapery falls behind the figure.
- Wealthy Bostonians spend their summers on exclusive Newport, Rhode Island, learning lawn tennis on a court marked out like an hourglass, wide at the base lines and narrow at the net.
- Boxer John L. Sullivan is developing a reputation in Boston for hitting his opponents so hard, they accuse him of "kicking like a mule"; his next fight will be against American champion Paddy Ryan for a purse of $5,000.

HISTORICAL SNAPSHOT
1880–1881

- Singer sold 539,000 sewing machines, up from 250,000 in 1875
- The new census declared that the United States now had 100 millionaires
- A&P operated 95 grocery stores from Boston to Milwaukee
- The plush Del Monte Hotel in Monterey, California, opened
- Halftone photographic illustrations appeared in newspapers for the first time
- Writer Mark Twain produced the first piece of telephone fiction, in which he described his reaction to the experience of listening to only one end of a telephone conversation conducted by someone else
- To make the invention of the electric light bulb practical, Thomas Edison created his own factory staffed by 133 men, turning out 1,000 lamps a day
- Midwest farmers burned their recently harvested corn for fuel; the price being paid for corn was less than the cost the railroads were charging for shipment east
- President Garfield was assassinated by Charles J. Guiteau, a disgruntled office-seeker
- According to fashion magazines, the "waist ideal" for women was 18 inches; well-dressed ladies wore corsets supported by whalebones to attain the standard
- *Scientific American* lauded the telegraph for having promoted "a kinship of humanity"
- French intellectuals proposed that the 24-hour day be scrapped in favor of a measurement system which divided the day into 10 equal segments
- The Supreme Court ruled that the 1862 federal income tax law was unconstitutional
- The Diamond Match Company was created
- The Southern Pacific Railway linked New Orleans with San Francisco
- The Barnum and Bailey Circus was formed
- Marshall, Fields & Co. stores were created through a reorganization
- Chicago meatpacker Gustavus F. Swift perfected the refrigerator car, allowing Chicago-dressed meat to be shipped to the East Coast
- The national population was increasing by one million people per year, due to immigration
- Only two percent of New York homes had water connections
- New York's Brooklyn Bridge was under construction

1880 ECONOMIC PROFILE

Daily Income, Standard Jobs

Bricklayers $2.68

Carpenters and Joiners $2.15

Engineers, Stationary. $2.48

Farm Labor $1.25

Firemen $1.37

Hod Carriers $1.82

Marble Cutters $2.40

Painters $2.49

Plasterers $1.81

Plumbers $3.37

Stonemasons $2.58

Selected Prices

Book $0.10

Business Cards. $0.05

Cake of Colgate's Harness Soap $0.35

Cologne $0.25–1.00

Cotton Seeds $0.10
Dickson Fertilizer, One Ton $40.00
Dinner Knives, One Dozen $3.00
Dress Silk Cloth. $0.80
Fine White French China,
        149-Piece Set $30.00
Fruit, Wine and Jelly Press $3.00
Hair Wave $6–12.00
Hotel Room. $1.00
Little Hop Pills, Headache
        Nonprescription Drug $0.25
Louisiana State Lottery
        Ticket. $2.00
Mason & Hamilton
        Baby Organ $22.00
Pocket Watch. $12.00
Sewing Pattern. $0.20
Shaving Soap $0.12
Tooth Extraction $0.25
Violin $5.00

The Development of the Telephone

- Alexander Graham Bell's patent application in March 1876 gave him the first claim to the telephone.
- Bell spent most of 1876–77 giving demonstrations around the country of the new "wonder" in large concert halls, sometimes borrowing telegraph lines for long-distance calls; customers were charged $0.25 to attend the lecture and hear the new invention operate.
- After one lecture hall exhibition, the *Providence Press* said, "It is indeed difficult, hearing the sounds out of the mysterious box, to wholly resist the notion that the powers of darkness are somehow in league with it."
- Bell's telephone demonstration during the Centennial Exposition in Philadelphia took place on the same day General George Custer and his men made their last stand at the Little Big Horn River.
- Commercial telephone service began in 1877, the same year Rutherford B. Hayes was sworn in as the new president.
- In May 1877, the Bell Telephone system began offering telephones for $20 a year for social purposes and $40 a year for business.
- Initially, the company leased pairs of telephones for simple two-point communications, commonly between two buildings of a business, or a business and a home.
- The first phone service consisted of a private line run between the Boston office of two young bankers and the home of one of them in Somerville, three miles away.
- By November, the system had 600 subscribers.
- Standard equipment rented to the customer consisted of a single piece of wood, which served as both the transmitter and receiver; power was supplied by a permanent magnet inside the device.
- The Bell Telephone Company itself was formed on July 9, 1877, at which time 5,000 shares were issued.
- Inventor Alexander Graham Bell only accepted 10 shares; the bulk of his share went to his soon-to-be wife and his two business partners; his assistant, Thomas Watson, received 499 shares.
- Two days later, Bell married Mabel Hubbard, his business partner's daughter, a deaf student he had tutored.
- In 1878, both Congressman James A. Garfield and humorist Mark Twain had telephones installed.

Advertisement: Bell Telephone Company, May 1877, offering two telephones and a line connecting them for $20.00 a year for social purposes and $40.00 a year for business:

"The proprietors of the Telephone...are prepared to furnish Telephones for the transmission of articulate speech through instruments not more than 20 miles apart. Conversation can easily be carried on after slight practice and with occasional repetition of a word or sentence. At first listening to the Telephone, though the sound is perfectly audible, the articulation seems to be indistinct; but after a few trials the ear becomes accustomed to the peculiar sound."

- Mark Twain told the installers, "Here we have been hollering 'shut up' to our neighbors for centuries, and now you fellows come along and seek to complicate matters."
- The usefulness of the telephone was greatly increased in 1878 with the development of a workable exchange, making it possible to switch calls among any number of subscribers rather than simply provide direct connections between two or three.

To control costs, the Board recently terminated its contract with inventor Alexander Graham Bell.

Letters from Alexander (Aleck) Graham Bell to his parents and friends, describing his struggles to invent the telephone:

November 23, 1874:
"The idea to which I allude is an instrument by which the human voice might be telegraphed without the use of a battery at all.... The vibrations of a permanent magnet will induce a vibrating current of electricity in the coils of an electromagnet."

March 18, 1875, following a visit with Joseph Henry, the first secretary of the Smithsonian Institute and the nation's most widely respected electrical theorist:
"I set the instrument working and he sat at a table for a long time with the empty coil of wire against his ear, listening to the sound. I felt so much encouraged by his interest—that I determined to ask his advice about the apparatus I had designed for the transmission of the human voice by telegraph. I explained the idea and said, 'What would you advise me to do—publish it and let others work it out—or attempt to solve the problem myself?' He said he thought it was the 'germ of a great invention' and advised me to work on it myself instead of publishing. I said that I recognized the fact that there were mechanical difficulties in the way that rendered the plan impractical at the present time. I added that I felt that I had not the electrical knowledge necessary to overcome the difficulties. His laconic answer was—'GET IT.' I cannot tell you how much those two words have encouraged me."

"July 1, 1875, after a day of experimenting with an early version of the telephone which produced muffled, but unmistakable speech over a wire:
"This afternoon, on singing in front of a stretched membrane attached to the armature of an electromagnet—the varying pitch of the voice was plainly discernible at the other end of the line (300 feet) with no battery or permanent magnet being employed.

The vibrations were not mechanically conducted, but were produced by magnetoelectricity occasioned by the vibration of the armature of the electromagnet. When the sounds are received upon another stretched membrane—instead of a steel spring which can only vibrate at certain pitches—it is highly probable that the 'timbre' of the voice may be perceived. I feel that I am on the threshold of a great discovery."

March 10, 1876, on the day the newly constructed liquid variable-resistance transmitter was tested— resulting in the words, "Mr. Watson, come here, I want to see you" travelling over a telephone line— he wrote his father:
"Articulate speech was transmitted intelligibly this afternoon. I have constructed a new apparatus operated by the human voice. It is not, of course, complete yet—but some sentences were understood this afternoon. . . . I feel that I have at last struck the solution of a great problem—and the day is coming when telegraph wires will be laid on to houses just like water or gas—and friends will converse with each other without leaving home."

- The first exchange, devised by George W. Coy of New Haven, connected 21 subscribers who were called by name rather than number.
- Almost immediately, the original teenage male operators were replaced by women who were more patient, ladylike and less prone to cuss the customers when frustrated by the equipment.
- Additional exchanges opened rapidly across the nation, many opened by rival Western Union.
- A key business decision was the company's determination that Bell Telephone, as the exclusive builder of telephones, would lease the instruments and license local providers of telephone service.

Western Union fought tenaciously for control of telephone services nationwide.

- Bell's father-in-law, who was also his business partner, made the decision to rent telephones rather than sell them, based on his experience leasing shoemaking machines.
- This business decision allowed Bell to control both the service and the customer's equipment.
- Bell Telephone attracted franchisees from around the country to use their own capital to rent telephones, string wires, build switchboards and sell interconnections.
- Bell collected a fee for providing the instruments and technical advice.
- By July 1878, about 10,000 Bell instruments were in use nationwide.
- That same year Western Union, with telegraph offices already established nationwide, began selling telephones designed by Thomas Edison and Elisha Gray, prompting lawsuits.
- The most valuable asset Bell Telephone owned was its patents.

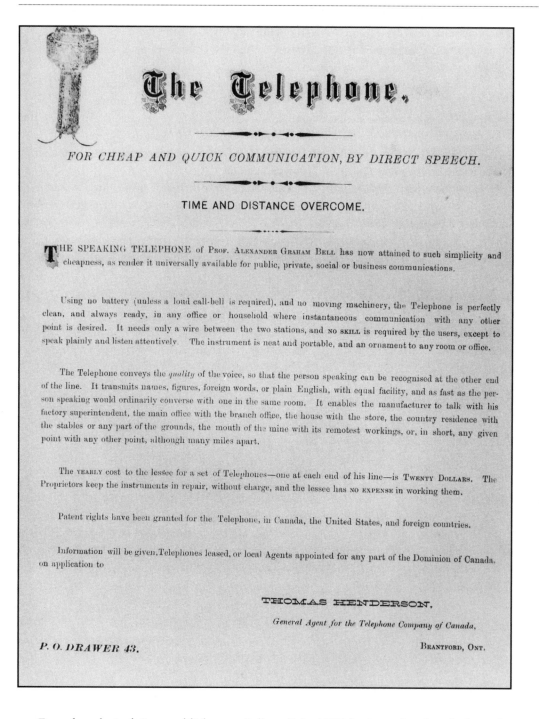

The Telephone.

FOR CHEAP AND QUICK COMMUNICATION, BY DIRECT SPEECH.

TIME AND DISTANCE OVERCOME.

THE SPEAKING TELEPHONE of Prof. Alexander Graham Bell has now attained to such simplicity and cheapness, as render it universally available for public, private, social or business communications.

Using no battery (unless a loud call-bell is required), and no moving machinery, the Telephone is perfectly clean, and always ready, in any office or household where instantaneous communication with any other point is desired. It needs only a wire between the two stations, and NO SKILL is required by the users, except to speak plainly and listen attentively. The instrument is neat and portable, and an ornament to any room or office.

The Telephone conveys the *quality* of the voice, so that the person speaking can be recognised at the other end of the line. It transmits names, figures, foreign words, or plain English, with equal facility, and as fast as the person speaking would ordinarily converse with one in the same room. It enables the manufacturer to talk with his factory superintendent, the main office with the branch office, the house with the store, the country residence with the stables or any part of the grounds, the mouth of the mine with its remotest workings, or, in short, any given point with any other point, although many miles apart.

The YEARLY cost to the lessee for a set of Telephones—one at each end of his line—is TWENTY DOLLARS. The Proprietors keep the instruments in repair, without charge, and the lessee has NO EXPENSE in working them.

Patent rights have been granted for the Telephone, in Canada, the United States, and foreign countries.

Information will be given, Telephones leased, or local Agents appointed for any part of the Dominion of Canada, on application to

THOMAS HENDERSON,

General Agent for the Telephone Company of Canada,

P. O. DRAWER 43.

BRANTFORD, ONT.

- Even though rival Gray publicly gave Bell credit in 1877 for inventing the telephone, he and Western Union sued Bell for the patent rights.
- Short on cash and clout to fend off a company as powerful as Western Union, Bell and his backers offered to sell the patent rights to the Western Union Company for $100,000; the offer was declined.
- Instead, Western Union decided to put Bell and his company out of business by setting its own phone rates so low that the Bell system could not compete profitably.
- Founded to exploit the invention of telegraphy, Western Union had $41 million in capital and a network of telegraph wires, making it ideally suited to take over the telephone business.

- To acquire new capital and save the Bell company, the founders decided to relinquish control to a group of aristocratic Boston capitalists; those who paid cash for their stock were awarded two votes per share versus one vote per share for the patentees.
- Thanks to the feverish work of two Boston attorneys, Chauncey Smith and James J. Storrow, the Bell patents were upheld by the courts, blocking Western Union's efforts.
- By 1879, Western Union conceded all patent rights to Bell Telephone; Bell agreed not to enter the telegraph business and agreed to pay some fees to Western Union.
- By 1880, Bell Telephone had 60,000 phone subscribers and a monopoly on the telephone business; one in every 1,000 people owned a phone.
- That same year, the board terminated all payments to inventor Alexander Graham Bell; the men who had been most closely associated with inventing the telephone were no longer a part of the company.
- After being asked to leave the company that carries his name, Bell, along with his wife Mabel, sold their remaining shares of stock to put them modestly into the millionaire class.

1892 Family Profile

Silver mining has built John Gustin's fortune and the town of Leadville, Colorado; Gustin is convinced that America will always need silver, even if the government repeals the Sherman Silver Purchase Plan. He and his wife, Lucille, have no children.

Income: His holdings are valued at more than $800,000.

Life at Home

- John and Lucille live in a 13-bedroom mansion built by craftsmen imported from England and Scotland; most of the materials were also brought from England to ensure authenticity.
- Gustin is very proud of Leadville, which has become a bustling city almost overnight, and hates the eastern press for mentioning the brothels and bars that come with a mining town.
- Down Main Street, at stores such as Zaitz Mercantile and the surrounding shops, he has the best of everything because so much wealth has come into Leadville and Denver, thanks to mining.
- He likes to boast to snobbish East Coast friends, "I can buy anything I desire, from a buggy to a hat to smoked meat to a cocktail—anything you have in New York."
- When they don't believe him, he sends them articles from the newspapers of Leadville; the city has seven papers, all eager to fully describe the annual balls, dinners and elaborate wedding dresses of the city's brides.
- Lately he has been urging Lucille to return to playing the piano; to encourage her, he recently ordered a Baldwin shipped from the East.
- He plans to put the piano in the music room; maybe then he can get rid of the Turkish leather couch she bought in England.

The Gustins live in a 13-bedroom mansion built by craftsmen imported from England and Scotland.

During a trip abroad, Lucille saw the famous actor Forbes-Robertson.

- At a recent party, several of their neighbors bragged about going into the wilderness for a camping trip—complete with servants.
- Lucille enjoyed hearing her friends talk about the joys of "roughing it" in a tent, but she plans to continue sleeping on her soft mattress stuffed with feathers.
- John loves his work, while Lucille loves to travel, particularly to Paris, where she frequently shops in the finest stores.
- To fit into French society, she is intensely studying the French language, despite a deep Irish accent; in France, she has poured money into the Blerancount Museum, with its great art collection and Franco-American historical documents.
- During her many trips abroad, she has been entertained by the rich and famous, including Sir Thomas Lipton, the tea millionaire, in England.
- She was also able to attend a play starring the famous actor Forbes-Robertson as Romeo.
- At home, the better ladies of Leadville have been promoting Valentine's Day celebrations; this year all of the women ordered elaborate valentines from New York and Germany, competing with each other for the grandest design.

Roughing it in the wilderness is a current fad the Gustins think is silly.

- The men are reluctantly going along.
- Lucille has selected a three-dimensional valentine featuring a hot air balloon.
- Her energy and her husband's fortune have significantly swelled the building fund of the Cathedral of the Immaculate Conception.
- The well-organized Catholic Church is a focus of social programs and power within the community.

Life at Work

- Born in Pennsylvania, John came West following the advice of newspaper publisher Horace Greeley in 1877, who advised, "Go West, Young Man."
- He wanted to "grow up with the country."
- He tried farming in Nebraska and worked in the quartz mines of the Deadwood gulch, finally making his way to Leadville at the time of the big miners' strike.
- During his early years in Colorado, he staked a claim to several mines, but was forced to abandon them because of financial difficulties.
- While serving as superintendent to the Smith and Moffat, he discovered a new silver vein, receiving part ownership as a reward.
- Today, Gustin is the largest owner of the Ibex Mining Company and a minority stockholder in several other mines in the area.

Lucille's three-dimensional valentine features a hot air balloon.

In a town dominated by miners, Gustin is considered a friend of the miner.

- His honesty has attracted capital when others were wanting; many men of wealth like to be associated with him.
- He has loaned money to more than one western miner who was in need; repayment often comes in the form of silver stock certificates.
- Several deals have been completed at the elegant New York Club, which serves as a gentleman's gambling parlor.
- Unconcerned about the federal government's efforts to reduce its silver consumption, Gustin believes that the nation will always need silver.
- In 1889, the price of silver had dipped to $0.93 an ounce, but climbed again in 1890 when Congress doubled the amount of silver purchased by the federal government.
- The Silver Purchase Act requires the Department of the Treasury to purchase 4.5 million ounces of silver at market prices every month.
- Farmers and others in debt believe that an unlimited amount of cheap silver in the monetary system is desirable for solving their economic woes.
- Many East Coast financiers are more wedded to the gold standard, and believe the Sherman Silver Purchase Plan is a colossal waste of money.
- After John came West, he often voted for the Republican ticket, but he has shifted his politics in recent years to being a Populist.
- He believes that many of the tenets of the newly formed Populist Party are so sound that they will survive even if the party does not.

Preamble of the National Populist Party Platform, 1893:

"The national power to create money is appropriated to enrich bond-holders; a vast public debt payable in legal-tender currency has been funded into gold-bearing bonds, thereby adding millions to the burdens of the people.

Silver, which has been accepted as coin since the dawn of history, has been demonetized to add to the purchasing power of gold by decreasing the value of all forms of property as well as human labor, and the supply of currency is purposely abridged to fatten usurers, bankrupt enterprise and enslave industry. A vast conspiracy against mankind has been organized on two continents, and it is rapidly taking possession of the world. If not met and overthrown at once, it forebodes terrible social convulsions, the destruction of civilization and the establishment of an absolute despotism."

- The third-party Populist platform calls for a national currency—safe, sound and flexible—issued by the general government only, a graduated income tax, government ownership of railroads and telegraph lines, and the abolition of land monopolies.
- To attract the labor vote, the Populists are also calling for the eight-hour day and restrictive immigration laws.
- Gustin is known as the miner's friend and has often come to the aid of injured miners or their families when he was aware of their needs.
- In Leadville, mining camps are divided ethnically: The Cornish, who learned the skill of smelting in England, live in Jacktown near the smelters; to the east, the Finns all cluster.
- At Horace Tabor's Little Pittsburgh and Chrysolite Mines, only men of English origin are hired.
- Many of the men also support families back East or in their country of origin; this year, the Leadville post office processed 13,352 U.S. money orders totaling $201,346 and 2,195 international money orders valued at $59,724.

Life in the Community: Leadville, Colorado

- Gold was discovered in 1858 along the banks of the Cherry Creek, near Denver.
- Within months, more than 10,000 men descended upon the area to pan for gold, which was difficult to mine because of an abundance of black sand.

Leadville is proud of its many fine, well-constructed buildings.

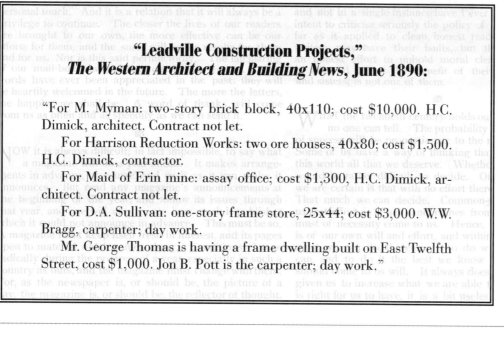

"Leadville Construction Projects," *The Western Architect and Building News,* June 1890:

"For M. Myman: two-story brick block, 40x110; cost $10,000. H.C. Dimick, architect. Contract not let.

For Harrison Reduction Works: two ore houses, 40x80; cost $1,500. H.C. Dimick, contractor.

For Maid of Erin mine: assay office; cost $1,300. H.C. Dimick, architect. Contract not let.

For D.A. Sullivan: one-story frame store, 25x44; cost $3,000. W.W. Bragg, carpenter; day work.

Mr. George Thomas is having a frame dwelling built on East Twelfth Street, cost $1,000. Jon B. Pott is the carpenter; day work."

Leadville is considered a marvel of the present age because of its growth.

- In 1875, two men sent a sample of this sand for mineral content tests, which showed it was 40 percent lead and contained up to 40 ounces of silver per ton.
- By 1877, Leadville was in the midst of a silver boom.

A fire department was created to protect the city's many new buildings.

- Set in the upper Arkansas River Valley in the center of Colorado, Leadville has an elevation of 10,200 feet, giving it the distinction of being the highest incorporated city in the United States.
- To the east stands the Mosquito Range, and to the west, the Sawatch, home of the two highest peaks in the state.
- Winter arrives in mid-October and stays until May; in between, more than 200 inches of snow will have fallen.
- The town of Leadville was incorporated in 1880, named for the secondary metal in which the silver was found, but nicknamed the "Magic City" and "Silver City" for the metal that provided its wealth.
- Since 1880, the railroad has connected Leadville to the rest of the world; as a result, businesses such as the Delaware Hotel are booming with new customers.

"Government should not support the people," President Grover Cleveland said, after vetoing a congressional appropriation of $10,000 in seeds for Texas farmers:

"I do not believe that the power and duty of the general government ought to be extended to the relief of individual suffering which is in no manner properly related to the public service or benefit. . . . The lesson should constantly be enforced that though the people support the government, government should not support the people."

The mining town of Leadville supports fine stores, grand hotels and dozens of brothels.

"Life in Leadville," *Leadville Chronicle Annual*, 1892:

"The correspondents of eastern papers are accustomed to representing that Sunday is a carnival day in Leadville; that the stores are open; that the saloons, the gambling houses and the questionable places of amusement flourish as on no other day; that inebriety staggers along the streets, and that sensuality parades in gorgeous apparel through all the thoroughfares. Through such assumptions and misrepresentations, with the amplifications of a readily resourceful imagination and the colorings of a gorgeous fancy, the correspondents are able to manufacture wonderfully entertaining letters that exactly suit the preconceived ideas and notions of the great mass of eastern readers. The fact is, however, that the Sabbath is well-observed in Leadville as in any other western city of life and push. The truth of the matter is that in all the great cities of the West, and especially the New West, the pushing impulses of enterprise, emulation and ambition are so strong and untiring that they scarcely permit men to stop for one day in the seven. They indeed almost push the people out of the restraining hold and beyond the controlling power of early teachings, early associations and early impressions. However, it is no uncommon thing to hear a rough, muscular miner retort to a blasphemous, arguing infidel: "See here, mister, my mother used to believe the Bible, and I'll be damned if I'll hear it abused."

- The city directory of 1879 read, "The city of Leadville is one of the marvels of the present age. Two years ago it had no existence, while today it has long streets and broad avenues many miles in extent, with large and handsome buildings on every side. As recently as August 1877, only six rude log cabins were to be found where today, well-designed edifices can be counted by the thousand."

- The same directory lists an array of businesses in the town: four assay offices, three bakeries, five boardinghouses, two booksellers and stationers, seven boot and shoe merchants, three carpenters, three carpet dealers, eight civil and mining engineering offices, nine clothing stores, 18 law firms, five meat markets, 10 physicians, 25 saloons, one scenic painter, one undertaker and three theaters.

- A visitor recently noted, "We can look up its length possibly two miles. It was a crawling mass of horses, mules, wagons and men. It looked impossible to get through, but we made it in about two hours."

- The quality of the city's Opera House attracts excellent, eastern acts entertaining throughout the West, thanks to the management's habit of paying the actors in silver.

- Gas lighting, installed in 1879, is also a draw, giving the Opera House and the streets of the city a soft glow.

- Currently, the population of 30,000 is just a few thousand shy of rival Denver's.

- Like many of the silver mine owners, Gustin believes that the brothels and bars along State Street provide a safe place for their miners to let off steam, although he is concerned that too many prostitutes on the streets will hurt the city's reputation.

- The climate of Leadville is blamed for "an uncontrollable desire for mountain dew," or liquid refreshment, in the city.

- The *Leadville Chronicle* says, "Other localities have their vegetarians, but Leadville has her whisketarians. It requires no more self-control for total abstinence here than elsewhere, provided people care to exert it, but a general spirit of recklessness pervades the air and few care to combat it."

- Leadville has three hospitals; St. Vincent's is the most prominent, opened in 1879 by a band of Sisters of Charity from Leavenworth, Kansas.

- St. Vincent's recently added a new operating room that is bright and cheery, "being tiled most artistically while the walls have an enamel finish."

- The hospital is operated by three doctors and eight sisters; the hospital serves 5,667 Catholics and 3,122 non-Catholics; nationalities include 2,677 Irish, 2,133 Americans, 713 Germans, 478 English, 169 Austrians, 69 Polish, 60 Welsh, 409 French Canadians, 62 Bohemians, 454 Swedes, 402 Italians, 361 Scots, 89 Norwegians, 68 Russians and 61 Swiss.

HISTORICAL SNAPSHOT
1892–1893

- American industry was benefiting from the 1890 decision by Congress to increase tariffs on foreign goods from 38 to 50 percent, making U.S. manufactured items less expensive

- New York City boss Richard Croker's fortune was estimated to be $8 million, not including his own railway car and a $2.5 million stud farm

- An improved carburetor for automobiles was invented

- The first successful gasoline tractor was produced by a farmer in Waterloo, Iowa

- Chicago's first elevated railway went into operation, forming the famous Loop

- The $1 Ingersoll pocket watch was introduced, bringing affordable timepieces to the masses

- The General Electric Company was created through a merger

- Violence erupted at the steelworkers' strike of the Carnegie-Phipps Mill at Homestead, Pennsylvania

- President Benjamin Harrison extended for 10 years the Chinese Exclusion Act, which suspended Chinese immigration to the United States

- The United States population included 4,000 millionaires

- The name Sears, Roebuck & Company came into use

- Pineapples were canned for the first time

- Diesel patented his internal combustion engine

- The Census Bureau announced that for the first time in America's history, a frontier line was no longer discernible; all unsettled areas had been invaded

- The first automatic telephone switchboard was activated

- Cream of Wheat was introduced by Diamond Mill of Grand Forks, North Dakota

- New York's 13-story Waldorf Hotel was opened

- The first Ford motorcar was road tested

- The Philadelphia and Reading Railroad went into receivership

- Wrigley's Spearmint and Juicy Fruit chewing gum were introduced by William Wrigley, Jr.

1892 ECONOMIC PROFILE

Daily Income, Standard Jobs

Bricklayers $3.68
Carpenters and Joiners $2.63
Engineers, Stationary. $2.72
Glassblowers $5.15
Hod Carriers $2.24
Marble Cutters $3.38
Painters $3.43
Plasterers $3.20
Plumbers $3.58
Stonemasons $3.90

H.C. Merwin,
Atlantic Monthly, 1892

"The upper class, with notable exceptions, is without high aims, without sympathy, without civic pride of feeling. It has not even the personal dignity of a real aristocracy. Its sense of honor is very crude. And as this is devoted to selfish spending, so the business class is devoted to the remorseless getting of money."

"Costly Gifts for a Bride, Nuptials of John Jacob Astor and Miss Ava Dowle Willing," United Press, February 18, 1891:

"PHILADELPHIA, Feb. 17—Miss Ava Dowle Willing, daughter of Mr. and Mrs. Edward Shippen Willing, was married to Mr. John Jacob Astor, of New York, at 1 o'clock this afternoon.

The wedding ceremony, which was witnessed by about 150 of the immediate relatives and close friends of the Astor and Willing families, was performed by the Rev. William Nelson McVickar, rector of the fashionable Episcopal Church of the Holy Trinity, at the beautiful home of the bride's parents on South Broad Street.

The fact that the wedding was celebrated in Lent was not allowed to detract from the brilliance of the occasion.

At the wedding breakfast the bridal table was set with 18 covers. The dining room itself was ornamented with whole chimes of wedding bells. Everything about the table was in pure white, only white bride's roses, white orchids and white violets being used.

A reception was held from 3 to 5 o'clock, and between those hours the house was filled with representative society people of Philadelphia, New York, Boston, Washington, Baltimore and other leading cities.

No Philadelphia bride ever received presents as magnificent as those sent to Miss Willing. Their aggregate runs high up in the hundreds of thousands of dollars. The groom's gift was a tiara of diamonds, possibly unsurpassed by any in America. His father gave a double bowknot of diamonds, from which hangs a pendant of huge brilliance about the size of a nickel. He also gave a diamond necklace and crescent of diamonds and sapphires some four inches in length.

The principal gifts of Mrs. Astor were five diamond stars, each as large as a silver half-dollar. These jewels were enclosed in a massive box of solid silver. Mrs. Astor also gave eight silver dishes, each about three feet in length.

Mr. and Mrs. Orme Wilson sent a pair of magnificent silver candelabra over a yard long. Mr. and Mrs. J. Coleman Drayton's presents were two silver dishes of exquisite open work. Mr. and Mrs. Roosevelt sent a large centerpiece of silver. Altogether, there were upwards of 300 presents.

The wedding tour consists of a trip South, the bride and groom keeping their immediate destination secret. On March 23 they will sail for Europe."

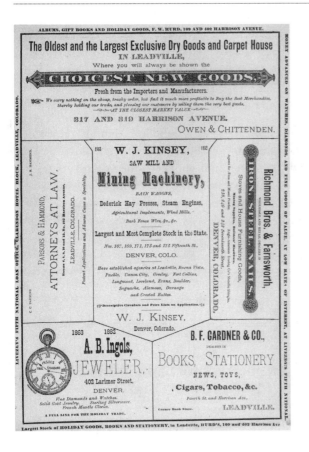

GOOD MORNING! Have you used PEARS' SOAP?

Selected Prices

Boy's Hat. $0.25
Candy, One Pound $0.80
Diaper, One. $0.65
Horse Muzzle $2.50
Hotel Room $2-2.50
House Paint, One Can. $0.25
Instant Chocolate $0.75
Lactated Baby Food. $0.25
Magazine $0.10

An Essay on the Present Distribution of Wealth in the United States, by Charles B. Spahr, 1896:

The Rich and the Poor in 1890

Estates by Annual Income	Number of Families	Aggregate Wealth	Average per Family
Wealth Classes			
$50,000 and over	125,000	$33 billion	$264,000
Well-to-Do Classes			
$5,000 to $50,000	1,375,000	$23 billion	$16,000
Middle Classes			
$500 to $5,000	5,500,000	$8.2 billion	$1,500
Poorer Classes			
Under $500	5,500,000	$0.8 billion	$150

Money Order $0.05–0.20
Oil Heater $12.00
Perfume $1.00
Plant Sprinkler. $0.75
Printing Press. $5.00
Shingles, 1,000 . . . . $2.50
Shoes, One Pair. $1.00
Suit, Man's $0.75–7.00

Symphony Orchestra Ticket $0.25–1.00
Tomato Seeds.................... $0.15
Turban $0.98
Undergarments $2–3.00
Wig $6.00
Writing Paper $0.75
Safety Deposit Box Rental,
    One Year $4–12.00

"A Rich Man's Grievance," *The Naiad, A Monthly Journal of Christian Education*, December 1892:

"The people who have the most trouble in selecting and buying holiday presents are those who have the most money. Nearly all of their friends are rich, and no present can surprise or gratify simply because it is costly. It must be unique and exquisitely beautiful, to provoke more than languid thanks. A rich man thus unburdens his mind of what he calls a grievance:

'Here I am worth $200,000; my friend Jones is worth a million; Smith counts his property at half a million; my neighbor Robinson pays taxes on $300,000. All of them have all the conveniences and luxuries that money can buy. Their wives and children are supplied with everything they need or wish. It is folly for me to buy a Christmas present, expecting by it to give them any special pleasure. They will thank me kindly, and next year would no doubt send me a present that costs twice as much as mine.

'What possible pleasure can I feel when Jones sends me for a holiday gift a volume of Shakespeare that costs $100? Or how much self-denial does it cost me to buy my wife the handsomest gold watch to be found at the jewelers?

'I have gone into the shops during Christmas week, and watched the poor people who are getting little gifts that cost $0.25 or a dollar, and I have actually envied them, knowing how much pleasure such a gift would bring to both giver and receiver.

'There are some things that riches cannot buy. One is the keen delight that comes from the exercise of self-denial in giving. That is the property of the poor. The rich know nothing of it. If there is any time in the year when I heartily wish that I were a poorer man, it is during the holidays, when so many other people are wishing they had more money.'

There is truth in this, and poor people with small purses but big hearts ought to be encouraged by it. That pair of mittens that you are knitting in the few minutes snatched from household work and drudgery, done at night when you are tired from the day's duties, will give more pleasure to you and your son than if they cost nothing more than the money expended in a mere purchase.

That simple toy, bought with hard-earned wages, will gratify your child. The children of the wealthy are not gratified by the most elaborate inventions.

Gifts that are made by loving hands are always more prized than gifts purchased with money; and the rare pleasure experienced by the poor in the presents they receive is born of the relish that comes because presents are few. And the highest joy of Christmas time does not come from the power to give costly presents, but from that loving self-denial which makes the poor rich in warm hearts and generous feelings, and in the keen realization of that spirit of which the Savior Himself spoke, when He said, "It is more blessed to give than to receive."

1897 FAMILY PROFILE

Mr. and Mrs. Fairmont were each left millions by their parents in stocks, bonds and real estate, so neither has needed to hold a job in years; they enjoy good wine, trips to Europe and 10-course dinners with friends in their Fifth Avenue home in New York City.

Income: The family wealth is estimated to be in excess of $37 million.

Life at Home

- Their home is always well-stocked with rare French wines; it is Roger Fairmont's claim to fame that he knows his wines and serves only the best.
- One of the couple's greatest pleasures is giving elaborate dinners, served on gold plates in a room filled with a forest of roses and orchids.
- Dinners begin at the continental hour of eight, and all menus for the 10-course meals are in French.
- Roger and his wife, Vivian, particularly like to begin the feast with terrapin soup matched with the perfect French wine.
- Sequent courses include beef larded with truffles, a confection of sweetbreads, paté de foie gras, and canvasback duck, plus imported asparagus, mushrooms and artichokes; a sorbet would then cool the stomach before a serving of French cheeses and desserts.
- For these events, they hire additional servants; Roger believes it is unseemly to have more than 20 servants on permanent staff at any one time.
- During dinner, discussion always turns to Europe, giving the Fairmonts the opportunity to mention their "latest discovery."
- Currently, they are collecting European oil paintings and highly ornate French furniture, because they believe that little in America is old enough to be worth owning.

Roger Fairmont serves only the best to his guests.

Vivian recently purchased a canopy bed.

- Vivian's latest purchase is a huge canopy bed decorated with ebony veneer on a mahogany background, finished with gold leaf inlay.
- She also picked up a silver urn with detailed engravings, simply because it was so lovely, even though it was "a local piece" made by a New York City silversmith around 1850.
- Rarely do they mention that they employ three men to scour Europe for them to purchase the finest paintings, furniture and jewelry; they may not have the money of the Astors or the Vanderbilts, but with a sharp eye and ready cash, they can acquire world treasures first.
- Besides, they wish to be discreet; they are very concerned about attracting the kind of unwanted attention that befell the Bradley-Martins, who gave a charity ball earlier in the year, inviting 1,200.
- Guests were invited to dress in Louis XV period costume, and the press was alerted of the grand event, which required hundreds of servants and coachmen.
- On the day of the party, the guests came—kings and queens, lords and ladies; one gentleman was even dressed in full armor that cost more than $10,000 to buy.
- All were served lush food and wonderful wine, and the hosts provided 400 carriages to transport guests, along with three bands to contribute nonstop music.
- Unfortunately, the press and city moralists were outraged at the extravagance during the current recession, to the point that the Bradley-Martins eventually left the city for Europe, where they would not hear the criticism.
- The Fairmont house is perfectly situated to observe parades and celebrations down Fifth Avenue.

On impulse, Vivian recently bought a silver urn, despite its being a "local" piece, simply because it was so lovely.

- The couple is also close enough to Central Park to enjoy an afternoon of ice skating, when there are not too many people around.

- Roger is increasingly uncomfortable with the "new wealth" coming into the neighborhood, and was especially disturbed that the home of patent medicine king "Sarsaparilla Townsend" was recently demolished to build an Italian mansion made mostly of marble; the home is too extravagant for words.

- Vivian has even heard people brag that they bought a painting because it was the right size for their room rather than being the best possible painting to acquire; some families seem happy to buy even American art from the Hudson River School of artists.

- As a result, the Fairmonts often escape the city to spend time on their yacht, which has a full crew year-round; they spend approximately $75,000 a year on the vessel's care and upkeep.

- Their teenage children are currently in Paris, where they have developed a taste for exquisitely designed clothing and French champagne.

- Their 17-year-old daughter has fallen in love with cycling and now owns half a dozen bicycles, along with dozens of riding outfits.

Their daughter has fallen in love with cycling.

In addition to touring Europe, they have discovered the wildlife of Africa.

- When they sent her to France, they were hoping she would fall in love with a count or duke, whose European title might add prestige to their wealthy name.
- Roger is not sure he is ready—financially—for his daughter to marry; at a recent Vanderbilt wedding, the bride received from her mother a set of pearls that once belonged to Catherine the Great, and more than $2.5 million in railroad stock from her father.
- When travelling, in addition to touring Europe, they now find that visiting the animals of Africa brings them great pleasure.
- They are thinking of adding to their home so they will have room to mount and display some of the rarer specimens.
- For now, Vivian must be content with wearing coats made from exotic furs otherwise unseen in New York.
- Their love of nature runs so deep, they are thinking about making a major contribution to the New York Botanical Gardens.
- Soon they plan to visit the wilds of North Carolina for a stay at the home of George Vanderbilt, whose 30,000-acre estate is known as Biltmore; the gardens were designed by Frederick Law Olmstead, and the home itself is considered the most astonishing American home of its time.
- Roger recently ordered a 12-gauge hammerless gun with 30-inch Whitworth steel barrels made by the Parker Company so he can shoot birds with the Vanderbilts while he is down South.
- This Christmas, the Fairmonts are debating what theme to employ on their traditional, 16-foot-tall Christmas tree; for years, Vivian has ordered one-of-a-kind, German-made

Their teenage children are currently in Paris.

Christmas ornaments for their evergreen, including several designed to look like their children.

- She is considering a display of stained-glass ornaments to commemorate the 22-foot-tall Tiffany windows she and her sisters gave to St. Michael's Church in honor of their parents.

Life at Work

- Vivian's grandfather established the family's penchant for producing extraordinary wealth through his early entry into the fur trade.
- From there, he expanded into silks, spices and tea, eventually gaining near-monopolistic control of natural resources as diverse as the sandalwood forests of Hawaii and the otter population in Alaska.
- Much of his early income was then invested in New York real estate and the creation of a food business.
- His New York holdings and financial clout were sufficient to allow city officials to expand roads and services into his property.
- Roger's money comes from the early days of the Civil War, when his father secured government contracts to supply clothing, food and supplies to the army.
- Within two years, the elder Fairmont's factories had been completely converted to manufacture materials for the Union Army; his ability to respond quickly to the government's new demands allowed him to make millions in the process.

At Christmas, she orders one-of-a-kind ornaments that resemble her children.

"The King's Daughters," Edited by Mrs. Margaret Bottome, *The Ladies' Home Journal*, June 1897:

"I heard yesterday of a dainty little lady who was standing on the dock by the side of a distinguished-looking gentleman, and their attention was attracted to the trouble of a woman with a child in her arms, who would not pass on as she was commanded to do. No one could understand a word the woman said. One after another, of different nationalities, went up to her, but she did not understand either French or German any better than she did English. The officer became impatient, and was about to lay hands on her when the beautiful little lady bounded away from her escort and in a moment stood by the side of the woman, and the face that had shown such terror and anguish was soon wreathed in smiles. After a few moments' conversation with her, the little lady turned to the crowd and said, 'She is from Honolulu. Her husband was to meet her at this steamer. She hasn't a cent with her and she feared to move till her husband came.' A young man with the badge of the Salvation Army said, 'Come lads, let us all give ten cents apiece to the poor woman,' and hands went into pockets and more than ten cents came from a good many, and the poor woman was comforted, and felt less friendless and alone."

- Today, much of the couple's yearly income is derived from ownership of the tenements of the Bowery and lower edges of the East River, where Vivian's family had purchased land years before.
- The dramatic rise in immigration has made every building valuable; some of the houses have been cut into 10 units accommodating up to 10 people per room.
- During the summer, overcrowding and unsanitary conditions give rise to cholera and yellow fever outbreaks.
- Roger has placed a corporation in charge of his wife's tenant houses to maintain the property and collect the rents.
- Unfortunately, the couple has found that most of the newly arrived immigrants are uncivilized savages; the extensive renovations demanded by the city and progressive reformers would only result in more vandalism, and as such, the improvements are a waste of time where immigrants are concerned.
- Years before, through his longtime connection to William Tweed, Vivian's father sat on the city's tenement housing committee; as a result, little legislation was passed.
- Unlike his father-in-law, Roger has avoided all such civic activities, convinced that no good can come from them.
- In addition, the poor's obsession with "millionaire watching" makes him uneasy and he would like to avoid publicity.
- To make his family less conspicuous, he has asked the coachman to stop using the red carpet when his carriage arrives at restaurants and the theater.
- Vivian sends the servants out to buy *Truth* magazine every week so she can see the elegant pictures and read stories about New York's more prominent "400," but still agrees

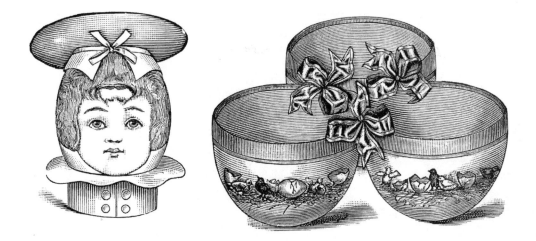

with her mother that a woman's name should only appear in the newspaper twice in her lifetime—when she marries and when she dies.

- She also loves the new, graceful illustrations being drawn by Rose O'Neill, although some issues are getting too serious for her.

- Roger is appalled that the Women's Rights movement seems to be gaining steam among New York's intellectuals; its leaders are female pests who are "simply loathsome dealers in clack," he believes.

- Today, he is once again investing in the stock market, thanks to tips from friends; only through timely information was he able to sell all of his stock in the Philadelphia and Reading Railroad, before its failure helped trigger the "Panic of 1893," which actually lasted several years.

- More than 15,000 businesses failed, including 158 national banks.

- Fearing that the unemployment lines, soup kitchens, crop failures and widespread anger at trusts would turn to violence, the family spent most of 1894 and early 1895 in Europe.

- They considered it a well-deserved "second honeymoon."

Life in the Community: New York City

- New York is fascinated by its wealthy, who are growing more conspicuous about displaying their wealth.

- Since 1894, P.F. Collier's *Once A Week* magazine has been photographing the homes of New York's 400 wealthiest citizens, featuring one each week; the series is extremely popular.

- Some newspapers are offering photographers up to $100 for pictures of the city's wealthiest residents.

- Recently, *Munsey's Magazine* called the number of Anglo-American weddings—of wealthy Americans to titled English—"epidemic," and accused the newly wealthy of falsely seeking respectability.

- Early each morning, servants of the city's elite line up along the docks near West Washington Market to buy oysters for the "the lady's" breakfast.

The Fairmonts enjoy acquiring furniture as they travel through Europe.

The Astor home helped set the standard for the rest of New York.

- The New York Telephone Company now operates 12 telephone exchanges, each with operators lined up at 250-foot-long switchboards; the women are referred to as "Hello Girls."
- Delmonico's, one of New York's finest restaurants, now has 10 locations, including one on Fifth Avenue and 44th Street, near the Fairmonts' home.
- The homes of the Astors and the Vanderbilts set the standard for the city.
- A race to bigger and fancier homes is under way in New York; some are now costing more than $3 million to build.
- For some, the real place to subtly establish wealth is in Newport, Rhode Island, where old money is safe from the newly rich—people whose money came from patent medicines, chewing gum, copper and tobacco.
- The Vanderbilts' cottage in Newport includes 110 rooms, 45 bathrooms, and a garage that can accommodate 100 cars.
- The home includes elaborate stables for their horses, which sleep in linens embroidered with the house crest.

HISTORICAL SNAPSHOT
1897

- Mail Pouch tobacco was introduced

- Thorstein Veblen developed the key concepts that would appear in his book, *Theory of the Leisure Class*, summed up by the statement: "conspicuous consumption of valuable goods is a means of reputability to the gentlemen of leisure"

- Continental Casualty Company was founded

- Radical Emma Goldman, advocate of free love, birth control, homosexual rights and "freedom for both sexes," was arrested

- The Royal Automobile Club was founded in London

- John Davison Rockefeller, worth nearly $200 million, stopped going to his office at Standard Oil and began playing golf and giving away his wealth

- The Presbyterian Assembly condemned the growing bicycling fad for enticing parishioners away from church

- Motorcar production reached nearly 1,000 vehicles

- Nearly 150 Yiddish periodicals were being published, many of which advocated radical labor reform, Zionism, and even anarchism, to obtain reform

- Wheat prices rose to $1.09 per bushel

- Republican William McKinley was sworn into office as America's 25th president; manager businessman Mark Hanna had raised $7 million for McKinley's campaign, compared with the $300,000 raised by opponent William Jennings Bryan

- Prospectors streamed to the Klondike in search of gold

- Boston's H.P. Hill used glass bottles to distribute milk

- Jell-O was introduced by Pearl B. Wait

- The Winton Motor Carriage Company was organized

- Dow Chemical Company was incorporated

"The Luxury of Ocean Travel," Advertising Supplement, *The Cosmopolitan, An Illustrated Monthly Magazine*, March 1897:

"There is a favorite saying, particularly among the good, old-fashioned people, that they do not intend to go to Europe until there is a bridge built across the Atlantic. There probably will never be an opportunity to cross the ocean this way, but the trip has, in these modern days, been made so easy, so comfortable and so short, that it has become a pleasure instead of a trial, a matter of recreation instead of a hardship.

Ships of immense size, constructed of iron and steel, propelled by enormous horsepower and furnished luxuriously, ply back and forth between New York and Europe with the regularity of express trains, and, the records show, with much less danger to life and limb.

This is particularly true of the service maintained by the *North German Lloyd*, the largest steamship in the world, and the one that has for many years carried more passengers between New York and Europe than any other line.

The ships employed in what is known as the North Express Service of the *North German Lloyd*, the *Havel*, the *Spree*, the *Lahn*, the *Trave*, the *Aller* and the *Saale*, are veritable floating hotels of the magnificent type. Structurally, they stand for the highest science attained by modern shipbuilding. Mechanically, they represent the most improved types of marine engineering skill, and as regards accommodations for passengers, they are unsurpassed by any ships floating.

Several of them, notably the *Saale* and the *Trave*, have recently undergone extensive improvements. New and more powerful engines and boilers of greater capacity have been added, increasing their speed very materially. Wooden awning decks have been built over the promenade decks, so that there should be a complete protection from the sun, rain and flying spindrift. The lifeboats have been elevated, leaving the long and wide promenade deck unobstructed from end to end. Changes have also been made in the interior arrangements, which have materi-ally increased the size of the smoking rooms, and the ladies' and the dining saloons. Similar changes will be made before the opening of the tourist season in the *Lahn*, so that the entire fleet will be in excellent condition to meet the demands upon it during the coming spring, summer and autumn.

The *North German Lloyd* maintains a double weekly Express Service between New York and Bremen, in addition to its popular all-the-year-round line to Genoa, via Gibraltar and Naples. It is, therefore, the only line that offers travelers the much-appreciated opportunity of going to Europe by one route and returning by another, thus avoiding the necessity of retracing one's steps to the point of landing. This plan enables the tourist to enjoy a much wider view of Europe without increasing the cost of ocean transportation....

The Express steams of the *North German Lloyd* sailing from New York on Saturdays touch first at Cherbourg, France, proceeding from there directly to Bremerhaven. This service is maintained for the convenience of travelers desiring to reach Paris or points in Switzerland and Central Europe in the quickest possible time and by the shortest route. It avoids the necessity of crossing the often vexatious English Channel in small steamers, and shortens the time between New York and the French capital about 12 hours. At Cherbourg, the *North German Lloyd* drops anchor in the beautiful harbor, and passengers and baggage are transferred to the quay upon the company's commodious tender. Special trains meet each steamer, reaching Paris in six hours. Passengers desiring to visit Germany or points in the northern central portion of Europe find Bremen a convenient point from which to begin their travels. It is one of the chief cities of Germany and railroads radiate in every direction. It is also one of the most interesting cities in Europe, far-famed for its handsome public buildings, its historical associations and beautiful park."

THE YOUTHS COMPANION

oston, Mass., February 17, 1898.   *Copyright, 1898, by Perry Mason & Company.*   VOLUME 72. NUMBER 7.
$1.75 A YEAR. SINGLE COPIES 5 CENTS.

Frieda Fairfax, Writer.

IN SEVEN CHAPTERS.— CHAPTER II.

THE night and the next day passed uneventfully. Frieda and her new acquaintance what she should have done if he had not chanced to be upon the train to tell her what she ought to do. She wondered, too, if care like that came often into people's lives, out in

Frieda raised herself obediently. "It will be something new if it does that for me," she said, "but it was sweet of you to think of it."

She swallowed the tasteless white dust, and sank back on her pillow with her eyes closed. It had almost killed her to sit up. Peggie Harrison's hand rested a moment on the hot forehead with its rippling waves of soft brown hair, and then she stole quietly from the room.

Frieda was grateful to her—more grateful than words could say—at being left to wrestle with her suffering alone. The hoof-beats of

on the side of the bed. "Now that is strange and I had on my seven-league boots. Of cou you could not possibly have been asleep."

"Of course not," assented Frieda, with laugh. "Oh, you dear thing, how can I than you for that powder? What is it? I mu have it—lots and lots of it."

Her new friend crossed her little tan sho finished off with the leather leggings of bicycle costume, and nodded sagely. "The you go," she said, "you're just like any oth little goose. Give you an inch, and so for

1898 NEWS PROFILE

"Brave Deeds of Locomotive Engineers," by Ray Stannard Baker,
***The Youth's Companion*, February 17, 1898:**

"It was a hot day in August, 1894. Three trains were bound northward over the Missouri River Railroad to Fort Custer, then the terminus of the line. The first was a construction train, with a load of telegraph poles for the road beyond the Little Big Horn. Behind it rattled the 'dust express,' otherwise a gravel-train, Rankin, engineer. The third train, which left Sheridan an hour or more after the other two were under way, was called an express train, but in reality was only the division superintendent's 'explorer' with a pair of talked-out officials, an inquisitive stockholder or two and a few friends of theirs.

Rankin leaned from the cab window of the locomotive of the gravel-train with the greasy visor of his 'dinky-cap' drawn down over his face. The boiler-head within simmered and stewed, and the cab was hotter than a kitchen on baking day.

Outside, the ragged Montana buttes burned in the sunshine. L. Larson, the big fireman, was swaying steadily from the coal-tender to the 'glory-hole' of the firebox. Larson wore a red woolen undershirt which was open at the breast and burned brown on the back with cinders. The sleeves were gone, and the lumpy muscles of his arms glistened with perspiration. His face was black with soot. There was a good-humored gleam in his blue eyes; but for these eyes he might have been taken for a Negro. On the run from Sheridan, Larson shoveled 10 tons of coal into the red-hot firebox, but at the end of the day he was ready to heave a car-wheel with any man on the line.

All the forenoon, Rankin had been catching momentary glimpses of his companion train toiling on ahead. Usually it was only a vanishing blur of yellow in a mist of dust, but it was a dear relief from the dead monotony of plain and mesa-bush and burning sunshine. About noon his train came to the curve near the bottom of Crow Grade—called because it ran through the land of the Crow Indians. Larson was double-firing for the long climb, and Rankin joggled on his arm-pad and watched for the train ahead. He expected to see the cars of telegraph poles just mounting the summit two miles away.

With a hitch and quiver, the engine shot around the curve. For a moment Rankin stared blankly up the track. Sometimes an engineer's eyes play him sad pranks. 'Larson!' he shouted, his finger tightening on the throttle bar. The fireman's shovel rang on the iron floor,

and he sprang to the cab window. Up Crow Grade, 'teetering' and swaying like a ship on a choppy sea, two carloads of telegraph poles were plunging down the track. The construction train had burst a coupler. On the front of the first car Jack Oliver, the brakeman, frantically waved his blue jacket and twirled the brake-wheel to show it was useless.

All this flashed instantly on Rankin's eyes. He knew that in less than two minutes the runaway cars would crash into his train, but his hand was steady and firm as the brass throttle lever. He drew on the whistle cord. There was a single biting blast—it meant 'down-brakes—hard.' Then he drove the throttle forward and reversed the engine. Underneath, the wheels screeched a shrill protest, and showers of sparks flew upward. The trainmen on the cars behind were straining hard at the brake-wheels. They did not know the danger, but they felt the thrill in Rankin's signal.

'Going to jump?' asked Larson, as the train shuddered to a standstill. A good engineer never deserts his train while there is a shadow of hope. Rankin had formed his plan instantly. The curve, which he had just made, was dangerously sharp. Once behind it—if only he could get behind it in time—the train would, perhaps, be saved, for the runaway cars, coming at terrific speed, would probably leap the rails and go tearing down the embankment. It was a slim chance, but Rankin took it.

'Fire away there,' he shouted to Larson. Without a word, the big fireman bent to his work. He might have jumped—some firemen would—but Larson was as much a part of the engine as was the piston rod.

"HE SPRANG TO THE RUNNING-BOARD."

Seconds were precious. Yet the train seemed barely to crawl—a baby could have toddled faster.

Up the track the runaway cars loomed big and near. The jar of their wheels sounded above the noises of Rankin's train. Poor Oliver was crouching and waiting his fate. His hair blew loose in the wind and he clung to the broken wheel with all the desperation of despair.

Rankin's locomotive was on the curve. Only a few feet more and it might be safe. The throttle was wide open and the stack belched fire. Larson grasped the cab window with tense muscles, as if to help the struggling engine.

Now the friendly embankment cut them off; they had made the curve. Rankin looked across the boiler-head at Larson, and laughed nervously. But they still watched with horrified interest to see the telegraph cars leap the embankment.

Far below there was a dry stretch of rocky gulch, covered, as if with fur, with tufts of prairie grass. It was a full 50 feet straight downward. They caught a glimpse of Jack Oliver clinging to the brake—the cars crashed into the curve. The inner wheels leaped in air and spun like a child's top. There was the shrill screech of steel grinding on steel.

Suddenly the runaways righted themselves with a quiver, twitched around the curve, and still on the rails, came thundering down the grade.

'They've made it!' said Larson, from somewhere deep down in his chest.

For a moment, neither Rankin nor his fireman stirred. Their danger, once averted, was more terrible for being unexpectedly renewed. They had lost their chance of jumping, for the train was now banking at runaway speed. There seemed no possible way to escape.

'Give her the fire!' shouted Rankin. 'We'll make a run for it!'

The speed of the telegraph cars had been somewhat checked at the curve. Rankin's plan now was to drive back under full steam to the upgrade a mile away on the opposite slope. Here the runaways must slacken their speed. It would be a desperate race, and Rankin felt that the chances were against him. What if his own train should jump the track, or what if he could not keep away from his grim pursuer?

Rankin leaned from his window and looked back along the line of reeling red cars, which seemed to run in a trough of dust. And then he stretched further out, with the perspiration starting fresh on his face. Behind there, just around the edge of a brown butte, was the fleecy white smoke of a passenger engine. The division superintendent's train was coming. He had not dreamed that train could be so near. At his present speed he would drive into it in less than a minute.

Rankin swung back to his place. His train had attained nearly the speed of the runaway cars. He deliberately pushed the throttle forward and shut off the steam. The indicator finger leaped to a figure that would have made a master mechanic's blood run cold; but he must save the passengers.

Larson looked up questioningly. Had Rankin lost his senses?

The telegraph cars were now scarcely a hundred feet away. Their grease-boxes had taken fire, and were blazing up like so many smoky torches. They rocked and jarred and soared, as if eager for the onset; and yet Rankin slowed his train.

The front of an engine has no bumper for receiving a heavy impact. Rankin knew that if the cars struck the pilot with any force the load of poles would probably be driven forward and brush off the whole top of the locomotive—car, crew and all—and an explosion might follow the collision.

'Larson,' shouted the engineer.

The big fireman straightened up, drawing his arm across his dripping face.

'Go out on the pilot and couple those cars to the engine.'

Larson had two tow-headed babies at home in Sheridan, but he did not hesitate. From the cab window he sprang to the running board and darted the length of the heaving engine. One foot on the steam-box, a firm grasp of the flag-rod, and he slid down to the pilot. He braced his left foot between the bars; one hand was gripped like a vice above, while the other poised the heavy coupling rod.

Below him, the blurred, gray track-bed flowed outward dizzily, and the air was full of fly-ing sand and cinders. It required every atom of the fireman's mighty strength to keep his place on the pitching pilot.

Rankin had opened the throttle again. The impact must not be a pound too heavy. He could not see Larson, but he felt his danger. What if there was a ring in the front bumper of the car, so that the fireman could not make the coupling?

At that instant, Rankin was hurled heavily forward, but he regained himself with a bound. Oliver, the brakeman, was waving his arms and signaling down-brakes. Rankin saw tears of relief streaming down his dust-covered face.

They stopped, with every wheel burned, less than a hundred yards from the passenger train. The officials, blanched about the lips and stammering with excitement, came stum-bling forward. They found Rankin pottering over his running-bars with his hooked-nose oil-can. The big fireman was calmly doing up a crushed thumb with a bit of cotton waste.

Of course they thanked Larson and Rankin, and I believe their salary was increased on the next payday; but there are some things for which money cannot pay."

1900–1909

The first decade of the twentieth century was marked by dramatic innovation and keen-eyed energy as America's men and women competed to invent a better automobile, mass market soft drinks or configure the right land deal that would propel them into the millionaires' mansions so frequently described by the press. At the same time, the number of inventions and changes spawned by the expanded use of electricity was nothing short of revolutionary. Factories converted to the new energy force, staying open longer. A bottle-making machine patented in 1903 virtually eliminated the hand-blowing of glass bottles; another innovation mechanized the production of window glass. A rotating kiln manufactured in 1899 supplied large quantities of cheap, standardized cement, just in time for a nation ready to leave behind the bicycle fad and fall madly in love with the automobile. Thanks to this spirit of innovation and experimentation, the United States led the world in productivity, exceeding the vast empires of France and Britain combined.

In the eyes of the world, America was the land of opportunity. Millions of immigrants flooded to the United States, often finding work in the new factories of the New World—many managed by the men who came two generations before from countries like England or Germany or Wales. When Theodore Roosevelt proudly proclaimed in 1902, "The typical American is accumulating money more rapidly than any other man on earth," he described accurately both the joy of newcomers and the prosperity of the emerging middle class. Elevated by their education, profession, inventiveness, or capital, the managerial class found numerous opportunities to flourish in the rapidly changing world of a new economy.

At the beginning of the century, the 1900 U.S. population, comprising 45 states, stood at 76 million, an increase of 21 percent since 1890; 10.6 million residents were foreign-born and more were coming every day. The number of immigrants in the first decade of the twentieth century was double the number for the previous decade, exceeding one million annually in four of the 10 years, the highest level in U.S. history. Business and industry were convinced that unrestricted immigration was the fuel that drove the growth of American industry. Labor was equally certain that the influx of foreigners continually undermined the economic status of native workers and kept wages low.

The change in productivity and consumerism came with a price: the character of American life. Manufacturing plants drew people from the country into the cities. The traditional farm patterns were disrupted by the lure of urban life. Ministers complained that lifelong churchgoers who moved to the city often found less time and fewer social pressures to attend worship regularly. Between 1900 and 1920, urban population increased by 80 percent compared to just over 12 percent for rural areas. During the same time, the non-farming work force went from 783,000 to 2.2 million. Unlike farmers, these workers drew a regular paycheck, and spent it.

With this movement of people, technology, and ideas, nationalism took on a new meaning in America. Railroad expansion in the middle of the nineteenth century had made it possible to move goods quickly and efficiently throughout the country. As a result, commerce, which had been based largely on local production of goods for local consumption, found new markets. Ambitious merchants expanded their businesses by appealing to broader markets.

In 1900, America claimed 58 businesses with more than one retail outlet called "chain stores"; by 1910, that number had more than tripled, and by 1920, the total had risen to 808. The number of clothing chains alone rose from seven to 125 during the period. Department stores such as R.H. Macy in New York and Marshall Field in Chicago offered vast arrays of merchandise along with free services and the opportunity to "shop" without purchasing. Ready-made clothing drove down prices, but also promoted fashion booms that reduced the class distinctions of dress. In rural America the mail order catalogs of Sears, Roebuck and Company reached deep into the pocket of the common man and made dreaming and consuming more feasible.

All was not well, however. A brew of labor struggles, political unrest, and tragic factory accidents demonstrated the excesses of industrial capitalism so worshipped in the Gilded Age. The labor-reform movements of the 1880s and 1890s culminated in the newly formed American Federation of Labor as the chief labor advocate. By 1904, 18 years after it was founded, the AFL claimed 1.676 million of 2.07 million total union members nationwide. The reforms of the labor movement called for an eight-hour workday, child-labor regulation, and cooperatives of owners and workers. The progressive bent of the times also focused attention on factory safety, tainted food and drugs, political corruption, and unchecked economic monopolies. At the same time, progress was not being made by all. For black Americans, many of the gains of reconstruction were being wiped away by regressive Jim Crow laws, particularly in the South. Cherished voting privileges were being systematically taken away. When President Roosevelt asked renowned black educator Booker T. Washington to dine at the White House, the invitation sparked deadly riots. Although less visible, the systematic repression of the Chinese was well under way on the West Coast.

The decade ushered in the opening of the first movie theater, located in Pittsburgh, in 1905. Vaudeville prospered, traveling circuses seemed to be everywhere, and America was crazy for any type of contest, whether it was "cute baby" judging or hootchy-kootchy belly dancing. The decade marked the first baseball World Series, Scholastic Aptitude Tests, the subway, and Albert Einstein's new theories concerning the cosmos. At the same time, the $1 Brownie Box camera from Eastman Kodak made photography available to the masses.

1900 Family Profile

As the largest stockholder in the Daly Bank and Trust Company, Jerome Hill keeps an office on the top floor of the seven-story office building at the center of the Butte, Montana, business district. He is a rich man in a state of rich men, thanks to copper.

Annual Income: $250,000; his holdings are worth more than $1.1 million.

Life at Home

- The Hill family lives on the west side of Butte, Montana, a neighborhood of huge Victorian homes owned by the city's élite.
- The family employs two Irish servants—one as a cook, the other as a maid and nanny to their two boys.
- The house runs a strict schedule: Monday is wash day; Tuesday is for ironing; Wednesday is for general cleanup; Thursday is for cooking and Friday is the big cleanup day.
- On Fridays, the beds are changed, all the rooms cleaned and dusted, and the kitchen and bathrooms scrubbed.
- Jerome's wife, Penelope, and their daughters have recently been on an extensive shopping trip to obtain appropriate calling dresses, bike riding outfits, dresses for the theater season and, of course, a few new tea gowns for when they come home tired and weary from an afternoon of shopping or visiting.
- After all, as members of western society, the newspaper often describes what clothing they wear, as well as their comings and goings.
- Although the girls can select bicycling, tennis and rainy day styles, most women's apparel still features ankle-length or

Jerome Hill has come to enjoy French wines during his travels to Europe.

A young lady's complete wardrobe includes calling dresses and bike riding outfits.

On trips, they buy whatever they like, including this Japanese porcelain and bronze Doré mounted center bowl and a Hunzinger hall seat (right).

longer hems; "the proper skirt length is just showing the tip of the shoe," fashion magazines decree.

- Penelope belongs to the West Side Shakespeare Club and is president of the Plant and Pray Garden Club.
- She is also interested in the work of the Women's Christian Temperance Union, but has not joined its ranks; her husband is concerned that many of the saloon owners who have accounts at his bank will take offense.
- Also, Jerome and Penelope have come to enjoy French wines during their travels to Europe, and are pleased that Lisa's Grocery in downtown Butte now carries some of France's best wines.
- On trips, they have bought whatever they liked, from a Japanese porcelain and bronze Doré mounted center bowl, to a Hunzinger carved cherry and gilt hall seat.
- To give their home a more comfortable feel, Penelope recently added two new wicker chairs made by Heyward Brothers and Wakefield Company.

- Jerome is planning to give his wife an oriental carpet from Joseph David's store for her birthday; the carpet is large enough to cover the 20' x 30' dining room.
- The pantry is well-stocked with glass jars containing dried beef, pigs' feet, tripe, lambs' tongues, oysters and fish, ready to supplement any meal.
- These glass jars, made by Culcutt's, have glass lids that prevent the food from ever touching metal.
- To celebrate his lifelong membership in the Elks, each morning Jerome uses a shaving mug decorated with the emblem of the fraternal organization.
- Twice a week, he drops by the corner barber for a $0.15 shave and a peek at the city tabloids, like *Police Gazette*.
- He also enjoys the atmosphere and gossip of the barber shop, where dozens of fellow businessmen drop by; "it is amazing," he likes to say, "what you can learn if you only listen."
- In his vest pocket he keeps a small, silver, engraved cigar cutter to light his signature Havana cigar; he believes that

The two boys are cared for by a nanny.

Recently, they added wicker chairs to give their home a more comfortable feel.

chewing plug tobacco is low-class, and is disgusted when the men display their talent for spitting accurately into the brass spittoons.

Life at Work

- Jerome Hill's greatest skill, he likes to say, is good timing and good friends; more than a decade ago, he helped create a bank, backed by the right people, in a town poised to grow dramatically.
- Since then, he has always remembered who owns the bank—the stockholders—and has been careful only to lend money when he was 100-percent sure of getting it back.
- Lately, he has also felt that his participation as a partner in a bank-funded real estate deal allows him to lend his expertise to the project and create a winning proposition for everyone.
- Across the West, many banks closed temporarily when the silver market collapsed during the 1890s, but copper kept Butte going.
- Currently, a pitched battle is raging between the copper kings of Montana; Hill is backing W. A. Clark, with whom his family vacations in Europe.
- The fight between Marcus Daly and W. A. Clark began in 1882 when Clark, learning that Daly was considering a site for his smelter operation on Warm Springs Creek, hastily bought up the water rights and made Daly pay dearly.
- In subsequent years, Daly and Clark have used their wealth to buy and sell political offices, organize labor actions and fight over territory.
- Jerome likes to say he could "wallpaper Vanderbilt's ballroom" with the worthless stock certificates floating around Butte.
- Miners, who gamble daily with their very lives, also enjoy gambling with their money—making most of them poor credit risks.
- Unions dominate, and the workers call the community the "Gibraltar of Unionism" because everyone from the theater usher to the mine hoist engineer belongs to a labor union.
- Men from the Butte Miners' Union first organized the Western Federation of Miners in 1893.
- Workers are currently pressing for shorter hours, insisting they only want to wear a "copper collar" down in the hole eight hours a day.
- Hardrock mining is one of the most dangerous occupations in the world because of the amount of drilling and blasting required.
- Currently, more than 5,000 Butte men work in the underground mines, which are set in deep shafts famous for high temperatures, falling rocks and structural faults.
- As mines grow deeper, conditions deteriorate; temperatures rise over 110 degrees, more water pours into the workings and the ground shifts more.
- Unstable rocks capable of falling on a miner are called "druggans" after Larry Druggan, the local undertaker.
- In the mines, some miners wear water-resistant clothing to prevent the copper water from dripping on them and causing sores; in other parts of the mine, the temperatures are so high that miners wear little to no clothing.
- The smell of the deep mines is particularly memorable; both human and animal excrement mingle with sweat, blasting powder, rotting food and tobacco.
- To demonstrate to friends in New York the progressive nature of his bank, Jerome recently insisted that all of his clerks begin using typewriters—even when writing out orders by hand would be faster.

"You can do business with anyone, but you can only sail a boat with a gentleman."
—Businessman J. P. Morgan

To demonstrate the progressive nature of his bank, Hill insists that all his clerks use typewriters.

- The first commercially produced typewriter, the Sholes and Glidden Type Writer in 1874, was difficult to use and produced tiny, uneven letters; today's models, especially the Daughterty Visible, are excellent for conducting serious business.
- Unlike other typewriters, the Daughterty Visible is a front-stroke instrument, which allows his clerks to see what is being written, while it is being written.

Life in the Community: Butte, Montana
- Butte claims to be the largest mining camp in the world, "with a somewhat scattered population of 45,000"; it is the world's greatest silver-producing camp and the second-largest copper producer, behind only the Lake Superior districts.
- As a mining city, Butte, Montana, has been shaped by its largely male work force, described as "stridently male, blusteringly profane, boisterous and boastful."
- According to the 1900 census, men still outnumber women four to one.
- Some call Butte the "richest hill on earth," because of its treasure trove of copper ore, largely controlled by the Anaconda Company—one of the most powerful corporations in the country.
- Conceived in the full flush of the industrial revolution, Butte grew helter-skelter into a major city almost overnight.
- The city was originally organized around gold and silver mining; Butte's silver wealth rivals that of Leadville and Aspen, Colorado, the Coeur d'Alene Valley in Idaho, and Virginia City, Nevada.
- Called the "Pittsburgh of the West" because of the large-scale extraction of metallic ores, Butte was incorporated in 1879; two years later, the Union Pacific Railroad had completed a line from northern Utah to Butte.
- When the silver market collapsed after the repeal of the Sherman Silver Purchase Act of 1893, Butte's fortunes continued thanks to copper.

"Butte and Some of the Big Men There," *The Denver Times*, September 18, 1899:

"Butte has become the metropolis of Montana and a city of supreme importance, says a correspondent. Were the Butte mines to close down for six months, there would be a copper famine in Europe and in America. Every industrial center on the globe would be affected thereby to a revolutionary extent, for Butte produces almost 25 percent of the world's copper. Butte is, therefore, an industrial center whose fortunes are entwined not with those of Montana alone, but with the fortune of the whole commercial and industrial world. . .

The site of the present city 25 years ago was a hamlet of wooden shacks and cabins, where perhaps a thousand frontier folk had congregated. They had been drawn thither by the fame of Montana's gold fields, or in search of adventure, or perhaps to acquire immunity for past misdeeds. The nearest railroad was in Ogden, 400 miles away, and Montana's communication with the outside world was carried on through stages over roads where the brigand and the bandit were not unknown, or by means of those picturesque stern-wheel steamers of the Missouri which have utterly disappeared before the iron horse of civilization. . .

W. A. Clark now wears the toga of the senatorship of the great republic. He has built a palace by the Hudson at fabulous cost, and is adorning it with art treasures fit only for the palaces of mighty monarchs.

I am not sure, but Senator Clark today ranks among the very wealthiest men on earth, for, besides his enormous wealth in Butte, he owns the United Verde of Arizona, apparently the most fabulously rich copper mine the world has ever known. The needy, but sturdy, pioneer who faced the wilderness a generation ago is now transformed into a Croesus, a senator, an art connoisseur, envied and courted for the power and influence his boundless wealth bestows.

Marcus Daly is, of course, the mining king of Montana. His career is more dramatic than even W. A. Clark's, and he has accomplished things stranger than the wildest dreamer or the romancer. He is the head of the greater copper combine, which is trying to amalgamate all the mines of Butte into one colossal concern. This is a consummation, from an economic standpoint, which is eminently desirable. If Marcus Daly winds up his mining career by effecting this vast amalgamation, it will be an achievement of vast importance to the industrial world. But I am not at all certain that it will be given him to effect his achievement. He is showing signs of age. That constitution of iron seems to me to be weakening under the strain that has rested on it for a generation or more. The eye is clear and the brain is as active as ever, but I can detect in Mr. Daly a longing for repose. His heart is yearning for rest in the bosom of his family amid his park, his gardens, his groves, his cattle, his horses and his dogs. This is why I think Mr. Daly will not crown his career by the achievement of merging into one all of the mines of this marvelous mining camp of Butte. This will undoubtedly be accomplished, but its accomplishment needs more years and vigor and youth and strength than Mr. Daly now has at his disposal."

- The timing was good; America's demand for copper to support the electrical revolution was rising.
- Currently, the cost of mining copper is high and the smell of the city is distasteful; foul sulphurous fumes constantly spew from smelters or float from open heaps of roasting ore.
- Often, dense smoke forces Hill and his family to walk the streets with sponges and handkerchiefs over their mouths.

His greatest skill, he likes to say, is good timing. He has also made good friends, many of whom helped him start a bank more than a decade ago.

- Yet most business people in the city agree with the *Butte Miner*, "The thicker the fumes, the greater our financial vitality."
- W. A. Clark likes to say the fumes are a disinfectant that kills germs, and the arsenic in the smoke gives Butte women their beautiful pale complexions; tuberculosis is common in the city.
- The immigration of Irish miners has marked Butte as one of the most Irish cities in the United States; currently, the miners represent 25 percent of the country's Irish population, a higher percentage than in any western city.
- The best-known Irishman is Marcus Daly, owner of the Anaconda Mines, and one of the "Copper Kings" fighting for control of the town.
- Of 5,369 working-class Irishmen living in Butte in 1900, 3,589 work in the deep mines, while most of the rest work as pumpmen, blacksmiths and carpenters supporting the work of the mine.
- Approximately half of the Irish residents are single men living in boardinghouses.

"Republican Party," *Helena Semi-Weekly Independent,* **January 19, 1900:**

"Behind every special complaint there is a general principle that is offered. There are in the United States today many concrete causes of social discontent, and these find expression in political movements aimed at mitigating or removing them. The important thing for the American people to realize is that these causes have a common origin; that these movements are directed against the same opponent, and that relief against any individual evil is possible only through the combined efforts of the opponents of each, respectively. To some men the money question seems paramount; to some, unjust taxation; to others, the regulation and control of monopolies; to yet others, the danger of adopting an imperial colonial policy.

But in back of each of these questions stands the organized greed of modern society. Its object is always the same—the acquisition of unjust power. The methods employed in each case are identical—force and fraud. All have combined in securing the same representative and champion—the present leadership of the Republican Party.

This party stands today for the flat opposite of everything it formerly professed. It was once for bimetallism. It is now for the gold standard. It gave birth to the greenback, which it is about to destroy. It originated the national banks as a financial assistance to the government. Its first national platform appealed for the support of citizens in favor 'of restoring the action of the federal government to the principles of Washington and Jefferson.' Forty-four years afterward, it is engaged in an open and contemptuous violation of each and every one of these principles."

- The Irish are so important to the city that the local newspaper has refused to run want ads with the notation "NINA," meaning "No Irish Need Apply"; many eastern newspapers use the four-letter designation routinely.
- The surnames of Harrington, Murphy and Sullivan are common, as are the first names of John and Mary in Dublin Gulch, where most of the Irish live.
- Baseball is a current passion, with fiercely contested games between families and neighbors in the Gulch.
- Finns, Serbs, Croatians and Italians are now flooding the city to compete with the Irish and Cornish miners for jobs.
- Most of the newcomers have little mining experience; often these "bohunks" are assigned to the most dangerous sites that more experienced miners avoid through seniority.
- Because more than half of the city's residents are foreign-born, many speak English only sparingly.
- Most were drawn to the "Treasure State" of Montana by the promise of the mines, and go underground with little or no preliminary training.
- Reflecting its rapid growth through immigration, approximately 88 percent of the population is under 45 years old and only 2.2 percent is older than 65.
- Butte revels in its reputation as a wide-open town; saloons, gambling halls and brothels operate 24 hours per day in the red-light district known as the Cabbage Patch.

HISTORICAL SNAPSHOT
1900

- President William McKinley used the telephone as part of his re-election campaign; he was the last Union soldier to be elected president
- Nationwide, 13,824 motorcars were on the road
- Hamburgers were introduced by Louis Lassen in New Haven, Connecticut
- The number of advertising agencies in New York City increased from 44 in 1870 to more than 400
- Firestone Tire and Rubber Company was founded based on a patent for attaching tires to rims
- John Davison Rockefeller's wealth was estimated to be $200 million
- A dinner party in New York attracted publicity when cigarettes rolled in $100 bills were given to guests before dinner
- The cost of telephone service fell dramatically as more companies offered a 10-party line, allowing that many customers to share one line
- The United States led the world in productivity, based on gross national product, producing $116 billion compared with $62.2 billion in Great Britain, $42.8 billion in France and $42 billion in Germany
- 30,000 trolley cars operated on 15,000 miles of track across America
- Cities like New York and San Francisco had one saloon for every 200 people
- Louis Comfort Tiffany opened his first glass studio in New York
- America's economic boom entered its fourth year; inflation was at 0.1 percent
- Cigarette smoking was extremely popular and widely advertised, particularly by American Tobacco
- Excavation had begun on the New York subway system
- The U.S. railroads were charging an average of $0.75 per ton-mile, down from $1.22 in 1883
- Because of job instability, approximately 30 percent of all workers were out of work for some period during the year
- Wesson Oil, Uneeda Biscuits and the American Legion all made their first appearance
- Automobile manufacturer Ransom Olds sold 425 cars during the year
- The U.S. College Entrance Examination Board was formed to screen college applicants using a Scholastic Aptitude Test
- The Junior League of the New York Settlement House attracted young débutantes to serve the less fortunate
- Puerto Rico, obtained in the Spanish-American War in 1898, was declared a U.S. territory
- A tidal wave in Galveston, Texas, killed 4,000 people
- The U.S. Navy bought its first submarine

1900 ECONOMIC PROFILE

Annual Income, Standard Jobs

Average of all Industries, Excluding Farm Labor	$490.00
Average of all Industries, Including Farm Labor	$438.00
Bituminous Coal Mining	$0.20/Hour
Building Trades, Union Workers	$0.37/Hour
Clerical Workers, Manufacturing and Steam Railroads	$1,011.00
Domestics	$240.00
Farm Labor	$247.00
Federal Civilian	$940.00
Federal Employees, Executive Departments	$1,033.00
Finance, Insurance and Real Estate	$1,040.00
Gas and Electricity Workers	$620.00
Lower-Skilled Labor	$459.00
Manufacturing, Payroll	$0.15/Hour
Manufacturing, Union Workers	$0.34/Hour
Medical/Health Services Workers	$256.00
Ministers	$731.00
Nonprofit Organization Workers	$652.00
Postal Employees	$0.37/Hour
Public School Teachers	$328.00
State and Local Government Workers	$590.00
Steam Railroads, Wage Earners	$548.00
Street Railway Workers	$604.00
Wholesale and Retail Trade Workers	$508.00

Selected Prices

Alcohol, Whiskey, per Quart	$1.00
Bedroom Suite, Hardwood	$21.00
Bicycle, Lady's	$8.95
Buggy, Acme Royal Top	$54.90
Buggy Whip, Six-Inch	$0.69
Camera, Delmar Folding	$3.75
Child's Overcoat	$2.50

Dance Lessons, Five Private,
　Four Class $5.00
Man's Shirt, Madras $0.94
Paint, Ready Mix, per Gallon $0.98
Parasol, China Silk $1.25
Petroleum Jelly, per Jar $0.04
Piano, Upright..................... $59.45
Rattle Pacifier $0.09
Refrigerator, Holds 125 Pounds
　of Ice $27.50
Silverware Set, 26 Pieces $4.95
Soap, Palmolive, per Bar $0.05
Talking Machine, Graphophone
　Grand $257.00
Tombstone, Marble, 3' 8"........... $29.00
Woman's Dress, Percale............. $4.88

"Helena Wholesale Market," *Helena Semi-Weekly Independent,* March 6, 1900:

Pillsbury Best Flour, per 100 Pounds $2.85
Dakota Flour, per 100 Pounds...................... $2.20
Montana Soft Wheat Flour, 100 Pounds........ $1.80
Montana Hard Wheat Flour, 100 Pounds......... $2.00
Cornmeal, White, per 100 Pounds $1.75
Bacon, Choice Breakfast, One Pound $0.11
Heavy Hams $0.11
Medium Hams $0.12
Lard, Prime Leaf, per Pound $0.09
Fruits and Vegetables:
Canned Tomatoes, Western, Case $2.50
Canned Tomatoes, Eastern, Case.................... $2.85
Dried Peaches, Unpeeled, per Pound $0.12
Apricots, Evaporated $0.14
Prunes, per Pound $0.10
Lemons, per Box $2.75
Bananas, Bunch... $2.75
Potatoes, 100 Pounds.................................. $0.99
Beets, 100 Pounds...................................... $0.85
Carrots, 100 Pounds................................... $0.85
Rutabagas, 100 Pounds................................ $0.75
Celery, Dozen $0.30
Onions, 100 Pounds.................................... $2.00
Apples, Box.. $2.00

America in 1900

- The U.S. population totaled 76,094,000; 30,160,000 (or 40 percent) lived in urban areas, defined as communities of 2,500 or more.
- America's population had increased 300 percent since 1850.
- The Census Bureau counted 56,595,000 native-born whites, 10,214,000 foreign-born whites, 8,834,000 African-Americans, 237,000 Native Americans and 114,000 Asians.
- New York, Pennsylvania, Illinois, Ohio and Missouri ranked as the top five largest states in the Union.
- New York, Chicago and Philadelphia all had populations in excess of one million.
- Nationwide, America claimed nearly 4,000 millionaires.
- These millionaires represented less than 1/10,000 of one percent of the population, but controlled 20 percent of the nation's wealth.
- A typical immigrant's tenement apartment, housing up to 10 people, was approximately 375 square feet.
- Elementary and secondary schools nationwide boasted 16.8 million pupils; the average annual salary in public schools was $325, while the average expenditure per pupil per year was $17.
- Nationwide, the illiteracy rate was 10.7 percent.
- The life expectancy was 47.3 years; white life expectancy was 47.6 years, while non-white life expectancy was 33.0 years, and 16 of every 100 children died before their first birthday.

"Electric Motor Vehicles," *Scientific America*, 1899:

"The wonderful development of electricity within the past few years, for power purposes, and its great economy, adaptability, and usefulness in that line, as shown by its universal adoption for the propulsion of street railway cars, also clearly demonstrates its superiority as a convenient and easily controlled power for motor vehicles, which are becoming so popular.

While the well-known trolley car takes its power through the overhead and underground wires and conductors from an inexhaustible source of electricity, the motor vehicle is limited to the charge or amount it will carry, in consequence of the fact that it is intended to travel in places and over roads where there is no continuous outside supply of electricity. Hence, the means of storing electricity economically in the form of batteries is now one of the problems which is undergoing development.

New ideas are constantly being worked out, and it is confidently expected improvements will continue by which greater efficiency will result. At present, changes have been made in the construction of storage batteries whereby a surprisingly large quantity of active material is put into a small space, and this accounts for the neater appearance electric motor vehicles now possess over former designs. It is also a fact that the aggregate weight of battery for the amount of current discharge obtained is less than formerly.

The factor of weight is one of the features in electric vehicles that practical men are working to overcome, and it is said that whenever a storage battery or a system of storing the electric current is invented, by which the weight of the battery is greatly reduced, there is certain to be an impetus given to the electric motor vehicle industry which has never been thought of."

Proper dress is critical for all sporting events.

- Heart and kidney disease were the leading causes of death, followed by influenza and pneumonia, tuberculosis, gastrointestinal diseases, cancer, diphtheria, typhoid, malaria, measles, whooping cough and suicide.
- Within the U.S., there were 350,000 reported cases of typhoid fever, resulting in 35,000 deaths.
- One in seven homes had a bathtub; one in 13, a telephone.
- More than 2.4 million mules provided tractor power to the nation's farms.
- More than 100 people were killed in motor vehicle accidents that year, 155 more were executed by the state, and 115 lynched by mobs.
- In 1899, Republican President William McKinley became the first American president to ride in an automobile.
- Trains so dominated travel and transportation that one arrived and departed from Chicago every four minutes.
- The average wage was $12.74 per week, or $0.22 per hour; the average work week was 59 hours.

- It cost $10 to cross the Atlantic from Europe to the United States by steamship in steerage, the lowest-cost passage.
- Nationwide, 8,000 automobiles were registered and driven on fewer than 150 miles of paved roads, while trolley cars boasted 22,577 miles of track; the powerful railroads controlled 93,368 miles of track.
- The Atlanta Constitution declared, "Government is no longer a vehicle for the enforcement of human rights, but an agency for the furtherance of commercial interests."
- It is estimated that one percent of the population controlled more than half of the national wealth.
- Approximately 431 million acres of virgin land were put under cultivation during the past 30 years—more land than in the nation's entire history.
- Wheat, cotton and corn production was up 150 percent over 1870.
- The total number of books published during the year reached 4,490, while the total number of daily newspapers was 2,220.
- Approximately 18 per 1,000—or 800,000—people owned a telephone; telegraph messages sent per 1,000 numbered 217.
- Members of Congress were paid $5,000 a year; cabinet members and the vice president of the United States all made $8,000 annually, and the president earned $50,000.
- In all states, women were prohibited from voting, and in some states, an unescorted female could be refused, by law, a meal at a restaurant or a room at a hotel.
- *Independent Magazine* insisted, "Men want a girl who has not rubbed off the peach blossom of innocence by exposure to a rough world."
- Magazines touted the ideal man as being 5'10" inches tall, weighing 150 pounds, with a 36" chest, a 32" waist and 11" feet.
- Nationwide, more than 100,000 saloons operated, supplied by 3,000 breweries and distilleries.
- In Boston and Chicago, half the male population paid a daily visit to a favored neighborhood bar.
- America's women adorned themselves with a great variety of clothing, spending more than $1 billion a year; $14 million was spent on corsets alone.
- Thousands of egrets and herons were hunted annually to supply the current fashion demand for ladies' hats adorned with bird feathers; the fledgling Audubon Society protested the slaughter.
- Journalist Richard Harding Davis opined, "What I like most in men is the ability to sit opposite a mirror at dinner and not look in it."
- The assortment of cars at the first American auto show, held in New York in 1900, was dominated by electrics—cars powered by battery, and steamers—autos which featured steam engines.

1901 News Profile

"Housekeeping in a Millionaire's Family," by M. E. Carter, *The Ladies' Home Journal*, January 1901:

"In the mansion of a modern millionaire, the most interesting feature is the invisibility of the housekeeping machinery. Everything runs with precision, and one never sees 'the wheels go round.' By nine o'clock in the morning every department is immaculately clean and in perfect order, except the bedchambers, where those who dwell in the lap of luxury may still be slumbering; or, perchance, they may be breakfasting in lovely grandeur. Millionairedom lies abed late—the feminine part especially, to whom 'beauty sleep' is an imperative necessity. In a great house, whatever the size of the family proper, two or 10, it matters not, a certain number of servants is always requisite to insure the proper conduct of the affairs of the household. If the people live elegantly and entertain frequently, the department of service must be composed of skilled hands, who are inmates of the house. The chef and butler only may sleep out. They usually have families and homes of their own. On the first floor, the butler—with three or four men in livery—finds continuous occupation for all. It is not uncommon to assign to him the responsibility of the first floor, including dining room, library, billiard room, salon, reception room and halls. Furnished with a staff of men, a parlormaid and a pantrymaid, he is held responsible for the cleanliness and order of that part of the house—the pantry, of course, included. He defers to the managing housekeeper, but, if he be competent, she gladly leaves him in full sway, only giving him a quiet hint now and then. The butler has care of the silver also.

The Butler Is an Important Personage

Upon the butler devolves the closing of the house at night, unless there be a private watchman within doors patrolling from nine o'clock until daylight. It will be seen that he must be a man of some executive ability, and able to command the respect of his subordinates. Otherwise, he cannot hold his post. Sobriety is an absolute requirement in a butler. He must write in a good hand, and be capable of keeping simple accounts. Through him passes money for many odd daily calls that must be met promptly—expressages, extra postage, extra cab hire and countless items that cannot go on monthly bills. He writes the daily menu

cards for the dinner table, which are indispensable whether the family dine alone or are entertaining guests. The care of the flowers usually belongs to him. He has his own refrigerator for keeping them fresh as they arrive in large quantities two or three times a week from the country greenhouse. He has another refrigerator for the table butter and cream that also are sent from the country. Sometimes the refrigerator will be arranged in compartments for the storing of fruits in the same icebox. Those table delicacies not passing through the chef's cuisine belong to the butler's charge, candies included. The table and all its appointments come under his supervision. Excepting those times when large dinners are given, the butler arranges all the floral decorations. The florist is engaged for dinners above 14 covers. He brings the centrepiece arranged in sections fitting together; he also furnishes the boutonnieres for the masculine guests, and leaves English violets and rose geranium floating in the finger bowls.

A dining room ready for a banquet is a spectacle to dazzle eyes unwonted to such display. Picture to yourself a round table—seating 24 diners comfortably—all glorious in white and gold, lit by 30 wax candles held aloft in golden candelabra, the light softened by delicate silken shades harmonizing in the color of the flower decorations, the centre a mass of choice exotics and waving ferns, and disposed about the table bouquets and luscious fruits along, it may be truthfully said, with every known device to tempt the appetite and charm the eye.

A Woman Superintendent Is the Head

The butler's business during a dinner is to announce the guests as they arrive, announce the dinner to madam and direct the entire dining room service. Each man is assigned certain duties. A quiet discipline necessarily characterizes the whole management of men and things. During the meal, whatever one it may be, the pantrymaid, with necessary assistance, is occupied 'washing up.' When the table is deserted all the dishes, except those of the last course, and the glasses are cleansed and put in their places, ready for the next entertainment, which is never distant. One man's special duty as the meal proceeds is to 'run it in' as each course arrives from the chef. Thus, system and order are maintained.

A palatial home—where the rites of hospitality are constantly observed—is a mammoth establishment requiring a perfect apportionment of work, with ample facilities for its accomplishment. To this end an experienced, well-bred and well-educated woman superintendent becomes a necessity. Her position is no sinecure. Where she is not in evidence an appalling state of things is found behind the scenes.

The Chef Is the Autocrat of the Kitchen

The kitchen of a large private establishment is presided over by a chef, with two or three women as aids. The chef is rear-admiral in his department. One of the women acts as second cook. She gets the servants' breakfast and any early family meal. She must be competent. Upon her rests the responsibility of preparing the home-made bread and cake. With all his accomplishments, the chef finds his Waterloo when these are demanded. It is a constant struggle in these houses to secure nice, old-fashioned, simple food, unless there is a woman employed who is versed in its production.

The chef gets $100 a month, usually, and manifold commissions. He occupies a unique position. The heads of the house are often deferential to him. His office has many emoluments. The second cook receives from $25 to $30 wages, but only remains long enough to be graduated under the chef. Then she is up and away, able to command, in less pretentious places, $50 or $60 monthly. In the culinary department, one kitchenmaid stands all day at the sink cleaning the utensils used by the chef and the cook.

The Baltimore Belle Who Made
The Most Brilliant Match of Any Girl in America

BEING THE FOURTH PART OF "A STORY OF BEAUTIFUL WOMEN"

By WILLIAM PERRINE

CHARLES CARROLL, of Carrollton: in the land from which his grandfather fled in terror his granddaughter now reigns a queen." Such was the joyous toast which Bishop England proposed at a banquet in South Carolina on the Fourth of July, 1827, when the venerable Carroll, whose Irish ancestors had settled in Maryland in the days of the English Revolution, had become the only surviving signer of the Declaration of Independence.

It was then that Americans were reading with wondering eyes the stories which came from Ireland of the regal magnificence with which one of their countrywomen was dazzling the British people; how she had become the wife of the brother of the foremost of British soldiers, and how the court of the newly wedded pair at Dublin Castle rivaled the brilliancy of royalty itself. She was called "The American Queen of the Irish Court," and in no capital of Europe would her flatterers allow that there was a woman who surpassed her in the elegance of her bearing and in the accomplishments of a sovereign. Indeed, she was only one of a group of sisters whom Europeans hailed as "The American Graces." Their mother, a daughter of Charles Carroll, had married Richard Caton, a poor English gentleman of handsome face and presence, who became a merchant after his arrival in this country. She herself bore the reputation of being one of the most attractive women of her day, and the graceful figure, the comely neck, the profusion of hair, the bright eyes and the winsome smile which are shown in her portrait amply bear witness to her womanly charms. Indeed, to her might not unfittingly be applied Macaulay's famous description of "Saint Cecilia, a beautiful mother of a beautiful race." Her brother, too, had married a well-known beauty, Harriet Chew, a sister of two of the belles of the Mischianza, and of the Caton girls it was said, as Joseph Shippen wrote of their aunts:

> "With either Chew such beauties dwell,
> Such charms with each are shared,
> No critic's judging eye can tell
> Which merits most regard.
> 'Tis far beyond the painter's skill
> To set their charms to view,
> As far beyond the poet's quill
> To give the praise that's due."

Most famous of the four girls was Marianne, or Mary, who at the age of eighteen was married in Baltimore to Robert Patterson, brother of Betsy Patterson, the first wife of Jerome Bonaparte. When the couple went to England, together with Elizabeth and Louisa Caton, they created a profound impression on London society at a time when it was dominated by the Prince Regent, and when the Duke of Wellington was in the height and flush of his military glory. In the English court Mrs. Patterson attracted the admiring eye of the Prince himself, who marveled at her as an American beauty. She easily adapted herself to English manners and customs, as her sisters also did, and in no long time she became a conspicuous figure among the choicest women of England. The victor of Waterloo, who time and again complimented her as an ornament of her sex, proudly lavished upon her all the honor which hospitality could suggest.

Hardly less eminent than the Duke before the Battle of Waterloo had been his brother, the Marquis of Wellesley, with whom Mrs. Patterson, after the death of her husband in Baltimore, in 1822, and her return to England, was soon destined to attract the gaze of Europe. Wellesley at this time was sixty-three years old and a widower. He had sat in Parliament, had been Governor-General of India, had put down Indian rebellions, and had exhibited in high degree the qualities of a successful ruler, as well as of a military chieftain.

In the spring of 1825 it was announced in Ireland, where Wellesley was Lord Lieutenant, that he was engaged to her, and it was noted in the United States as a curious coincidence that while one American girl had married the brother of Napoleon, another, and she her sister-in-law, should marry the brother of Napoleon's conqueror.

"She has made," said Madame Bonaparte, in a half-envious, half-querulous letter at this time, "the greatest

DRAWN BY LUCIEN DAVIS

"WITH MEASURED AND STATELY TREAD THE VICE-ROYAL PAIR ADVANCED TO A THRONE SURMOUNTED BY A CANOPY OF SCARLET AND GOLD"

5

Regaling the inner man is a continuous function with the new rich. Regarding supplies, the white-tiled cold room—where the chef guards the beef, mutton and game stored there—looks as if it might belong to a good hotel rather than the refrigerating room of a private family. An ice plant on the place furnishes all the ice used throughout the house. In making the ice, filtered water is used. People of wealth wage war upon microbes, but as their tiny enemy is ubiquitous, and the battle is confined to their own homes, his miteship comes off victor every time.

A relatively provident chef always buys in large quantities. He must know just how long each piece hangs. The cool room is a sanctum visited only by the chef—who holds the keys—the cleaner, and a few privileged ones. The chef reigns in his own province. His closets of flavoring essences, coloring mixtures, molds, and whatnot, would completely puzzle the uninitiated. His needs are limitless, his orders always honored.

Filling the Millionaire's Market-Basket

The other stores in these houses are seldom large. A messenger calls daily for orders that are immediately filled. The telephone and messenger boys are ever ready for any emergency. This method insures freshness in those things where it is most desirable. The chef and the butler each have their lists ready; duplicates are given to the housekeeper, who keeps these to compare with the books delivered to her once a week. She makes payments monthly. There are some nonperishable things that she keeps in large quantities on hand. The daily orders are delivered directly to those who will use the articles. Each chief of any department becomes responsible for what is charged to his or her province. This simplifies the distribution. An experienced woman immediately detects any excessive ordering and makes inquiry about it. In the home of the millionaire, the aggregate consumption of food of all sorts is enormous. It disappears like dew before the morning sun. Unquestionably, there is great and unavoidable waste where the style of living is commensurate with enormous wealth.

A Small Fortune Expended on Linen

The basement floors of these houses are tiled in white to insure cleanliness. In this respect, perfection can only be assured where everything in floors, walls and woodwork will reveal dirt. Sunlight or electrical illumination also forbid any unsightly corners. Aesthetic ones know that absolute cleanliness is a greater necessity than lavish luxury. In her home, my lady may trail about in white satin and daintiest underwear with scarcely a sign of dust on her raiment. Early, every stairway, hall and balustrade is carefully gone over by an expert hand with clean brushes, feather dusters and soft cloths. There must be no speck to be found in remote corners. It is the business of each domestic, in his or her own department, to sponge out daily every window-sill, thus forestalling the collection of dust in those places, to blow in later. Broom-bags and hardwood polishers are in constant requisition.

The purity of a palatial home forms its chief charm, outranking pictures, statuary, gold or silver ornaments. Each housemaid reigns supreme on her own floor. No one else can, with impunity, meddle with her or her tools. Her implements are kept in a closet separately her own, no careless one presuming to borrow from her domain without the fact being apparent to anyone familiar with the house. Each floor has its implements marked by name and by a color belonging to it exclusively. Military discipline prevails and preserves order.

In the linen room, each set tied up with beautiful ribbons, are piles of embroidered, lace-bordered pillowcases; matching sheets also decorated with French needlework half a yard deep; countless dozens of towels embroidered 18 inches deep; guest sheets costing $250 apiece; and immense damask cloths that required special loom building for their weaving.

Twenty-four diners can surround a table covered with one of these cloths. There are others smaller, with point Venise borders, insertion and monograms, too costly for one to presume to guess the price. The bath towels are worthy of mention, so luxurious are they in texture and size, and sometimes exquisite in color. They seem too beautiful for the bathrooms until you visit the latter: Mexican onyx trimmings, with silver and gold mountings; bathtubs sculptured out of solid blocks of spotless marble. Axminster rugs which are laid on the floors harmonize perfectly with the contents of the linen room."

1907 Family Profile

Jacob Heller is a wealthy wholesale wine merchant who is rebuilding his company after 2.5 million gallons of wine were lost during the 1906 San Francisco earthquake and fire.

Annual Income: $65,000 this year; his net worth is approximately $500,000, including property.

Life at Home

- A native of New York City, Heller came West 18 years ago with the financial backing of a group of fellow Jewish merchants.
- He was planning to stay in California only a short time, but was intrigued by the possibilities and openness of the state.
- Rarely on the West Coast did he hear the slur, "kike," first invented by German-American Jews to deride Russian Jews whose names ended in "ki."
- He was married in an orthodox ceremony to Judith, a woman who had grown up in Sacramento.
- He and Judith have three children, all girls; he sometimes believes they, not he, run the household, but says little.
- His oldest daughter has become obsessed with taking pictures with a Kodak Brownie camera; Jacob finds it hard to sit down to do anything enjoyable without the camera appearing, and though he complains, he secretly enjoys the game.
- On trips he is overwhelmed by the luggage and ornate hatboxes required for the four women and girls in his house;

A native of New York, Jacob Heller came West 18 years ago.

His daughters change their dresses five or six times each day.

all insist on changing their dresses and accessories five or six times a day, yet no one outfit can be seen twice during one weekend.

- Like teens across the country, two of his daughters enjoy puzzles and board games, especially those related to travel, that challenge the mind.

- At the time of the earthquake last year, the Hellers lived on California Street in a three-story wooden home decorated with handcrafted furniture made of Koa from Hawaii, and native artifacts from Fiji made of teak, all of which Jacob and Judith collected on their travels.

- The night before the quake, on April 17, 1906, they had attended the opera, in which Enrico Caruso sang the role of Don José in Bizet's *Carmen* to a delighted San Francisco audience; Judith remembers that the lobby of the opera house on Mission Street glittered that night with brocade and jewels, along with the aroma of quality perfumes and more than a hint of a good Havana cigar.

- At 5:13 a.m. the next day, life in San Francisco changed.

- That morning, within their home, the chandeliers began swaying back and forth, part of the elaborate molding of the ceiling cracked, the grandfather clock in the upper hall fell on its face and the brick chimney buckled at the roof line and fell.

"Indoor Portraiture," *The Camera, A Practical Monthly Magazine for Photographers*, May 1908:

"No doubt you will read this title calmly. It will raise no feelings of excitement in your mind, nor will you be led to wonderment. Indoor photography is too common a thing. In that commonness lies one of the pities of the age in which we live; surrounded by wonders and marvels on every hand, we accept them in a most matter-of-fact way, not because they are wizardlike, but because they are not rare. Indoor portraiture, like the rest of photography, is common because it is easy. Indoor things which are hard are the few—the things which anyone may do are common, usual, for all of us. And indoor portraiture is easy and common, not that science is easy, but because the manufacturers of photographic appliances have designed, improved and made simple that which is inherently neither simple nor easy. . . .

Given the ability to manage a camera and sensitive material with ordinary skill—ability to focus, to expose the plate, to develop it and make a print—the development of the artistic side means only time and patience and study."

Two of his daughters enjoy puzzles and board games that challenge the mind.

- Jacob checked first on his family, then turned his thoughts to his business.
- Not realizing the severity of the damage, he believed that on his way to work, he would stop at a plumbing and carpentry shop to arrange for repairs.
- Only later, while checking on his warehouse, did he comprehend the extent of the structural damage to buildings and the size of the fire roaring throughout the city.
- The need to protect his family, including Judith's parents and cousins, became all-consuming.
- Jacob and the maid went back into the house and carried out stacks of blankets, then took the family wagon to Golden Gate Park where they found an empty tent and unrolled their bedding.
- Following the earthquake, the children were not allowed to reenter the house.
- The first evening in the park, few people slept; the peacocks in the nearby aviaries screeched all night, while tongues of orange flame could be seen from the park as they destroyed the city.
- Returning toward their home the next morning, the Hellers passed many strange sights: a woman carrying an empty birdcage, baby carriages filled with possessions, and boxes attached to roller skates.
- Immediately, Jacob took his family south to San Mateo, using huge Percheron horses to pull the wagon carrying the 12 members of his extended family.
- Judith gathered what she needed and cared about, packing items as varied as a silk rug from India and the rest of the season's opera tickets, but not the family silver.

Eastman Kodak Company
ROCHESTER, N. Y., *The Kodak City.*

THE 4A SPEED KODAK

1/1000 OF A SECOND.

A camera in which especial adaptability to high speed work is combined with the convenience and simplicity of the Kodak Cartridge system.

The Speed Kodak is fitted with our Kodak Focal Plane Shutter with a range of automatic exposures from 1/5 of a second to 1/1000 of a second.

This shutter differs from the ordinary between the lens shutters, in that it operates as nearly as possible to the surface of the sensitive film, and is built in the camera body. The shutter consist of a cloth curtain, with a series of adjustable apertures, any one of which can be made to pass across the face of the film as desired.

The speed of the exposure is regulated by the width of the aperture in the curtain, and a tension spring in one of the rollers upon which the curtain is wound.

This shutter possesses two very great advantages over all other types.

It is the only shutter with which it is possible to make extremely short exposures, such as are absolutely essential in arresting the motion of rapidly moving objects, in fact anything calling for an actual exposure,

Camera Back open showing shutter curtain.

(1)

His oldest daughter is obsessed with taking photographs.

As she fled the earthquake and fire, Judith slipped on underneath her coat a Victorian 18-karat gold bracelet made with emeralds, pearls, and diamonds.

- Underneath her spring coat, she slipped on a Victorian 18-karat gold bracelet made with emeralds, pearls and diamonds; it was her husband's gift on their fifteenth wedding anniversary.
- As they were leaving the city, they saw opera star Caruso and his baggage on a high, one-horse wagon dashing by at top speed.
- The Hellers reached Ocean View that night and were able to sleep indoors, though they slept little, waking often to the sensation of aftershocks.
- Once they reached San Mateo, a cousin who lived in Oakland sent her automobile to pick up the family, who stayed with her for three weeks.
- During those early weeks, fearing the worst, they bought enormous stocks of cereals and dry beans, which the family has not been able to completely consume a year later.
- Within a week of the quake, they learned that their home was unfit for use and must be torn down; they found a house in North Berkeley, where they now live.
- Determined to leave the past year behind, they joined the city's elite in a wide variety of celebrations designed to usher in the new year.
- Their favorite was the 1907 new year festivities for the annual New Year Cotillion of the Entre Nous Club at the Palace Hotel.
- The children have been made to join a reading club to refocus their minds; Judith is proud that her daughter Hannah is so interested in reading.

The earthquake destroyed much of San Francisco, including Heller's warehouse.

- Hannah has not disclosed how hard her heart beats when she reads the love scenes of Elinor Glyn's current bestseller, *Three Weeks*.
- The morning of the earthquake, Heller made his way to his place of business, a massive warehouse at Beale and Mission Streets.
- Dozens of his employees were already gathered, including the woman who operates the telephone.
- Nothing could be done as they watched the six-story building, each floor piled with whiskey and wine, catch fire and burn violently.
- Since then he has gotten capital from his original backers in New York; in exchange, they own more of the West Coast operation.
- Within six weeks of the tragedy, they shipped hundreds of cases of whiskey and wine by rail from the East—an expensive way to supply the West Coast; the shipments arrived ahead of many others and were sold immediately at inflated prices.
- For weeks following the quake, the city restricted the sale of intoxicating liquors—only making the demand stronger for Heller's quality product when it arrived.
- With increased shipments, most by steamship, the prices he charges have come down.
- New Year's celebrations were particularly profitable; the people of the city were ready to move forward from the quake in every way possible.
- Most of Heller's employees were glad to be back at work and earning money; two people left the area completely, determined never to experience an earthquake again.

Life in the Community: San Francisco, California

- Many refugees are still living in tents, one year after the earthquake and great fire that ravaged the city.
- The bubonic plague has broken out, and 77 of the 160 victims have died; to stop its spread, two million rats have been killed with poison and 6.5 million square feet of concrete flooring has been poured to eliminate their breeding grounds.
- The unsanitary conditions also have resulted in an epidemic of intestinal worms; many families rely on Keyes' Anti-bilious Worm and Stomach Powders, advertised as being "Best in the World for Children when Feverish or Constipated."
- In the year since the disaster, 8,000 building permits have been issued; $100 million has been spent on reconstruction, employing more than 50,000 men.

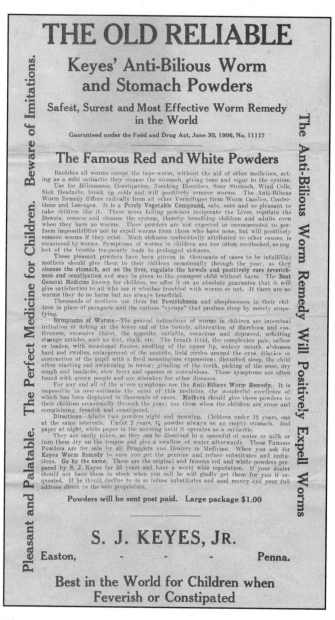

The unsanitary conditions unleashed an epidemic of intestinal worms.

San Francisco, As It Was. As It Is. And How to See It,
Helen Throop Purdy, San Francisco, 1912:

"Before the ashes had ceased falling, every available house on the street was rented. One man advertised, 'My rent receipt for my present location is dated April 20, 1906.' Such high rents were offered for the houses, that every fortunate owner could afford to move out and live on his income elsewhere. Doctors, lawyers and dentists opened offices on the upper floors, the lower were filled with shops of every variety, and Fillmore Street became for a time the main retail street. It soon bore the aspect of a country fair. All sorts of booths, tents and hastily erected sheds filled the vacant lots and street corners. Lunch wagons and counters close to the sidewalks offered refreshments, and 'pop,' lemonade and all sorts of soft drinks, to allay the thirst of throats parched by mortar-dust and ashes. Spielers at the corners cried out their wares. It was pandemonium. All saloons were closed and no liquor could be had except on the prescription of a physician, countersigned by General Greely. As a consequence San Francisco was free from crime as it had never been before. The next phase of shopping accommodations was when the larger firms opened in houses. Some of the merchants and bankers used their own homes; others rented houses, mostly on the west side of Van Ness Avenue. . . .

It was a curious experience to enter a store by a marble vestibule, find yourself in a beautiful hall, with a carved oak staircase and stained-glass windows, to have the goods you desire brought to you from the pantry or sideboard drawers or from the library shelves, to have them spread before you on a beautiful great dining table, around which not long before wit and beauty had made merry; or, in another room, to be served at a hastily improvised pine counter, while feet pressed the rich velvet carpet and your eyes rested upon the fine oil paintings which had not yet been taken from the walls. If you wandered up the stairway to look at suits or coats, perhaps you were asked to step into the bathroom to be fitted. It was a topsy-turvy land, but in a few months Van Ness Avenue became a delightful shopping street. . . .

It was a sight to stir the heart and warm the blood—yes, to bring a lump to the throat—to walk up Van Ness Avenue on a sunny afternoon. From the pole which surmounted each building waved one or two flags and a pennant, all flying straight in the afternoon western breeze. The pennant bore the name of the store or firm, one flag was the Stars and Stripes and, if there were two, the other marked the nationality of the owners; the flags of all nations mingled with our own. Flying gaily the whole length of the avenue, they symbolized triumph over disaster, and proclaimed to the world the spirit which sent the merchants back down to the old locality three and a half years after the desolating fire."

- Spreckel's Call Building is nearing completion; the lower floors were opened within a month after the fire, while the upper floors are being refinished.
- Even though Market Street is now bustling with activity, businessmen prefer to receive gold and silver coins for their goods rather than bank notes.
- United Railroads has been accused of destroying its cable cars to obtain higher insurance payouts; San Francisco's mayor was found guilty of extortion.

HISTORICAL SNAPSHOT
1907

- Congress raised the head tax on immigrants to $4 as a record 1.29 million immigrants arrived in the United States
- Pepsi-Cola sales increased from 8,000 gallons in 1903 to 104,000 gallons
- The Forest Preservation Act set aside 16 million acres in five states
- The Protestant Episcopal Convention condemned the removal of "In God We Trust" from the new gold coins
- Alabama and Georgia adopted prohibition laws
- Taximeters, imported from France, appeared in New York City
- The Great Arrow Car was sold for $4,500; advertisements did not bother to list the price
- Periodicals warned the nation about "nickel madness" in an attempt to control the wild popularity of the new short movie features being shown across the nation in thousands of tiny nickelodeons
- Nationwide, an economic crisis was building with the collapse of the New York Stock Market and runs on the banks
- Sears, Roebuck distributed three million copies of its spring catalogue
- Francis Benedict discovered how the body consumed itself in starvation after fats, carbohydrates, and finally protein were metabolized
- The Cadillac was advertised for $800 that year, a Ford Model K was $2,800, and a horse sold for $150 to $300
- Movie projectionist Donald H. Bell founded Bell and Howell Company, a pioneer in the development of motion picture photography and projection
- The world's largest steamship, the *Lusitania*, set a record by racing from New York to Ireland in five days, 54 minutes
- The first canned tuna fish was packed in California
- Surgeons discovered that patients recovered faster and with few complications if they became mobile shortly after surgery
- Oklahoma became the forty-sixth state in the Union
- President Teddy Roosevelt limited Japanese immigration; California agreed to allow resident Asians' children to attend school again
- During the Second Hague Peace Conference, 46 nations established the rules of war in the future, including giving notice to those to be attacked
- Rube Goldburg cartoons, Neiman Marcus, Prince Albert tobacco, Armstrong linoleum and spray-paint guns all made their first appearance

1907 ECONOMIC PROFILE

Annual Income, Standard Jobs

Average of all Industries,
   Excluding Farm Labor $593.00
Average of all Industries,
   Including Farm Labor $542.00
Bituminous Coal Mining $0.29/Hour
Building Trades, Union Workers . . . $0.51/Hour
Clerical Workers,
   Manufacturing and
   Steam Railroads $1,091.00
Domestics $316.00
Farm Labor $319.00
Federal Employees, Executive
   Departments $1,094.00
Finance, Insurance and
   Real Estate $1,180.00
Gas and Electricity Workers $623.00
Lower-Skilled Labor $442.00
Manufacturing, Payroll $0.18/Hour
Manufacturing, Union Workers . . . $0.40/Hour
Medical/Health Services
   Workers $306.00
Ministers $831.00
Nonprofit Organization Workers $741.00
Postal Employees $0.40/Hour
Public School Teachers $431.00
State and Local Government
   Workers $694.00
Steam Railroads, Wage Earners $661.00
Street Railway Workers $658.00
Telegraph Industry Workers $635.00
Telephone Industry Workers $412.00
Wholesale and Retail Trade
   Workers $593.00

Selected Prices

Camera, Kodak (without Lens) $50.00
Carbon Paper, 25 Sheets $0.50
Chicks, Barred Rock, White Leghorn $0.25
Cloth, Black Taffeta, Yard $1.10
Coat, Man's Raccoon Fur $47.50
Dining Table, Oak $11.25
Eyeglasses, Man's $1.98
Fishing Rod $1.29
Hotel Room, Lenox Hotel, per Day $1.50
Magazine Subscription, One Year,
   Financial Forum $1.00

Peanuts, Salted, Half Pound	$0.21
Petticoat	$1.39
Railroad Ticket, per Mile	$0.03
Razor, with Leather Case	$3.50
Talking Machine, Wurlitzer	$29.50
Theater Ticket	$0.25–$0.50
Toothpaste	$0.25
Typewriter Rental, Monthly	$2.00
Watch, Elgin, Pocket	$8.15
Water Heater	$198.00

Approximately two thirds of San Francisco was destroyed by the earthquake and fire.

The San Francisco Earthquake and Fire of 1906

- Economically, San Francisco began 1906 as an exceedingly prosperous city.
- Businesses were profitable enough to underwrite the arts extensively.
- Immediately after the earthquake and fire, and for weeks following, money had little value; society drifted into primitive conditions in which food and shelter came first.
- Those who had laid in the largest stock of foodstuffs on the first day of the disaster were considered wealthy in subsequent days.
- Simple kitchen utensils, dismissed the week before, were now highly prized.
- In all, about two thirds of San Francisco was destroyed; more than 450 people died, and the 250,000 left homeless were everywhere; the grass was their bed, the clothing on their backs their only protection against the penetrating ocean fog or the chilling dew of the morning.
- Fresh meat was impossible to find; canned foods and breadstuffs were the only victuals in evidence.
- Every vacant space in the safe zones was occupied, even the crowded cemeteries, where women of high social position passed nights.

- Hundreds of other homeless women and children slept in the hay on the wharves or on the sand lots near North Beach, with no protection from the chilling winds of the bay.
- Strategists directing the fire-fighting operations attempted to use the wide streets as firebreaks, but the blaze often jumped the street, driven by the wind.
- In desperation, the firemen torched the wooden mansions, which lined the east side of Van Ness Avenue, as fuel for a backfire.
- Kerosene was poured over exquisite, irreplaceable furniture and torched to create the backfire; the gamble worked, thanks to a west wind that sprang up.
- It was impossible to obtain a vehicle, except at exorbitant prices; one merchant agreed to pay $50 an hour for a teamster, horses and wagon.
- Others charged $40 for carrying trunks just a few blocks.
- The Bank of Italy's A. P. Giannini, who was able to remove the assets and records from his bank before they were consumed by the advancing fire, reopened his bank almost immediately, loaning money to the cash-strapped of the community.
- Sugar magnate Rudolph Spreckel volunteered as a special officer to assist the firemen trying to stop the blazes.
- Relief stations for the homeless were established by the general committee at Golden Gate Park, Presidio and San Bruno Road.

Firemen torched many buildings to create a backfire.

Ferry Building from the Bay at night, San Francisco.

Thanks to years of prosperity, many elegant homes have been built in San Francisco.

- Mrs. Hugh Crum, a wealthy property owner who lost all her income-bearing property to the fires, gave half of her remaining cash—$10,000—to the Relief Committee for distribution to others.
- To feed the hungry, grocery stores were entered by the police and their goods confiscated for distribution.
- When looting became epidemic in the disaster area, General Frederick Funston, commanding officer of the Presidio, declared the city under martial law.

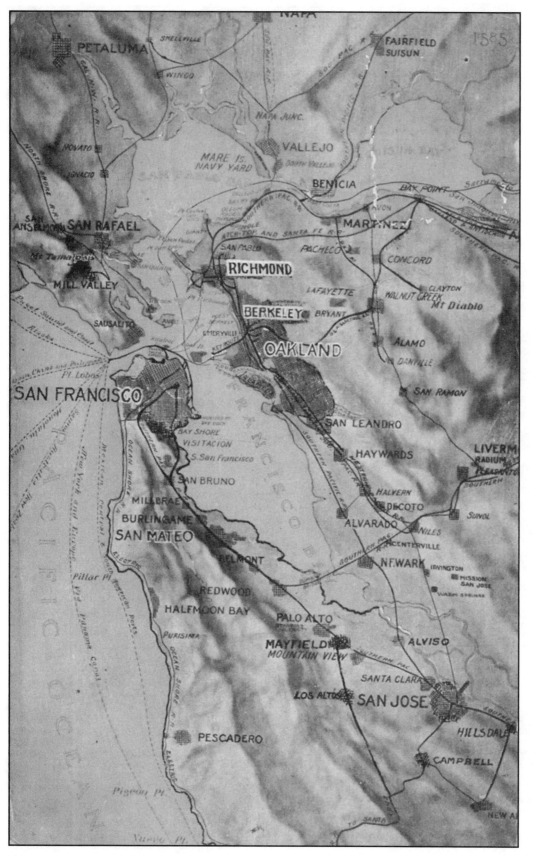

The earthquake of 1906 impacted a wide area.

"My Reception in America," by Fu Chi Hao, M.A., *The Outlook*, August 10, 1907:

"America has always been a very sweet and familiar name to my ears, because I have been told by my American friends that it is the only free country in the world, the refuge of the oppressed and the champion of the weak; so I have had a great affection for this country since my childhood days. I had an idea for a great many years that America was the best nation on the earth, and a good friend of China. . . .

There is a close connection between America and China. The modern invention of steamboats brought these two nations nearer together. The great Pacific Ocean served as an indestructible tie. It is America that sent out her missionaries and merchants to China early in the nineteenth century, to instruct her people and help her to open the long-closed doors, and thus to get into contact with the new civilization of the twentieth century. We of China owe a great debt to America, especially during the Boxer uprising of 1900. It is largely due to America that China stands intact as she is today. Without America China might have been divided among the European nations seven years ago. Certainly America is China's best friend.

Don't be shocked if I tell you that, after six years of careful study and close observation, and after the personal treatment I have received from your country, my attitude toward America is totally changed. America is not so good a friend to China as I had mistakenly thought, because in no part of the earth are the Chinese so ill-treated and humiliated as in America.

I hope I shall not be misunderstood. I have no hard feeling whatever against the American people. I can sincerely say that some of my best friends are Americans, and I have a great many sympathetic friends all over the country. But I do hate the misinterpretation of the Chinese exclusion law by your government. The original idea of the law is lost. The officials on the Pacific Coast have made it their special business to find errors in the papers of every Chinese who comes to this country, so as to send them back, whether they are laborers or not.

Pardon me if I give you a brief review of the personal treatment I received from America a few years ago. In the fall of 1901 a college-mate and

289 — *Going to Market, Chinatown.*

myself were brought by an American missionary to this country, with the hope of getting an American college education which would enable us to take part in the uplifting of China in the near future. Glad indeed were we when the steamer *Doric* entered the Golden Gate on September 13, 1901. The peril of the water, the seasickness on the boat, were both ended. Christian America was reached at last. Our hearts were full of anticipation of the pleasure and the warm welcome we were going to receive from our Christian friends.

I was very much surprised to learn, after waiting several days on the steamer, that the passports which we had with us were not accepted by the American Government. There were several objections to the papers. In the first place, we ought to have got them not from Hi-Hung-Chang, the highest and most powerful official in North China at that time, but from his subordinate, the Customs Taotai, the Collector of the Port at Tientsin. In the second place, our papers were in the form of passports, while the law of this country requires certificates. The careless American consul at Tientsin had made still other mistakes and omissions in his English translation. We learned that we were denied the privilege of landing, and were to go back to China on the same steamer one week later.

I wish I could end the story with the deportation, but fortunately, or, if you please, unfortunately, our friends in this country did their best to have us stay. Letters and telegrams began to fly to the Chinese Minister and the Secretary of the Treasury Department in Washington. We were finally allowed to stay in the detention shed where the *Doric* left for China.

The detention shed is another name for a 'Chinese jail.' I have visited quite a few jails and state prisons in this country, but have never seen any place half so bad. It is situated at one end of the wharf, reached by a long, narrow stairway. The interior is about one hundred feet square. Oftentimes they put in as many as two hundred human beings. The whitewashed windows and the wire netting attached to them added to the misery. The air is impure, the place is crowded. No friends are allowed to come in and see the unfortunate sufferers without special permission from the American authority. No letters are allowed either to be sent out or to come in. There are no tables, no chairs. We were treated like a group of animals, and we were fed on the floor. Kicking and swearing by the white man in charge was not a rare thing. I was not surprised when, one morning, a friend pointed out to me the place where a heartbroken Chinaman had hanged himself after four months' imprisonment in this dreadful dungeon, thus to end his agony and the shameful outrage."

Editorial: "Wretched Street Car Service, Growing Conviction That It Is the Result of Deliberate Policy," *San Francisco Chronicle*, January 1, 1907:

"The conduct of the United Railroads in destroying its cable lines, under color of authority, obtained, as appears by the sworn statement of its own officers in adjusting its insurance, upon statements utterly false, has made every resident of San Francisco its enemy. Its gross disregard of public rights in tearing up miles of streets and leaving them impassable for months has created a public feeling whose effects the corporations will feel for years. In spite of its assertions that the car service is as good as it can give with the number of cars which it is possible to obtain, too many people see cars standing idle in the barns, while the public is waiting in vain for transportation, to make it possible to believe them. Especially is that true when comparison of their declarations that the cable machinery was ruined, with their sworn statement to the insurance companies, proves them to be unworthy of belief. Now that we know, by the testimony of United Railroads themselves, that the public might long ago have been riding comfortably on the cable cars, there is less disposition than ever to quietly submit to the outrageous overcrowding and delays which we now endure. The people of Oceanside have voted to employ counsel and endeavor to ascertain whether the public has any rights which its public service corporations are bound to respect."

1909 FAMILY PROFILE

Edward Pierson, a 48-year-old former attorney, is one of the principal partners of Coca-Cola Bottling Company, begun 10 years ago. Today, there are 379 Coca-Cola bottling plants in the United States.

Annual Income: $100,000; his net worth is more than $1 million.

Life at Home

- The son of a wholesale grocer, Edward Pierson attended the University of Virginia, worked in a bank, operated a stone quarry and ran a hosiery mill before attending law school.
- After graduating in 1887 from the Cincinnati Law School, he moved to Chattanooga, Tennessee, to practice law.
- When war with Spain erupted a few years later, Pierson was sent to Cuba to serve as chief clerk in the office of the Assistant Army Quartermaster.
- There, during his stay in Manzanilla, Cuba, he purchased a Cuban-bottled soft drink called Pina Fria.
- The carbonated pineapple drink was delicious and reminded him of how much he enjoyed the cold, carbonated drink of Coca-Cola from the soda fountain back home.
- When he returned to Chattanooga, he discussed the idea with several friends; one even suggested that a bottled Coca-Cola would be a great addition to any baseball game.
- The product was growing in popularity, carried a distinct trade name, and could be manufactured and distributed inexpensively.

Edward Pierson has built his fortune on bottling Coca-Cola.

Coca-Cola by the glass is gaining popularity.

The idea for a bottled soft drink came to Pierson while in Cuba.

- When the men approached Asa Candler, the president of Coca-Cola, to get the exclusive rights to bottle the drink, Mr. Candler was not enthusiastic.
- Only when Candler was assured that they would take full responsibility for bottling the drink, and that he would not be bothered by his venture, did he agree.
- The men gained the right to bottle Coca-Cola anywhere in the United States except New England, Mississippi and a part of Texas; these exceptions were made to protect distribution agreements made years before.
- The agreement, which established Pierson's company and wealth, was only six hundred words long.
- Even though he is worth more than $1 million on paper, old habits never die: he continues to be careful with his money when purchasing for himself, and also likes to spend his money locally; currently, Hardie and Caudle on Market Street is running a special on $3.50 pants on sale for only $1.98.
- An important indulgence is his automobile; the entire family enjoys a Sunday drive, even with the hazards of blown tires and rough roads.
- Dora, Edward's wife, is leading a group of women from the Music Club to erect a new auditorium in Chattanooga, because they believe the present structure is not in keeping with the city's dignity.

Life at Work

- Edward Pierson has the national franchise to sell Coca-Cola bottled drinks in the Middle Atlantic States and Pacific Coast, while his partner has the Southeast, Southwest and Midwest.
- Edward likes using amber bottles to sell Coca-Cola.
- Most of his contracts with franchise bottlers are for two years.
- Since 1901, he has established bottling plants in cities throughout his territory, including major cities such as Chicago, Cincinnati and Los Angeles.
- Today there are 379 Coca-Cola bottling plants in the United States, allowing Edward and his partners to receive compensation every time a bottle of Coca-Cola is sold.
- After gaining an agreement from Asa Candler in 1899, Pierson established an office on Market Street and spent about $5,000 to equip a soda-water bottling plant on Patten Parkway.
- One of his partners formerly worked for Edward's father-in-law, producing and marketing the famous female disorder patent medicine "Cardui" and Black Draught.
- Since Pierson and his partners had neither the money nor the manpower to cover the country themselves, they

A wide variety of items were created to promote the new taste sensation.

The entire family enjoys a Sunday drive in the country.

sold franchises, buying the syrup from Coca-Cola and selling it, with a slight markup, to the bottlers—allowing all the partners to profit on every bottle of Coca-Cola sold.

- To get stores to accept the new bottles, many companies agreed to deliver five cases and only charge for four.
- In exchange, the Coca-Cola Company created oilcloth streamers to go over the front door of the stores with the words, "Ice Cold Coca-Cola for Sale Here."
- Initially, the franchises were called "parent bottlers," and many did very well.
- It is told that, in 1902, Crawford Johnson went to Birmingham, Alabama, with $12,000 in borrowed cash and a borrowed mule named Bird to establish a bottling plant; within a year he was able to move to larger quarters and buy Bird.
- By 1904, the annual sale of Coca-Cola syrup reached one million gallons, produced in 123 plants nationwide.
- By 1909, the standard bottle is carrying the Coca-Cola trademark in script form on one side and a paper label on the other.
- Many are now manufacturing bottles using the script trademark on the shoulder of the bottle so it can be more readily seen by the consumer.
- Nationwide, ingenious methods are being employed to increase the visibility of Coca-Cola, including playing cards, pocketknives, desk clocks, matches, purses and other novelties.

IS THIS YOU?

LADIES! If you suffer from headache, backache, sideache, pains in limbs and joints, falling feeling, bearing-down pressure pains, pains low down in stomach, numbness, nervousness, irregular functions, and feel weak, miserable, unable to attend to your household or social duties,—if you suffer from any of these symptoms of

FEMALE TROUBLE

you are surely sick, and need the health-giving assistance to be found in Cardui, or Woman's Relief.

This is the woman's medicine, about which you have so often heard,—but have you ever tried it?

If not, it would be worth your while to see if it is not, perhaps, the very medicine you need for your trouble.

Remember that Cardui's reputation for being a good female remedy is based on what it has done for other women.

Its success, in benefiting sick women, after other methods of treatment had failed, has shown that it is a medicinal preparation of strictly scientific value, for such cases of female sickness as are due to disorder of the womanly organs.

If you suffer, then, from any female complaint, you are earnestly urged to take

WINE OF CARDUI

Mrs. Rosa B. Trice, of Pittsburg, Tex., writes:
"Two years ago, the birth of my baby left me in a very bad state. I suffered with very bad backache, headache, swollen stomach, and pain low down in my side, in my ovaries. I was awful pale and weak and for 11 months I did not come around.

"I tried many remedies without relief; my doctor could not help me; I only got worse. I could hardly sleep at night and thought I should have to have an operation, but at last began to take Cardui.

"The first bottle did me good.

"I am now on my sixth bottle. My ovaries hardly ever hurt me now, my whites are cured and I am better than I have been in the past five years."

Cardui is for sale by all reliable druggists, in $1 bottles, with full directions for use, in seven languages.

Try it.

THE CHATTANOOGA MEDICINE CO.
Chattanooga, Tenn.

- Competitors are everywhere: Moxie in the Northeast; Dr. Pepper débuted in Waco, Texas; Hires Root Beer was bottled first in Philadelphia and Pepsi-Cola was organized in New Bern, North Carolina.
- Many competitors are playing off the Cola name, including Celery Cola, Koca-Nola, Gay-Ola, Roxa-Kola; other competitors include Iron Brew, Phospho-Crew and Marrowfood.
- Nationwide, all bottlers will produce 65 million bottles of soft drink in 1909.
- Extensive efforts are under way to find suitable bottles and bottle caps, as are experiments to find a liner for the inside of bottle caps.
- In keeping with the Pure Food Laws, advertisements now feature the words, "Purity Our Motto," and "No Hands Touch It."
- Also, anti-Coca-Cola crusades were mounted, fueled by rumors of the drink's harmful effects.
- For a short time, the army prohibited the sale of Coca-Cola at post exchanges.
- Coca-Cola has recently built a new factory at the corner of Marietta and Magnolia Streets in Atlanta at a cost of $250,000; the building, constructed of reinforced concrete with concrete floors, is already being called an architectural masterpiece.
- From 1886 to 1894, Coca-Cola was only dispensed at soda fountains; Joseph August Biedenharn of Vicksburg, Mississippi, was the first person to bottle the drink.
- At the time, Biedenharn was selling several thousand gallons of Coca-Cola syrup annually through his candy company to customers throughout the state.
- Bottling the drink was simply a way to get his product into the rural areas where soda fountains were scarce.
- The first bottles contained six ounces and were packed upside down in wooden cases to keep the wire and cork caps in place.
- A case of Coca-Cola was $0.70, while a case of soda-water sold for $0.60.

Life in the Community: Chattanooga, Tennessee

- Chattanooga is also the home of Wine of Cardui, a "woman's relief" medicine sold by all druggists for $1 per bottle; according to *Cardui Fashion Magazine*, published in Chattanooga for women nationwide, a complete home treatment for women includes Wine of Cardui, Thedford's Black Draught for the liver, and Cardui Wash, an antiseptic.
- Chattanooga ministers are calling on their congregations to provide relief funds to the stricken Sicilians, injured in an earthquake; on the first day of the drive, the "philosophers" of the Mountain City Club announced a contribution of $36.
- The city is watching with fascination the development, by a local inventor using a lightweight engine, of the Hemstreet flying machine; recently, 5,000 people went to see his latest creations.

Umbrella Rock — Lookout Mountain, Chattanooga, Tennessee   115

Photo by W. M. Cline Co.   65091

- The job-starved city is excited by rumors that W. J. Oliver will soon begin work on building the Ooltewah track for the Chattanooga Railroad; contracts may run as high as $8 million.
- Efforts to build a tuberculosis hospital in the city are going at full speed; the Women's Club is giving everyone an opportunity to donate $1 toward the purchase of land.
- The Imperial Café, Chattanooga's largest restaurant, is closing, forced out of business, its owners say, by the new prohibition laws in Tennessee.
- Although it is illegal to serve liquor, whiskey manufacturing continues in the city.
- The White Oak Distillery is currently selling four quarts of Hamilton Company Corn for $2.50; Tennessee residents may order from White Oak Distillery by writing E. R. Betterton and Co. in Cincinnati, Ohio.
- Ads are also appearing in the *Chattanooga Daily Times*, advertising, "Cascade Pure Whisky, Physicians everywhere recommend Cascade for medicinal purposes because of its purity and quality," with ad notes saying, "All shipments made in securely packed, plain boxes—nothing of any kind on the box to indicate the contents."
- Items listed in the "Lost" column of the newspaper include, "Basketball in alley back of Y.W.C.A. gymnasium Monday night," a "White Pomeranian dog, either in station at Chattanooga or off baggage car Southern Railroad Train, No. 14," and "Lost—Between Broad and Cedar Streets, silver mesh purse, with 'Billy and Fred' engraved. Ten small coins inclosed. Finder please telephone Main 2854."
- Now that telephone business has increased, Postal Telegraph and Cable Company is fighting in court for the right to erect its own lines between Chattanooga and Knoxville; the company currently leases the wires of the Cumberland Telephone Company.

CURRENT JOKE:

First Man: Did you hear about the man who named his Ford after his wife?
Second Man: How funny!
First Man: Not at all. After he got it, he found he couldn't control it.

FROM SIGNAL POINT, SIGNAL MOUNTAIN, CHATTANOOGA, TENN.   B-143

- The city has seen a number of the new Model T Fords crowd the streets; now being sold for $850, the cars are being purchased by doctors, lawyers and businessmen who can't bring themselves to pay $2,000 for an automobile.
- Visitors to the city from Atlanta often stop to buy candlewick bedspreads, also known as turfed bedspreads, which are displayed along the roadways for tourists to buy.
- The city's hopes of developing a steel industry and becoming "the Pittsburgh of the South" died in the 1890s, so city fathers are focusing on textiles as a way to bring jobs to the city.
- A new religious community, although small, is attracting attention because of its affinity for snakes; started in the town of Grasshopper, the Church of God with Signs Following After has formed around the last verses of the Gospel of Mark: "And these signs shall follow them that believe: In my name shall they cast out devils; they shall speak with new tongues; they shall take up serpents; and if they drink any deadly thing, it shall not hurt them; they shall lay hands on the sick, and they shall recover."

Competitors are everywhere, vying for the new soft drink market.

HISTORICAL SNAPSHOT
1909

- Railroads were the nation's largest industry, employing 1.7 million people
- The number of persons engaged in "professional service" reached 4.4 million, more than double that of the same category in the 1890 census
- Composer Gustav Mahler was serving as principal conductor of the Metropolitan Opera in New York
- The poverty line, under which about 40 percent of workers lived, was pegged at $660 a year
- Radical labor leader Frank Little was sentenced to 30 days in prison in Spokane, Washington, for reading aloud the Declaration of Independence
- Paul Ehrlick's discovery of Salvarsan 606, a miracle cure for syphilis, was hailed as both a medical blessing and an enticement to sin
- Missouri's Christian Endeavor Society attempted to ban movies that displayed kissing
- A skeptical Wall Street refused to list any automobile shares on the New York Stock Exchange
- The average man earned $15 for a 58-hour week; approximately 42 percent, or $326, was spent annually on food
- The National Negro Committee, formed in 1909, became the NAACP, founded by Jane Addams, John Dewey and W.E.B. Du Bois, its only black officer
- On the last day of 1908, Wilbur Wright's airplane stayed in the air two hours and 20 minutes; as 1909 drew to a close, the nation boasted 40 civilian pilots
- Nationwide, more than 10,000 nickelodeons existed, charging $0.05 for an hour of one-reel movies, vaudeville routines and an occasional dog act
- The Flexner report condemned U.S. medical schools as being inferior to European schools, launching a $600 million medical reform effort
- The term "progressive" came into usage to describe the reform movements battling the power and privilege of the wealthy, government corruption, unsafe labor conditions and the plight of the poor
- Reflecting the increased sales of parlor pianos, more than two billion copies of sheet music were sold; ragtime was at its peak
- Beta Theta Pi boasted the largest number of fraternity members in America with 116,000, while Phi Beta Phi was the largest sorority, at 15,404
- Clark University president Stanley Hall invited Sigmund Freud and Carl Jung to receive honorary degrees
- A bison refuge was established near Boise, Idaho
- The wealthiest Americans included the Vanderbilts, Goulds, Astors, Rockefellers, Morgans, Mackays, Havemeyers, Fields, Belmonts, Whitneys, Leitners, Goelets, Lorillands, Carnegies and Armours

1909 ECONOMIC PROFILE

The national consumer expenditures (per capita income) in 1909 were:

Auto Parts, Gas and Oil	$1.96
Auto Purchases	$1.85
Clothing	$30.00
Food	$81.43
Furniture	$3.25
Housing	$61.48
Intercity Transport	$2.97
Local Transport	$5.12
Personal Business	$9.61
Personal Care	$2.88
Physicians and Dentists	$4.15
Private Education and Research	$4.59
Recreation	$9.49
Religion/Welfare Activities	$9.05
Telephone and Telegraph	$0.91
Tobacco	$6.33
Utilities	$4.00
Per Capita Consumption	$318.42

Annual Income, Standard Jobs

Average of all Industries, Excluding Farm Labor	$594.00
Average of all Industries, Including Farm Labor	$544.00
Bituminous Coal Mining	$0.28/Hour
Building Trades, Union Workers	$0.45/Hour
Clerical Workers, Manufacturing and Steam Railroads	$1,136.00
Domestics	$420.00
Farm Labor	$328.00
Federal Employees, Executive Departments	$1,106.00
Finance, Insurance and Real Estate	$1,263.00
Gas and Electricity Workers	$618.00
Lower-Skilled Labor	$443.00
Manufacturing, Payroll	$0.15/Hour
Manufacturing, Union Workers	$0.39/Hour
Medical/Health Services Workers	$326.00
Ministers	$831.00
Nonprofit Organization Workers	$741.00
Postal Employees	$0.38/Hour
Public School Teachers	$476.00

Women's Secrets, or How to be Beautiful, by Grace Shirley:

"The Teeth:

That the parting of rosy lips should disclose uneven, unhealthy, discolored teeth is a sin for which parents are almost entirely responsible. The care of a child's teeth is one of the most important duties of motherhood, and criminal carelessness alone can cause this duty to be neglected...

Always use the best tooth powder that it is possible to obtain, as it will be found that the best is not always the cheapest.

If the teeth, the eyeteeth especially, are inclined to be too yellow, a little powdered pumice stone on a bit of linen will remove it effectually.

When the proper tooth powder or other dentifrice cannot be procured, use a little pure olive castile soap and tepid water. Never put very cold or very hot water upon the teeth, as it is more likely to crack the enamel. A few simple recipes for the care of the teeth and gums may be found useful:

Precipitated chalk, 1 pound
Powdered orris root, 0.5 pound
Powdered camphor, 0.5 pound

Reduce the camphor to a fine powder by adding a little alcohol and rubbing in a mortar. Sift through muslin and bottle, taking care to keep it tightly corked.

An excellent toothpaste is made as follows:

Peruvian bark, 1 scruple
Powdered orris root, 1 scruple
Powdered charcoal, 1 scruple
Tincture of myrrh, 0.5 drachm
Add sufficient clarified honey to form a paste"

State and Local Government
   Workers...................... $696.00
Steam Railroads, Wage Earners $644.00
Street Railway Workers............. $671.00
Telegraph Industry Workers........ $622.00
Telephone Industry Workers........ $430.00
Wholesale and Retail Trade
   Workers...................... $561.00

Selected Prices

Alcohol, Whiskey, Rye, per Gallon...... $3.15
Automobile, Rambler Model 44 .... $2,250.00
Cigar $0.05
Coffee Pot, One Pint $1.25
Cold Cream, per Jar $0.35
Cruise, to the Orient; 80 Days $300.00
Dentist, Fillings $1.00
Eggs, per Dozen.................... $0.30
Hat, Man's Deluxe $6.00
Horse Race $0.50
Hotel Room, Richmond, Virginia,
   per Day $1.50
House, Rental, Seven Rooms,
   per Month $19.00

Iron Stove $19.50
Lawn Mower $6.50
Playing Cards, Bicycle $0.25
Sanitarium, 10 Days' Care . . . . $30–$60.00
Sewing Machine $9.85
Stockings, Ladies', Silk $4.50
Tooth Soap $0.25
Violin, Student $15.00

The History of Coca-Cola

- Coca-Cola traces its roots to May 8, 1886, the same year the Statue of Liberty was unveiled in New York harbor.
- Atlanta pharmacist John Styth Pemberton is credited with creating the popular soft drink, taking a jug of his new reddish-brown syrup to Willis E. Venable, the manager of the soda fountain at Jacobs' Pharmacy.
- Venable's soda fountain was an impressive 25 feet long and considered one of the most popular of the day.
- The new drink was named after two of the constituents of the new product, coca and cola.
- The first advertisement for Coca-Cola appeared in *The Atlanta Daily Journal* three weeks later calling the new soda fountain drink, "Delicious, Refreshing, Exhilarating, and Invigorating."
- A competitor, who ran an advertisement the same day, was "the marvelous Moxie Nerve Food on draught at H. C. Beerman's Soda Water Palace."
- During the first year, only 25 gallons of the syrup, enough for 3,200 drinks, was sold, earning Pemberton approximately $50; that same year he invested $73.96 in advertising.
- In July 1887, because of ill health, Pemberton offered to sell a two-thirds interest in the Coca-Cola formula for $1,200 and retire his debts of $283.39.
- By December, the Coca-Cola formula had been sold again for $1,200.
- The resulting firm of Walker, Candler and Company then acquired the remaining one third of the rights from Pemberton for $550, using funds advanced by Asa G. Candler.
- By August 1888, Candler bought out his partners and became the sole proprietor of Coca-Cola.
- Through his drugstore, he sold Coca-Cola and several other proprietary products including Botanic Blood Balm, Delectalave, and Everlasting Cologne.
- By 1890, when Candler's businesses were grossing $100,000 annually, the 38-year-old businessman sold his other interests to devote his time to developing Coca-Cola.
- In 1892, the Coca-Cola Company was formed and 500 shares of stock were issued with a par value of $100.
- The company grew rapidly, and after 1896, the dividends were as high as $3,000 dollars per share, or 30 times the par value of the stock.
- Early advertisements claimed the drink "Cures Headaches. Renews the exhausted brain and body caused by excessive mental and physical labor, loss of sleep, etc."
- In 1896, the company's publicity campaign was costing $80,000 a year and Coca-Cola syrup for soda fountains was sold outside the United States, including Canada and Hawaii.

- By 1898, Candler reported the sale of 214,000 gallons of Coca-Cola syrup, and by 1901, the total had risen to 370,877 gallons with a 26 percent, and then a 45 percent, increase in sales the following two years.
- Coca-Cola in bottles was featured in newspaper advertising for the first time in 1902.
- At the same time, the National Bottlers' Association was calling for federal legislation to prevent bottlers from stealing each other's soft drink bottles and reusing them.
- In 1905, glass blowers in Terre Haute, Indiana, sent out a circular calling for their friends and families to break all bottles before throwing them away, preventing their reuse and creating more work for bottle blowers.
- During the annual meeting in 1909 of the American Bottlers' Protective Association, the convention opposed the sale of any soft drinks made from extractives of the cola nut and the coca leaf, and containing caffeine, though little was said about the growing problem of unsanitary conditions in many bottling plants nationwide.
- By 1909, each share of Coca-Cola stock was worth more than $10,000.

Advertisement: "Carbonators for Dispensers," *Practical Druggist* **and** *Review of Reviews*, **January 1902:**

"The tendency of the times is toward elimination of expenses and the consolidation of profits. Many soda-water dispensers are already combining the two profits of the carbonator and dispenser by making their own charged water. The time is coming very soon when every soda-water dispenser will be operating an automatic carbonator in direct connection with his foundation. It is done today in all of the large stores and in many of the small ones. It requires no extra space, as the apparatus can be placed on a shelf; it need require no belted power; it needs no attendance or attention, not even oiling; it supplies automatically the sharpest kind of charged water at uniform pressure in an unlimited flow as needed; and, finally, it doubles the present profits of the dispenser. It is the dispenser's great opportunity to double his profits simply by doing now what he must do soon."

CHICAGO.

During the past month the wholesale drug trade of this city saw the high water mark of its fall business. From now on the volume of orders will somewhat diminish until the tide of spring business begins to rise directly after the holidays. For the balance of this year the burden of transacting a successful season's business rests upon the retailer.

Wholesalers and manufacturers generally seem well satisfied with the fall business. Almost without exception they report that they have transacted a greater volume of business than a year ago. This is encouraging in view of the fact that other lines of trade have not enjoyed as great prosperity. Orders, however, have been small, but many. Stocks are not being completed but instead the tendency is to buy as few goods as possible and still maintain an up-to-date store. Mail orders are very much in evidence.

Nevertheless an attitude of great optimism pervades the trade. Times are merely slow, not bad, and there seem to be excellent prospects of good times ahead. Accordingly business is merely held in check, not depressed; and a great store of latent energy is accumulating.

C. R. D. A. Quarterly and Executive Board Meetings.

The regular C. R. D. A. quarterly and monthly executive board meetings were held in the Northwestern University building on October 10, the board meeting in the afternoon and the association in the evening.

At the board meeting, Chairman Holthofer of the U. S. P. and N. F. committee reported that his committee had this year determined upon circularizing the entire list of 3,000 physicians in Cook county instead of upon having the various druggists suggest the names of physicians whom each wanted the literature sent to, as heretofore. In order to enable the committee to carry out this purpose an appropriation of $350 was made to be added to a similar amount then in the hands of the committee.

A counter wrapper and blotter system was officially endorsed.

Greater promptness in the payment of rebates in the rebate plan of securing price-protection was urged, and the matter referred to the jobbers' committee, which later reported it would confer with the jobbers on the subject without delay.

The advisability of employing a fire insurance adjuster will be submitted to a special committee appointed for the purpose.

National Committeeman Zuber reported that the Boehm plan of price-protection would be the first to be considered by the national committee at its meeting in December to which will be invited representatives from the proprietary association and the wholesalers' association.

The quarterly meeting of all the C. R. D. A. members held the same evening, drew a splendid attendance.

President Hoelzer, reviewing the work of the preceding (this) quarter in his address, cordially thanked the association members for their loyal support in taking the "C. R. D. A. Special" to the Niagara Falls convention, especially in view of the efforts on the part of the A. D. S. to make its "special" the official conveyance. Mr. Hoelzer strongly resented the slurring inference cast upon the officers of the C. R. D. A. by the official organ of A. D. S. and stated his position in clear and unmistakable language. He had a few encouraging remarks to make in connection with the work of the U. S. P. and N. F. committee. He closed with a statement to the effect that he would not be a candidate for re-election under any circumstances.

Secretary Light's report for the third quarter showed receipts amounting to $3,481.97 and expenditures amounting to $3,369.98 leaving a balance for the quarter of $111.99. Accordingly with the fund carried over from the preceding quarter there was on September 30 $1,424.29 in the Northwest bank and $32.99 in the secretary's hands.

Chairman J. P. Crowley of the executive committee reported that the advertising committee was just about to start on its fall campaign. In the course of his remarks he also took occasion to approve the action taken by the executive board in voting a regular remuneration to the chairman of the U. S. P. and N. F. committee.

Chairman Mahaffey of the jobbers' committee reported that very few complaints had been entered and that it seemed to be the almost universal opinion that conditions were wholly satisfactory.

Two resolutions were adopted—one making the executive board "consist of the officers and nine trustees," and the other reading as follows:

"Resolved, That the president instruct the executive committee, or appoint a special committee of nine members, three from each of the geographical divisions of the city, viz., North, West

Annihilator of Space

To be within arm's reach of distant cities it is only necessary to be within arm's reach of a Bell Telephone. It annihilates space and provides instantaneous communication, both near and far.

There can be no boundaries to a telephone system as it is now understood and demanded. Every community is a center from which people desire communication in every direction, always with contiguous territory, often with distant points. Each individual user may at any moment need the long distance lines which radiate from his local center.

An exchange which is purely local has a certain value. If, in addition to its local connections, it has connections with other contiguous localities, it has a largely increased value.

If it is universal in its connections and inter-communications, it is indispensable to all those whose social or business relations are more than purely local.

A telephone system which undertakes to meet the full requirements of the public must cover with its exchanges and connecting links the whole country.

The Bell Telephone System annihilates space for the business man to-day. It brings him and any of his far-away social or business interests together.

AMERICAN TELEPHONE AND TELEGRAPH COMPANY
AND ASSOCIATED COMPANIES

One Policy,   One System,   Universal Service.

Changing America: 1909

- Approximately nine million immigrants had come to America since 1900—about the entire population of the country in 1820.
- New York City had more Italians than did Rome, more Jews than in Warsaw, more Irish than in Dublin and more blacks than in any city in the world.
- Fully one seventh of the population of the United States was foreign-born.
- In Boston, Chicago, Cleveland, New York, Philadelphia, Pittsburgh and St. Louis, the foreign-born and children of the first generation outnumbered the native population.
- Cities were growing so rapidly, the poorest areas held upwards of 600,000 people per square mile.
- The Committee on Congestion of Population in New York found the average annual wage among 339,221 workers was $543.17, $257 less than the $800 a year they declared to be a minimum standard of living.

A new pipe dream.

"Poppy and Her Aunt Lucie," a fictional short story by Anne Story Allen, *The Ladies' World*, August 1910:

"When Elwood Markham decided to marry he cast about in his mind for a suitable wife.

'Here I am,' he said to himself, 'established in business, sound in mind and body, and with enough leisure to enjoy a certain amount of travel. Above all, it is, when you come to think of it, a man's part in life to found a family, to think not of himself alone, but of those who come after him.'

Having said this to himself, Mr. Markham stretched his well-shod feet a trifle nearer the fire, leaned back more negligently in his chair and yawned.

'You are a self-made man, Markham, and you have not botched your job (chuckle, chuckle). You started with rather less than the proverbial penny, and here you see yourself a millionaire; and if you care to raise your eyes to the mirror, above you—ah, that is right—you see yourself still a young man, albeit your locks are whitening at the temples. And vastly becoming it is, too (ha, ha)! You are the president of the Adjustable Stopper concern, its founder, director, principal stockholder and general boss—forgive this flippancy.

'And who is the inventor of this wonderful Adjustable Stopper? Elwood Markham, who saw the need, the empty gaping necks of countless stopperless bottles, and recognized the futility of bottles without stoppers, and who filled the gap of gaps? Elwood Markham. Think of the homes that today are supplied with Adjustable Stoppers just because you had the sense to think about it and the genius to invent the stopper. Or rather, don't bother to think of those homes, but let your mind dwell on those fat bank accounts of yours, of this house, your horses, your motors, your steady and increasing incomes. Oh, Elwood Markham, think of yourself and have a bully old time.'

And the man in front of the fire stretched his toes once more toward the genial warmth and relaxed even more comfortably into the padded leather of his big chair.

'In all the circle of your acquaintances, whom do you know as great as yourself,' asked his thoughts, 'tell me candidly.'

A delightful little wriggle crept down Markham's spine, and he almost spoke aloud: 'No one.'

'Ah,' cried his thoughts. 'To be sure! No one! And who, may I ask, among the women you know, is in the slightest degree worthy of becoming your wife?'

And Elwood Markham's chest puffed itself out, and his eyes flashed up at the mirror above him; he put a white hand up to the silver locks that made his temples look intellectual, and except for his innate modesty, would have cried out to the four walls of the room: 'No one!' "

"New York Fashion Hints," by May Manton, *Cardui Fashion Magazine*, Chattanooga, Tennessee, 1907-08:

"This season's fashions promise to be exceedingly attractive as well as varied. There is every evidence that the short walking skirt will continue in favor, and there are a number of smart models shown for the tailored costumes that make every woman's standby. For these, long sleeves will be the rule and a rather simple finish. Cutaway coats of all lengths will have great vogue and every variation of the plaited skirt will be seen, although plain gored ones also will be worn in the heavier materials. Applied bands promise to retain their vogue whatever form the skirt may take. For the lightweight materials of the early season, the kilted models will undoubtedly be popular, but heavier materials become a burden when so made, and skirts with fewer plaits will be given the preference for these. In addition to the cutaway coats, there will be a number of half-fitted ones with box fronts worn, and the long coat of general use that can be slipped on over any gown is promised extended favor. This last will be noted both loose and semi-fitted, and makes an altogether desirable garment, whichever form may be chosen."

1910-1919

America was booming during the second decade of the century, and economic excitement was in the air. Anything seemed possible to those who had money to invest or the resources to explore the possibilities. America's upper class now enjoyed the world's finest transportation—by train and automobile—and spent considerable time discovering new forms of entertainment. At the same time, an emerging middle class was showing that it was capable of carrying a greater load of managerial decisions, freeing factory owners and stockholders to travel, experiment, and study ways to cure the ills of the poor. Millions of dollars were poured into libraries, parks and literacy classes designed to uplift the immigrant masses flooding to American shores. America was prospering and, at the same time, the country's elite were reevaluating America's role as an emerging world power which no longer had to look to Britain for approval.

Immigration continued at a pace of one million annually in the first four years of the decade. Between 1910 and 1913, some 11 million immigrants—an all-time record—entered the United States. The wages of unskilled workers fell, but the number of jobs expanded dramatically. Manufacturing employment rose by 3.3 million, or close to six percent in a year during the period. At the same time, earnings of skilled workers rose substantially and resulted in a backlash focused on protecting American workers' jobs. As a result, a series of anti-immigration laws was passed culminating in 1917 with permanent bars to the free flow of immigrants into the United States. From the beginning of World War I until 1919, the number of new immigrants fell sharply while the war effort was demanding more and more workers. As a result, wages for low-skilled work rose rapidly, forcing the managerial class—often represented by the middle class—to find new and more streamlined ways to get the jobs done—often by employing less labor or more technology.

In the midst of these dynamics, the Progressive Movement, largely a product of the rising middle class, began to shape the decade, raising questions about work safety, the rights of individuals, the need for clean air and fewer work hours. It was a people's movement that grasped the immediate impact of linking the media to its cause. The results were significant and widespread. South Carolina prohibited the employment of children under 12 in mines, factories, and textile mills; Delaware began to frame employer's liability laws; the direct election of U.S. Senators was approved; and nationwide communities argued loudly over the right and ability of women to vote and the need and lawfulness of alcohol consumption.

During the decade, motorized tractors changed the lives of farmers, and electricity extended the day of urban dwellers. Powered trolley cars, vacuum cleaners, hair dryers, and electric ranges moved onto the modern scene. Wireless communications bridged San Francisco to New York and New York to Paris; in 1915, the Bell system alone operated six million telephones, which were considered essential in most middle class homes as the decade drew to a close. As the sale of parlor pianos hit a new high, more than two billion copies of sheet music were sold as ragtime neared its peak. Thousands of Bibles were placed in hotel bedrooms by the Gideon Organization of Christian Commercial Travelers, reflecting both the emerging role of the traveling "drummer" or salesman and the evangelical nature of the Progressive Movement.

Yet in the midst of blazing prosperity, the nation was changing too rapidly for many—demographically, economically, and morally. Divorce was on the rise. One in 12 marriages ended in divorce in 1911, compared with one in 85 only six years earlier. The discovery of a quick treatment for syphilis was hailed as both a miracle and an enticement to sin. As the technology and sophistication of silent movies improved yearly, the Missouri Christian Endeavor Society tried to ban films that included any kissing. At the same time, the rapidly expanding economy, largely without government regulation, began producing marked inequities of wealth—affluence for the few and hardship for the many. The average salary of $750 a year was rising, but not fast enough for many.

But one of the biggest stories was America's unabashed love affair with the automobile. By 1916, the Model T cost less than half its 1908 price, and nearly everyone dreamed of owning a car. Movies were also maturing during the period, growing rapidly as an essential entertainment for the poor. Some 25 percent of the population, including many newly arrived immigrants, went weekly to the nickelodeon to marvel at the exploits of Charlie Chaplin, Mary Pickford, and Douglas Fairbanks, Sr.—each drawing big salaries in the silent days of movies.

The second half of the decade was marked by the Great War, later to be known as the First World War. Worldwide, it cost more than nine million lives and swept away four empires—the German, the Austro-Hungarian, the Russian, and the Ottoman—and with them the traditional aristocratic style of leadership in Europe. It bled the treasuries of Europe dry and brought the United States forward as the richest country in the world.

When the war broke out in Europe, American exports were required to support the Allied war effort, driving the well-oiled American industrial engine into high gear. Then, when America's intervention in 1917 required the drafting of two million men, women were given their first taste of economic independence. Millions stepped forward to produce the materials needed by a nation. As a result, when the men came back from Europe, America was a changed place for both the well-traveled soldier and the newly trained female worker. Each had acquired an expanded view of the world. Yet women possessed full suffrage in only Wyoming, Colorado, Utah, and Idaho.

The war forced Americans to confront one more important transformation. The United States had become a full participant in the world economy; tariffs on imported goods were reduced and exports reached all-time highs in 1919, further stimulating the American economy.

1910 NEWS PROFILE

"The Problem of the Millionaire," by Henry Waldorf Francis, *Overland Monthly,*
San Francisco, California, September 1910:

"The indiscriminate denunciation of the millionaire solely and simply because he is a millionaire, and without regard to his personality or the use he makes of his wealth, is as senseless and without justification as it would be to rage against dynamite or strychnine because they can be employed in illegal, dangerous and nefarious operations.

This is the era of the railroad, the steamship—even the aeroplane—not of the stagecoach, the brig and the gas balloon. It is the era of 'big things.' Modern enterprises require large capital and the corporation, and it is well to remember that but for corporations and capitalists we would not have the railroad, the trolley, the telegraph, telephone—any of the wonderful mediums of communication and transportation that have revolutionized life and thought, and compared to which the marvels, as we once thought them, wrought by Aladdin's Lamp are mere commonplaces. Since we are—or the majority of the public is—opposed to the Government (The Nation) engaged in enterprises of a business character, the Panama Canal excepted, we can look nowhere but to private sources for improvements and progress not only in business matters, but in such scientific and eleemosynary lines as great hospitals and colleges, for research into the causes of diseases, crushing diseases out and a hundred other benefits to humanity. Under our system of government and with our jealous limiting of its powers, the United States would never have reached the remarkable state of development it has, and individually we would in many important respects be helpless indeed, and certainly would not be enjoying the fruits of modern inventive genius. For these things are indebted to aggregations of private capital, their development being beyond the means of any single individual, even if any single individual had been or would be willing to assume the risk that always attends a new departure from beaten paths. To accept the benefits which aggregated capital confers and then to not only denounce it but seek to destroy it—not its results—oh, no, we will keep them!—simply because it is capital, certainly looks like the height of ingratitude.

The choice is between capitalism and socialism, and beautiful as the theories of socialism undoubtedly are, until socialism can formulate some better scheme of distribution than is comprehended by 'from everyone according to his ability, to everyone according to his needs,' it will never win the majority of people to its support. The tendency is to 'bear the ills we know rather than fly to those we know not of.' Admitting the possibility of being able to tell whether one is always giving 'according to his ability,' needs are changing things, largely imaginary and born of contrasts—and who is to determine what my needs are—why I should be satisfied with a cotton suit instead of an all-wool one, and do not need the latter as much as the next man, etc., etc.? Plainly, for any man or body of men to impose their ideas of my needs upon me without regard to my own notions on the subject would be exercising despotic power. This is the question—the question of the willing subordination of the individual, of envy and Self—with the aided solution of distribution—that socialism will have to offer some better, more explicit, commend-itself-to-the-reason answer before it is likely to be adopted to the extent its ultra advocates preach and urge it. The writer is not opposing socialism in toto, because in a very large measure he believes in it, and that it is practical, and he realizes as everyone with eyes and a modicum of sense and feeling must, the terrible inequalities prevailing under our present social system, and that there is something, somewhere, radically wrong with it, becoming daily more and more intolerable, and which being wrong cannot endure. Only the Right can defy time; nothing that is Wrong can, although its righting may be slow and tedious, and its seeming triumph often. It is probably true that all of us are more or less, consciously or unconsciously—that is to say, all of us who have to struggle for existence and earn it by the sweat of our brow—prejudiced against the possessor of wealth. We do not forget what the old copybook of our school days sought to impress upon us that 'money is the root of evil.' The copybook, however, was misleading. It is not the use, but the abuse of money that is the root of evil; and the copybook would have been more accurate if it had said, 'GREED is the root of evil.'

But while the ambition to acquire wealth is laudatory rather than condemnatory, it is entirely plain that the millionaire can and often does use the power it gives him to oppress the people, and that the public should be protected against the wealth it creates being employed for purely selfish ends, and mere accumulation—against, for instance, such ways of using it as 'cornering' or attempting to 'corner' any of the necessaries of life—a crime in every civilized country in the world except the United States—corrupting public officials or private persons, or for any purpose detrimental to morality and the public interest. It is entirely within constitutional legislative domain to accomplish this; in other words, it is within the power of the public itself, whenever it becomes wise and united enough to assert itself and subordinate the individual to the community.

The greatest danger lies in the inactive increase in wealth—this is to say, its continual compounding in the mere course of time without labor on the part of the owner or any return to the community. This results from the privilege of disposing of property by will and creating trusts thereunder—a privilege that should be greatly limited. It should not be possible for a millionaire to so tie up his estate that when his unborn or infant grandson comes into possession of his legacy it will amount to 20, 30 or 50 times the original amount. This is only another system of the primogeniture, and in its effects is even more pernicious to society. Prevent this and one of the great evils of millionaires—the dead in effect dominating the living—will disappear. Let the millionaire enjoy honestly every dollar he earns while living, but limit the amount he may devise or bequeath to heirs or individuals or for other than public purposes—which can be done, among other ways, by death and inheritance taxation—and absolutely stop the now common practical suspension of ownership. Let him divide his wealth while living if he pleases—divided wealth returns ultimately and comparatively quickly to the public—but prevent his making money for others while he is in the grave. It will be necessary, of course, to guard against the evasion of laws made to this end. This can be done. Contrary to the general prevailing idea, there is no constitutional right to make a will. It is wholly a statutory privilege, and any state legislature could revoke it altogether any

day it saw fit, and oblige all property to pass under a statute of distributions—a fact every lawyer is or ought to be fully aware of. Other safeguards against the millionaire acquiring too great or oppressive power are a progressive income tax, progressive inheritance taxes, progressive taxes upon him generally on the correct theory that he requires and receives greater public protection and should pay a higher rate. In taxing he should follow the fire insurance companies dividing into ordinary, hazardous and extra hazardous risks and increasing the premium or rate accordingly as the individual has more at stake and requires more public protection. Coming to corporations, while they should not be hampered or their usefulness impaired or restricted by unwise or prejudiced legislation, and should not be set down as sinners and public enemies, because some of them have been and are, any more than

we should all be regarded as thieves because we have jails, they should be under strict Government supervision, limited as to the amount of dividends they may pay—allowance being made for improvements and depreciation liberally—and any surplus earned beyond fair returns should go into the Government treasury as a tax upon the franchise. In the case of railroads and other corporations of similar character, where the earnings exceed a fair return upon the investment after deductions for maintenance, depreciation and improvements, and the surplus has been taken as a tax in the manner stated, the toll charged to the public should be reduced, and in the event the reduced toll should fail to prove sufficient, then the Government should refund out of the surplus theretofore taken as a tax enough to make good the loss. In this way stockholders as well as the public would be protected and there would be no more 'melon cutting' at the community's expense. . . .

Money is like everything else: it can be used and it can be abused. It is for the public, which has the power whenever it sees fit to apply it, to enact such legislation as will prevent individual wealth from being oppressive, and it is not necessary to 'kill the goose which lays the golden egg' but to control the goose. France, England, Germany, by old age pensions, accident and other compulsory insurance, tenement and labor legislation, progressive income, death and inheritance taxes—and the new English Budget will even cover the 'unearned increment' in land—have been and are pointing out the road of progress—the road, if he would but see it, in which lies the security of the millionaire, the safeguard against violent revolution, the allaying of that 'class prejudice' in which there is so much danger. This legislation is beyond question 'socialistic' in its character and nature, but it is practical socialism that benefits society, and to which no one not entirely dominated by Greed and Self can with reason object. It is the United States—the United States that we have proudly held up as an example for the world—'the refuge for the oppressed'—that lags far, far behind in guarding and promoting the welfare of its citizens in every civilized country except Russia! (If Russia can be classed as civilized!) How long is this condition to last?"

1913 FAMILY PROFILE

Henry Jorgensen, already wealthy through Michigan copper and lumber investments, became a major player in the manufacture of Oldsmobile automobiles and engines before selling out in 1908 to travel with his wife Phoebe, enjoy life on the eastern shore of Maine and explore his new passion, rediscovering his heritage in Scandinavia.

Annual Income: The Jorgensens are currently living off their investments; the total assets of the family are more than $1.5 million.

Life at Home

- The Jorgensens live in Detroit in a 5,000-square-foot, three-story home with buff-colored brick trimmed with red sandstone.
- The hip roof is covered with green slate, and in the corners are impressive, Victorian towers.
- The interior of the house has paneled walls, decorated ceilings and marquetry floors with four-tone borders throughout; the house also features on the first floor a music hall, a separate library and complete study.
- A mural of a partially draped woman swinging on a garland of flowers is painted in the arched stairwells leading to the second floor, where it blends with the 18-foot stained glass window.
- The second story, which has 10 bedrooms, features a walnut-paneled music room dominated by a large pipe organ, which Phoebe takes great pride in playing for her children, grandchildren and guests.

Henry Jorgensen enjoys investing in new inventions and ventures.

Phoebe enjoys playing the pipe organ for her grandchildren.

- The floor of the massive room is covered with an oriental rug from Turkey.
- In recent years, Henry has added an "automobile room" to the house at the right rear of the first floor; the trade journal *Automobile* pointed out that with the rapidly growing popularity of the automobile, future houses might contain a similar room.
- Born in 1840 in Lansing, Michigan, Henry took an early interest in politics, winning office in the Michigan House of Representatives before running unsuccessfully for statewide office in his late 20s.
- Leaving southern Michigan in 1869, he went to Copper County in the state's upper peninsula, where he made a fortune.
- Beginning modestly enough as a merchant in Houghton, he participated in the organization of several copper mining companies.
- To keep the copper moving, he put his energy into expanding the transportation resources of the area and was successful in bringing to completion the Portage Lake and Lake Superior ship canals.
- He also helped organize two railroads, the Marguette, Houghton and Ontonagon and the Copper Range.
- When he was approached at the turn of the century by a friend about investing in horseless carriages, he was 59 years old, already rich and in semi-retirement.

Henry made a fortune in Michigan's upper peninsula.

- Initially, he regarded horseless carriages as an interesting idea requiring relatively little capital—about $10,000—even if the risk was high.

- The creation of the Olds Motor Company to manufacture the Oldsmobile automobile and the Olds engine also allowed him to work with one of his two sons.

- His son joined the company in 1899, becoming president after founder Ransom Olds left in 1904 in a dispute over control.

- Because Henry was always focused on work and promoting the economy of Michigan, he and Phoebe rarely traveled during his working years.

- One of the family's first trips abroad was an excursion to England two years ago to attend the coronation of King George V, following the death of King Edward VII.

- The long, luxury steamboat ride across the ocean provided Henry with lots of "thinking time," so they now take two cruises a year, frequently visiting Denmark, Sweden and occasionally Russia.

- He believes his great-grandfather came from Copenhagen, so he has hired a university professor to research the records.

- Henry and Phoebe also enjoy spending summers at their home on the eastern shore of Maine, which is good for his health, and where they can relax, walk the harbor area and visit the beaches.

Coronation of King George V. Procession passing through Whitehall.

One of the family's first trips abroad was to attend the coronation of King George V.

Four of a Kind raising a pair.

The Jorgensens enjoy spending summers at the shore.

Quicksteps through Scandinavia, by S.G. Bayne, 1908:

"We were not long making the run across the North Sea to Norway, and when we anchored in the harbor of Christiansand on a Sunday morning, we found the people in the gayest of attire going to church in boats, all bent on having a good time, and from what we could see they were certainly having it. Here the local fishermen supplied us with fresh sole right out of the fjord, and they were 'fjoine.' Some of our passengers left us to make their way up the coast, and we went on to Christiania, situated at the head of a long and beautiful fjord of the same name. We spent a delightful day in the capital among a gay and light-hearted crowd, all anxious to make it a delightful day for their visiting friends, the Scandinavian-Yankees. A crowd of two thousand people came to see us off and cheer us on the way. Just as we were moving out, King Edward VII and his wife passed into the harbor in their gorgeous new yacht. This yacht has four smokestacks in gold-leaf and black; the stairs leading down to the water are covered with velvet carpet in purple and gold; she sports the Royal Standard on her stern pole, and a pair of British battleships trail her as a convoy. Cleopatra's barge held the record for splendor for many long centuries, but I doubt if she could do that today with this craft in sight. Our vessel, the *Hellig Olav*, is a big thing in Norway, and so the King and Queen came on deck and saluted us, while we returned the compliment by playing 'God Save the King' as we passed out into the open sea. The Queen visits her mother and sister every summer, and Christiania is the port at which she lands, finishing the trip to Denmark by rail.

Our last port of call was Copenhagen, and after steaming through the Skager Rack and the Cattegat we had a look at Hamlet's castle at Elsinore, where the ghost used to 'visit the glimpses of the moon.' There was some kind of a convention of Hamlet's descendants and relatives going on in Copenhagen, and we could not get a room at any of the big hotels, but found quarters at the 'King of Denmark,' a small place which, while some distance from the local bowery, was still good enough for us."

- They often take the grandchildren and great-grandchildren to the shore with them, along with a handful of servants and nannies.
- One of their newest obsessions is the sound produced by the new and vastly improved phonographs now on the market; they have one at each of their homes.

Life at Work

- Jorgensen has made a fortune in Michigan copper and lumber in the years following the Civil War; for the past few years, he has been investing in real estate in Detroit and in new inventions that catch his fancy.
- In 1897, he was connected to Ransom Olds of Lansing, Michigan, through a friend who had already put money into the company.
- Olds desperately needed capital to keep alive his dream of making an affordable automobile, known as the Oldsmobile.
- Originally from Lansing, Henry has a long history of partnering with friends for investment purposes; in the 1880s, he was part of a group of investors who started City National Bank.

- Initially, in 1897, he came into the Olds company with four other investors who each put in $10,000; 18 months later he became the dominant player in the new company and active in its running.

- By 1899, the nominal capital in the company was $350,000, of which $200,000 was paid in; a total of $400 was invested by Olds himself, the rest by Jorgensen.

- To help Henry watch his investment, his son was named secretary and treasurer of the new company.

- As a businessman, Jorgensen's initial interest was in the Olds gasoline engine, which was already selling well; he was also intrigued by the possibilities of the horseless carriage.

- At first, he did not like the other term gaining popularity, a French term that his partner Ransom Olds favored, automobile.

- The investment in the Oldsmobile was often vexing for investor and inventor alike.

- Inventor Ransom Olds found that inviting others to invest brought much-needed capital, but unwanted advice, as well; he was often frustrated that outside investors were men who wanted to make money from a product about which they knew little or nothing.

- During an early board meeting, Olds was told, "We want you to make one perfect horseless carriage." Ultimately, the minutes of the meeting reflected a desire to make a "nearly perfect" carriage.

- A master at publicity, Olds promoted his new car constantly; in 1897, Olds' brother Wallace gained nationwide headlines when he drove the company's one motor vehicle from Lansing to Grand Lede and back, making the 12-mile return trip in one hour and 15 minutes.

- By 1901, the Oldsmobile was one of the biggest names in the fledgling industry; the car sold for $650 at a time when an imported, top-of-the-line French automobile cost up to $17,000.

Eugene Cooley, reflecting his decision in 1897 to be an early investor in the Oldsmobile:

"Here was a contrivance that would run on the road by means of power developed within itself. I did not see any great possibilities for it, but nevertheless any contrivance that would do that I felt was worthy of some encouragement. I am sure I did not see any great future for the invention, and I do not think others did, but we felt that if developed, the power vehicle would have some sales and that a business possibly could be developed which would show a profit. I am free to say that I had not the faintest vision of what was eventuated in the automobile business."

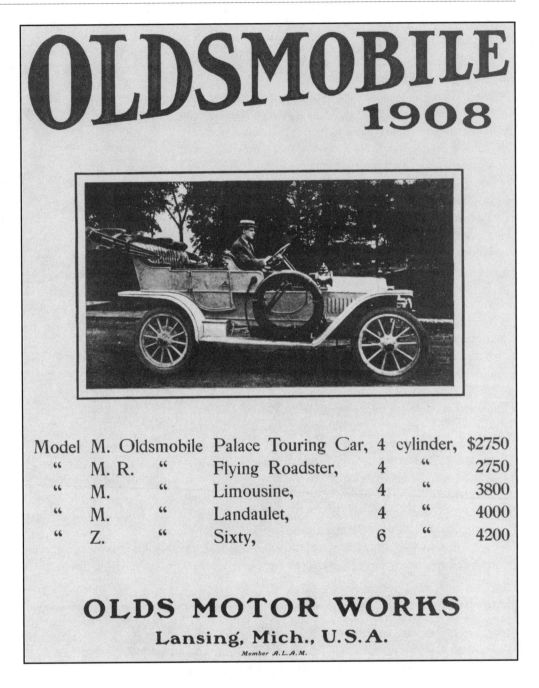

OLDSMOBILE 1908

Model	M.	Oldsmobile	Palace Touring Car,	4	cylinder,	$2750
"	M. R.	"	Flying Roadster,	4	"	2750
"	M.	"	Limousine,	4	"	3800
"	M.	"	Landaulet,	4	"	4000
"	Z.	"	Sixty,	6	"	4200

OLDS MOTOR WORKS
Lansing, Mich., U.S.A.
Member A.L.A.M.

- By 1902, the Olds company had selling agents throughout the East and Midwest, plus a few in the South and West.
- The Olds dealer in Denver, Colorado, reported that he sold 15 cars in the first four weeks of the year, six to doctors.
- That year, the company sold 3,700 vehicles; by 1903, Oldsmobile ads referred to "5,000 satisfied" customers.
- The nation's total automobile output in 1903 by all companies was 9,000 cars.
- Sales for the Oldsmobile totaled $2.3 million in 1903, up five times over the sales results of $410,000 in 1901.
- The curved-dash Olds was the talk of the industry.

- To conserve cash while growing so rapidly, Olds Motor Works insists that the burden of funding salaries at the factory be passed along to the dealer.

- Dealers' deposits often pay half the sum necessary to bring out a full year's production; in turn, to get their cash back as rapidly as possible, dealers require that their customers pay cash also.

- Olds believed that selling on credit only encouraged customers to be careless with a car they do not own and are paying for in installments.

- Working together, Olds, Jorgensen and his son streamlined the business, especially the manufacturing process; in January 1904, *Scientific American* singled out the Olds Motor Works as an operation that exemplified the new trend in automobile manufacturing.

- Unfortunately, by the time the article appeared, Ransom Olds had left the company in a battle of wills.

- Believing that the Oldsmobile runabout was beginning to be regarded as an inferior product, Henry wanted to replace the inexpensive model with a bigger, heavier, more expensive vehicle which was more reliable.

- Olds blamed the problems on inexperienced repairmen who did not understand the complexity of an automobile.

- Upon leaving, Olds created a new company and a new car, the REO, representing Ransom E. Olds' initials; Henry and his son, however, continued to manufacture Oldsmobiles.

- By 1907, both the REO and the Oldsmobile were being manufactured in a factory in Lansing, Michigan, creating fierce competition.

- According to *Motor Age*, "Everyone works either for one or the other of the two motorcar factories, has a friend who does or knows a friend's friend who expects soon to be employed. So strong is the rivalry between the two factories, however, that the man who leaves skimmed milk at the door of the Olds employee knows better than to solicit trade from the family whose breadwinner dallies with an envelope from the REO paymaster."

- By 1908, REO's sales soared well ahead of Oldsmobile, which produced only 1,000 cars that year.

- Henry pumped more than a million dollars into the firm to keep it going, but in November 1908, he, his son and the stockholders accepted an offer from William Durant to merge Olds Motor Works with a new company known as General Motors—a merger which handsomely rewarded the Jorgensen family.

- Henry enjoys dabbling in "inventions of progress"; he also has investments in a local automobile brake company called Lockheed Brakes.

After Ransom Olds left the company, he created the REO.

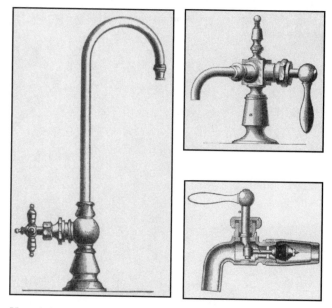

Henry's interest in inventions extends to bathroom fixtures.

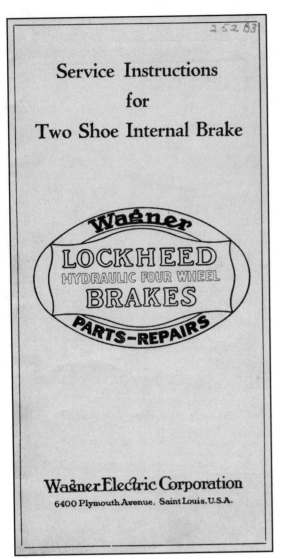

Service Instructions
for
Two Shoe Internal Brake

Wagner
LOCKHEED
HYDRAULIC FOUR WHEEL
BRAKES
PARTS-REPAIRS

Wagner Electric Corporation
6400 Plymouth Avenue, Saint Louis, U.S.A.

Henry enjoys dabbling in inventions of progress such as Lockheed brakes.

- His interest in inventions even extends to bathroom fixtures; to the enormous frustration of his wife, he keeps changing the faucets in the bathroom, experimenting with the latest ideas in compression valves versus fuller ball valves.
- He is particularly interested in the Sanitary Movement, which is pushing for greater bathroom cleanliness and focusing on the use of porcelain-enameled iron bathtubs and sinks, along with the elimination of extensive use of microbe-harboring wood in the bathroom.

Life in the Community: Detroit, Michigan

- Detroit was founded in 1701 by Antoine de la Mothe Cadillac as Fort Pontchatrain on the Detroit River, and for more than 100 years was the most important military and trading station on the Great Lakes.
- Real development of Detroit began after the War of 1812; by 1830, it was the fifty-third largest city, and by 1910, the nation's ninth and growing.
- From 1900 to 1910, while the population of the state of Michigan grew 16 percent, the city of Detroit increased 63 percent to 492,695 inhabitants.
- Key industries of the city include pharmaceutical manufacturing, most notably Parke, Davis and Company; the paint and varnish industry, which began in the 1890s; and automobile manufacturing.

The growing immigrant population has forced merchants to prepare packages in various languages.

The owner of the V-63 Five Passenger Sedan travels in an atmosphere of richness and refinement.

Its beautiful Cadillac-Fisher Body, appointed with the care used in decorating an exquisite drawing room, affords every facility for the convenience and comfort of its passengers.

But the dominant appeal of the Sedan, as of all V-63 models, is its extraordinary performance.

Its harmonized and balanced V-Type eight cylinder engine—Cadillac's greatest contribution to automotive progress in recent years—functions with a smoothness and quietness new to motoring.

To the speed and power of this engine is added the safety of Cadillac Four Wheel Brakes—and these qualities, combined with instant acceleration and exceptional ease of control, inspire the one who drives with a sense of complete road-mastery.

Cadillac invites you to approach the V-63 Sedan with great expectations, and is confident that a single ride will convince you of its surpassing quality.

CADILLAC MOTOR CAR COMPANY, DETROIT, MICHIGAN
Division of General Motors Corporation

- Currently, 29 separate companies manufacture 30 different makes of passenger cars, trucks and tractors; another 129 companies are devoted exclusively to the manufacture of parts and accessories.

To the great frustration of his wife, Henry keeps changing faucets in the bathroom.

- In addition, Detroit supplies 95 percent of the state's meat products and 86 percent of its structural steel.
- In all, Detroit's factories are valued at more than $254 million, and are supplied by 15 railroads with a combined capacity of 2,989 cars.
- Currently, railroad service in and out of Detroit is seriously hampered by a bottleneck of line connections through Toledo, where terminals have been so congested during much of the year that losses are being sustained by Detroit shippers.
- Outbound freight by steamship is currently 250 million pounds annually, with the potential for more.

Sheet music by writer Irving Berlin is everywhere.

- The growing immigrant population has forced many merchants to prepare signs and instructions in various languages; directions are written in both English and German for Gooch's Mexican Pills, good for stomach, liver and bowels.
- Across the city and the state, sheet music by writer Irving Berlin is everywhere; his songs range from love songs titled "Snookey Ookums" to tales of the "Devil's Ball."
- The campaign for good roads continues to rage; every new car owner becomes "a voter for good roads," *The Ford Times* says.
- Motorists have the American Automobile Association, which became a powerful lobbying force, although many groups seeking quality roads do not want federal assistance;

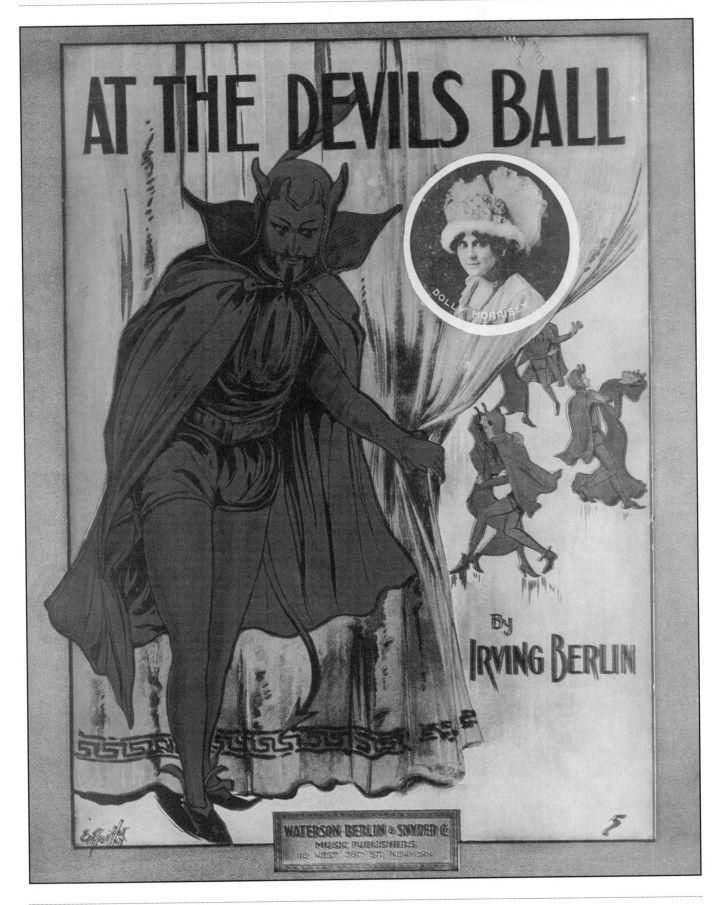

Henry keeps a picture of his two daughters on his desk.

the *Engineering News* says, "It needs but the slightest knowledge of Congressional methods and precedents to perceive that the first grant of federal aid to highway work will be the opening of a drain out of the Treasury which may easily menace national solvency."

- The fiscal 1913 Post Office Appropriation Bill includes a grant of $500,000 in federal aid for the improvement of rural post roads, provided each federal dollar is matched two for one by the states.

- At the Jorgensens' other home, along the eastern shore of Maine, the very wealthy residents of Long Island and Bar Harbor are actively talking about "giving back" to the poor, partly to make sure America's working class does not rise up in revolt against conspicuous wealth.

- Andrew Carnegie, who popularized the concept of giving through the "gospel of wealth," says money must be used to ease the social ills of the world.

- Banker Jacob H. Schiff is said to demonstrate this "gospel" through the giving of least 10 percent of everything he makes to Jewish and non-Jewish causes; wealthy lawyer Louis Marshall believes in giving through the Talmudic doctrine, "Twice blessed is he who gives in secret," so all his gifts are given anonymously.

- But the very rich are also finding creative ways to celebrate and get into the press; Mrs. W. Watt Sherman gave her daughter Mildred a party in which a huge swan floated on an artificial lake surrounded by 1,300 guests, and when the débutante took her bow, the giant swan exploded, scattering 10,000 pink roses into the air.

- At Newport, Norman R. de Whitehouse recently hired the U.S. Navy to assist with the coming-out party of his daughter Alice; warships moored offshore used their search lamps to light up the dance floor so everyone could enjoy an extended evening of dancing under the stars.

"It is a disgrace to die rich."

—Multimillionaire Andrew Carnegie, who gave away $25 million in 1913 alone.

Historical Snapshot
1913

- John D. Rockefeller established the Rockefeller Institute with an initial donation of $100 million
- National black leader Booker T. Washington advocated black economic reform through education rather than political change
- Approximately 18 percent of American households had telephones
- The new federal income tax was imposed on income of more than $3,000, affecting 600,000 of the nation's 92 million people
- Oscar Hammerstein reentered the opera world and began construction of the American National Opera building
- The 55-story concrete and steel Woolworth skyscraper, costing $13.5 million, was completed in New York City
- The growing popularity of phonographs and records made entertaining easier
- Albert Schweitzer opened a hospital in Lambarene, French Congo
- Zippers, in use since 1891, and the new dance, the Fox Trot, both gained in popularity
- Baseball player Ty Cobb won his seventh batting title
- Henry Ford pioneered new assembly line techniques at his car factory
- Alice Paul founded the National Women's Party; when 5,000 suffragettes marched down Washington's Pennsylvania Avenue, 40 women were attacked and injured by opponents
- R.J. Reynolds created Camel cigarettes, the first modern blended cigarette; the package featured "Old Joe," a dromedary in the Barnum and Bailey circus
- Clarence Crane introduced peppermint Life Savers to balance slow chocolate sales during the summer months
- The B'nai B'rith founded the Anti-Defamation League to fight anti-Semitism
- U.S. output equaled 40 percent of the world's total production, up from 20 percent in 1860
- The Fletcherism fad, which stressed the need to chew one's food thoroughly, swept the nation
- Congress strengthened the Pure Food and Drug Law of 1906
- Athlete Jim Thorpe was stripped of his Olympic medals when it was discovered that he had earned $15 playing semipro baseball in 1909
- Brillo Manufacturing Corporation was founded
- The monthly Consumer Price Index, the Geiger counter, the erector set and Quaker Puffed Rice and Wheat all made their first appearance
- President Woodrow Wilson called the Chinese revolution the most significant event of our generation
- Leonardo's *Mona Lisa*, missing since 1911, was discovered in France

1913 Economic Profile

The national consumer expenditures (per capita income) in 1913 were:

    Auto Parts, Gas and Oil $3.44
    Auto Purchases $4.21
    Clothing. $29.52
    Food. $90.34
    Furniture $3.47
    Housing. $62.78
    Intercity Transport $3.32
    Local Transport. $6.13
    Personal Business. $9.86
    Personal Care. $3.08
    Physicians and Dentists. $3.94
    Private Education and Research $4.97
    Recreation $10.06
    Religion/Welfare Activities $8.44
    Telephone and Telegraph $1.13
    Tobacco $7.39
    Utilities. $4.64
    Per Capita Consumption. $336.95

Annual Income, Standard Jobs

    Average of all Industries,
        Excluding Farm Labor $675.00
    Average of all Industries,
        Including Farm Labor $621.00
    Bituminous Coal Mining. $0.32/Hour
    Building Trades,
        Union Workers $0.56/Hour
    Clerical Workers in
        Manufacturing and Steam
        Railroads $1,236.00
    Domestics $357.00
    Farm Labor $360.00
    Federal Employees, Executive
        Departments. $1,136.00
    Finance, Insurance and
        Real Estate $1,349.00
    Gas and Electricity Workers $661.00
    Lower-Skilled Labor $536.00
    Manufacturing, Payroll. $0.21/Hour
    Manufacturing, Union Workers ... $0.43/Hour
    Medical/Health Services Workers..... $357.00
    Ministers $899.00
    Nonprofit Organization
        Workers. $802.00
    Postal Employees. $0.45/Hour

Public School Teachers $547.00
State and Local Government
    Workers. $779.00
Steam Railroads, Wage Earners $760.00
Street Railway Workers. $704.00
Telegraph Industry Workers $717.00
Telephone Industry Workers. $438.00
Wholesale and Retail Trade
    Workers. $685.00

Selected Prices

Automobile, Maxwell Mercury. $1,150.00
Baseball $0.10
Bed, Mahogany $39.50
Cake Turner, Steel $0.02
Cloth, Mohair, per Yard $0.36
Crayons, Pack of 28 . . . . $0.04
Diaper Cover, Waterproof. $0.35
Dress, Girl's $1.65
Gloves, Ladies', Lined $0.23
Hair Barrette $0.49
Hotel Room, Boston Puritan,
    per Day $2.00
Nightgown. $0.99
Phonograph Record $0.65
Steamship Ticket, San Francisco–
    Los Angeles $12.00
Suitcase $4.00
Sweater Coat, Man's $2.48
Theater Ticket (*The Merry
    Widow*) $0.50-2.00
Toupée, Man's $21.65
Union Suit $0.48
Vacuum Cleaner $46.75

The History of the Oldsmobile

- Ransom E. Olds was born in Geneva, Ohio, in 1864, 10 months after Henry Ford.
- His father operated a successful machine shop in Lansing, Michigan, where Ransom worked both as mechanic and bookkeeper.
- Like so many of his age, he was fascinated with the concept of a self-propelled carriage; eventually he would acquire 30 different patents.
- In 1886, Olds built his first automobile, a three-wheeled steam-powered car.
- Four years later he built another, larger steam-powered automobile, which was sold to a British patent-medicine company for $400.
- The company shipped the vehicle to Bombay, India, but it never arrived; the ship sank en route.
- His third automobile, a gasoline-powered carriage, was built in 1896, the same year the Duryea brothers sold their first automobile and began the American automobile industry.

The curved dashboard was an immediate hit.

- In 1897, Olds formed the Olds Motor Vehicle Company and the Olds Gasoline Engine Works; he sold four cars that year.
- In 1899, when he brought in additional investors, the Olds Motor Works was created and the company was moved from Lansing to Detroit, Michigan, becoming the first car company to move to that city.
- In 1901, Olds designed an automobile in which the floor curved up to form the dashboard.
- The new vehicle, carrying the Oldsmobile name, featured a seven-horsepower, single-cylinder engine with two forward gears and one reverse, and was steered by a tiller; the new car was an immediate hit.
- Advertising for the car bragged, "there's nothing to watch but the road."
- With a simple press of the foot on the gas pedal, the marvelous new invention would run "whether your machine shall go at a snail's pace or at varying speeds limited only by your desires."
- The top speed was approximately 20 miles per hour, depending on the quality of the road.

- In October 1901, race car driver Roy Chapin drove it from Detroit to the New York Auto Show in a hail of publicity over the new car; a New York City dealer took orders for almost a thousand of the new vehicles.
- The following year, Ransom Olds accepted a challenge from famous auto racer, Alexander Winton, for a test of machines; they competed on the beach at Daytona, Florida, capturing more publicity and establishing that city as one of America's premier racing centers.
- By 1904, when the Oldsmobile was selling for $650, the company was selling 5,500 cars annually.
- In a dispute with his key investor, Olds resigned from the company that carried his name.
- By 1908 William C. Durant, the founder of General Motors, acquired the Oldsmobile name; Ransom Olds was never associated with the Oldsmobile again.

1915 FAMILY PROFILE

Stuart Ramsdell and his wife Charlotte both trace their roots to the founders of Virginia. The son of a wealthy Virginia landowner, Ramsdell currently serves as president of the Association of Seaboard Air Line Railway Surgeons, as well as chief surgeon for the Railway. Their oldest child is attending the exclusive prep school, Groton.

Annual Income: Approximately $60,000 a year, including Stuart's salary as chief surgeon and revenues from the 11,000 acres they inherited.

Life at Home

- Both Stuart and Charlotte claim membership to the First Families of Virginia, which is restricted to individuals who are "lineal descendants of an ancestor who aided in the establishment of the first permanent English colony, Virginia, 1607–1624."
- Charlotte loves to point out—especially when in New England—that her forebears arrived on American shores 13 years before the *Mayflower* even landed.
- As important, of the 105 men in the original Jamestown, Virginia, expedition of 1607, 35 carried the all-important status of gentleman, whereas the settlers who came aboard the *Mayflower*, she likes to say, were "just hard-working people—hatters, tailors, merchants, wool combers, weavers and the like."
- A graduate of Princeton and a railroad executive, Stuart is less inclined to make fun of the Yankees he meets.
- On weekends, they love to go fox hunting; Charlotte especially enjoys the aristocratic pageantry of this equine fashion show, while Stuart likes putting away the problem of automobile carburetor adjustments for the joys of sitting astride a well-trained, powerful horse.
- She lives for the formal balls in Petersburg, Richmond and Washington, which they are frequently invited to attend.
- Recently, they attended a society ball in Washington, where she met Countess Cellere, wife of the Italian ambassador, and Mme. de Riano, wife of the Spanish ambassador.

The Ramsdells' oldest son is attending Groton.

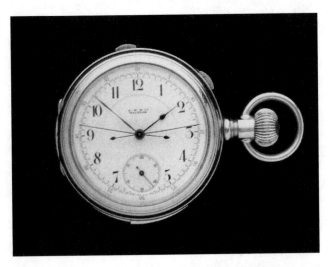

Stuart Ramsdell loves the precision embodied in his Waltham pocket watch.

- Mme. de Riano was wearing a golden-brown satin gown with drapery of gold-brocade chiffon; her hat was trimmed with black goura.
- Charlotte felt well-turned-out in her gown of dark blue chiffon, with falling folds over soft blue silk and trimmed with cream and dark blue lace; she topped her look with a smart hat of shiny black straw, with a wreath of natural-tone dahlias.
- During the same trip, they attended the very private marriage of Mrs. Mabelle Swift Moore, widow of Mr. Clarence Moore, a victim of the *Titanic* disaster three years earlier; she married Axel Christian Preheu Wickfeld.
- Like many of the more professional men who work around the railroad, Stuart loves precision, embodied in his gold-case Waltham pocket watch—a gift from his father upon Stuart's graduation from medical school; not only is the watch very accurate, it has buttons on the edge of the case to activate two separate stopwatch hands, useful in recording events or counting a pulse.
- Their oldest son attends Groton, one of the most aristocratic of New England's private schools.
- Groton's founder, the Reverend Peabody, was connected to one of the oldest families of New England, while the school's chief financial banker was multimillionaire J. Pierpont Morgan.
- Groton is well-known for its educational quality and its ability to be a spiritual extension of a well-born boy's own family.
- Upholding the belief that a Spartan lifestyle builds character, Groton directors require that undergraduates sleep in unheated cells without doors, wash up in long, communal black sinks with cold water and eat meals often featuring cold poached cod and "sure-death hash."
- Groton boys wear stiff white collars and black patent-leather pumps to dinner; no one is allowed to stand with his hands in his pockets, and close friendships are discouraged.
- A favorite form of punishment is known as pumping, during which an erring student is taken into the lavatory and literally pumped full of water.
- Former U.S. president Teddy Roosevelt, a Groton graduate and a bold leader, is often cited by the school as the type of leader the school produces.

Life at Work

- Last year, 10,150 people were killed and more than 190,000 injured on railroads in the United States.
- Stuart Ramsdell is pushing for every railroad to employ a surgical staff, and insisting a "surgical organization is of paramount importance today to the successful operation of trains."

DOMESTIC BILL OF LADING.

(Form 14.)

SOUTHERN EXPRESS COMPANY.

Express Forwarders.

Insured by SOUTHERN EXPRESS COMPANY
for to except against loss occasioned by the public enemy-
only,
For the Company,
Insurance, $

$6 —

Saffups SC June 2? 1874

Received, from Z Phillips

One Package — *Sealed and said to contain*

Six Dollars

Addressed Jilu + Dickenson

Richmond Va

Upon the special acceptance and agreement that this Company is to forward the same to its agent nearest or most convenient to destination only, and there to deliver the same to other parties to complete the transportation—such delivery to terminate all liability of this Company for such package; and also, that this Company are not to be liable in any manner, or to any extent for any loss, damage or detention of such package, or of its contents, or of any portion thereof, occasioned by the acts of God, or by any person or persons acting or claiming to act in any military or other capacity in hostility to the Government of the United States, or occasioned by civil or military authority, or by the acts of any armed or other mob, or riotous assemblage, piracy, or the dangers incident to a time of war, nor when occasioned by the dangers of railroad transportation, or ocean, or river navigation, or by fire or steam, unless specially insured by this Company, and so specified in this receipt. In no event is this Company to be liable for a greater sum than that above mentioned, nor shall it be liable for any such loss unless the claim therefor shall be made in writing, at this office, within thirty days from this date, in a statement to which this receipt shall be annexed, (and the shipper and owner hereby severally agree that all the stipulations and conditions in this receipt contained shall extend to, and enure to the benefit of, each and every Company, or person, to whom the SOUTHERN EXPRESS COMPANY may entrust or deliver the above described property for transportation, and shall define and limit the liability therefor of such other Company or person.)

Freight, 25 ilo Pd   *For the Company,* Shuck

- With the increase in locomotion speed, accidents are increasing, resulting in more injuries and death; a train such as the Twentieth-Century Limited can now speed between Chicago and New York in 20 hours.

- Stuart has come to believe that once a railway accident occurs, the early and careful transportation of the victim is necessary in a large majority of injuries, because there is more shock from railway injuries than from any other class of accidents.

- Even though the idea is new, he thinks that administering first aid will decrease deaths by controlling bleeding and trauma.

- He is also insisting that every train and every station have a "First Aid Package," including instructions on how to use the medicine in the box, along with the proper use of a stretcher.

- He supports a rule that all employees should be examined every five years and be required to pass the same physical exam used by the army and navy; the union management is fighting the concept, believing it will be used to eliminate workers.

- The company that employs Stuart, The Seaboard Air Line Railway Company, was chartered in 1900 as the successor to the Richmond, Petersburg and Carolina Railroad Company, which owned the 102-mile line from Richmond, Virginia, to Norlina, North Carolina.

- Charlotte's family was a major stockholder in the predecessor company, and profited handsomely from the sale.

- The company's 18,949 railroad cars include 143 passenger and 284 freight locomotives.

There were 190,000 injuries from railroad accidents last year.

Speech: "Traumatic Neurasthenia," by Joseph M. Burke, M.D., Chief Surgeon of Association of Seaboard Air Line Railway Surgeons:

"The reasons impelling me to present you with this paper on 'traumatic neurasthenia,' or 'railway spine,' is that long experience in my official capacity compels me, in justice of the railways I service, to give you some facts by which you may be guided, and which will prove helpful to you in the differentiation of the true condition from mythical fake cases.

The appalling frequency with which juries render large verdicts against railroads is abhorrent and abominable; in fact, their prejudices cannot be removed by any testimony the company presents, and the conclusion must necessarily be, therefore, that they do not believe one iota of the evidence sworn to by any of the medical witnesses produced by a railroad. There are no doubt some exceptions to this general rule, and it may be that the verdicts against railroads could be condoned because of the impression made on juries by the glib tongue of a 'shyster lawyer' or an 'ambulance chaser,' who will have the assistance of some unscrupulous fool or knave, or maybe, one who could, if he would, be an ornament to our ranks, but is shrewd and cunning and swears on the stand without compromise, that physical neurasthenia is a mental condition, there is something material existing which is unexplainable, and at the same time will openly admit the verdict of the jury as rendered will determine the amount of his fee. We can readily, therefore, put the blame of the prejudices existing among jurors on the educated and better class of people, as without their assistance and coaching, action in law would rarely be had.

It is true the antipathy toward railroads was originally infused within the minds of the general public by the demagogic, petty politicians, who would proclaim that the wealth of the railroads was in the hands of the few, and that this wealth would someday grind every man, woman and child into smithereens. Such statements

were and are now believed by some persons, without their reasoning for one minute that but for the railroads we would be as barren as when Columbus discovered this great land of ours. Each and every one should gratefully recognize that our progress and civilization are indebted to that wealth which serves as so helpful an adjunct to our well-being in everyday life.

The railroads are daily paying out large sums of money to persons who get something for nothing, and this is due to the circumstances enumerated above. This condition, in my opinion, will continue unless the U.S. Government intervenes through the Interstate Commerce Commission and appoints an unbiased, non-political commission of competent physicians to decide whether a person is injured or not."

- The Bureau of Railway Economics reports that net operating income of the U.S. railroads increased 21.3 percent in the East; operating revenues per mile of line averaged $1,191 nationwide.
- Currently, the railroads are opposing a plan by the postmaster general concerning payment for mail transportation.
- Stockholders recently gathered in Petersburg, Virginia, to approve the merger between the Seaboard Air Line and the Carolina, Atlantic & Western Roadway; the new company is called the Seaboard Air Line Railway Company.
- Twelve railroad executives in New Haven, Connecticut, including William Rockefeller, are now being tried in federal court for conspiracy to monopolize railroad, steamship and trolley transportation traffic in New England.

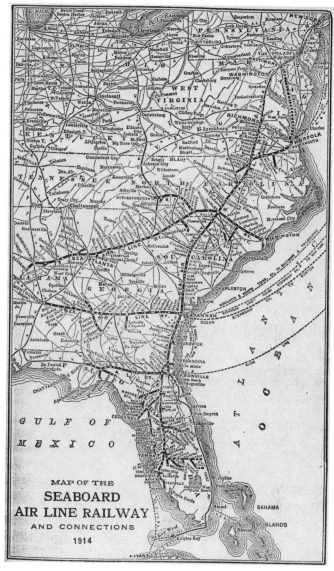

MAP OF THE
**SEABOARD
AIR LINE RAILWAY**
AND CONNECTIONS
1914

Life in the Community: Petersburg, Virginia

- Recently, the Daughters of the American Revolution moved a solid rock basin from the banks of the Appomattox River to Central Park so it can be better displayed; tradition says Pocahontas was "wont to take her morning bath" in the basin.
- Within a mile of the city limits is the site of the Battle of the Crater, which took place during "our late unpleasantness," as city fathers like to say.
- It was there that Union Colonel Pleasants, under General Grant, conceived the idea of digging a tunnel under the Confederate works; on July 28, 1864, 8,000 pounds of gunpowder exploded, blowing up the works and killing 284 Confederate soldiers.
- Despite the 300-foot-wide breach, the Federals were repulsed by the Confederate soldiers led by Mahone; Congress is now considering the purchase of Crater Farm and adjacent land for the creation of a National Battlefield Park.
- The city holds Old Blandford Cemetery within the city limits, where 30,000 Confederate dead "are sleeping their last sleep," according to W.E. Poole, acting mayor of the city.
- Located on Market Street is the Wallace House, where General Grant and President Lincoln discussed the terms of surrender prior to General Grant's meeting with General Lee at Appomattox.
- Petersburg acquired the sobriquet of the "Cockade City" during the Battle of 1812 after President Madison thanked a company of Petersburg men for their gallantry, saying they had won for their city "the proud appellation of the Cockade City of the Union."
- The comic strip *Bringing up Father* is a favorite across the city; nearly everyone claims to know someone like the newly wealthy Jiggs, who can't seem to leave his immigrant worker roots behind, or his wife Mary, who can't wait to use their newfound wealth to unlock the doors of society.
- Another favorite is the vaudeville shows that combine live entertainment with moving picture shows—many of which feature westerns or comedies.

"I am sick to death of this shriek for women's rights. It is doing more harm than good among women. I wish all women felt as I do; I have more rights now than I can properly attend to."
—Actress May Irwin

A TREMENDOUS SUCCESS
Wonderful Boy.

Lyric by
MERCEDES LORENZE.

Music by
JAS. T. DUFFY.

FOR SALE BY ALL DEALERS

- The city leaders are discussing, again, the installation of an electric streetcar or trolley; the first in the nation was created by engineer Julian Sprague from nearby Richmond, Virginia, in 1887.
- Now that war is under way in Europe, everyone is talking about when and if America should join the fight; many in Petersburg believe this is a European matter best settled by Europeans.
- Some say the war will be good for American business; the banking community believes that world commercial and financial leadership may be "thrust within its grasp by war."
- A columnist for *Life* magazine says, "It is being whispered, for instance, that the war is going to kill feminism and cubism, and all the other strenuous and angular isms and bring the good old simple life back into favor."
- Thanks to predictions of very favorable crop production, most of which would be shipped by rail, many of the "better" people of Petersburg are aggressively buying railroad stocks; the earnings of the New Haven Railroad are expected to be strong, thanks to the shipping needs of industries doing war business in New England.
- Throughout Southern states such as Virginia, economic optimism is high in the expectation that cotton prices will be good; Fairfax Harrison, president of the Southern Railway Company, says, "At current prices the profit to the farmer on a bale of cotton is probably greater than in some years."

"Ripley Says the World as a Whole is Getting Poorer," *Wall Street Journal*, May 22, 1915:

"E.P. Ripley, president of the *Atchison*, says to the *Wall Street Journal*: 'The European war situation is no worse than I thought it would be by this time when I went to California last fall for the winter. The world as a whole is getting poorer. The balance of trade at the moment is much in our favor, and some of us are getting much richer on account of others' misfortune, but does that mean our permanent good? I cannot conceive it so.

'Many things are in our favor now, however, among them being the saving of many millions by keeping our rich people at home. Europe is consuming an enormous amount of foodstuffs at high prices, and may do so for another year. The immediate result is prosperity for a small portion of our people and disaster to another and quite considerable portion. If we should be drawn into the war, the sort of prosperity which the war has given to us would shrink rapidly. But I cannot see any excuse for our being drawn into it.'"

City leaders are discussing the installation of an electric streetcar for the town.

Traveling shows often include Petersburg on their schedules.

"Do You Know That—" *Royster's Almanac*, 1915:

"There are 7,397,533,000,000 tons of coal in the world, according to a careful estimate by the editor of *Coal Age*.

Apples, pears, lemons, oranges and limes are of great value in improving a muddy complexion. Raw tomatoes have a fine effect on the liver.

The amount of iron ore mined in the United States last year is officially estimated at 58 million to 60 million long tons, a new high record.

If new gas mantles be dipped into vinegar and hung up to dry before being placed upon the gas fixtures, they will give a more brilliant light and last longer.

A famous German physician proves that infantile paralysis is often carried from one household to another by domestic animals, such as chickens, ducks and steers.

The railroads of Great Britain kill in accidents, for which the passenger is in no way responsible, one passenger for every 72 million carried, while those of the United States kill one for every 4.9 million passengers carried."

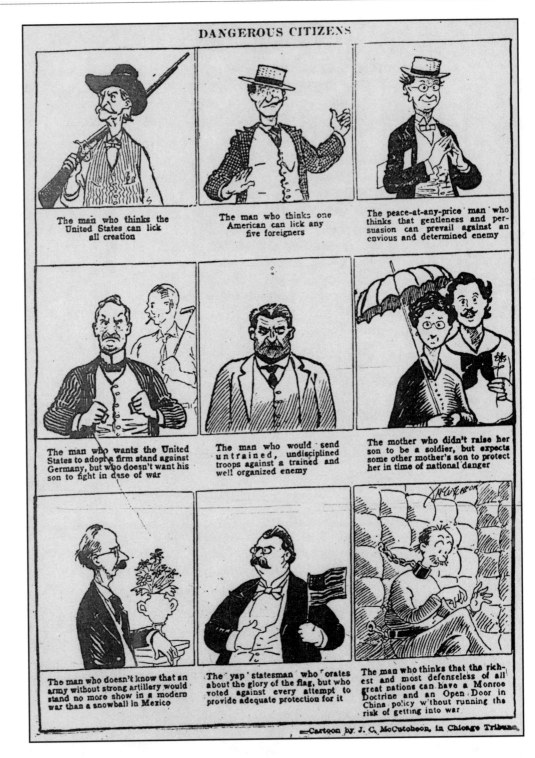

- Advertisements appearing in the local newspaper tout the use of radium on plants and grass lawns to make them grow better; the Radium Fertilizer Company claims radium will increase vegetable yields by 39 percent.

HISTORICAL SNAPSHOT
1915

- The Vanderbilt family now had 17 houses around the country, valued at more than $1 million each
- More than one million socialists were demanding the overthrow of capitalism, which was exploiting America's labor
- Approximately 40 percent of America's labor force worked 12 hours a day, sometimes seven days a week
- Nevada's divorce reform legislation required only a six-month residency to take a legal action
- Margaret Sanger was arrested and imprisoned on obscenity charges for publishing *Family Limitation*, concerning birth control
- Since 1874, approximately 39 Italian Americans had been lynched for alleged crimes; often when faced with a crime, the police rounded up all Italians for questioning
- South Dakota abolished the death penalty
- Jane Addams led a group of 80 women to The Hague to protest the First World War
- The one millionth Ford automobile rolled off the assembly line
- On the advice of a public relations consultant, millionaire John D. Rockefeller handed out shiny new dimes to bystanders wherever he went to soften his image as a ruthless oil tycoon
- Nearly half of the U.S. population lived in a "dry" territory where alcohol could not legally be sold
- The U.S. was outraged after German submarines attacked U.S. passenger liners and merchant ships, resulting in deaths
- In response to worldwide war needs and high market prices, U.S. farmers produced a record one billion bushels of wheat
- The disposable scalpel, gas mask, transatlantic call, Brooks Brothers and the International Fingerprint Society all made their first appearance
- The success of D.W. Griffith's 12-reel movie, *The Birth of a Nation*, proved the financial potential of long films; admission was $2
- The U.S. Commission on Industrial Relations reported that, "In large cities, up to 20 percent of children are undernourished and poor children die at three times the rate of the middle class; only one third of children finish elementary school, and less than 10 percent graduate high school"
- With the First World War under way in Europe, making importing difficult, consumers embraced a "Made in America" fad, though the very wealthy continued to import goods from Paris

1915 Economic Profile

The national consumer expenditures (per capita income) in 1915 were:

Auto Parts, Gas and Oil	$3.44
Auto Purchases	$4.21
Clothing	$29.52
Food	$90.34
Furniture	$3.47
Housing	$62.78
Intercity Transport	$3.32
Local Transport	$6.13
Personal Business	$9.86
Personal Care	$3.08
Physicians and Dentists	$3.94
Private Education and Research	$4.97
Recreation	$10.06
Religion/Welfare Activities	$8.44
Telephone and Telegraph	$1.13
Tobacco	$7.39
Utilities	$4.64
Per Capita Consumption	$336.95

Annual Income, Standard Jobs

Average of all Industries, Excluding Farm Labor	$687.00
Average of all Industries, Including Farm Labor	$633.00
Bituminous Coal Mining	$0.38/Hour
Building Trades, Union Workers	$0.59/Hour

"Mail Order vs. Country Store," *Wall Street Journal*, May 1915:

"Is the country store doomed to go, because of the pressure which is being brought to bear upon it through the mail order houses? The advocates of the fixed-price method of retailing regard the rural village shop as one of the vital links in the merchandising economy of a farm community. Yet here comes along a rural witness against it, charging the village or country store with being the cause of much of the decay in farm life. 'I charge the country store with being a nuisance on three charges,' writes a Pennsylvania farmer to the Department of Agriculture. 'One of these is the abominable loafing system it tolerates; another is the debasing language used among the loafing clientele; and the third is the neglect of the home duties by the men, leaving the burden to fall on the womenfolk to the impairment of the health and the stability of the home.'"

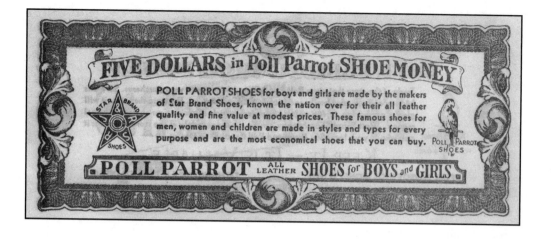

Clerical Workers in
Manufacturing and
Steam Railroads $1,327.00
Domestics $342.00
Farm Labor $355.00
Federal Civilian $940.00
Federal Employees, Executive
Departments. $1,152.00
Finance, Insurance and
Real Estate $1,040.00
Gas and Electricity Workers $620.00
Lower-Skilled Labor $905.00
Manufacturing, Union Workers . . . $0.34/Hour

"Women Students Spend More than Men at University of Wisconsin Despite Their Free Amusements," *Washington Post*, May 15, 1915:

"Women students spend more than men at the University of Wisconsin, and the same is probably true of other coeducational state universities. Less than $500 a year is spent by the average Wisconsin University student, and that suffices to carry him through in comfort, according to a comprehensive survey that has recently been made at the Madison institution. . . .

The fact that women spend considerably more than men students may occasion some surprise when it is recalled that women at state universities are exceptionally well-treated by men students as far as amusements and entertainment go, so that the average 'coed' is not often obligated to purchase her own tickets to football or the theater, and she seldom pays for a dance."

Manufacturing, Payroll $0.15/Hour

Medical/Health Services

    Workers $381.00

Ministers $730.00

Nonprofit Organization Workers $652.00

Postal Employees $0.38/Hour

Public School Teachers $328.00

State and Local Government

    Workers $590.00

Steam Railroads, Wage Earners $548.00

Street Railway Workers $604.00

Wholesale and Retail Trade

    Workers $510.00

Selected Prices

Automobile, King Motor Car $1,350.00

Boots, Man's $21.00

Baby Blanket $0.75

Baby Shoes $0.50

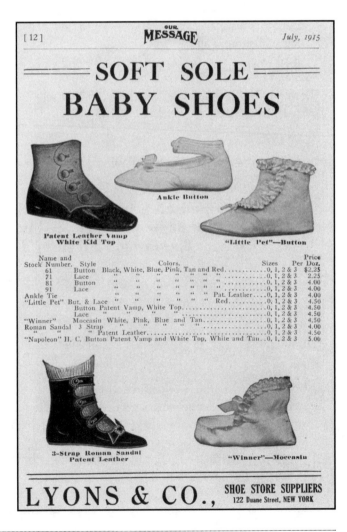

Canvas Shoe Cleaner	$0.25
Card Game, Rook	$0.42
Chair, Reclining	$37.00
Corset, Woman's	$1.59
Electric Radiator	$5.75
Macaroni, Skinner's	$0.25
Mousetrap	$0.02
Newspaper, Annual Subscription	$12.00
Player Piano	$397.00
Purse, Mesh, Silver Plated	$7.50
Raincoat, Woman's	$10.98
Seeds, Burpee's	$0.25
Settee, Leather	$96.50
Shotgun, Remington	$32.70
Tuition, Raymond Riordon School, per Year	$800.00
Typewriter, Corona	$50.00

The Outlook Magazine, on the Woman's Suffrage parade down Fifth Avenue, New York, in 1915, witnessed by 250,000 people:

"I didn't walk in New York's first suffrage parade because my mother wouldn't let me. Next year, in 1913, I wanted to march, but my husband asked me not to. This fall I decided that it was 'up to me' to suffer for democracy.

Three o'clock on the afternoon of October 23, and a glorious day. Every band in greater New York and some beyond blows like the breeze today. First it's 'Tipperary,' and then 'Tipperary' again, and once more, 'Tipperary.'

After 50 false alarms, suddenly down the line comes the signal, 'Make ready.' Quickly we slip into place. The marshals look us over, straighten out bends and kinks, and then as the band strikes up, begin to count time, 'Left, left, left!' My heart is thumping louder than the band. Dear heaven, we're there!

By the time we had gone two blocks I had forgotten everything I had expected to feel. All my girlhood, Mother had repeated that a lady should never allow herself to be conspicuous. To march up Fifth Avenue had promised to flout directly one's early training. I was mistaken. There's no notoriety about it. When it's done along with twenty-five thousand other women, nothing could seem more natural. Embarrassment is left at the street corner, and one is just a spar, a singing, swinging part of a great stream, all flowing in the same direction toward the same goal. . . .

As we marched along I did not see the crowd. I never heeded the many policemen battling with the encroaching throng. Once when we were marking time, an indignant woman burst through the sidelines and demanded of an over-worked officer, 'How can I get to the Grand Central Station in time to take my train?' 'Well, ma'am,' he drawled, 'I don't see any better way than for you to fall into line and march there.' 'What, I in a suffrage parade!' she shrieked. 'I won't so demean myself,' and flounced away. Another time I'd have thought that funny, but as we took up our procession I wondered what she meant. Thousands and thousands of women walking in protest before the bar of public opinion—could that be an unworthy thing? Could this, my new elation, multiplied twenty thousandfold, carry no impression on those who watched? Would even a czar of autocratic Russia dare to disregard so great a demonstration of his people?"

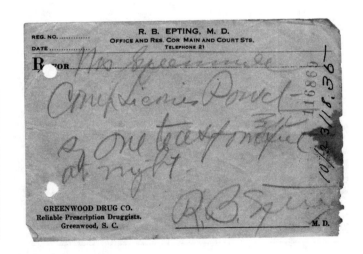

"Entertainment Ideas for New Year's," by Laura A. Smith,
Today's, **January 1914, An Immigration Party:**

"IMMIGRATION PARTY
Will Land at Ellis Island, U.S.A.
(date)
Wear the costume of some foreign land.
Prepare to show your money to the Inspectors,
Uncle Sam and Columbia,
Host and Hostess

Lay a gangplank from the street to the porch where the immigrants are to be 'inspected.' As they enter this hall they pass some blue-capped inspectors who ask them why they have come to the United States and other questions that will call forth witty answers, ask them to show their 'money,' and pass them on to white-clad 'doctors.' They turn little flashlights into the eyes of the immigrants and bid them stick out their tongues, then the immigrants pass into the United States. Here Uncle Sam, Columbia, a colored Mammy and other characters greet them. Uncle Sam's hand is a glove filled with cotton which collapses when one shakes hands with him. Columbia's hand is greased and Mammy's kiss leaves a smudge of burnt cork on the face. Baseball players, Indians, confidence men, suffragettes (militant) and other friends can help greet the immigrants when the crowd is a large one. Each newcomer receives a little flag to pin on her costume when she has become a citizen of the United States."

A
Christmas
Wish

When I think of the pies and
the puddings you make
And all of the hundreds of steps
that you take
With hands ever skillful
no pains do you spare
To make all those happy who
chance to be there
May your life be quite rosy
and read like a book
And give as much pleasure
as the good things you cook

"Baby's Upbuilding," by Edith V. Hart, *Child Betterment*, *The Official Organ of the National Child Welfare League*, June 1914:

"Baby comes into the world a helpless, dependent creature, with no habits, and no impressions. That into which his mind is to develop is plastic—like a wax record, ready to retain such impressions as are made upon it. But on the future of your infant boy or girl you place great store. You try to lift aside the veil of the years unborn and see the wonderful success of your own flesh and blood.

As a mother, your very tenderness and love may handicap the child. The fostering care you bestow upon your little one may induce weakness, bad habits, and disease and retard physical and moral growth through all after-years."

Child Betterment

10 Cents Per Copy   JUNE, 1914 $1.00 Per Year

Published Monthly *as the* Official Organ *of* the National Child Welfare League.

Help the children. Childhood today means manhood tomorrow. Manhood is the basis of the republic which directs the future of the race and nation.

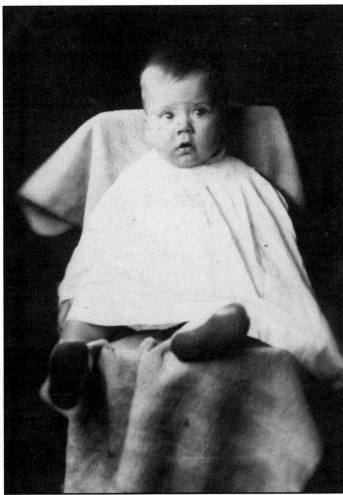

The Child Betterment League discouraged mothers from giving too much love that might handicap the child and create bad habits.

1919 FAMILY PROFILE

As the heiress to a lumber fortune and wife of a Presbyterian minister, Agnes Forcelle has had the benefit of traveling with her family to Hawaii as missionaries and to Paris as first-class tourists. They have one daughter, Martha, who has announced her engagement.

Life at Home

- The Forcelle family lives in Chevy Chase, Maryland, near Washington, D.C., where Agnes's husband Albert serves as a Presbyterian minister.
- Three years ago, Agnes's mother passed away, leaving an estate of more than $300,000, which has increased the family's economic freedom considerably.
- Agnes's grandfather had made a fortune first in the timber industry, later redoubling his wealth through real estate as the vast land holdings he had acquired for timber became valuable to developers near rapidly growing cities and towns.
- Because her parents had always shared their wealth generously, for most of the past two decades Agnes has traveled to Europe for vacations with her husband and their only daughter.
- Their daughter Martha, now 25, has completed her education at George Washington University and has begun her master's degree.
- Unmarried, she still lives at home, but travels widely with great skill and aplomb—often with her mother.
- Recently, she announced her engagement to a local businessman, but before she is married, she and her mother plan to repeat their 1913 grand tour of Europe with one last trip together, now that the war is over.
- The entire family enjoys traveling when time permits.

Agnes Forcelle is heiress to a lumber fortune.

Martha loves to travel.

- As one of 12 children from a middle-class family in Springfield, Massachusetts, Albert in his younger years did not have the wealth to travel on his own.
- After graduation from Yale in 1878, he spent two years as principal of Connecticut's Rockville High School, then entered Yale Divinity School, graduating in 1885 and spending the next two years touring the world as a guide, tutor and companion to a wealthy young man.
- As the daughter of a wealthy timber magnate, Agnes grew up traveling; she has been to England a dozen times, has visited India, and dreams of Japan.

This couple has traveled extensively throughout their marriage.

- From upstate New York, where her father's timber interests and paper mills were located, she fell in love with New York theater as a child, and often returns to New York City for Broadway plays and opera.

- She is proud to be a member of both the Colonial Daughters and the Society of Mayflower descendants, tracing her lineage through William Bradford, who was the second signer on the Mayflower Compact.

- Their daughter Martha went to Miss Hall's, a private boarding school, and hated the experience.

- During the war, when foreign travel was restricted, they traveled the United States collecting art pottery—a passion that appeals to many well-to-do American women they know.

- The current popularity of these ceramic vessels, which are created for beauty rather than utility, is driven by a rebellion against the machine-made anonymity of mass-produced objects.

- In their quest for pottery, the Forcelles have taken the train to New Orleans, where they bought several pieces of Newcomb pottery depicting a misty moon shining through moss-draped trees; they particularly like the work because it is an outgrowth of the art and design department of Newcomb College, the women's college of Tulane University.

- On another trip, they went to Chicago to buy Roseville pottery, made in Ohio and New York, and found a three-handled vase glazed one color inside and unglazed outside, made by Louis C. Tiffany.

The beauty of Newcomb pottery is a rebellion against machine-made, mass-produced objects.

While in Hawaii the Forcelles learned the language and collected crafts.

- During that trip, they visited the theater and opera, and bought several very subtle Tiffany bowls which had leaves and flowers etched into a monochromatic finish.

Life at Work

- During his many years as a Presbyterian pastor, Albert has served for five years in churches in upstate New York and Allston, Massachusetts, near Boston; four years in Hawaii; then 13 years in Rye, New York, before taking his current pulpit in Chevy Chase, Maryland.
- During World War I, their home had been a center for visiting pastors and soldiers, as well as a refuge for the Korean government in exile, a dangerous political position; the Japanese government currently has a price of $300,000 on the head of dissident Syngman Rhee.
- Albert enjoyed studying at Yale and often returns; from the pulpit, he enjoys telling how in 1638 the Rev. John Davenport and the merchant Theophilus Eaton founded the New Haven Colony to establish a Puritan "Bible State," in which "the word of God shall be the onely rule to be attended into in ordering the affayres of government."
- He particularly feels at home at Connecticut Hall, Yale's first foray into the Gothic Revival architectural style.
- Currently, a building program is under way at his church in Chevy Chase by a builder who is a local man and a friend of Albert known for his ability to construct meaningful worship space using only the finest stone.
- During the flu epidemic of 1918 several children of the parish died within days of each other; their parents and grandparents have all contributed funds for an expanded Sunday School building in their memory.
- Albert is also working on outreach programs with the women of the church who want to help the starving people of Armenia, formerly a part of the extensive Turkish Empire; now that World War I has ended, many countries are calling on the United States to act as their guardians.
- Prior to the war, his church was actively engaged in the Christian Helpers League, designed to help down-and-out men who were often alcoholics.
- Working with other Presbyterian churches in 1915, the League provided meals to 11,352 people, baths to 4,834, clothing to 64, medical care to 102 and jobs to 100; records show that 5,442 of those served also attended religious services.
- Even earlier, while in Rye, New York, Albert secured contributions from property owners to build sidewalks and improve the looks of the public library.

November 15, 1919   LESLIE'S WEEKLY   747

America Feeding Starving Armenia

Photographs by DONALD C. THOMPSON, LESLIE'S Staff Correspondent

The "Flour Line" in Erivan, with an Armenian representative of the American Relief Administration weighing out flour to the children who come with tickets. The weights on the scales are stones. The A. R. A. makes its investigations in advance and distributes tickets to the needy families in order that each may get its portion and not more than its portion. These photographs are from the land which asks the United States to act as its guardian, a responsibility which our official missions of investigation seem to think unwise. Armenia was formerly an important part of the very extensive Turkish Empire.

Three starving Armenian boys applying for admission to a relief station in Erivan. The boy on the left is in the last stages, as is shown by his emaciated body and the "starvation face" so familiar in the Near-East. The boy in the center has been living on grass and roots, with a distended stomach as the result. Thousands of children are in this distressing condition and other thousands have been brought through the summer by American flour. To continue relief for 150,000 undernourished little bodies the Commonwealth Fund of New York has just given $750,000 to the American Relief Administration.

Armenian children in the public park at Erivan, being entertained by Miss Gertrude Pearson, of Oak Park, Chicago, who is a genius in telling pantomime stories. At this particular moment she is giving the girls a mental picture of the American skyscrapers, in spite of the handicap of not being able to speak the very difficult Armenian language.

"The Street of Little Coffins" is one of the pathetic spectacles seen in Erivan. The death-rate has been so high that it was found necessary to have "dead

Greek refugees making bread at a station in the neutral zone between the new republics of Armenia and Georgia. The woman at the board in the fore-

His church is raising money for the people of Armenia.

- Before the turn of the century, the Forcelles lived in the newly acquired U.S. territory of Hawaii, where Albert was serving as a Presbyterian missionary.
- While there they learned some of the language, collected furniture made by local craftsmen and learned to fish from outrigger crafts; they also welcomed the American troops passing through during the Spanish American War.

Washington society is attempting to regain its footing.

Life in the Community: Chevy Chase, Maryland

- With the war over, Washington society is attempting to regain its footing.
- President Woodrow Wilson remains incapacitated following his stroke, and Mrs. Wilson devotes all of her time to his care.
- Belgian and British nobility have dressed up the season recently by visiting Washington.
- A reception for H.R.H. Edward Albert, Prince of Wales, held at the Congressional Library "brought out the gowns and jewels," according to the *Washington Post*; Cora, Countess of Stafford, the former Mrs. Colgate of New York, arrived in white satin with diamond tiara and corsage ornaments, and Lady Newborough, who has been passing the past few months with American friends, wore "black velvet on modish lines, with diamonds and pearls."
- Albert and Agnes, in recognition for what they had done during the war, were honored by a personal invitation to the White House by Mrs. Wilson, prior to the President's illness.

"Apartment House Sold," *Washington Post*, November 16, 1919:

"A four-story apartment building at 3516 Connecticut Avenue was sold last week by Harry Wardman to Morris Cafritz for $80,000. The building, which is located just above the Cleveland Park car stop, contains 14 apartments, six of which have four rooms and the remaining eight three rooms. The structure was completed for occupancy October 1. The annual rent is about $9,200."

The Vice President and Mrs. Marshall

request the pleasure of the company of

Rev. & Mrs. Birnie

on Monday evening

February Twenty first

at half after nine o'clock

Dancing   *The New Willard*

This couple enjoys frequent invitations to the White House.

- Women's clubs, created for the purpose of mind improvement, continue to study key issues such as English and French women's war work, prohibition and national efficiency
- General John J. Pershing is still basking in the glow of his victory, even though recently, Ohio Representative Sherwood attracted a firestorm of criticism for suggesting that Pershing was "not on the firing line during the great battles of the western front."

"Society News," ***Washington Post,*** **November 16, 1919:**

"There was an exodus of débutantes and other young people to the White Sulphur for the weekend, parties being made up as soon as it was hinted that the prince was going to be there.

The short and historic visit of the Prince of Wales in Washington has left much-elated the buds of this season and last, who were in the several private parties given for him. Many of the débutantes frankly admit that they hardly know whether they are on their heads or their heels when dancing with a real, delightful prince of the royal blood. This prince left behind a number of personal gifts and souvenirs, which will be cherished probably through many generations. They range all the way from gold purses and silver cigarette cases, to autographed photos of himself, both framed and otherwise. A number of the people with whom he had been thrown together during his visit, and who entertained him, called at the Belmont home just before his departure for the train on Friday night to bid him farewell."

"With the Allies on the Rhine," by Charles Victor, *Leslie's Weekly*, November 15, 1919:

"I wonder how many people thought, when we went into the war, that any part of the American army would be stationed for 10 years on the banks of the Rhine? Very few, I am sure. And not many more, probably, have a very clear idea of the nature of this 'occupation.' Officially, of course, the occupation has one purpose: to enforce the provisions of the treaty of peace. With a hostile army in this country at all times ready for action, it is safely expected that the defeated enemy will be rather particular about 'paying up' promptly. But, as a matter of fact, the army is not, strictly speaking, a hostile one, and its military duties are destined to be perfunctory. Unofficially, however, its presence in the country is bound to have a considerable influence, and incidentally, to bring about consequences that were neither foreseen nor intended by those who decreed the occupation.

These effects, to some extent apparent today, after 12 months, are bound to vary greatly in different zones, according to the temperaments of the nations involved, and according to the policies of their authorities. I have just had an excellent opportunity to observe these differences at close range.

The policy of the British is perfectly clear from the moment you arrive in Cologne. Aside from the primary purpose of the occupation, their objectives are frankly commercial. As soon as the bars of the blockade were let down, the British government considered that it was its particular duty to help British businessmen into Germany as fast as it was physically possible. There is not the slightest attempt to hide this purpose. The corporal in charge of the passport control at the railroad makes you 'show cause' before he allows you to enter the town. If your job is anything but 'business' you are shoved aside, for Cologne is too crowded to accommodate mere pleasure-seekers, journalists, and such-like. . . .

The French are busy at Mayence making the Germans understand that they—the French— are the victors. They have old scores to settle and they propose to settle them here and now. Their policy is not commercial, but political, as their protection of the 'Rhenish Republic' of Dr. Dorten indicates. In the English and American zones harmless army newspapers are published, recording the doings and diversions of the boys; in the French zone there appears a handsomely illustrated weekly, in German and French, recording the latest achievements of the separatists, and 'stimulating French interest in Rhenish affairs.' While the British examine the passports of foreigners, letting the Germans pass without control, a ferocious-looking Algerian in Coblenz scrutinizes every native that attempts to pass the gate. . . .

The American policy is less easy to define. Strictly speaking, we have no policy at all, except to fulfill our engagements with our Allies, irksome as they may be. Our 'Watch on the Rhine' is a purely military action, carried out strictly in conformity with the rules of war, with the minimum amount of discomfort to the natives and no material advantages to ourselves. In the early days of the armistice, when Cologne and Mayence were centers of illicit trading with the enemy, when one truckload of goods after another was smuggled across the 'neutral zone,' and when unscrupulous officers were said to grow rich on bribes, Uncle Sam stood guard over the morals of his men so that not a single case of nefarious dealing could be held against them. The Germans, who abetted this practice for their own benefit, now say that every French officer is a 'schieber' (profiteer), but are obliged to admit the Americans were proof against all temptation."

FIRST IN THE FIGHT— ALWAYS FAITHFUL— BE A U.S. MARINE!

- General Pershing is also popular with America's mothers; the normally unsentimental general gave the celebration of Mother's Day a boost in 1918 by ordering all his commanding officers to have "every officer and soldier in the American Expeditionary Forces to write home on Mother's Day."

"Same Pay for Loan Flyers," *Washington Post*, March 25, 1919:

"As a result of the attempt of some flying 'aces' to commercialize their fame by asking fancy prices, the Treasury Department has been flooded with requests from aviators anxious to pilot the captured German planes in the 'victory loan' campaign. A great number have offered their services 'to Uncle Sam, for nothing.' The department, however, ruled yesterday that all will be paid and all the same amount. They will receive the amount paid aviators in the army service, which is, at the maximum, about $250 a month.

'We have a surplus of crackajack aviators now,' said a Treasury official. 'What we are short of is planes. Many of the aviators have exhibited a splendid patriotic spirit by offering to defray their own expenses. One man who tendered his services explained "that in private life [he was] a minister".'

Women provided America's "manpower" during the war.

- The soldiers were instructed to write "Mother's Letter" on the envelopes so the Army Postal Service could spot them more easily and speed them home.
- According to the *Stars and Stripes*, one transport alone carried approximately 1.4 million letters from France to the United States that year.
- Pershing also took time to thank the women who worked to aid the war effort.
- During the war, women took a critical role in book drives to create libraries overseas, and even gathered peach stones to combat the effects of poisonous gases; seven pounds of pits were needed to filter a single gas mask, and a million men required masks.
- Many women's groups are now turning their attention to widespread starvation in Europe and the threat of socialism taking hold in America.

Historical Snapshot
1919

- President Woodrow Wilson went to the Peace Conference at Versailles and proclaimed America's idealism: "Tell me what's right and I'll fight for it"
- While in Colorado promoting the League of Nations, Wilson suffered a paralyzing stroke on his left side
- The inflationary rate was down to 8.9 percent from 13.5 percent; because of the war, unemployment remained at 1.4 percent
- Labor unrest was intense, the worst since the 1890s; an August tally showed 300,000 workers on strike
- After 110 days of striking, steelworkers in Gary, Indiana, returned to work unsuccessful in gaining recognition from U.S. Steel
- The attorney general brought an injunction to halt a United Mine Workers strike
- An actors' strike for recognition of Actors' Equity closed theaters in New York, Philadelphia, Boston and Chicago
- A nationwide plot to mark the Communist May Day with mail bomb assassinations was thwarted when 16 packages were held at the post office for insufficient postage; the intended victims included millionaires John D. Rockefeller and J.P. Morgan
- The American landscape boasted more railroad tracks than any country in the world
- Standard Railway Time became federal law with the Standard Time Act of 1918, establishing five time zones
- The United States first experimented with daylight-savings time
- Created as a war measure, a 10-percent excise tax on a variety of goods, including soft drinks, was still in effect
- When 45,000 strikers threatened to paralyze Seattle, Washington, the mayor set up machine guns and threatened anyone who attempted to take over the city's facilities
- Thirty-one-year-old Conrad Hilton invested his lifetime savings of $5,000 on the Mobley Hotel in Crisco, Texas
- States ratified the Eighteenth Amendment prohibiting the sale of alcohol, starting in 1920
- The dial telephone, the Communist Party of America, a nonstop flight from New York to Chicago and the Drake Hotel in Chicago all made their first appearance
- Henry Ford gained full control of Ford Motor Company by repurchasing the Company for $105 million
- Prices were up 79 percent over 1914; adjusting for inflation, wages had risen only 14 percent in industry and 25 percent in agriculture

1919 ECONOMIC PROFILE

The national consumer expenditures (per capita income) in 1919 were:

Auto Parts, Gas and Oil	$17.27
Auto Purchases	$12.44
Clothing	$55.52
Food	$177.53
Furniture	$6.97
Housing	$76.98
Intercity Transport	$5.43
Local Transport	$7.78
Personal Business	$19.83
Personal Care	$5.88
Physicians and Dentists	$9.52
Private Education and Research	$7.19
Recreation	$20.64
Religion/Welfare Activities	$13.92
Telephone and Telegraph	$1.93
Tobacco	$13.67
Utilities	$6.76
Per Capita Consumption	$579.57

Annual Income, Standard Jobs

Average of all Industries, Excluding Farm Labor	$1,272.00
Average of all Industries, Including Farm Labor	$1,201.00
Bituminous Coal Mining	$0.34/Hour
Building Trades, Union Workers	$0.57/Hour
Clerical Workers in Manufacturing and Steam Railroads	$1,999.00
Domestics	$538.00
Farm Labor	$706.00
Federal Civilian	$971.00
Federal Employees, Executive Departments	$1,520.00
Finance, Insurance and Real Estate	$1,099.00
Gas and Electricity Workers	$556.00
Lower-Skilled Labor	$991.00
Manufacturing, Union Workers	$0.37/Hour
Manufacturing, Payroll	$0.15/Hour
Medical/Health Services Workers	$606.00
Ministers	$759.00
Nonprofit Organization Workers	$677.00
Postal Employees	$0.38/Hour
Public School Teachers	$377.00

Mother's Cereal Spoon
DOMINION PATTERN
Oneida Community

Par Plate

FREE For Ten Mother's Oats Coupons

This is the cereal spoon for eating oatmeal and other cereals. It is a happy medium in size—larger than a teaspoon and smaller than a dessert spoon. Beautiful in design, closely resembling Sterling Patterns. It is full standard A 1 plate, with best nickel silver base.

Guaranteed by us for period of ten years.

MOTHER'S OATS, RAILWAY EXCHANGE, CHICAGO

This coupon not good after Jan. 1, 1918

State and Local Government
Workers $640.00
Steam Railroads, Wage Earners $600.00
Street Railway Workers. $610.00
Telegraph Industry Workers $601.00
Telephone Industry Workers. $392.00
Wholesale and Retail Trade
Workers $508.00

Selected Prices

Bloomers, Ladies' $0.90
Bookcase, Oak w/Glass Doors $8.00
Chewing Gum, Wrigley's,
Box of 25 Packs. $0.73
Cigarettes, Pack. $0.18
Clock, Wall $5.22
Cough Drops, Luden's. $0.05
Dress, Woman's $5.48
Golf Bag, Canvas. $3.45
Hat, Man's. $5.00
Land, 180 Acres, Wisconsin $9,000.00
Phonograph. $65.95
Phonograph Record $1.50
Puffed Wheat. $0.15
Rug, 6' x 9' $43.50
Rum, Bacardi, per Fifth. $3.20
Soap $0.07
Suit, Child's $2.95
Swing, Rock-a-Bye Baby $1.00
Tobacco $0.15
Work Shirt, Man's $0.75

The estate of Agnes Forcelle's mother:

CASH:

Cash on Deposit, Fifth Avenue Bank		$ 5,800
Currency, Gold		$ 10

STOCKS:

Santa Clara Lumber	1,529 Shares	$76,475
American Telephone and Telegraph	102 Shares	$13,132
Casin Company of America	100 Shares, Preferred	$ 4,000
Casin Company of America	150 Shares, Common	$ 300
Sargent Engineering Company	18 Shares	No Value
Forest Land and Mill Company	60 Shares	$ 585
New Niquero Sugar Company	81 Shares	$ 2,025
Cuban-American Sugar Company	40 Shares, Preferred	$ 3,520
National Sugar Refining Company	305 Shares, Preferred	$29,890
Georgia Coast and Piedmont Railroad	62 Shares	No Value
Adirondack Timber and Mineral Company	100 Shares	No Value
Hudson County National Bank	40 Shares	$15,200
Hudson County Gas Company	50 Shares	$ 6,600
Newark Consolidated Gas Company	125 Shares	$12,000
Wilson Transit Company	40 Shares	$ 4,200
North Jersey and Pocono Mountain Ice Company	3 Shares	No Value
Fajardo Sugar Company	250 Shares	$13,750
Brooklyn Union Gas Company	60 Shares	$ 7,620
State Line Telephone Company	30 Shares, Preferred	No Value
State Line Telephone Company	117 Shares, Common	No Value
United States Steel Corporation	15 Shares, Preferred	$ 1,605
United States Steel Corporation	19 Shares, Common	$ 1,121
West India Company	10 Shares	Unknown
Great Eastern Telephone Company	30 Shares	No Value

BONDS:

New Niquero Sugar Company	10 Bonds of 1,000 each	$ 9,000
U.S. Steel Corporation	2 Bonds of $1,000 each	$ 2,000
Manhattan Railway	1 Bond of $1,000	$ 900
Denver and Rio Grande Railroad	1 Bond of $1,000	$ 1,000
Pacific Coast Company	1 Bond of $1,000	$ 990
Newark Consolidated Gas Company	10 Bonds of $1,000	$10,150
Interborough Rapid Transit Company	2 Bonds of $1,000	$ 2,080
Cuban-American Sugar Company	5 Bonds of $1,000	$ 4,500
Newark Gas Company	5 Bonds of $1,000	$ 6,200
Hudson County Gas Company	12 Bonds of $1,000	$12,120
North Jersey and Pocono Mountain Ice Company	15 Bonds	$10,500
Pacific Telephone and Telegraph Company	2 Bonds of $1,000	$ 1,975
Westinghouse Electric and Manufacturing Company	1 Bond of $1,000	$ 1,000

REAL ESTATE:

No. 16 East 65th Street, New York		$75,000

The entire family loves to travel in style.

Letters home from Martha Birney, during her tour of Europe, 1919:

"Here we are in mid-sea, or rather a bit more than half over, for tomorrow we see Gibraltar and Friday we should be in Algiers. We were delayed two days in sailing and six hours on the pier waiting for our passports to be visaed, but at last we were off and really the sea has treated us most kindly. It has been cold and quiet. We are six at a table, a dear old Frenchman that was naturalized and fought in our Civil War and a professor from Weslyian who is going to study the antiquities in Greece. Father says that with the vigor he displays here onboard ship the ruins had better look out when he gets there. He walks as much as 40 miles a day at home, on the ship, 10 with his feet and at least 16 with his arms.

This boat is French and mine has been so little used that the first few days I would lie awake nights wondering what the femme de chambre was saying to the garçon outside my door. It has returned somewhat and now I lie awake to hear the delightful things the Americans say who attempt a foreign tongue. Even my dear father had a mishap. He always takes a warm bath followed by a cold sponge. The other morning I awoke to hear him in the hall yelling, 'easy frud.' Of course the boy thought he meant his bath was cold and turned on more hot. This only increased his tone and finally I heard him bellow, 'Lucia, come here, I've had my hot bath and now I cannot make this fellow fix the cold so it will run. . . .'

We landed at Ponta Delgada and I assure you the sight of dry ground was heaven to me, although the crossing has not been rough at all but the sea surely grows boring. We walked in the lovely gardens and saw calla lilies and Wandering Jew growing wild and the japonicas were trees instead of potted plants and they were all covered with their lovely cardinal blossoms. Our Portuguese was limited and they did not speak French, but one is always rich when one can get 1,400 rais (their coin) for a dollar and money is a universal language. . . .

Here I am in Rome where I found your letter and indeed I was glad to hear that all was well with you and yours. Various postals will have told you my different whereabouts. We were in Naples for a week staying with people we had known in America, and so of course we had to make the best of things, but I am sure you would have been amused if you could have seen us when they informed us there was only one bath and it was in the kitchen, so if one wanted a bath please to let them know in advance so they could be given a holiday. It was so cold in our rooms that we had to go to bed every moment that we were not out, for the temperature was only 40 and there was no heat of any kind. I used to wear two sets of underclothing in order to dress for dinner and then I always wore my fur on top for, of course, the houses are those old palaces and they are built of stone with very thick walls which hold the dampness and the cold. They like it because it keeps them cool in summer and the Neapolitans do not mind wrapping up in numerous layers in winter.

We came to Rome Wednesday and have been very comfortable here in a hotel built for foreigners which is heated and supplied with sufficient plumbing. We have been sightseeing, resting and generally thawing out since, and now I am seated in my bed in a room decorated in true Italian style with so many mirrors that one sees oneself everywhere, and it is a bit discouraging before one has done one's hair. Ever sincerely your friend, Martha."

P.B. - BORDEAUX — Le Pont de pierre et l'Eglise St-Michel

1920–1929

The years following the Great War were marked by a new nationalism symbolized by frenzied consumerism. By 1920, urban Americans had begun to define themselves—for their neighbors and for the world—in terms of what they consumed. The car was becoming universal—at least in its appeal. At the dawn of the century, only 4,192 automobiles were registered nationwide; in 1920, the number of cars had reached 1.9 million. Simultaneously, aggressive new advertising methods began appearing, designed to fuel the new consumer needs of the buying public. And buy, it did. From 1921 to 1929, Americans bought and America boomed. With expanded wages and buying power came increased leisure time for recreation, travel, or even self-improvement. And the advertising reinforced the idea that the conveniences and status symbols of the wealthy were attainable to everyone. The well-to-do and the wage earner began to look a lot more alike.

Following the Great War, America enjoyed a period of great expansion and expectation. The attitude of many Americans was expressed in President Calvin Coolidge's famous remark, "The chief business of the American people is business." The role of the federal government remained small during the period and federal expenditures actually declined following the war effort. Harry Donaldson's song "How Ya Gonna Keep 'Em Down on the Farm after They've Seen Paree?" described another basic shift in American society. The 1920 census reported that more than 50 percent of the population—54 million people—lived in urban areas. The move to the cities was the result of changed expectations, increased industrialization, and the migration of millions of Southern blacks to the urban North.

The availability of electricity expanded the universe of goods that could be manufactured and sold. The expanded use of radios, electric lights, telephones, and powered vacuum cleaners was possible for the first time, and they quickly became essential household items. Construction boomed as—for the first time—half of all Americans now lived in urban areas. Industry, too, benefited from the wider use of electric power. At the turn of the century, electricity ran only five percent of all machinery, and by 1925, 73 percent. Large-scale electric power also made possible electrolytic processes in the rapidly developing heavy chemical industry. With increasing sophistication came higher costs; wages for skilled workers continued to rise during the 1920s, putting further distance between the blue-collar worker and the emerging middle class.

Following the war years, women who had worked men's jobs in the late 'teens usually remained in the work force, although at lower wages. Women, now allowed to vote nationally, were also encouraged to consider college and options other than marriage. Average family earnings increased slightly during the first half of the period, while prices and hours worked actually declined. The 48-hour week became standard, providing more leisure time. At least 40 million people went to the movies each week, and college football became a national obsession.

Unlike previous decades, national prosperity was not fueled by the cheap labor of new immigrants, but by increased factory efficiencies, innovation, and more sophisticated methods of managing time and materials. Starting in the 'teens, the flow of new immigrants began to slow, culminating in the restrictive immigration legislation of 1924 when new workers from Europe were reduced to a trickle. The efforts were largely designed to protect the wages of American workers—many of whom were only one generation from their native land. As a result, wages for unskilled labor remained stable; union membership declined and strikes, on average, decreased. American exports more than doubled during the decade and heavy imports of European goods virtually halted, a reversal of the Progressive Movement's flirtation with free trade.

These national shifts were not without powerful resistance. A bill was proposed in Utah to imprison any woman who wore her skirt higher than three inches above the ankle. Cigarette consumption reached 43 billion annually, despite smoking being illegal in 14 states and the threat of expulsion from college if caught with a cigarette. A film code limiting sexual material in silent films was created to prevent "loose" morals, and the membership of the KKK expanded to repress Catholics, Jews, open immigration, make-up on women, and the prospect of unrelenting change.

The decade ushered in Trojan contraceptives, the Pitney Bowes postage meter, the Baby Ruth candy bar, Wise potato chips, Drano, self-winding watches, State Farm Mutual auto insurance, Kleenex, and the Macy's Thanksgiving Day Parade down Central Park West in New York. Despite a growing middle class, the share of disposable income going to the top five percent of the population continued to increase. Fifty percent of the people, by one estimate, still lived in poverty. Coal and textile workers, Southern farmers, unorganized labor, single women, the elderly, and most blacks were excluded from the economic giddiness of the period.

In 1929, America appeared to be in an era of unending prosperity. U.S. goods and services reached all-time highs. Industrial production rose 50 percent during the decade as the concepts of mass production were refined and broadly applied. The sale of electrical appliances from radios to refrigerators skyrocketed. Consumers were able to purchase newly produced goods through the extended use of credit. Debt accumulated. By 1930, personal debt had increased to one third of personal wealth. The nightmare on Wall Street in October 1929 brought an end to the economic festivities, setting the stage for a more proactive government and an increasingly cautious worker.

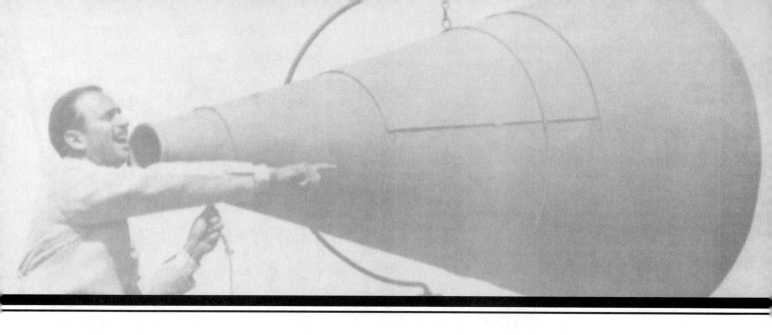

1922 FAMILY PROFILE

Beautiful, tough and driven, Gwendolyn Price is nearing the top of the silent movie star world, due to her mother's ambition, her fabulous good looks and her husband's business savvy. They have no children.

Annual Income: Approximately $650,000; currently, Price commands $50,000 to $100,000 per movie and is able to make four to five movies a year; her husband, Walter Zarnov, will make $350,000 this year through movie productions and the management of several movie stars.

Life at Home

Gwendolyn Price has gained stardom in silent movies.

- Gwendolyn and Walter live west of Los Angeles in a sprawling 3,800-square-foot home complete with an Olympic-size pool where Walter exercises; since they both work in the movie industry, they live near the studio, but still enjoy a mountain view.
- Recently, they purchased a Daniels automobile from "back East" that gives them the look they both desire, since the car is not only expensive—something he likes; it is also very sexy—something she likes.
- Gwendolyn began appearing in movies in 1910 when she was only 14 years old, driven by a very determined mother and a desire to be famous.
- One of three daughters, she is now gaining fame, along with her sister, in the movie industry; their mother had taken the three girls to Hollywood with the expressed purpose of their being movie stars.
- The girls knew little of their father, who left them and their mother before the sisters made their first movie.
- Like many of Gwendolyn's contemporaries, "she came from nowhere and nothing," according to the movie magazines.

The couple's 3,800-square-foot home offers a mountain view.

- For many young actresses, movies are viewed as a way out of poverty.
- When she was featured in the 1911 hit, *An Old Man's Love Story*, her head of thick black hair, full bosom and seductive beauty launched her career, and by 1914, movie scripts were being written around her talent and name.
- That same year, at 18 years old, she married a Russian immigrant who had created a fortune in movies, first as the owner of a chain of movie houses, and later as a movie producer; he is 19 years her senior and she calls him Daddy.
- After their marriage, her husband established a Hollywood-based production company to feature his wife's skills and those of her sister.
- For the past five years, her movies have featured not only her natural beauty, but dozens and dozens of fabulous outfits; women often go to her movies to marvel at the latest fashions she displays on the screen.
- Her roles range from traditional women to exotic, ethnic characters; in recent movies she has played an Asian maiden; the daughter of one of the first families of Virginia fated to marry the wrong man; a Russian in a movie titled *New Moon*, and in *Isle of Conquest*, she is shipwrecked with a man who hates women.
- Her older sister often plays in comedies; they find their parallel careers complementary and rarely compete with one another for attention.
- Her youngest sister, who has only managed to land small parts in a handful of moving pictures, recently married movie star Buster Keaton.

Life at Work

- Gwendolyn belongs to a tiny group of highly celebrated movie actresses who have come to symbolize the romantic ideals of the nation; she is flooded with fan letters, while girls across the nation emulate her clothing, hairstyles and her "way with men."

Recently they purchased a Daniels automobile from "back East."

- Although during the early years she worked an arduous dawn-to-dusk schedule to get parts, her fame is now said to rival that of "America's Sweetheart," Mary Pickford, who is earning more than $100,000 per picture.

- Like many of her fellow movie stars, she is small at only five feet tall, and often plays with leading men who are only six to eight inches taller.

- Her adoring fans see her as a woman with one foot in the 1890s and the other in the 1920s; in a recent movie, she was shown driving her roadster at top speed while planning her "radiophone" dance for the coming evening—a scene displaying both her "new woman" role as the driver of a powerful automobile, and her "old" role of wife, focusing her attention on social events.

- Since her career began, she has appeared in more than 200 movies and can now name her price, often up to $100,000 per picture.

- Silent movies are about emotion and action, and she is talented at displaying both without speaking; title cards displayed throughout the movies provide the viewers with an ongoing conversation, relaying historical information, mood, dialogue and often wit.

- She loves her job, and worships the money she has made as a movie star; having money and power makes her wonder why so many movie directors demand that female actors appear so childlike, helpless and frightened while waiting for heroic men to save them.

- One reason she can command high salaries was the creation of the star system, which began in 1913 when actors began demanding screen credits for their work, allowing them to command higher and higher wages as the public demanded to see their favorite stars.

Her roles range from the exotic to the traditional.

Life in the Community: Hollywood, California

- In 1910, Hollywood, California, was a quiet, country town near Los Angeles, dominated by lemon groves, churches and a few sprawling estates.

- Four years later, Hollywood claimed 52 moviemaking companies which spent $5.7 million a year to crank out more than a thousand miles of developed film annually.

- The area also offered scenic lands for the shooting of cowboy movies, majestic backdrops such as the Pacific Ocean, and the availability of mountains and deserts only a day away.

- The ability to concentrate production into factory-like studios and integrate virtually all aspects of production allowed Hollywood-produced movies to be shot more quickly, at less cost, with more control.

Fans across the country emulate Gwendolyn's fashions and "way with men."

"It was an age of miracles, it was an age of art, it was an age of excess, it was an age of satire."
—Writer F. Scott Fitzgerald

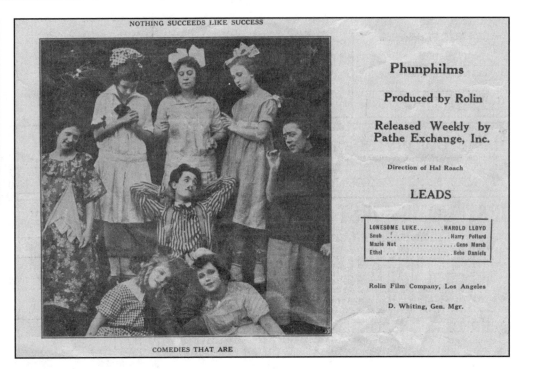

- The Hollywood system became the model worldwide and its products and stars, such as Charlie Chaplin and Mary Pickford, became cultural icons.
- Currently, Hollywood-produced movies dominate worldwide; World War I dramatically reduced the ability of many European producers to compete with American films.
- Nationwide, Americans are enjoying all types of entertainment—motion pictures, baseball and boxing are all drawing record crowds.
- Everyone wants to be in the movies and in Hollywood, so the Chamber of Commerce is currently buying newspaper ads to discourage young women from coming to Hollywood—"the land of broken dreams"; the advertisements plead, "Please don't try to break into the movies."
- Even the great escapologist Harry Houdini has made films to display his greatest stunts; unfortunately, his ability to escape from impossible situations is irrelevant on the screen where the stunts can easily be faked.
- Nationwide, more than 20,000 cinemas are now open, 2,000 of which are picture palaces for the showing of exclusive, first-run movies of "feature length," running about 90 minutes.
- Picture palaces are architectural marvels, designed to capture attention, with many featuring colossal electric signs that can be seen for miles, while interior decorations often showcase opulent chandeliers and classical drapery on walls and entrances, plus elegant furniture; many offer free child care.

Even Harry Houdini is doing movies to display his greatest stunts.

HISTORICAL SNAPSHOT
1922

- Seventeen-year-old Clara Bow won a fan magazine contest for "The Most Beautiful Girl in the World," while Charles Atlas won the "World's Most Perfectly Developed Man" contest
- During his third trial, movie star Roscoe "Fatty" Arbuckle was exonerated of starlet Virginia Rappe's murder, but not before his name was sullied in a highly publicized sex trial
- The self-winding wristwatch, Checker Cab, Canada Dry ginger ale, and State Farm Mutual auto insurance all made their first appearance
- California became a year-round source of oranges
- Automobile magnate Henry Ford, who earned $264,000 a day, was declared a "billionaire" by the Associated Press
- Radio station WEAF objected to airing a toothpaste commercial, deciding that care of the teeth was too delicate a subject for broadcast
- The first commercially prepared baby food was marketed
- The U.S. Post Office burned 500 copies of James Joyce's *Ulysses*
- The mah-jongg craze swept the nation, outselling radios
- Protestant Episcopal bishops voted to erase the word obey from the marriage ceremony
- Movie idol Wallace Reid died in a sanitarium of alcohol and morphine addiction
- Thom McAn shoe store introduced mass-produced shoes sold through chain stores for $3.99 a pair
- Hollywood's black list of "unsafe" persons stood at 117
- Radio was a national obsession; people stayed up half the night listening to concerts, sermons and sports
- Syracuse University banned dancing
- A cargo ship was converted into the first U.S. aircraft carrier
- Publications for the year included T.S. Eliot's *The Waste Land*, F. Scott Fitzgerald's *The Beautiful and the Damned* and H.G. Wells's *The Outline of History*; Willa Cather won the Pulitzer Prize for *One of Ours*
- The tomb of King Tutankhamen, in the Valley of the Kings, Egypt, was discovered
- New York's Delmonico's Restaurant closed
- The first mechanical telephone switchboard was installed in New York
- Broadway producer Florenz Ziegfeld forbade his stars to perform on radio because it "cheapens them"
- In describing the new "flapper," *Vanity Fair* reported, "She will never . . . knit you a necktie, but she'll go skiing with you. . . . She may quote poetry to you, not Indian love lyrics but something about the peace conference or theology"

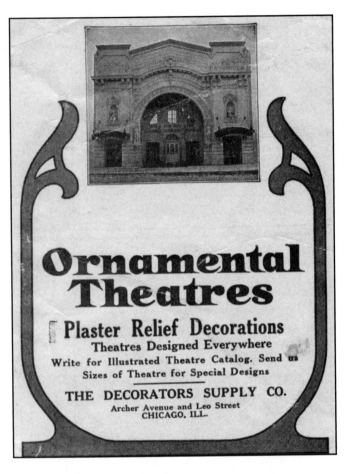

1922 ECONOMIC PROFILE

The national consumer expenditures (per capita income) in 1922 were:

Auto Parts, Gas and Oil $15.03
Auto Purchases $10.66
Clothing. $56.45
Food $128.14
Furniture $6.36
Housing. $89.20
Intercity Transport $5.16
Personal Business $17.95
Personal Care. $5.55
Physicians and Dentists. $6.50
Private Education and Research $6.87
Recreation $19.05
Religion/Welfare Activities $12.57
Telephone and Telegraph $2.35
Utilities. $7.63

Annual Income, Standard Jobs

Average of all Industries,
    Excluding Farm Labor. $1,305.00
Average of all Industries,
    Including Farm Labor $1,201.00
Bituminous Coal Mining. $0.86/Hour
Building Trades, Union Workers. . . $1.11/Hour
Clerical Workers in
    Manufacturing and
    Steam Railroads. $2,067.00
Domestics $649.00
Farm Labor $508.00
Federal Civilian $1,694.00
Federal Employees,
    Executive Departments $1,625.00
Finance, Insurance and
    Real Estate $1,932.00
Gas and Electricity Workers $1,343.00
Lower-Skilled Labor $807.00
Manufacturing, Union Workers . . . $0.87/Hour
Manufacturing, Payroll. $0.49/Hour
Medical/Health Services Workers. $912.00
Ministers $1,622.00
Nonprofit Organization Workers . . . $1,446.00
Postal Employees. $0.76/Hour
Public School Teachers. $1,206.00
State and Local Government
    Workers $1,316.00

Steam Railroads, Wage Earners..... $1,591.00
Street Railway Workers $1,436.00
Telegraph Industry Workers $1,110.00
Telephone Industry Workers $1,064.00
Wholesale and Retail
    Trade Workers $1,261.00

Selected Prices

Alarm Clock $2.50
Automobile, Buick $1,175.00
Brassiere...................... $0.79
Cigarette Case, Silver $11.72
Condensed Soup, Campbell's $0.12
Crib $17.50
Dresser, Walnut $98.00
Electric Percolator $7.15
Fountain Pen, Waterman............ $7.50
Hat Box $5.00
Hotel Room, New York, per Day $3.00
Mouthwash, Listerine $0.79
Permanent Wave Hairstyle $15.00
Piano, Steinway................... $875.00
Riding Breeches, Man's............. $12.00
Steamship Ticket, New York to Boston .. $5.19
Swimming Lessons $5.00
Tennis Racquet $10.50
Tie, Silk $0.39
Waffle Iron...................... $4.00

By 1920, the motion picture business was the fifth largest industry in America.

The Development of Hollywood

- The movie industry's move to California was inadvertently begun by Thomas A. Edison, who invented movies in 1889 and held patents on the equipment and processes.
- To maximize his income and control the use of his patents, as well as the price charged, in 1909 he and several other companies created a trust known as the Motion Picture Parents Company, allowing him to monopolize the film business, which was then conducted largely along the East Coast.
- Eventually, for their own survival, most moviemakers, including Vitagraph, Selig, Essanay and Biograph, signed with the trust, which focused on two-reel, 15-minute stories and showed little interest in long-format movies.
- The independent producers who did not join soon found that movie cameras became impossible to buy, mysterious accidents plagued their studios, and few movie houses would show their films; the Edison-controlled trust decreed that theaters showing independent films would be cut off completely.

"Silent Cinema, 1895–1929," *The Oxford History of World Cinema*:

"The Hollywood production system was not invented, but evolved in response to a number of felt imperatives, of which the most important was the need for a regular and consistent profit. A pioneering role, however, can be ascribed to producer Thomas Ince, working at Mutual in 1913. The standard studio working procedure, as devised by Ince, involved a studio boss, the film's director, and a continuity script. Once Ince, as head producer, had approved a project, he assigned available building for filming, and commissioned writers and production artists to create the necessary script, sets, and costumes. Backup systems, such as an internal police force to keep out crowds, or firefighters to assist when sets burned, meant that by the early 1920s studio lots, covering many acres, operated as veritable subcities within the urban environs of Los Angeles.

Studio bosses planned a programme of films a year in advance. Sets were efficiently used over and over again, and adapted for different stories. Art directors designed and constructed sets; casting directors found talent; makeup artists perfected the glamorous movie look; and cinematographers were picked to shoot scripts as written. Time was of the essence, so actors were shuttled from film to film. Often multiple cameras were used for complicated shots (for example, a battle-field sequence) to avoid having to stage them twice. And always present was the continuity clerk, who checked that, when shooting was completed, the film could be easily reassembled."

- To escape the power of the trust, independent producers began moving to Los Angeles, which offered not only good weather, cheap land and non-union labor, but also steady sunshine for year-round shooting.
- In 1913, when director Cecil B. de Mille began shooting his first movie, *The Straw Man*, he was shot at twice by snipers; the master copy of his film was destroyed by saboteurs and he began carrying a pistol.
- Although the harrassment and violence continued in California, the shift to the West Coast was permanent.
- In Hollywood, however, the warring continued as studios also began competing for talent; at that time the names of most actors and actresses were kept secret to hold their salaries down to a standard $5.00 a day.
- Mary Pickford and her independent producer Carl Laemmle of Imp Studios broke with this tradition, creating the first major silent movie star; with the use of careful lighting, a curling iron and outsized sets designed to make her look smaller, she was able to remain a coy young maiden of 16 for many years.
- She quickly became the best-loved actress in the world; by 1916 she was making $10,000 a week.
- *Picture-Play* magazine complained that year that "salaries of players are, without a doubt, the greatest drain on the producers' bank

Miss America of 1925, Adrienne Dore. Mostly she furnished atmosphere for scenes of the Montmartre. Left: Adrienne in "The Wild Party."

The one and only Parisian honey (by way of Montreal), Fifi D'Orsay, with that big brute Victor McLaglen in "Hot for Paris." McLaglen has gone on up the cinemaladder, Fifi is appearing in night-clubs.

Left: Minnesota's pride, who rose to greatest heights on Broadway; whose ex-husband, Sidney Blackmer, surpassed her on the screen; who appeared in "Faust" last year; was making "South Sea Rose" when this picture was taken... who? Lenore Ulric, of course!

By the 1920s, the movies were responsible for creating dozens of "stars" each year.

accounts. This can be readily realized when one brings to mind the single man who draws a salary that is nearly seven times that of the President of the United States—Charlie Chaplin. Mr. Chaplin alone costs the Mutual Company $520,000 a year, and when his contract was signed he received an additional bonus of $150,000."

• That year nearly 25 million people a day were paying from $0.05 to $0.25 to view a movie; gross revenues from ticket sales reached $735 million.

"Married Women in Industry, Radio Talks on Women in Industry," by the United States Women's Bureau, broadcast over radio in 1923:

"Most persons think of wage-earning women as youngsters from 18 to 25 years old, who are working for a few brief years in industry until they are fortunate enough to meet some young men who marry them and they live happily ever after.

That is just what does happen to a good many young women, as we all know. But it does not happen, by any means, to all women wage earners. There are many thousands of women in industry who never marry but keep on working through all their lives. A woman in a factory in Indiana stated that she had been making gingham aprons in that factory for more than 40 years. Besides such women who have worked steadily in industry, there are many thousands more who get married, stop work for a while, and then go back to the factory to help out with family expenses, or, in some cases, to take the places of husbands whom sickness or death has removed from the ranks of the breadwinners.

These are the women the bureau wants to tell you about, so that you may get a better idea of who goes to make up the great group of women wage earners, and so that you will know more of the human problems which must often be dealt with by these women who wait on you in stores, who make your clothes, prepare your food, and help to make almost every article you use, from a toothbrush to a railroad train.

It is an easy matter to find out how many married women are wage earners. In 1920 there were 1,920,281 married women who were gainfully employed. The census, which is taken every 10 years, tells us that. But the census does not tell us very much about them. The Women's Bureau wanted to find out more details of those women, so the records which the census had taken in 1920 for all the women in one industrial town were studied, and it was found that about half the women who were breadwinners were married women. There were about 4,000 married women earning money in this one community. When examined closely the records disclosed something that seems very important. Nearly two thirds of

them were mothers who had children less than five years old. The bureau wanted to find out how these mothers managed to take care of the children and do other work at the same time, so the census records were looked at again to see whether any light on the subject could be discovered. It was found that about half of these mothers of young children earned money at home by taking in boarders or doing laundry or some other form of work which did not oblige them to leave home, so they could look out for children and work at the same time. But the other half went out to work and spent their days in mills making woolen and worsted cloth, and in factories making handkerchiefs and other manufactured articles. Wonder arose as to what became of those little children while their mothers were away from home all day; and because there was no other way to find out, agents were sent to visit as many of these families as they could.

During these visits, among every five women one was found who was working at night and looking out for her children during the daytime, and one who just left the children alone at home to look out for each other. Sometimes the father worked at night and cared for the children in the daytime while their mother was away, and sometimes the neighbors or the landlady or relatives kept an eye on the children. Only one woman in 20 had someone who was paid especially to care for her young children while she was away at work.

Does this give you a picture of the pressure under which women are working in industry? Can you see all these mothers leaving home at 6:30 or 7:00 in the morning after they have washed and dressed the children and fixed their breakfast and lunches? Can you see these mothers working all day, and can you imagine their thoughts as they wonder whether the children are all right and whether someone has seen to all the many things little children need? And at the end of the day's work in factory or mill, can you picture the homecoming of these mothers, and the tasks which await them?"

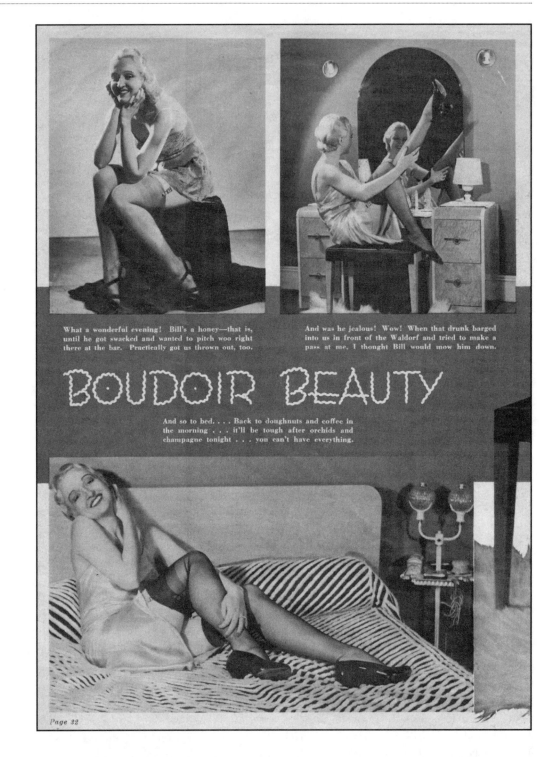

What a wonderful evening! Bill's a honey—that is,
until he got swacked and wanted to pitch woo right
there at the bar. Practically got us thrown out, too.

And was he jealous! Wow! When that drunk barged
into us in front of the Waldorf and tried to make a
pass at me, I thought Bill would mow him down.

BOUDOIR BEAUTY

And so to bed. . . . Back to doughnuts and coffee in
the morning . . . it'll be tough after orchids and
champagne tonight . . . you can't have everything.

Page 32

- By 1920, the motion picture business had become the fifth largest industry in America; only railroads, textiles, iron and steel, and oil were larger, while the automobile industry was sixth.
- The cost of producing a film rose from $500 in 1910 for a one-reel short to more than $20,000 for a two-hour feature.

Theatre Magazine
review of *Tarzan of the Apes*, 1918:

"*Tarzan of the Apes*, with Enid Markey and Elmo Lincoln, is above all else different, wherein its success should lie. We are, all of us, tired of looking at society, sex, allegorical and historical pictures, and it is a relief to view a picture, with a unique jungle story, in which the hero is kidnapped as a child by apes and brought up by them. Add some exciting jungle scenes, apes in great quantity, the appearance in jungleland of Jane Porter in the person of Enid Markey and you have a closeup of *Tarzan of the Apes*."

• In 1915, D.W. Griffith's three-hour extravaganza, *Intolerance*, required 15,000 extras and cost $1.9 million to make; though critics called it "the highest achievement which the camera has recorded," the public didn't understand the complex plot and the film was largely a bust.

Hollywood and fashion are frequent partners.

"The First Oyster-Purification Plant," *The Literary Digest*, February 16, 1922:

"Certified oysters will soon be in as much demand as certified milk. Processes for the sterilization of the oyster, already noted in these pages, have already passed the experimental stage, and a commercial plant, endorsed by city, state and federal health authorities, is now in successful operation near New York. Apparently no one need contract typhoid from eating oysters in the future, no matter what may be the character of the location of the beds where they have been grown. The purifying plant alluded to above is described in *The Nation's Health* (Chicago) by William Firth Wells of the New York State Conservation Commission, who had charge of the earliest experimental work on the process. 'It is unfortunate for oyster culture that these estuaries are also valuable harbors, about which population concentrates and pollutes the tidal waters.'

He goes on: 'Thus many of the finest grounds are restricted by public health regulations, and so any efficient and reliable method of purification should concern sanitarians as well as the shellfish industries. During the past year the first practical plant has been certified by the New York State Conservation Commission, thus, it is believed, marking the establishment of this process as a part of the oyster industry. Fifteen thousand bushels of oysters have been purified commercially, marketed with the approval of the authorities, and consumed by an appreciative public.

'The operation of this plant represents the consummation of successful scientific, commercial, and administrative studies. The underlying principles were carefully worked out during 1914–15 at the Fisherman's Island, Virginia, experiment station in charge of the writer. It was discovered that shellfish closed tightly in the presence of considerable excess of free chlorine, thus protecting the interior tissues from its effects, but permitting the sterilization of everything exterior to the shells; and secondly, that shellfish kept in pure salt water rapidly eliminate by their natural functions all interior contaminating materials accumulated on the tissue surfaces.'"

1924 FAMILY PROFILE

Seventy-year-old Garrett Cooper has invested so much of his money, energy and life in guiding the growth of Tulsa, Oklahoma, that he is considered the unelected mayor of this oil boom-built community. A millionaire thanks to the boom, he currently devotes his time to civic projects on behalf of Tulsa. His wife died three years ago.

Annual Income: He lives on the interest from his assets of more than $13.5 million.

Life at Home

- Throughout his long career in Tulsa, Garrett Cooper has operated a mercantile store, served as postmaster, founded a bank, been a Board of Education member and a Sunday School superintendent, as well as president of the Old Commercial Club.
- The love of his life, his wife Nell, whom he met during a trip to Atlanta, Georgia, kept her job as a third-grade school teacher years after he had made his first million.
- Since her death three years ago, he has turned her bedroom into a shrine to her memory, cherishing pictures of her as a young woman, when they first fell in love, and though the couple had no children, they jointly reveled in the potential of the community to be a great city.
- Many call Cooper "Mayor," and even though he has never officially held the position, few civic leaders would attempt a project without getting his support in advance.
- He and Nell came to Tulsa with little when the community was still small and struggling.
- Drawing on his experience, he opened a small store catering to the largely male population of oilmen who were continually drilling holes in search of the liquid, which has become a precious commodity due to the dramatic increase in the sale of automobiles and gasoline engines.

Garrett Cooper is the unofficial mayor of Tulsa, Oklahoma.

Garrett and Nell came to Tulsa when it was a small, struggling community.

- Even when money was scarce, Nell backed his decision to give certain oil wildcatters store supplies on credit in exchange for a portion of their drilling discoveries; this decision and his flair for leadership have made him millions.

- He currently lives in an old section of town in a house he and his wife built at the turn of the century; most of the homes around his were built later and are much larger, owned by men who have become wealthy during the past two decades, thanks to oil.

- Last year was particularly satisfying to his neighbors: oilman Harry Sinclair's horse Zev won the Kentucky Derby and oilman Josh Cosden's horse Martingale came in second; Cosden was disappointed with second place, having won the Derby in 1921 with his horse Paul Jones.

- Garrett and Cosden have been friends since Josh came from Baltimore around 1912 with the dream of supplying the emerging automobile market with lubricants and cheaper gasoline.

- Cosden had little and borrowed a lot from Garrett's mercantile store; four years later, when Cosden acquired $12 million from Wall Street to build a refinery, Garrett was paid back handsomely for his generosity and patience.

- The newspapers have speculated that Cosden is worth more than $50 million, but Garrett has always been careful with his money and would not even think of building a home similar to his friend's, which is known throughout the state as a showplace, featuring an indoor swimming pool and garden braced by two clay tennis courts built with soil imported from France at a cost of $10,000.

- A founding member of the Tulsa Commercial Club, begun in 1901, Garrett has been in the center of the city's most critical decisions since the oil boom began on June 25, 1901, with Sue Bland No. 1 at Red Fork, just across the Arkansas River from Tulsa.

- Almost overnight the area was teeming with adventurous oilmen, investors, speculators, gamblers, wildcatters, geologists and lease hounds, all eager to wrestle wealth from the black gold.

- So much oil was being produced so rapidly, for a short period crude oil dropped to an all-time low price of $0.03 per barrel.

- Oil companies worked off the surplus by marketing their products to railroads, shippers, sugar refiners, breweries and other businesses as a cheap alternative to coal; they also began selling gasoline to automobile owners, who were then a small, wealthy niche market.

- The Commercial Club played a key role in creating the additional infrastructure needed to cope with the oil boom: railroad facilities, bridges, hotels, banks and housing.

- One of its first steps in 1902 was for 50 of the businessmen in the club, including Garrett, to collectively pledge $12,000, plus several miles of free land, to persuade the railroad to include Tulsa on its planned route from Muskogee to Pawhuska, and though for many, the individual amounts pledged exceeded their personal assets, when the railroad traffic arrived, the payoff was tremendous.

- This type of unified "Tulsa Spirit" was used repeatedly during the past two decades to encourage and guide growth; for example, in a similar move, Garrett invested in a private effort to build a bridge from Tulsa to the Red Fork oil development after a city-wide bond effort failed.

- The impact of the bridge on the city was immediate; Cooper and his fellow investors not only improved Tulsa's access to the oil fields, their real estate and oil holdings escalated in value.
- As Cooper's reward for his leadership, several oilmen deeded him a portion of their annual production.
- The city is also working on plans to build an airport; oil and aviation seem to go together for men who love risks and are always in a hurry, and as a result, W. G. Skelly, founder of Skelly Oil company, is prepared to organize Spartan Aircraft Company to build planes.
- Currently, Garrett's energy is going into erasing the embarrassment Tulsa suffered last year when Governor J. C. Walton declared marshal law in the city after the Ku Klux Klan engaged in mob violence and numerous whippings; as a result, 150 National Guardsmen have been assigned to the city.
- Many business and political leaders in the state are members of the KKK, so Garrett has been visiting them privately to ask that they control the Klan for the sake of Tulsa.
- Unemployment is rising and lawlessness after World War I has become more pronounced, including labor fights, clashes between racial groups, bank robberies and mob whippings.
- Klan violence has become common against women who wear their hair or skirts short, Jewish merchants who open on Sundays, foreigners who do not speak English and students who speak out.
- Recently, Garrett rewarded himself for a lifetime of work by buying a new Cadillac V-63, a five-passenger sedan; he loves its size and beauty, and knows that, with a car like this, if he becomes too ill to drive himself, he can always hire a chauffeur.

Life at Work

- Now in his seventies, Garrett Cooper opened one of the first mercantile stores in Tulsa.
- Honest and hardworking by nature, he was trusted by the community with their purchases and later with their cash, when he helped establish one of the first banks in the area.
- Like many Tulsa merchants, he preached a simple motto: "A dollar's worth of honest goods for a dollar in money."
- Garrett is attempting to promote further growth around the concept of the "Tulsa Spirit"; a recent newspaper story quoted him as saying, "Tulsa just didn't happen. While the settlers were all poor, I do not believe the Creator ever put down in one place so many pioneers with the vision of state and city buildings as had Tulsa's first citizens. Indian and white man, Jew and Gentile, Catholic and Protestant, we worked side by side, shoulder to shoulder, and under these conditions the Tulsa Spirit was born and has lived and God grant that it never dies. As we start this new year of 1924, may the spirit of the pioneer—the spirit that built Tulsa—prevail as of yore."

Oil has fueled the growth of Tulsa.

- Because one of his many current projects is the development of air travel to Tulsa, he chaired an aviation land site committee formed in 1917 by the Tulsa Chamber of Commerce.
- As a result, within two years Tulsa bought land four miles east of the city and developed its first airfield, operated by barnstormer Duncan A. McIntyre.
- By 1919, McIntyre Airport was the second largest commercial airfield in the United States and the only one with runways both lit for night flights and long enough for two-passenger airplanes.
- It was a grand moment for Garrett and Nell to watch America's first air shipment of goods over an interstate route—from Tulsa to a factory in Kansas City, Missouri—leave McIntyre Airport.
- As a result, August Henry M. Hickam, Director of the National Air Service in Washington, D.C., added Tulsa as a regular stop for all transcontinental mail and military flights, securing the future role of air travel in Tulsa.
- Air travel also helped Tulsa become the unchallenged leader of the oil industry; since World War I, executives from all parts of the world have been travelling to northeastern Oklahoma for training in the latest techniques of producing and marketing petroleum.
- A recent report of the Chamber's Aviation Committee indicates that "a great public airport" is now needed if the city is to stay at the forefront of aviation.
- Garrett and his friends, not entirely satisfied with the speed and urgency shown by the Chamber, are now raising money to buy the necessary land for an enlarged airport.

Life in the Community: Tulsa, Oklahoma

- Recently, the Tulsa Regional Commission was organized to devise a city plan for promoting future expansion.
- The commission is attempting to eliminate serious handicaps retarding future expansion, such as the haphazard growth of subdivisions outside the city limits.

Many of Garrett's partners have been friends since the turn of the century.

ADVERTISEMENT: Maple Ridge Addition, a Tulsa Subdivision

"Maple Ridge exemplifies the highest residential development in Oklahoma with colonial-type architecture predominating . . . . Permanency, with quiet good taste, is the ruling motive—no garish waste of money for mere show's sake. Rather, the homes of Maple Ridge are the fruition of the plans of years, now made possible of realization through the city's growing prosperity. And the growth of Tulsa follows no rule. It is the marvel of our neighbors in that it never hurries, yet never halts."

- The plan being studied provides for railroad terminals, parks, a civic center and control of subdivisions both within the city and those extending three miles beyond the city limits in all directions.
- The International Petroleum Exposition, established last year in Tulsa, is bringing the city fame as the home of the "World's Fair of the Oil Industry."
- The community has come a long way in a short time; by the end of 1882, Tulsa's entire commercial district consisted of Hall's General Store, Bullette Brothers' Store, Perryman Brothers' Store, Archer's Furniture and Hardware, Chauncey Owen's Boarding House and one physician, Dr. W. P. Booker.
- When Tulsa was officially incorporated as a City of the Creek Nation on January 18, 1898, the population totaled 1,100 and the citizenry was almost entirely white as a result of the 1889, 1891 and 1893 land runs.
- In 1900, this former Indian meeting place was a hamlet known as Tulsey Town, still consisting of a single dirt street lined with buildings; the population was 1,340.
- The community's entire freight business for the first week of 1900 was listed as, "Receipts: One car—bran; Shipments: Two cars—hogs; One car—sand; One car—mules."

The University of Tulsa, 1921–1923, by Guy Williams:

"Howard Archer had been appointed (football) coach. A good team and a strong schedule awaited him, but he was concerned that there was no official name for the team. They had been referred to as "Kendallites," "Tigers," and other titles; that year they were called the "Yellow Jackets" because of the yellow-gold color of their uniforms. Archer wanted a distinctive name. He had been impressed by the Georgia Tech-named "Golden Tornado," which implied a wave of power, and he chose "Golden Hurricane." The name in part was related to the jerseys. The team voted to approve the name, and it became the official name of all the athletic teams."

WHO has not sailed a pirate ship or looked for treasure lands! · · · Those boyhood dreams return once more to the man who sits at the wheel of his LaFayette · · · His is the sense of command of every situation · · · He may lay his course to match his mood and whim. Doors to new motoring pleasures are opened to him. Trails once forbidden are easily mastered. Travel is glorious and secure.

Steadily the conviction that the LaFayette is one of the world's finest motor cars is finding wider and wider acceptance as the experience of LaFayette owners becomes known

LaFayette Motors Corporation, *Milwaukee, Wisconsin*

LAFAYETTE

- The newspaper carried a story saying that Chief Frank Corndropper would soon give his daughter May in marriage and receive in return the groom's gift of several hundred ponies.
- Then in 1902, oil was discovered, and by 1910, the population had reached 18,182; agrarian Tulsa quickly evolved into oil-town Tulsa.
- Within a decade, more than 100 oil and gas companies were established, employing 15,000 field workers and averaging $15,000 in royalty payments per month.
- In the single year of 1911, nationally and locally based firms drilled 4,986 wells at a combined cost of $11 million, losing only $800,000 on 675 speculative sites that produced dry holes; of the 114 petroleum companies in the state, 95 located their home offices in Tulsa.
- At the same time, the Mayo Brothers constructed a five-story building downtown—widely considered the "finest building in Tulsa"—setting a standard for others to follow.
- By the beginning of World War I, the city boasted 72 miles of paved streets; 32 passenger and freight trains arrived and departed daily, and tourists had the choice of 20 hotels—two of which were six stories high.
- Thanks to the oil money, everything was new; in the year 1920 alone, Tulsa spent $3 million paving 110,243 square miles of streets.
- Currently Tulsa's population is 110,000, enough both to rival Oklahoma City and be listed nationally with other cities that claim more than 100,000 people.

"Riches End the Frontier," *Then Came Oil*, **by C. B. Glasscock, 1938, quoting oilman Josh Cosden, who made and lost millions in the oil fields:**

" 'When a man plays for high stakes every day of his life for years, when he races horses, fights economic and political hazards, and lives constantly up to the limits of his energies and his physical, intellectual and material resources, it burns him up. I have lived that way, and I have enjoyed it.' . . .

'I found on the Oklahoma frontier in the early days of oil the greatest lure and the finest human social drama in the history of America. The lure of oil is the most romantic business in history. It is a business on the highest plane because in finding and producing oil, we are taking from the earth a hidden natural resource of great value to humanity. We are hurting no one, and are helping many.' "

- Construction is proceeding at a torrid pace; the residence of Richard Lloyd Jones, publisher of the *Tulsa Tribune*, has raised a few eyebrows with its modern lines and a "strange and startling beauty that fits naturally into a setting unconscious of a past."
- The Boston Avenue Methodist Church, which Garrett attends, has recently completed its fourth expansion program with architecture so distinctive, it is known internationally.

"The Oil Exposition Is an Immense Exhibit," *The Oil and Gas Journal*, October 2, 1924:

"Developing in 18 months from an idea into the largest exposition ever held by a single industry, the International Petroleum Exposition stands as a monument to the tremendous scope and power of the business of oil exploration, the production of crude petroleum, the refining of the crude into hundreds of distinctly useful products and the transportation and marketing of oil in every part of the world.

The Exposition, which opens in Tulsa on Thursday, occupies 7.5 acres of space; the size of it can better be imagined by mentally envisioning the great display as in one building. To house the show under one roof, with one big aisle, and the exhibits grouped along both sides of the aisle, would require a building that would occupy more than 20 city blocks. With the outside exhibits it would string even farther.

It occupies more space and will have a greater number of exhibits than was contained in the great machinery hall at the World's Columbian Exposition in Chicago, which was housed in the largest building ever built up to that time. . . .

Many entirely new tools, devices and instruments which manufacturers have held back for this occasion will be shown for the first time, and improvements on well-known articles of oil industrial equipment will be first noted by the crowds who attend the big oil and gas show."

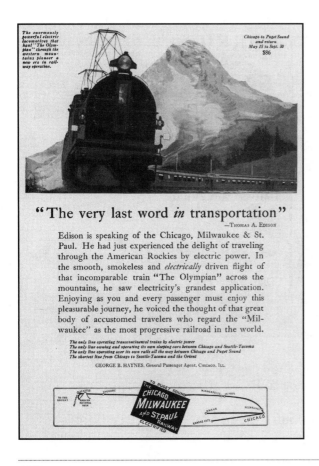

The enormously powerful electric locomotives that haul "The Olympian" through the western mountains pioneer a new era in railway operation.

Chicago to Puget Sound and return
May 15 to Sept. 30
$86

"The very last word *in* transportation"
—Thomas A. Edison

Edison is speaking of the Chicago, Milwaukee & St. Paul. He had just experienced the delight of traveling through the American Rockies by electric power. In the smooth, smokeless and *electrically* driven flight of that incomparable train "The Olympian" across the mountains, he saw electricity's grandest application. Enjoying as you and every passenger must enjoy this pleasurable journey, he voiced the thought of that great body of accustomed travelers who regard the "Milwaukee" as the most progressive railroad in the world.

The only line operating transcontinental trains by electric power
The only line owning and operating its own sleeping cars between Chicago and Seattle-Tacoma
The only line operating over its own rails all the way between Chicago and Puget Sound
The shortest line from Chicago to Seattle-Tacoma and the Orient

GEORGE B. HAYNES, General Passenger Agent, Chicago, Ill.

- The city now boasts a critical item missing for many years—a satisfactory water system—thanks to a $7.5 million expenditure to bring water from the Spavinaw Hills, 65 miles to the northeast.
- At the same time, Tulsa purchased the land surrounding Lake Spavinaw to protect the water from pollution and then began building public recreational facilities, including picnic tables and cabins, and providing boats for hire; the availability of water also means that ice can be provided for the Tulsa Ice Oilers, the city's professional hockey club.
- Three years ago, when the Presbyterians relinquished their exclusive control of Henry Kendall College, it was chartered as the University of Tulsa; as part of the transition, the church still directs the policy of its Department of Religion and requires Bible courses for nearly all students.
- Recently, when the 400-plus students returned to campus, they found that the wooden gymnasium had been removed and the lumber used to erect four temporary buildings—two for classrooms, one for music and the fourth for storage.
- Garrett loves to attend the football games, especially last season when the Golden Hurricanes of the University of Tulsa went undefeated.

It is now the custom of many Tulsa women to visit vacation resorts for six weeks each summer.

- In 1923, a special technical department was formally launched at the public Carnegie Library, creating a comprehensive collection of information on the petroleum industry.
- Nationwide, as well as in Tulsa, the custom of women going to vacation resorts for six weeks in the summer is now common; the comic magazine *Judge* created a "Summer Widowers Number" devoted to the subject.

HISTORICAL SNAPSHOT
1924

- Concerns arose that the increasing number of telephones would lead to the elimination of regional dialects and the reduction of written records for historians to study

- College football, thanks to stars such as Galloping Ghost Red Grange, was so popular it surpassed boxing as a national pastime

- Ernest Hemingway gained national recognition when he joined in the running of the bulls at Pamplona, Spain

- African-American actor Paul Robeson was threatened by the KKK when he was featured in the play *All God's Chillun Got Wings* as the black husband of a white woman

- News programs became more prominent on radio, challenging the popular all-dance-music programs

- A popular GOP convention drink was the "Keep Cool with Coolidge" highball, consisting of raw eggs and fruit juice

- Henry Ford paid $2.467 million in federal income taxes

- Dime magazines such as *Detective Story* and *Western Story* increased in circulation to half a million

- Walt Disney created a cartoon named "Alice's Wonderland"

- The permanent wave, contact lenses, Beech-Nut Coffee, Wheaties and college marriage courses all made their first appearance

- The U.S. Supreme Court declared unconstitutional an Oregon law requiring all grammar school-aged children to attend school

- Gangland king Diom O'Banion was buried in a $10,000 bronze casket; 20,000 attended the funeral

- The Methodist Episcopal General Conference lifted its ban on theatergoing and dancing

- Commercial laundry use increased 57 percent during the past 10 years

- The newest places to hide liquor included shoe heels, flasks form-fitted to a woman's thigh, folds of coats and perfume bottles

- The first Macy's Thanksgiving Day Parade delighted thousands as it made its way down Central Park West in New York City

1924 ECONOMIC PROFILE

The national consumer expenditures (per capita income) in 1924 were:

Auto Parts, Gas and Oil	$22.66
Auto Purchases	$20.82
Clothing	$62.04
Food	$160.59
Furniture	$9.49
Housing	$98.89
Intercity Transport	$4.95
Local Transport	$9.13
Personal Business	$27.33
Personal Care	$7.79
Physicians and Dentists	$10.94
Private Education and Research	$7.72
Recreation	$24.52
Religion/Welfare Activities	$11.31
Telephone and Telegraph	$5.88
Tobacco	$13.13
Utilities	$9.82
Per Capita Consumption	$619.45

Annual Income, Standard Jobs

Average of all Industries, Excluding Farm Labor	$1,434.00
Average of all Industries, Including Farm Labor	$1,434.00
Bituminous Coal Mining	$0.72/Hour
Building Trades, Union Workers	$1.31/Hour
Clerical Workers in Manufacturing and Steam Railroads	$2,239.00
Domestics	$741.00
Farm Labor	$382.00
Federal Civilian	$1,762.00
Federal Employees, Executive Departments	$1,776.00
Finance, Insurance and Real Estate	$1,997.00
Gas and Electricity Workers	$1,552.00
Lower-Skilled Labor	$1,095.00
Manufacturing, Union Workers	$0.99/Hour
Manufacturing, Payroll	$0.49/Hour
Medical/Health Services Workers	$916.00

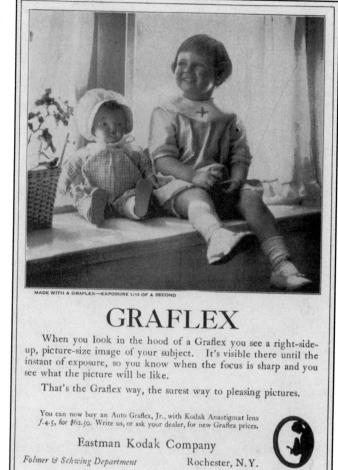

Ministers $1,826.00
Nonprofit Organization
  Workers $1,578.00
Postal Employees............... $0.87/Hour
Public School Teachers........... $1,299.00
State and Local Government
  Workers $1,377.00
Steam Railroads,
  Wage Earners $1,597.00
Street Railway Workers $1,565.00
Telegraph Industry Workers $1,161.00
Telephone Industry Workers $1,108.00
Wholesale and Retail Trade
  Workers $1,416.00

Selected Prices

Airline Ticket, Los Angeles
  to San Francisco $50.00
Cape, Mink $55.00
Cigarettes, Pall Mall $0.30
Dance Lessons, per Couple $1.00
Eyelash Treatment, Maybelline........ $0.75
Golf Bag......................... $6.50
Insecticide, Licecil $1.00

Lawnmower $18.00
Magazine, *Life*, One-Year
   Subscription...................... $5.00
Nonprescription Drug,
   Milk of Magnesia $0.39
Refrigerator, Kalamazoo............. $27.95
Ring, Black Pearl $3,500.00
Sewing Thread..................... $0.09
Shoes, Child's Keds $0.75
Stationery, 24 Sheets
   w/Envelopes...................... $1.50
Straight Razor $2.90
Suitcase, Black Enameled Buck........ $6.00
Talking Machine, Victrola $125.00
Work Shoe, Man's, all Leather $3.45

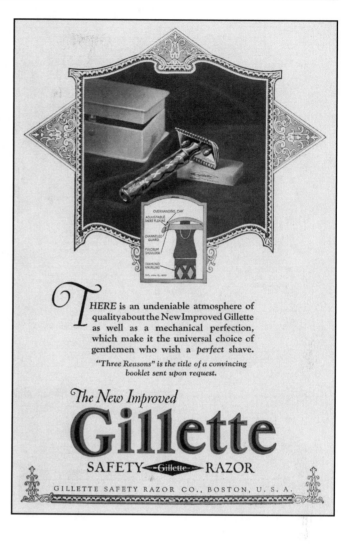

1927 Family Profile

The Ormsby family divides its time between Palm Beach, Florida, and Philadelphia, Pennsylvania, where Harriet Ormsby is the reigning hostess of the city.

Income: The family assets total more than $38 million.

Life at Home

- The daughter of wealthy parents, Mrs. Ormsby married well and was widowed at age 44 when her husband died of a heart attack while participating in a polo match.
- The next year, while crossing the Atlantic on a cruise with her daughter, Harriet met a widower and the two immediately fell in love.
- Martin Ormsby is an investment banker who has spent most of his life handling the family's affairs, not unlike her first husband, who was also very active in commercial development.
- Originally from New York City, Martin moved to Philadelphia following the wedding, which was attended by former president William Taft; Ormsby has since taken riding lessons and joined the Rose Tree Hunt.
- Even though main-line Philadelphia wealthy matrons have shunned the Ormsbys' display of wealth and party giving, Harriet, who is notorious for her parties, is determined to become the city's reigning hostess; she keeps detailed scrapbooks of every event, including seating charts and menus.
- Her jewelry collection resembles a jewelry store; many of her favorite necklaces are displayed on mannequins on a dressing table, and her diamond tiara is so heavy, she occasionally complains to the servants that it gives her a sore neck.
- Built at a cost of $1 million, their home in Palm Beach, Florida, is a 50-room Georgian colonial mansion with quarters for 30 servants and a garden room accommodating 200 dinner guests.
- Their 145-room Philadelphia home, comprising 2.5 acres, cost $3 million to construct over a five-year period and boasts 45 bathrooms, 12 elevators, an indoor gym, swimming pool, squash and tennis courts and an icemaking plant capable of producing a ton of ice a day.

The Ormsbys' 145-room Philadelphia home boasts 45 bathrooms and 12 elevators.

Thirty-six-year-old Geoffrey is currently living at home following his divorce.

- The house is staffed by 45 servants and includes its own telephone switchboard and operator, a bakery, tailor, barber shop and movie theater; 70 gardeners tend the 300 acres of landscaped grounds, while two chauffeurs care for the family's six cars, including four Packards.
- The Ormsby family also has a house at Bar Harbor, Maine, where they swim and socialize in the summertime.
- When their daughter made her début at age 18, the 600 invited guests were entertained by four orchestras.
- That night, Harriet presented her daughter with a $1.5 million pearl necklace once owned by Catherine the Great of Russia.
- Her 36-year-old son Geoffrey is currently living with them following his divorce from an automobile heiress.
- Married after a two-month courtship, he and his bride entertained more than 2,000 guests at a reception at the palatial Grosse Point home of her parents as guards watched over the $100,000 pearl necklace worn by the bride, a wedding gift from her father.
- The bride's mother gave the couple a wedding present of $100,000 in silver.
- Following the wedding, the bride and groom made their getaway under an archway of roses to the waiting 243-foot family yacht, with its crew of 60, after which the couple took a year-long honeymoon, visiting Europe and Asia, and sailing around the tips of both South America and Africa during the year.
- Geoffrey's tendency toward liquor and other women was overlooked until he lost millions of his wife's money attempting to control the Florida resort market; a quiet divorce was arranged by her father.

"Financial Questions That Women Ask Me,"
by Mrs. William Laimbeer, *The Delineator*, June 1928:

"The term speculative investment has lured many a person to ruin. Perhaps if they had good judgment they might have pulled out with profit. The woman today who feels the urge to buy common stocks with a view to appreciation must do it at her own risk.

It is a recognized fact that some common stocks offer large opportunities for profit over a period of years, but it is also true they possess great possibilities of loss. In order to minimize the risk when one reaches a stage in the investment program where common stocks can be considered, diversification of commitments as to industry, company and location is the proper procedure. The general order of common stocks is—railroads, public utilities and industrials, re-

spectively. This is because railroads and public utilities are least affected in the way of earnings from operation by changing conditions in economics and finance.

In purchasing common stock it is well to be sure on one point: That the company has a large earning power over and above dividend requirements and that it has an excellent dividend record over a long number of years. During periods of inflation or rising commodity prices, greater earnings result, particularly for industrial companies, and these earnings are usually passed on to the stockholder in the form of increased dividends. During periods of depression, dividends in common stocks are sometimes passed over altogether."

Following the divorce, Geoffrey's wife divides her time between her house in Michigan and the developing resorts of Palm Beach, Florida.

A love of golf is sweeping the nation.

Life at Work

- Harriet has convinced her husband Martin that they should invest in opera; she has seen what the promotion of the Metropolitan Opera in New York has done for the social position of the Belmont family, especially August's second wife Eleanor, and believes it will do the same for her in Philadelphia.
- She also feels it will help overcome the talk of her son Geoffrey's divorce, which caused a recent slight by Philadelphia society; she was stung by a snub from the aristocratic Mrs. Alexander Williams Biddle, who is very adept at ignoring those she does not believe to be in her class—no matter how much money they have.
- Recently, several important parties have come and gone without an invitation to the Ormsbys.
- Martin has little interest in parties, his focus being on golf and the potential for building golf courses near every major city; having recently toured golf courses in three states to learn more about proper design, he was particularly impressed with a course he saw in Augusta, Georgia.
- He also visited courses in Florida, but due to the recent embarrassment caused by his stepson, he is avoiding the Palm Beach scene: during a party at the home of Marjorie Merriweather Post, which featured animals loaned by the

Martin has a keen interest in building quality golf courses.

Ringling Brothers and Barnum and Bailey Circus, Geoffrey caused a scene by becoming so intoxicated, he attempted to ride one of the elephants, causing an animal stampede that destroyed the food tables, knocked down a small building and resulted in several women being hurt.

- He was asked to leave and does not expect to be invited back; upon reflection he is convinced there is room for a "second Palm Beach" for people who are more fun-loving.
- When the time is right, Geoffrey wants to invest in Florida again; he believes that his losses in land development there were simply bad luck, and besides, he now has the experience to learn from his mistakes.
- No one could have predicted that the northern press would attack the Florida land boom at the same time a railroad strike stopped the flow of materials and a hurricane that killed 400 made everyone skittish.
- Now that Geoffrey is again unattached, his taste for show girls, café society and heiresses is being fully tested; he plans a trip to Paris soon to see "what is new."
- His theory of life is simple: "If you've got it, flaunt it"; he rarely reads books and hates magazines, saying, "Life is an open book," although every morning he avidly reads the sports pages of the newspaper to see how his teams are doing.
- Rarely a day goes by that he does not place a bet on a baseball game or boxing match; he is convinced the American League is more corrupt, so he places most of his money on National League teams.
- He considers London his second home, where he keeps an apartment complete with two cars; he loves showing off his British driver's license.

Life in the Community: Palm Beach and Philadelphia

- Movie theaters in Palm Beach and Philadelphia are installing air conditioning, which requires an apparatus taking up the entire basement to house more than 15,000 feet of heavy-duty pipe, giant 240-horsepower electric motors, and two 1,000-pound flywheels.
- Though in the past, the theaters have simply closed during the summertime because of the heat, summer is becoming the peak moviegoing season nationwide because of air conditioning and the construction of elaborate movie palaces.
- In Florida, increased railroad construction has dramatically increased the number of people visiting Florida even in the face of the collapse of the real estate boom.
- Last year alone, 2.5 million tourists visited Florida, some coming by airplane, since the state now has nine airports.

"Passages," *Town and Country Magazine*, April 1, 1926:

"DePolignac, Princess Edmond (Winnaretta Singer), that famous and formidable daughter of the Singer who so fortuitously sold us sewing machines, passed through New York from her visit to Florida, where she has been surveying the fantastic and magic real estate activities of her brother, Paris Singer. She is one of the few Americans to have accomplished the rare feat of establishing a salon. Much of the new music we have heard in the public concert halls of New York has had its premiere in the private music room of her Paris home. Many artists are grateful for the eager impulse her patronage has afforded them."

Luxury cruises now feature elegant meals, fashion shows and the latest entertainment.

- Jacksonville remains Florida's largest city, but Miami has moved from fourth in 1920 to second place.
- During the land boom, which peaked in 1925-26, the *Miami Herald* was the world's largest newspaper in terms of advertising linage, with one issue setting a record by publishing 22 sections containing 504 pages.
- The state of Pennsylvania is debating the merits of erecting a statue to the memory and works of Boies Penrose, the city boss who became one of the nation's most powerful United States senators.
- One of the Ormsby family's social friends, Albert Coombs Barnes, is gaining considerable fame for his collection of modern art including more than 1,000 paintings displayed in a French Renaissance palace within a 12-acre park in Merion, a suburb of Philadelphia.
- Harriet secretly agrees with Philadelphia's elite who have branded his extensive collection of Renoirs, Van Goghs, Matisses and Pascins as simply ugly; many suggest publicly that he is simply a rich collector somewhat deficient in his artistic knowledge and taste.

HISTORICAL SNAPSHOT
1927

- More than 40 percent of all American households now had a telephone
- The ticker tape parade for pilot Charles Lindbergh in New York consumed 18 tons of phone books, newspaper and ticker tape; the city spent $16,000 to clean up after the celebration
- Twenty million cars were on the nation's highways, up from 13,824 at the turn of the century
- The per capita consumption of crude oil reached 7.62 barrels
- Peanut butter cracker sandwich packets were sold under the name NAB by the National Biscuit Company for $0.05 each
- Massachusetts passed the nation's first compulsory automobile insurance legislation
- Transatlantic telephone service between London and New York began at a cost of $75 for three minutes
- The Conover Company advertised: "Why drown your soul in a greasy dishpan? The greatest gift of electricity to the modern housewife is the Conover Electric Dishwasher"
- Film producers added sound sequences to silent movies and called them "part talkies"
- The Model A Ford replaced the Model T and featured four colors (including Arabian Sand), a self starter, rumble seat and shatterproof windshield; since 1908, Ford had sold 15 million of the retired Model T automobiles
- The Al Capone gang netted $100 million in the liquor trade, $30 million in protection money, $25 million in gambling, $10 million in vice and $10 million in the rackets
- The original manuscript for Lewis Carroll's *Alice's Adventures Underground* was sold for $75,000
- Broadway roared; in all, a record 268 plays were performed
- Black leader Marcus Garvey, who was convicted of mail fraud in 1923, had his sentence commuted and was deported to the West Indies
- Sears and Roebuck distributed 15 million catalogues to American homes
- The car radio, Borden's homogenized milk, Volvo, the Literary Guild of America, A&W Root Beer and the all-electric jukebox made their first appearance
- A national survey reported a "loosening" in manner and morals; Mrs. Bertrand Russell defended "free love" and Judge Lindsey advocated trial marriages
- To abide by prohibition laws, restaurants hired detectives to search customers for hip flasks and bottles before serving ice and ginger ale
- Despite extensive protests at home and abroad, Sacco and Vanzetti were executed
- The average salary reached $1,312 a year; teachers made an average of $1,277, lawyers took home $5,205 and factory workers averaged $1,502

Palm Beach fashion was sweeping the nation.

> "Society consists of people of common interests who know one another and like to be with one another. It is simply people who prefer to be with their own kind."
>
> —Elsa Maxwell

1927 ECONOMIC PROFILE

The national consumer expenditures (per capita income) in 1927 were:

Auto Parts, Gas and Oil	$20.48
Auto Purchases	$16.76
Clothing	$63.92
Food	$153.89
Furniture	$9.43
Housing	$95.09
Intercity Transport	$4.77
Local Transport	$9.45
Personal Business	$31.67
Personal Care	$8.75
Physicians and Dentists	$11.03
Private Education and Research	$8.46
Recreation	$26.39
Religion/Welfare Activities	$12.16
Telephone and Telegraph	$6.33
Tobacco	$13.58
Utilities	$10.33
Per Capita Consumption	$626.45

Annual Income, Standard Jobs

Average of all Industries, Excluding Farm Labor	$1,487.00
Average of all Industries, Including Farm Labor	$1,380.00
Bituminous Coal Mining	$1,342.00
Building Trades, Union Workers	$1,719.00
Domestics	$756.00
Farm Labor	$387.00
Federal Civilian	$1,907.00
Finance, Insurance and Real Estate	$2,019.00
Gas and Electricity Workers	$1,558.00
Manufacturing, Payroll	$1,534.00
Medical/Health Services Workers	$931.00
Nonprofit Organization Workers	$1,647.00
Public School Teachers	$1,393.00
State and Local Government Workers	$1,488.00
Steam Railroads, Wage Earners	$1,687.00
Street Railway Workers	$1,549.00
Wholesale and Retail Trade Workers	$1,573.00

"You'd think he'd start using Marlin Blades!"

GUARANTEED BY THE MARLIN FIREARMS CO.

SAVE TIME and MONEY on SHAVING

HERE'S HOW...

Selected Prices

Baseball Bat, Louisville Slugger. $2.00
Book, *Winnie the Pooh* $2.00
Ceiling Fan, Hunter. $52.00
Concert Ticket, Washington . . . . $1–$2.00
Funeral Expenses. $935.00
Golf Clubs, MacGregor $78.00
Hunting Coat, Man's $3.50
Ironing Table, Daisy $2.35
Lipstick, Tangee. $1.00
Pistol, Six-Shot, Revolver $12.00
Pocketknife, Remington $3.50
Shoes, Woman's, Snakeskin $22.50
Soap, Bar $0.57
Tissue, Scott. $0.25
Tool Chest, Stanley $15.00
Toaster, Toastmaster $12.50
Vase, Imported Japanese $1.25
Wheelbarrow. $6.25
Wristwatch, Man's 14-Karat Gold $38.50

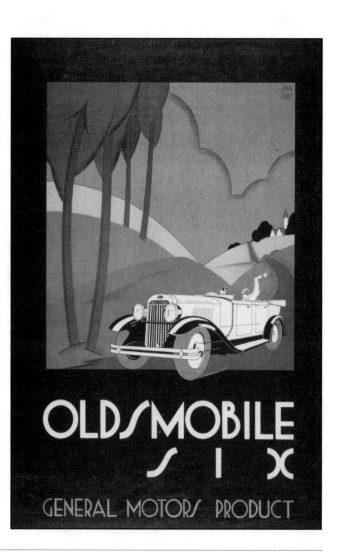

OLDSMOBILE SIX

GENERAL MOTORS PRODUCT

"Undercover," an Interview with Bruce Bielaski by John B. Kennedy, *Colliers*, August 13, 1927:

"'In the fight against booze smugglers there have been flagrant cases of local authorities cooperating not with us but with the bootleggers,' declares A. Bruce Bielaski, recently chief of the federal forces in the Atlantic seaboard war of wits between the government and the rum barons.

Then this ex-official of a Republican administration adds: 'I believe that a shrewd politician like Governor Smith could, if he wanted to, enforce prohibition.'

When Hippy Werner, henchman for the Providence rum syndicate, stepped scowling into Coast Guard regional headquarters he was eagerly received. Hippy was sore on the syndicate. They had done him dirt. Revenge!

'They're bringin' a load tomorrow night,' whispered Hippy, 'on the British trawler *Minerva*, from Barbados. Four thousand cases of Scotch. The boat's due at Warwick Beach at two in the mornin'. They're protected by Coast Guard X-3. Now you guys go get 'em. I'm through.'

Hippy's scowl was realistic; it seemed permanent. He withstood the cold gleams of doubt.

The government men thanked him. The next morning when the *Minerva* snorted up the channel, the mid-New England Coast Guard was concentrated to intercept her, and yowling cockney seamen found themselves betrayed after assurance that they'd go unmolested. The *Minerva* was found to have 1,000 cases in her hold—all dolled up in the authentic Scotch bottles with straw overcoats. Disappointing, but substantial. Hippy had told part of the truth.

When the bottles revealed no Scotch, but an inferior concoction of fuel oil and watered alcohol, the government sniffed suspiciously.

Later they discovered that while all available Coast Guard forces were out watching for the *Minerva*, an armada of schooners had landed

elsewhere on the Rhode Island coast with the biggest importation of rum in months!

So much for the sincerity of Hippy Werner's scowl. The incident was humiliating. But —

To Hippy Werner's superiors in Providence there went one day a captain in the Coast Guard, disgruntled and gloomy. He complained that he had been put under suspicion by the government men and that if he got the blame he might as well get the game. The syndicate paid the captain something in advance, with rosy promises of reward if the adventure succeeded. Their trawlers, loaded to the limit with authentic Scotch and Canadian ale, had no sooner got within view of shore than the captain, ostensibly protecting them, showed his guns, the government swarmed from his hold, and the biggest capture in months was made.

There are typical high spots in the continuous crossplay of strategy between the rum importers and the federal undercover forces. It's up to the government to match the ingenuity of the crafty gentlemen who play every card in the pack of human cupidity and guile to land their shipments.

A. Bruce Bielaski, who operated the New York undercover headquarters for two years, speaks frankly for the first time on the war of wits between government and bootleggers.

'The spectacular cases are few. The job of catching the rum gangs is mainly routine,' he says, 'and exasperating. Enforcement is on the defensive, resisting invasion most of the time. . . .' Bielaski initiated and supervised scores of successful raids, uncovered seagoing corruption in the U.S. Coast Guard, and received scores of letters threatening limb, life and reputation—and forming an impressive array of unsolicited testimonials to his efficiency.

A medium-size, plump, affable, youngish man, with a clean-shaven face that has never known in 15 years of federal detective work the melodramatic adjunct of false whiskers, this son of a Methodist minister of Polish ancestry was drafted into the prohibition service to be Eastern field marshal of the cleanup campaign planned by General Lincoln C. Andrews early in 1925. He returned last spring to the quiet, downtown law practice which he had deserted to serve the government . . . returned with a sense of relief which an intelligent man experiences who has tackled a thankless, hopeless job.

This he brands it, not with the dulled enthusiasm of one who went brightly into his first crusade to find the disillusionment that is part of all crusading. He had turned three successful jobs for the government, one in his youth, as chief of the Bureau of Investigation on Mann Act cases; another as special assistant to the attorney general in the federal bucket-shop roundup in 1909; and the third as head of espionage during the height of the enemy propaganda wave in the war.

'Those jobs,' he says, 'were conclusively successful. Public opinion was solidly behind the Mann Act and the bucket-shop prosecutions, and approved the drive against enemy propaganda. These campaigns were well-conceived and energetically executed. We got results because everywhere we received assistance from the local authorities, who supported us in a common cause.

'But in the fight against booze smugglers, my experience has been the opposite. Save in one instance, that of Police Commissioner George V. McLaughlin in New York City, local authorities have not regarded prohibition enforcement as of any concern to themselves. Indeed, there have been flagrant cases of their cooperating not with us but with the bootleggers. . . .

'When I was told in the spring of 1925 that I was wanted at an important conference with General Andrews, I went to that meeting in the right mood. The picture painted to me was one of a serious and unflagging effort to check liquor smuggling and the illicit diversion of grain alcohol, to fight bootlegging by reaching for the higher-ups. It seemed an attractive picture. Although I had been out of the federal service for some years, it was apparent to me that prohibition enforcement could have progressed under

resolute administration. So, knowing something of General Andrews, I accepted the appointment.

'In everything I did I had the help and encouragement of General Andrews. No bureau chief could be more inspiring to his aides. But after nearly two years of it I learned that A LARGE PERCENTAGE OF OUR POPULATION DOES NOT CONSIDER TRAFFIC IN LIQUOR AS HEINOUS AS A VIOLATION OF ALMOST ANY OTHER FEDERAL STATUTE.

'We discovered that the extension of the rum line from a three-mile limit to a 12-mile limit, or one hour's steaming from shore, had little perceptible effect. The legal boundary was meaningless if the Coast Guard supposed to patrol it was venal—AND IT WAS. . . .'

Spying activities among the personnel of the Coast Guard, riddled with graft, covered so much flagrant crookedness that Bielaski himself wryly admits conditions were farcical. 'I have read a dozen or more cases in the official records. They are all alike, differing only in detail of quantity in bribes and identity of the bribe taker. Captain Nicholas Brown, skipper of the patrol boat No. 126, confessed that he received bribe money regularly and "slipped some of the money to higher-ups in the Coast Guard service. . . ." Captain Frank J. Stuart of No. 129 confessed his "career of crime lasted two months. In that time I pocketed thousands of dollars in bribes. I got $2,000, a year's pay, just to let several fishing boats land liquor on Fort Pond Bay, near Montauk, Long Island."'

Keep your vacation with a Kodak

For the good times you'll like to remember—your Kodak will not let you forget. Keep your Kodak handy.

EASTMAN KODAK COMPANY, ROCHESTER, N. Y., *The Kodak City*

A little tinker gets just as smudged as a big one –

P-G

The largest-selling soap in the world

"Dr. Cadman on the Moral Plight of Youth," *The Literary Digest*, January 14, 1928:

"Youth's wild scramble for pleasure and pursuit of pagan gods, about which there have been such great outcry by distracted elders, are traceable to the lack of piety in the home, to the surrender by the very elders who make complaint of those moral restraints and gentle urgings of which Burns sang in his immortal 'Cotter's Saturday Night.' So says Dr. S. Parkes Cadman in an article prepared by request for *The American Review of Reviews*, in which he tells us that the young people of today are essentially what their predecessors have been, that 'they too nearly resemble their parents to be saints, and are too much like themselves to be anything but human.' When we recall, he says, the widespread demoralization and anarchy which ensued after the war, 'in which fatuous promises of "a new world fit for heroes and heroines to live in" turned to dust and ashes in the mouths of those who made them, we ought not be surprised that social stability was severely shaken, or that a universal slump in authority has seriously impaired home supervision and religious guidance.' Yet that is exactly what has happened; the surprise of the older generation has not been about its own sins of omission, but about youth's sins of commission.

Dr. Cadman, who is so well-known as hardly to need introduction, is president of the Federal Council of Churches of Christ in America, and millions listen to him over the radio every Sunday. Now he gives us a profound and considered analysis of the moral situation in which the world found itself in the years after the war, in which we thought we had discovered moral salvation and a salve for all our sins. . . . Whether true or not, it is generally taken for granted that the younger generation of today is the worst in the cradle of the race. Dr. Cadman acknowledges that conditions are bad, but he sees a saving remnant, at least, in which most of us are born.

Like most prophets of all time, Dr. Cadman looks to the home as the unit of civilization, as the nucleus of all that is permanently good in the history of man. 'If parentage is noble,' he tells us, 'so is its progeny; if it is treacherous to its trust, the consequences fall upon the children.' But in too many homes the old pieties have been abandoned. 'They have been forsaken,' Dr. Cadman tells us, 'at a crisis when mechanical and materialistic elements assert themselves on every side, with the result that much shallowness and cynicism mar the zest for life, and youthful but prematurely stale souls become inert and useless before their fight has well begun. Neurosis, depression, crime, and even suicide ravage youth unfortified by domestic religion and its faith in a righteous and loving God.

'The old Biblical formulas are not accepted by modern youth; secularism has had some sort of triumph; materialism has been overstressed, the attainments of science have been used too much to promote physical welfare and comfort, and the new learning and much of current literature are too much devoted to inculcating an individualistic philosophy of life.' "

Many believe that "the younger generation of today is the worst in the cradle of the race."

1928 NEWS PROFILE

"Little Lost Sheep—Modern youth is groping its way toward higher levels of understanding. Such is the firm faith expressed by the great English preacher Maude Royden, in an interview with Myra Mason Lindsey," *McCall's Magazine*, **April 1928:**

" 'The wild revolt of youth—I am speaking of only the feminine part of it here—with its hip flasks, its gin-mad parties, its roadhouse revels and its even more radical departures from the path of convention followed by its mothers, is the last gasp of the old system of woman's slavery to man, of the ancient idea that he was lord and master of the universe, superior to her in every way and therefore, to be imitated. When woman first advocated suffrage, certain militant leaders among them sought to prove their equality with men by lopping off their hair, wearing breeches and swaggering in a manner that they thought suggestive of bravery and masculinity. But women like that and haircuts like that have, mercifully for the rest of us, developed along lines more natural and beautiful and original.

'And so will hip flasks pass and gin-mad parties and roadhouse revels and their complementary evils. These violent social convulsions are only more modern, more widespread symptoms of the same general imitative malady, which, by its every epidemic form, should serve to immunize the world from its further ravages. There will be, of course, other epidemics, as civilization moves along, for we cannot grow properly, cannot learn to be wise unless we have first suffered for our own foolishness.

'Those young folk whom Judge Lindsey describes in his recent book, *The Companionate Marriage*, and in earlier writings and whom other students of our present social order are painting in much the same colors, are insisting upon their right to do wrong. They want to be free as men have always been and they are daring the world to stop them. They are determined to be wicked no matter how much it may hurt. Men, of course, have always had enough moral rope to hang themselves and these young women and girls of ours want to discover whether they can play with the same coils and still escape the noose. This is what they call "freedom." They do not know that it is only a pitiful lack of imagination, a blind and sleeplike following of the footsteps of someone else!'

This is the diagnosis of A. Maude Royden, one of the greatest preachers and sociologists of her generation. Miss Royden, absent during the past three months from her congregation

Maude Royden

in Guildhouse, London, has been preaching and lecturing in the United States where she is so widely known and loved. As she sat in the long, book-walled study of the house of her New York publisher and talked, she seemed to see 'quite through the deeds of men' and beyond them into the promise of God, and those deeds would someday be wiser and kinder and lovelier. The daughter of a baronet, with all the graces and exquisite culture of the British aristocrat, and with an education in science and literature rounded off at Oxford, she still has not been appalled by the brutal contracts of living which she encountered while she worked and preached in the slums of Liverpool and London, scenes of misery and savagery and human failure as would have horrified eyes of shorter vision or a spirit of weaker faith. Instead she gained a vision and a faith so profound and understanding that she has been able to make the miracles of Christ as credible and simple to a materialist as to a mystic, a vision and a faith that sees in every new discovery of science but another revelation of God to the ever-awakening spirit of man. She believes that humanity is on a long upward march to human betterment and that it has been for millions of years, and that 'an ocean of truth lies unexplored before us,' and that that truth shall make us free.

She believes that no matter how great God is, 'our idea of him is inadequate.' She believes 'that each age, each nation, each individual is great, not in proportion to the special love of God, but in his own ability to respond to that love.'

She recognizes the recklessness and image-breaking of modern youth and yet she is not discouraged and not afraid!

'The World War broke open the chrysalis of our vague unrest, tearing loose the bonds of our old standards and loosening upon the world young human butterflies that must taste every flower, whether it yield honey or gall,' Miss Royden continued. 'It brought on much talk about the rights of people and peoples, and these children whose exploits were not burdening the public mind have, like many of the unthinking young before them, interpreted liberty as the right to do as they please, no matter whom that might displease or injure. The blame of all this cannot be laid at the door of the parents, except in individual cases. It is rather the product of the age. Science is moving too rapidly for the multitude; it will take time for this to be absorbed and translated into the common life.'

In her ministry, Miss Royden receives the confidences and the agonized confessions of thousands of persons every year. Many of these come, she says, from young women who have found that the primrose path to 'a good time' ends in a labyrinth bristling with thorns and brambles. They are beginning to awake and to pay the price of that awakening. Thus, painfully, they are growing into a deeper comprehension of the values of life. 'I will not let my daughters behave as my mother has let me,' she wailed.

'It may take another generation to check the general stampede. It may take even longer. It may not take so long. But checked, it will then have served its social purpose,' Miss Royden emphasized.

She does not, however, hold with Judge Lindsey that the terrible conditions he describes are universal. They may have reached the plague stage but they have, by no means, felled everybody. The strongest and most protected among our young folk have escaped, are escaping, just as the strongest and most protected among them physically avoid diphtheria and scarlet fever and infantile paralysis. She respects Judge Lindsey's honesty and sincerity. But she regards *The Revolt of Youth*, the book which preceded his more recent and even more startling one, as 'a tissue of falsities from beginning to end,' not in the specific facts and cases which he cites, but in the interpretation he puts upon them.

'Why,' she exclaimed, 'he seems to see nothing wrong in a girl's deliberately deceiving her parents by palming off her own baby upon them as the child of another. He even condones it. I myself have great respect for a girl who, if she has got into trouble, does not snake off into a corner like a cat to give birth to young, but has the courage and the character to bring it up as her own and tell the truth about it.'

Miss Royden takes issue also with Judge Lindsey's prescription for a companionate marriage. She realizes that he does not mean that term as trial marriage but as a perfectly legal contract. But even so, she disapproves of it. Its idea of economic independence for the wife, of her having no claim upon her husband until there are children, of their pledging themselves to practice birth control until they decided to have those children, is a dangerous one. It would lessen their responsibility toward themselves, each other, their marriage and society in general. They would interfere with their growing personal unity and would tend to heighten selfishness rather than diminish it, making it harder for them rather than easier to reach the final basis of family marriage, as Judge Lindsey calls the old-fashioned variety we have always known, with children and a common purpose and a common income."

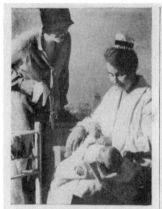

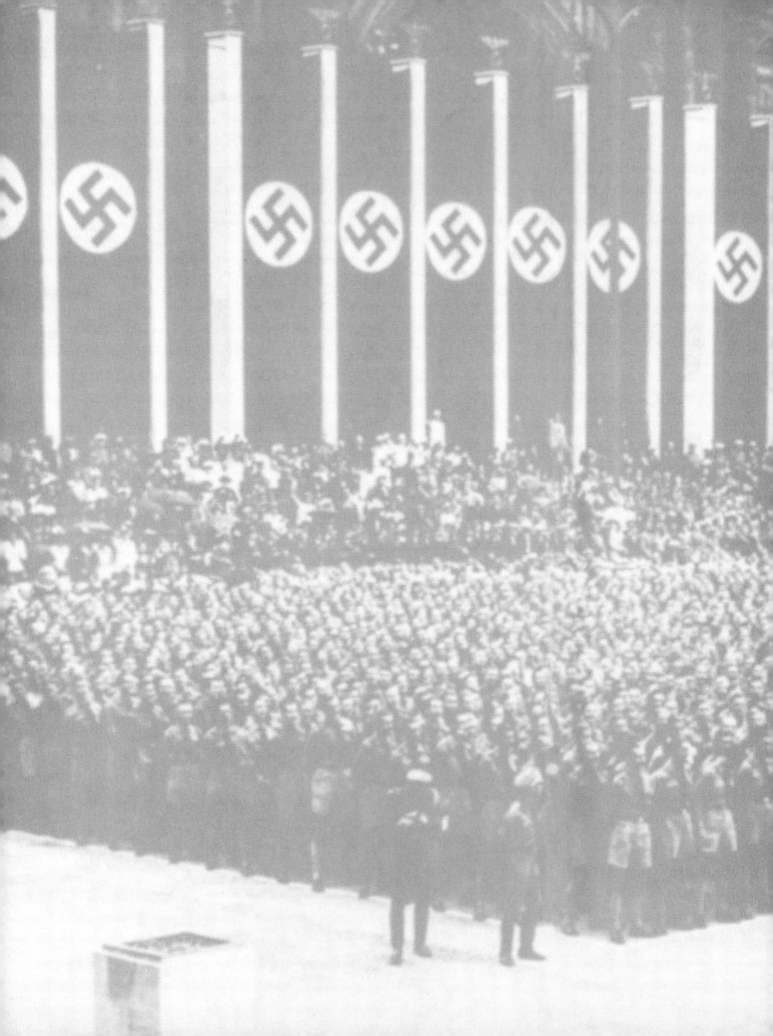

1930–1939

Few Americans—including the very rich—escaped the devastating impact of America's longest and most severe depression in the nation's history. Banks failed, railways became insolvent, unemployment rose, factories closed and the upper class moved out of the biggest houses in town. Economic paralysis gripped the nation. Promising businesses and new inventions stagnated for lack of capital and customers. By 1932, one in four Americans was jobless. One in every four farms was sold for taxes. Five thousand banks closed their doors, wiping out the lifetime savings of millions of Americans—rich and poor.

The stock market sank into the doldrums. In urban areas, apple sellers appeared on street corners. Bread lines became common sights. The unemployed wandered from city to city seeking work, only to discover the pervasive nature of the economic collapse. In some circles the American Depression was viewed as the fulfillment of Marxist prophecy—the inevitable demise of capitalism.

President Franklin D. Roosevelt thought otherwise. Backed by his New Deal promises and a focus on the "forgotten man," the president produced a swirl of government programs designed to lift the country out of its paralytic gloom.

Roosevelt's early social experiments were characterized by relief, recovery, and reform. Believing that the expansion of the United States economy was temporarily over, Roosevelt paid attention to better distribution of resources and planned production. The Civilian Conservation Corps (CCC), for example, put 250,000 jobless young men to work in the forests for $1.00 a day. By 1935, government deficit spending was spurring economic change. By 1937, total manufacturing output exceeded that of 1929; unfortunately, prices and wages rose too quickly and the economy dipped again in 1937, driven by inflation fears and restrictions on bank lending. Nonetheless, many roads, bridges, public buildings, dams, and trees became part of the landscape thanks to federally employed workers. The Federal Theatre Project, for example, employed 1,300 people during the period, reaching 25 million attendees with more than 1,200 productions. Despite progress, 10 million workers were still unemployed in 1938 and farm prices lagged behind manufacturing progress. Full recovery would not occur until the United States mobilized for World War II.

While the nation suffered from economic blows, the West was being whipped by nature. Gigantic billowing clouds of dust up to 10,000 feet high swept across the parched Western Plains throughout the 'thirties. Sometimes the blows came with lightning and booming thunder, but often they were described as being "eerily slight, blackening everything in their path." All human activity halted. Planes were grounded. Buses and trains stalled, unable to race clouds that could move at speeds of more than 100 miles per hour. On the morning of May 9, 1934, the wind began to blow up the topsoil of Montana and Wyoming, and soon some 350 million tons were sweeping eastward. By late afternoon, 12 million tons had been deposited in Chicago. By noon the next day, Buffalo, New York, was dark with dust. Even the Atlantic Ocean was no barrier. Ships 300 miles out to sea found dust on their decks. During the remainder of 1935, there were more than 40 dust storms that reduced visibility to less than one mile. There were 68 more storms in 1936, 72 in 1937, and 61 in 1938. On the High Plains, 10,000 houses were simply abandoned, and nine million acres of farm turned back to nature. Banks offered mortgaged properties for as little as $25 for 160 acres and found no takers.

The people of the 1930s excelled in escape. Radio matured as a mass medium, creating stars such as Jack Benny, Bob Hope, and Fibber McGee and Molly. For a time it seemed that every child was copying the catch phrase of radio's Walter Winchell, "Good evening, Mr. and Mrs. America, and all the ships at sea," or pretending to be Jack Benny when shouting, "Now, cut that out!" Soap operas captured large followings and sales of magazines like *Screenland* and *True Story* skyrocketed. Each edition of *True Confessions* sold 7.5 million copies. Nationwide, movie theaters prospered as 90 million Americans attended the "talkies" every week, finding comfort in the uplifting excitement of movies and movie stars. Big bands made swing the king of the decade, while jazz came into its own. And the social experiment known as Prohibition died in December 1933, when the Twenty-first Amendment swept away the restrictions against alcohol ushered in more than a decade earlier.

Attendance at professional athletic events declined during the decade, but softball became more popular than ever and golf began its drive to become a national passion as private courses went public. Millions listened to boxing on radio, especially the exploits of the "Brown Bomber," Joe Louis. As average people coped with the difficult times, they married later, had fewer children, and divorced less. Extended families often lived under one roof; opportunities for women and minorities were particularly limited. Survival, not affluence, was often the practical goal of the family. A disillusioned nation, which had worshipped the power of business, looked instead toward a more caring government.

During the decade, United Airlines hired its first airline stewardess to allay passengers' fears of flying. The circulation of *Reader's Digest* climbed from 250,000 to eight million before the decade ended and *Esquire*, the first magazine for men, was launched. The early days of the decade gave birth to Hostess Twinkies, Bird's Eye frozen vegetables, windshield wipers, photoflash bulbs, and pinball machines. By the time the Depression and the 1930s drew to a close, Zippo lighters, Frito's corn chips, talking books for the blind, beer in cans, and the Richter scale for measuring earthquakes had all been introduced. Despite the ever-increasing role of the automobile in the mid-1930s, Americans still spent $1,000 a day on buggy whips.

1931 Family Profile

Quentin Chappel of Oberlin, Ohio, his wife Edna and their daughter Pauline are experiencing the devastating financial impact of the stock market crash of 1929, after he had heavily invested money in the future of airplane travel; they are now bankrupt.

Life at Home

- The October 1929 stock market crash has forced desperate measures upon this family; Quentin Chappel is now selling the family home in Oberlin, Ohio.
- During the 1920s, they often traveled in style; since the crash, Quentin has been convinced that the market will recover and his family's lifestyle of luxury and frequent travel will return.
- Unfortunately, his investments have only gotten worse.
- Their 50-year-old house was built in the Italianate style and includes more than 24,000 square feet of living space.
- He has boasted for years—to practically everyone he met—that their home is the largest private residence in the city.
- It is a magnificent structure built in the mid-1870s by a prominent New Orleans banker who moved to Oberlin after making a fortune during the Civil War by financing blockade runners; he kept his fortune by investing in British sterling rather than in Confederate currency.
- Quentin inherited the house from Edna's father and had it redecorated by Louis Comfort Tiffany in 1910; in all, it has 35 rooms and 24 fireplaces.
- Over the main staircase, the domed ceiling rises 75 feet high, paneled with alternating strips of walnut and satinwood, and containing sliding pocket windows to give access to a three-level side piazza.

During the 1920s the Chappels often traveled in style.

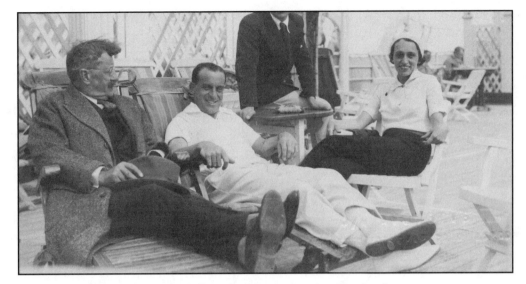

Quentin married well, investing his father-in-law's money in railroads and real estate.

Pauline has been forced to postpone her plans for touring Europe.

- The dining room is on the first floor, and the music room on the second floor; the library has built-in black walnut bookcases and mahogany crown moldings.
- Their daughter Pauline is devastated that her débutante party will not be at the Ritz-Carlton in New York, where the ballroom rental is $1,500, the minimum meal $3.00 per person, and the orchestra $1,000—extra if the party goes beyond 2 a.m.
- She has also been forced to postpone plans for a tour of Europe next year—something she has dreamed about for years.
- During the good times, Quentin was convinced that air travel represented the future, and the family often took luxury trips in airplanes styled after the finest trains, offering room for pool games, a place to have their hair done at 125 miles per hour and elaborate sleeping quarters.
- On a lark, they even took a trip to New York one weekend to see comedian Will Rogers perform; to keep up with business, Quentin brought along a secretary to type letters he dictated along the way.
- He spends a lot of his time reading economic journals to determine his next steps, and humor magazines like *Life*, which seem to lift his spirits.

Life at Work

- Quentin married well, investing his father-in-law's money in railroads and real estate, and from 1925 to 1928, his millions made millions in the market; his friends said he had the "Midas touch" for making money.

Before the crash, he was infatuated with the possibilities offered by luxury airplane travel, including an on-board beauty parlor, pool tables and full office facilities.

- He was especially bullish on Seaboard Air Line, traditionally considered a railroad stock, because the company appeared to be positioned as a great aviation stock; he thought it had tremendous growth potential.
- One of the reasons stock prices were so high in 1929, Quentin believes, was that there weren't enough stocks to go around, creating a "scarcity value."
- He also believes in buying stock in big companies; since the turn of the century, hundreds of small companies had formed into giant firms such as United States Steel Corporation, International Harvester, International Nickel and American Tobacco.
- Each merger and combination reduced or eliminated all competition, in turn reducing price competition which, he felt, gave them great potential for making their stockholders wealthy.
- Many of the companies in which he invested also moved toward centralized management during the period; Montgomery Ward, Woolworth and American stores were all viewed as great stock buys because of their ability to control huge markets.

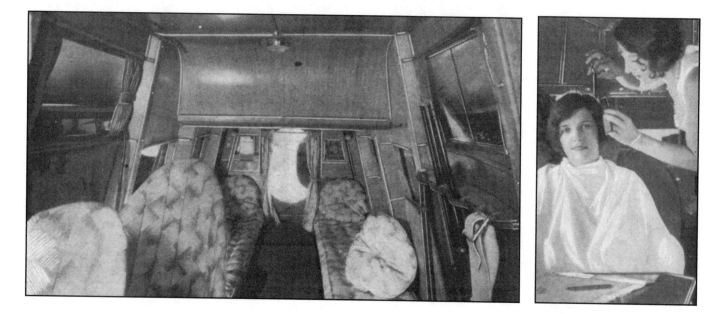

On a lark, the Chappels took a trip by airplane to see Will Rogers perform in New York City.

- During the past few years, he was particularly infatuated with the opportunities offered by investment trust companies, which originated in England and Scotland, becoming popular in the United States around 1921; by 1927, 160 were in existence.

- In 1927 and 1928, another 140 and 186, respectively, were formed, and in 1929, they were being promoted at the rate of one each business day.

- In 1927, the trusts sold to the public $400 million in securities, marketing approximately $3 billion in stock by 1929; at the time of the crash, money in the investment trusts exceeded $8 billion.

- Their popularity was driven by the feeling that Wall Street brokers, professors and American capitalists had the inside track on wealth, and by investing through them, literally everyone could be wealthy one day.

- In 1928, Quentin bought into a trust at $75 a share just before it zoomed to $99 a share; instead of selling, he bought more and the stock rose to $125 in the heady days of 1929.

- Today the stock is worth $0.75 a share, if any buyers can be found at all.

- Following his dramatic losses during the October stock market crash, Quentin supported his family by selling pieces of their home's furniture and fixtures.

- He has already sold the Minton tile from 22 of the 24 fireplaces, but is holding on to a favorite English-made Minton tile in the library fireplace, which depicts 17 scenes of plays by William Shakespeare.

John Kenneth Galbraith, "In Goldman Sachs We Trust," *The Great Crash, 1929*:

"Knowledge, manipulative skill, or financial genius were not the only magic of the investment trust. There was also leverage. By the summer of 1929, one no longer spoke of investment trusts as such. One referred to high-leverage trusts, low-leverage trusts, or trusts without any leverage at all.

The principle of leverage is the same for an investment trust as in the game of crack-the-whip. By the application of well-known physical laws, a modest movement near the point of origin is translated into a major jolt on the extreme periphery. In an investment trust, leverage was achieved by issuing bonds and preferred stock, as well as common stock to purchase, more or less exclusively, a portfolio of common stocks. When the common stock so purchased rose in value, a tendency which was always assumed, the value of bonds and preferred stock of the trust was largely unaffected. These securities had a fixed value derived from a specified return. Most or all of the gain from rising portfolio values was concentrated on the common stock of the investment trust which, as a result, rose marvelously.

Consider, by way of illustration, the case of an investment trust organized in early 1929 with a capital of $150 million—a plausible size by then. Let it be assumed, further, that a third of the capital was realized from the sale of bonds, a third from preferred stock, and the rest from the sale of common stock. If this $150 million were invested, and if the securities so purchased showed a normal appreciation, the portfolio value would have increased by midsummer by about 50 percent. The assets would be worth $255 million. The bonds and preferred stock would still be worth only $100 million; their earnings would not have increased, and they could claim no greater share of the assets in the hypothetical event of a liquidation of the company. The remaining $125 million, therefore, would underlie the value of the common stock of the trust. The latter, in other words, would have increased in asset value from $50 million to $125 million, or by 150 percent, and as the result of an increase of only 50 percent in the value of the assets of the trust as a whole.

This was the magic of leverage, but this was not all of it. Were the common stock of the trust, which had so miraculously increased in value, held by still another trust with similar leverage, the common stock of that trust would get an increase of between 700 and 800 percent from the original 50-percent advance. And so forth. In 1929 the discovery of the wonders of the geometric series struck Wall Street with a force comparable to the invention of the wheel."

- As both an avid golfer and a man desperate to see the stock market get back on track, he keeps in his office a cartoon from the *Oberlin News Tribune* showing Uncle Sam hitting a golf ball down the economic fairway.
- At the very least, he is pleased that America is preparing to repeal the Eighteenth Amendment outlawing alcohol sales, so that he can drown his misery legally.

Life in the Community: The Village of Oberlin, Ohio

- Oberlin, Ohio, is the home of Oberlin College, the first in the nation to provide coeducational classes.

- A recent study shows that a third of the college's 1,400 students are currently employed to defray the cost of college; of the 475 working students, half have dormitory board jobs, while the rest work in private homes firing furnaces, mowing lawns and caring for children.
- Despite the pressures of the depression, the Oberlin Village council recently set the salaries of its key officials for 1932, stating the city manager would make $4,200 per annum, night policemen—$1,200, and fire chief—$1000; they also declared that "labor shall be paid at a rate not to exceed $0.85 per hour."
- During the year, the council completed construction of the new water line from the dam in Kimpton to provide Oberlin with "plenty of water in years to come so there will be no shortages in dry seasons."
- Last year the police began providing 24-hour service; as a result, they made 101 arrests during the year, impounded 10 dogs, found 63 doors unlocked, investigated three stolen autos (recovering all) and seven stolen bicycles (recovering five), and replaced seven traffic signal bulbs.
- The city's volunteer fire department answered 37 calls; nine were in response to sparks on the roof of a home, six for a chimney burning out and one for an electric iron catching fire.
- The community spends a total of $87,000 annually on municipal services, up from $64,000 just two years ago.

Editorial, "What Do You Think of This Plan for Discussing the Eighteenth Amendment?" *Oberlin News Tribune*, January 1, 1931:

"Whenever an important issue confronts the country, every community includes two classes: those who do care and those who don't care how it is decided.

Just now the prohibition issue is regarded by many as the most vital question before the American people, and the conviction is generally that it will be decided within the next two years. How many are there in Oberlin who don't care how it is settled?

Those who do care include wets, drys and doubters. While the wets comprise a large number of persons with whom personal appetite, social standing or financial advantage outweigh every other consideration, there are many having no axe to grind, who favor the repeal or modification of the Eighteenth Amendment from the most unselfish motives, being persuaded that some other plan will produce better results for the people as a whole. Such persons—and their number seems to have been increasing within the last few weeks—are just as anxious to get and circulate the facts in the case as are the most ardent drys. Then why cannot these two groups in Oberlin join hands with the honest doubters in an intensive scrutiny of the arguments for and against the Eighteenth Amendment? Not the arguments of the brewers and bootleggers, not those of lawless society leaders, nor yet those of bigoted dyed-in-the-wool drys, but of thoughtful, unselfish, patriotic students of history both ancient and modern as it is related to this problem.

It seems as if some plan should be found for community co-operation in our search for the truth about prohibition. When we read an article

of special merit we wish that everybody else might read it too, but to hand or mail a single copy to one person after another is a discouragingly slow process, and to persuade all our fellow townspeople to subscribe to our favorite journals is impossible, even if desirable. The question has arisen whether it would not be practicable to have a representative committee of capable and patriotic citizens which would receive such articles

from anyone finding them and condense them for our own local paper, as articles are condensed for the *Readers' Digest*, or at least skim the cream of them for us by at least mentioning, of course, where the whole article could be found.

Would such a plan be feasible? Would it help us to an intelligent decision on this issue? W.T.C.U. Committee"

- At H. G. Klermund, the Ford dealer, prices have been reduced; a DeLuxe Roadster is now $475, a price cut of $45, and a Sport Coupe is only $500, down from $525.
- Oberlin, like many communities throughout the nation, is observing the eleventh anniversary of the passage of the Eighteenth Amendment, prohibiting the sale of alcohol.

- According to a recent story in the *Oberlin News Tribune*, the prohibition of liquor sales has "increased the national purchasing power by $6 billion a year by diverting a major portion of the old saloon keepers' receipts to more useful channels."

- The "useful channels" listed by the newspaper include, (1) it has reduced poverty from drink to a negligible minimum; (2) it has given at least three million boys and girls a chance to attend high school from homes that could not have afforded it in the saloon era; (3) it has added hundreds of millions of dollars of value to the great dairy industry and has aided agriculture generally; (4) it has bettered the condition of the army of workers by doing away with "Blue Monday," which was a regular bugbear of the manufacturers of the old days, decreasing quality and quantity once a week because of Saturday night carousals that lasted over until Tuesday.

HISTORICAL SNAPSHOT
1931

- The top one percent of Americans held a 44-percent share of all personal assets in America
- Major publications continued to predict the impending arrival of television into American homes
- Fish frozen and packed in cardboard containers as soon as it had been caught was being sold in Canada
- Bird's Eye frozen foods were sold nationwide for the first time
- Inflation for the year was at a negative 4.4 percent; prices on most goods were falling
- Efforts to repeal prohibition, the Eighteenth Amendment of the Constitution, were under way in numerous states
- With the depression ongoing and car sales stagnant, two of three workers in Detroit, Michigan, were out of work
- Four men were killed during a bitter coal miners' strike in Harlan, Kentucky
- Al Capone was convicted of tax evasion and sentenced to 11 years in prison
- National income was down 33 percent since 1929; payrolls dropped 40 percent
- Safeway Stores reached their peak of expansion with 3,527 stores
- Lucky Strike cigarettes outsold its rival Camel for the first time
- Silent film extra Clark Gable appeared in the movie *A Free Soul* and gained instant stardom
- A photoelectric cell was installed commercially for the first time
- Infrared photographs, air conditioners, the Schick electric dry shaver, Beech-Nut baby food, Alka Seltzer and stockings in transparent mesh all made their first appearance
- Lucky Luciano organized the Mafia into federated families
- The rate of admission to state mental hospitals for the past year was triple the rate from 1922 to 1930
- Nearly 6,000 cases of infantile paralysis struck New York
- Midwestern farmers were helpless against an invasion of grasshoppers that destroyed 160,000 miles of pristine farmland
- The New York Waldorf-Astoria Hotel opened

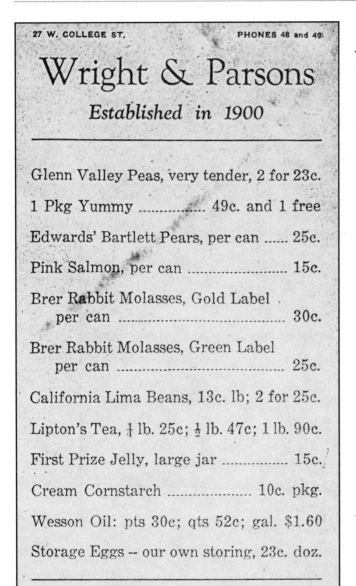

1931 ECONOMIC PROFILE

The national consumer expenditures (per capita income) in 1931 were:

Auto Parts	$3.22
Auto Usage	$30.61
Clothing	$45.91
Dentists	$3.22
Food	$118.41
Furniture	$6.44
Gas and Oil	$12.08
Health Insurance	$0.81
Housing	$84.58
Intercity Transport	$2.42
Local Transport	$7.25
New Auto Purchase	$8.86
Personal Business	$25.78
Personal Care	$8.05
Physicians	$6.44
Private Education and Research	$5.64
Recreation	$26.58
Religion/Welfare Activities	$5.64
Telephone and Telegraph	$4.83
Tobacco	$12.08
Utilities	$22.55
Per Capita Consumption	$487.73

Annual Income, Standard Jobs

Average of all Industries, Excluding Farm Labor	$1,406.00
Average of all Industries, Including Farm Labor	$1,298.00
Bituminous Coal Mining	$723.00
Building Trades	$907.00
Domestics	$584.00
Farm Labor	$355.00
Federal Civilian	$1,895.00
Federal Employees, Executive Departments	$1,549.00
Federal Military	$1,164.00
Finance, Insurance and Real Estate	$1,858.00
Gas and Electricity Workers	$1,600.00
Manufacturing, Durable Goods	$1,127.00
Manufacturing, Nondurable Goods	$1,352.00
Medical/Health Services Workers	$919.00
Miscellaneous Manufacturing	$1,230.00
Motion Picture Services	$2,175.00

Nonprofit Organization
Workers $1,653.00
Passenger Transportation
Workers, Local and
Highway. $1,500.00
Personal Services $1,136.00
Public School Teachers. $1,463.00
Radio Broadcasting and
Television Workers. $2,732.00
Railroad Workers. $1,661.00
State and Local Government
Workers $1,497.00
Telephone and Telegraph
Workers $1,436.00
Wholesale and Retail Trade
Workers $1,495.00

Selected Prices

Automobile, REO $795.00
Binoculars $33.48
Camera, Kodak 6-20. . . . . $20.00
Clock, Gilbert $5.95
Croquet Set $3.98
Dinner Plates, Semi-Porcelain,
Dozen $0.84
Flowers, 20 Tulips. $1.10
Girdle, Woman's $1.74
Hair Color Treatment, Bottle $1.29
Light Bulbs, Package of Eight $1.00
Magazine, *Popular Mechanics*,
Monthly. $0.25
Marshmallows, Kraft, Box of 200 . . . . . $0.65
Radio, Philco. $20.00
Rug, 9' x 12' Velvet. $14.95
Sanitary Napkins, Kotex, Dozen $0.85
Shave Cream, Colgate $0.25
Valentines, 16 Cards $0.25
Washing Machine $57.95
Wristwatch, Lady Elgin. $25.00

The Depression

- During the decade of the 1920s, the sale of automobiles, electrical appliances, radios, refrigerators and other durable goods skyrocketed.
- This higher standard of living was made possible through the efficiency of the machine age, which brought prices down, and by the extended use of credit, which made immediate purchases based on future earnings possible.
- To make as many sales as possible, merchants made installment credit easier and easier to obtain; as a result, debt accumulated faster than wealth expanded.

- By 1930, the debt of the country had increased to one third of its wealth; in addition, millions of Americans who had become familiar with the procedure of investment through their purchase of Liberty Loan bonds during World War I were more comfortable buying stocks.

- Spurred by visions of dazzling gains, millions poured into the stock market.

- From 1927 to 1929, prices on the stock exchange soared; the Dow Jones high in 1926 was 162, while the high in 1929 was 381.

- Preceding the crash of 1929 were several key events, including the collapse of the Florida land speculation boom in 1926, the failure of 6,000 (or one fifth) of the nation's banks (many in rural areas), and the severe problems of several vital industries, including agriculture.

- To further exacerbate the problem, in 1927 the Federal Reserve system began an easy money policy by reducing discount rates, partly to aid business and to help foreign nations; the policy encouraged increased speculation.

- The Federal Reserve Board attempted to correct the situation by raising the discount rate; by December 1928 the call-loan rate reached 8.6 percent, but speculation continued.

- When the crash came on October 29, 1929, more than 16 million shares changed hands.

- The stock of General Electric Company dropped 47 points, American Telephone and Telegraph fell 34 points, and Westinghouse Electric and Manufacturing Company went down 35 points.

- By the end of 1929, stockholders had lost $40 billion in paper values, or more than the total cost of World War I, to the United States.

"Looking down on the World from the Tallest Skyscraper,"
***Popular Mechanics*, January 1930:**

"Workmen have laid the last piece of steel framework for the Chrysler building in New York, which, when completed, will be the tallest habitable structure in the world at present. It rises for more than 800 feet, overtopping the 792 feet of the Woolworth building. From the dome of the $15 million structure, every point on Manhattan can be seen. One of the unusual sights is the Chanin building nearby which, when viewed from the Chrysler building, has a startling modernistic effect, which is hardly to be expected in a skyscraper."

- The stock market crash began the impoverishment of millions of Americans, the demoralization of business and the growth of unemployment.
- Other nations experienced the misery and suffering at approximately the same time, largely as a result of the policies enacted following World War I; by 1930, the depression was worldwide.
- Throughout the United States, factories closed down, an increasing number of banks failed, prices of commodities sank, foreign trade languished, railroad loadings declined and railways became insolvent.
- By 1930, more than three million workers were unemployed, and by 1932, the figure stood at more than 12 million; during the same two years, 5,102 banks failed, setting a new record.
- Congress rejected President Herbert Hoover's proposal to save money by reducing the salaries of government officials, and opposed a general sales tax.
- Instead Congress sought to solve the problem by increasing income tax rates, raising postage rates and taxing items such as amusements, bank checks, stock sales, automobiles, gasoline, oil, tires, matches and refrigerators.

"Guess we'll have to sell the farm, Maria —can't raise nothin' here!"

The Front Drive— And Why?

By H. F. BLANCHARD

WITHOUT question the most radical development in a quarter century of American automobile building is the advent of front-drive passenger cars.

While front drive is new to most owners, the principle itself is lost in the dim past of unwritten history. Vehicles propelled by animal power have had front drive ever since man first learned to use animals for hauling. The only notable exception is the wheelbarrow which is without doubt a much more recent invention than the drag or its successor, the two-wheeled cart of ancient times.

Nor is the front-drive automobile new in itself. It would be difficult to say who built the first one, but at least it can be stated that the first front-drive car to attract attention in this country was a racing machine built and driven about 1905

by Walter Christie, a New York engineer. Other Christie racing cars followed, and all were quite successful.

About three years ago, Harry Miller, well-known Pacific coast builder, produced a front-drive racing car which handled so well at high speed, especially on turns, and looked so smart, that many were prompted to raise the question, "Why

Above, Front-Drive Mechanism of the Miller; Below, Unit Power Plant of the Cord, Showing Engine, Transmission, Differential, Front Axle, Brake Drums, Spring Suspension and Steering Universal Joints

not front-drive passenger cars?" Thus it was automobile racing, or rather the success of Miller's front-drive racing cars, that fanned up in this country the present interest in the front-drive question.

Is front drive better? Is rear drive out of date? Will all cars at some time in the future be driven from the front? The automotive industry is divided as to the answers to these questions. A certain enthusiastic minority gives an emphatic "yes" to all three. The majority, however, answer "no," while others take the

A Front View of the Front-Drive Cord, Showing Some of the Mechanism, and Clearly Indicating the Difference in Proportions between the Front-Drive and Rear-Drive Cars

middle ground, remarking, "we shall see." Even after all the arguments for and against have been carefully weighed, it is still impossible to say just how popular front drive will eventually become, because nobody can accurately measure public reaction. In short, just how will the public at large appraise the advantages and disadvantages of front versus rear drive after it has become thoroughly acquainted with the features of both? This article will be devoted to a discussion of the question to assist each reader in forming his own opinion.

Those who favor front drive emphasize the following structural advantages: drive at the front where it logically should be; a 100-per-cent unit power plant; a lower car with a lower center of gravity; straight frame siderails (without a kick-up at the rear axle) which provide an ideal foundation for the body; reduced unsprung weight, especially at the rear where a simple I-beam rear axle replaces the conventional pressed-steel rear axle containing the differential assembly, and elimination of the long propeller shaft.

Those who prefer rear drive reply that

these advantages are not important, and certainly not sufficiently important to warrant the extra expense and complication, not to mention the necessarily longer wheelbase and resultant increased weight.

In reply, the front-drive proponents insist that theirs is the simpler construction; that all the major units are bolted together to form an integral whole; that the long propeller shaft is eliminated with its tendency to vibrate; that the relatively complicated rear axle is replaced by an I-beam; that the differential assembly is removed from the road and placed up on the frame, and that, in consequence, the bevel pinion and ring gear may be made as heavy as desirable for maximum silence, since so doing does not add to the unsprung weight.

Rear-drive engineers point out that only one or two universals are required with their construction, whereas four to six are necessary with front drive; comparing front and rear-drive cars point for point, front drive is more complicated and more expensive, including such minor details as gearshift mechanism, starter-crank mechanism, and so forth.

"How Safe Is Flying?" by John Draper, *Popular Mechanics*, January 1930:

"Hitherto unwritten stories of heroism, of single-handed battles against the forces of nature and of the thrills of flying, have been brought to light by a questionnaire sent by *Popular Mechanics* magazine to more than 8,000 licensed pilots to learn their actual experience with lightning.

Many of the pilots contended that lightning could not strike an airplane in flight, although it is positively known that eight balloons have been destroyed by lightning in the past nine years. While Zeppelins have been struck more than 100 times, none has been wrecked in this way, the nature of their metal framework probably being responsible for their immunity.

In all the history of aviation, the only verified case of lightning striking an airplane in flight was reported as follows: 'While flying from Paris to London with 14 passengers, Mr. F. L. Barnard had an alarming experience. He ran into a thunderstorm over Picardy, between Beauvais and Poix. Suddenly there was a loud report as a flash of lightning struck the machine. A large piece of fabric on the lower plane was burnt, the compass was put out of action, and one engine started to miss, as apparently the permanent field of one of the magnets had been upset. On examination, it was found that, in addition to the hole in the fabric, one of the main spars was scorched, all of the bonding was fused and one of the ailerons damaged.'

There have been other, although not verified, cases of crashes attributed to lightning. In 1928 the deaths of Capt. Emil Carranza, Mexican flying ace, and Morris M. Titterington, inventor of the earth-inductor compass, were believed due to bolts. In the same year a mail plane plunged to earth with its motor wide open during an electrical disturbance. Although no positive proof that this was due to lightning could be obtained, observers believe the pilot was stunned by a bolt. The same is true of a navy plane which plunged into lower Chesapeake Bay in 1927. The naval board which investigated the crash reported 'its belief that the lightning flash stunned both pilots in the ship to such a degree that they could not recover in time to save the plane and that it went in uncontrolled.'

With mail and passenger planes now covering 84,656 miles daily, C. M. Keys, president of the Transcontinental Air Transport, recently quoted figures showing that there were 6,500 persons killed in 1928 as a result of the operation of the railways, or one fatality for 172,768 train miles. In the same year, there were 368 persons killed in civil aviation or one fatality for 191,800 plane miles, a slightly better record than was made by the railways. The Actuary Society of America, insurance risk experts, reported that there is only a 4,000-to-one chance of an accident when riding with a licensed pilot over a scheduled passenger route. They found that in 1928 only 13 passengers were killed out of the 50,000 carried in such flights.

'The forces of nature cannot be eliminated, but they may be balanced, one against another,' Count Zeppelin once said. Mr. Keys now declares that 'aeronautical science has progressed to the point where the only uncontrollable factor is weather, which in final analysis remains the major cause of interrupted transportation both on land and sea.'"

Accuracy keeps them flying

Speed—endurance—dependability— we marvel at the performance of present day airplane motors. The perfection of these powerful engines is a true tribute to modern engineering skill.

At the factory — if motors are to withstand the terrific strain of high speeds, every part must be accurately fitted. Cylinders, crankshafts, bearings — all must be accurate within exceedingly close limits.

At the airport—here rigid inspection and accurate repair are necessary. If motors are to stand the grind of regular schedules, original accuracy must be maintained.

In the factory, at the airport — wherever performance depends upon precision, you will find Brown & Sharpe Tools. Their dependability is the by-word of all skilled mechanics.

Copy of our Small Tool Catalog No. 31 sent on request. Address Dept. P. M., Brown & Sharpe Mfg. Co., Providence, R. I., U. S. A.

Brown & Sharpe Tools
"WORLD'S STANDARD OF ACCURACY"

Micrometer No. 11RS   Steel Rule No. 300   Outside Spring Caliper No. 811   Vest Pocket Speed Indicator No. 746   Inside Micrometer No. 264

Will Rogers provides entertainment to millions during the difficult years of the depression.

MAY 1935   The American LEGION MONTHLY   25 CE

1935 News Feature

"Revolution in the Air," by Samuel Taylor Moore,
The American Legion Monthly, May 1935:

"In 1924, Samuel Taylor Moore, flying under the auspices of the *American Legion Weekly*, was America's first coast-to-coast airplane passenger. The round-trip journey occupied 66 hours of actual flying time but consumed altogether some three weeks and required the use of three airplanes. One ship came to grief in a Nebraska haystack; another was condemned at San Francisco after a hazardous passage of the Rockies. A few weeks ago Mr. Moore made the Atlantic-to-Pacific-and-back trip, but with a difference, and what a difference! In the accompanying article he presents a vivid comparison between 1924 and 1935.

'Lunch time.

Manhattan skyscrapers were scattering their hungry tenants into the concrete canyons swept by a bitter winter gale as our big Douglas airplane, its portside motor still dripping champagne from its christening, rose from Newark Airport heading slightly west by south at close to two hundred miles an hour.

Washington, D.C., was returning to bureau desks from the noon meal as we glided to a landing there for refueling before resuming our journey.

Memphis, Tennessee, was sitting down to dinner as we said goodbye to one pair of pilots and a pretty stewardess and greeted their successors.

Little Rock, Arkansas, was leaving for the movies that evening as the city flashed by in a broad pattern of tiny yellow lights six thousand feet below, and Dallas, Texas, was sauntering home to bed when we paused briefly at Love Field before the next hop into Fort Worth (call it West Dallas if you like a fistfight).

Eleven hours from lunchtime in the East to bedtime in the plains country—and despite the most comfortable seats imaginable and three opportunities to stretch our legs on the ground for 15-minute intervals, muscles were getting cramped. So we went to bed—yes, to bed—on another type of transport plane, a Curtiss-Wright Condor.

The cabin into which we transferred suggested nothing so much as a contracted railroad Pullman coach with seats facing one another until an attractive porteress (with some help from a broad-shouldered co-pilot) converted each section into conventional double berths, upper

and lower. Though somewhat narrower than their rail counterparts, in length each berth was all that could be desired. My own six feet found perfect comfort. Other accommodations were in keeping—immaculate sheets, clothing nets, baggage racks, heavy green curtains to insure all the privacy one could wish. But this ingenious plane offered even extra gadgets—individual controls for ventilation and heat in each berth.

Already the sound of deep breathing (and one unmistakable soprano snore) told that two weary air travelers were taking time by the forelock. Then we were off, and ensconced in the soundproofed cabin, the roar of the twin motors came to the passengers as a sleep-inducing lullaby. Abilene's desert lights came into view through a lifted window curtain sometime after midnight as the rest of us, pajama-clad, prepared to join the sleep squad.

None of us knew when a fourth crew took over our ship on the four-thousand-foot plateau of El Paso, Texas, with the lights of Juarez, Mexico, twinkling across the Rio Grande, but most of us were stirring as the green and red tiles of Tucson bungalows reflected the first rays of an undecided sun playing African dodger in dark clouds that brushed bare, brown mountain peaks on the desert horizon.

Phoenix, Arizona, as well as ourselves, had just had her face washed by a sky full of soggy nimbostratus clouds when, still pajama-clad, I stepped out for waiting orange juice and coffee from the tray of a pretty stewardess. Then we resumed flight over more bare mountain peaks and monotonous desert floor, save where the spread of bright green squares beside irrigation ditches told how man's ingenuity had made the desert bloom in midwinter.

Now, according to a printed timetable of our airplane, we should have been drinking orange juice and hot coffee while leaving behind us the San Bernardino Mountains and approaching the coast, while dictating our respective orders for more substantial breakfast items to our newest stewardess for radio transmission ahead to our Los Angeles destination. But the same type of clouds that were wetting Phoenix had shut down solidly the Sierra pass known as San Gorgonio, extending on either side, so we made an intermediate landing at the desert airport of Indio. For more than three hours, resting in a cozy air station, dining on sandwiches and the American-grown dates which are a source of Indio's pride, we waited for the ceiling to lift. Then a radio message bade us to be on our way again—a friendly wind had swept the pass clear.

As a result, instead of breakfasting with Los Angeles that morning, we had a hearty lunch with Hollywood. Yes, we were six hours late when we landed at Grand Central Air Terminal in Glendale, California, at 1:00 p.m. instead of the scheduled 6:45 a.m. the day following our departure from New York City. But even so, I insist it was a good trick.

Now the air-transport company which performed that trick, with all the speed one could possibly ask, with all the physical comforts and conveniences any reasonable mind could imagine, with all the dependability consistent with safety, is not the first airline regularly (in total, several times daily) to whisk travelers from the Atlantic to the Pacific between one sun and the next.

The flight I summarize was conducted by one of the three air-transport concerns now offering fast service across the continent. Enclosed in draft-free, soundproofed cabins where conversations may be carried on in normal tones, it is to be emphasized that passengers experience complete relaxation, even to cigarettes and cigars, as they hurtle through the skies at approximately two hundred miles an hour.

And now, by way of contrast, let's go back 10 years.

To the best of my knowledge and belief I was the first civilian passenger to cross the American continent by air. Certainly I was the first civilian to be flown from New York to San Francisco over the pioneer transcontinental air route organized by an epic band of intrepid pilots and engineers of the United States Air Mail, which began operations a mere decade past.

A summary of that memorable journey shows that while our 5,500-mile flight took just under 66 hours of flying, actually the round trip extended over three weeks and required three airplanes to complete. To be fair, 10 of the 21 days spent on the haphazard voyage were idled away awaiting new airplanes when the first two of our craft were washed out, one demolished in a crash, the other claptrap crate condemned after a half-dozen forced landings from one side of the Continental Divide to the other.

Now our actual flying time of 66 hours 10 years ago was the approximately scheduled elapsed time for the mail to cross and recross the continent. That is, it included the time required for the transfer of mail from an incoming ship to another one awaiting, fuel tanks full, motors warmed, new pilot ready for a takeoff on his two hundred- to four hundred-mile relay, much as the historic Pony Express buckos threw mail pouches from one rider to the next. But air schedules 10 years ago were observed almost entirely in the breach. What with cancellations on account of weather, due largely to lack of information, a complete absence of communications other than visual between plane and ground, the only navigational aids a magnetic compass and feeble light beacons supplementing landmarks, the uncertainty of schedules in our first organized air transport is not to be wondered at. Three years after its beginning, little progress was to be observed. In Hollywood, in the winter of 1927, corresponding with my family in Massachusetts, ordinary first-class mail beat airmail letters across the continent as often as not.

Earlier that year, by relinquishing his cockpit in a mail plane for the hazardous adventure of flying from New York to Paris nonstop, a lanky, blond youngster caused the unloosening of pocketbooks which made possible this revolution in air transport.

When 10 years ago I flew from what is now Roosevelt Field at the Presidio of San Francisco, not only did my pilot fly under the same mechanical handicaps as those hampering the mail pioneers, but he faced also an edict against night flying by civilians.

The advances in seven short years are too numerous to describe in detail. They may be summarized only. Staunch, commodious hangars of steel and concrete have replaced the flimsy, corrugated iron shelters which almost weekly were being burned down or blown down. Passenger stations, ranging from cozy bungalow types to structures of architectural impressiveness comparable to first-class railroad stations, dot the nation.

The nomad civilian flyer has expert servicing crews at his beck at every organized airport, not to mention the expert technicians serving transport planes at every air terminal, or the big plane repair shops reminding one of the railroad roundhouse in their mechanical completeness at Chicago, Kansas City, Fort Worth. Amazing new navigational instruments, complete weather information, and, equally important, such radio marvels as two-way voice communications between flying planes and ground, and radio beams, functioning much as steel rails guide crack trains, have made schedules mean something—though it must be admitted perfection remains elusive. . . .

Let us compare the vehicles of yesterday's flight with today's. Six years after the Armistice, air-minded America was still flying in war-surplus planes. They cruised at 85 to 90 miles an hour mostly behind Liberty engines. Pilot and passenger (one only) sat topside with heads above the fuselage squirming uncomfortably on an uneven seatpack-type parachute, or were forced to lean forward if wearing one of the even more uncomfortable backpack types (and parachutes had been in common use then only a year). For long flights special clothing was necessary, fur-lined teddy bears—or leather jackets with heavy underwear beneath—not to mention fur-lined boots and gauntlets also lined with fur in cold weather. The head was ensconced in a close-fitting helmet with chin strap and goggles, for cockpit cowlings provided only a minimum of protection against the propeller blast, and the sting of rain and snow when the elements were at play. Goggles protected one's eyes from the constant gale of slipstream. But worst of all was the undeadened beat of the motor's roar and the propeller's scream. Stuff one's ears with cotton batting as one would, motor deafness was inescapable.

Such acute discomforts have been conquered. Today's air traveler wears the same clothing in flight as on the ground. Thanks to perfect heating systems, he removes his hat and overcoat once the plane takes off. Even the pilot wears a uniform suggesting that of a railroad conductor rather than a grease-streaked locomotive engineer. Extra engines capable of maintaining flight, should another fail, make parachutes unnecessary.

There is no air blast in a modern transport cabin—in fact, should a meandering draft threaten one with the snuffles, it is a proper subject for complaint. Deeply upholstered, lounge-type chairs with plenty of leg room remind one of a favorite chair at home. Conversations are carried on in a normal voice. Against changes in pressure due to high-altitude flying, which may affect certain persons in other ways than the hearing sense, many precautions are taken, notably gradual descent from rarefied air to that of ground pressures. . . .

You'll like flying today. The wild pilot of war days has vanished. In his place you will find a solicitous young man at the controls, a conservative air engineer who will not "hang his ship on the prop" for a takeoff, execute vertical banks in making turns, or sideslip into an express-elevator landing for the benefit of pretty ladies who may be his charges. He and his co-pilot, under penalty if need be, are taught to handle aircraft as though every passenger was a nervous old lady in black, or a curmudgeon of a rich grandfather who hasn't yet named the pilot as his heir. You'll find yet another helpmeet on most modern planes, the stewardess. She'll serve you a tasty lunch as you fly, with delicacy and dispatch, light your cigarettes, or mind the baby if need be. She and her sisters now number a hundred—but her work is a story in itself.' "

1936 FAMILY PROFILE

Twenty-four-year-old Susannah Wainwright is the heiress to a sugar and tobacco fortune created during the days of the great trusts; she is married and building a home in Hawaii where she can be away from the glaring eyes of the social set of Palm Beach, Florida, and Bar Harbor, Maine.

Annual Income: She has already inherited more than $150 million, with more to come on her thirtieth birthday; Edmund, her husband, lives on a small trust fund from his grandfather and an allowance from his new wife.

Life at Home

- Susannah was married two years ago, when she was 22; to avoid publicity and reporters, the marriage plans were kept secret, and only family members were invited.
- Friends of the bride arranged for the marriage license to be issued without her going to the municipal building or appearing in person.
- During the weeks before the wedding, she went on a shopping trip in New York City to buy dresses for her honeymoon, purchasing 50 in all.
- She then flew in a private plane to Palm Beach, Florida, for a party before returning to New York for the wedding.
- The couple was married by a Supreme Court Justice they had never met, in a ceremony that took place before a roaring fire in the spacious, heavily draped downstairs library of her New York mansion.
- She wore a simple blue crepe dress and hat for the wedding, which lasted five minutes and omitted the word "obey" from the vows.
- After the ceremony, two private chauffeurs, each driving Rolls-Royces, took the couple, a dozen suitcases and Susannah's personal maid to the awaiting honeymoon ship, the *Conti di Savoria*, which sailed for the

Susannah Wainwright is the heiress to a sugar and tobacco fortune.

Edmund is the son of a wealthy Philadelphia family.

Orient on a tour that included the Mediterranean, Egypt, Baghdad, India, Siam, Java, China, Japan, the Philippines and finally, Hawaii; the trip was designed to last 24 months, but lasted only 13.

- Susannah financed the entire trip; they learned while on the ship that Edmund's check for the initial honeymoon expenses had bounced.
- Ten years older, Edmund is the son of a wealthy Philadelphia family and is interested in making his name in politics; he has never worked.
- While on their honeymoon, he met a former girlfriend in Naples and had an affair while his new wife was shopping for more dresses.
- During the trip, Susannah fell in love with the Taj Mahal and hired a Delhi architect to draw up plans in the style of a Mogul temple.
- The plans included the construction of dozens of tessellated windows and doors inlaid with jade, agate, malachite, lapis lazuli and mother-of-pearl.
- The construction in India of each door required six men working for three months; the doors will be shipped, along with the windows and walls, to her new home in Hawaii.

They have been captivated by the beauty of Hawaii.

- While in India, the couple took a 500-mile detour to Wardha where Mahatma Gandhi granted them an audience; Susannah was deeply impressed by the Holy One, especially his views on the emancipation of Indian women.

- During the fourth month of the honeymoon, when train travel became too grueling, she hired a private railroad car to calm her nerves and make the trip more pleasant; when the couple reached Singapore, she was admitted to the hospital for rest from "the fatigue of her honeymoon travels."

- Once discharged, she went on a shopping spree, spending $5,000 in a matter of hours on clothing, Chinese-style satin brocade pajamas, two-century-old Chinese ivory carvings, lingerie and jewelry.

- In Bangkok the couple purchased $20,000 in ancient rugs, in addition to nearly $300,000 in jade, a five-foot bronze monkey, a marble sunken bathtub and a huge ruby on a heavy gold chain.

- In Bali they hired a private yacht to take them to the Philippines, where the honeymooners were invited to tea with Mrs. Arthur Rubinstein, wife of the pianist.

- The couple next visited Japan and then, to end their 18,000-mile trek, sailed to Hawaii, where she found freedom from the social expectations of the United States, particularly the social set of Palm Beach, Florida, and Bar Harbor, Maine; she decided to go no further.

- Since they arrived, she has taken hula lessons and is learning how to surf from Duke Kahanamoku, Olympic swimming champion and sheriff in Honolulu, who is providing

While in India she purchased rugs, jade and statues.

She is making plans to attend the 1936 Olympics, which are in Germany.

her with personal surfing instructions; his stories about the 1920 Olympics, where he introduced the flutter kick style of freestyle racing, have inspired her to make travel plans to attend the 1936 Olympics in Germany.

- When she wrote to her friends about the joys of surfing, they thought her silly; few on the East Coast of the United States thought standing on a board in the middle of a rushing tide sounded fun or stylish.

- Her wealth comes from the tobacco and sugar businesses created at the turn of the century by her grandfather, who enjoyed a near monopoly for many years, although she has no interest in the business or where the money came from; currently, she is spending most of her time building a new home on the Island.

- Her husband has decided to return to the mainland; he considers himself an expert on economics and believes he can help President Roosevelt end the depression.

- Before he left, he and Susannah went to the Big Island where they climbed to the top of Mauna Loa.

- Only occasionally does she return to the United States, where she has three homes.

- Her most recent trip was to Palm Beach for the birthday of her new father-in-law, whose highly exclusive party was restricted to a select 350 of his closest friends.

- Now, two years into their marriage, Susannah and Edmund continue to travel, but separately; since the wedding, they have covered 500,000 miles, but seldom are both of them in the same city.

- The couple did attend the coronation of King George VI of Great Britain together, a grand royal spectacle, and enjoyed seats next to the royal family.

- In Palm Beach rumors are rampant that the marriage is over and that divorce is expected shortly.

Islanders welcome the rich, whom they view with amusement.

Life at Work

- Currently, Susannah is putting all her energy into building her new home in Hawaii; using her money, they purchased a 4.5-acre plot for $100,000 in the residential section of Black Point near Diamond Head, on land formerly owned by Honolulu businessman Ernest H. Wodehouse, who had paid $16,000 for the land at the turn of the century.

The views from Susannah's new home in Hawaii are magnificent.

- Hawaii is becoming the playground for other American blue-bloods, including railroad heir George Vanderbilt, tinplate heir Henry Topping, Pennsylvania steel magnate B. Barton Singer, Jr., and Fleishmann yeast heir Christian Holmes.
- Lavish cottages have sprung up near Diamond Head, which is becoming known as "Millionaire's Row"; in the midst of a worldwide depression, the islanders welcome the rich with amusement.
- Publisher Roy Howard has dubbed the Hawaiian islands "The American Riviera"; many of the wealthy live on fortunes created when monopolistic trusts were legal and even encouraged by government policy.
- In 1900, the tobacco trust boasted of owning 92.7 percent of the cigarette market, 80 percent of snuff, 62 percent of plug tobacco and 59 percent of smoking tobacco; thanks to trusts, the number of millionaires in America doubled from 1900 to 1902 to 8,000.
- In addition to elaborate homes, depression-era dollars are being lavished on private zoos, tropical gardens, aviaries and glassed-in aquarium walls.
- Susannah loves the informality of the islands; no one is scandalized when she wears pants out to dinner.
- Edmund is working hard to incorporate the doors and designs she bought in India into their Hawaii palace and focusing on his political career.
- To assist him in his effort to gain the attention of President Roosevelt, Susannah gave $50,000 to the Democratic Party.
- To improve his political network, the couple also threw an elaborate dinner dance for 500 at a friend's townhouse on East 72nd Street in New York, where thousands of orchids and hundreds of palm trees were brought in from her grandfather's country estate as decoration for the event.
- In addition, Edmund is working on an economics book which he believes Simon and Schuster will be happy to publish.
- One of his political advisors is William Randolph Hearst, whose California home resembles a Spanish castle, hung with seventeenth-century Flemish tapestries and occupying 350,000 acres, where Hearst raises American buffalo, giraffes, zebras, camels and ostriches on the grounds; within his private zoo, he has lions, tigers, panthers and chimpanzees.
  - The castle is often filled with the Hollywood set who come to party; no one is allowed to bring his or her own personal maid or valet to the home—individual servants are assigned to guests once they arrive.

Life in the Community: Honolulu, Hawaii

- Despite a rising tide of tourism, the economy of the territory is still dependent on pineapples, sugar cane and fishing, and many Hawaiians still gather much of their food from the ocean.
- American law became definitive in Hawaii in 1900 under President William McKinley when he named Sanford B. Dole the first governor of the territory.
- During the 1890s, the labor policy of the major sugar plantations determined the population mix of Hawaii, as plantation owners brought in many Asian workers, mostly Japanese, who by 1920 comprised 43 percent of the population.

The economy of Hawaii is still based on fishing and agriculture.

- These workers were supplemented by more than 100,000 Filipinos, imported as plantation laborers starting in 1907, and even later, by workers from Portugal.
- Another key element of Hawaiian society, especially Honolulu in the 1930s, is the presence of American sailors; since Pearl Harbor is the home of the Pacific fleet and Schofield Barracks is the biggest army post in the United States, approximately 20,000 men are currently stationed in Hawaii, making the military a key economic force on the islands.
- The building of a dry dock at Pearl Harbor involved a payroll of $60,000 a month for 10 years; the development of the harbor was an undertaking second in cost only to the Panama Canal.
- In addition, small-business owners, from taxi operators to barbers, to tattoo artists and nightclub owners, make a killing whenever the fleet is back from maneuvers or the enlisted men of Schofield come to town with their pay, although, as in many military towns, the dividing line between servicemen and residents is clearly marked and rarely crossed.
- Living in Honolulu also requires an understanding of the diverse Asian culture; newcomers to Chinatown often miss the different dialects of Chinese spoken and do not understand that the two main groups of Chinese immigrants, the Punti and the Hakka, have little time for each other.
- It is also easy to miss that most of the Japanese came from the southern area of Japan and wish to be distinguished at all times from the Okinawans, the minority immigrants who came from the Ryukyu Islands.
- Further, a Korean does not want to be mistaken for either a Chinese or a Japanese, and all wish to be distinguished from the late arrivals from the Philippines, who separate themselves according to three divisions—Tagalog, Visayan and Ilocano.
- Despite years of discussions concerning statehood for Hawaii, the racial mix of the island is causing problems in Congress.
- Currently, the threat of full-scale war in the Pacific between Japan and the United States is in the air; about 30,000 of Hawaii's Japanese hold dual citizenship.

HISTORICAL SNAPSHOT
1936

- Approximately 38 percent of American families had an income of less than $1,000 a year
- Ford unveiled the V-8 engine
- Recent advances in photography, including the 35 mm camera and easy-to-use exposure meters, fueled a photography boom
- The population of America reached 127 million
- *Life* magazine began publication, claiming in an early issue that one in 10 Americans had a tattoo
- New York's Triborough Bridge opened, with a toll of $0.25
- The National Park Service created numerous federal parks and fish and game preserves; in all, 600,000 acres were added to state preserves
- Mercedes-Benz created the first diesel-fueled passenger car
- The WPA Federal Art Project employed 3,500 artists who produced 4,500 murals, 189,000 sculptures and 450,000 paintings
- A Colorado farmland survey showed that half of the 6,000 farmhouses in one area had been abandoned
- Dust storms denuded large portions of the farmland of Kansas, Oklahoma, Colorado, Nebraska and the Dakotas
- A sleeper berth from Newark to Los Angeles cost $150; the New York Fifth Avenue double-decker bus fare was between $0.05 and $0.10
- Margaret Mitchell's book, *Gone with the Wind*, sold a record one million copies in six months
- A *Fortune* magazine poll indicated that 67 percent of readers favored birth control
- Seven million women paid more than $2 billion for 35 million permanents
- The photo-finish camera, bicycle traffic court, screw-cap bottle with pour lip, the Presbyterian Church of America and Tampax all made their first appearance
- Congress passed the Neutrality Acts designed to keep America out of foreign wars
- A revolt against progressive education was led by Robert M. Hutchins, president of the University of Chicago
- Molly Dewson of the National Consumers' League led a fight to gain the appointment of more female postmasters
- The first successful helicopter flight was made
- The "Chase and Sanborn Hour," with Edgar Bergen and Charlie McCarthy, and "The Shadow," starring Robert Hardy Andrews, both premiered on radio

1936 Economic Profile

The national consumer expenditures (per capita income) in 1936 were:

Auto Parts	$3.12
Auto Usage	$39.01
Clothing	$42.13
Dentists	$2.34
Furniture	$6.24
Gas and Oil	$14.82
Health Insurance	$0.78
Housing	$63.97
Intercity Transport	$2.34
Local Transport	$6.24
New Auto Purchase	$14.82
Personal Business	$24.18
Personal Care	$7.02
Physicians	$5.43
Private Education and Research	$3.90
Recreation	$23.40
Religion/Welfare Activities	$7.02
Telephone and Telegraph	$3.90
Tobacco	$11.70
Utilities	$23.40
Per Capita Consumption	$483.69

Annual Income, Standard Jobs

Average of all Industries, Excluding Farm Labor	$1,226.00
Average of all Industries, Including Farm Labor	$1,146.00
Bituminous Coal Mining	$1,103.00
Building Trades	$1,178.00
Domestics	$506.00
Farm Labor	$351.00
Federal Civilian	$1,896.00
Federal Employees, Executive Departments	$1,112.00
Federal Military	$1,152.00
Finance, Insurance and Real Estate	$1,713.00
Gas and Electricity Workers	$1,615.00
Manufacturing, Durable Goods	$1,376.00
Manufacturing, Nondurable Goods	$1,210.00
Medical/Health Services Workers	$851.00
Miscellaneous Manufacturing	$1,298.00
Motion Picture Services	$1,896.00

Nonprofit Organization
    Workers $1,465.00
Passenger Transportation
    Workers, Local and Highway $1,433.00
Personal Services $940.00
Public School Teachers $1,329.00
Radio Broadcasting and
    Television Workers $2,223.00
Railroad Workers $1,724.00
State and Local Government
    Workers $1,433.00
Telephone and Telegraph Workers . . $1,420.00
Wholesale and Retail Trade
    Workers $1,295.00

Selected Prices

Airline Fare, New York to Chicago $44.95
Automobile Battery $16.95
Basketball $3.59
Bath Salts, Elizabeth Arden $4.50
Bed, Louis XIV w/Mattress $345.00
Dog, English Cocker Spaniel $50.00
Dress, Maternity $2.98
Flashlight $0.55
Guitar $8.45
Hotel Room, Boston, per Night $4.00
Itch Relief, Absorbine Jr $1.25
Man's Suit, all Wool $13.95
Motor Yacht, Elco 53 . . . . $26,300.00
Paintbrush, 4" $0.90
Pocket Telescope $1.00
Refrigerator, Cold Spot $169.50
Sausage, Country Style, Pound $0.20
Wall Clock, Regulator $6.98
Water Hose, 25' $3.00
Windows, Andersen Casement $10.03

Franklin D. Roosevelt, campaign speech, presidential election, 1936:

"For 12 years this nation was afflicted with hear-nothing, see-nothing, do-nothing government. Never before in our history have these forces been so united against one candidate as they stand today. They are unanimous in their hatred of me—and I welcome their hatred."

"What Sort of People Are Getting Divorces?"
by Farnsworth Crowder, *McCall's*, February 1936:

"The obvious and easy answer is—all sorts of people. The butcher, the baker, the candlestick maker, the banker, the broker, the slavey and stoker, all rub shoulders in the echoing halls of the divorce courts. The fellowship of disillusion knows no class lines.

But an easy answer is not always correct, and a sweeping cynicism is almost sure to be wrong. All sorts of people, it is pleasant to report authoritatively, are not getting divorces; it only seems so.

The names on the casualty lists are drawn, to be sure, from every profession and every social stratum, but there is a telltale family resemblance among most of the unhappy wights who cannot stay put in marriage.

It is only recently that case histories have been examined scientifically to determine why American husbands and wives do not continue as husbands and wives. From these examinations there emerges, illuminatively, a composite picture of the individual who is a likely candidate for divorce.

Let's describe him. He is a native-born Protestant, childless and without property. He lives in a furnished house or flat in the western part of the United States. He is below par in health. He is contemptuous of old-fashioned standards. He (or she) is inclined to be bossy, uncooperative, self-centered, conscious of his own ego and indifferent to his partner's. His conception of love is immature. He has not been able to progress beyond the heated lightning of romance to an affectionate sharing of common destinies.

This, sketched in roughly, is the picture of the man or woman who keeps Reno alive. True, it is a synthetic portrait, but it is built up from the researches of two men who, without theses to prove or causes to advocate, have sought to isolate the realities of divorce. One is Dr. Paul Popenoe, who directs the trail-blazing Institute of Domestic Relations in the domestically rest-less city of Los Angeles. The other is Professor William Ogburn, the University of Chicago's renowned student of social trends and the problems of the American family.

Dr. Popenoe acts as father confessor to thousands who have become shoaled on marital reefs, and it was to bring sense out of confusion that he posed the question: What sort of people are getting divorces? He began to query his consultants and then, as the mass of information grew, to codify the answers.

From the answers collected, however diverse and contradictory, there emerges not only the picture of the dissatisfied husband and wife, but also a pretty definite map of the hazards of the marriage partnership. The whirlpools, the rapids, the shallows are all marked out on the blueprint—here, plotted out, are the dangers a wary couple may avoid. It is difficult to give specific advice on marriage, but this sweeping injunction seems reasonable enough: Consider the divorced, and then go thou not and do likewise! Don't live as they do, don't be what they are.

From the way they live and the way they are, emerges a decalogue for youth at the altar, a Ten Commandments of Marriage. No one can keep all these commandments, but everyone can keep some of them. There is nothing adamant about the code. Marriage is a patchwork of compromises and concessions at best. To those who avoid divorce and separation I say—edit the decalogue to fit your own ground rules.

1. Stay out of the West: This is not a warning to shy clear of Nevada. Reno's notoriety has bred a fallacy: that people in large numbers rush to the lax-law state to file for divorce decrees. Well, they don't. The number who do so is negligible. Eight in every 10 decrees are issued to couples who were married in the very state they are seeking divorce. So Reno (with less than three decrees out of every 100 granted) bulks far larger in the news than it does in the statistics.

(continued)

"What Sort of People Are Getting Divorces?" *(continued)*

But the West appears, nevertheless, to be rough on matrimony. The famous sun that's a little brighter, the ready smile that's a trifle wider and the larger heart that's a trifle warmer do not, in fact, make marriage even a little solider. On the contrary. The riskiest place, geographically, to contract a marriage is on the Pacific slope; the safest place, the middle Atlantic seaboard....

2. Don't live in a metropolis. Marriage flourishes better in the smaller city, in the towns and the country. In 1930, in Chicago, separation and divorce were twice as fatal as death to family unity....

3. Don't be childless. When a man and a woman hold hands, we call it romance. When that linkage, with its mutual self-absorption, is broken and a child enters the chain, we have a family and its strongest link is likely to be that smallest mortal. Professor Ogburn makes the statement that 'Families without children may almost be classed as a different type of family. Such situations affect the activity of wives in and out of the home and have a bearing on the stability of the marriage.' How much of a bearing may be judged from the fact that from 1900 to 1930, the percentage of broken homes among families without children was nearly three times as large as the percentage with children.

4. Own things. Possessions—furniture, a house, land—are mooring posts. Couples adrift, unattached to material things, are in danger of drifting apart....

5. Don't scorn to do the things your grandparents did. That may seem futile advice, because it is impossible to battle or decry the influence of a mechanical civilization. The home as a factory vanished because it could not meet the stiff competition from the outside. Industry clamors for the chance to do for you what grandma did for herself—knead the bread, do the laundry, bake the beans, churn the butter, sew the clothing and put up the pickles.

6. Avoid being bossy. A short time ago Dr. Popenoe conducted a study of 2,600 marriages

that had stood the test for five years. One thing he wanted to know about was this matter of who wears the pants. Can a family have two heads? He found that it not only can but does 'in more than one third of the educated families in America; and such families are happier than any other kind.' The figures leave no doubt 'that a democratic co-partnership is associated with the greatest happiness; that man-dominated marriages come next in this respect; and that marriages dominated by the wife show a definitely smaller percentage of happiness than do the other two.'

7. Give your partner's ego room to breathe. There is a jingle that runs:

Though in wedlock
He and she go
Each maintains
A separate ego . . .

8. Keep biologically up to par. Dr. Popenoe is the authority for the statement that 'divorcés are, on the whole, biologically inferior to the happily married part of the population.' What does he mean? For one thing, that they show a higher frequency to nervous breakdown. For another, that they are more temperamentally unstable. For a third, that they have a shorter life expectancy....

9. Don't be a matrimonial illiterate. Most people are still married by ministers who pronounce the state 'holy' and solicit God's blessing upon it. A pastor who averages over a hundred marriage services a year says that they fill him with melancholy forebodings, that time and again he wanted to stand with his fingers crossed in his prayer book 'for the union won't be holy and the prayer won't be holy and the prayer won't help much. The eager kids don't know what it's all about. They are matrimonial illiterates.'

10. Love your mate. Love, like Life, like Spirit, is impossible to define. 'Life is one damned thing after another; love is two damned things after each other.' "

Towering Diamond Head looms prominently over developing Honolulu.

Hawaiian Journey, "Hawaii Calls":

"There must be millions of Americans who, as children in the 1930s and 1940s, remember tuning in to a radio program called 'Hawaii Calls.' They would await that thrilling opening moment when the soft wash of the surf on the beach and the haunting sound of the conch-shell trumpet could be heard. The swaying palms, the sandy beach, the blue sky, and the colorfully costumed Hawaiian singers gathered on the shore could be seen in the mind, stimulated by the 'magic of radio.' More than anything else, 'Hawaii Calls' was responsible for popularizing Hawaiian music on the mainland and in other parts of the world, where it was heard by shortwave radio.

The music played on the program was known as 'hapa-haole,' or half-white, music. These songs sung in a Hawaiian style consisted of mostly English words with a few Hawaiian words thrown in for spice and color. Some, including 'Sweet Leilani' and 'My Little Grass Shack,' became world-famous. The program and its performers presented the kind of Hawaiian entertainment that they felt the outside world wanted to hear. Often the performers sang Hawaiian songs in the Hawaiian language, but the overall emphasis was on the hapa-haole music so popular at the time."

1939 Family Profile

Inventor and businessman Owen Verheil sold his frozen vegetable food business and processing plant 10 years ago for $22 million; he has been thinking about new inventions that are now possible with the capital from his sale.

Annual Income: Approximately $250,000 from investments; his net worth exceeds $6 million.

Life at Home

- Ten years ago, Owen Verheil sold his frozen food business for $22 million, receiving about $5 million for his life's work, including patents; during the past decade, he has devoted himself to improving science and his fellow man.
- Curious by nature and adventurous by habit, he has traveled extensively in Alaska, Greenland and Sweden, mostly to talk with scientists about the preservative qualities of cold temperatures.
- His current new passion is objects made in jade; it delights him that for centuries the Chinese used a single calligraphic character to denote both "jade" and "treasure."
- He is intrigued by the familiar attraction between jade and human flesh; while in Hong Kong he visited the Kowloon Jade Market and returned home with a tiny carved figure he carries in his pocket.
- He enjoys cooking, gardening, inventing, playing Chinese checkers with his grandchildren and entertaining the smartest men and women in the world.
- He loves to experiment, even with the foods he cooks, recently serving his guests porpoise meat, whose flavor he

Owen Verheil currently has a passion for objects made of jade.

Emily devotes her time to their six grandchildren.

    compares to that of canvasback duck; he has also enjoyed trying beaver tail, polar bear, lion tenderloin and "the front half of a skunk."

- When he wants to get away, he often goes to the movies alone, enjoying the corny puns in shows like "No Snooze is Good Snooze"; his favorite actress is Claudette Colbert.
- He was born in 1886, one of eight children; his father, a New York attorney, owned a farm in Long Island, New York, where Owen spent his summers enjoying countless hours tramping along the seashore.
- A loner by nature, Owen had little interest in organized sports; he attended Amherst College, but dropped out his sophomore year because of shaky family finances.
- His first job was as a naturalist with the United States Department of Agriculture's Biological Survey, collecting specimens of the animal and bird life in New Mexico and Arizona.
- In 1912, he took a six-week cruise to Labrador with a medical missionary and stayed to trap and breed black foxes, which were bringing $18,000 to $45,000 a pair in the United States.
- Unfortunately, two years later when he was ready to ship his foxes out of the country, the Newfoundland government intervened, ending his chance to make a fortune.
- During the trip he first saw food frozen rapidly by extreme winter cold, noticing that duck and caribou meat preserved in this manner retained its taste; he compared food frozen during the warm spring to food frozen during the dead of winter and concluded that winter-frozen meat was smoother and more appetizing.

- When he returned to Labrador in 1916 with his new wife Emily, he decided there should be vegetables in the house, so he bought a barrel of cabbages; when the temperature dropped to 10 degrees below zero, he took the cabbage outside and froze it in sea water, after which, whenever the family wanted leafy vegetables, he went out and chopped loose a head of cabbage.
- Currently, they live outside Bangor, Maine, in a home he bought in 1931—a Georgian colonial-style country estate that includes 145 acres.
- The seven bedrooms give them enough room for their six grandchildren, three boys and three girls; the massive living room, anchored by a French 1760s white-limestone fireplace, is excellent for entertaining guests, arguing about science or solving the world's political problems with the best minds in the area.
- Recently, they took a two-day trip to the New York World's Fair, which made him excited about the progress under way; it was so large and sprawling they would have quickly become lost without their map.
- Despite their wealth, Emily is most comfortable in her traditional role as wife, mother and grandmother, occasionally skipping trips with her husband to stay home and quietly knit, decorate the house and entertain their grandchildren.
- It brings her great pleasure to make clothes for the grandchildren, as it did when she made clothing for her own children during the early years of her marriage.
- Last year, Owen purchased a Rolls-Royce large enough for all the grandchildren and hired a chauffeur, even though Emily is embarrassed by the mere thought of having a chauffeur, let alone to carry grandchildren around.

Life at Work

- Owen Verheil currently holds more than 30 United States and foreign patents, mostly related to food preservation; selling his business a decade ago has freed him to experiment with new ways to preserve food.
- Since 1936, he has concentrated much of his effort on creating nutritious, portable foods for soldiers, as it is obvious to anyone who travels that the European war will include the United States soon.
- During their last trip abroad, they attended a play in London, participated in a lecture at Oxford and then were in the Hague, Netherlands, for the celebration of the queen's fortieth anniversary of her coronation; Emily loved the white cape the queen was wearing during the parade.
- Owen's experiments with food preservation range from ways to more efficiently seal food and its flavors to methods of grinding up food for rapid freezing so it can be economically shipped in bulk.

To escape, he often goes to the movies alone; Claudette Colbert is his favorite actress.

The Verheils' Georgian colonial-style home includes 145 acres.

The couple recently spent two days at the sprawling New York World's Fair.

- In 1922 he began his company with $7.00, with which he bought salt, ice and an electric fan, and worked out of a corner of the Clothel Refrigerating Company of New York.
- His goal was to create a fish-freezing plant; his first freezer consisted of a funnel-shaped can which was filled with food and then submerged in brine.
- Next he developed a freezer using narrow cans equipped with automatic loaders, which could process 2.5- to five-pound blocks of food by submerging the containers in a tank of frigid calcium chloride brine; unfortunately, when the finished frozen food was loaded into cans, producing airspace, it failed.
- He discovered that shipping frozen foods required special containers that only he seemed interested in developing; balsa wood proved too expensive, so he turned to a fiberboard shipping carton that cost only $0.01 per pound.
- The patent for the new shipping container with good insulating quality was his first.
- By 1928, about one million pounds of fruits and vegetables were frozen.
- He sold his company to the Postum Company in 1929 for $22 million; $20 million was paid for his patents and only $2 million for other assets.
- He is glad he remained in the industry, focused on perfecting the freezing of food—despite all the challenges; he often likens the frozen food industry to a small infant—plenty of noise at one end and an absolute lack of control on the other.
- In 1930, the Postum Company began marketing frozen foods, based on his patents, featuring frozen peas and spinach in their vegetable line and raspberries, loganberries and cherries in the fruit line.
- When the new frozen foods were offered, a salesman in Springfield, Massachusetts, said it was not an easy sell: "It took about five minutes to fast-talk a reluctant housewife into buying a package of peas at $0.35"; most housewives were more interested in price than in convenience.
- In the beginning, the main selling theme was "quick frozen versus cold storage."
- By 1933, only 516 frozen food retail outlets had been established nationwide; many grocery stores were reluctant to spend large sums on expensive refrigerator capacity for an unproven product.
- An editorial in a 1938 edition of *Quick Frozen Foods*, a publication for the supermarket industry, campaigned for self-service cabinets, in which shoppers could select the frozen foods without the assistance of a clerk.
- Many in the industry are convinced that frozen foods are "a passing fad," that is "too expensive to handle."

- The principal brands are Bird's Eye and Honor Brand, followed by Bodle, Little America, Hershey, Cedergreen, and Dulany Fairmont.
- To improve distribution, several major companies have contracted with the American Radiator Company to manufacture boxes that can be placed in stores on a monthly payment basis.
- Currently, a shift is taking place within the frozen food industry toward retail-sized packages; for the first time one third of the strawberries packed and sold are going into consumer sizes.
- Strawberries, which once had been a bulk item used primarily by bakers and ice cream makers, have became a retail leader for ready-to-eat desserts in the home.
- This year, a total of 268 million pounds of fruits, poultry, meats and seafood will be shipped as frozen foods.
- Locker plants currently account for most of the frozen food business; today there are 3,000 plants and new ones are opening at a rate of 50 a month.
- This year marked the first Frozen Food Association meeting, which was held in Chicago.
- California Consumers Corporation is experimenting with frozen whole orange juice.
- The biggest pre-cooked innovations of the year came from the Postum Company, under the Bird's Eye label, featuring chicken fricassee and a cross-cut steak.
- Competitors are offering brick soups, cooked and frozen creamed chicken, beef stew and roast turkey with dressing.

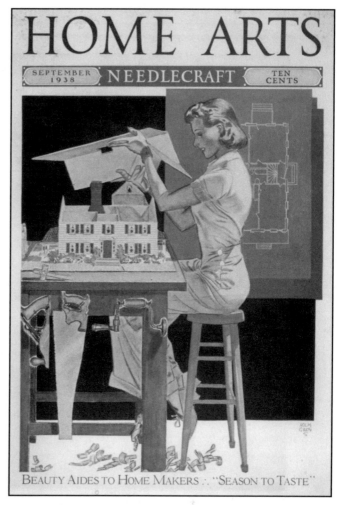

Last year, Owen purchased a Rolls-Royce large enough for all the grandchildren.

During their last trip abroad, Emily enjoyed seeing the Queen in her white cape.

- Since the industry must sell a concept, not a price, a typical advertisement reads, "It's October. The fresh asparagus season closed months ago. Yet today we offer you quick frozen asparagus, actually field fresher than the king can get in the middle of the season. Here's why—asparagus changes fast after cutting. The sugars turn quickly to starch. Stringy fibers develop. Even in season, your average asparagus may take up to three days to reach your table. By that time it's but a dry copy of the green shoots the farmer cuts in the field"; the price of frozen asparagus is $0.29 for a 12-ounce box.

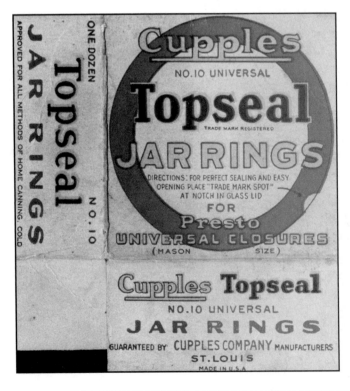

- Currently, 2,641 people earn a total of $1.5 million in the industry created by Owen's inventions.
- The industry is still struggling with distribution issues; most railroads only use salt and ice to keep the frozen food at the appropriate temperature, and many railroad men believe that transporting fresh food is more profitable than shipping frozen food.

Life in the Community: Bangor, Maine
- Bangor is the third largest city in Maine, nestled along the Penobscot River.
- Twenty-three miles from deep sea anchorage and at the head of the tidewater, Bangor established its place early on as the logging capital of America; it was the place where hard-drinking, deepwater sailormen mixed with the rough, backcountry loggers.
- Thanks to its early wealth, more than 80 residences are over 100 years old; Charles Bulfinch, who assisted in designing the nation's capital, laid out the city's streets in 1830.

"Business and Finance," *Time*, April 3, 1939:

"Manhattan reporters last week journeyed to the docks to count cases of gold being unloaded from the *Queen Mary*. They counted 355 cases, thus estimating that the *Queen* brought in some $20 million. This was presently dwarfed by a shipment on the *Manhattan* estimated at $56 million, the largest ever. At the week's end, four other liners were on the way from frightened Europe with $75 million more to add to the $15,007,517,132.83 (57 percent of the world's monetary supply) in gold already admittedly in the U.S. Treasury's hands.

As usual when the golden tide laps high on U.S. shores, reporters went to see Secretary of the Treasury Morgenthau. As usual, he pooh-poohed the idea of inflation. But though he said the gold was not affecting U.S. economy, it was amply clear that the continued European crisis was. Markets are nervous. Businessmen cut their buying for the future so low that three new indexes of inventories published by the National Industrial Conference Board touched the lowest point since May 1937. Most cheerful fact of the week (to businessmen): the sales ratio of twin beds to double beds was up from one-to-10 in 1936 to one-to-five."

- Between 1840 and 1880, lumber barons constructed lavish homes in the city, some of which were lost in the massive fire of 1911.
- Currently, the Pine Tree State has 39,000 farms, more than Connecticut, New Hampshire and Rhode Island combined.
- Potato farmers are fighting to maintain their position as the nation's top producer of potatoes, battling Alaska and Idaho for the honor.
- Three of every 10 dollars earned by Maine farms come from potatoes; six of every 10 dollars come from lumbering, paper and furniture manufacturing.
- Maine is the nation's largest producer of toothpicks, creating 100 million daily; since 1914, the state has also been the nation's largest producer of wood pulp.
- Owen and Emily's only son attended Bowdoin College in Brunswick; incorporated in 1794, the men-only institution is known nationally as a "Little Ivy League" school.
- Portland is serving as the naval operating base for the North Atlantic fleet; naval destroyers routinely convoy precious supplies to Great Britain, North Africa and Murmansk, USSR.
- The state's population stood at 694,466 in 1900; today it boasts 847,226.
- During the last election in 1936, Maine and Vermont were the only two states of the 48 that did not cast the presidential majority vote for incumbent President Franklin D. Roosevelt.

HISTORICAL SNAPSHOT
1939

- The average wage nationwide was $0.62 per hour, or $22.30 a week
- Clark Gable and Vivien Leigh starred in the movie *Gone with the Wind*, which lasted three hours and 42 minutes and cost $4.2 million to make
- The opening ceremonies of the New York World's Fair were televised and featured President Franklin D. Roosevelt
- German leader Adolph Hitler branded modern art degenerate and auctioned a number of museum works; many masterpieces passed into American museums and private collections
- Eight million men and women were still unemployed
- Newsreels, like "The March of Time," gained importance as worldwide events such as the invasion of Finland were documented
- Fifty-eight percent of Americans told the Gallup poll organization that the United States would be drawn into the war; 65 percent favored boycotting Germany
- Marian Anderson gave an open-air concert before 75,000 people in Lincoln Memorial Park after the Daughters of the American Revolution, who owned Constitution Hall, barred her from performing there because she was African-American
- *Reader's Digest* announced that its circulation had risen from 250,000 in 1930 to eight million
- Clara Adams became the first woman to fly around the world
- Sixty thousand German immigrants had arrived in America since 1933
- Because of the war, the Finns ceased shipping cheese to the United States
- Air-conditioned automobiles, electric slicing knives, the marketing of nylon stockings and legislation to regulate pinball machines all made their first appearance
- Cooperstown was established as the site for the Baseball Hall of Fame
- The Social Security Act was amended to allow extended benefits to the aged and widowed, minors and parents of a deceased person
- The production of chickens and turkeys by American farms set a new record
- The United States led the world in candy production, with 16 pounds consumed per person
- President Roosevelt ordered U.S. ports and waters closed to foreign submarines
- The minimum wage was $0.25 an hour for a 44-hour week

1939 Economic Profile

The national consumer expenditures (per capita income) in 1939 were:

Auto Parts	$3.82
Auto Usage	$39.69
Clothing	$45.03
Dentists	$3.05
Furniture	$6.87
Gas and Oil	$16.79
Health Insurance	$1.53
Housing	$71.74
Intercity Transport	$3.05
Local Transport	$6.87
New Auto Purchase	$12.21
Personal Business	$24.42
Personal Care	$7.63
Physicians	$6.87
Private Education and Research	$4.58
Recreation	$26.71
Religion/Welfare Activities	$7.63
Telephone and Telegraph	$4.58
Tobacco	$13.74
Utilities	$23.66
Per Capita Consumption	$511.34

Annual Income, Standard Jobs

Average of all Industries, Excluding Farm Labor	$1,346.00
Average of all Industries, Including Farm Labor	$1,266.00
Bituminous Coal Mining	$1,197.00
Building Trades, Union Workers	$1,268.00
Domestics	$544.00
Farm Labor	$436.00
Federal Civilian	$1,843.00
Federal Employees, Executive Departments	$1,137.00
Federal Military	$1,134.00
Finance, Insurance and Real Estate	$1,729.00
Gas and Electricity Workers	$1,766.00
Manufacturing, Durable Goods	$1,479.00
Manufacturing, Nondurable Goods	$1,263.00
Medical/Health Services Workers	$908.00
Miscellaneous Manufacturing	$1,337.00
Motion Picture Services	$1,971.00

STATEMENT
CONCERNING
FINNISH-RUSSIAN RELATIONS
AND THE
CIRCUMSTANCES LEADING TO
THE INVASION OF
FINLAND
BY THE UNION OF SOVIET SOCIALIST
REPUBLICS ON NOVEMBER 30, 1939

*Based on Official Documents published by
The Ministry for Foreign Affairs of Finland*

LONDON
PUBLISHED BY SIMPKIN MARSHALL, LTD.
at 4 Stationers' Hall Court, London, E.C.4
To be purchased through any bookseller or newsagent
Price 3d. net

The drumbeat of war is present throughout Europe.

Nonprofit Organization Workers . . . $1,546.00
Passenger Transportation
   Workers, Local and Highway $1,569.00
Personal Services $1,034.00
Public School Teachers. $1,403.00
Radio Broadcasting and
   Television Workers. $2,427.00
Railroad Workers. $1,877.00
State and Local Government
   Workers $1,569.00
Telephone and Telegraph Workers . . $1,600.00
Wholesale and Retail Trade
   Workers $1,360.00

Selected Prices

Aspirin, Bayer $0.59
Bicycle, Goodyear $43.95
Book, *Ripley's Believe It or Not* $0.85
Disinfectant, Lysol. $0.83

CHARLES STARRETT
in
"Ridin' The Outlaw Trail"

A COLUMBIA PICTURE

Fishing Reel $8.25
Fountain Pen $1.00
Hair Tonic, Wildroot $0.47
Kitchen Range $76.95
Paper Pattern for Dress $0.15
Pressure Cooker $7.45
Sewing Machine with Console $23.95
Shirt, Man's Chambray $0.69
Shoe Polish $0.14
Soap, Woodbury's, Three Cakes $0.25
Suit, Boy's $4.98
Tinkertoys $0.67
Tire, Goodyear $18.75
Tobacco, Pipe, Chesterfield $0.39
Wedding Ring, Man's 14-Karat Gold $4.98

"Ready for New Clothes for School," by Marilyn Madison, *Home Arts—Needlecraft*, September 1938:

"Begin today to plan what the children will have new for school. Be practical in your selections, and plan a wardrobe that will not need to have consideration from you every school morning. . . .

A thrifty mother of my acquaintance says, 'I buy shoes first, then socks right for the shoes. Then I buy sweaters and berets or caps. Next, I select the material for skirts or buy shorts or pants to go with the sweaters. Then I choose fabrics for dresses and blouses to give desired variety. Of course, I do all this to a planned color scheme so that each child looks as though thought has been given to his or her clothing.

'For the girls and the boys, when I have chosen styles in dresses and blouses right for them, I plan to make at least three garments in each style, varying the fabric and trimming so that each has individuality. I cut all garments one day, do my machine work all in one day, and then take my time with the finishing. There is less of this to do since I use slide fasteners in every garment I make. The children like them and they cut dressing time in half. . . .'

In making clothes to fit, I'd like to say a word about clothing for the 10- to 14-year-olds. By all means plan for becomingness in sewing for girls of these ages. No set rule can be put down, because some girls are chubby, some lanky, some large or small for their ages; so consider well the style and the fabric. Strive for simplicity. Tailored effects are safest, usually. Remember that bright, attractive clothes prove a real stimulus to a girl's pride, and, when sewing for these ages, listen to their whims and try to please them. The sooner a girl begins to know what she wants in a dress, the sooner she will express individuality and good taste. Dresses for a 10- to 14-year-old girl are no more difficult to make than for a two to six, but they do need more consideration as to individual becomingness. . . .

Hand embroidery is being emphasized this season, also bias-binding trims, loads of rickrack in all widths and colors, and colored and plain slide fasteners. Cotton having dark backgrounds and bright designs is as popular for winter as are the wool crepes and challis. Novelty plaids go in many of the pleated skirts."

1940–1949

The dramatic, all-encompassing nature of World War II dominated the lives and economies of Americans. As Americans became consumed by the national war effort and the need for rapid production of war materials, fortunes were made. America quickly shifted from the role of passive observer to fierce warrior following the bombing of Pearl Harbor in December 1941.

People from every social stratum either signed up for the military or went to work supplying the military machine. Even children, eager to do their share, collected scrap metal and helped plant the victory gardens that symbolized America's willingness to do anything to defeat the "bullies." In addition, large amounts of money and food were sent abroad as Americans observed meatless Tuesdays, gas rationing and other shortages to help the starving children of Europe.

Business worked in partnership with government; strikes were reduced, but key New Deal labor concessions were expanded, including a 40-hour week and time and a half for overtime. As manufacturing demands increased, the labor pool shrank, and wages and union membership rose. Unemployment, which stood as high as 14 percent in 1940, all but disappeared. By 1944, the U.S. was producing twice the total war output of the Axis powers combined. The wartime demand for production workers rose more rapidly than for skilled workers, reducing the wage gap between the two to the lowest level in the twentieth century.

From 1940 to 1945, the gross national product more than doubled, from $100 billion to $211 billion, despite rationing and the unavailability of many consumer goods such as cars, gasoline, and washing machines. Interest rates remained low, and the upward pressure on prices remained high, yet from 1943 to the end of the war, the cost of living rose less than 1.5 percent. Following the war, as controls were removed, inflation peaked in 1948; union demands for high wages accelerated. Between 1945 and 1952, confident Americans—and their growing families—increased consumer credit by 800 percent.

To fight inflation, government agencies regulated wages, prices, and the kind of jobs people could take. The Office of Price Administration was entrusted with the complicated task of setting price ceilings for almost all consumer goods and distributing ration books for items in short supply. The Selective Service and the War Manpower Commission largely determined who would serve in the military, whose work was vital to the war effort, and when a worker could transfer from one job to another. When the war ended and regulations were lifted, workers demanded higher wages; the relations between labor and management became strained. Massive strikes and inflation followed in the closing days of the decade and many consumer goods were easier to find on the black market than on the store shelves until America retooled for a peacetime economy.

The decade of the 1940s made America a world power and Americans more worldly. Millions served overseas; millions more listened to broadcasts concerning the war in London, Rome, and Tokyo. Newsreels brought the war home to moviegoers, who numbered in the millions. The war effort also redistributed the population and the demand for labor; the Pacific Coast gained wealth and power, and the South was able to supply its people with much-needed war jobs and provide blacks with opportunities previously closed to them. Women entered the work force in unprecedented numbers, reaching 18 million. The net cash income of the American farmer soared 400 percent.

But the Second World War extracted a price. Those who experienced combat entered a nightmarish world. Both sides possessed far greater firepower than ever before, and within those units actually fighting the enemy, the incidence of death was high, sometimes one in three. In all, the United States lost 405,000 men and women to combat deaths; many suffered in the war's final year, when the American army spearheaded the assault against Germany and Japan. The cost in dollars was $350 billion. But the cost was not only in American lives. Following Germany's unconditional surrender on May 4, 1945, Japan continued fighting. To prevent the loss of thousands of American lives defeating the Japanese, President Truman dropped atomic bombs on the Japanese cities of Hiroshima and Nagasaki, ending the war and ushering in the threat of "the bomb" as a key element of the Cold War during the 1950s and 1960s.

Throughout the war, soldiers from all corners of the nation fought side by side and refined nationalism and what it meant to America through this government-imposed mixing process. This newfound identity of American GIs was further cemented by the vivid descriptions of war correspondent Ernie Pyle, who spent a considerable time talking and living with the average soldier to present a "worm's eye view" of war. Yet, despite the closeness many men and women developed toward their fellow soldiers, spawning a wider view of the world, discrimination continued. African-American servicemen were excluded from the marines, the Coast Guard, and the Army Corps. The regular army accepted blacks into the military—700,000 in all—only on a segregated basis. Only in the closing years of the decade would President Harry Truman lead the way toward a more integrated America by integrating the military.

Sports attendance in the 1940s soared beyond the record levels of the 1920s; in football the T-formation moved in prominence; Joe DiMaggio, Ted Williams, and Stan Musial dominated baseball before and after the war, and Jackie Robinson became the first black in organized baseball. In 1946, Dr. Benjamin Spock's work, *Common Sense Baby and Child Care*, was published to guide newcomers in the booming business of raising babies. The decade also discovered the joys of fully air-conditioned stores for the first time, cellophane wrap, Morton salt, daylight-saving time, Dannon yogurt, Everglades National Park, the Cannes Film Festival, Michelin radial tires, Dial soap, and Nikon 35mm film.

1942 FAMILY PROFILE

George Staub and his brother Frederick successfully shifted the focus of their already lucrative construction business to shipbuilding as World War II began. Comfortable, but not rich before the war, they have expanded their fortune dramatically, thanks to contracts issued by Roosevelt. George and his wife Constance recently adopted a seven-year-old girl and her five-year-old brother.

Annual Income: $250,000 a year, including bonuses; George's net worth is more than $3 million.

Life at Home

- Born in 1892, George Staub grew up in the central Texas town of Belton.
- He started a small construction and road-building business in 1914, and Frederick joined him in the business in 1922.
- Since that time, the two brothers have always worked together, complementing each other's strengths and weaknesses.
- Six years older than Frederick, George has a forceful personality, acts decisively, and is the leader in most respects; a prominent state politician calls him a "bulldozer."
- He is highly practical and driven, with a gift for sizing up talent quickly.
- Frederick, who is more sophisticated and less abrasive, was trained as an engineer and is the creative half of the team.

George and Frederick Staub began working together in 1922.

The Staubs recently adopted two children, who thought their new home looked like a hotel.

1865   1942

A style as American as the red, white and blue feather in the band—with emphasis on quality and accent on wear. This is another Stetson original, made by the exclusive Stetson Vita-Felt process, shown in the new "Freedom Blue" color.

The STETSON *Eagle* $7⁵⁰

OTHER STETSONS $5 TO $25 • STETSON HATS FOR MEN AND WOMEN • ALSO MADE IN CANADA

George rarely leaves the house without his Stetson hat.

- He talks with a slight speech impediment—a characteristic he uses to put people at ease and contrast himself with his hard-charging brother.
- Since the beginning, the brothers have agreed to share an equal financial interest in business ventures; though they often argue—and loudly—about politics, business strategies and personnel matters, disputes over money are rare.
- During the Depression days of the 1930s, they won the contract for the Marshall Ford Dam west of Austin on the Colorado River, giving them the experience they needed on a major project, so when the military buildup for the Second World War began, they were ready.
- George rarely leaves the house without his John B. Stetson hat made of the finest felt, the belly fur of a Canadian beaver.
- Frederick's family still lives in Austin, where he travels each weekend to see his three daughters; currently, he uses a surplus DC-3 airplane for his trips to ease the stress of wartime travel.
- George's wife Constance considers herself a partner in his career; it is her job to manage the demands of the household, provide emotional support, and even serve as his replacement at many cultural, social and civic affairs; as a symbol of her independence, she does not wear her wedding ring.
- She suffers from chronic bronchial problems and uses a bed that tilts up when she finds breathing difficult; she also keeps a container of oxygen by the bed.
- The seven-year-old girl they recently adopted had been abandoned by her parents; once the child understood that George and Constance wanted to adopt her, she told them about her younger brother, who was also in a foster home, and they adopted him, as well.
- In their 50s, the Staubs suggested that their children call them Uncle George and Aunt Connie.
- An avid reader since childhood, Constance wants to give the two children the best possible education.

Life at Work

- George and Frederick have worked hard and planned carefully to be where they are today; currently, they operate an immense shipyard near Houston, Texas.
- They are also building a massive shipyard near a major naval base in Corpus Christi, Texas.
- The government contracts, requiring thousands of workers, are worth more than $300 million.
- On June 11, 1940, with the threat of war looming, but before the bombing of Pearl Harbor, the Navy approved a contract supporting a naval air station at Corpus Christi, Texas.

- Two days later President Franklin Roosevelt signed a cost-plus-fixed-fee contract for $23.3 million with the Staubs' company and two others; the total contract was $125 million.

- That same day, Roosevelt also approved funding for 10,000 planes, 18,000 pilots and 22 new combat vessels.

- George had worked for months to secure this contract, which originally called for the construction of four patrol craft, or subchasers, costing $2.5 million.

- George conducted frequent conversations with U.S. Congressman Lyndon Johnson, who sat on the Naval Affairs Committee.

- The concrete for the first new facility was poured five weeks later on July 26, 1940, and the first cadets began training at the partially completed base in April 1941.

- The base was 60 percent complete only eight months after the contract was approved and eight months ahead of schedule.

- Construction on the 2,000-acre site required building a 20-mile-long railroad line to transport heavy materials, while fresh water had to be trucked to the site by an outside contractor because local water contained such a high salt content.

- Staub Contracting Company also experienced labor disputes; two employees filed a complaint with the National Labor Relations Board claiming company officials engaged in anti-labor union practices.

- The company's movement into defense-related projects reflected the growing importance of military construction as the nation slowly came to grips with the prospects for American involvement in the war.

- As Congressman Johnson said, "When you consider that we are now training only 500 pilots annually and need to increase the figure immediately to 10,000, you can realize the possibilities for Texas."

- After the Corpus Christi project—completed on time and at a reasonable cost—Staub Contracting Company took over the shipbuilding operation of an overburdened Houston contractor.

- Though experienced in construction, they knew nothing about shipbuilding, but their decision to begin mirrored the character of George and his company: bold, creative and willing to take the risk of any complex project, large or small.

- Because of the considerable financial exposure involved with the new venture, the brothers formed a new company expressly for the purpose of shipbuilding, but almost immediately they discovered that few workers in the Houston area were experienced in the industry, so they pulled workers from many different fields.

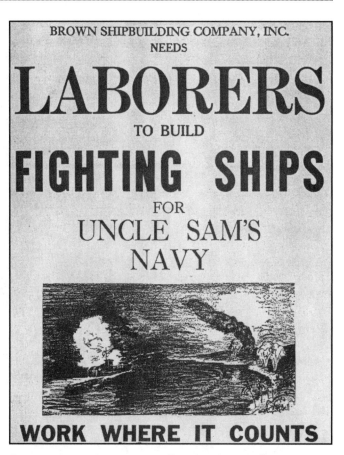

Once war began, America's war effort geared up rapidly.

Before World War II, the United States was only training 500 pilots a year.

The Staub brothers slashed the cost of building ships.

- They also found the existing shipyard inadequate and had to buy 156 acres, at $1,000 per acre, to build a new one; to create the equipment needed, they salvaged heavy machinery and tools from various other ventures.
- The cost of ships built by their company has been slashed by two thirds, and they are now competing favorably with the giant Bethlehem Steel for new contracts.
- Currently they have 23,000 people working in two shipyards; at Yard A, women are restricted to clerical and technical occupations, while at Yard B, they are given jobs as expediters, burners, welders and loftsmen.
- Blacks at both yards are employed only in unskilled positions.
- The first ship completed, a PC-565, was the first PC (patrol craft) from any yard to sink a German submarine.
- Recently, the brothers received additional shipbuilding contracts, including one for the Navy's new, compact, 300-foot destroyer escort, designed to battle the U-boats plaguing Allied ships in the Atlantic.
- George is intensely loyal to his workers, demanding loyalty in exchange, and passionately believes that people who work for him should not be forced to join a union as a condition of labor; he feels that he—not an outside union—is the best judge of his workers' needs.
- He also believes that non-union labor is more flexible, more efficient and, at times, less expensive than union labor.
- Unlike most contractors who lay off construction workers whenever a project is completed, the brothers keep their employees on the payroll, with many working on annual contracts; this policy allows them to retain quality workers, build loyalty and take on new projects quickly.
- The demands of the war require a typical work week of 48 to 56 hours.

The company newsletter, Victory Dispatch, *carries the compliments of ship commanders.*

- To keep everyone motivated and production high, the company is producing a newsletter called the *Victory Dispatch*, which often carries compliments from ship commanders concerning the superior quality of the company's warships.
- Staub Contracting is widely believed to build the best ships at the least cost of any shipyard under contract in the Navy; one of its latest innovations is the creation of swinging scaffolds, which move as ship construction progresses.
- Recently, the Navy awarded the company the "E" (for Excellence) pennant, signifying the determined effort of the brothers to rapidly develop a shipyard capable of producing ships vital to the Allied war effort.
- During 1942, U.S. merchant shipbuilding was one of the few industries to reach the ambitious production goals set by President Roosevelt at the beginning of America's entrance into the war.
- Aircraft production fell short by 12,000, or 20 percent, in 1942, as did tank and anti-aircraft programs.
- Shipbuilders nationwide produced 746 vessels during the year totaling eight million tons—90,800 tons above the President's quota.
- In December alone, U.S. shipyards shattered all world records by delivering 1,999,300 tons of ships, almost double the production in all of 1941 and 36 percent of the peak year for World War I.

Speech delivered by President Franklin D. Roosevelt at the Tomb of the Unknown Soldier in Washington, DC, Armistice Day, November 11, 1942:

"My Fellow Americans: Here in Arlington we are in the presence of the honored dead, and I think that we are accountable to them—accountable to the generations yet unborn for whom they gave their lives. . . . Today Americans and their British brothers in arms are again fighting on French soil. They are again fighting against a German militarism which transcends a hundred-fold the brutality and barbarism of 1918. The Nazis of today and their appropriate associates, the Japanese, have attempted to drive history into reverse—to use all the mechanics of modern civilization to drive humanity back to conditions of prehistoric savagery. They sought to conquer the world, and for a time they seemed to be successful in realizing their boundless ambition.

They overran great territories, they enslaved, they killed.

But today we know, and they know, that they have conquered nothing. Today they face the inevitable, final defeat. Yes, the forces of liberation are advancing. Britain, Russia, China and the United States grow rapidly toward full strength. The opponents of decency and justice have passed their peak.

And as a result of recent events—very recent—the United States and the United Nations forces are being joined by large numbers of the fighting men of our traditional ally, France. On this day of all days, it is heartening for us to know that the soldiers of France go forward with the United Nations."

- Staub Contracting is being praised widely; one story reads, "The brothers form a type of two-headed businessman, with the energies and vision of two different men possessing complementary talents."
- Every day, after the company closes at 5:15, executives gather for social hour at Houston's Lamar Hotel's Suite 8-F, which was furnished by their wives and features simple elegance rather than showy antiques; its main features are its warmth, its history of political deal-making, and the guarantee of a good book to read.
- It is the place where the most respected leaders in town meet to plan the future—from their annual trip to the Kentucky Derby to the decision of which political candidates to support.
- The "8-F Crowd," as they are known, believe fervently in the creation of a "healthy business climate" in their region, and are always focused on helping Houston grow; often their discussions center around philanthropy and the role of the wealthy in making Houston a better place.
- It is not uncommon for politicians, businessmen or fellow contractors to stay at the Suite while visiting Houston.
- George likes to say privately, "By day, I'm a contractor, by night a politician"; his skill at working behind the scenes is widely admired.

Life in the Community: Houston, Texas

- Although it contains only five percent of the U.S. population, Texas is contributing seven percent of the armed forces and has suffered seven percent of the casualties.
- The high enlistment rate is believed to grow from Texas's wild West cowboy image.

AIR EXPRESS TONNAGE GAINS 93.6%

"The impetus given by the war to AIR EXPRESS operations...is indicated in figures for the first ten months of 1942 showing a rise of 93.6 per cent in pounds carried...Despite release of about half of commercial air-line equipment to the Army early in the year, nevertheless, by rearrangement of schedules, increasing plane hours a day, and stepping up plane maintenance and servicing, air lines are equaling and even surpassing pre-war performance."

Excerpt from *New York Herald Tribune*, January 11, 1943

Although you do not need a priority to ship by AIR EXPRESS, if you have war production shipments requiring priorities, they will be granted. Phone Railway Express Agency, AIR EXPRESS DIVISION, or any air line

NOW IN ITS 16th YEAR AIR **EXPRESS**

Division of RAILWAY EXPRESS

- In the two decades preceding the war, the movie industry has indelibly linked the state with the image of the Old West, even though Wyatt Earp and Doc Holliday operated primarily in Arizona, and Billy the Kid in New Mexico, while the James and Dalton gangs came from Missouri.

- The cost of living has risen 20 percent in two years, with the price of food alone rising 34 percent.

- Roosevelt signed a $15 billion appropriation in October for the construction of more than 14,000 naval planes and 25 aircraft carriers.

- The annual base pay of a rear admiral in the United States Navy is $8,666, including bonuses for 12 years of service; a lieutenant with more than 10 years' service makes $2,400.

- A profit of $24 million, or 22 percent, on the construction of ships for the federal government is not "grossly in excess," according to a ruling by the United States Supreme Court, which says, "The ships built by Bethlehem cost the government less than other comparable ships built by other shipbuilders."

- Recently, Oveta Culp Hobby of Houston was appointed by the President to form and then command the Women's Army Auxiliary Corp (WAAC)—the first official unit of female soldiers in the nation's history.

President Roosevelt has signed a $15 billion appropriation for additional planes and ships.

- Because nylon stockings are becoming unavailable with the war on, women are covering their legs with stocking-colored makeup and drawing lines down the backs to resemble seams.
- New construction of homes has virtually stopped, since all building materials are being diverted to the shipyards and the war effort.
- Recently, the Texas legislature approved $500,000 for a cancer hospital in Houston.
- Summer concerts are being staged at the Miller Outdoor Theater and are so successful there is discussion about their becoming an annual event of the Houston Symphony.
- The Museum of Fine Arts is staying open despite the shortages; its collection of works by Frederick Remington, donated by Ima Hogg, is one of the largest in the nation, and contains 53 oils, 10 watercolors and the bronze *Bronco Buster*.
- The Texas legislature is considering a bill that would prohibit the blind from driving automobiles.
- African-Americans in Houston, led by black dentist Dr. Lonnie Smith, are suing for the right to vote in the Democratic primary, when most Texas elections are decided.

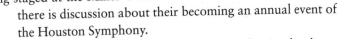

A *New Yorker* cartoon, reflecting wartime rationing, shows two world-weary young blondes meeting over a martini:

"Oh, you know. It was the old, old story. He plied me with presents—butter, sugar, nylons. . . ."

HISTORICAL SNAPSHOT
1942

- U.S. casualties during 1942 totaled 8,192 killed, 6,335 wounded and 43,562 missing
- World War II casualties worldwide among all sides topped 20 million for the first three years, with one quarter dying from their wounds; civilian deaths approached one million
- In a worldwide radio broadcast, British Prime Minister Winston Churchill declared that the British would use poison gas against Germany if Hitler did so in Russia
- The national debt passed $100 billion for the first time in history
- Single men 18 to 35 and married men 18 to 26 were eligible for the draft
- Congress passed an anti-inflation bill to stabilize prices, wages and salaries while war was under way
- A poll of radio editors selected Bob Hope and Jack Benny as the year's top performers; in children's programming, "Let's Pretend" was first and the "Lone Ranger" second
- An American-built four-engine bomber flew 2,200 miles from Newfoundland to Great Britain in six hours, 40 minutes
- New Year's Day was proclaimed a National Day of Prayer
- The lights in New York's Times Square and across the nation were dimmed at night so that ships at sea were not betrayed to U-boats
- Bill Mitchell was posthumously restored to the rank of major general
- The first attack on the American mainland was launched by a Japanese submarine, which fired approximately 25 shells at an oil refinery near Santa Barbara, California
- More than 900 translators/censors were hired in the New York Post Office to examine foreign mail
- Eighty war movies were made
- President Franklin D. Roosevelt had four sons fighting on the front lines
- Enrico Fermi secretly achieved a controlled nuclear fission reaction at the University of Chicago; in a coded message, he told President Roosevelt, "The Italian navigator has entered the new world"
- Blacks lodged complaints about discrimination in the armed forces, particularly in the Navy
- The Nobel Prize ceremonies, discontinued in Stockholm since 1939, took place at a dinner at the Waldorf Astoria in New York City
- The Japanese executed three fliers captured during General Doolittle's raid on Tokyo
- RCA Victor sprayed gold over a recording of Glenn Miller's "Chattanooga Choo Choo" when it sold more than one million copies, creating the first gold record
- Actress Carole Lombard and 20 others died in a TWA transport crash; she was on a tour selling war bonds

1942 ECONOMIC PROFILE

The national consumer expenditures (per capita income) in 1942 were:

Auto Parts	$2.22
Auto Usage	$26.69
Clothing	$63.03
Dentists	$3.71
Food	$210.59
Furniture	$9.64
Gas and Oil	$19.28
Health Insurance	$1.48
Housing	$83.05
Intercity Transport	$5.19
Local Transport	$7.42
New Auto Purchase	$0.74
Personal Business	$25.21
Personal Care	$10.38
Physicians	$7.42
Private Education and Research	$5.93
Recreation	$34.85
Religion/Welfare Activities	$9.64
Telephone and Telegraph	$5.93
Tobacco	$17.05
Utilities	$28.92
Per Capita Consumption	$656.98

Annual Income, Standard Jobs

Average of all Industries, Excluding Farm Labor	$1,858.00
Average of all Industries, Including Farm Labor	$1,778.00
Bituminous Coal Mining	$1,715.00
Building Trades, Union Workers	$2,191.00
Domestics	$706.00
Farm Labor	$769.00
Federal Civilian	$2,265.00
Federal Employees, Executive Departments	$1,632.00
Federal Military	$1,485.00
Finance, Insurance and Real Estate	$1,885.00
Gas and Electricity Workers	$2,040.00
Manufacturing, Durable Goods	$2,292.00
Manufacturing, Nondurable Goods	$1,654.00
Medical/Health Services Workers	$1,063.00
Miscellaneous Manufacturing	$1,540.00
Motion Picture Services	$2,124.00

Nonprofit Organization Workers ... $1,482.00

Passenger Transportation Workers,
Local and Highway $1,990.00

Personal Services $1,199.00

Public School Teachers........... $1,512.00

Radio Broadcasting and
Television Workers............. $2,667.00

Railroad Workers................. $2,303.00

State and Local Government
Workers $1,574.00

Telephone and Telegraph
Workers $1,715.00

Wholesale and Retail Trade
Workers $1,608.00

Selected Prices

Alka Seltzer, Eight Tablets............. $0.24

Automobile, DeSoto Deluxe $1,010.00

Billfold, Amity Leather $2.50

Blended Whiskey, Seagram's, Fifth $2.70

Camera, Eastman Brownie $2.56

Deep Freezer $225.00

Drapery, Chintz, One Yard $4.00

Globe............................ $2.95

Golf Shoes $4.99

Hotel Room, Atlantic City $6.50

Ice Cube Tray $1.50

Peanut Butter..................... $0.41

Rouge, Coty Air-Spun............... $0.50

Shoes, Child's Saddle Oxford $1.69

Slack Suit, Woman's $6.95

Soda Pop, Coca-Cola, Six-Pack $0.25

Theatre Ticket, *Porgy and Bess*........ $2.75

Wallpaper, per Roll $1.50

America's Industry Goes to War

- Only a year after the attack on Pearl Harbor, the arms production in America reached 49,000 planes, 32,000 tanks and self-propelled artillery, 17,000 anti-aircraft guns and 8.2 million tons of merchant shipping.
- This production surpassed the total output of the Axis powers, including Germany, Italy and Japan.
- A highway 1,671 miles long from Dawson Creek, northwest of Edmonton, Alberta, to Fairbanks, Alaska, was hewn out of the wilderness by 10,000 soldiers and 2,000 civilian workers in approximately six months.
- The 24-foot-wide road was built at a rate of eight miles a day and involved bridging 200 streams.

"1943 Hairpin Supply to Be One Fourth of 1941," *The World Almanac, 1942:*

"Miss and Mrs. America will have to get along with one new bobpin in 1943 for every four they had in 1942. In an amendment to the earlier order cutting the 1942 production of these pins to half of what it was in 1941, the WPB reduced the 1943 production to one quarter of the 1941 consumption. The WPB said that based on the 1941 consumption the order would have about 5,700 tons of steel for the essential war purposes. The amendment also prohibited the bulk sale of bobpins and hairpins, and provided that no more than 100 pins might be included in one package. Formerly, only hairpins were covered by the restriction."

- Meat rationing in the United States limited Americans to 2.5 pounds per week, to include beef, pork, veal, lamb and mutton; exempt from restrictions were hearts, kidneys, livers, sweetbreads and meat from heads, tails and feet.
- By comparison, the average Briton was restricted to 31 ounces of meat a week.
- To meet the manpower needs of the war, women poured into the work force, holding 30 percent of non-agricultural jobs.
- Despite a no-strike pledge from CIO president Philip Murray, almost 300 new strikes were called each month.
- The governor of New York signed a bill giving the State Industrial Commissioner the right to suspend the operation of labor laws for a six-month period and enabled both men and women to work as many as seven days a week.
- The United States Supreme Court ruled that a sit-down strike by sailors is mutiny even if the ship was at a dock in port.
- The United States Treasury "loaned" 40,000 tons of silver for the manufacture of bus-bars, the main conductors of electric generating plants, freeing up the use of copper.
- The War Production Board banned the use of iron and steel in more than 400 civilian products, including pie plates, clock cases, mailboxes and fountain pens.
- A patent was awarded to Charles T. Jacobs for a device that kept the ice in a cocktail shaker from diluting the "dividend."
- Women bought trousers at a rate 10 times higher than the previous year.

Letter from Lewis P. Walker, 3147 Copper Street, El Paso, Texas, to his sister, December 12, 1942:

"The last letter I received from you was dated May 27; it was interesting and I was glad to hear—sorry I did not answer sooner but it looks like I never catch up. We are all well and Lewis is still at Duke—he will be a junior after the first semester after being there only one and one half years. This was made possible by going to school this summer. He is a good student and makes fine grades. I think he is going to be a real man if he is not killed in action. He is now in the Enlisted Reserve Corps. I am proud he did not wait to be drafted. Do not know how soon he will be called but he seems to think he will be able to stay in school until June. His Christmas holidays back here are very short—no time to come home, so we are leaving tonight to meet him in New York City for that period. We will be in Spartanburg [South Carolina] for only one week—from the third to the tenth of January, so it looks like I will not have a chance to see you this time. ... Merry Christmas and best wishes from all of us. Sorry I cannot write more but my time is very limited now.

Much Love, Lewis."

Leading magazines in the United States and the number sold (in millions) monthly in 1942:

Life 5.5
The Ladies' Home Journal 4.9
The Saturday Evening Post 4.5
McCall's Magazine 4.5
Woman's Home Companion 4.2
Family Circle 4.0
Better Homes and Gardens 4.0
Woman's Day 3.8
Look 3.8
Collier's 3.7
Good Housekeeping 3.5
American Home 3.0

"Don't shove, Elmer, there's no shortage of War Bonds," smiled Elsie

"At Last You Can Have a Passionate Kiss from Deanna Durbin,"
Screen Guide, April 1941:

"Passion in a kiss is not something you can turn on or off like Rudy Vallee on the radio—especially if your name is Deanna Durbin and you never kiss off-screen unless you mean it. That's why this scene from *Nice Girl* took a whole morning to film.

Director William Seiter had this situation to get across: Deanna is the good girl who gets a little reckless and takes a trip to New York with Franchot Tone. On her return, she goes to a party, where old friend Walter Brennan gets up and announces without warning that Deanna and Tone are engaged. As soon as Franchot comes on the scene, she runs to him, kisses him and gives him a whispered explanation. Catching on, Franchot stage whispers, "Jane, my own, my precious!" And they really kiss.

Several rehearsals and takes were necessary before this brief incident was on film to Seiter's satisfaction. For this is the first time Deanna has ever been kissed on-screen by somebody who really knows his business. That preliminary encounter with Bob Stack in *First Love* is hardly to be reckoned in the same class, even though Stack wins her heart again by the fadeout of *Nice Girl*.

Put yourself in Deanna's shoes—or Franchot's—and notice the progress of the kiss: first anticipation; he takes the aggressive; she has a moment's qualms, but decides to cooperate, with the enjoyable result seen below. It's something like a golf swing—start slowly, then follow through and stay with it!"

1946 Profile

Julius Costello has followed in the footsteps of his grandfather, who was an early inventor, investor and entrepreneur in the business of having fun—pioneering ways for Americans to relax by playing pool, bowling or motoring in the country. Thirty-one and never married, Julius enjoys traveling, selling new ideas and collecting billiard tables, many dating back to 1875.

Annual Income: As a major stockholder in the Brunswick Company, his annual dividends alone allow him an income of more than $100,000, an amount similar to his salary.

Life at Home

- Julius Costello lives outside Chicago in a 24-bedroom house built during the boom years following the Civil War.
- The paneled music room has been converted into a bar complete with a giant mirror, walnut counter and a dozen billiard tables, including his collection of Brunswick tables—some originally designed and built by his grandfather, Leo, a close friend and business partner of John Brunswick.
- For more than 75 years, Brunswick has been associated with leisure time activities, building elegant bar fixtures, inlaid billiard tables and bowling alleys.
- Julius's favorite is The Monarch, made in 1875 and inlaid with California laurel, burl ash, French walnut, birds-eye maple, ebony and mahogany.

Julius Costello's company supplied equipment for the lavish pool parlors of the 1920s.

He recently purchased an Italian Baroque secretary.

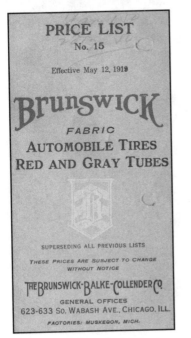

The company's products once included tires.

- The tables, the bar and his staff of six are kept busy every Friday night when business partners, friends and investors gather at his sprawling house, decorated with furniture discovered on travels around the world.
- A recent purchase was an Italian Baroque bone- and ivory-inlaid walnut secretary from the early eighteenth century.
- At work he concentrates on sales and searches for new ideas; restless, adventurous and rich, he is willing to take risks.
- His drive helped Brunswick take the lead role in providing America's soldiers throughout the world with recreations—centered around bowling alleys and billiard tables—and has even learned French to make certain that Amsterdam merchants are not cheating him.
- During the past five years, 13,000 billiard tables and 3,000 bowling alleys have been provided to USO and military clubs and bases around the globe.
- When possible, he takes time off to think, often while hunting in Alaska or fishing in the Andes.
- John M. Brunswick built his first billiard table in 1845 in Cincinnati; like the cabinets, tables, chairs and carriages he was making at the time, it was another wooden item—an experiment for which he hoped to create a market.
- Leo Costello, Julius's grandfather, possessed skills as a craftsman, inventor and sales manager that made him invaluable to the young company.
- In 1884, the company began manufacturing bowling equipment; the two pastimes seemed to go together naturally, and frequently, both pool tables and bowling alleys were sold to the same proprietor.
- Although for years saloonkeepers used both games to attract thirsty customers, the Brunswick Company helped forge a solid union among booze, billiards and bowling.
- That same year, the capital stock of the Brunswick-Balke-Collender Company increased to $1.5 million, and by 1904, the company was the largest billiard equipment operation in the world, so successful that cities from throughout the Midwest submitted offers to attract the company to their town; Muskegon, Michigan, was the winner.
- When the Prohibition movement reduced the sale of bar fixtures and beverage coolers by $4 million, the company refocused on its other business lines: billiards, church furniture and bank interiors.
- The company continued expanding; Brunswick-Balke-Collender began producing the "Whale-Bone-Ite," the first rubber toilet seat to replace the rigors of wooden seats.
- It also jumped into the automobile tire business and the building of tall, inlaid phonograph cabinets, for which the Edison Phonograph Company was its principal client.
- Yet, even with all the additional products, the company's financial foundation was still built around its billiard tables produced in eight plants around the country.
- In the mid-1920s, there were more than 42,000 poolrooms in the United States, 4,000 in New York alone; in other cities, lavish parlors became minor urban landmarks and tourist attractions.
- To meet these demands, Brunswick owned more than a thousand acres of hardwood timberland near Lake Superior and its own slate quarries in Vermont and Pennsylvania.
- Annually it produced more than 400,000 pool cues.

- When the Depression came, the company shrank in size dramatically, losing $1 million a year by 1935.
- With the arrival of the Second World War, the ever adaptable Brunswick provided pool tables for USO clubs and military centers, in addition to Brunswick-built parachute bomb flares, aircraft fuselages, landing skids for air force gliders and self-sealing fuel cells for floating mines; by 1942, total sales had reached $20 million.

Life at Work

- Currently, more than 18 million Americans crowd into bowling alleys annually to spend an estimated $200 million a year for the privilege of assaulting a formation of hardwood pins, with most of this activity taking place on Brunswick lanes.
- Many of today's most avid fans are soldiers who learned to love the game while serving in the military.
- The unsavory air, which hung over bowling alleys and the bars where most of them were located, was dispelled, thanks to improved lighting, a more inviting environment, and established game standards; bowling is now rapidly becoming America's top spectator sport.
- *Life* magazine claims bowling is the most popular of all participant sports.

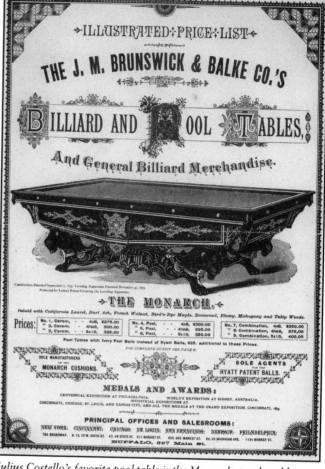

Julius Costello's favorite pool table is the Monarch, produced by Brunswick.

"Our Monarch Cushions," The J.M. Brunswick and Balke Company's Illustrated Price List, 1881:

"In buying the table the cushion is the most important item. It is to the billiard table what the mainspring is to the watch. The bed may be level, the frame strong, the cloth the finest, the balls true, the cues perfect, but if the cushion is defective, the table is practically worthless. After making numberless thorough experiments, spending much time and money in the last 36 years, The J.M. Brunswick and Balke Co. pronounce the Monarch Cushion the best ever invented or now in use. Its composition is their secret, its value their customer's gain. They control one of the largest rubber factories in the United States; it manufactures the Monarch Cushion exclusively for them, and makes no cushion for any other firm. India Rubber varies more in cost and quality than any other article in the building or outfitting of a billiard table. Cushions are made for from $1.00 to $1.50 per pound, the same as used in car springs, but the Monarch Rubber Cushions for the J.M. Brunswick and Balke Co.'s billiard tables, while made of the purest and finest rubber, cost far more than others, because of the combinations used to make them perfect."

By 1904 Brunswick was the world's largest manufacturer of billiards equipment.

- Approximately one third of all bowlers are women, many of whom participate in weekly league games that keep them at the alleys 32 weeks a year.
- In some ways, the reformation of the bowling image began with Prohibition; when saloons were outlawed, bar proprietors who had installed bowling alleys to attract drinkers turned their attention to serious promotion of the sport.
- In 1927, the city of Chicago alone boasted more than 400,000 bowlers.
- In April 1946, a private bowling alley was installed in the White House by President Harry Truman, who knocked down seven pins with his first ball.
- Fashionable Vassar College has added bowling to its intramural collegiate sports program.
- Recently, competitor American Machine and Foundry Company introduced an automatic pinsetting machine called the pinspotter, which Julius believes will ultimately fail because, although pin boys are getting more difficult to find and hire, he feels machines cannot replace these icons of America's lost innocence, even if the boys often sass back the customers or heckle the ladies.

Life in the Community: Muskegon, Michigan

- Muskegon, Michigan, was a quiet town when the Brunswick Company built a new factory there in 1906.
- Already a prosperous firm with sales offices in a half-dozen American cities, Canada and Mexico, Brunswick was recruited by numerous cities determined to attract a major new manufacturing facility.
- Grand Rapids, Michigan, was the front-runner in 1904, before Charles Hackley and Thomas Hume presented the case for Muskegon, a community of only 25,000 people, whose streets were paved with sawdust.

"Striking Back," *Fortune Magazine*, February 1946:

"To the proprietor, league play is the bread of business. With the help of the American Bowling Congress, he has raised his one-time shadowy, sideshow enterprise to the substantial level of Main Street's tidiest merchants. In fact, few U.S. little businessmen can claim a comparable stability.

Just because a bowling alley may stay open all night and its neon lights wink at late stragglers along a lonesome street, it should not be misjudged; luring an odd dollar or two from the casual, impulsive wayfarer is insignificant to its business. Hours ago—roughly between 6:00 and 11 p.m.—it may have earned its daily cost from the steady, booked-in-advance patronage of league bowlers. The transient or 'open' bowling is largely so much velvet. In a 16-bed alley, for example, the economies of a day's operation might work out something like this. At 6:00 p.m. all the alleys will be taken over by teams in industrial and business leagues who have come directly from plant or office. Each man of a five-man team bowls three 'lines' at $0.25 a line (a line is 10 frames and there are two balls to a frame), which is $3.75 per team. Their games take about two and one half hours to complete. At 8:30 p.m. the after-dinner social and church leagues will begin to play, continuing until about 11:00. The alley's total take from these scheduled activities will be $120, roughly equal to the day's operating expenses. But before 6:00, the alley was doing a fair though probably not capacity business. From noon on, it was visited by women's groups, high school children, milkmen, (whose playtime is 2:00 p.m.) and others. And after 11 p.m. comes more open bowling—many casual customers, policemen and firemen at midnight, night shift workers and cab drivers at 3:00 or 4:00 a.m. Some alleys have a ratio of 60 percent league to 40 percent open bowling."

- Originally only 100,000 square feet, the plant now covers more than one million square feet and produces a wide variety of products.
- By 1944, the United States was producing more than 40 percent of the world's arms; the normal work week was increased from 40 to 48 hours.
- The 200,000 American women who joined the armed services in World War II received equal pay, which was good enough to trigger a huge migration of country and small-town girls toward the large urban areas and defense plants to obtain jobs.
- The concern about moral laxity at many factories, especially ones near freewheeling military bases, prompted the creation of "Dorothy Dixes"; their job was to serve as counselors and chaperones for young women whose morality might be compromised.
- The factories also organized industrial bowling leagues to bolster morale, encouraging more women to bowl.

World War II triggered a migration of women into urban areas.

"Good Times A-Coming, Twentieth Century Fund Experts Study Economic Past and Present to Forecast a Rosy U.S. Future," *Life*, May 5, 1946:

"While the U.S. has been going through four of the most hectic years in its economic history, 27 economic experts have been studying the merry-go-round and trying to make some sense out of it. Last week their work, which deserves some such circus word as "gargantuan," was published by the highly respected Twentieth Century Fund, endowed by the late Edward A. Filene, Boston merchant.

Its commonplace title, *America's Needs and Resources*, could not quite conceal that here was an exhilarating study of what a free people had done, were doing, could do. Americans for the first time in history harnessed machine power. And now they stood on the brink of a new epoch of shorter working hours, higher incomes, better, more rewarding ways of life. Indicative of the extreme range of the study are miscellaneous facts, such as: we now spend as much on movies as on religion; that our use of canned fruit multiplied four times between the wars; that we now consume 20 percent less beer than 25 years ago; that we lost 10 times more in gambling machines in 1944 than in 1929; that use of snuff was more prevalent in rural areas; that our diets contain at least three dozen chemicals and that the tendency is to spend less for clothes and more for beauty treatments. . . .

The secret of our past attainment and our future prosperity is clearly revealed by the study as the ability to produce more because we have the machines to help. The machine has taken over the work of man and beast. Our working hours, which were 70 a week a century ago, were reduced to 47 in 1944. Yet the 1944 worker turned out over three times more production than the 1850 worker. . . .

The study is also valuable in disclosing the futility of fearing and resisting the machine as we did in the mid-1930s. The inventive spirit that designs the machine always ends up creating more jobs than it eliminates. Canal boatmen and livery stable workers gave way to railroaders and filling-station attendants. And so the examples go. Technological progress has not only raised living standards with new and infinite varieties of products; it has also made it possible to expand greatly the number and proportion of persons in gainful occupations. They have increased by 50 million in the last 75 years. And the average family is materially benefited. The Fund used 'mineral energy' to signify power from water, coal, gas and oil. Translated into 'machine power,' this energy is now 300 to 1,000 times cheaper than the sweat of a man's brow. But any skeptic who believes mineral energy has already been fully exploited needs to be given only one word: uranium."

- While most of America's recreational sports were forced to march to the beat of war shortages, the Brunswick Company was asked to play a critical role in entertaining the troops at home and abroad.
- In 1940, America claimed 12 million bowlers; today, the number is close to 18 million.
- Brunswick is not the only corporation whose success is tied to the army; Philip K. Wrigley persuaded the military that chewing gum was an essential war material, and at the request of the army (and despite sugar rationing) he supplied a stick of gum for every pack of K, or combat, rations.
- Wrigley also supplied gum to war workers in arms factories by convincing management that chewing gum meant fewer trips to the water fountain or smoking area.

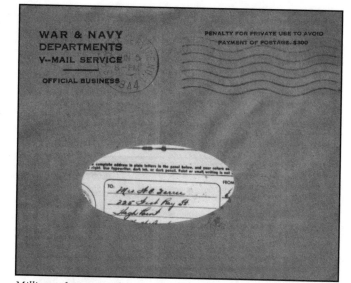

Millions of miniature letters were shipped stateside via V-mail.

- At the same time, advertisers used the war effort to sell products even when supplies were low, as in the case of Life Savers, which distributed fliers that read, "If your dealer doesn't have your favorite LIFE SAVERS flavor, please be patient; it is because the shipment he would have received has gone to the Army and the Navy."

To conserve paper, song sheets were reduced in size.

- A more aggressive note was struck by an advertisement boasting that because bomber crews had to have their intake of Vitamin C, "maybe your canned Florida grapefruit juice is OVER NAZI ROOFTOPS TONIGHT!"
- Cigarette manufacturers had made minimal profit selling their product to the government at cut-rate prices, but from 1940 to 1946 the annual production of cigarettes rose from 19 billion to almost 40 billion.
- Chesterfield, Camel and Lucky Strike were hard to obtain in the states, but soldiers returned from the war convinced that smoking national brands made them better Americans.
- Throughout the war, rationing was common; even song sheets with optimistic titles, such as "In the Land of Beginning Again," were printed in a smaller size to "cooperate with the government to conserve paper during the war."

HISTORICAL SNAPSHOT
1946

- The U.S. gross national product topped $211 billion, double the GNP of 1928
- With World War II now ended, commercial supplies of penicillin began appearing
- Ballpoint pens, first introduced during the war, cost $12.50 each
- The auction of Franklin D. Roosevelt's stamp collection brought $211,000
- Strikes idled 4.6 million workers, resulting in a loss of 116 million man-days; it was the worst stoppage since 1919 at the end of the First World War
- U.S. college enrollment broke new records with more than two million students, including thousands of former GIs
- The size of the military was reduced from 11 million to one million in one year
- With sugar no longer on the ration list, the sale of ice cream took on fad proportions
- French designers created a sensation with the introduction of the bikini in Paris
- Tide washing powder and Timex watches were both introduced
- Hunt Foods established the concept of "price at time of shipment" in its contracts with customers
- The U.S. birth rate soared to 3.4 million, up from 2.9 million the previous year
- Dr. Benjamin Spock's book, *The Common Sense Book of Baby and Child Care*, was published, written while in the Navy Medical Corps in charge of severe disciplinary cases
- RCA's 10-inch television sold for $374
- African-Americans voted for the first time in the Mississippi Democratic primary
- Ektachrome color film was introduced by the Kodak Company
- Oklahoma City offered the first rapid public treatment of venereal diseases
- French's instant potatoes, electric blankets, the FDR dime, auto-bank service, mobile telephone service, Fulbright awards and automatic clothes dryers all made their first appearance
- Gangster Bugsy Siegel and his mob opened the Flamingo in Las Vegas and began building the "entertainment capital of America"
- Albert Einstein and a group of nuclear scientists formed the Emergency Committee of Atomic Science to advance the peaceful use of atomic energy
- President Truman ended all price and wage controls except on rent, sugar and rice

1946 ECONOMIC PROFILE

The national consumer expenditures (per capita income) in 1946 were:

Auto Parts	$9.90
Auto Usage	$67.19
Clothing	$106.79
Dentists	$5.66
Food	$334.54
Furniture	$15.56
Gas and Oil	$24.05
Health Insurance	$2.83
Housing	$100.43
Intercity Transport	$7.07
Local Transport	$13.44
New Auto Purchase	$14.15
Personal Business	$33.29
Personal Care	$14.85
Physicians	$12.73
Private Education and Research	$7.78
Recreation	$60.12
Religion/Welfare Activities	$14.85
Telephone and Telegraph	$9.19
Tobacco	$24.05
Utilities	$35.36
Per Capita Consumption	$1,072.76

Annual Income, Standard Jobs

Average of all Industries, Excluding Farm Labor	$2,529.00
Average of all Industries, Including Farm Labor	$2,473.00
Bituminous Coal Mining	$2,724.00
Building Trades, Union Workers	$2,537.00
Domestics	$1,411.00
Farm Labor	$1,394.00
Federal Civilian	$2,904.00
Federal Employees, Executive Departments	$2,490.00
Federal Military	$2,279.00
Finance, Insurance and Real Estate	$2,570.00
Gas and Electricity Workers	$2,697.00
Manufacturing, Durable Goods	$2,615.00
Manufacturing, Nondurable Goods	$2,404.00
Medical/Health Services Workers	$1,605.00
Miscellaneous Manufacturing	$2,442.00

Motion Picture Services $2,978.00
Nonprofit Organization Workers . . . $2,070.00
Passenger Transportation
    Workers, Local and Highway $2,886.00
Personal Services $1,881.00
Public School Teachers. $2,025.00
Radio Broadcasting and
    Television Workers. $3,972.00
Railroad Workers. $3,055.00
State and Local Government
    Workers $2,093.00
Telephone and Telegraph
    Workers $2,413.00
Wholesale and Retail
    Trade Workers $2,378.00

Selected Prices

Adding Machine $120.00
Board Game, Ouija $1.59
Bookcase Desk, Chippendale
    Mahogany $565.00
Cereal, Nabisco Honey Grahams $0.27
Child's Car Seat. $1.98
Cigarettes, Carton $1.34
Coffee Maker, Electric. $29.00
Cuff Links, 14-Karat Gold $47.50
Dormitory Trunk. $20.34
Dry Cleaning, per Piece $0.50
Electric Floor Polisher, Johnson's $44.50
Figurine, Meissen $250.00
Girdle, Bestform $7.50
Hammer, Craftsman $1.39
Lawnmower $127.50
Movie Ticket $1.00
Organ, Hammond $1,300.00
Paint, Glidden, One Gallon. $4.98
Railroad Ticket, Chicago to
    Washington, Round-Trip $25.30
Tie, Hickey-Freeman $3.50

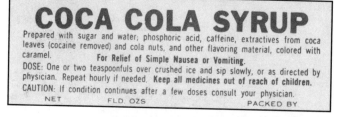
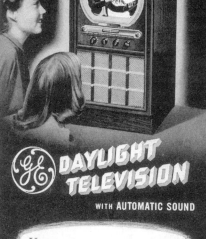

The Business of Bowling

- Today the American Bowling Congress exerts a near-total control over standards, rules and public image issues.
- No equipment company would dream of building an alley for public use that didn't conform to the A.B.C.'s strict specifications: a minimum 15-foot approach, an alley bed 62 feet 10.125 inches long and not less than 41 or more than 42 inches wide.
- Alley maintenance is also rigidly policed by the A.B.C.; if any area of the lane is more than 40/1,000 of an inch from being truly level, league play is ruled out for that facility.

- To get into the bowling alley business requires a total capital investment of about $4,000 per pair of alley beds, or $16,000 for a modest, eight-alley establishment.
- Under the credit terms offered by Brunswick, a down payment of $7,000 would be required, with the balance to be paid over approximately five years.
- A reasonable gross might amount to $15,000 for a 10-month year.
- Expenses, including rent at $0.35 per square foot, depreciation at eight percent, and maintenance at around $5 per alley per operating week, could come to fairly $10,000 per year, leaving a profit of $5,000.
- The formula is so successful, Brunswick has not been forced to uproot a single alley in the past 10 years.

Approximately one third of all bowlers are women, many of whom bowl in weekly leagues.

"You Can Drive a Car with Atom Power," *Science Digest*, October 1946:

"A certain uneasiness arising from the fact that an atom-powered automobile may also be a potential atomic bomb and a source of deadly radiation will be spared future automobilists if a novel idea for 'atomic storage batteries' is perfected.

It may not be necessary to put atomic bomb elements into the motors of automobiles or airplanes, because uranium energy can be stored in more stable elements simply by subjecting them to intensive neutron radiation.

Radioactive elements produced in this way will provide a constant source of heat to be used in small power generators, and will be completely free from the possibility of atomic explosion, according to Dr. George Gamow, professor of theoretical physics, George Washington University, in his book *Atomic Energy in Cosmic and Human Life*.

Since their radioactive elements would be chosen for their relative freedom from dangerous radiation, the atomic fuel tank would not be burdened with tons of protective lead shielding.

The only drawback to this suggestion, aside from expense, consists in the power waste involved. Such atomic storage batteries produce energy in a steady flow from the moment they are 'charged.' Thus, it would be impossible to 'shut off the engine' of this type of atom-powered car. Atomic motors of this type would be more apt to find use in public vehicles running a large percentage of the time, high-speed aircraft, and possibly spaceships, than as motive power for private cars."

"X-Ray Shoe Gadget Banned in New York," *Science Digest*, October 1946:

"Most New York stores with x-ray shoe-fitting machines have discontinued their use in accordance with a Health Department ban established because of the potential danger involved, according to Milton Amsel in P.M.

'Since competent authorities have stated that there is a danger where these machines are involved,' said Dr. Israel Weinstein, Commissioner of Health, 'we must insist that any operator be as qualified as men in x-ray laboratories. X-rays are potentially dangerous, and in order to safeguard everyone, the Health Department feels that x-rays should not be used promiscuously.'

Manufacturers of x-ray shoe machines deny that danger exists in their products, pointing out that they are completely insulated and use only small amounts of x-rays.

One department store shoe buyer was asked about the value of the x-ray machine on his sales floor. 'Oh, it's only a selling gadget,' he replied."

"America's Shameful Treatment of Her Teachers," by Joy Elmer Morgan, *Read*, Pick of the Month's Best Reading, May 1946:

"Years ago, when I was a boy on my grandfather's farm in Franklin County, Nebraska, and attended school in old district 46, I had a truly great teacher by the name of Jennie Collins.

Mrs. Collins was a widow with three children of her own. The farmers built her a little cabin as a home and a one-room school. Year after year she taught us—pupils of all ages and sizes—and she taught us for the munificent sum of $90 a month for nine months, $360 a year.

Jennie Collins never won any medals or acquired fame or got rich, but she knew how to awaken ambition and arouse purpose in her pupils. Without her inspiration I should never have lifted my eyes to the wider horizons that led to normal school, state university and beyond.

Remember Ethel Barrymore in the play, *The Corn is Green*, and Bette Davis in the film of the same name? Such teachers are priceless and can never be paid enough because everything they get they put back into helping others. There are millions of such unknown teachers who made this country what it is.

But how do we, in turn, repay these teachers? Shamefully!

Indicative of the exploitation of our teachers today is the significant fact that only a few teachers in the armed forces are returning to their old jobs. One, a navy lieutenant, explains why:

'A month before I enlisted in the navy, my morale received a sharp shock and I decided never to return to teaching. The school's most notorious delinquent and numskull, a boy of 17 who worked in a nearby shipyard, came to my class, flaunted his weekly paycheck for $90 and thumbed his nose at me. At that time I was getting one third that amount for teaching eight hours and coaching the baseball, basketball and football teams for three more hours a day.'

Though this naval officer still loves teaching, he owes it to his wife and two children, he declares, not to resume a career which has entangled so many other fine men and women into a lifetime of poverty. . . .

One Alabama principal had a janitor named George who could neither read nor write. George abandoned his job as janitor to accept one in industry at $80 per week. George later returned to ask the principal to assist in filling out his income tax report, whereupon it was discovered that George was paying more income tax than the principal, a Ph.D. . . .

In Helena, Montana, which boasts of the best salary schedules in the state, we find the following: A plumber receives $96 a week; a beginning teacher, after spending thousands of dollars and years of study to qualify, receives $31 per week. . . .

In 1944 some 44,000 teachers were being paid less than $800 for the school year; 254,000, less than $1,200. Is it any wonder that more than 250,000 teachers have left teaching since Pearl Harbor and that enrollment in teachers' colleges has dropped 50 percent?

This decline in enrollment in teachers' colleges and schools of education is one of the most serious aspects of the problem. It means that the teacher shortage will be prolonged. Only a fraction of those who left the schools for the army and war industries ever return to teaching."

BY

LT. COL. GREGORY (Pappy) BOYINGTON, USMC

1946 News Profile

"I'll Buy the Drinks, Boys," by Lt. Col. Gregory (Pappy) Boyington, USMC, *True Magazine*, January 1946:

"When the now-famed 'Black Sheep' Squadron of the Marine Corps took off on its first aerial combat, one of the young pilots said: 'We still need smoothing out. Only one thing is holding us together, and we know it will pull us through—it's our faith in Pappy.'

'Pappy' is Lt. Col. Gregory Boyington, born 32 years ago in Coeur d' Alene, Idaho.

The Black Sheep Squadron, put together from 'has-beens' and 'orphan' pilots, fought only two tours of combat duty but came home with a blazing record of 199 enemy planes destroyed or damaged. One man inspired that record—Boyington.

During his brief but spectacular service in the South Pacific, Pappy shot down 28 Japanese planes and was credited with nine probables. Pappy vanished on his last flight, January 3, 1944, just after he had smashed the combat pilot record. He was given up for dead and his squadron was broken up. Twenty months passed, during which time Pappy was posthumously awarded the Congressional Medal of Honor and the Navy Cross. In August 1945, American navy officers entering the Omori prison camp near Yokohama found the missing ace, ending his long stay in Jap prison camps.

The Marine Corps has publicly acknowledged that Pappy was not only a deadly marksman, a clever fighter and a fine tactician, but a beloved leader who inspired his men to unforgettable deeds. As Major General James T. Moore, USMC, said: 'The kind of spirit that the Black Sheep have is what wins battles.'

The wristwatch is new and shiny. On the back there is an inscription: 'To Gramps from his Black Sheep. 9-12-45.'

I am 'Gramps,' sometimes known as Pappy. The Black Sheep are my boys, the greatest marine fighter squadron in the world. The date is this peace-bringing year of 1945. They gave me the watch at a dinner recently—a party none of them ever expected to attend. They came to San Francisco from Marine bases scattered all along the California coast, 21 guys who fought the Nips with me. I was supposed to be dead.

They had memorial services for me one January morning almost two years ago at Espiritu Santo. So long, Pappy, rest in peace. More than once I had told them: 'If I'm missing don't believe it. I'll turn up to buy the drinks in San Diego.' Getting killed was always the least of my worries. But I didn't really expect to get it, and so that's why I told them. They probably remembered those words when they went to my 'funeral.' Poor Pappy—he cussed a Zeke once too often.

But I'm not dead, and I've got a new watch to prove it. I haven't any gray hair, and I still get around without crutches. But I can't blame them for calling me 'Gramps,' because most of the Black Sheep were fuzzy high school lambs when I got into the Marines 10 years ago.

And that's where the story really starts—1935.

As far back as I can remember, I had always wanted to fly with the Marines.

I got my wings in 1937 and spent the next four years at the Naval Air Station in Pensacola.

Like many other Marine pilots, I was itching to get into the air and fight.

They sent me right out to the Solomons area, as executive officer of VMF Squadron 122, based at Henderson Field on Guadalcanal.

Those were desperate days, as the nation knows. Guadalcanal had been regained, the first little link in that long bloody chain to Tokyo. I arrived there busting with the fever to fight; I knew the Nips and their treachery and their tactics, and hoped for immediate action.

But I was jinxed. The hunting season at Guadalcanal was over, and I got eye strain from trying to spot a Zeke.

Then, while taking it easy in a rest area, I broke my leg. Everything happens to me, I thought bitterly, and sometimes I wished I could get along without legs. Breaking a leg in a combat zone is worse than a trapeze artist slipping in the bathtub. So there I was with the Marines, hotter than a gas plate—and I had to break a leg.

'Major,' the doctors said, 'you're all through.'

'Through with what?' I snapped.

'Combat flying.'

'Like hell I am.'

And I meant that. I had gloomy visions of myself glued to a swivel chair for the rest of the war. But about that time the dice started rolling sevens. There was in existence then a pilot replacement pool at Espiritu Santo in the New Hebrides. Most of the men in the pool were orphans, fliers without squadrons of their own, for one reason or another. Coincidentally, there was a new squadron needed immediately. I wanted that squadron and I wanted to train it myself.

An old friend of mine happened to be at Espiritu Santo then, Major Stanley Bailey of Harvey, Illinois. Stan and I had been roommates at Pensacola, and we both had the same feeling of impatience. Together we fumed and fretted around Wing Command headquarters, demanding that something be done.

'Okay,' they said at last, 'the old Squadron 214 has just completed a tour of the Russells. You can take that number and start a new one—and you're on your own!'

I named Stan as executive officer and we started handpicking our pilots. Some of the boys were green and you could only guess what they would do under pressure. Some had been eased out of the other squadrons, I recall, because they 'weren't good enough for combat flying.' Some had been ill or hurt or left behind when their squadron moved on. All of us felt as unwanted as the proverbial baby left in a basket on somebody's doorstep.

That feeling was so strong that one of them proposed that we call ourselves, 'Boyington's Bastards.'

It seemed appropriate, but I was afraid it wouldn't help the gang, and we finally compromised on the name 'Black Sheep.' Someone suggested that in ancient England a certain type of shield denoted illegitimacy, so we used that idea in designing our insignia. It was a black-bordered shield with a wide diagonal black stripe. We placed a miniature gull-winged corsair at the top and a flop-eared black sheep and black stars below. I like to think that there are Japanese who will never forget that trademark—and there are no less than 97 Nip pilots who didn't even get a chance to talk about it."

1948 FAMILY PROFILE

Already a successful New York architect, Bartholomew Holmes is part of a United States Government-sponsored delegation spending a year in England assisting in postwar restoration. Holmes is married with two children, one of whom has joined him for the tour of Britain's most damaged cities.

Annual Income: $1 a year for supporting this effort; his family's net worth exceeds $10 million.

Life at Home

- Bartholomew Holmes is currently touring England with a team of 25 Americans, giving advice, inspecting buildings and working with the British government to solve its housing shortage.
- An architect by training, he has spent the past few years redeveloping sections of New York, including the launching of many projects in which he and his father were direct investors.
- He is being paid $1 a year plus expenses for his work in England, and is one of two African-Americans on the trip who both gained encouragement from former First Lady Eleanor Roosevelt to take a visible role in the mission.
- He was shocked when he arrived in London to find block after block of flattened rubble created by consistent German bombing of the nation's cities.
- In Kent, southeast of London and within the flyway of the German attack planes, he met with a farmer whose land contained 93 bomb holes.
- In general, the British economy is in shambles; since August 1945, Britain has wrestled with the task of reallocating resources, rebuilding industrial potential and restoring exports.

Bartholomew Holmes is assisting in the restoration of Britain.

The ancient stained glass of Britain's cathedrals was removed and stored during the war.

- Throughout the country, government officials are terrified of repeating the mistakes of World War I, which resulted in high inflation and massive unemployment.
- He is unsure that the new Labour government, which replaced Winston Churchill's Conservatives in July 1945, is experienced enough for the job of restoring the economy; its pledge in 1945 to build four million houses over a 10-year period is already way behind schedule.
- He believes that the United Kingdom is more interested in preserving tradition than in solving the housing shortage.
- Bartholomew's family traces its roots and wealth to Chicago, where his Civil War-era grandfather established a lucrative business transporting hogs; Chicago's strategic position as a transportation hub gave him an opportunity to profit from the hogs, and later beef, flowing through the city's slaughterhouses.
- Later his two sons, using the profits of the business, went into the printing business just as the African-American migration to northern cities began; the brothers did extremely well supplying news, advertising and print jobs to Chicago's growing middle class.
- Bartholomew's father, sensing a rising tide of racism in Chicago, sold the printing business to white investors after the First World War and moved to New York City.
- His son has spent his entire adult life in New York, except for his undergraduate years at Harvard.
- Along with his father, Bartholomew bought depressed properties in New York and created new housing developments; the quality of their work attracted the attention of city and federal officials, helping father and son easily attract investment capital for bigger and bigger projects.
- Recently, his 17-year-old daughter Joyce joined the group during her summer break, and has been amazed, not only by the destruction, but also by the dreariness of English fashion.
- She resents the stereotype harbored by British boys that American Negro girls are loose, so she sticks close to her father's touring group whenever possible.

Life at Work

- When the American delegation arrived in England, an early stop was St. Paul's Cathedral, which stands by the Thames River in London.
- Although German planes throughout the Second World War had flown along the river at night and bombed London, the ancient cathedral, designed by Sir Christopher Wren in the 1600s, miraculously survived.
- St. Paul's Fire Watch was restarted in 1939 with more than 300 people from around the world who volunteered to protect the church from incendiary bombs dropped by the German war planes.
- Up to 40 people would sleep in the cathedral at night; known as "kickers," they would literally kick bombs off the roof and grounds of the cathedral to keep it safe—an enormous task because of the many complex angles on the roof and hundreds of corners and crannies where an incendiary bomb could lodge and start a fire.

The dome of St. Paul's Cathedral rising out of the morning mist served as a symbol of hope during the dark days of the blitz.

- Over time, St. Paul's Cathedral stood as a visible symbol of hope for many Londoners; if they could see the dome of St. Paul's the morning after an air raid, it fueled their courage to fight on.
- After London, Holmes is touring Exeter, Bath, Norwich, York and Canterbury—all traditional spots before the war.
- The German air raids of these cities were nicknamed the "Baedeker raids" from the assumption that the popular Baedeker tourist guidebooks had been consulted when the list of German targets was drawn up.
- In other parts of England, fourteenth-century abbeys and churches are covered in scaffolding to replace elegant stained-glass windows, many of which were taken out during the early days of the war and stored in the buildings' crypts.
- Despite the enthusiasm for new ideas and different ways to develop the countryside, Britain has little money for the programs Holmes would like to undertake.
- Privately, he hopes he can duplicate his success in New York while allowing the government to take a substantial level of risk.
- Unfortunately, British wartime expenditures on troops and munitions were paid for through the transfer of British securities to creditors rather than in cash payments—creating ongoing obligations.

Beat 'FIREBOMB FRITZ'

BRITAIN SHALL NOT BURN

BRITAIN'S FIRE GUARD IS BRITAIN'S DEFENCE

- To repay these obligations and finance the necessary imports for recovery, exports must be increased quickly.
- The abrupt termination of the Lend-Lease arrangements with the United States now requires that future supplies be paid in American dollars, further pinching Britain's resources and forcing the Labour government to juggle its internal and external priorities.
- To increase domestic demand too quickly would threaten the export drive and absorb greater imports, putting the balance of payments at risk; thus, much of the nation's consumer goods such as clothing, food and coal are still restricted—years after rationing has been lifted in the United States.
- In fact, the number of consumer expenditures subject to rationing in Britain has actually risen since 1946.
- In June 1946, the British armed forces stood at more than two million people; today only 810,000 are still in the armed services, with more returning every day, while approximately 1.3 million women have left war-generated factory jobs.
- Yet, the coal shortage of 1947 that threatened the very stability of the new Labour government was caused largely by a shortage of labor in the mines; returning war veterans were unwilling to return to the pits, preferring jobs above ground.
- Holmes believes that the much discussed aid from the United States under the Marshall Plan will give the country the capital injection it needs to consider new proposals like his.
- This is particularly important since the country is now moving in what he believes is a dangerous direction—nationalization—under which industry is brought into public ownership to be run and controlled by the government.
- The goal is to ensure that industry works in the interest of the country as a whole rather than for the profit of individuals.
- Bartholomew is surprised that the Conservative Party has not taken a more aggressive stance against what he considers a socialist action.
- Currently, more than 1.5 million workers, employed by the Bank of England, the National Coal Board, Cable and Wireless, British Transport Commission and British Electrical Authority, are all nationalized.

Life in the Community: London, England
- The Second World War was the least unexpected war in history.
- Britain began to prepare in 1935 when it became clear that Hitler was leading the German people toward the attempted mastery of Europe; in 1937, the Air-Raid Precaution Act made preparations compulsory.
- As the outbreak of war drew nearer, important buildings throughout Britain were protected from bomb blasts by being faced with sandbags.
- The film *Wuthering Heights*, starring Merle Oberon and Laurence Olivier, was on at the Regal Cinema and a Shirley Temple film, *The Little Princess*, was showing at the Arts Theater in the city of Cambridge when Hitler's troops invaded Poland in September 1939.
- On September 7, 1940, the first night of the blitz in London, nearly 2,000 people were killed or wounded.

Diary entry of a Bristol woman, November 24, 1940:

"Jerry is here early tonight. Siren went five minutes ago. Yes, he's here all right. Some bombs are being dropped and fire has started already to the east of us. I've got a nasty feeling in my tummy, too, at this moment. God grant it is going to be all right for us. 11.05 p.m. same night: we've been through hell. Never have I experienced anything like it. Tummy still wobbly. Fires and bombs everywhere. Went to the cellar at first, but couldn't settle down, so went to the sitting-room. We didn't need any light for the room was lit up with the glare of the fires. Wine Street looks as if it is no more. Fires all seemed centred in that direction, though up the hill at the back of our place there are fires also. One looks like the Princess Theatre. Our sitting-room-window woodwork is so hot you can hardly bare your hand on it. The house rocks as the bombs drop."

- At the height of the blitz, approximately 177,000 people slept in the underground tube stations of the city; nightly bombings were so frequent Londoners began wearing a lapel badge reading, "Don't tell me, I've got a bomb story, too."
- Shops and offices closed early to allow their workers time to get home before the air-raid warning sirens sounded.
- Much of the damage to Britain's major cities came in the last years of the war, thanks to the German's V-1 revenge weapon, a mechanically guided, pilotless aircraft launched by a 180-foot catapult, first used in 1944 one week after D-Day in Europe.
- By 1943, 90 percent of single women and 80 percent of married women were engaged in war work.
- England has been changed by the war effort and the passage of more than 1.5 million GIs (Government Issue) through Britain.
- In all, more than 80,000 GIs took home British brides.
- American GIs were better paid than British soldiers and had access to the base PX, where Lucky Strike Cigarettes, razor blades of prewar quality, and chocolate were available.
- To escape the claustrophobic atmosphere at home, people went to the movies in droves, lining up for hours to attend movies; 25 to 30 million tickets were sold each week.
- Though the most popular were the adventure films, especially Westerns and musicals from the United States, *Gone with the Wind* played in London's West End nonstop from the spring of 1940 to the spring of 1944.

Marriage ceremonies continued to be held despite the bombing and destruction.

Historical Snapshot
1948

- A Gallup poll reported that 94 percent of Americans believed in God
- Inflation drove nearly all costs up; clothing expenses rose 93 percent from 1939 to 1948, while a house priced at $4,440 in 1939 had risen to $9,060
- Both Baskin-Robbins and McDonald's began operations
- Nationwide, 50 cities banned comic books dealing with crime or sex; psychiatrist Fredric Wertham charged that heavy comic-book reading contributed to juvenile delinquency
- President Harry Truman ordered racial equality in the armed forces
- Jack Benny sold his NBC radio program to CBS for a reported $2 to $3 million; the IRS then claimed 75 percent for personal income taxes
- New York began a fluoridation program for 50,000 children
- A transistor developed by Bell Telephone Laboratories permitted miniaturization of electronic devices such as computers, radios and television
- Gerber Products Company sold two million cans and jars of baby food weekly
- Dial soap was introduced as the first deodorant soap
- One million homes had television sets
- Garbage disposals, heat-conducting windshields, Nestlé's Quick, Michelin radial tires and Scrabble all made their first appearance
- The Nikon camera was introduced to compete with the Leica
- 360,000 soft-coal workers went on strike, demanding $100 per month in retirement benefits at age 62
- Dwight D. Eisenhower requested a move by the Democratic Party to draft him as a candidate for president of the United States
- Peter Goldmark of CBS invented a high-fidelity, long-playing record containing up to 45 minutes of music
- Ben Hogan won the U.S. Open and was the top PGA money winner with $36,000
- A new liquid hydrogen fuel was created that was touted as having the potential to send men to the moon
- The Dow-Jones Industrial Average hit a high of 193
- The United Nations passed the Palestine Partition Plan, creating the State of Israel
- Mahatma Gandhi was assassinated by a Hindu extremist

1948 ECONOMIC PROFILE

The national consumer expenditures (per capita income) in 1948 were:

Auto Parts	$8.87
Auto Usage	$105.71
Clothing	$114.57
Dentists	$5.46
Food	$369.64
Furniture	$19.09
Gas and Oil	$32.74
Health Insurance	$5.46
Housing	$122.08
Intercity Transport	$6.82
Local Transport	$13.64
New Auto Purchase	$34.09
Personal Business	$38.87
Personal Care	$15.69
Physicians	$16.37
Private Education and Research	$10.23
Recreation	$66.15
Religion/Welfare Activities	$15.69
Telephone and Telegraph	$10.91
Tobacco	$27.28
Utilities	$45.01
Per Capita Consumption	$1,192.79

Annual Income, Standard Jobs

Average of all Industries, Excluding Farm Labor	$2,999.00
Average of all Industries, Including Farm Labor	$2,933.00
Bituminous Coal Mining	$3,388.00
Building Trades, Union Workers	$3,125.00
Domestics	$1,500.00
Farm Labor	$1,541.00
Federal Civilian	$3,256.00
Federal Employees, Executive Departments	$2,949.00
Federal Military	$2,676.00
Finance, Insurance and Real Estate	$2,954.00
Gas and Electricity Workers	$3,223.00
Manufacturing, Durable Goods	$3,163.00
Manufacturing, Nondurable Goods	$2,892.00
Medical/Health Services Workers	$1,918.00
Miscellaneous Manufacturing	$2,808.00
Motion Picture Services	$2,964.00

Nonprofit Organization Workers ... $2,334.00

Passenger Transportation
    Workers, Local and Highway $3,101.00

Personal Services $2,120.00

Public School Teachers........... $2,538.00

Radio Broadcasting and
    Television Workers............ $4,234.00

Railroad Workers............... $3,611.00

State and Local Government
    Workers $2,593.00

Telephone and Telegraph
    Workers $2,776.00

Wholesale and Retail Trade
    Workers $2,832.00

Selected Prices

Bacon, One Pound.................. $0.59

Bedspread, Chenille................ $3.99

China, Haviland, 100 Pieces........ $250.00

Chinese Checkers $0.95

Corn Remover, Freezone............. $0.16

Dye, Rit $0.25

Flying Lessons $2.00

Harmonica........................ $1.79

Hat, Man's Stetson $12.50

Magazine, *Jack and Jill*, 10 Months $1.98

Manicure Set $15.00

Mink Coat $1,650.00

Playpen $11.98

Radio, Silvertone................. $11.75

Record Cabinet $13.50

Soap, Woodbury's $0.23

Television, GE 16 .... $189.95

Tricycle $5.98

Washing Machine, Kenmore........ $119.95

Water Heater, Presto $4.98

Britain during the War

- As war loomed in 1938, the government distributed 38 million gas masks house to house to British families.
- Gas masks became a regular feature of children's wear; they carried them to school, hauled them to the bomb shelters and, when adults were not around, they blew air into the masks so the side would flap and produce rude sounds.
- To show solidarity, the Queen has created a "limiting mark" on her bathtub to indicate the approved level of water permissible.
- To provide protection from the bombing, millions of residents erected "Anderson Shelters," which served as bunkers against the raids and were designed to accommodate six people.

- To support the war effort, household aluminum pots were collected from homes throughout the United Kingdom and melted to make Spitfire fighter planes, while ornamental railings were stripped from the nation's parks to make ships and tanks.
- Starting in 1941 and lasting throughout the war, the countryside of Britain was populated with German and Italian prisoners of war, who were used to work the fields.
- To meet coal shortages within the country, more than 15,000 young boys were assigned by the national service to work in the mines instead of in the army.
- At Christmastime, British carol singers were told not to ring bells in case they were confused with air-raid signals; in many cities, traditional midnight Christmas mass was cancelled because of the difficulty of blacking out the huge church windows during the service.
- The war effort required widespread rationing, including bans on automobile and bike tires, hot-water bottles, beach balls and rubber floor mats.

The Legacy of War, Keeping Left, Labour's First Five Years and the Problems Ahead, by a group of members of Parliament, 1948:

We need not here do more than list the problems which arose from the war itself.

i) War damage, including shipping losses and obsolescence, had depreciated our capital assets by £3,000 millions. We had sold overseas investments to the tune of over £1,000 millions, and we had mortgaged the bulk of the remainder against external debts (sterling balances), which had increased by well over £3,000 millions.

ii) On the other hand, the average standard of living, thanks to the artificial stimulus of Lend-Lease, had only dropped about 15 percent, and this had been offset for most people by wartime fair shares. The man in the street, with high wages, subsidised prices and no unemployment, felt secure, well-off and entitled, by the role Britain had played in defeating the Nazis, to a 'good time' as soon as the war was over. He did not realise that, for the first time since the Industrial Revolution, Britain was a nation without anything in the kitty.

iii) The U.S.A. came out of the war with a 50-percent increase in its industrial potential and a 16-percent increase in its standard of living. Moreover, as the 'arsenal of democracy,' she had built cargo ships and transport planes, while we, nearer the front line, built destroyers and fighters. This made the disparity still more grave. America was not only 10 times more powerful, but could also turn over more quickly to peacetime production.

iv) Our recovery was possible only if world trade revived. But our exports had sunk by two thirds. War had paralysed our European markets and sources of supply, and the Far East was in a ferment. The cold war was still further aggravated by this problem. Politically and economically, we were linked with the U.S.A. But economic interests demanded that we should also trade with the Eastern bloc, since it needed our capital goods and could provide us with some part of our needs in foodstuffs and raw materials.

These postwar problems, however, were merely the immediate expression of a long process of world revolution. By 1945, Europe had finally ceased to be the centre of world politics and become one of the objects of dispute between two non-European powers. Simultaneously, the centre of world finance had shifted to Washington. London was still the capital of the single biggest trading area in the world; but the sterling area could not recover out of its own resources. This is one of the many reasons why, however much we dislike it, we had in the end to take sides in the Cold War."

- Kleenex was virtually unobtainable, and toilet paper was perennially scarce; in 1943, shoes were rationed, with civilians eligible for two pairs a year.
- To deal with the increased pressure to move soldiers and war materials rapidly, the railroads finally made the switch from steam-powered locomotives to diesel engines.
- The BBC broadcast its programming in 24 languages to support the resistance movements in countries such as France, Norway and Denmark, even broadcasting coded messages, such as "Barbara's dog will have three pups," to inform resistance workers of the arrival of three refugees.

"Meals on Wheels," by Margaret Cooper, *Worcestershire Countryside Magazine*, July-September 1948:

"Four days a week in wintertime and well on into the spring, the Women's Volunteer Society in Worcester takes hot dinners to old-age pensioners. In Stourbridge there is a similar system three days a week, and at Malvern, a notoriously scattered series of communities, the hot food is delivered to local centres whence the old people or their more robust relatives fetch on a cash-and-carry basis.

If you are around eighty it stands to reason that to queue for a meal is out of the question, and if you live alone in an almshouse, one person's rations do not go very far. On the other hand, hot food at British Restaurant prices is very welcome.

It happened to be a bitterly cold spring morning when the pictures were taken, and it was clear enough what a blessing this voluntary service is.

At the kitchen in St. Martin's Gate, which supplies the British Restaurants of Worcester, three W.V.S. workers loaded a small van with containers of hot meat pie, potatoes, greens, gravy, and milk pudding, and then bestowed themselves inside as well.

Away went the van to Berkeley's Almshouses, where one of the 'crew' walked briskly along the two rows of houses knocking on doors and calling out 'dinners.' Doors opened, heads and shoulders wrapped in shawls came out, trembling old hands knotted with age and rheumatism held out clean plates and pie

dishes. One dear old man collected his nearest neighbor's dishes and trotted off to the van outside the gates, where the remainder of the crew busied themselves serving out the food, ladling the gravy carefully over the vegetables, and noting in a book the payments of the customers."

Meals on Wheels, supported by the British Restaurant, are providing much needed meals to the elderly and persons living in almshouses.

Teas on the Cathedral lawn are once again a feature of life in Worcester.

"Friends of Worcester Royal Infirmary," *Worcestershire Countryside Magazine*, October–December 1948:

"Nothing rouses more fury in the average open-air citizen of Britain than the discovery that his favorite footpath has suddenly been closed. In wartime he will patriotically suppress his indignation, and leave the barbwire entanglements alone, but as soon as the emergency is past, he (and his children, and his dog) will take strong measures to open up that path, possibly during the night since no one ever seems to see the actual tearing-down of rails, cutting of wires, and destruction of notice boards. Landowners generally are more particular about respecting the rights of way over routes sanctified by long tradition and usage, but now and then someone takes an unfair advantage, or decides that it is in the public interest to stop a footpath and grow some vulnerable crop where strollers used to enjoy themselves; and then the baffled and bewildered pedestrian writes a caustic letter to the county council.

It is well to know that the Worcestershire County Council intends to protect public rights in this direction, and that its members are especially asked to inspect footpaths in their area, consult with parish councils, and report to the county council on any obstructed footpath which they may find, and should it prove that a real wrong has been done, the county council can and will take legal action."

1950–1959

As the 1950s began, the average American enjoyed an income 15 times greater than that of the average foreigner. Optimism and opportunity were everywhere. The vast majority of families considered themselves middle class; many were enjoying the benefits of health insurance for the first time. Air travel for the upper class was common, and the world was their oyster. America was manufacturing half of the world's products, 57 percent of the steel, 43 percent of the electricity, and 62 percent of the oil. The economies of Europe and Asia lay in ruins, while America's industrial and agricultural structure was untouched and well-oiled to supply the needs of a war-weary world.

In addition, the war years' high employment and optimism spurred the longest sustained period of peacetime prosperity in the nation's history. A decade of full employment and pent-up desire produced demands for all types of consumer goods. Businesses of all sizes prospered. Rapidly swelling families, new suburban homes, televisions, and most of all, big, powerful, shiny automobiles symbolized the hopes of the era. During the 1950s, an average of seven million cars and trucks were sold annually. By 1952, two thirds of all families owned a television set; home freezers and high-fidelity stereo phonographs were considered necessities. Specialized markets developed to meet the demand of consumers such as amateur photographers, pet lovers, and backpackers. At the same time, shopping malls, supermarkets, and credit cards emerged as important economic forces.

Veterans, using the GI Bill of Rights, flung open the doors of colleges nationwide, attending in record numbers. Inflation was the only pressing economic issue, fueled in large part by the Korean War (in which 54,000 American lives were lost) and the federal expenditures for Cold War defense. As the decade opened, federal spending represented 15.6 percent of the nation's gross national product. Thanks largely to the Cold War, by 1957, defense consumed half of the federal government's $165 billion budget.

This economic prosperity also ushered in conservative politics and social conformity. Tidy lawns, bedrooms that were "neat and trim," and suburban homes that were "proper" were certainly "in" throughout the decade as Americans adjusted to the post-war years. Properly buttoned-down attitudes concerning sexual mores brought stern undergarments for women like bonded girdles and stiff, pointed, or padded bras to confine the body. The planned community of Levittown, New York, mandated that grass be cut at least once a week and laundry washed on specific days. A virtual revival of Victorian respectability and domesticity reigned; divorce rates and female college attendance fell while birth rates and the sale of Bibles rose. Corporate America promoted the benefits of respectable men in gray flannel suits whose wives remained at home to tend house and raise children. Suburban life included ladies' club memberships, chauffeuring children to piano and ballet classes, and lots of a newly marketed product known as tranquilizers, whose sales were astounding.

The average wage earner benefited more from the booming industrial system than at any time in American history. The 40-hour work week became standard in manufacturing. In offices many workers were becoming accustomed to a 35-hour week. Health benefits for workers became more common and paid vacations were standard in most industries. In 1950, 25 percent of American wives worked outside the home; by the end of the decade the number had risen to 40 percent. Communications technology, expanding roads, inexpensive airline tickets, and a spirit of unboundedness meant that people and commerce were no longer prisoners of distance. Unfortunately, up to one third of the population lived below the government's poverty level, largely overlooked in the midst of prosperity.

The Civil Rights movement was propelled by two momentous events in the 1950s. The first was a decree on May 17, 1954, by the U.S. Supreme Court which ruled "that in the field of public education the doctrine of 'separate but equal' has no place. Separate educational facilities are inherently unequal." The message was electric but the pace was slow. Few schools would be integrated for another decade. The second event established the place of the Civil Rights movement. On December 1, 1955, African-American activist Rosa Parks declined to vacate the White-only front section of the Montgomery, Alabama, bus, leading to her arrest and a citywide bus boycott by blacks. Their spokesman became Martin Luther King, Jr., the 26-year-old pastor of the Dexter Avenue Baptist Church. The year-long boycott was the first step toward the passage of the Civil Rights Act of 1964.

America's youths were enchanted by the TV adventures of "Leave It to Beaver," westerns, and "Father Knows Best," allowing them to accumulate more time watching television during the week (at least 27 hours) than attending school. TV dinners were invented; pink ties and felt skirts with sequined poodle appliqués were worn; Elvis Presley was worshipped and the new phenomena of *Playboy* and Mickey Spillane fiction were created only to be read behind closed doors. The ever-glowing eye of television killed the "March of Time" newsreels after 16 years at the movies. Sexual jargon such as "first base" and "home run" entered the language. Learned-When-Sleeping machines appeared, along with Smokey the Bear, Sony tape recorders, adjustable shower heads, *Mad Comics*, newspaper vending machines, Levi's faded blue denims, pocket-size transistor radios, and transparent plastic bags for clothing. Ultimately, the real stars of the era were the Salk and Sabin vaccines, which vanquished the siege of polio.

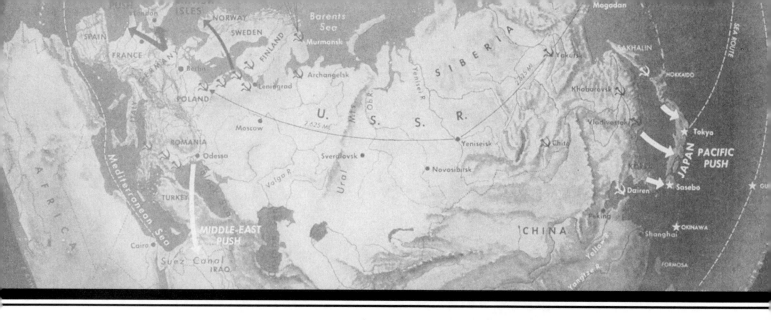

1950 NEWS PROFILE

"The Nature of the Enemy," Editorial, *Life*, February 27, 1950:

"The Elemental Fact of 1950

This is the age of obliteration. Formal war between the possessors of nuclear weapons means the obliteration of society as most of humankind—Communist and non-Communist—now knows it. Therefore it is necessary to avoid war, to control nuclear weapons and to fashion a formula for permanent peace.

Opposed to these necessities is the elemental fact of 1950: The enemy of the free world is implacably determined to destroy the free world.

This enemy cannot surrender and cannot make peace. The makers and leaders of Stalinist thought have said again and again and again that the object of Soviet Communism is 'the victory of Communism throughout the world.' They have also said that this victory is essential to the safety and welfare of the Soviet Union itself. Their own system is so grounded upon this objective that it has become a driving necessity; to abandon it would be to invite the collapse of their system and the destruction of themselves.

There can be no compromise and no agreement with Soviet Communism. It is not merely that Soviet Communists refuse to fulfill agreements. It is that they use compromise and agreement to destroy those with whom they compromise and agree. Any compromise, any agreement can only be, so far as the Communists are concerned, a further stage in the war which they continually wage.

Every relevant act and attitude of Soviet Communism during the first years of the atomic age compels the conclusion that any atomic agreement acceptable to the Communists would be used by them as every agreement has been used—to further 'the victory of Communism throughout the world.'

When and in what situations Soviet Communism will proceed from informal war to shooting war is unpredictable. It is conceivable that the Soviet Communists will not choose shooting war as the method of final decision. Stalin himself has often expressed contempt for war ('imperialist war,' of course) as a solution. But the military power of the Soviet Union is a vaunted instrument of world Communism. Its propagandists continually boast of the Soviet Union's military might. What they studiously avoid is any predefinition of the situation

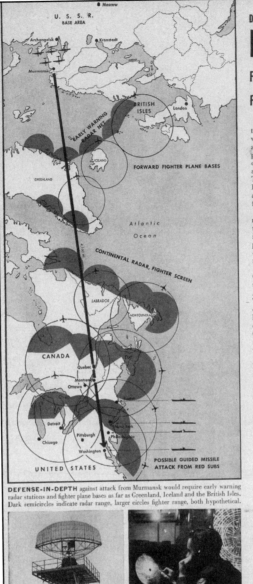

DEFENSE-IN-DEPTH against attack from Murmansk would require early warning radar stations and fighter plane bases as far as Greenland, Iceland and the British Isles. Dark semicircles indicate radar range, larger circles fighter range, both hypothetical.

Danger of War CONTINUED

HOW MUCH FOR RADAR?

FULL PROTECTION IS TOO COSTLY, BUT WE MUST HAVE FAR MORE THAN OUR PRESENT SKIMPY WARNING NET

Early in World War II, long before our own coastal civilian defense volunteers began getting excited about yellow, blue and red "alerts," Britain put to work a device that made the human eye of the air-raid spotter strictly secondary. Scanning the skies with its own electronic eyes, radar could spot an airplane many miles away and register its position, speed and course as a "blip" on its own retina or scope. A sort of television camera, transmitter and receiver all in one, radar sought out ships behind smokescreens, airplanes behind haze. This superhuman vision gave it a tremendous function in national defense, beginning with the Battle of Britain: to detect, up to the limit of its range, approaching flights of hostile aircraft, and thus gain precious time for defense forces to intercept the enemy.

Like the atomic bomb, radar once was in effect, but no longer is, an Allied monopoly. Along Russia's coast, from Vladivostok north to the Arctic and west to Murmansk, the Soviets have presumably thrown a radar network functioning in depth. It is probably perfectly good radar, backed up by good fighter plane defenses (p. 20). By contrast, the U.S. has radar warning stations around only a handful of strategic areas and right now has no modern squadrons of night fighters ready to scramble on any warning they may get.

As one hesitant step toward creating a warning system worthier of the name, Congress last year authorized $85.5 million for a partial radar screen around the U.S. and then neglected to appropriate any money. As a firmer step the Air Force took $50 million, which it could ill afford, to get the program going. The money came out of its hide in across-the-board cuts which meant, among other things, a reduction in pilot flying time. In effect, of course, this was robbing Peter to pay Paul in the hope that Peter could temporarily afford it. Another $50 million has been requested for the coming fiscal year, and last week Canada, whose air would be invaded first in any attack from the north, announced it was spending several millions more to extend its own thin radar net with stations near Halifax, Toronto and Vancouver.

The cost of an airtight radar screen of possibly more than 100 stations around North America is probably out of sight for both countries: to build one station in the far North and get it into round-the-clock operation with a 200-man crew costs over $3 million. Within the defense establishment there is argument over where to place the basic core, which is all we can afford of the needed radar defense-in-depth (map at left). Should B-36 bases and atomic installations get top priority against atomic attack, or should industrial areas get it? We shall probably have to compromise on a half measure of protection for both, for even a $17.5 billion military budget would provide only enough radar to assure critical areas a minimum warning time.

The pictures on these pages give some idea of how complicated an aircraft warning system can get. Besides its restless antennae and flickering scopes and well-protected operations rooms and human spotters between its far-flung stations, it even requires men who can write backward (opposite page). It also calls for fighter planes and antiaircraft guns, if its warnings are to result in anything besides panic. How the U.S., which was relatively rich in such items at the end of the war, is doing with regard to them now is shown on pages 28 and 29.

SEARCH ANTENNA (left) at a radar station sweeps horizon like a lighthouse beam, picking up signals bouncing back from the surrounding terrain. Target entering the antenna's range shows up as a "blip" or light pattern on the face of the radar scope (right).

HEIGHT ANTENNA (left), which will be mounted on a steel platform like the search antenna, rocks back and forth like a rocking chair. It indicates the altitude of approaching planes as light patterns which are painted on the "height-finder" radar scope (right).

in which Soviet Communism would resort to shooting war (except attack upon the Soviet homeland). Therefore, the strategists of the free world cannot calculate with certainty that this or that choice, decision, situation will make for shooting war or avoid shooting war. All-out war is never predictable. But it is always possible.

This week *Life* appraises the military defenses of the U.S. in the light of the military capacity of the Soviet Union. This appraisal is undertaken in awareness that the problem of U.S. defense is not entirely a military problem. The American people could make no worse

Danger of War CONTINUED

WORK-HORSE FIGHTERS right now are the 600-mph F-80s. Squadrons of them are now based in Alaska (*above*), in Germany and Japan. F-80 was the Air Force's first operational jet, flown experimentally before the end of last war. We have 1,500 of them.

EARTH-BOUND BOMBERS, old B-29s, veterans of the Pacific war and of questionable strategic value in modern aerial warfare, are preserved in webby plastic coverings and are stored in scattered areas. Some have been demoted for shipment to England.

LIGHT BOMBERS of the class of these 500-mph high-altitude B-45s could deliver a heavy bomb tonnage on Russian supply lines if based in Alaska, the Middle East and England. B-45 is replacing older vintage light bombers—but slowly. We have less than 50.

FASTEST FIGHTER in operation is F-86, which holds official world's record of 670.9 mph. Able to reach 40,000 feet within five minutes, it will soon be our chief weapon for stopping enemy bombs. These are from 4th Fighter Group, Langley Air Force Base, Va.

HOW MUCH AIRPOWER?

WE HAVE SOME GOOD PLANES BUT NOT ENOUGH OF THEM

The airplane sky-writing its vapor-trail signature across these pages is the world's best intercontinental bomber. The six-engine B-36 is the plane upon which the Air Force relies to deliver the weight of our retaliatory attack (for the U.S. never attacks first and cannot have the advantage of surprise) on any enemy. We have fewer than 60 of these great strategic weapons on hand, plus slightly over 100 on order. If war should come between now and 1952, we would have to rely mainly on the B-29 of World War II, a once-great bomber and big enough to tote an atomic bomb but now obsolescent and mothballed (*left*). We would have only sample copies of the B-47, the first big jet bomber. Against us Russia

F-89 IS NEW NEEDLE-NOSED NIGHT FIGHTER

could send 350 B-29-type bombers which they are building at the rate of nearly 200 a year, and they may have a counterpart of the B-36 on the way. Our ability to intercept an aerial attack is limited for the same reason our ability to launch one is limited: because our modernization program is geared to the level of 48 air force groups, dictated by President Truman, instead of the 70 groups requested by airmen and authorized by Congress. We have fewer than 10 interceptor air groups equipped with such speedy, high-flying planes as the F-86 and F-84, and have none with all-weather, night-fighting F-89 (inset *left*) or the long-range, bomber-escorting F-90 (inset *right*), both twin jets. At our present level of purchasing we may not even have an up-to-date 48-group force in 1952 but only about 30 groups. Our aerial armament lags behind the transonic and supersonic planes that carry it. The fighter pilot's great speed actually works against him,

F-90 IS LONG-RANGE PENETRATION FIGHTER

giving him too little time to sight and fire conventional guns. Much more research money is needed to extend the range or the sighting and firing time of weapons and to perfect air-to-air target-seeking missiles that can be launched from greater range and without accurate sighting. An additional $1.5 billion is needed in the Air Force budget to restore existing groups to full strength, to bolster procurement to a rate that will provide a 70-group air force in two years and to give that force adequate armament. A billion and a half dollars is a lot of money, and $13.5—or $17.5—billion is enough to buy a wondrous lot of things if it did not have to be spent to buy peace and/or preparedness. But the need for spending is almost beyond argument (see editorial on following pages).

mistake than to assume that there is safety in military defense alone, however massive and costly the defense may become.

Then why undertake such an appraisal?

First, although there is no sure safety in military defense alone, there is sure ruin in any miscalculation or neglect of military defense.

Second, the wisdom and adequacy with which the officials who are in charge of the U.S. policy calculate the defense necessities of the time provide a measure of the wisdom and adequacy with which they calculate the total necessities of the time.

The net showing of our report is that the defense necessities of the U.S. have been avoidably underestimated by the President, by his Secretary of Defense and (to the extent that they have participated in final policy decisions) by the chiefs of the military services. Not in extenuation of these officials but to indicate the scale of the turnabout in attitudes and policies now required, this must be added:

The official estimate of U.S. defense necessities has on the whole been welcomed by the U.S. Congress, the public and the press. The dominant desire has been to let the postwar economy run its course toward full civilian abundance. Most everybody had come to realize that the U.S. was in something called 'the world conflict,' that the conflict might even be called a kind of war and that a certain amount of dollars and goods had to be put up for the fight against Communism, which most everybody had come to detest. But hardly anybody really thought that the U.S. was really in a real war, a war for survival that might cut into the civilian economy and take more out of it than the U.S. has as yet been willing to pony up.

Now, chunk by chunk, the walls of illusion are falling away. . . .

The Supreme Question: How Strong Is Freedom?

We have said, the free world must know its enemy. But knowing the enemy is not enough.

The free world must know itself. It must know—it must never forget—that its freedom and its strength are one. Without freedom it cannot have strength. Without strength it cannot preserve freedom. Without the will for freedom it cannot have the strength of freedom.

At this hour of this age these are not empty words. They have a very present meaning for free men, and especially for free Americans who guard the source and center of the free world's strength.

The danger and the power of obliteration on a nuclear scale are new to mankind. Only now, five years after Hiroshima, is the prospect coming home in its full meaning to Americans. As it must for all men, it will affect the lives, the ways and the standards of Americans. The supreme question—and the sooner it is spelled out the better—is whether it will alter the American idea and the American love of freedom.

The national habit, the good habit, is to say as a matter of course that freedom is something to enjoy, to defend, if need be to die for (though preferably not in person). The habit and the idea of freedom have been stronger than any force yet arrayed against them. Are they stronger, will they be stronger than the prospect and power of obliteration? The accustomed 'what is life without freedom?' takes on an unaccustomed meaning when there is the prospect of no life. What price the free life in the free society, free men will ask, if to defend freedom is to risk all life and all society?

These are the questions, this is the risk that Americans will be living with until further notice."

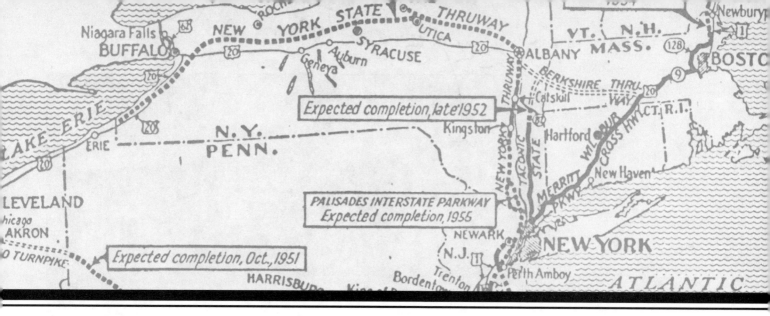

1951 Family Profile

Giulio Filetra is an Italian immigrant who has worked for Lionel Train Company, America's largest toy manufacturer, for 40 years, rising to the role of secretary-treasurer and major stockholder. He and his wife, Giovannina, have eight children and nine grandchildren.

Annual Income: Giulio's salary is approximately $50,000, plus a $25,000 bonus; his Lionel stock holdings exceed $3 million.

Life at Home

- Born in Italy, Giulio Filetra emigrated to America at the turn of the century, seeking opportunity.
- Like many Italians, he left his wife and two children behind, planning to return home a wealthy man; instead, he found America to his liking and brought his family to New Jersey.
- Trained as an engineer, Giulio found employment at the Lionel Train Company, which was just emerging as a major player in the production of toys.
- Through the years he obtained a major portion of stock, bonuses and patents, enabling him to be independently wealthy; currently, he is considered the number two man behind Joshua Lionel Cowen, with the power to make or break an idea.
- He rules with an iron hand, confident in his every decision, but at home, the tight-fisted economy he employs at work disappears under the assault of giggling grandchildren who, along with his wife and children, can talk "Papa" into almost anything.

The Filetra's music room has been converted into a model railroad dreamland.

- Even though the home office is in New York City, the manufacturing facilities are in New Jersey, where the Filetra family has a home in nearby Livingston.

Their oldest grandson attends Hotchkiss School in Lakeville, Connecticut.

- To the amazement of his neighbors, his home even has a small outdoor waterfall and pond, beside which Giovannina enjoys sitting in the late afternoons.
- The music room on the second floor, which was originally designed as a ballroom, is covered with train tracks, scenery and prototypes; a Lionel production engineer spends one day a week maintaining the tracks and implementing new ideas.
- At night, Giulio uses the elaborate setup to think through problems encountered during the day.
- With his blessing and financial support, their oldest grandson, Joseph, attends the exclusive Hotchkiss School in Lakeville, Connecticut, headed by George Van Santvoord.
- For decades, the school has prided itself on the development of character in its broadest sense; Van Santvoord likes to point out that both the Talmud and the Koran have something to say about character.
- Sunday services range from the traditional Church of England services to lectures by a rabbi or priest.
- Joseph agrees with the school's philosophy that it is more important to know why a war was fought than to memorize the actual dates it occurred.
- On the subject of morality, Van Santvoord teaches, "One way to decide whether an act is moral or immoral is to ask yourself what the world would be like if everybody did it."
- The Duke, as Van Santvoord is called, emphasizes one rule, "Be a gentleman," and even offers prizes for the most tastefully decorated dormitory rooms.

Hotchkiss: A Chronicle of an American School, by Ernest Kolowrat, with contributions from Stephen Birmingham, C. D. B. Bryan and John Hersey, 1992

"As distinguished a niche as Archibald MacLeish (1911 Hotchkiss graduate) would attain as a lawyer, professor, statesman and America's poet laureate, another Chicago boy of approximately the same vintage would ultimately play a more pervasive role in the annals of the Hotchkiss School.

To his classmates he was known as Bert. When Bert entered as a prep in 1909, he was already eighteen because of the circuitous route by which he had come to the school. Only the previous year, he had been a runner for a Chicago bank, and in his spare time emptied spittoons and otherwise helped out at a bar owned by his stepfather. (His father had died some years before.) It was on one of his bank errands for the commodity exchange that the hard-working youth chanced on a Princeton graduate known as Captain Bradley, who had founded a small farm school for orphans where Bert had spent some time a few years earlier. Captain Bradley had just returned from a Princeton reunion at which one of his classmates had told him about the promising New England boarding school where he was a master. Best of all, Captain Bradley said, the school offered scholarships, and he would help Bert apply through that Princeton classmate—who turned out to be Dr. J.J. 'Doc' Robinson. Determined not to miss this chance of a lifetime, Bert ironed his one suit so assiduously that during the long journey East by train, he repeatedly checked if the seat of his pants had not dropped out. He arrived in fine form, only to be told by the splendidly clad headmaster that he would have to take examinations in English, history, Latin and algebra. Whereupon the young man said he would be glad to take the first two, but as for Latin and algebra, he did not even know that such subjects existed. Whether or not he took any exams at all is unclear, but when Bert found out that he did not qualify, he asked the headmaster if there was any job he could fill around the school. He needed the money for train fare back to Chicago.

If some of the foregoing details have been distorted by time, the rest of Bert's saga is amply documented. Dr. Buehler let the boy stay and Albert William 'Bert' Olsen graduated with the class of 1913 and later married a sister of a classmate and future Nobel laureate, Dickinson Richards; the couple's son would become the school's fifth headmaster and lead Hotchkiss through the two most tumultuous decades of its history. 'Dr. Buehler will always be something of a hero in my book,' says A. William Olsen, Jr., '39. 'I judge that underneath all the pomposity was a heart just about as big as he was.'"

Life at Work

- Already the biggest toy manufacturer in the world, Lionel Train Company has experienced phenomenal growth since the Second World War ended.
- Its signature toy, a train set, has been considered one of the "must-have" Christmas gifts for boys during the past several years; the company will sell nearly three million toy engines and freight cars this year alone.
- In 1949, company sales hit a record $15.2 million; today, only two years later, sales are more than $28 million.
- Orders for 1952 are anticipated at more than 620,000 engines and 2.5 million freight cars; the nation's actual working railroads currently have 43,000 locomotives operating, hauling 1.8 million freight and passenger cars.

His home includes a small outdoor waterfall and pond.

- Lionel's ability to manufacture engines that produce real smoke has captured the imagination of America's men and boys; other recent innovations include realistic knuckle couplers, radio wave transmitters that control individual cars and a detailed model of the Pennsylvania Railroad's 20-wheel steam turbine locomotive.
- While World War II was under way, no production facilities in America could be spared for such frivolities as electric trains; now, after five years of war, rationing and a ban on toy manufacturing, the race is on to feed America's luxury-deprived appetite for fun.

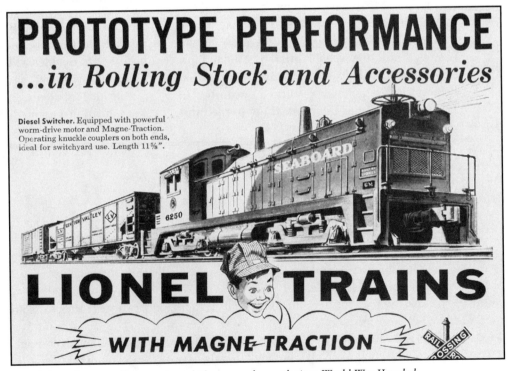

Lionel Train Company has experienced phenomenal growth since World War II ended.

- To attract a wider market, Lionel trains are emphasizing realism at a lower price, and Giulio, always exacting in his standards of design and manufacture, loves getting the details right.

- His management control extends to the lives of his managers outside work; distrusting ostentatious living of any kind, he frowns on managers who drive cars more expensive than a Ford.

- Also, he discourages anyone from buying summer homes at the seashore, believing that the bosses should never get too far removed from the workers.

- Small, dynamic and explosive, he often pits his managers against each other, believing that competition among them will produce better ideas and inventions.

- As a result, Lionel's management style fosters infighting, not only for the creation of ideas, but for who will get credit for new inventions and developments.

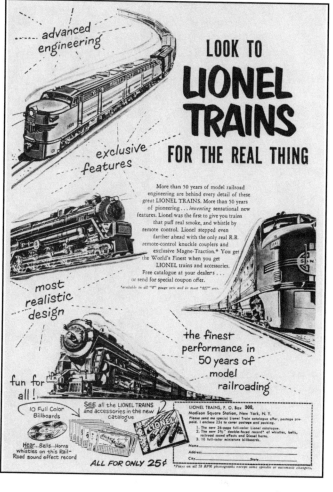

Lionel takes great pride in getting the details right.

- Giulio believes this dynamic tension improves the creative process; "If everyone agrees with everyone," he likes to say, "nothing moves forward."
- Much of the staff thrives on this highly competitive environment, despite the backbiting and disputes it causes.

The company recently hired baseball great Joe DiMaggio as its spokesman.

- Recently, the company hired as its spokesman Lionel train fan and famous New York Yankee baseball player Joe DiMaggio, who is making $125,000 to appear on 13 episodes of the *Lionel Club House* television program, broadcast on Saturday afternoons.
- This bold move by the company is attracting an even wider audience to Lionel train sets—especially now that the cost of one is falling.
- While manufacturing war materials for the army, Lionel learned how to create parts in plastic without harming quality; as a result, Lionel now uses plastic for freight and passenger cars and diesel locomotive bodies, which can be molded with more surface detail and at a lower cost than with metal.
- Lightweight plastic cars also allow an engine to pull a longer train—a must for many train families.
- Annually, children pore over the company's catalogs, dreaming of building the ultimate city through which to drive their smoking, puffing train.
- Since the 1930s, the catalogs have featured fathers and sons setting up and running the trains together, an important marketing device for this company.
- Many soldiers returning home from war aboard a passenger train speculated about how to bond with the children they'd left behind.
- In addition, the wide use of trains to transport troops and move supplies during the war has triggered a new familiarity and romance with train travel in America.

Collector's Guide to American Toy Trains, by Susan and Al Bagdale:

"Lionel's catalog was probably the most influential of all the sales devices used to promote toy trains. Children waited eagerly for its appearance each year, and it did much more than provide a list of trains and accessories. The child's imagination could go wild as he plotted his role as chief engineer of his very own railroad. Each and every decision was something to agonize over and dream about to make sure the best choices were made whether children were spending their allowances, their paper route money, or were choosing Christmas or birthday gifts."

- The war even gave a brief comeback to the beloved but inefficient steam locomotive, both for train lovers and lovers of toy trains.
- Today, only the Sears, Roebuck catalog is more widely read than the annual Lionel Train Company book.

- Throughout the war, Lionel planned for the moment the postwar newborns would reach the age of six—when parents often buy their child a toy train; this year is the sixth year since the war ended and the troops returned home.
- In addition to trains, the company manufactures a wide variety of accessories such as cattle cars and corrals.
- Employing a vibrating platform, the company enables cattle literally to move from the cattle car into the corral and back into the car using small feelers on the bottom of the plastic cows' hooves.

Life in the Community: Livingston, New Jersey

- Teenagers in this community are looking forward to Halloween when they are allowed to paint the broad display windows of the area merchants; merchants supply the brushes and watercolor paint, and are offering prize money totaling $250 to the young artists who produce the best works.
- To lure customers, many New Jersey-based stores are currently engaged in "price wars"; bargain items include electric mixers, toasters, summer suits and typewriters.
- Livingston and the surrounding communities are wrestling with the need to eliminate unfair trade practices in the servicing of television sets, and are considering an ordinance that would require city licenses for all television repairmen.

"Roads Linking the Northeast Will Mean Safer and Faster Travel by 1954," *The New York Herald Tribune*, October 21, 1951:

"Road planners have come a long way since the invention of the automobile, and the superhighways, some completed and some under construction, which eventually will link New England, New York, New Jersey and Pennsylvania, loom as the last work in highway development.

Intersections are seldom used. In their place are elaborate interchanges with long extra lanes where cars turning into and out of the stream of high-speed traffic can accelerate or slow down. Most of the superhighways are divided arteries, their turns are gentle and banked, and there are no steep grades. Speed limits range up to 70 miles per hour.

Not only have the engineers come a long way in road planning, highway financing has changed from a state operation to private authorities which raise funds from bond issues.

The roads are therefore paid for through tolls, which average $0.01 a mile.

The scheduled completion dates of most of the arteries have been estimated with the defense program and probable material shortage in mind. Some of the roads are in a good position and will get materials easily because plans were completed and approved before steel and other necessary materials became scarce. Others feel the pinch and have made allowances in their schedules. . . .

The 118-mile New Jersey Turnpike, portions of which will open next month, will link up with the New York State Thruway a few miles north of the George Washington Bridge. Downstate, it will meet a spur of the Pennsylvania Turnpike, and further along it will connect via the new Delaware Memorial Bridge south of Wilmington, with routes to Washington and the South."

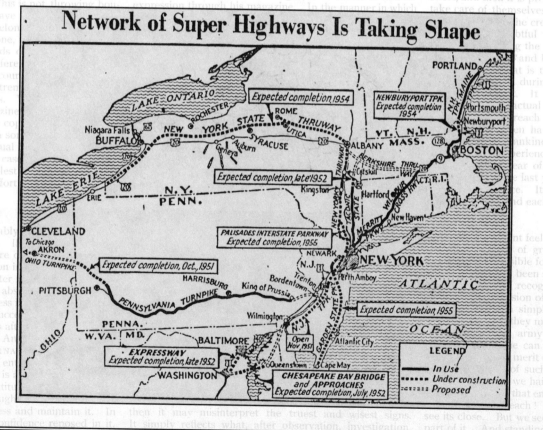

Network of Super Highways Is Taking Shape

Today 15.5 million homes have a television set, up from 8,000 in 1946.

- The local newspaper routinely reports the number of new polio cases nationwide; in the first week of June, 87 new cases were discovered compared with 78 the previous week.
- In Newark, the failure of the legislature to enact a law making bingo legal for charitable and church purposes is a key campaign issue, along with inequalities in the New Jersey Turnpike toll rates.
- A network of superhighways is taking shape, promising to link New England, New York, New Jersey and Pennsylvania.
- America's move into the suburbs has sparked a renewed interest in sewing as a family activity.
- Nationwide, there is an explosion in commerce as more Americans buy national brands and expect fresh fruit even out of season.
- Television is consuming the evening hours; 15.5 million American homes have television sets, up from 8,000 in 1946.
- Several of the coffee shops in this train-loving town run hamburgers and ice cream sodas up and down their lunch

"Cowen in Profile," by Robert Lewis Taylor, *The New Yorker*, December 13, 1951:

"Joshua Lionel Cowen, a small, bustling, choleric man of 67, is perhaps the country's most progressive and farsighted railroader. A magnate of exceptional and refreshing immodesty, he considers his contributions to the industry at least as impressive as those of the run-of-the-mill pioneers like James J. Hill and E. H. Harriman, and he feels that Robert R. Young (president of the New York Central), although shooting in the right direction, is still pretty much an upstart. Cowen is Chairman of the Board of the Lionel Lines, some of whose terminals are separated by as much as 30 feet.... At times he has served—together with important officials of other railroads, like the Pennsylvania and the Baltimore and Ohio—on the boards of large corporations, and he gives up-to-date methods a clamorous endorsement.

'Look alive!' he once shouted at the meeting of the board of an insurance company. 'Keep moving. Never stand still. You stand still and you're moving backward. It's the same in everything. If you're a railroader,' he added, directing a somewhat bilious glance toward a couple of railroad members on the board, 'you need to keep your tracks in shape, put out new engine and car models, work up other modern equipment—in short, step out of the 1890s....'

The chairmen of many corporation boards try to maintain a certain detachment from routine operations; Cowen, who is crazy about toy electric trains, even after 47 years, cannot take them or leave them alone. Separated from his plant for very long, he gets jumpy and tense.

Cowen is short, standing just over five feet five, and has a ruddy complexion and gray hair. For his years, he appears uncommonly youthful. Some of his friends think he looks like ex-Governor Lehman, but other authorities have described him as resembling an anxious cherub. Cowen's harassed expression can be traced to his longstanding suspicion that the A.C. Gilbert Company, his only major business competitor, is trying to make good trains, too. Although the Lionel Company is by far the largest of the toy train manufacturers and has symbolized the industry for two generations, Cowen regards anybody's appearance in the field as rash and highly presumptuous.

He has always felt that the children of America were looking over his shoulder as he worked. Furthermore, he has, he thinks, the viewpoint of a child himself, and he thus keeps a detached but automatic check on his progress. This picture of Cowen looking over his own shoulder while seated at his desk provides the best explanation of Lionel's somewhat exalted niche in the toy train world. Any sacrifice of excellence for expediency would tax his conscience severely, and might even age him out of his juvenile viewpoint."

counters on Lionel trains, which stop to let patrons remove their orders, after which the trains return down the track and back into the kitchen again.

- Military hospitals are using fancy train layouts as occupational therapy for disturbed veterans; playing with trains helps them both relax and learn to make decisions in cooperation with others.
- Recently, an elaborate Lionel train layout was sent to the Berlin World Youth Festival, at the request of West Berlin mayor Dr. Ernst Reuter, who wanted an exhibit that would extol the American way of life.

HISTORICAL SNAPSHOT
1951

- Nationwide 3.8 million people played golf on approximately 5,000 courses, comprising 1.5 million acres of land
- North Korean forces crossed the thirty-eighth parallel, took Seoul, and rejected American truce offers
- Color television was first introduced
- H&R Block, formed in 1946 in Kansas City, began offering tax preparation services when the IRS stopped preparing people's taxes
- Margaret Sanger urged the development of an oral contraceptive
- The Univac computer was introduced
- The Metropolitan Life Insurance Company reported a link between being 15 pounds overweight and dying younger than the average life span
- Massive flooding covered more than a million acres of land in Oklahoma, Kansas, Missouri and Illinois
- The Twenty-second Amendment to the U.S. Constitution passed Congress, limiting the service of the president to two terms
- The latest census reported that eight percent of the population was more than 65 years old, up from four percent in 1900
- For the first time in history, women outnumbered men in the United States; Washington, D.C., had the highest percentage of single women (27 percent), while Nevada had the lowest (13 percent)
- Julius and Ethel Rosenberg were sentenced to death for espionage against the United States
- President Truman dispatched an air force plane when Sioux City Memorial Park in Iowa refused to bury John Rice, a Native American who had died in combat; his remains were interred in Arlington National Cemetery
- Sugarless chewing gum, dacron suits, pushbutton-controlled garage doors, telephone company answering service, college credit courses on TV, and power steering all made their first appearance
- Charles F. Blair flew solo over the North Pole
- Entertainer Milton Berle signed a 30-year, million-dollar-plus contract with NBC
- New York and other major cities increased the cost of a phone call from $0.05 to $0.10

1951 Economic Profile

The national consumer expenditures (per capita income) in 1951 were:

Auto Parts	$9.72
Auto Usage	$143.24
Clothing	$113.42
Dentists	$6.48
Food	$393.42
Furniture	$20.74
Gas and Oil	$39.54
Health Insurance	$5.83
Housing	$157.49
Intercity Transport	$6.48
Local Transport	$12.96
New Auto Purchase	$55.74
Personal Business	$46.02
Personal Care	$17.49
Physicians	$17.49
Private Education and Research	$12.31

"Dr. Earnest Diehter, New York Consulting psychologist, told the Pacific Council of the American Association of Advertising Agencies convention that he has conducted six exhaustive studies to find out why people drink. His findings: 'To get drunk.' "

MODEL RAILROAD CHARACTERS: **The Dope**

"I thought it would be more realistic and true to prototype, so instead of cutting a tunnel hole in the partition with a chisel and hammer, I tried a scale explosion with dynamite!"

Recreation $75.83
Religion/Welfare Activities $16.85
Telephone and Telegraph $14.26
Tobacco $29.17
Utilities $51.20
Per Capita Consumption $1,348.79

Annual Income, Standard Jobs

Average of all Industries,
  Excluding Farm Labor $3,526.00
Average of all Industries,
  Including Farm Labor $3,452.00
Bituminous Coal Mining $3,762.00
Building Trades $3,774.00
Domestics $1,588.00
Farm Labor $1,568.00
Federal Civilian $3,924.00
Federal Employees, Executive
  Departments $3,189.00
Federal Military $2,788.00
Finance, Insurance and Real Estate . . $3,356.00
Gas and Electricity Workers $3,851.00

An article in 1952 in *All Aboard*, the Lionel house organ, told all about the advantages of dealer displays and how they were put together. Although self-promotional, naturally, it still makes interesting reading now.

LIONEL APPETIZERS—Photo above shows one of the scenic displays that was mass-produced this year to stimulate that urge to buy Lionel Trains and accessories. They'll be in action throughout the nation from now until Christmas.

Displays Boost Lionel Sales

It takes mass production selling to move mass production goods in sufficient quantity to keep assembly lines running. So, Lionel's Display Department is one of the busiest sections of the plant at this time during the fall, and that probably is one of the reasons that the demand for miniature trains has required a continuing expansion of production facilities in excess of anticipated needs. In fact, it is many years since the firm has been able to meet consumer demand despite constant expansion.

It is an unusual youngster, be he six or sixty, who can pass a display of Lionel Trains in action without pausing, fascinated by their realism. And once they have arrested his attention, if he leaves without placing an order, it's a cinch he will be back soon to purchase a set or additional equipment to add to his pike.

Displays Help Keep Assembly Lines Busy

Dealers have learned the magic effect of these displays as a merchandising tool, and demand for scenic layouts has grown steadily year after year. Now nearing the fulfillment of its 1952 schedule, the department has produced thousands of standard displays to be sold, at cost, to stores throughout the country. This service is provided by the company to help its merchants keep Lionel assembly lines in full production.

Four standard layouts were made this year and produced in large quantities. Scores of other layouts were manufactured to meet the specific needs of individual dealers. Some occupy entire show windows and utilize virtually every item produced by the company. Other huge displays are provided for large department stores, to be witnessed by thousands of potential customers daily. Many are so large they must be shipped in sections. The manufacture of displays, unlike that of trains and accessories, cannot be spread over the major portion of the year. En-

tirely new layouts must be designed annually, and that is a time-consuming procedure. Then, when designs are completed and have been accepted, demand must be determined. The price of a display hinges upon costs, and quantity is an important factor in determining that item.

Consequently, most displays are produced in the late summer and early fall. This year the department was able to utilize considerable space in uncompleted portions of the new building. The additional space helped keep their production on schedule.

Joseph Donato is in charge of the Display Department, assisted by William Bonanno, who doubles in planning packaging. Their normal working force is small but, at the peak of the season as many as forty are employed. As their work tapers off displaced employees are welcomed by other departments to help fill the demand those realistic scenic displays have helped to create.

Meanwhile the department goes back to thinking about next year's designs and filling last-minute orders for special merchandising set-ups to help maintain Lionel's leadership in the field.

ADDITIONAL HELP in stimulating sales will be provided by these smaller displays, designed to provide maximum sales help where space is limited.

FOR LIONEL FOLKS   Page Five

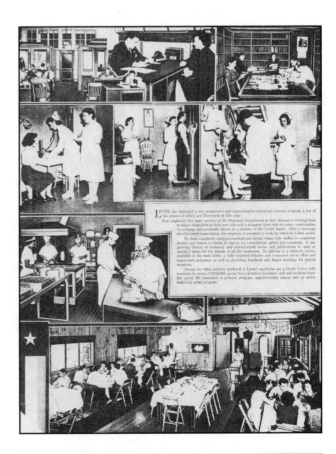

Manufacturing, Durable Goods $3,862.00

Manufacturing, Nondurable
    Goods...................... $3,386.00

Medical/Health Services Workers ... $2,143.00

Miscellaneous Manufacturing...... $3,240.00

Motion Picture Services.......... $3,269.00

Nonprofit Organization Workers ... $2,720.00

Passenger Transportation Workers,
    Local and Highway $3,489.00

Personal Services $2,355.00

Public School Teachers........... $2,998.00

Radio Broadcasting and
    Television Workers............ $5,017.00

Railroad Workers................ $4,163.00

State and Local Government
    Workers $2,758.00

Telephone and Telegraph
    Workers $3,253.00

Wholesale and Retail Trade
    Workers $3,171.00

Selected Prices

Automobile, Chevrolet Corvette	$3,156.00
Baby Lotion, Johnson's	$0.49
Buffalo Bill Costume	$2.98
Card Table and Chairs	$49.75
Cotton Swabs, Q-tips	$0.98
Doll, Tiny Tears	$7.95
Dress, Woman's Cotton	$15.00
Fabric, Yard	$3.06
Hair Dryer	$21.50
Mixer, GE	$34.95
Pinking Shears	$3.95
Pipe Tobacco	$0.15
Refrigerator, Admiral	$189.95
Shortening, Crisco, One Pound	$0.31
Stapler	$2.60
Toaster, Automatic	$21.95
Toothbrush	$0.60
Wedding Ring, Man's	$6.75
Wieners, Oscar Mayer, One Pound	$0.49
Wrestling Ticket	$2.60

"Marriage Is a Way of Life,"
by Amy A. McGregor, *Nautilus Magazine*, March 1951:

" 'I wish I weren't married; then I'd be able to afford a car.'

The young man who made this statement is not at all dissatisfied with his wife; he is more than ordinarily proud of his little girl. But the fetters of married life chafe him. So does the constant sacrifice—the doing without something he would like to have, and could afford if he were single. In truth, he is dissatisfied with marriage itself.

The squabble over sex education has distorted and overemphasized the physical side of marriage. Some preparation for the responsibilities of marriage is given to our young girls, but that also is physical. It is important to learn to budget one's earnings, to learn to care for a house, to look after the welfare of a small baby, to sew, to cook and to do the various things which promote physical well-being. But of what use is a spic-and-span house, a healthy, happy baby, a well-balanced budget, or a well-cooked meal, if the husband always refers to things he would like to have but cannot because he is married? Would anyone in his right mind call that a happy marriage?

If it is important that a girl be taught such details appertaining to the physical side of marriage, how much more important is it that both boys and girls should be taught the one most obvious lesson they will need for marriage: the art of living together?

The family group, on which our present civilization is based, is supposed to teach this lesson. But our modern news items, particularly those concerned with juvenile delinquency and divorce, testify that it does not. From the other members of his family, the child is supposed to receive his first true impressions of the world, and his first contacts with it. From that group, he should learn the fine art of living with others, and be made aware that the universe does not center directly about him.

Instead, what happens? The child is born, and immediately becomes the pivot around which the household revolves. The parents can deny him nothing, and the whole routine of the household is disrupted to fit his pleasure, instead of gradually fitting the child into the already established routine.

As he grows older, there is an eager rush to keep him from realizing the world of reality. He is fed with fairy stories and tales of the world as his parents imagine it should be. Each idle wish is fulfilled as if by magic, even though the parents have to go without necessary comforts for themselves.

When he enters adolescence, he is thoroughly self-centered. He really knows nothing of the world. His ideas of his playmates are based on the world of make-believe in which he has lived all these years. Physically, he is becoming aware of himself as never before, and this tends to make him even more self-centered. At the same time, he feels the need of companionship from those of his own age, and is unable to meet them on an equal footing. Is it any wonder that the process of growing up is so difficult? Is it any wonder that the divorce rate soars to even higher levels each year?"

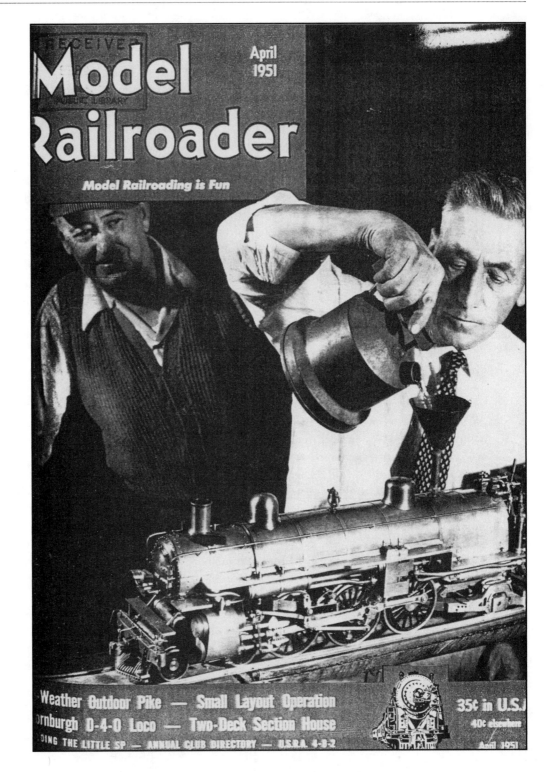

1955 Family Profile

After making a fortune running illegal rum during the prohibition era, Eddie Curran moved into loansharking and gambling. Today, he legally operates a casino in Las Vegas, a city open to opportunity, gambling and tourists eager to part with their money. Twice divorced, Curran has three grown children.

Annual Income: His casino operations earn him more than $400,000 a year.

Life at Home

- For the past six years, Eddie Curran has lived in an apartment on the top floor of his Las Vegas Strip resort; although smaller than his home in Detroit, his apartment has everything, including room service on demand.
- Notoriously a poor sleeper, the 24-hour nature of the hotel gambling business suits him well; when he can't sleep, he simply goes downstairs to watch the showgirls perform and gaze over his vast gambling operation.
- After years of operating in the shadow of the law, Curran enjoys being licensed to operate a "legit" business in Las Vegas.
- He has run the resort since 1949, taking over the building after its owner got into financial straits.
- When Jack, his son from his first marriage, recently came to visit and play the crap tables, it was Eddie's chance to show him that Las Vegas' future was as a resort city, not just a gambling center.

Eddie Curran (seated) is promoting the growth of tourism in Las Vegas.

Curran says, "If you wanna get rich, make little people feel like big people."

- While Jack was in town, Eddie and a fellow resort owner talked about building a golf course near the Desert Inn with an entrance on Paradise Road, the street just east of the Strip, so that other casinos could benefit from it as well.
- Most of the other resort owners hate the idea, because they want visitors to gamble in their casinos, not play golf, but Eddie believes Las Vegas needs a wider spectrum of entertainment to attract more tourists and families.
- He tells Jack repeatedly, "If you wanna get rich, make little people feel like big people."
- Although five additional resorts are being discussed on the Strip, Eddie, now 60 years old and rich, does not fear competition; what he wants now is respectability.
- His resort features landscaped lawns and gardens graced with palm trees and an elegant waterfall near the front entrance, plus a variety of distractions including a pool, health club, horse stables and shops.
- His only problem is income taxes; knowing that his tax return will be reviewed carefully, he is taking great pains to include all of his income—and experiencing great pain at the amount he must pay—more than 90 percent of his reported income.

Life at Work
- The Las Vegas scene lives on connections; it is a personal world where everyone knows everyone else, and who butters whose bread.
- When the newspaper announces that the new owners of a Strip hotel are "Miami Hotel-men," it means the owners enjoy the confidence of Miami-based mobster Meyer Lansky, who coordinates a substantial part of the mob investment on the Strip.

Las Vegas is slowly moving away from its cowboy image.

- Even children can walk the Strip and declare which casinos are operated by the Chicago mob, or which hotels are run by the Detroit mob.
- Curran is closely tied to mob money in Detroit and Cleveland.
- He believes that Las Vegas must expand its image and offer entertainment beyond gambling if it is to have a long and prosperous future.
- A stickler for professionalism, he recruited to run his resort experienced hotelmen who learned the ins-and-outs of running a casino from some of Curran's business partners from Detroit.
- The Las Vegas Strip began taking shape in 1941 when Californian Thomas Hull opened a resort—not a hotel—featuring expansive gardens, a large swimming pool and a rustic-looking casino and restaurant.
- He located the facility, known as El Rancho, beyond the city limits in an area called the Strip to escape an onerous city tax burden.
- In 1942, The Last Frontier opened a mile south of El Rancho; thus, the Strip began, but gambling was still a localized, small-time activity.
- In 1944, the county's licensing agency, the Liquor and Licensing Board, started the year by approving 214 gaming applications, mostly from the owners of bars, cafés, liquor stores, markets and other small businesses requesting slot machines.
- However, when mobster Bugsy Siegel took over the building of the Flamingo Hotel, he had a vision for a national gambling constituency that was married to a deep access to capital.
- The Flamingo was the brainchild of Billy Wilkerson, who wanted to retreat from the sawdust-covered floors and cowboy motifs that had dominated Las Vegas, and transform the city into the Beverly Hills of the desert.
- The Flamingo Hotel was planned as an elegant resort that would appeal to a fashionable crowd; to accomplish this goal Wilkerson needed a partner who had capital, i.e., Bugsy Siegel.

"Federal Income Taxes," *Information Please Almanac*, 1955:

Rate Table for Joint Returns

If Your Taxable Income Is:	Your Tax Is:
4,000 – 7,999	800 + 22% of excess over 4,000
8,000 – 11,999	1,680 + 26% of excess over 8,000
12,000 – 15,999	2,720 + 30% of excess over 12,000
16,000 – 19,999	3,920 + 34% of excess over 16,000
20,000 – 23,999	5,280 + 38% of excess over 20,000
24,000 – 27,999	6,800 + 43% of excess over 24,000
28,000 – 31,999	8,520 + 47% of excess over 28,000
32,000 – 35,999	10,400 + 50% of excess over 32,000
36,000 – 39,999	12,400 + 53% of excess over 36,000
40,000 – 43,999	14,520 + 56% of excess over 40,000
44,000 – 51,999	16,760 + 59% of excess over 44,000
52,000 – 63,999	21,480 + 62% of excess over 52,000
64,000 – 75,999	28,920 + 65% of excess over 64,000
76,000 – 87,999	36,720 + 69% of excess over 76,000
88,000 – 99,999	45,000 + 72% of excess over 88,000
100,000 – 119,999	53,640 + 75% of excess over 100,000
120,000 – 139,999	68,640 + 78% of excess over 120,000
140,000 – 159,999	84,240 + 81% of excess over 140,000
160,000 – 179,999	100,440 + 84% of excess over 160,000
180,000 – 199,999	117,240 + 87% of excess over 180,000
200,000 – 299,999	134,640 + 89% of excess over 200,000
300,000 – 399,999	223,640 + 90% of excess over 300,000
400,000 and higher	313,640 + 91% of excess over 400,000

- When the Flamingo opened in 1946, it quickly became the place to be, where black-chip ($100-chip) gamblers flocked to enjoy its 105 lavish rooms, spectacular three-story waterfall and tuxedo-clad staff; the building was even air-conditioned.
- Its opening was followed by the Desert Inn in 1950, the Sands in 1952 and the Riviera in 1955.
- Within hours of Siegel's murder in 1947, Moe Sedway, Morris Rosen and Gus Greenbaum entered the hotel's lobby to announce they were taking over—making Las Vegas' image as a center of sin even uglier.
- The city's image, however, has improved in recent years through the hiring of top-flight entertainment talent; Nat King Cole, Pearl Bailey, Dean Martin, Jerry Lewis and Lena Horne have all appeared on the Strip.
- For Noel Coward's opening-night show, Frank Sinatra chartered a private plane to fly in Judy Garland, the Bogarts and the Nivens; also present at the show were Zsa Zsa Gabor and Joan Fontaine.

Currently, 10 resorts, 35 hotels and 250 motels operate in Las Vegas to handle tourists who wish to gamble.

- Coward was pleased by the reception of the stars, but also by his ability to amuse ordinary audiences who flocked to his shows from Kansas, Nebraska, Utah and Illinois.
- Currently, 10 Strip resorts, 35 hotels and 250 motels operate in Las Vegas, attracting tourists who will spend $164 million this year.

Life in the Community: Las Vegas, Nevada

- The largest city in the only state in the nation that permits casino gambling, Las Vegas has developed a reputation as a town designed and built to accommodate the pleasures of high rollers.
- Located in the scorching desert of southern Nevada with little industry and less water, Las Vegas nonetheless lures millions seeking excitement.

> "It seems clear to the committee that too many of the men running gambling operations in Nevada are either members of existing out-of-state gambling syndicates or have had histories of close association with the underworld characters who operate these syndicates. The licensing system which is in effect in this state has not resulted in excluding the undesirables from the state but has merely served to give their activities a seeming cloak of respectability."
>
> —Sen. Estes Kefauver, 1951

- The city's rise from the desert floor is marked by many from the day that mobster Benjamin "Bugsy" Siegel arrived in 1945 and began transforming Las Vegas into a national center for gambling, which in the absence of any competing industries has rapidly become the culture of the city during the past decade.
- Tourists relish the "bad boy" image of a city built around gambling and openly funded by the underworld.
- It is an image promoted by U.S. Senator Estes Kefauver's investigation into organized crime, resulting in the televised interrogation of many of Eddie Curran's associates—to their embarrassment and Curran's.
- Sen. Kefauver's investigation showed that thousands of phone calls were routinely made to relay bets to all parts of the country, violating the laws of the other states; most of these calls were made by out-of-state bookies who wished to lay off money in Las Vegas for their own benefit or for that of syndicate members.
- The state legislature promptly drew up new rules which forbade the horse parlors to have more than one phone installed.
- Also, as a result of the national investigation, the Nevada Gaming Control Board was created to administer the gaming industry of the state, principally in Las Vegas.

> "I figured it this way. If people will take a trip out into the ocean to gamble, they'll go to a desert, too—especially if it's legal and they don't have to worry about getting pinched. So one day I drive into Nevada looking for a nice desert spot and I picked this one because the price is right and it's on the main road to L.A."
>
> —Bugsy Siegel, 1946

- Recently the Gaming Board ruled that every stockholder of a gaming establishment had to be licensed by the Board, virtually eliminating corporate ownership of casinos; designed to ensure that "undesirable elements" would not operate casinos, the ruling effectively eliminated publicly held companies from investing in gambling, making the city even more dependent on underworld capital and the Teamsters pension funds for its growth.

- The Kefauver Committee also created a wave of national reforms; as other localities elected administrations pledging to wipe out illegal gambling, more capital flowed to Nevada, and Las Vegas in particular.

- Critics say Las Vegas packages itself around the moment, making it a city with no past or future; others say this image simply underscores the malleability of a city determined to survive.

- Its formula is simple, city leaders say—Las Vegas offers a time-out from daily life for people who, though respectable back home, can come to this city and cut loose; all bets are off as visitors indulge in a core of pleasures that they could acquire at home only with the risk of embarrassment, stigma or even arrest.

- For most residents, the Strip and local life are separate; while tourists revel in the gambling and showgirls, locals pride themselves on the quality of the Little League, Girls Scouts and high attendance levels at churches and synagogues.

Locals live in the never-never land of all-night gambling, working as dealers, croupiers, pit bosses, change girls or cocktail waitresses.

Las Vegas offers a time-out from daily life for many out-of-towners.

- Clergymen often find that the need to expand their buildings conflicts with the source of new capital; as one Methodist minister says, "There is no way a church in Las Vegas can avoid benefiting from gambling. We are here building a new church that will cost $220,000. We already have $40,000. Thirty thousand came from a man who owns the property on which the Golden Nugget gambling hall is situated. Without this income he could not give this amount of money; therefore, it derives from gambling. What can I do about it? I'll tell you. Nothing."
- Many of the locals live in the never-never land of all-night gambling, working as dealers, croupiers, pit bosses, shills, change girls or cocktail waitresses.

- Generally, beautiful cocktail waitresses make up to $15,000 a year; an ordinary dealer takes home $100 to $150 a week, doubling his take during the busy holiday seasons when tips are more frequent.

- The pit boss, who supervises a group of dealers, averages $50 for an eight-hour shift, and even the lowly shill, the come-on guy who uses the house's money, makes a decent wage averaging up to $10 a day.

- Many also live well on unreported tip income, saving on income taxes.

- Nevada was acquired by the United States in 1848 after the country's war with Mexico, and was largely ignored until the discovery of gold and silver at Comstock Lode in 1859.

- Thousands rushed to the state to get rich quick, resulting in territorial status in 1861 and statehood three years later.

- By the 1880s, the mines were exhausted, and by 1900, the population of the state had fallen by a third.

- A new silver and gold discovery at the turn of the century brought new miners, expanded railroads and, fairly quickly, economic collapse once again.

- Then in 1931, with the depression under way, the silver mines exhausted and illegal gambling the only business that seemed to make money, the Nevada state legislature saw the wisdom of legalized gambling.

- To further stimulate tourist travel to the state, the legislature also reduced the residency requirement for divorce to six weeks; some claim the "Four Horsemen" of the state economy are gambling, drinking, marrying and divorcing.

- In those years before World War II, Reno, in northern Nevada, was the nation's biggest gambling center.

- After the Second World War, Las Vegas took prominence, thanks to its being within driving distance of Los Angeles, the spreading use of air conditioning and the resort model created by Bugsy Siegel.

- In general, other industry has not been actively recruited as Norman Biltz, Reno politician and real-estate tycoon explains, "Nevada must be kept small. Let industry go elsewhere.

Locals pride themselves on the quality of the city's Little League, Girl Scouts and churches.

"Entertainment Tourism," *Devil's Bargains*, by Hal Rothman:

"Disneyland reached for the public in the same manner as did Las Vegas. Disneyland and its followers placed the visitor at the center of the story in a manner eerily reflective of Las Vegas; they promised complete experience, as did Las Vegas. . . . In this way, Las Vegas and Disneyland shared enormous parallels. Founded in 1954, Disneyland became the epitome of entertainment tourism at a time when Las Vegas could not compete in the mainstream marketplace. Disneyland offered the same sort of refraction of experience as did Las Vegas, but through a lens focused directly on the heart of the baby boom generation. Disneyland offered a form of cultural and heritage tourism—some say indoctrination—along with its scripted entertainment. Like Santa Fe and Aspen, Disneyland created an identity; it became static and immutable in a way that Las Vegas could not afford to be. Disneyland invented faster rides. Las Vegas reinvented itself time and again."

Large industrial payrolls bring large families, which cost more money in taxes for public services."

- However, of Nevada's 17 counties, only two, Washoe, where Reno is located, and Clark, in which Vegas thrives, are benefiting from the gambling.
- Vegas, at the southern tip of the state, is considered a sort of "economic plumb-bob" that represents a rich potential—like having a wealthy relative who might do you some good one day.

Las Vegas packages itself around the moment, with no past or future.

- When the other 15 counties, which do not have widespread gambling, began talking about a state gaming tax hike, 50 Nevada assemblymen and state senators were invited to the Strip by Vegas owners.
- There the gamblers explained their position over fine food and free floor shows; one senator stayed on for a month, studying the situation.
- When the proposed tax bill reached the senate, it died, failing even to come up for a vote.
- The other key element in the Las Vegas economy is nuclear research; four years ago the U.S. Atomic Energy Commission conducted its first above-ground nuclear test in southern Nevada, at the proving grounds of Nellis Air Base.
- When the white puffball rose in the sky in January 1951, gamblers rushed out of the casinos to watch the desert sky glow in the light of an artificial sun.
- The nuclear test brought more business and prestige to the town; soon, swimsuits and wedding cakes were fashioned after a mushroom cloud, hairdressers designed "atomic hairdos" and restaurants served "atomburgers."

Historical Snapshot
1955

- The Ford Foundation gave $50 million to private colleges to raise faculty salaries
- The minimum wage was raised from $0.75 per hour to $1.00 per hour
- Oveta Culp Hobby, Health, Education and Welfare secretary, opposed the free distribution of the Salk vaccine to poor children as "socialized medicine"
- Racial segregation on interstate buses and trains was ordered to end
- The population explosion that followed WWII hit the schools, resulting in extensive teacher and classroom shortages
- The construction of suburban shopping centers and motels increased dramatically as Americans moved out of the cities; by this year, 1,800 shopping centers had been built
- Disneyland opened in Anaheim, California
- The electric stove for home use, the *Village Voice*, *National Review* and Revlon "no-smear" lanoline lipstick all made their first appearance
- The two labor unions—the American Federation of Labor and the Congress of Industrial Organizations—merged to form the AFL-CIO
- The Kellogg Company introduced Special K cereal; Procter and Gamble sold Crest with fluoride for the first time
- The Whirlpool Corporation merged with Seeger Refrigerator Company and began producing refrigerators, air conditioners and cooking ranges
- The three makers of soap, Procter and Gamble, Lever Brothers and Colgate-Palmolive, spent a total of $64 million on TV advertising to sell their products
- The University of California reported that more than a billion copies of comic books were sold yearly, costing $100 million—four times the book budget of all U.S. public libraries
- National City Bank merged with First National Bank, both of New York, to form the third largest bank in America
- The Salk vaccine was successful in preventing polio
- Hollywood developed a passion for shooting movies in Spain, filming 10 major American movies there during the year
- The United Automobile Workers union forced Ford and General Motors to pay workers a modest weekly sum during layoffs
- Noel Coward reportedly earned $40,000 a week to entertain at a "gambling joint" in Las Vegas
- The United Nations celebrated its tenth anniversary
- A Cadillac dealer in Dallas, Texas, reported that 97 percent of the cars he sold were air-conditioned
- Former President Harry Truman was paid $600,000 for his memoirs

1955 ECONOMIC PROFILE

The national consumer expenditures (per capita income) in 1955 were:

Auto Parts	$9.68
Auto Usage	$193.01
Clothing	$118.59
Dentists	$9.08
Food	$414.46
Furniture	$26.62
Gas and Oil	$52.03
Health Insurance	$8.47
Housing	$208.14
Intercity Transport	$$6.66
Local Transport	$11.49
New Auto Purchase	$83.49
Personal Business	$58.69
Personal Care	$22.39
Physicians	$22.99
Private Education and Research	$15.13
Recreation	$87.73
Religion/Welfare Activities	$21.18
Telephone and Telegraph	$18.76
Tobacco	$30.86
Utilities	$61.72
Per Capita Consumption	$1,560.43

Annual Income, Standard Jobs

Average of all Industries, Excluding Farm Labor	$4,224.00
Average of all Industries, Including Farm Labor	$4,128.00
Bituminous Coal Mining	$4,470.00
Building Trades	$4,607.00
Domestics	$1,874.00
Farm Labor	$1,498.00
Federal Civilian	$4,801.00
Federal Employees, Executive Departments	$3,774.00
Federal Military	$3,237.00
Finance, Insurance and Real Estate	$4,005.00
Gas and Electricity Workers	$4,757.00
Manufacturing, Durable Goods	$4,737.00
Manufacturing, Nondurable Goods	$4,134.00
Medical/Health Services Workers	$2,488.00
Miscellaneous Manufacturing	$3,789.00

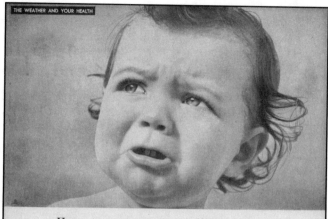

More vintage tobacco makes PHILIP MORRIS so popular with younger smokers

Gentle, more delicate in flavor...for those with keen young tastes

Maybe you've noticed it yourself...PHILIP MORRIS seems to have a way with younger smokers. That's because their fresher, unspoiled tastes are quick to appreciate the special qualities of gentleness and delicate flavor that vintage tobacco offers. Follow Young America's lead. Enjoy PHILIP MORRIS— King Size or Regular—in the convenient Snap-Open pack.

Philip Morris

Motion Picture Services $4,330.00
Nonprofit Organization
    Workers $3,291.00
Passenger Transportation
    Workers, Local and Highway $4,142.00
Personal Services $2,766.00
Public School Teachers $3,608.00
Radio Broadcasting and
    Television Workers $6,250.00
Railroad Workers $4,701.00
State and Local Government
    Workers $3,447.00
Telephone and Telegraph
    Workers $4,153.00
Wholesale and Retail
    Trade Workers $4,616.00

Selected Prices

Air Freshener $0.49
Baseball Glove $9.95
Bath Towel $0.95
Candy, Tootsie Roll $0.05
Coca-Cola $0.05
Chandelier, Crystal $425.00
Cooker, Presto $12.95
Eyeliner, Max Factor $1.50
Flashlight Battery $0.14
Guitar, Washburn $27.50
Hotel Room, Ritz Carlton,
    Boston $9.00
Lighter, Zippo $4.75
Listerine Antiseptic $0.79
Mattress, Simmons $79.50
Outboard Motor, Johnson $430.00
Shoes, Child's Buster Brown $6.99
Suit, Man's Botany 500 . . . . $59.50
Transistor Pocket Radio $75.00
Typewriter, Electric $209.35
Watch, Timex Boy Scout $9.95

Tourism in Nevada

- In the 1890s, recreational tourism was largely defined as a pursuit of the wealthy, who could afford to hire private train cars for hunting trips into the wilderness, often supported by elegant hunting lodges operated by the rich for the rich.
- Even the development of the ski industry and the emergence of pre-World War I resorts such as Sun Valley in

Idaho or Aspen, Colorado, in the years after the war were largely elite activities.

- Only 10,000 Americans called themselves avid skiers in 1935 and most of those lived in the East.
- By 1945, more than 200,000 people had experienced the joys of skiing and were searching for more slopes to conquer.
- As the infrastructure that supported travel developed and roads stretched across the horizon of the American West, tourist camps and motor courts arose to meet the needs of the traveling middle class.
- The independence offered by the private automobile democratized travel and the industry of tourism, which boomed after the Second World War.
- The growth in population and employment opportunities in the post-World War II era, as well as technological innovations such as air travel and air conditioning, further fueled a highly mobile population, determined to see all of America.
- During the war, the population of the West grew substantially, attracted by new, war-related industries from shipbuilding to steel production, but rationing on goods and travel restricted Americans' ability to spend the money they earned from these industrial jobs.

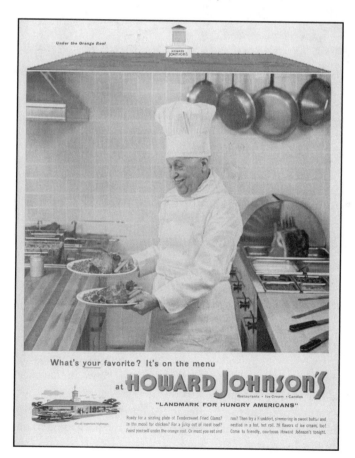

- The end of the war changed all that; as early as 1945, millions of returning soldiers on their way home took side trips to the great icons of the American West—the Grand Canyon, Grand Teton and Yellowstone—traveling mostly by car.
- After World War II, a solid symbol of middle-class status was automobile ownership, which, coupled with the expanded popularity in the late 1940s of two-week annual vacations, made the availability of national park campsites as rare as the American eagle.
- An affluent, mobile America was determined to be entertained during its leisure time allotment, and out of this desire came another form of entertainment, the packaging of unreality in places like Disneyland theme park.

Gambling—How It Is Run, by Ed Reid:

"While gambling jobs are rewarding moneywise, the boredom that sets in comes from doing the same thing day in and day out. Dullest of all is the work of the shill. His shift consists of nothing more than putting down and picking up silver dollars with absolutely no interest in whether he wins or loses, since he can do neither.

The sole concern of the pit boss is to see that no one, customer or dealer, cheats anyone else. Once in a great while he gets a chance to capture a laugh, as in the case of Sherlock Feldman, colorful pit boss at the Sands Hotel. During an exciting roll of the dice, with frenetic tourists jumping up and down and whooping (which is usually what happens when the visitors start winning from the house), one portly gentleman with false dentures yelled a little too loudly. His teeth popped out and landed on the green felt of the dice table.

Quick as a flash, the agile mind of Sherlock acted. He whipped his hand to his mouth, pulled out his own false teeth and plopped them down on the table beside those of the astonished tourist. "You're faded," he yelled as everyone screamed with laughter that did not stop for a week as the story circulated around Vegas. . . .

Cheaters are heartily disliked, whether they be dealers or players, and they are given scant shrift when caught. However, in one case, another rich story gained circulation after a cheater was caught in the act. He had approached a crap table with a pair of loaded dice and every intention of putting them in play. He put his money down and called for the croupier or stickman to pass him the house dice. The idea was to substitute the loaded dice for the ones given him by the casino.

This he tried to do as he shook the dice in his closed fist and yelled that baby needed a new pair of shoes. He threw the crooked dice on the table, confident that he had made the switch unnoticed. To his and everyone's vast astonishment three dice rolled out on the table, each one a five.

The stickman's eyes widened, then calmly he reached out his curved wand and flipped two of the dice back to the cheater. 'Okay, Bub, your point is 15; let's see you roll it!' he said as the player turned green."

- Thanks to television and its many "westerns," the romance of the West was ignited nationwide.
- Most of the tourism was clustered between Memorial Day in late May and Labor Day in early September, when children were not in school.
- Tourism was especially welcomed in communities where industrial changes or played-out mines had left workers idle; most tourism employment requires no special skills, save a willingness to be gracious and attentive.

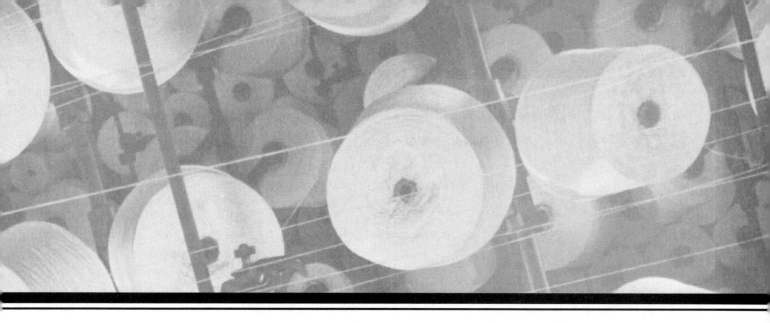

1957 Family Profile

For five generations, Wilton Hayslett's family has been in the cotton business, building expertise and wealth. Today, Hayslett is a highly successful cotton broker, married to a woman whose family owned thousands of acres of farmland; they devote their time to the Baptist Church, the Billy Graham crusades and the ever changing cotton business.

Annual Income: His annual income will be about $75,000 this year; their assets include several thousand acres leased for farming and approximately $1 million earned through the sale of her family's land.

Life at Home

- A cotton broker for the past 30 years, Wilton Hayslett knows that little is predictable about this profession and the fluctuating price of cotton; therefore, he demands consistency at home.
- Every morning he rises at 5:00 a.m., as did his father and grandfather, both farmers, and goes for a walk.
- When he returns he expects his breakfast to be ready and the newspaper on the table.
- His wife Bonnie normally prepares eggs, bacon, juice, fresh fruit, biscuits and grits.
- It is the only meal of the day she prepares; the family cook is in charge of the big noonday meal and assists with the evening meal before she leaves each night.
- After breakfast, Wilton dresses in a white shirt, black suit, black tie, black shoes and a hat; his apparel does not vary whether he is going to work, church or a funeral.

Wilton Hayslett has been a cotton broker for 30 years.

The cotton industry has been an important part of Gulf Port's history.

- Wilton and Bonnie eat together at 1:00 p.m. every afternoon he is in town; afterwards he takes a 20-minute nap.
- He is home by 6:00 p.m., unless he is ushering at church or helping raise money for the Boy Scouts; as a teenager, he was an Eagle Scout.
- Their only child, a 30-year-old son, is severely mentally retarded and has been institutionalized since he was 12.
- Because Wilton was born and raised on a cotton farm near Gulf Port, Mississippi, going into the cotton business seemed only natural.
- Bonnie's family, also in the cotton business, owned thousands of acres of land, some of it acquired around 1815.
- Through the years, Wilton and Bonnie have quietly sold off pieces of property as the Gulf Port community has grown.
- Today the clubhouse for the country club's golf course stands on the exact spot where her grandfather built his first cabin 100 years ago.
- In addition to the cook, the Haysletts employ a gardener and two maids.
- One of the maids, a black woman named Etta, was raised with Bonnie on the family farm after both Etta's parents were killed in a farming accident; she has worked her entire life as a maid for Bonnie.
- Wilton believes that something must be done to help the Negro; many of the laborers and all of his servants are black, and most have little more money or status than they had two decades ago.
- He does not believe integration is the solution, though he knows it is inevitable; he feels, rather, that Booker T. Washington had the answer: education.
- Although he rarely talks about it, he and his wife have paid for three of his gardener's children to attend Morehouse College in Atlanta; they also helped Etta's only daughter go through secretarial school.
- A member of the downtown Baptist Church, Wilton believes that too many young people are straying from religion to chase money and good times; not enough people want to work hard anymore.
- He and his wife are proud that they tithe to the church, giving away 10 percent of their income; the west window of the church is dedicated to Wilton's mother, who passed away a dozen years ago.
- When not worrying about the changing price of cotton, he focuses on his other love, supporting the Billy Graham crusade.
- He recently served as a volunteer during the Madison Square Garden crusade; one of thousands of assistants, he has volunteered five times in the past two years as a counselor.

"God in the Garden" *Time*, May 27, 1957:

" 'Hear the word of the Lord, ye rulers of New York; give ear unto the law of our God, ye people of New York.' The words were the prophet Isaiah's—about Sodom and Gomorrah—but the voice was the Southern smoothness of Billy Graham coming over the 18 loudspeakers in Manhattan's Madison Square Garden. The voice beat upon more than 18,000 people—seekers and servers of the Lord as well as the merely curious—and it etched itself upon the sliding ribbons of the tape recorders set up by radiomen. The evangelist of the mid-century set out last week on his toughest 'crusade'—to bring salvation to New York's eight million sinners.

If the heart of the crusade is Madison Square Garden, its head is a seven-room suite in Times Square where 35 permanent staff members, 30 temporary employees and more than 200 volunteer clerical workers control a hectic, complex organism. Automatic typewriters clack out letters appealing for prayer; duplicating machines roll out instructions and memorandums. On wall maps of New York, the U.S. and the world, red, blue and green pins and tape spot churches (1,510 in Greater New York) and prayer groups supporting the campaign. Staff members: 1) channel the activities of 108,415 'prayer partners' in the U.S.; 2) keep tabs on 158,817 'prayer partners' in 48 other countries; 3) ride herd on the 'active' cooperating ministers, the 'partial supporting' ministers and the 'undecided' ministers; 4) process applications for blocks of seats ('Lancaster, Pennsylvania, wants 2,000').

Long before the crusade began, the personal counseling staff signed up 4,000 applicants in 11 centers throughout the city for a nine-week course in Scripture, how to apply Bible lessons, how to handle people's problems. (Among the carefully drawn-up list of traits that disqualify applicants for counseling posts: inability to communicate, argumentative or surly attitude, unkempt appearance, and halitosis.) Of the 4,000 applicants, 3,800 stuck the course to the end,

2,143 qualified as counselors, and 350 were held in reserve. The counselors are evangelist Graham's shock troops.

New Yorkers who came to the Garden for the beginning of the crusade last week—many in buses chartered by their own church organizations—had several surprises. First was the strange sensation of walking into the Garden without a ticket and, even stranger, being directed to a seat by a polite, quiet-voiced usher who seemed to know the difference between a shepherd and a sheepherder. Second was the clear air of the Garden's interior without its usual blue haze of cigarette smoke; hot-dog stands throughout the building were cigaretteless for the duration, and strips of cardboard covered the signs that normally announced 'BEER' (a checkroom was converted to a Bible shop). Third surprise was the crowd itself: quiet, well-dressed, all ages—there was nothing to distinguish it from the audience at the Radio City Music Hall.

And there was little to distinguish the atmosphere of what followed from that of a church. Choir director Cliff Barrows led a 1,500-voice mixed choir in the old gospel hymn, 'Blessed Assurance,' and then called upon the whole audience for 'All Hail the Power of Jesus' Name.' A Scripture lesson was read, an offertory prayer said, the collection taken (in delicatessen buckets of waxed cardboard, quieter than wood or metal). Suddenly, there was Billy Graham.

His handsome hawk face tanned beneath his wavy blond hair, his silk suit in faultless press as he paced and prowled the platform, waving, folding and pounding a limp-bound Bible, Graham was a new kind of evangelist, without the crowd-pleasing tricks of Billy Sunday or the trappings of Aimee Semple Macpherson. His evident sincerity, efficiency and unfaltering faith in his dependence on the power of God are far more important influences on the people who hear him than the things he says or the way he says them.

(continued)

"God in the Garden" (continued)

Those who heard him before found Graham at the start of his New York campaign a shade more subdued than usual. He was passionate, particularly when he expounded the sinfulness of man, his long arms hammering in all directions at the crowd, with the words: 'You are guilty! You are guilty! You are guilty!' He was warmly appealing, as when he offered the Gospel as balm for mankind's illness, as the solution for spiritual and personal problems. But each time he deliberately eased his listeners down again with a pulpit joke or a homely family anecdote—such as the time he bought his wife a bargain diamond which under the lens turned out to be flawed. 'God looks at you too with his magnifying glass and sees your faults.'

The most critical and moving part of every evening's preaching is the 'invitation'—when Graham calls for those moved to commit their lives to Christ and come forward to the platform. The moment is carefully planned: 'When asked to bow our heads and close our eyes, do so,' say the mimeographed instructions to counselors. 'Then open your eyes and watch as unnoticeably as possible . . . watch for those of your own sex and age who are responding, and accompany them to the front . . . DO NOT BLOCK THE AISLE AT ANY TIME.' Graham's words now vary little, from evening to evening, and he delivers them hunched forward over the lectern—tensely, urgently, often a trifle hoarsely:

'I'm going to ask you to do something that I've seen people do all over the world. I've seen the Congressman, the governor, the film star. I've seen lords and ladies. I've seen professors. I'm going to ask every one of you tonight to say: "Billy, I will give myself to Christ, as Savior and Lord. I want to be born again. I want a new life in Christ. I want to be a new creation in Christ tonight. I'm willing to come to the Cross in repentance." If you say that, then I'm going to ask you to do a hard thing. Nothing easy. The appeal of Communism today partially is because it's a hard thing. They demand great things. Jesus demanded no less.

'I'm going to ask every one of you to get up out of your seat—over here, in the balcony, everywhere—and come quietly and reverently. I don't want a person to leave the Garden, not one person. I'm not asking you to join a church tonight. I am not asking you to come to some particular denomination. I am asking that you need Christ, your heart is hungry for Christ.

'You may be a deacon or an elder, I don't know. You may be a Sunday school teacher. You may be a choir member. You may be an usher, but you need Christ tonight. Young man, young woman, father, mother, whoever you are, come right now. Just get up out of your seat and come now. Quickly right now, from everywhere you come, from up in the balconies all around, up here, back there. All of you that are coming, come right now, we're going to wait. You come on now.'"

- Proud to be a part of bringing salvation to New York's eight million sinners, he was especially pleased that he could accompany a called Christian to the front when it was time for the altar call.
- He is angry that the press seems so cynical about this great crusader's efforts to bring Christ to the world.

Life at Work

- The cotton industry is in the doldrums; since 1954, it has been difficult for cotton brokers to turn a profit.

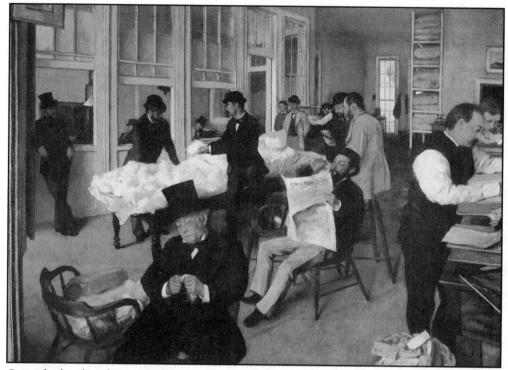

Cotton brokers have been part of the Southern culture for many years.

- To create more incentives for success, Weil Brothers Cotton has been issuing company stock to its top managers, who previously shared in the profits of the company through a bonus pool.
- Weil Brothers is also demanding that managers stay in constant touch with the head office to ensure a perpetual give-and-take of business intelligence and advice.

Today's brokers live in a world of constantly shifting prices and demands.

Mechanization has improved the profitability of cotton throughout the South.

- Wilton joined the cotton industry as an accountant in the late 1920s, discovering during his first months on the job that the manager of his office was juggling the books for his own personal benefit.
- Most recently, the manager had taken a heavy position in low-grade cotton, but kept the sale off the company books.
- Had the weather lived up to its wet and miserable expectations, he would have made a bundle, but when the skies brightened and low-grade cotton became scarce, he was unable to deliver what he had contracted for.
- When impatient textile mill managers immediately began calling the home office demanding the promised cotton, Weil Brothers launched an investigation with Wilton's help.
- His honesty and cooperation catapulted his career, and he was named manager of the office the next year; as a result, he never spent time as a "classer" of cotton, normally a critical requirement for any cotton broker.
- He believes in volume and will take calculated risks when he buys cotton if the volume is high enough to justify a quality return.
- Although casual about many issues, he believes that temperance is important, and does not trust anyone who regularly has a drink after work.
- He also thinks that idleness is demoralizing; during long summer days, before the cotton harvest is in, he invents jobs for his office personnel so they will not play checkers.

"Challenge to Cotton," *Time*, June 10, 1957:

"How much does the cotton support program cost taxpayers? Last week Lamar Fleming, Jr., board chairman of Anderson, Clayton and Co., the world's largest private cotton dealer, dug into Government figures and came up with the staggering total of $1.156 billion as the cost for this year. In a speech to the American Cotton Congress in Dallas, Fleming, a crusader for sound farm policies, pointed out that this equals more than $1,000 for each of the 850,000 farms on which cotton is grown.

Fleming's figures are underlined in a press conference in Washington where Agriculture Secretary Ezra Taft Benson took pride in the fact that his department this fiscal year is selling 7.5 million bales of surplus cotton abroad v. total U.S. cotton exports last year of 2.2 million bales. But Benson conceded that the Government will lose $530 million by selling cotton for an average $115 a bale v. the Government cost of $186."

- Simply to keep his staff busy, he will occasionally even send them around to visit farmers.
- No one questions his orders or his leadership, since his successful track record speaks for itself.
- In his ever changing world, within one hour he will put in a straddle order, bemoan the imminent collapse of western civilization, give a buy order to his stockbroker in New York, solicit donations for the Gulf Port United Way, make arrangements to testify in a court case and read a Bible reflection from a monthly publication sent to him by his church.

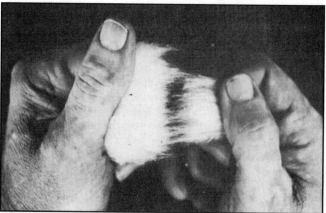

Learning to "class" cotton is an art.

- He also spends considerable time in the sample room where cotton samples, cut from bales in warehouses, are examined for color, trash content, staple (length) and character of fiber—the criteria that will determine the cotton's eventual use and relative worth.
- Cotton that has already been examined will pile up ankle-deep on the floor until it is swept away at the end of the day for resale as cotton waste; during the peak season, from September to March, visitors often remark that they feel like they are walking on clouds.
- The company was created by brothers Isidor and Herman Weil, Jewish immigrants from Germany who settled in Opelika, Mississippi.
- At that time the United States not only grew more cotton than any nation on earth, it spun most of it.
- Although important, length is not the only consideration when buying cotton, which comes in many variations of color, brightness, purity, resilience, tensile strength—all qualities that depend on the seed, vagaries of the weather, type of soil, and how the cotton was cultivated, harvested and ginned.
- Because the economics of the cotton business are firmly based on supply and demand, brokers like Wilton make money by estimating the demand for the various grades of cotton in relation to their probable availability—an exercise in educated guesswork that then determines what price to pay for the cotton based on what he can get for it.

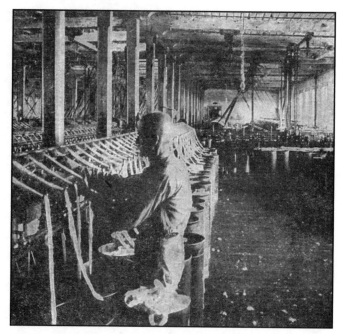

- Since the price of cotton often varies greatly from day to day, he can easily be wrong, but can reduce his risk by hedging his transactions on the futures exchange; at this company, a hedge is made on each purchase.
- Often, he will only agree to buy 10,000 bales of spot cotton if he can sell 100 contracts (of 100 bales each) on the futures market the same day at a profit.

Life in the Community: Gulf Port, Mississippi

- This city of 40,000 on the Mississippi Sound and the Gulf of Mexico has always tied its fortune to transportation and shipping, especially of cotton.
- Laid out in 1887 as the terminus for the Gulf and Ship Island Railroad, Gulf Port became the center for timber distribution.
- By the 1920s, the community was focusing on cotton—building warehouses, compresses and mills—eventually

Textile mills dominate the labor force of the South.

becoming a major seaport with deep-water access to the Gulf, capable of bringing in lumber, bananas, cotton and seafood.

• It also serves as a major port for sport fishermen seeking speckled trout, pompano, tarpon, redfish and shrimp.

• Like many men who grew up in Gulf Port, Wilton hunted extensively as a child, waiting especially for the months when migratory waterfowl such as teal, wood ducks, mallards and canvasbacks were in season.

HISTORICAL SNAPSHOT
1957

- The Federal Communications Commission approved American Telephone and Telegraph Company's plan to send U.S. programming to Cuba via a "scatter propagation" system, which deflected TV waves off particles high in the atmosphere and transmitted them over the horizon without a relay

- A record 4.3 million babies were born in the U.S.

- After three years of scientific experimentation costing $200 million, Great Britain dropped its first H-bomb off Christmas Island, 1,160 miles south of Hawaii

- Per capita margarine consumption exceeded butter for the first time

- *Sputnik I,* the world's first manmade earth satellite, was launched by the Soviet Union

- Allen Ginsberg's book *Howl* was seized by the police for being obscene

- The Everly Brothers' song "Wake Up, Little Susie" was banned in Boston

- On the third anniversary of the U.S. Supreme Court's Brown v. Board of Education decision, Bobby Lynn Cain graduated from Clinton High School (Tennessee), the first black in the state ever to graduate from an integrated school

- A University of Wisconsin study showed that 20 percent of Americans lived in poverty

- The first civil rights legislation since 1872 passed despite South Carolina Senator Strom Thurmond's record 24-hour, 18-minute filibuster

- The painkiller Darvon was introduced by Eli Lilly

- Philip Morris switched from its brown cigarette package to a more colorful one to meet the competitive demands of television advertising

- The terms "Asian flu," "meter maid" and "funky" all entered the language

- *Fortune* named Paul Getty the richest American, estimating his worth at more than $1 billion

- One in three women regularly went to a beauty shop; apricot- and silver-colored hair remained popular

- Volkswagen sold 200,000 Beetles

- The Massachusetts governor reversed the 1692 witchcraft convictions of six Salem women

1957 ECONOMIC PROFILE

The national consumer expenditures (per capita income) in 1957 were:

Auto Parts	$11.68
Auto Usage	$196.76
Clothing	$120.28
Dentists	$10.51
Food	$437.89
Furniture	$26.27
Gas and Oil	$59.55
Health Insurance	$9.34
Housing	$229.46
Intercity Transport	$7.01
Local Transport	$11.68
New Auto Purchase	$73.57
Personal Business	$66.56
Personal Care	$26.86
Physicians	$26.86
Private Education and Research	$18.09
Recreation	$92.25
Religion/Welfare Activities	$23.94
Telephone and Telegraph	$21.02
Tobacco	$33.28
Utilities	$67.73
Per Capita Consumption	$1,665.75

Annual Income, Standard Jobs

Average of all Industries, Excluding Farm Labor	$4,657.00
Average of all Industries, Including Farm Labor	$4,546.00
Bituminous Coal Mining	$5,086.00
Building Trades	$5,120.00
Domestics	$2,050.00
Farm Labor	$1,657.00
Federal Civilian	$5,203.00
Federal Employees, Executive Departments	$4,073.00
Federal Military	$3,439.00
Finance, Insurance and Real Estate	$4,314.00
Gas and Electricity Workers	$5,247.00
Manufacturing, Durable Goods	$5,207.00
Manufacturing, Nondurable Goods	$4,540.00
Medical/Health Services Workers	$2,612.00

Miscellaneous Manufacturing...... $4,195.00
Motion Picture Services.......... $4,745.00
Nonprofit Organization
    Workers...................... $3,533.00
Passenger Transportation
    Workers, Local and
    Highway.................... $4,449.00
Personal Services $2,999.00
Public School Teachers........... $4,085.00
Radio Broadcasting and
    Television Workers............ $6,756.00
Railroad Workers................ $5,416.00
State and Local Government
    Workers...................... $3,747.00
Telephone and Telegraph
    Workers..................... $4,471.00
Wholesale and Retail
    Trade Workers $5,119.00

Selected Prices

Butter, Pound...................... $0.79
Camera Film $0.43
Cat Food, Puss N' Boots $0.39
Chain, Swank Sterling Silver.......... $2.50
Cough Syrup $0.49
Eggs, Dozen...................... $0.58
Electric Iron...................... $9.88
Fry Skillet $15.95
Grandfather Clock, Antique........ $345.00
Lawn Sprinkler $6.50
Magazine, *Boy's Life*.............. $0.25
Milk, Quart...................... $0.60
Movie Projector................... $89.95
Pillow, Goose Down $14.97
Railroad Fare, Chicago to
    San Francisco................... $63.12
Shaver, Lady Norelco $24.95
Shirt, Man's, Arrow................. $5.00
Socks, Men's $0.37
Stereo........................... $129.95
Vodka, Smirnoff, Fifth $5.23

"The Cotton Surplus, New Hope for a Permanent Cure," *Time*, September 17, 1956:

"Old King Cotton has been sick for years and getting progressively worse. But now, for the first time since the Korean War, there are hopeful signs of recovery. In the 1956–7 marketing year the staggering cotton surplus, currently at an all-time record 14.1 million bales, is expected to level off or perhaps even decline a bit. More important, the Government is trying new medicines on cotton, all aimed at effecting a permanent cure in the years to come.

Last week the U.S. Export-Import Bank lent Japan $60 million to be used for importing more raw cotton from the U.S. The loan was one part of a broad program designed to boost both overseas and domestic consumption while holding down production. The goal for 1956–7 is a 20 percent to 25 percent increase over total cotton sales in 1955–6 by doubling exports to 4.5 million bales while keeping domestic consumption at last year's 9.2 million-bale level, or even increasing it. With flexible price support between 75 percent and 90 percent of parity, Agriculture Secretary Ezra Taft Benson hoped that minimum acreage allotments (17.4 million acres in 1957) and marketing quotas (11 million bales) will hold next year's crop to 13 million bales, or about this year's level. Furthermore, under the new soil-bank program Benson hopes that farmers will increase the number of acres taken out of production well beyond last year's 1,064,000-acre total. Though some cottonmen fear that only the poorest acreage will be allowed to lie fallow, and that farmers will produce as much as ever by working their remaining acres harder, most applaud the program.

The biggest battle will be fought in the world market, where the U.S. has been taking its worst beating. The U.S. hopes to dispose of much of the surplus by stepping up grants and loans to underdeveloped nations, selling the rest. Though the U.S. is flatly against 'dumping,' i.e., selling at any price, it has moved into world markets with a big program to dispose of some seven million bales of high-grade Government-owned cotton abroad at competitive world prices by subsidizing U.S. exporters, and has already sold three million bales. On the total, the U.S. stands to lose as much as $220 million (it paid $0.32 per pound for the cotton and can sell it for, at most, $0.25 per pound).

Heavy exports of cotton at world prices may reduce U.S. raw cotton supplies, but they will also boost foreign production of cheap finished textiles—to the detriment of competing manufacturers, who still pay U.S. prices. The Government's answer is still another program: textile exports will get a $0.0658-per-pound subsidy on cotton products made for export, and will thus be able to cut prices to compete in world markets.

While many cottonmen cry for higher tariffs or strict import quotas, the Administration is determined not to give in. Textilemen want protection, demand restrictions on Japan, which is 'flooding' domestic markets with cheap finished cotton goods, forcing the closing of some U.S. mills. Actually, Japanese exports to the U.S. are barely 2.5 percent of the U.S. cotton-goods market. Moreover, Japan is also one of cotton's best customers, buying $120 million worth of raw cotton last year from the U.S. To still the protests, the U.S. has worked out agreements for voluntary curbs, e.g., Japan has pledged to limit exports to the U.S. of cotton cloth blouses."

1960–1969

The 1960s were tumultuous. Following the placid era of the 1950s, the seventh decade of the twentieth century contained tragic assassinations, momentous social movements, remarkable space achievements, and the longest war in American history. Civil Rights leader Martin Luther King, Jr., would deliver his "I have a dream" speech in 1963, the same year President John F. Kennedy was killed. Five years later in 1968, King, along with John Kennedy's influential brother Bobby, would be shot. And violent protests against American involvement in Vietnam would be led and heavily supported by the educated middle class, which had grown and prospered enormously in the American economy.

From 1960 to 1964, the economy expanded; unemployment was low and disposable income for music, vacations, art or simply having fun grew rapidly. Internationally, the power of the United States was immense. Congress gave the young President John F. Kennedy the defense and space-related programs Americans wanted, but few of the welfare programs he proposed. Then, inflation arrived, along with the Vietnam War. Between 1950 and 1965, inflation soared from an annual average of less than two percent (ranging from six percent to 14 percent a year) to a budget-popping average of 9.5 percent. Upper class investors, once content with the consistency and stability of banks, sought better returns in the stock market and real estate.

The Cold War became hotter during conflicts over Cuba and Berlin in the early 1960s. Fears over the international spread of communism led to America's intervention in a foreign conflict that would become a defining event of the decade: Vietnam.

Military involvement in this small Asian country grew from advisory status to full-scale war. By 1968, Vietnam had become a national obsession leading to President Lyndon Johnson's decision not to run for another term and fueling not only debate over our role in Vietnam, but more inflation and division nationally. The antiwar movement grew rapidly. Antiwar marches, which had drawn but a few thousand in 1965, grew in size until millions of marchers filled the streets of New York, San Francisco, and Washington, DC, only a few years later. By spring 1970, students on 448 college campuses made ROTC voluntary or abolished it.

The struggle to bring economic equality to blacks during the period produced massive spending for school integration. By 1963, the peaceful phase of the Civil Rights movement was ending; street violence, assassinations, and bombings defined the period. In 1967, 41 cities experienced major disturbances. At the same time, charismatic labor organizer Cesar Chavez's United Farm Workers led a Civil Rights-style movement for Mexican-Americans, gaining national support which challenged the growers of the West with a five-year agricultural strike.

As a sign of increasing affluence and changing times, American consumers bought 73 percent fewer potatoes and 25 percent more fish, poultry, and meat and 50 percent more citrus products and tomatoes than in 1940. California passed New York as the most populous state. Factory workers earned more than $100 a week, their highest wages in history. From 1960 to 1965, the amount of money spent for prescription drugs to lose weight doubled, while the per capita consumption of processed potato chips rose from 6.3 pounds in 1958 to 14.2 pounds eight years later. In 1960, approximately 40 percent of American adult women had paying jobs; 30 years later, the number would grow to 57.5 percent. Their emergence into the work force would transform marriage, child rearing, and the economy. In 1960, women were also liberated by the FDA's approval of the birth-control pill, giving both women and men a degree of control over their bodies that had never existed before.

During the decade, anti-establishment sentiments grew: men's hair was longer and wilder, beards and mustaches became popular, women's skirts rose to mid-thigh, and bras were discarded. Hippies advocated alternative lifestyles, drug use increased, especially marijuana and LSD; the Beatles, the Rolling Stones, Jimi Hendrix, and Janis Joplin became popular music figures; college campuses became major sites for demonstrations against the war and for Civil Rights. The Supreme Court prohibited school prayer, assured legal counsel to the poor, limited censorship of sexual material, and increased the rights of the accused.

Extraordinary space achievements also marked the decade. Ten years after President Kennedy announced he would place a man on the moon, 600 million people around the world watched as Neil Armstrong gingerly lowered his left foot into the soft dust of the moon's surface. In a tumultuous time of division and conflict, the landing was one of America's greatest triumphs and an exhilarating demonstration of American genius. Its cost was $25 billion and set the stage for 10 other men to walk on the surface of the moon during the next three years.

The 1960s saw the birth of Enovid 10, the first oral contraceptive (cost $0.55 each), the start of Berry Gordy's Motown Records, felt-tip pens, Diet-Rite cola, Polaroid color film, Weight Watchers, and Automated Teller Machines. It's the decade when lyrics began appearing on record albums, Jackie and Aristotle Onassis reportedly spent $20 million during their first year together, and the Gay Liberation Front participated in the Hiroshima Day March— the first homosexual participation as a separate constituency in a peace march.

1961 FAMILY PROFILE

Wes Cameron, 42, has built his company into the world's largest Ford dealership through hard work, hard sell and personal TV pitches. He lives in Lincolnwood, outside Chicago, with his wife Violet and their three children.

Annual Income: $175,000 a year, including $150,000 from his Ford dealership and $25,000 from a separate leasing corporation; his multimillion-dollar investment portfolio provides him and his family with additional capital when needed.

Life at Home

- Wes Cameron has pushed, prodded and sold his way to his dream—creating the largest car dealership in the nation.
- Half Irish and half Italian-German, he is endowed with a natural enjoyment of people and a gift for conversation that together make him a natural salesman.
- Wes is a member of many charitable, civic and religious groups, appearing on TV talkathons for charity, and is a Roman Catholic layman; he also coaches a Little League team that won a district championship last year.
- He supports several religious causes in the area, and even provides clergymen with cars at cost.
- Annually, his dealership sponsors the Lake Michigan endurance swim as part of his $1 million annual advertising budget.
- He and his wife Violet live in a sprawling, nine-room ranch house in Lincolnwood, a Chicago suburb, with their son and two daughters.
- He also owns three motorboats, a summer home in the country and a winter home in Florida.
- His house in Lincolnwood includes a 30' x 60' swimming pool which he shares with neighborhood children, even hiring a lifeguard to watch over

Wes Cameron is endowed with a natural enjoyment of people and a gift for conversation.

Violet lives in a sprawling ranch house in Lincolnwood, outside Chicago.

them; though he built the pool for exercise, he also swims 44 laps every afternoon at the Illinois Athletic Club.

- He began his selling career at age eight, when he sold soda pop in his neighborhood; when he was 12, he took a paper route and an after-school job at a service station to help his mother and sister pay bills after his father died.

- He never went to college; instead, he first parlayed his fascination with cars into a job at a service station, then as owner of his own gas station.

- After serving time in the army during World War II, he took advantage of the car shortage in 1943 by setting up a used-car lot.

- In 1945, he bought a failing Ford dealership, but Ford gave the lucrative franchise to someone else, after which he opened a Hudson automobile dealership.

- While appearing on TV with other Hudson dealers to promote a wrestling match, he found his calling; his appearance was such a big hit, he took over the wrestling sponsorship and became one of the on-air personalities.

- After that came a TV variety show of his own, a barn dance and late movies, with Wes making his pitches at intermission.

- Before long, he was Hudson's number one U.S. dealer, selling more than 10 percent of the factory's products, but his eagerness brought both success and problems.

- When he began offering a "lifetime guarantee" against defective parts in his cars, customers complained that he met their objections by insisting that the parts were worn by age, not by defect.

- His aggressive salesmen were accused of illegal practices, including bushing—persuading the customer to sign a blank contract, then filling in numbers different from those agreed upon—and the file at the Chicago Better Business Bureau grew thick.

- When Wes saw that Hudson was not keeping up with the times by sticking to its backward styling, he switched to Ford.

Life at Work
- Wes has learned to take full advantage of the power of television, appearing in his own commercials to promote his dealership and, in the process, becoming a TV personality.
- A handsome man with curly blond hair and steely blue eyes, he possesses a voice that captures attention, whether he is speaking in person and on television.
- Standing 6'1", he ends his commercials by looking into the viewer's eyes and intoning the words, "God bless you."
- In a recent Chicago poll, he was more popular than national entertainers Ed Sullivan and Steve Allen.
- Rival dealers complain that their own mothers sing the praises of "that honest Mr. Cameron"; throughout Chicago he is known as the Courtesy Man.

Today's customer, he believes, is sharper, shrewder and better informed.

- Sales have consistently risen at this dealership since he took over the franchise, except during the recession of 1958.
- Today, sales are at a record $41 million a year, although the company's net earnings are $117,000, down 55 percent from last year, reflecting the narrow profit margin a dealer has in today's competitive market.
- In 1960, dealers nationwide averaged a $22 profit on each new car sold; as a result, dealer failures were up 43 percent.
- Wes's profit margin is higher, and he believes that dealers must be flexible; "If they can't sell a car for a $300 to $400 profit," he says, "they won't sell it. If we can only sell a car for a $50 profit this month, we have to sell it for a $50 profit. Maybe next month we'll take $40. Maybe the month after that it will be $100. We have to take what the market will bring."
- He is disdainful of efforts to create a factory-fixed fair price agreement, saying, "A lot of dealers are sitting around waiting to be legislated into making a living."
- Today's customer, he believes, is sharper, shrewder and better informed, with many realizing that dealers are overstocked and anxious to deal; as a result, haggling is in its heyday.
- Everyone wants a bargain; dealers are especially frustrated by buyers who shop around from dealer to dealer, using one salesman's figures to cut the price of another.
- Wes has a staff of 94 salesmen to cover the six-block-long dealership complex on Chicago's West Side.
- Personally selling more than 1,000 cars a year, he has an amazing memory for names and can make complete strangers comfortable in minutes.
- When selling, he plays shamelessly on nationalities: if the customer is Irish, he puts on a brogue; if the customer is Jewish or Italian, he has a few phrases to match.

Pure elegance...with a two-year/24,000 mile pledge of excellence*

Now America has a new kind of fine car, one that combines even greater luxury with 14 inches *less* length. Specifically designed for today's close-packed traffic, the new Lincoln Continental is slimmer, easier to park and handle. But its greatest achievement is in standards of quality and reliability...standards so high that it alone, among all American fine cars, is now warranted for two full years or 24,000 miles.

There are so many other pleasures to discover: Doors that open at the center-line for unusual ease of entrance. Contour-zoned seats cushioned with nearly twice the usual amount of foam rubber. The first *hydraulic* windshield wipers, silent and 50 percent more powerful. This country's only four-door convertible. America's largest V-8 engine—and biggest brakes.

This car is so advanced in design and durability it will keep right on revealing new virtues mile after velvet mile—but isn't that just the enduring kind of automobile you've wanted?

Lincoln-Mercury Division, *Ford Motor Company*,

*Ford Motor Company warrants to its dealers, and its dealers, in turn, warrant to their Lincoln Continental customers as follows: That for 24 months or for 24,000 miles, whichever comes first, free replacement, including related labor, will be made by dealers, of any part with a defect in workmanship or materials. Tires are not covered by the warranty; appropriate adjustments will continue to be made by the tire companies. Owners will remain responsible for normal maintenance service and routine replacement of maintenance items such as filters, spark plugs, ignition points and wiper blades.

LINCOLN CONTINENTAL

Last year his dealership led the nation in the number of cars sold.

- Last year his Ford dealership sold 21,000 cars—9,000 new and 12,000 used, more than any Ford dealership in the world; his secret: make every customer believe he is getting the same deal the salesman would offer his very own brother.
- To maintain the quality of his empire, he pays close attention to the details: during his daily tour, he looks in on the new car showroom to make sure it is clean and that sales are at a steady clip; in the service department, he leafs through service orders to detect any

ANNOUNCING THE 1961 FORD FALCON PICKUP

LOW IN PRICE – AMERICA'S LOWEST PRICED COMPACT PICKUP!

What a Falcon saves you on price* could keep your gas tank filled for thousands of miles! And there's more savings to come! Main underbody members are Zinclad-protected against rust and corrosion. Front fenders bolt on for ease of replacement—cost just $29.95 each. Insurance is as much as 15% less. Aluminized muffler lasts twice as long as ordinary types. You save on tires, on brakes, on oil . . . you name it and your Falcon saves it!

*Based on latest available manufacturers' suggested retail delivered prices.

LOW GAS COSTS – OVER 30 MILES PER GALLON IN CERTIFIED TESTS!

In certified tests by the country's foremost independent automotive experts, the Falcon pickup with 144 cu. in. Six scored as high as 38.3 miles per gallon! Average of all tests combined —hills and traffic, as well as moderate speeds on the level—was 30.5 mpg! Low oil costs, too —change it only every 4000 miles!

- Roomy comfort for 3 husky passengers!
- Rides, handles like a passenger car!
- High Falcon fashion inside as well as out!
- Optional Fordomatic Drive available!

1961 Falcon Ranchero, shown here in Montecarlo Red, is available in 8 handsome colors with Color-Keyed Luxury interiors.

ECONOMY NEVER HAD SUCH STYLE

NEW HIGH-PERFORMANCE OPTIONAL SIX!

For '61 Ford's new Falcon Ranchero offers a choice of two modern gas-saving engines — 144 Economy Six and, as an option, a new high-performance 170 Six. Both available with standard or Fordomatic transmissions. And thanks to the simplicity of their proven design, servicing is fast, low in cost!

See your Ford Dealer's Certified Economy Book . . . it proves

FORD TRUCKS COST LESS

LOW LOADING HEIGHT

Cargo-floor to the ground measures a scant 25.2 inches . . . that means easy loading. And what a load! The Falcon Ranchero packs 800 pounds into its big six-foot box! With tailgate flat, there's 7½ feet of load length—room to spare for just about any pickup job going! You can open or close the tailgate with just one hand . . . it locks tight and rattle-free automatically!

If Wes Cameron had his way, dealers would be consulted more often about new models being planned in Detroit.

patterns that might be a problem, and he also drops in on the repair waiting room to talk with customers so their stay will be more pleasant.

- "If you're in the automobile business today," he says, "and your only profit is from selling new cars, you aren't going to make money. You have to be in insurance, financing, repair—the whole ball of wax."
- If Wes had his way, dealers would be consulted more often when auto makers are planning new models, remarking, "If I have $4 million invested in my company, then I should be invited to see what I'm going to have to sell."
- Since 1951, America's new-car dealerships shrank from 47,000 to 32,000, with another 25,000 selling only used cars.
- New-car dealers offer a choice of 17 standard-sized cars and 89 compacts, most offering a variety of models, motors, options and accessories; it is possible to buy a Chevrolet in more than 100,000 different combinations.
- Since American dealers introduced compact cars, the sale of foreign automobiles has dropped dramatically, helping to drive the American economy, which is still showing signs of weakness.
- Currently, national inventories hover at one million cars; some dealers still have unsold 1960 models on their lots.
- To help spur sales, Ford has announced the new Falcon Futura, which features large hubcaps, an opulent interior, bucket seats, deep pile carpets and all-vinyl upholstery.

"Corvair Wins the Race for Chevy," *Business Week*, October 8, 1960:

"The man in the photograph on the cover is making and selling more motor vehicles than anyone else in the world. He is Edward N. Cole, vice president of General Motors Corporation and general manager of its Chevrolet Division. Although an engineer who spouts technical lingo at a hot-rodder's clip, this year he might easily be considered the cleverest marketing strategist in Detroit.

By the end of this year, Cole expects Chevrolet to have sold 2,085,000 cars and trucks, the greatest number in a single year ever sold by any factory. Chevy could even wind up about 300,000 cars ahead of Ford, for the greatest lead it has ever had.

In an auto year that has been somewhat weaker than originally expected, only Cole at Chevrolet and Matthew C. Patterson, boss of Chrysler's Dodge Division and its soaring Dart, are very far ahead of their 1959 sales. Plymouth and Rambler gains are less than half as big as those of Chevy and Dodge.

At Ford Division, General Manager James O. Wright had a completely redesigned standard-sized Ford for 1960 that even some GM people figured was going to sell exceptionally well. But the big Ford has dropped 40 percent in sales. Wright's compact Falcon has succeeded beyond the expectations of everyone. Still the combined Ford Division sales are off eight percent.

Because of the great number of lower-profit Falcons in total sales, Ford's profits have dropped. At Chrysler, the success of the smaller Dart and the compact Valiant also has had to be paid for in slipping profits.

Chevy's Year—Chevrolet's standard-sized car for 1960 was a cleaned-up 1959 design that has done better than the year before by a bare one percent. Yet, for the first seven months, total Chevy car sales are ahead of last year by about

15 percent. There's one reason: the compact, rear engine Corvair—the car that has been widely regarded as the poor relation among the Big Three small cars, the good idea that just didn't work.

Cole, as the saying goes, could cry all the way to the bank. If he had sold 202,000 Corvairs in the 1960 model year (which ended last month), he would have made a normal after-tax profit of something more than 20 percent on his investment; that's the basis on which Corvair prices were set. He actually sold 251,000, exceeding his 'standard volume' by a hefty 25 percent. He also shot 200,000 over his 1.3 million standard volume for the big car. And each car over the standard volume always nets a bigger profit than cars in the targeted production run. Cole's Corvair might be considered in some circles the equivalent of the theater's artistic flop, but it is an unquestioned financial success.

Alone among the Big Three, General Motors doesn't have to explain a slipping profit by pointing to swelling small-car sales. . . .

Ford Strategy—In their desire to be first in the compact class, Ford officials found themselves more concerned with American Motors Corporation's Rambler than with Chevrolet, for Rambler was the front-runner. Falcon got the heavy promotion, and right from the start Ford dealers were encouraged to cut the Falcon price to the bone.

This sends prospects streaming to Ford showrooms to examine the Falcon. When they got the salesman's offer of a trade on their own vehicles though, many lost enthusiasm. That was because the dealer, setting a rock-bottom price on the Falcon, couldn't afford an allowance so high as the owner thought he had coming. If the prospect was really interested in small cars, chances are he headed straight for a Chevy showroom; and right away he got a different pitch."

"The Arabian Bazaar," *Time*, March 24, 1961:

"Aggressive salesmen use so many tricks and traps to sell to the customer—ranging from legitimate gamesmanship to downright shabby conduct—that customers enter a showroom on guard. A sample of unscrupulous tactics:

The highball: The salesman offers an unrealistically high price for the customer's trade-in, then jacks up the price of the new car (often with accessories) to cover the too-high trade-in, or backs off altogether.

The lowball: The salesman quotes a rock-bottom price for the new car to win the customer, then later hikes up the price, declaring that a mistake has been made or that the quoted price was for another model.

The double dip: Two salesmen work on a customer, pretending to be in competition with each other. When the first salesman is turned down, another moves in with a better deal. Later, the two split the commission.

The bush: The salesman persuades the customer to sign a blank contract after he has agreed to certain terms, then fills in figures different from those agreed on, or adds additional costs for such fictitious items as delivery charges, handling costs and excise tax (which is already included in the price). The bush is illegal in some states.

A variation on the bush is to fill out the contract at the agreed-upon figures, sending the customer away satisfied. Then the salesman calls later and informs the customer that a mistake has been made and the car will cost more money—figuring that he will pay the difference rather than go through the whole haggle again. Some salesmen try to close a deal by insisting, 'I can only get it for you at this price today'—though they will be glad to quote the same price tomorrow. Another salesman rushes off into the back room to check the new, low, low price with his boss, but often simply goes for a drink of water. He comes back breathless, bearing the news that his boss has lost his mind and agreed."

- To compete, General Motors plans several new compact convertibles next year, and Pontiac will introduce the sporty, two-door Tempest Coupe.
- Detroit researchers believe that the economic mood of the nation is ripe for "the economic-luxury market."

Life in the Community: Chicago, Illinois

- The television program "The Untouchables," depicting the crime sprees of Chicago mobster Al Capone, is now in its third year and still stirring controversy as letters to newspapers rage against the image it is creating for Chicago and charges of defamation emerge from the estate of Al Capone.

CHICAGO: SHERATON-BLACKSTONE

Traditional host to celebrities and Chicago society, the stately Sheraton-Blackstone sets the pace for attentive service in an atmosphere of French Renaissance splendor. You'll find the modern comforts of your guest room highlighted by the superb appointments that distinguish all twenty-two floors of this gracious lakefront hotel ... apart from the hustle of the Loop yet near the city's fascinations. And the elegant *Cafe Bonaparte* is inspiration for a memorably festive evening.

Sheraton Corporation shares are listed on the New York Stock Exchange.   *Diners' Club Card honored for all hotel services.*

"Visitors yearn to believe Chicago wicked, if only because it makes them feel virtuous. Chicago is everybody's whipping boy."
—John Bartlow Martin, "To Chicago, with Love," *Saturday Evening Post*

- Yiddish-theater star Dina Halpern recently founded the Chicago Yiddish Theater Association, adding a new dimension to a growing theater scene in once-staid Chicago.
- The city is still celebrating its role in electing John F. Kennedy, America's first Catholic president, though accusations still abound that voter fraud, engineered by Chicago Mayor Richard Daly, was the only reason John Kennedy carried Illinois, and subsequently the nation, in a close vote.
- Chicagoan Ray Kroc recently bought Dick and Mac McDonald out for $2.7 million as part of his plans to further expand the McDonald's fast-food chain.
- The New English Bible, a product of 13 years of cooperative scholarship in Britain, has been a runaway bestseller; book dealers' orders in New York, Chicago and San Francisco have resulted in a fifth printing of the new version.

HISTORICAL SNAPSHOT
1961

- U.S. astronaut Alan Shepard became the first American in space on a suborbital flight that lasted for 15 minutes

- As the Cold War continued to heat up, President John F. Kennedy advised "prudent families" to have a bomb shelter; Civil Defense officials distributed 22 million copies of the pamphlet "Family Fallout Shelter"

- FCC Chairman Newton N. Minow called television programming "a vast wasteland—a procession of game shows, violence, audience participation shows and formula comedies about totally unbelievable families"

- Jack Lippes produced an inert plastic contraceptive, known as the intrauterine device, or IUD

- President Kennedy appointed a committee to study the status of women in America

- A Gallup poll of teenagers indicated that 74 percent believed in God and 58 percent planned to attend college

- The United States sent 4,000 servicemen to Vietnam to act as advisors to the South Vietnamese army

- Segregation on all interstate facilities was banned; the Congress of Racial Equality (CORE) organized Freedom Rides to integrate buses, trains and terminals

- The minimum wage rose from $1.00 to $1.25 per hour

- Congress passed legislation making airplane hijacking punishable by death

- New York Yankee baseball player Roger Maris hit 61 home runs in the newly expanded 162-game season

- John Steinbeck's *The Winter of Our Discontent*, Irving Stone's *The Agony and the Ecstasy*, Joseph Heller's *Catch 22*, and Harper Lee's *To Kill a Mockingbird* were all best-sellers

- Readers voted *Peanuts*, *Li'l Abner* and *Pogo* the best comic strips of the year

- The IBM Selectric typewriter, self-wringing mops, certificates of deposit and Coffee-mate all made their first appearance

- The twist craze, led by Chubby Checker, began

1961 ECONOMIC PROFILE

The national consumer expenditures (per capita income) in 1961 were:

Auto Parts	$14.15
Auto Usage	$207.41
Clothing	$125.21
Dentists	$11.43
Food	$462.19
Furniture	$26.13
Gas and Oil	$65.33
Health Insurance	$10.89
Housing	$278.73
Intercity Transport	$7.62
Local Transport	$10.89
New Auto Purchase	$65.87
Personal Business	$65.87
Personal Care	$33.21
Physicians	$32.12
Private Education and Research	$22.32
Recreation	$103.98
Religion/Welfare Activities	$29.94
Telephone and Telegraph	$26.13
Tobacco	$38.65
Utilities	$76.21
Per Capita Consumption	$1,856.92

Annual Income, Standard Jobs

Average of all Industries, Excluding Farm Labor	NR
Average of all Industries, Including Farm Labor	$4,961.00
Bituminous Coal Mining	$5,357.00
Building Trades	$5,938.00
Domestics	$2,356.00
Farm Labor	$1,929.00
Federal Civilian	$6,451.00
Federal Employees, Executive Departments	$4,812.00
Federal Military	$3,813.00
Finance, Insurance and Real Estate	$5,203.00
Gas and Electricity Workers	$6,390.00
Manufacturing, Durable Goods	$6,048.00
Manufacturing, Nondurable Goods	$5,250.00
Medical/Health Services Workers	$3,636.00
Miscellaneous Manufacturing	$4,753.00
Motion Picture Services	$5,871.00

Nonprofit Organization Workers ... $3,684.00
Passenger Transportation Workers,
    Local and Highway $4,966.00
Personal Services $3,810.00
Public School Teachers........... $4,991.00
Radio Broadcasting and
    Television Workers............. $7,384.00
Railroad Workers............... $6,440.00
State and Local Government
    Workers $4,721.00
Telephone and Telegraph
    Workers $5,793.00
Wholesale and Retail Trade
    Workers $5,932.00

Selected Prices
Air Conditioner, Admiral $158.00
Apples, Pound $0.10
Automobile, Corvair $2,850.00
BB Gun, Daisy.................... $12.88
Battery, Auto $7.88
Brassiere, Formfit $3.00

When the grand gesture is expected...
serve the scotch with the background

Martin's 12 Year Old Scotch

ALSO MARTIN'S FINE AND RARE (20 YEARS OLD). BLENDED SCOTCH WHISKIES, 4/5 QUARTS. 86.8 PROOF.
IMPORTED BY McKESSON & ROBBINS, INC., NEW YORK, N. Y. ©McK & R., 1960

NOW...

Discover the only records system that puts all the
facts you need in front of you, at the touch of a button!

Just push *one* button — and out pops a single slide with *all the facts you need* for sound decisions, speedy clerical procedures!

Flat in front of you — and clearly visible — is a range of vital information keyed for instant action with movable, colored signals!

Press again: in goes the old slide and out comes the new slide.

No longer must you guess at trends and usage . . . lose valuable time with old-fashioned vertical card

files and other manual systems.

And it is important to note that even though you may be planning to install a computer system — it cannot be effective without summary control records providing historical data on trends, averages and past performances.

High-speed Electro Kardex is used by a tremendous variety of businesses, both large and small. See how it can help *you* formulate sound decisions, speed up office procedures today.

HIGH-SPEED *Electro* **KARDEX**
by *Remington Rand Systems* DIVISION OF SPERRY RAND CORPORATION
122 East 42 Street, New York 17, N. Y.

Briefcase	$8.00
Can Opener, Electric	$8.44
Charcoal, 20 Pounds	$0.85
Child's Car Seat	$6.95
Cold Medicine, Contac	$1.49
Driving Lessons	$46.88
Lunch, Walgreen's	$0.49
Movie Ticket	$0.75
Pen, Parker-T-Ball Jotter	$1.98
Slacks, Man's Wool	$11.90
Stereo	$124.95
Subway Token, New York City	$0.15
Tape Recorder	$99.95
Water Heater	$229.95

"The Chosen Three for First Space Ride," by Loudon S. Wainwright, *Life*, March 3, 1961:

"Three men and their families stood on a beach near Cape Canaveral and waited to watch a rocket fired. In shorts and summer hats, carrying cameras and field glasses, the group looked like sightseers whose next stop might be Cypress Gardens or Marineland. But the men are not vacationers. They are astronauts from Project Mercury, the prime candidates for a violent, historic event.

Last week the world learned that one of these three would be chosen as the first American, and perhaps the first man, to be launched into space. Some time this spring either John Glenn or Virgil Grissom or Alan Shepard will climb into a small capsule on top of a redstone rocket and wait for the most awesome journey man has ever taken. It will be the same sort of dangerous mission on which, according to persistent and believable reports, one or more of Russia's cosmonauts have already died. The 15-minute ballistic flight will fling the chosen astronaut more than 100 miles high and then drop him and his capsule by parachute into the sea more than 200 miles away

from the launching point. Though all three men will be ready to go, the one finally chosen will not be named until just before the flight.

Glenn, Grissom and Shepard were picked for the first launch team by Robert Gilruth, director of the National Aeronautics and Space Administration's Space Task Group. In announcing his decision, Gilruth made one point emphatically clear: the other two astronauts will still play a big part of Project Mercury. They will be candidates for future rides in the capsule, including the project's climactic mission, an orbital flight three times around the earth."

"Playgrounds, The Boss of Taste City," *Time*, March 24, 1961:

"The American boy lies on his left side, dreaming.

Someday, when I have enough money, I am going to have a house with a massage room, a steam room, a bar, and a bedroom big enough for two 707s. The floor will be covered with a white rug four inches thick, with a polar-bear skin near the hi-fi. And the bed, oh, maneroonian, the bed will be adequate for an exhibition match between the Green Bay Packers and the Los Angeles Rams.

Downstairsville, there is a two-story, chandeliered, oak-paneled living room with teakwood floors and a trapdoor through which you can drop 12 feet into a kidney-shaped indoor pool. 'That,' I'll tell my visitors, 'is where we throw the old, discarded girls.' At the end of the pool is a waterfall, and you can swim through it two-sies into a dark, warm grotto which has wide ledges at the sides, softened with plastic-covered cushions.

The preposterous dream has materialized in a $400,000 Victorian house on Chicago's North State Street, complete from the half-acre bed to the woo grotto. No wonder its owner says, 'Life is beautiful.' He is Hugh Marston Hefner, 34, editor and publisher of *Playboy Magazine*, a sort of editorial whee, whose candy castle—aswarm with *Playboy*'s celebrated center-spread Playmates—symbolizes the expansion of his young empire into show business. Scarcely a year in operation, Hefner's members-only Playboy Key Club has become the largest employer of entertainment talent in Chicago and is the prototype of more girl-filled clubs to follow in virtually every major city in the country. Moreover, Hefner has just announced that in the fall he will start publishing a new biweekly magazine called *Show Business Illustrated*. 'Like *Playboy*, it will offer status, romance, and girls—all that a guy works for in our society.' Will S.B.I. be collecting plenty of sex? Down, playboy. 'If girls were the only motivation for buying our magazines,' says Hefner, 'they wouldn't sell. People would buy

sheer smut. We, on the other hand, are Taste City.'

Fundamental Things. Taste City has many flavors, and they can all be savored at Hefner's Playboy Club. All the customers have membership keys, the closest thing to a Phi Beta Kappa from Yale, and no one except a sick accountant seems to notice that all this costs $50 a key and $1.50 a drink. The place is aquiver with girls dressed as rabbits, the subtle symbol of *Playboy*. They wear more or less what field rabbits wear, and they have what Chicago businessmen call 'majestic mezzanines.' When an expense account walks in, a honey comes up to him and says, 'Good evening. I'm Barbara. I'm your bunny.'

But is she really? No, she is really Hefner's. All bunnies—many of whom have appeared in the magazine—are absolutely forbidden to date the customers. 'However,' says Hefner, 'that does not hold true for the boss.' What the customer gets is good entertainment. Also, according to Hefner, he gets status—merely by being there. 'Few status symbols are left in the world,' he says. 'Sure, these are material things, but awfully fundamental, and the sort of things that made this country prosper.'

Common Stock. Hefner, at any rate, has prospered. A Chicago accountant's son, he is a graduate of the University of Illinois, did freelance cartooning and whetted his appetite on *Esquire*'s staff before starting *Playboy* (now worth more than $10 million) with roughly $10,000 borrowed. In seven years, he has shot past *Esquire* (*Playboy*'s circulation is 1.1 million, *Esquire*'s, 859,000). Hefner's enterprises now push sterling silver Playboy cufflinks with bunnies on them, Playboy party kits, three Playboy-produced jazz LP albums, a weekly syndicated television show, and a new Playboy Travel Service, set up to run coeducational tours abroad that 'will include all those things that the hip guy wants to see: bullfights, sports car rallies—but no bunnies. . . .

Moving by Cadillac limousine or Mercedes-Benz 300 SL between his office and the house that flesh built, Hefner is actually a living promotion stunt, the most conspicuous playboy of the Middle-Western world. He has five servants who, in shifts, work 24 hours a day, sometimes dusting a framed share of Esquire common stock on his bathroom wall, over a sign that says 'In Case of Emergency, Break Glass.' As a precaution, he will set up a nationwide modeling school and agency, which will serve as a vast bunny farm. Having put a wife and two children behind him (he was divorced two years ago), Hefner claims he would make himself 'take a sanity test' if he should contemplate marriage again. Instead, he loves his work. 'My doctor says I do it "with a bright flame",' he boasts. Needless to say, he has never had a vacation."

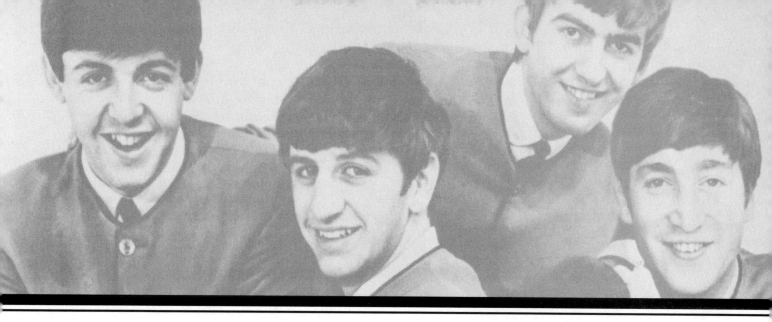

1964 News Profile

"Building the Beatle Image," by Vance Packard, *Saturday Evening Post*, March 21, 1964:

"What causes an international craze like the current Beatlemania?

Press agentry can only swell a craze. To get one started you need to bring into fusion five ingredients. This is true whether the craze involves Davy Crockett, Liberace or Elvis Presley.

Only three years ago it is doubted that any observer of pop culture would have picked the Beatles to inspire madness on both sides of the Atlantic. In 1961 the Beatles affected a beatnik look. They wore black T-shirts, black leather jackets, blue jeans and disheveled hair. In one picture taken of them that year they scowled at the camera as good beatniks would.

Then, along came Brian Epstein, an aristocratic-looking young Englishman who ran a record shop and soon became their manager. First he made them scrub, comb their hair and get into civilized clothing. Then little by little, by a combination of hunch, luck and design, he began exploiting the five ingredients that will create a craze.

First, the Beatles needed a symbol that would make them stand out in people's minds, a symbol such as the coonskin cap that Walt Disney gave to his Davy Crockett creation. For a symbol it was decided to exploit their already overlong hair. The Beatles let it grow longer and bushier, combed it forward—and then had it immaculately trimmed. The result was not only eye catching but evocative. Such hairdos were common in the Middle Ages and the new coiffure suggested the ancient roots of England.

A second ingredient necessary for a craze is to fill some important subconscious need of teenagers. Youngsters see themselves as subjugated people constantly exposed to arbitrary edicts from adult authorities. The entertainment world has developed many strategies to offer youngsters a sense of escape from adult domination. Television producers of children's shows sometimes make adult figures either stupid or villainous. The press agents for some teen stars publicize the stars' defiance of their parents. Teenage crooners relate with amiable condescension their support of their parents.

Rock'n'roll music, of course, annoys most parents, which is one of the main reasons why millions of youngsters love it. But the Beatles couldn't possibly hope to outdo Elvis Presley in appalling parents. Instead of open opposition, the Beatles practice an amiable impudence and a generalized disrespect for just about everybody. They succeed, happily, in getting

Beatle Ringo Starr enjoys his fame.

themselves denounced in some pretty high adult places. The Lord Privy Seal indicated his annoyance. And Field Marshal Lord Montgomery growled that the army would take care of those mop-top haircuts if the Beatles were ever conscripted.

But the Beatles—under Mr. Epstein's tutelage—also have put stress on filling other subconscious needs of teenagers. As restyled, they are no longer roughnecks but rather lovable, almost cuddly, imps. With their collarless jackets and boyish grins, they have succeeded in bringing out the mothering instinct in adolescent girls.

The subconscious need that they fill most expertly is in taking adolescent girls clear out of this world. The youngsters in the darkened audiences can let go all inhibitions in a quite primitive sense when the Beatles cut loose. They can retreat from rationality and individuality. Mob pathology takes over, and they are momentarily freed of all of civilization's restraints.

The Beatles have become peculiarly adept at giving girls this release. Their relaxed, confident manner, their wild appearance, their whooping and jumping, their electrified rock'n'roll pulsing out into the darkness makes the girls want to jump—and then scream. The more susceptible soon faint or develop twitching hysteria. (One reason why Russia's totalitarian leaders frown on rock'n'roll and jazz is that these forms offer people release from controlled behavior.)

A third ingredient needed to get a craze started—as Brian Epstein obviously knew—is an exciting sense of freshness. In an informal poll conducted through my offspring, who are at high school and college, I find that the fact that the Beatles are somewhat 'different'—something new in the musical world—made the deepest impression. Teenagers feel they are helping create something new that is peculiarly their own. And as my 15-year-old expert (feminine) explained, 'We were kind of at a lag with popular singers.'

The delivery, if not the music, is refreshingly different with the Beatles. Surliness is out, exuberance is in. Sloppiness is out, cleanliness is in. Self-pity is out, whooping with joy is in. Pomposity is out, humor is in.

A fourth ingredient needed to keep a craze rolling once it shows signs of starting is a carrying device, such as a theme song. The carrying device of the Beatles is found in their name. It playfully suggests beatnik, but it also suggests 'beat'—and the beat is the most conspicuous feature of the Beatles' music. It is laid on heavily with both drums and bass guitar. When the screaming starts, the beat still gets through.

Finally, a craze can succeed only if it meets the mood of the times. England, after centuries of cherishing the subdued, proper form of life, is bursting out of its inhibitions. There has been a growth of open sexuality, plain speaking and living it up. The Beatles came along at just the right time to help the bursting-out process.

What is the future of the Beatle craze in America? At this point it is hard to say. But the Beatles are so dependent upon their visual appeal that there is a question whether they can sustain the craze in their American territory from across the Atlantic. Another problem is that they are not really offensive enough to grownups to inspire youngsters to cling to them.

Frankly, if I were in the business of manufacturing mophead Beatle wigs, I would worry. Crazes tend to die a horribly abrupt death. It was not so long ago, after all, that a good many unwary businessmen got caught with warehouses full of coonskin caps when the Crockett craze stopped almost without warning."

1965 Profile

David Creswell's trained eye and playful imagination have led him in two distinct directions—architectural preservation and collecting African art. When he is not focused on redirecting the development of Baltimore, Maryland, he travels—often to Africa or Paris—to discover new artwork, much of it based on ancient African patterns, practices and spirits.

Annual Income: He lives on the earnings from his various investments, which exceed $50 million.

Life at Home

- David Creswell's three-story brownstone apartment in Baltimore was burglarized and badly damaged on New Year's eve.
- Although the apartment contained millions of dollars' worth of African art treasures, meticulously gathered over 20 years, the thief took only David's television set, silver and watches—and then spray-painted the walls and smashed many of the African masks.
- After years of being the guardian of architectural standards in Baltimore, he is shocked and disheartened that the city has paid him back in this way, and is spending much of the year in Paris, attempting to recover.
- Besides, in Paris he can enjoy the "culture of the world" without taking a plane anywhere, although he is planning a side trip to the Orient to satisfy his taste for authentic Asian food.
- To assure that he will have appropriate accommodations in Paris, he is keeping a rented apartment available there.

David Creswell has developed a passion for architectural preservation and African art.

Unity of the Universe dance masks from the Bateke tribe represent the harmonious union of the conflicting elements of the universe.

- Raised in a privileged environment, he came from a family whose fortune was made in banking and oil, and he grew up surrounded by impressionist paintings in his home.
- He went to prep school before attending Rhode Island School of Design.
- While he was a sophomore in college, his parents were both killed in a private airline crash; the courts ruled that the accident was the result of faulty airplane maintenance.
- In addition to the millions inherited from his parents' estate, he was awarded $28 million in compensatory damages from the accident.
- Settling in Baltimore, he worked briefly for an architectural firm before establishing his own company, which has been the platform for many of his crusades against the destruction of the city in the name of the "New Baltimore."
- He has also published a wide variety of books and essays on the architecture of the inner city, many of which are focused on saving the concept of inner-city neighborhoods—not simply preserving quality architecture.
- Even before his parents' deaths, he traveled extensively, living in a world dominated by ideas, images and visions—a unique blend of reality and fantasy that others might not immediately see.

"People of Paris," by Herbert Gold, *Holiday*, December 1965:

"Who can say anything about the people of Paris that is not immediately to be contradicted? They are kind and mean, generous and treacherous, graceful and ugly. We can all say that, and also say it about the people of any great city. But we can add one paradox that belongs to Parisians alone: they have contradiction worked more deeply into their blood and bones than the people of any other city in the world. The martyrs and the heroes survive in the memory of the lazy, the grubbing and the indifferent. The merely human live on in the sight of the extraordinary human.

Most visitors return from short stays in Paris shivering with hatred for the Parisians.

The rest leave Paris in despair of ever finding such vividness, such burning examples of both the exalted and the base. Les Flaneurs de Paris—the Strollers of Paris—is a worldwide secret society whose members are recognizable by the glaze of fever in their eyes, that disease known as *la nostalgie de Paris*, which renders life in other places dangerously dim.

When I rented a room from a spectral old widow in the 13th Arrondissement, she took an inventory that seemed to list, number and describe every fly speck on the wall. In advance she threatened to sue me for the slightest scratch or damage to her ruins. Quickly she established the normal condition between the Parisian landlady and tenant: war, terror and desolation. She promised me that the room was heated, but added that when winter came, the 'central heating' was supplied by the rising warmth from the cooking done on the floor below. She pointed a conspiratorial finger: 'Cook a lot.' All the same she tiptoed about to keep from disturbing my labors, and she left gnawed portions of her own lunch at my door with a rude shrug that made it impossible to thank her.

Everyone who has lived in Paris must resolve such puzzles. The romantic lady, truly kind, truly generous, picks your pockets on her way out. The lawyer gives of his time to explain the philosophy behind the Napoleonic Code, but when he is gone, your earlobes are missing. The concierge sniffs away your freedom. And yet, once you have made a friend in Paris, he is your friend forever. You are attuned; he receives the message. He knows when you are ill and sends flowers, soup and books. He tells you his troubles and expects to hear yours. Once you have moved past the meetings in cafés and restaurants to be admitted to his apartment, you have been admitted to the sacred center. You can nevermore shake him loose. He is your friend for life, and your life is wider, deeper, for knowing him.

Not long ago Paris was a walled city. The winding, twisting streets of the Marais and the Saint-Julien-le-Pauvre neighborhood are permanent evidence of the medieval compression and subtlety made necessary by the limits of walls. Some of the rock-shot emplacements of walls can still be seen alongside the new superhighways, which are shooting the city through with a briefly open air, which is immediately plugged up by automobiles. The psychology of the city is still beleaguered, walled up. The people are cautious. The loudest noises are within the self. Many rules are violated, but many rules remain. Within the limits of taste and tact there is the play of wit and malice, joy and freedom. But within. Within the limits, within the complications, within the soul of Paris, that paradise of misery and capital of hope. . . .

The typical schedule of the Parisian day consists of a joyous breakfast of bread and coffee, a mad conniving for money until noon, an outpouring of brotherhood between one and three as friends exchange gossip and ideas over lunch, hence more wrestling with power and the franc until five, then drink, and if possible, love between five and seven, and finally either a locking away into the sacred domicile or an avid roaming of the evening streets, depending on age, condition and disposition. This is not a life of stoic resignation. The Parisian tends to be a furious person, ribald, vengeful, joyous and miserable. A few thick-ankled women and ancient, worn-out gentlemen seem to have found peace in fishing or walking their animals, but the overarching sense of the city is that of insatiability."

David travels extensively to buy art.

- His publisher recently sat in on a witty conversation David had with a woman about how beautiful the gardens of Versailles were at the time of Louis XVI, but they were speaking in the present tense; only later did the publisher realize they were absolutely serious about having met in a previous life.
- David does not hesitate to rent gardens, or even entire buildings, as party settings for his friends; when his imagination is aflight, money is no object.
- His friends look forward to the charming, hand-drawn, whimsical Christmas cards he creates and mails each holiday season.
- Last year, the motif consisted of an intricate landscape with looming castles and futuristic, but highly detailed, trees; to give a festive look to the more than 1,500 cards created, he hired an artist to apply gold leaf to specific details of the drawing.
- David is delighted that rural French furniture style is capturing headlines in the U.S. this year; the Mediterranean influence of heavily distressed finishes on pecan, pine and cherry will be a "vast improvement for most Americans," he believes.
- He also likes the textured and colored walls being displayed in many of the more sophisticated magazines, and is having his home in Baltimore completely redone to wipe away the "sting of invasion" left by the burglary.

Life at Work

- During the past decade, David has consistently been a voice for neighborhood preservation as Baltimore wrestles with blight, corruption and an inferiority complex.
- He is a regular visitor—and often a loud voice—at zoning meetings where developers are petitioning for wholesale changes that often involve the leveling of entire neighborhoods.
- One of his books on neighborhood preservation is now considered a model "call to arms" for neighborhood organizations nationwide—especially those in urban areas.
- His ideas and writings often clash with the desire of the city's commercial establishment to create a "New Baltimore," often, he believes, at the expense of the old.
- He is unsure how he feels about the passage of the Housing and Urban Development Act, which expanded urban renewal and public housing while authorizing rent supplements for lower-income families; although the intent of the new law appears beneficial, experience has taught him that large, federally financed programs normally result in the bulldozing of entire neighborhoods in the name of progress.
- When his public voice is not being heard, he writes about preservation and tours the world collecting high-quality African art.
- He takes his passion for art seriously, spending days at the Musée de l'Homme, studying books and visiting galleries that display primitive art; he has traveled as far as Germany to buy one object in an auction.
- He is particularly fascinated by the concept of "total art," which calls attention to the beauty of ordinary household utensils as well as of ritual or religious articles, and does not hesitate to buy everyday objects such as arm and ankle bracelets, stools and headrests, in addition to very rare Dogon, puni, Kota, Fang and Baule sculptures.
- African sculpture is made by animists who confer a soul onto inanimate objects, even tools and spoons.
- Two years ago, David organized an all-Africa show in Paris, funding much of it himself, to demonstrate to the world the value and quality of primitive African art.
- He arranged for the display of 100 different objects from as many different tribes, spending thousands of dollars of his own money arranging and promoting the show, which in-

cluded a massive gala featuring African musicians and dance groups he flew in for the occasion.

- The show was well-attended, but poorly reviewed; many critics, especially those in the United States, believe that the rustic art of Africa has little to say to the modern world, denying that the work is art or fretting that it has not been signed or dated.
- The concept that a sculpture is not only anonymous, but that so little importance is attached to its age bothers many occidental collectors.
- David's most critical criterion for art is its intended use; the object must have been made not for tourists, but with a ritualistic significance.
- He also looks for African art that shows use and wear, rarely buying objects that are in pristine condition.
- He purchased his first piece of African sculpture when he was 26—two years to the day after his parents died in the airplane crash—and currently has more than 600 objects, including masks, jewelry, reliquaries, statues, beadwork and textiles, some of which are displayed in his home, the rest in storage.
- Many of the works came from French and Swiss collectors, but he often acquires art in Europe from immigrants who have left African colonies that have achieved nationhood.
- Two of his finest pieces were recently donated to the Louvre.
- A recent purchase is from Ivory Coast and depicts a female Baule Kpan mask, whose arresting, 18-inch-tall curved face, crowned by a high headdress of carved braids and chignons, has closed eyes, a long, straight nose and a small, oval mouth with teeth showing; David finds its simplicity arresting.
- The mask was once used as part of a masquerade, a day-long performance in which an entire village marked the death of a notable person or celebrated an important event.
- Another piece bought during the same trip is from Bakwele—a dance mask whose beauty comes from the omission of all irrelevant detail.
- Much of Africa's finest art left the continent or was destroyed years ago; in countries where Islam has been embraced, the destruction has been particularly devastating.

He organized an all-Africa show to demonstrate the value of primitive art.

Life in the Community: Baltimore, Maryland

- Longtime Baltimoreans feel their city is changing in positive ways, explaining, "We used to say, 'We hope you like our city, sir. But if you don't, you can go to the Devil.' We don't feel that way anymore."
- After seeing the city fade into the lengthening shadows of Philadelphia and Washington, and watching centuries-old companies merge with New York-based corporations, Baltimore is ready to change.

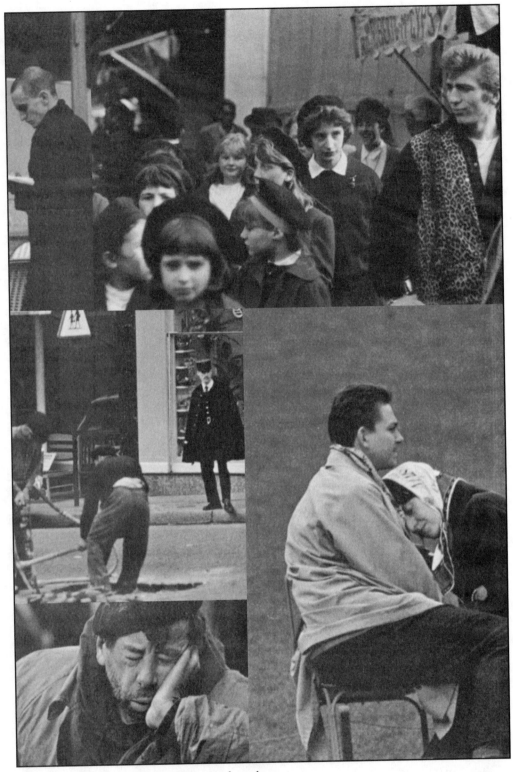

For many, Paris is a city of contradictions and puzzles.

- Local newspapers have campaigned against Baltimore's "branch-plant" status as the city's firms merge with companies such as General Electric, W.R. Grace and Olin Mathieson Chemical Company.

- Meanwhile, other Chesapeake ports have begun challenging the role of the Baltimore Port, long geared to the fortunes of the railroads that link it to the Midwest.
- As a result, more than $165 million is being poured into improvements, including trade missions to London and Brussels to drum up new international commerce for its piers.
- Commercial leaders love to talk about the "New Baltimore," symbolized by the $125 million Charles Center complex of commercial buildings.
- At the same time, two major office buildings comprising 600,000 square feet of office space have been built and are already enjoying an 80-percent occupancy rate.
- Most of the new building also means tearing down—often of once-elegant neighborhoods whose history is only a faint memory.
- David continues to use knowledge, history and a mischievous personality to force developmental compromises; "Not all change is bad, but neither is all change good," he often reminds the zoning board.
- Instead of attempting to stop major developments, he often looks for ways to redirect the destruction away from irreplaceable homes and buildings.
- Not all in Baltimore is changing, however; The Maryland Club, a sanctuary for the city's leaders, has yet to admit its first woman.

HISTORICAL SNAPSHOT
1965

- Americans purchased $60 million worth of prescription weight-loss drugs, twice the dollar amount spent just five years earlier
- "Flower Power" was coined by Allen Ginsburg at a Berkeley antiwar rally
- Quaker Norman Morrison immolated himself on the steps of the Pentagon to protest the U.S. military buildup in Vietnam
- Unemployment, at 4.2 percent, was at its lowest point in eight years
- The 1,250-room Washington Hilton opened in Washington, DC
- The U.S. Immigration Bill abolished national origin quotas
- Avis Rent-A-Car was acquired by International Telephone and Telegraph
- The Voting Rights Act, which eliminated literacy tests and provided federal oversight in elections, stimulated a dramatic increase in voting by African-Americans
- America's place in harvesting seafood fell from first in 1945 to fifth as the country became a major fish importer
- The robust business expansion, begun in 1961, continued without interruption, representing the longest period of economic expansion in peacetime since 1854
- The U.S. Supreme Court struck down a Connecticut statute forbidding the use of contraceptives and eliminated state and local film censorship
- Pope Paul VI visited the United Nations headquarters and delivered a message of peace
- After extended hearings on cigarette smoking, Congress required that cigarette packages carry the warning, "Caution: Cigarette smoking may be hazardous to your health"
- The amount Americans paid for prepackaged food increased $7.5 billion from 1940
- The birth rate fell to 19 per 1,000 people, the lowest since 1940
- Cereal packaged with fruits preserved through freeze-drying was introduced
- Miniskirts, Cranapple, Diet Pepsi, the Sony home videotape recorder and all-news radio stations made their first appearance
- Work began on a 150-mile commuter rail transportation system around San Francisco and Oakland, California
- Kraft foods sponsored the first commercial television program transmitted between the U.S. and Switzerland via the *Early Bird* communications satellite
- More than 70 percent of the world's orchestras resided in the United States
- The production of soft-top convertible automobiles reached a record 507,000
- For the first time since 1962, the administration did not ask Congress for a fallout shelter construction program
- The U.S. Public Health Service announced an ambitious program to eradicate syphilis in the United States by 1972

The beauty of the Bakwele mask comes from the omission of all irrelevant detail.

The Ritualism of African Art

- African ideology is often manifested in cults that aim to increase the life force of the tribal community.
- One of the chief methods of accomplishing this goal is through the ritual dance, whose chief appurtenance is the carved and decorated mask.
- Dances are held during funeral rites, at annual celebrations for the dead and at other occasions such as various rites of passage.
- Dance is central to these events, particularly in agrarian ceremonies, when animal masks may be worn to help unleash the force of nature connected with hunting, cultivation and animal husbandry, all critical to the tribe's survival.
- Dancing is believed to increase the power of the performers themselves.
- Departed elders are considered to be sharing in the performance and acting as powerful intermediaries or channels of power.
- When a man wears the mask of honor of a particular spirit, he is no longer himself but has temporarily become that spirit.
- Some masks are deliberately terrifying and are used to scare away strangers and women from initiation rites and other ceremonies of the various secret societies.
- Certain African art uses a minimum of detail to create abstract masks of enormous beauty.
- Others, notably those of the powerful Ekpo society of the Ibilio, are deliberately macabre.
- In other parts of Africa, a mythical being called Chi wara is traditionally believed to have taught the Bambara to cultivate grain; to celebrate, the young men dance in his honor after hoeing contests during the planting season.
- Images come in all forms, including those to celebrate womanhood in carvings from the Congo.

"Dining in the Far East,"
by Silas Spitzer, *Holiday*, December 1965:

"One bright morning not long ago, my wife and I left Australia on the Qantas jetliner *City of Darwin*, bound north from Sydney to Hong Kong and Tokyo. We were streaking high above the beaches of Queensland when a ginger-haired Australian sitting nearby started a conversation that inevitably got around to: 'What brings you Yanks so far from home?' We explained that we were on a gastronomical tour of the South Pacific and the Far East.

Like most strangers we meet on our travels, he assured us that he, too, had a passion for fine food. Twice a year he traveled to Japan on business. On the return trip he always stopped over at Hong Kong to 'eat some great Chinese food, the real thing, not the imitation stuff you get outside.'

Up to now we were listening with polite marginal interest, but his last words brought us briskly to attention. We were both addicts of Chinese cooking and longed for a taste of the wonderful stuff. We were heading to Hong Kong to appease that craving, but more important still, to determine how 'the real thing' compared with what we had eaten since childhood in Chinese restaurants back home. Would Hong Kong food taste even better? And would we find exciting new dishes unknown in New York and San Francisco?

The midday meal, our first on this airplane, surprised us with its studied elegance. Few restaurants on land could have improved upon the heavy linen, the fine silver and crystal, the superb butter, the crisp rolls and biscuits, or the dexterity with which this five-course meal was served. It started with caviar canapés and kangaroo-tail soup. Then a glass of dry champagne with a half-dozen briny Australian oysters, a Bordeaux-type red wine with the filet of perfectly roasted beef and a spot of cognac after the cheese and dessert. Steaming towels were passed twice during the meal, in the Oriental way. . . .

The ginger-haired Australian on the Sydney plane had obligingly scribbled the names of his favorite Hong Kong restaurants on the back of a menu. Frustrated by his spelling, we showed the list in turn to a room clerk, a barman, the doorman and a trim young policewoman who was checking parked cars outside the hotel. All these nice people grinned and chuckled in the friendliest manner, but in the end admitted they were stumped. As a last resort we interrogated an elderly, bearded Chinese who operated a money-changing bureau on a packing case in an alley off the Nathan Road. Pointing to one of the names on the list, he shouted instructions to a waiting cab driver, and soon we were bowling through narrow, teeming streets to 240 Woo Sung Street, where the restaurant called Tien Heung Lau lurked behind a gaudy red and gold façade.

Inside were several rambling rooms, drenched with ancient accumulated smells of many meals. Nearly all the guests were impassive-faced Chinese, hastily flipping food into their mouths from bowls held below their chins. In America, logically or not, one is cheered by the sight of Chinese customers eating in a Chinese restaurant. Here, in this dim and rather dingy interior, every chopstick wielder was Chinese. None seemed to be eating anything that resembled any dish we were familiar with. Our hopes of finding 'the real thing' rose sharply."

1969 Family Profile

Verne Cringely, a 54-year-old Nashville-based record producer, can proudly claim a long string of country hits resulting in wealth he never imagined as a child. Currently, his effort to downplay some of the roots of country music is causing controversy.

Annual Income: Approximately $250,000 a year, including fees from his recording studio, royalties on hundreds of recordings, and earnings from record projects currently under way; his total assets exceed $15 million.

Life at Home

- Three years ago Verne Cringely, already famous as a record producer of country music, converted an old barn near his home in Mount Juliet, outside Nashville, Tennessee, into a recording studio, which has become a magnet for musicians seeking stardom.
- His original plan was simply to open up a space for his oldest son to cut demo tapes and possibly throw a party or two.
- Since then, the entire operation has blossomed; this year 1,000 recording sessions will take place in the studio.

Record producer Verne Cringely has been a professional musician his entire adult life.

Nashville's WSM has been at the center of country music's growth since the 1930s.

Loretta Lynn and Patsy Cline have both recorded with Verne.

- Verne owns three homes—all in the mountains of the United States.
- His other two houses, one in Colorado and the other in North Carolina, are used by Verne and his wife Claudia only a few times a year; more often, they are lent out to friends.
- Verne enjoys the conveniences afforded by money, but is rarely affected by its presence.
- After years of producing and performing, he has the confidence and the wealth to not worry about impressing anyone but himself.
- He does have a fabulous ear for talent and loves to attract singers to his place.
- Building the studio has provided the perfect balance of professionalism and fun; most of all, he is in control.
- The building has many conveniences, especially its location to his house, but the resonant tin roof rattles during Tennessee thunderstorms, forcing recording sessions to stop until the rain abates.
- Despite his wealth, he is normally more comfortable dressed in flannel shirts and ripple-soled boots than in a coat and tie, and recently threw away all the ties he owned; most days, he drives a pickup truck to work.
- He doesn't hesitate to describe himself as a hillbilly.
- Claudia has a wide circle of friends, mostly outside the music industry; "One musician in the family is one too many," she often says.
- Few fully realize the amount of money he has made through the years, much of it accumulated from royalties on records he has produced.
- Many country records stay on the market for several years, especially those of superstars like Loretta Lynn, Patsy Cline or Kitty Wells—all his clients.
- Born in Macon County, Tennessee, in 1915, he began his life within 100 miles of Nashville, the home of country music.
- While Verne was recovering from an eye injury as a child, his father gave him a crystal radio, which opened his mind and ears to the musical worlds of both country and jazz.
- By the time he was 15, he was so obsessed with playing the piano, he quit school to perform with a local orchestra; he also taught himself to play guitar, harmonica and vibes.
- By 1935, when he was 20 years old, he won a position as an intermission player on radio station WSM in Nashville, making $5 per segment; the station and its music format were at the epicenter of country music at that time.
- Five years later, he graduated to the post of keyboardist and arranger with the 18-piece radio orchestra.
- During the 1940s, he led his own orchestra, often playing country club functions, at the same time learning the craft of country music and doing music-recording sessions at the radio station.

- One of his first recordings was "Blue Mexico Skies," sung by Zeke Clements.
- By 1947, he had joined a major record label as a pianist and arranger; the label's roster included Patsy Cline, Kitty Wells, Loretta Lynn and Conway Twitty.
- Within a decade, he became a record producer with a major label, managing some years personally to create 30 or more albums.
- Loretta Lynn's hit song "Don't Come Home A-Drinking with Lovin' on Your Mind" was recorded at Verne's studio two years ago.
- Recently, the Queen of Country Music, Kitty Wells, famous for her song "It Wasn't God Who Made Honky-Tonk Angels," taped five songs for an album in just three hours.
- He is proud that his son is now in the music business, and pleased his oldest daughter is not.

Verne has produced records by many of country music's greatest stars.

Life at Work

- The music business is tough: Verne likes to tell singers that having a big hit is like having to go to the bank with no money in it; "You wonder where the next is coming from."
- Now that he has converted the barn into a recording studio, he has more control over the sounds he wants to produce.
- A consummate professional, he still loves to describe his production style as being a referee for a bunch of musicians getting together and doing what comes naturally.
- Verne has a hands-on style, both managing the label and producing in the studio, and has been accused of micromanaging, but believes quality begets quality; he is known for choosing the right songs and coaxing the best possible vocal performances from his artists.
- His son and his brother both work for the company, often playing backup on many of the albums he creates.
- Frequently he must balance the demands of Nashville artists with the marketing ideas of New York backers.
- When New York music executives insisted that Patsy Cline's record "I Fall to Pieces" needed to have more of a "pop" sound, Verne added a string section; the record went on to sell millions.
- He has de-twanged other songs he has produced so they will reach a wider audience.
- For most recording sessions, he incorporates a team of musicians hired for a particular record, instead of using an artist's touring band.
- The studio musicians may work with five or six different singers during the week, adapting their style of playing each time.
- Critics say his studio musician formula has sucked the life out of country music, but Verne believes he has pumped the money back in.

Groups like the Jordanaires back dozens of stars, including Elvis Presley.

- For years the name of the artist, not the song, has dominated the industry, but that is now changing; he believes that the song itself should be the star, not the artist or the recording—even though he represents some of the biggest names in the business.
- At the same time, groups like the Jordanaires, who once backed Elvis Presley on many of his recordings, now work almost exclusively for record studios and stay off the road; at $85 per session, each singer can earn $65,000 a year singing in the studio by day and eating home cooking at night.
- Records Verne produces reflect his musical skills, honed through years of playing; when the record is complete the listener hears every instrument.
- What he likes best about the business is that everyone knows everyone else; throughout his career, he has worked with Kitty Wells, Brenda Lee, Patsy Cline, Loretta Lynn, Grandpa Jones, Burl Ives and Charlie Walker—all of whom have contributed to Verne's wealth and fame.
- Many people believe his greatest talent is discovering extraordinary voices and then letting them shine.

"First Angry Man of Country Music," by Tom Dearmore, *New York Times Magazine*, September 21, 1969:

"Why, on the threshold of the 1970s, is the United States reverting to its rurigenous music of the 1930s? To some observers it is almost a comic anomaly that country-western music, the backwoods balm of the Great Depression, should in this time of affluence, technological domination and blasé youth suddenly gain millions of converts among those who once were repelled by it.

Indeed, the country seems to have gone 'country' crazy: 'The Beverly Hillbillies' goes on and on, 'Hee-Haw' is a Sunday prime-time prize of CBS's and 'country' singers have now 'made the network' with their own shows and are recording with the Boston Pops.

Country-western string music was the cultural adrenaline of the thirties and forties in all the little Dullsvilles of the South, suffocating in the humid heat of Saturday nights when the bawling jukebox voices drifted out of slot-in-the-wall honky-tonks. It told of the slovenly, busted boozer, the flawless sweetheart, the fast trains that held some mystic promise, the hobo's death, the cowboy's loneliness. Twangy gospel pieces mapping the road to salvation (a railroad to the pearly gates in more than one instance) were on the same Wurlitzers with low-down music-to-swill-beer-by and the tearjerkers about home and mother. The form appeared in the twenties among the hillbillies and cotton pickers of the poor South—an amalgam of ancient folk balladry, Negro spirituals, fundamentalist gospel pop music and Prohibition jazz. It flowered in the early thirties when the farmers got their battery radios and heard songs both mournful and rousing from WSM in Nashville, wept as Jimmie Rodgers, 'The Singing Brakeman,' related how Hobo Bill died alone but smiling in a frigid freight car.

Many Americans despised it as the banal evocation of a tawdriness of life unworthy of notice, as a nasal cacophony, as ignorance put to music. But it now is not only rising in popularity at home, it is, as John Greenway points out in *The American West* (the magazine of the Western History Association), making headway abroad—it has devotees all over western Europe; there is a 'Tokyo Grand Ole Opry' on the air, featuring bands like Jimmy Tokita and His Mountain Playboys. American country singers have packed the London Palladium and drawn cheers in Hobart, Tasmania, equal to those in Nashville, Tennessee, the capital of country music."

• Currently, he is at the forefront of a movement that gives country music a softer sound by downplaying the steel guitar and country fiddles; he believes that steel guitars can be used as flourishes on some records rather than as the foundation of the song.

The move away from traditional country music is causing tension within the industry.

- This move toward "country pop" or "easy listening country" is causing tension between the artists who believe in the traditional honky-tonk or mountain music sound of country and those who see the softer sound as their way to fame and fortune.
- He denies that he is abandoning country music, insisting he is only updating the sound for modern radio audiences.
- Those in the business claim that a record producer is a creation of technology and art, managing the creative and practical sides of a recording.
- Verne loves doing it all; in Nashville today, it is not unusual for one person to have the authority to sign an artist to a major record label, authorize the budget and then produce the artist's record in a studio at least partially owned by that same individual.
- It is also not unusual for the producer to hold, through various means, at least part of the publishing rights on the songs—one of the reasons that in today's Nashville, the producer is the most powerful individual title in country music.
- Often entire records are cut in two or three days with no overdubbing; the vocals, instrumental solos and background harmonies are generally done at the same time the basic tracks are cut.

Life in the Community: Nashville, Tennessee

- Located inside the encircling ring of the Appalachian Mountains, Nashville has been the capital of country music for most of the century, becoming a candidate for that title after it started beaming out the WSM "Barn Dance" on November 28, 1925.
- The radio show, sponsored by an insurance company, featured performers such as Uncle Jimmy Thompson and Sam and Kirk McGee.

- The station acquired the Grand Ole Opry tag in 1927 when announcer George D. Hay, whose country program followed an hour of classical music, made a pun on the theme of grand opera.
- The Opry staged its first outdoor tent show in 1932, attracting 8,000 people at $0.10 a head.
- By 1941, when WSM (which stood for "We Save Millions," the insurance company's slogan) joined the NBC radio network, the Opry and Nashville obtained a wider audience.
- Featuring music with which rural America could identify, the Opry came to be heard across the nation and Canada.
- The first major artist to record in Nashville was Eddy Arnold in 1944.
- In 1950, Capitol Records was the first big label to begin a Nashville operation, and within 10 years, all of the major record labels had Nashville offices and studios.
- Today, Music Row is famous throughout the world, drawing millions of tourists to the city annually.
- Guidebooks comfort the uninitiated by saying, "You don't have to be a connoisseur of country music to get a kick out of Nashville's country music boom. It's interesting to observe simply as a phenomenon, like the Grand Canyon and Niagara Falls."
- A mandatory stop for country music fans is the Grand Ole Opry House, built originally as the Union Gospel Tabernacle and still equipped with the original, very hard tabernacle pews.
- Reserved seats to the Opry are $3; general admission—$2.
- WSM Music City Bus Tours on Saturdays takes visitors to the wooded clump where Gentleman Jim Reeves died in a plane crash, and to the homes of Webb Pierce, Tex Ritter, Skeeter Davis, Faron Young, Jim Ed Brown, Eddy Arnold, and, of course, Audrey Williams, widow of the legendary Hank.

Today, Music Row and its stars are famous throughout the world.

"We were so poor and everyone around us was so poor that it was the forties before any of us knew there had been a Depression."
—Record producer Chet Atkins, on growing up on his father's 50-acre farm in the Clinch Mountains near Luttrell, Tennessee

"Coast Rock Group at Fillmore East, Crosby, Stills, Nash and Young Offer Concerts in Debut," *New York Times*, September 21, 1969:

"Crosby, Stills, Nash and Young from Los Angeles played here for the first time this weekend with two nights of their unusual brand of polished folk rock.

The group appeared at the Fillmore East Friday and again last night. They are a collection of well-known musicians who banded together last year—David Crosby, formerly of The Byrds, Steve Stills, of the now-defunct Buffalo Springfield, and Graham Nash from The Hollies, a British group. Neil Young, another ex-Buffalo Springfield member, joined them a few months ago. They play both acoustic and electric guitars, and Mr. Stills and Mr. Young switch to piano occasionally during their concerts. This weekend they were accompanied by Dallas Taylor on drums and Greg Reeves on bass.

The group has a slick folk sound of exquisitely wrought local harmonies by the four leaders. They sing mostly their own material, bolstering their pretty voices with occasional brilliant flashes of hard, loud rock."

- For a $1 admission at the Country Music Hall of Fame and Museum, country's faithful can view a 10-minute color film on the history of country music, see how a record is made, peer into a recording studio and then look at the memorabilia of the stars.
- Sights in the Hall of Fame include Eddy Arnold's first guitar, the hat Minnie Pearl wore at her Opry debut, Earl Scruggs's banjo, and Gabby Hayes's boots.
- An entire display case is devoted to the relics salvaged from the 1963 plane crash that took the life of Patsy Cline; the case contains her favorite wig, mascara wand, hair brush and a battered, Confederate-flagged cigarette lighter that still plays "Dixie."
- But Nashville is more than country music, as many of its long-time residents are quick to say; the city prides itself on being a regional financial, wholesale and retail center, drawing customers from middle Tennessee, southern Kentucky, northern Alabama and northeastern Mississippi.
- It does not wish to lose that designation and become too heavily dependent on a single industry such as country music.
- Seven years ago the city of Nashville merged with the outlying suburbs to form a 535-square-mile metro government of half a million people.
- The move was made because the interior of the city was rotting: land values and rentals were dropping downtown, while few new buildings were being built.
- The metro government concept has sparked a boom in Nashville, including its Capital Hill project with a new domed auditorium.
- National Life and Accident Insurance Company, the South's biggest insurance company with $1.5 billion in assets, is constructing a 31-story, $15 million building near the capital complex.
- In addition, a $100 million downtown renewal program has been announced that will rebuild 14 city blocks.
- Banks such as Commerce Union and First American National are contemplating whole blocks as investment projects.

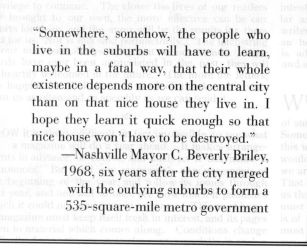

HANK WILLIAMS
JUST ME AND MY GUITAR

This collection conveys the conviction, emotional intensity, and vocal technique which earned Hank his legendary place in country music.

Nashville bus tours still stop at the home of Audrey Williams, widow of Hank Williams.

- The first attempt at creating a metro government in 1958 failed, opposed by center-city Democratic jobholders who feared the country crowd, black leaders who figured it would dilute their voting power downtown, suburban businessmen who feared higher taxes, and hard-core conservatives who viewed governmental centralization as part of a Moscow plot.
- By 1962, attitudes had changed and the move passed with a comfortable majority, forcing suburbanites to pay taxes for downtown problems and, therefore, to suddenly become interested in the solutions, according to city officials, who stress that Nashville's approach brings together all the human resources of the suburbs and the inner city.

"Somewhere, somehow, the people who live in the suburbs will have to learn, maybe in a fatal way, that their whole existence depends more on the central city than on that nice house they live in. I hope they learn it quick enough so that nice house won't have to be destroyed."
—Nashville Mayor C. Beverly Briley, 1968, six years after the city merged with the outlying suburbs to form a 535-square-mile metro government

HISTORICAL SNAPSHOT
1969

- Neil Armstrong, Buzz Aldrin and Michael Collins landed on the moon; Armstrong and Aldrin remained 21 hours, 31 minutes collecting nine pounds, 12 ounces of rock and soil
- Approximately 484,000 U.S. soldiers were fighting in the war in Vietnam
- President Richard M. Nixon announced the first withdrawal of 25,000 U.S. troops from SouthVietnam.
- Rock and Pop concerts drew millions as artists such as the Rolling Stones, the Who, Joan Baez, Jimi Hendrix and the Jefferson Airplane launched tours
- A copy of the first printing of the Declaration of Independence sold for $404,000
- "The Johnny Cash Show," "Hee Haw" with Buck Owens and Roy Clark, and "The Bill Cosby Show" all premiered on television
- Following student protests, universities nationwide made ROTC voluntary, or abolished the program altogether
- After weeks of debate, the delegates from the United States and Vietnam were only able to agree on the shape of the table to be used when South Vietnam and the National Liberation Front joined the talks
- Black militant defendant Bobby Seale was ordered bound and gagged by Judge Julius Hoffmann when Seale repeatedly disrupted the Chicago Eight trial
- The popularity of paperback novels detailing life in "today's easy-living, easy-loving playground called suburbia" skyrocketed
- Actor Richard Burton bought Elizabeth Taylor a 69.42-carat diamond from Cartier; the price was not revealed
- John Lennon and Yoko Ono married
- 448 Universities experienced strikes or were forced to close; student demands included revisions of admissions policies and the reorganization of academic programs
- *Penthouse* magazine, vasectomy outpatient service and automated teller machines all made their first appearance
- The 17-point underdog New York Jets, led by quarterback Joe Namath, upset the Baltimore Colts to become the first AFL Super Bowl winner
- Robert Lehman bequeathed 3,000 works valued at more than $100 million to the Metropolitan Museum of Art
- Bestsellers for the year included Philip Roth's *Portnoy's Complaint*, Jacqueline Susann's *The Love Machine*, Mario Puzo's *The Godfather*, and Penelope Ashe's *Naked Came the Stranger*
- To protest the Miss America contest, feminists dropped girdles and bras in the trash
- Hippie cult leader Charles Manson and "family" were charged with the Hollywood murders of pregnant Sharon Tate and three others
- The first draft lottery was held

1969 Economic Profile

The national consumer expenditures (per capita income) in 1969 were:

Auto Parts	$26.64
Auto Usage	$361.66
Clothing	$189.96
Dentists	$21.22
Food	$643.88
Furniture	$41.45
Gas and Oil	$101.15
Health Insurance	$20.72
Housing	$428.27
Intercity Transport	$18.26
Local Transport	$13.32
New Auto Purchase	$123.84
Personal Business	$144.07
Personal Care	$54.77
Physicians	$61.18
Private Education and Research	$54.77
Recreation	$196.86
Religion/Welfare Activities	$54.27
Telephone and Telegraph	$45.89
Tobacco	$48.35
Utilities	$105.09
Per Capita Consumption	$2,978.63

Annual Income, Standard Jobs

Bituminous Coal Mining	$8,582.00
Building Trades	$9,049.00
Domestic Industries	$7,230.00
Domestics	$3,543.00
Farm Labor	$3,646.00
Federal Civilian	$9,690.00
Federal Employees, Executive Departments	$7,010.00
Federal Military	$5,526.00
Finance, Insurance and Real Estate	$7,400.00
Gas and Electricity Workers	$9,316.00
Manufacturing, Durable Goods	$8,454.00
Manufacturing, Nondurable Goods	$7,257.00
Medical/Health Services Workers	$5,845.00
Miscellaneous Manufacturing	$6,620.00
Motion Picture Services	$8,318.00

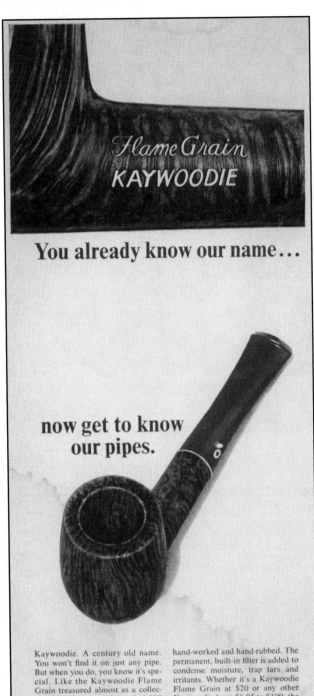

Nonprofit Organization
  Workers $5,138.00
Passenger Transportation
  Workers, Local and Highway $6,623.00
Personal Services $5,254.00
Private Industry, Including
  Farm Labor $7,237.00
Public School Teachers. $7,623.00
Radio Broadcasting and
  Television Workers. $10,085.00
Railroad Workers. $9,317.00
State and Local Government
  Workers $7,894.00
Telephone and Telegraph
  Workers $8,044.00
Wholesale and Retail Trade
  Workers $8,685.00

Selected Prices

Artificial Fingernails $0.49
Beer, Six-Pack $0.99
Boots, Men's Cowboy. $26.80
Car Wax, Simonize $0.99
Chaise, Redwood $25.95
Clock Radio $62.95
Coffee, Folger's, Two Pounds $1.27
Dancing Shoes, Child's Tap. $5.77
Electric Blanket $19.35
Encyclopædia, World University. $59.00
Guitar, Electric $199.95
Hair Spray $0.47
Ice Cream Maker, Electric. $27.95
Living Room Suite, Seven Pieces. $169.77
Pool Table, 8'. $334.50
Rider Tractor. $352.95
Rod and Reel, Zebco. $15.49
Shaving Cream, Gillette $0.59
Slide Projector $80.00
Stroller. $29.95

"Program for Non-White Jobs to Begin," *New York Times*, September 21, 1969:

"Arthur A. Fletcher, Under Secretary of Labor, said today that the Nixon administration had decided to require contractors on federally financed projects to make specific commitments to hire non-whites.

Mr. Fletcher told West Coast Negro leaders that the new policy would be announced officially Monday in Philadelphia.

He said the strict federal requirements would first be applied to projects involving federal money in the Philadelphia area and would be implemented in the San Diego, Los Angeles and San Francisco Bay areas 'within the next 30 to 60 days.'

Previously, the high-ranking Negro official said the Government required contractors to sign a nondiscrimination pledge but allowed them to arrive at the specific number of minority workers by themselves.

Under the new policy, supervisors of federal agencies that grant contracts will be required to make certain that sufficient non-white personnel are employed.

'We are using contract law to achieve a social end,' Mr. Fletcher told a news conference during the West Coast conference of the National Association for the Advancement of Colored People."

"The Game of the Name," by William Zinsser, *Life*, November 7, 1969:

"I keep losing American companies. Every week two or three more disappear, taking with them their names, their trademarks and my memories. It makes me nervous. Suddenly everyone is GAF or GAC or GCA. Or Dayco or Citgo or Armco. Or National General. National General what? Two adjectives and no noun. I miss the noun. I no longer know what business American businesses are in.

Remember Pittsburgh Plate Glass, the company that made plate glass in Pittsburgh? Now it's PPG Industries, presumably making ppg's. And where have you gone, Corn Products? I used to like to think of you making corn products. Now you're CPC International—unless that's somebody else—and I don't think of you at all. Or of any other company that took some commodity out of my life by burrowing into the alphabet. The shoe machinery went out of USM, the rubber out of Uniroyal. What can a man hang on to? Is the Minneapolis and St. Louis Railway

really MSL Industries, Inc.? And the Alaska Juneau Gold Mining Company really A.J. Industries, Inc.? Say it ain't so! Did railroaders push West and prospectors push north to die in a desert of initials? Did founders found businesses to serve real needs that would later be hidden behind fake names? Take the American Molasses Company. I doubt if there's a man or boy who doesn't like to picture a company that's sitting around all day making molasses. Well, that picture's over. The firm vanished, and when I found it again it was SuCrest. What's SuCrest to me, or me to SuCrest?

I don't even insist on knowing exactly what a company does—all I ask is a decent clue. I've never understood for instance, how the Air Reduction Company makes any money reducing air, but that's evidently what it does and I think of it with fondness. Not so the National Cylinder Gas Company, which I guess made gas, or cylinder gas. Now it's Chemetron. And I'm Apathy Industries, Inc."

1970–1979

The Vietnam War finally came to an end during the decade of the 1970s, only to spawn spiraling costs that set off several waves of inflation. The result was an America stripped of its ability to dominate the world economy and a nation on the defensive. In 1971, President Richard Nixon was forced to devalue the U.S. dollar against foreign currencies and allow its previously fixed value to "float" according to changing economic conditions. By year's end, the money paid for foreign goods exceeded that spent on U.S. exports for the first time in the century. Two years later, during the "Yom Kippur" War between Israel and its Arab neighbors, Arab oil producers declared an oil embargo on oil shipments to the United States, setting off gas shortages, a dramatic rise in the price of oil, and rationing for the first time in 30 years. The sale of automobiles plummeted, unemployment and inflation nearly doubled, and the buying power of Americans fell dramatically.

The economy, handicapped by the devaluation of the dollar and inflation, did not fully recover for more than a decade, while the fast-growing economies of Japan and western Europe, especially West Germany, mounted direct competitive challenges to American manufacturers. The value of imported manufactured goods skyrocketed from 14 percent of U.S. domestic production in 1970 to 40 percent in 1979. The inflationary cycle and recession returned in 1979 to disrupt markets, throw thousands out of work, and prompt massive downsizing of companies—awakening many once-secure workers to the reality of the changing economic market. A symbol of the era was the pending bankruptcy of Chrysler Corporation, whose cars were so outmoded and plants so inefficient they could not compete against Japanese imports. The federal government was forced to extend loan guarantees to the company to prevent bankruptcy and the loss of thousands of jobs.

The appointment of Paul Volcker as the chairman of the Federal Reserve Board late in the decade gave the economy the distasteful medicine it needed. To cope with inflation, Volcker slammed on the economic brakes, restricted the growth of the money supply, and curbed inflation. As a result, he pushed interest rates to nearly 20 percent—their highest level since the Civil War. Almost immediately the sale of automobiles and expensive items stopped.

The decade also was marred by the deep divisions caused by the Vietnam War. For more than 10 years the war had been fought on two fronts: at home and abroad. As a result, U.S. policy makers conducted the war with one eye always focused on national opinion. When it ended, the Vietnam War had been the longest war in American history, having cost $118 billion and resulted in 56,000 dead, 300,000 wounded, and the loss of American prestige abroad.

The decade was a time not only of movements, but of moving. In the 1970s, the shift of manufacturing facilities to the South from New England and the Midwest accelerated. The Sunbelt became the new darling of corporate America. By the late 1970s, the South, including Texas, had gained more than a million manufacturing jobs, while the Northeast and the Midwest lost nearly two million. Rural North Carolina had the highest percentage of manufacturing of any state in the nation, along with the lowest blue-collar wages and the lowest unionization rate in the country. The Northeast lost more than traditional manufacturing jobs. Computerization of clerical work also made it possible for big firms such as Merrill Lynch, American Express, and Citibank to shift many of their operations to the South and West.

The largest and most striking of all the social actions of the early 1970s was the women's liberation movement; it fundamentally reshaped American society. Since the late 1950s, a small group of well-placed American women had attempted to convince Congress and the courts to bring about equality between the sexes. By the 1970s, the National Organization for Women (NOW) multiplied in size, the first issue of *Ms. Magazine* sold out in a week, and women began demanding economic equality, the legalization of abortion, and the improvement of women's role in society. "All authority in our society is being challenged," said a Department of Health, Education, and Welfare report. "Professional athletes challenge owners, journalists challenge editors, consumers challenge manufacturers . . . and young blue-collar workers, who have grown up in an environment in which equality is called for in all institutions, are demanding the same rights and expressing the same values as university graduates."

The decade also included the flowering of the National Welfare Rights Organization (NWRO), founded in 1966, which resulted in millions of urban poor demanding additional rights. The environmental movement gained recognition and momentum during the decade starting with the first Earth Day celebration in 1970 and the subsequent passage of the federal Clean Air and Clean Water acts. And the growing opposition to the use of nuclear power peaked after the near calamity at Three Mile Island in Pennsylvania in 1979. As the formal barriers to racial equality came down, racist attitudes became unacceptable and the black middle class began to grow. By 1972, half of all Southern black children sat in integrated classrooms, and about one third of all black families had risen economically into the ranks of the middle class.

The changes recorded for the decade included a doubling in the amount of garbage created per capita from 2.5 pounds in 1920 to five pounds. California created a no-fault divorce law, Massachusetts introduced no-fault insurance, and health food sales reached $3 billion. By mid-decade, the so-called typical nuclear family, with working father, housewife, and two children, represented only seven percent of the population and the family size was falling. The average family size was 3.4 persons compared with 4.3 in 1920.

1972 Family Profile

Oliver Pitt, the 22-year-old grandnephew of the founder of Wrigley's Chewing Gum, is working for the company that made his family rich; as a recent college graduate with a degree in engineering, he is working on the next generation of computers for the company.

Annual Income: Oliver earns $16,000 a year working for the company, in addition to over one half million dollars in income he makes from a $16 million trust fund.

Life at Home

- Oliver Pitt loves Chicago and couldn't wait to return after graduation from The Massachusetts Institute of Technology in Cambridge.
- He recently purchased—using some graduation money—an 1880s warehouse in Chicago's "near-Loop" area, planning to create loft apartments in the huge old building.
- The five-story brick building with broad windows was once used as a manufacturing facility; its hardwood floors, which he had refinished, show the ancient holes where machinery had been bolted to the floor.
- He especially loves the way the 12-foot ceilings create a liberating sense of spaciousness and independence.
- The building, like several on the block, has been used for warehousing since the 1950s, when manufacturing techniques began demanding more flexible space.
- Oliver believes the renovation of this building and the revitalization of the area will be an important contribution to the city.
- While New York City actively encourages residential use of lofts, it is a brand-new concept in Chicago, where current zoning laws restrict residential use above the first floor of loft buildings.
- The city has nearly 300 commercial loft buildings containing 25 million square feet of space; the greatest concentration is just north of the Loop in

Oliver Pitt is working on the next generation of computers for Wrigley's Chewing Gum.

Today's for January, 1914   Page 27

Millions of bright teeth and eyes are longing for *clean, pure, healthful*

WRIGLEY'S SPEARMINT

It's constant aid to children's teeth, appetites and digestions.

THE FLAVOR LASTS

WRIGLEY'S SPEARMINT PEPSIN GUM

THE FLAVOR LASTS

CHICAGO

Wm Wrigley Jr Co

Be sure you get **WRIGLEY'S** See the name before you buy. *Avoid imitations made to deceive you.*

BUY IT BY THE BOX

Chew it after every meal

a district loosely defined by the lake, the Chicago River, the North Branch and Chicago Avenue.

- Raw space, unimproved since it was built, rents for $0.90 to $1.50 per square foot; space with improvements goes for a maximum of $2.80.
- Oliver is currently engaged to a woman he met in college, Judy Kimbro, who is working on Wall Street in New York.
- She has clearly and repeatedly stated her desire to have her own career and retain her maiden name after their marriage—an attitude that is causing considerable friction; he wants a modern wife, but not too modern.
- To keep his relationship with Judy alive, he makes frequent phone calls and writes letters, but feels a distance growing between them.
- He has even experimented with sending little sketches and poems over fax machines he bought for each of them, but the transmission can take 10 to 15 minutes a page, spoiling the spontaneity and fun of the pictures.
- He is currently living in an apartment purchased by his mother as an "investment" while he completes the renovations of the loft; the eight-room flat has double French doors that open off his second-floor bedroom, allowing the sounds of the city to rush in.
- His mother has furnished the apartment with Mission oak she found in a secondhand store; he has supplemented her purchases with a large art deco armoire and two Tiffany lamps from the turn of the century.
- The apartment is close enough for him to hear jazz wafting from a nearby club where he loves to go at night.
- After four and a half years away at M.I.T., he was more than ready to return to the Midwest and his beloved Chicago.
- He was also happy to return to a city that understands the need for America to fight for its place in the world, including defeating the communists in Vietnam.
- Although he was number 10 in the draft board's lottery, he did not join the military because of his 4-F status, caused by arthritis.
- His family doctor provided the draft board with a letter saying he was unable to enter combat without taking his daily medication; the draft board provided him with a deferment without his having to participate in the induction process, where the normal military physical is given.
- In Chicago he feels at home, particularly now that he has taken a job with Wrigley.
- He grew up hearing tales about his famous granduncle, William Wrigley, who was known for his advertising audacity.
- Around the turn of the century, Wrigley obtained the number and address of every telephone subscriber in the United States and mailed each one a sample package of gum.
- A few years later, with a recession threatening, he increased his advertising, spending $250,000 in New York City alone, knowing his ads would have more impact during slow times.
- As important, he focused his advertising on a handful of flavors such as Juicy Fruit, Spearmint and Doublemint, dumping flavors such as peach, blood, banana and vanilla pepsin.
- Today, the company spends one seventh of its total income, or about $25 million, on advertising, most of it continuing to focus on a basic message: "Chewing gum is enjoyable

The Wrigley family has been part of the growth and development of Chicago for many years.

and relaxing, a pleasant, inexpensive way of winding down that you can enjoy almost anywhere."

- In his household, which included 26 rooms on three stories near the lake, Uncle Wrigley was a legend.
- His mother, heiress to the Wrigley wealth through her mother, loved to tell stories around the dinner table, especially when Oliver's father was present; she didn't think her husband had as much get-up-and-go as her uncle had, and didn't mind if people knew it.

Life at Work
- Oliver's office is in downtown Chicago, only a few miles from where he grew up.
- Although officially a trainee, he reports each week to his cousin William Wrigley, the 39-year-old grandson of founder William Wrigley, Jr.
- A third-generation, family-managed corporation, all Wrigley makes, they like to say, is "gum and money."
- Currently, 32 billion sticks of chewing gum disappear into American mouths each year.

Chicago has grown and prospered during the past decade.

- In 1970, Americans spent $272.8 million on chewing gum.
- Forty-five percent of the gum chewed in America comes from Wrigley, which grossed $176 million last year, for satisfying America's "non-addictive habit."
- Ninety percent of the sugar content—and, as such, its taste—is gone in the first 10 minutes.

"All about a Subject You Can Sink Your Teeth into," by Norman Mark, *Today's Health*, November 1972:

"It's harmless to your health, sloppy underfoot, ecologically neutral, popular through the ages when people feel deprived or anxious, and no longer a sign of vulgarity. It's . . . chewing gum, a welcome grind for the famous and unknown alike.

Phosphates are removed from laundry detergents and something else is put in that may be just as bad; small cars pollute less, but some studies find that people in them suffer more injuries in accidents; rats thrive on cereal boxes but grow thin on the cereal.

In such an improbable and dangerous world, fit more for machines than for humans, it's important to celebrate those rare occasions when we are greeted with pleasant surprises instead of nasty ones. So celebrate this: There is good news about chewing gum, that bane of parents and schoolteachers for the last generation or two. Both the gum manufacturers and a growing number of dental researchers agree that gum chewing is virtually harmless. Better yet, there is even evidence that chewing sugarless gum may be of some value in reducing cavities.

But before we get further into what gum does and does not do to your teeth, we have to admit that anywhere outside the mouth it is sticky stuff. It does no good for the soles of shoes and it looks ugly whenever it lands in public after it has been chewed. (Authorities on gum also point out that it doesn't retain much flavor if left on the bedpost overnight . . .)

An average-sized stick of gum has only a little sugar and fewer than nine calories. But gum chewing increases the saliva in your mouth, which washes the sugar into your stomach along with many particles of food. So gum doesn't do much one way or another for your teeth.

But current studies offer preliminary indications that gum might someday benefit those who chew it. At the Eastman Dental Center in Rochester, New York, a team headed by Basil G. Bibby, D.M.D., Ph.D., is trying to learn which snack food causes the most decay. So far, Dr. Bibby says, the evidence shows that chewing gum does less harm to your teeth than hard and chewy candies, cookies, cakes and doughnuts.

'You hang on to that word moderation,' Dr. Bibby says. 'If you must have sugar, you might as well take it in gum as from a stick of candy or a cookie. A stick of gum is less destructive than a cookie, for instance. And the sugar in a carbonated beverage is less destructive than that in a candy bar . . . .'

If scientists could add some decay-fighting substance to gum, it could make a powerfully healthy habit. But saliva, which washes away the sugar in gum, also washes away almost everything else, including the dozens of additives scientists have been adding, unsuccessfully, to gum for decades. One new experiment in this area, however, does look promising.

Sidney B. Finn, D.D.S., professor of dentistry at the Dental Research Institute of the University of Alabama, is experimenting with a new phosphate—sodium trimetaphosphate—that has reduced tooth decay in test animals by about 60 percent. It has been added to gum chewed by 600 children in the Florida School for the Deaf and Blind in St. Augustine. We should know the results of Dr. Finn's research in about two years, after which we may have a chewing gum additive that can also cut down on decay."

- Early on, Oliver decided that he was not interested in sales or management, but found his calling in college with the emergence of computers; he believes he can help turn Wrigley into a model of efficiency through the magic of computer technology.
- He is even talking about the day all employees will have computers on their desks; some people at work, particularly those who don't type and don't care to learn, are convinced that this will not be necessary.
- Currently, the company is using General Electric computers, which recently exited the data processing business, and most of the executives believe that now is the logical time to switch to IBM, which dominates the U.S. market.
- Oliver wants to take another look at a small, $100 million sales company on the West Coast known as Intel.
- Unfortunately, Intel's earnings are suffering from too much growth and many in the Wrigley company are convinced that Intel will not be around in a decade, when they will need to update their equipment.
- Many believe Sperry-Rand or Control Data will be IBM's primary competitor in the future.
- Wrigley is now attempting to expand its product use into the workplace; a recent psychological study widely circulated within the company reports that a secretary who chews gum is 19 percent more efficient than one who doesn't, and tends not to tap her feet or squirm in her chair while typing.
- Since Wrigley believes that gum belongs in the office, twice daily a woman walks through the Wrigley building with a tray of gum, encouraging everyone to take a stick or two; on Fridays, employees are permitted to take a couple of packs home for the weekend.
- Oliver appreciates the missionary zeal for gum chewing at Wrigley, but has banned gum from the processing room, fearing that a misplaced wad will gum up his always-temperamental computers.

Life in the Community: Chicago, Illinois

- Chicago is known for many things, but Oliver places its pizza and jazz high on his list of favorites.
- A perfect night, especially when his fiancée is visiting, includes a trip to Pizzeria Uno and a swing by a jazz club.
- At Pizzeria Uno's, the cradle of Chicago-style pizza, his favorite is a deep-dish cheese and sausage; another favorite restaurant for the couple is Chez Paul, where he asked Judy to marry him.
- Opened in 1969 by Bill Contos, Chez Paul offers first-class service with Wedgwood china, Baccarat crystal, linens on the tables and food worthy of the setting.
- The night Judy was engaged, she had terrine of pheasant with pistachios, veal normande and asparagus hollandaise; neither of them can remember what he ate that night.
- When she is in town, the next stop after dinner is always music, often to a small jazz club that caters to Chicago natives who grew up enjoying the city's unique style of music.
  - Chicago jazz grew out of the work of trumpeter Bix Beiderbecke, who was nurtured by an enthusiastic and understanding audience in the 1920s.
  - Beiderbecke and his band, The Wolverines, started the white jazz movement, which blossomed in Chicago through other groups as well, such as The Austin High Gang.
  - This was further enhanced by the work of Jelly Roll Morton, who played his piano in the city for nearly five years.

> "Nothing great was ever achieved without enthusiasm."
> —William Wrigley, Jr.

Chicago jazz grew out of the work of trumpeter Bix Beiderbecke.

- Oliver goes to a show at the club near his house several times a week after work, always limiting himself to two drinks before going home.
- His father used to take him there, and would often be asked to sit in with the band to play his smooth, sweet clarinet—one of Oliver's fondest memories of his dad.
- Two years ago, his father died; he had been drinking and drove his car into a tree while traveling at a very high rate of speed, leaving no skid marks on the road.

Historical Snapshot
1972

- Intense U.S. bombing of North Vietnamese cities resumed after peace talks broke down.
- The Supreme Court ruled that the death penalty was "cruel and unusual punishment"
- The number of fast food establishments increased from 1,120 in 1958 to 6,784 in 1972
- Sears reprinted its 1903, 1908 and 1927 catalogs after its 1902 edition sold 400,000 copies
- Singer Frank Sinatra was subpoenaed by a House committee on crime and denied all Mafia connections
- David Bowie introduced glitter rock
- The Watergate burglary that would eventually lead to the resignation of President Richard Nixon occurred during the 1972 presidential campaign
- First-class postal rates rose to $0.08 per ounce
- Marlon Brando starred in *Last Tango in Paris*, the first graphically erotic movie featuring a major star
- *The Godfather*, *Deliverance*, *Sounder* and *Deep Throat* all opened in movie theaters
- The average taxpayer paid the government $400 for defense, $12 to fight the war in Indochina, $40 to build roads, $30 to explore space and $315 for health activities
- The annual per capita consumption of beef reached 11 pounds
- *Life* magazine ceased publication; *Ms.* magazine began
- Acupuncture treatment centers, pocket calculators, the Polaroid SC-70, and electronic lock and key systems using plastic cards all made their first appearance
- The Massachusetts Supreme Court ruled unconstitutional the law prohibiting the sale of contraceptives to single persons
- After 3,242 performances, *Fiddler on the Roof* closed; it was the longest-running show in Broadway history
- Hot pants in mini lengths filled the fashion scene
- Einstein's prediction of a time difference in a moving clock was validated
- Palestinian terrorists from the Black September movement invaded the Israeli housing compound at the Munich Olympic Games; 11 Israeli athletes died in the ensuing shootout
- *Jonathan Livingston Seagull* by Richard Bach, *August 1914* by Alexander Solzhenitsyn and *I'm O.K., You're O.K.* by Thomas Harris were all bestsellers
- The Dow-Jones Industrial Average reached 1,036 during the year

1972 Economic Profile

The national consumer expenditures (per capita income) in 1972 were:

Auto Parts	$38.11
Auto Usage	$460.70
Clothing	$225.83
Dentists	$26.68
Food	$755.11
Furniture	$45.55
Gas and Oil	$116.25
Health Insurance	$28.59
Housing	$534.07
Intercity Transport	$24.77
Local Transport	$16.19
New Auto Purchase	$150.55
Personal Business	$183.42
Personal Care	$61.46
Physicians	$79.09
Private Education and Research	$71.94
Recreation	$244.88
Religion/Welfare Activities	$72.42
Telephone and Telegraph	$59.08
Tobacco	$58.75
Utilities	$131.02
Per Capita Consumption	$3,658.00

Annual Income, Standard Jobs

Bituminous Coal Mining	$11,323.00
Building Trades	$10,747.00
Domestic Industries	$8,794.00
Domestics	$4,478.00
Farm Labor	$3,900.00
Federal Civilian	$12,596.00
Federal Employees, Executive Departments	$10,331.00
Federal Military	$8,603.00
Finance, Insurance and Real Estate	$8,861.00
Gas and Electricity Workers	$11,420.00
Manufacturing, Durable Goods	$10,747.00
Manufacturing, Nondurable Goods	$8,636.00
Medical/Health Services Workers	$7,499.00
Miscellaneous Manufacturing	$7,800.00
Motion Picture Services	$8,882.00

Nonprofit Organization Workers $6,088.00

Passenger Transportation Workers, Local and Highway $7,496.00

Personal Services $6,268.00

Private Industry, Including Farm Labor $8,634.00

Public School Teachers $9,284.00

Radio Broadcasting and Television Workers $11,575.00

Railroad Workers $11,991.00

State and Local Government Workers $8,898.00

Telephone and Telegraph Workers $10,518.00

Selected Prices

Basketball $4.98

Book, *The Joy of Sex* $12.95

Cassette Tapes, Three-Pack $1.99

Coloring Book $0.10

Condoms, Trojan, Nine-Pack $3.00

Cruise, Orient, Four Months $3,105.00

Eggs, per Dozen $0.39

Eye Drops, Visine $0.99

Fabric Softener, Downy $0.99

Jacket, Man's Leather $80.00

Jeans, Woman's Corduroy $4.88

Jewel Case, Gucci $99.00

Life Vest $20.59

Nonprescription Drug, Excedrin $0.89

Pajamas, Child's $5.49

Pepper Grinder, Cartier $35.00

Soap, English Leather $2.00

Theatre Ticket, *Hair* $12.00

Valise, Leather and Canvas $175.00

Wig, Human Hair $29.99

"The Data Processors' Big Bets on the Future," *Fortune*, January 1972:

"Sperry-Rand's Univac Division moved to fortify its position in the computer industry in November by buying a major part of RCA's operations. At first glance, the purchase seems an eminently sound one. One computer consultant, Isaac L. Auerbach of Philadelphia, says, 'Univac has bought a hunting license with an inside track on RCA's customers at effectively no cost because it will be getting income from the leasing business.' The agreement calls for Sperry to make a $70 million cash payment for RCA's customer base, which includes some 1,000 computers, mostly leased, of 500 clients.

So, for a maximum of $130 million, Sperry is buying $1 billion in equipment that produces about $250 million in annual revenues. When combined with the Univac Division (whose machines valued at $3.2 billion produce revenues of $700 million a year), the acquisition increases Sperry-Rand's share of the domestic market's installed computers from 4.8 to 8.4 percent. That leaves Sperry-Rand in second place, followed by Honeywell, which bought General Electric's installations, with 6.8 percent, Control Data with 4.1 percent, Burroughs, 3.7 percent, and National Cash Register, 2.4 percent. But IBM, with a U.S. market share of 69.9 percent and an annual research-and-development budget of $500 million, still dwarfs the combined strength of the five companies.

J. Frank Forster, 63, Sperry's chairman and chief executive officer, acknowledged that, in buying the RCA installations, his eye was on the future. To survive the next decade in this concentrated, capital-intensive business, Sperry must show that it has the technology and marketing muscle to compete with IBM. The industry's revenue growth is now forecast at about 10 percent annually, instead of the 20 percent annual growth of the sixties. That means a greater degree of concentration on replacement business—a good number of machines installed in the fifties and early sixties have now become obsolete. Forster believes that if Sperry can convert half of RCA's customers to Univac systems when their equipment becomes obsolete in the mid-1970s, he will then have a formidable sales base.

Whether this gamble will pay off is, of course, impossible to gauge. The departure of GE and RCA from the business has left a lot of their old computer customers nervous. In making a choice of new equipment, they will need a lot of reassurance that the vendor will be around to service their expensive installations."

Chewing Gum through the Ages

- Humans have always compulsively chewed non-food items of some kind; down through history they have nibbled on their own fingers and, if agile enough, their toenails.
- Betel nut is a favorite in Asia, whale blubber is chewed in the Arctic and chicle in South America.
- The ancient Greeks, who were advanced in so many ways, favored sap from the mastic tree.
- American colonists munched on spruce tree resins, and later, on sweetened paraffin wax.
- H.L. Hollingsworth of Columbia University concluded in 1939 that gum chewing is a form of "retrogression to the entire erotic patterns of infancy" and a means of "suppressing the biting instincts" left over from prehistoric man.
- Modern gum is a relatively recent product; according to one legend, General Santa Ana, conqueror of the Alamo, brought chicle to Manhattan in 1869.
- Then president-in-exile of Mexico, he was looking for ways to make money and happened to meet Thomas Adams, an American merchant and part-time inventor.
- Santa Ana showed Adams how to chew the dried sap of the sapodilla tree that grows in the jungles of the Mexican Yucatan peninsula.
- Adams's first efforts at transforming the sap into a useful rubber failed; then, with the help of his 12-year-old son, Adams boiled the chicle until it was soft, rolled it in sugar and thus created Adams New York Chewing Gum—Snapping and Stretching.
- Unfortunately, the sapodilla tree, the source of the sap, resists cultivation, preferring to flourish in the jungles of Mexico, Guatemala and British Honduras.

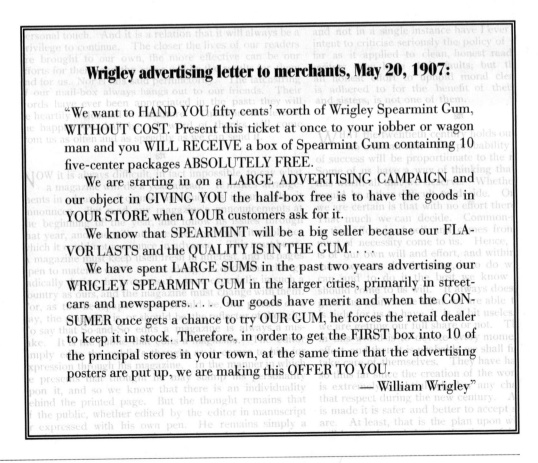

Wrigley advertising letter to merchants, May 20, 1907:

"We want to HAND YOU fifty cents' worth of Wrigley Spearmint Gum, WITHOUT COST. Present this ticket at once to your jobber or wagon man and you WILL RECEIVE a box of Spearmint Gum containing 10 five-center packages ABSOLUTELY FREE.

We are starting in on a LARGE ADVERTISING CAMPAIGN and our object in GIVING YOU the half-box free is to have the goods in YOUR STORE when YOUR customers ask for it.

We know that SPEARMINT will be a big seller because our FLAVOR LASTS and the QUALITY IS IN THE GUM.

We have spent LARGE SUMS in the past two years advertising our WRIGLEY SPEARMINT GUM in the larger cities, primarily in streetcars and newspapers. . . . Our goods have merit and when the CONSUMER once gets a chance to try OUR GUM, he forces the retail dealer to keep it in stock. Therefore, in order to get the FIRST box into 10 of the principal stores in your town, at the same time that the advertising posters are put up, we are making this OFFER TO YOU.

— William Wrigley"

- To obtain the sap required climbing 70 feet in the air, where the sap flowed best, all the while avoiding poisonous snakes, malaria-bearing mosquitoes and the chicle fly, which can cause cancerous growths in the ears and nose.
- Today most gums have a synthetic base, eliminating the need to brave life-threatening dangers for a stick of gum.
- Chewing gum has appeared in a variety of forms through the years, including Love Gum, Fight the Red Menace Gum, Forbidden Fruit and Ox Heart Peppermint gums, and even Peerless Chips by the Texas Gum Company.
- Throughout history, the sale of chewing gum has increased when people were deprived or anxious; sales zoomed, for example, during Prohibition, World War II, and after the 1964 U.S. Surgeon General's report linking smoking to cancer.
- Today, advertising is being used to increase gum's popularity; Americans are urged to stretch their coffee breaks with gum, and some teachers even offer gum as a reward for good work.
- Wrigley prides itself on the fact that its gum has not changed size or shape; a stick of gum today is the same weight it was 70 years ago.
- However, the packaging has changed through the years; the air has been squeezed out of the package to get a tighter wrap, so the gum will have a longer shelf life—approximately six months.

Because there's nobody else like them.

You don't buy life insurance for yourself. You buy it for them. Your wife. Your kids. Because they're unique. And they need financial security.

With an Equitable policy, you have the assurance of knowing you've given them that security.

But you have something else that's important, too.

The help of an Equitable Agent. An Agent whose training and skills are all dedicated to you and your individual insurance needs. Needs that are different from anybody else's.

Because to you, there's nobody else like your family.

But to the Equitable Agent, there's nobody else like you. **THE EQUITABLE**

The Equitable Life Assurance Society of the United States, N.Y., N.Y.

There's nobody else like you.

"Women Against Themselves," *The Humanist*, by Miriam Allen deFord, January/February 1971:

" 'Women were better off when the only taste they got of the competitive world was in cutting each other's throats over a cup of tea.'

'Women are already ahead, and the best they can get out of "liberation" is a setback.'

'Woman respects man for his strength . . . Should a wife become her husband's equal, she would lose some of that respect and he would lose his self-respect.'

'I don't care for women's liberation. I prefer the strong arms of my husband around me.'

'I would rather that my husband have more prestige at his career, and I be only the lady of the house.'

'Everything about us man has made—not woman. Women have got to be kidding when they say they want to help run the world. They are fighting a losing battle if they hope to equal men.'

These are all actual quotations from women of our own time and place. One is from that sterling example of shrinking femininity: Shirley Temple Black.

When women marched for equal rights last August, a female group in New York gave 'Adam's Rib' awards to men 'for discriminating against women,' and a St. Louis dissident proposed that the semicentennial celebration of women's suffrage be transformed into 'be nice to a man day.'

Why?

How do these women, who don't want to be considered fully responsible human beings, with equal rights and opportunities in a democratic society, get that way? Why does a psychologist conclude from a study of college women that 'women are prejudiced against female professionals and . . . firmly refuse to recognize them as the equals of their male colleagues'? Why does Leslie

Ford remark that 'women would rather be taught by a third-rate man than a first-rate woman'?

It goes back a long, long way, and it's going to take more than demonstrations and conferences to undo it. And since in this country women make up 53 percent of the population, and most men are indifferent or opposed, we'd better try to understand those Women Against Themselves.

Theirs is the view of the female sex as secondary, ancillary, what Gillian Tindall calls 'the humble we-live-only-through-men attitude.' Woman to them is primarily sexual, a walking incubator, her true function to serve men and rear children. You can't call them Aunt Thomasinas, for (aside from the fact that people who think Uncle Tom liked being a slave have never read *Uncle Tom's Cabin*) I have never heard of a slave who approved of and advocated slavery. Nor were there any German Jews who thought the Nazis were right and that Jews deserved to be put in concentration camps and gas chambers. Nor, outside of mental hospitals, are there any destitute people who consider their poverty the proper order of society and who would rather be poor than prosperous.

Yet here we have a sizable proportion of articulate American women who honestly believe that they are inferior, that the male should be dominant, that the husband and father should be the family 'king,' that wives should obey their husbands, and that marriage should be a dictatorship instead of a partnership. They also believe that women ought to be paid less than men for the same work (otherwise they might pull all wages down, and then they themselves would have less to spend), that women ought not to aspire to administrative or executive jobs, and so on, through all the rest of the tenets of the patriarchal system."

"At Last, the Year of Real Recovery," *Time*, January 10, 1972:

"A year from now, most Americans will be earning more than they are today and enjoying the first real gain in buying power since 1968. The outlook for the economy in 1972 can be summed up simply: growth. Old-fashioned, rapid, sustained growth. Best of all, real growth in incomes, jobs, profits, sales and production, rather than the illusory rise in dollar totals that comes with inflation.

That's the unanimous opinion of *Time*'s Board of Economists, and of most other analysts as well. They are not predicting a boom. Too many machines and people will remain idle for 1972 to qualify for that description. Instead, the economists foresee the type of gains that the nation used to enjoy routinely in the first year of recovery from recession, but that somehow eluded it through all the fireworks of that otherwise spectacular economic year, 1971.

In terms of fundamental economic change, 1971 was easily the most exciting and eventful year since the early 1930s. Domestically, a Republican president who had preached the glories of free enterprise climbed on first with a rigid wage-price freeze, then comprehensive controls of the kind usually associated with all-out war. His actions took the U.S. economy into a new world in which it is difficult to envision any administration ever again proclaiming that private wage-price decisions are none of its business. . . .

Yet, in terms of the numbers that mean the most to businessmen, workers, consumers and investors, 1971 was a distinctly disappointing year. Real gross national product—the value of output minus the cost of inflation—rose by an anemic 3, about half the rise that is normal for the first year of recovery from recession. The rate of price increases declined only slowly after the freeze, averaging around 4 for the year v. 5.5 in 1970. Unemployment climbed to a peak of 6.2 in May, and hung stubbornly close to that level for most of the year. The combination of unemployment and inflation frightened consumers into a particularly wary mood, and the deficit budget that Nixon unfurled early in the year—in another philosophical defiance of G.O.P. tradition—proved insufficient to spur the spending necessary for prosperity. . . .

The economic momentum should accelerate, making 1972 the year of real recovery. New government stimulation of the economy is one main reason. The tax cuts just signed into law will worsen the nation's budget squeeze, but will put an extra $8 billion of spending power into the pockets of consumers and businessmen. The Labor Department plans special training and public-employment programs to fit 262,000 Vietnam veterans into civilian jobs."

1976 News Profile

"Housing for the Aged in Suburbia: Even the Affluent Find It Hard to Keep Up," by Wendy Schuman, *New York Times*, April 18, 1976:

"In Freeport, Long Island, an 80-year-old homeowner puts off insulating his freezing bathroom. 'I have to eat, I have to pay my taxes and oil bills,' he said. There is just no money left over for improvements, however necessary.

In White Plains, a widow of 68 sleeps on a fold-out sofa in her son's den. Living with five grandchildren is difficult, she says. 'I'm always in the way.' But with a $260-a-month income from Social Security, she simply cannot afford to move out.

Once a prosperous Manhattan couple with two boats and a weekend apartment on Long Island, Edward Futterer and his wife now live in a project for the low-income elderly in Islip. 'Our retirement money just went,' said Mr. Futterer, 78. 'I suppose we didn't expect to live so long.' There are 1,200 people on the waiting list for the 180 apartments in Mr. Futterer's project.

Many elderly residents of New York's suburbs—whatever their income level while they were working—have become poorer since retirement. A large number who live on fixed incomes, usually Social Security and pension payments, can barely make ends meet. Some have seen their savings depleted by high inflation. In the affluent suburbs of Long Island, Westchester and parts of Connecticut, old people frequently pay from half to three quarters of their income just for housing.

Indeed, no aspect of life in the suburbs is more difficult for the elderly than housing. Even those in higher income brackets are becoming more and more watchful of their savings. At Heritage Hills, a newly built adult community in Somers, New York, salesmen record more condominium buyers taking mortgages and using their capital for investment.

Both the Heritage group and another major builder of retirement communities, Leisure Technology, report that while condominium prices get higher, the age of purchasers is getting younger. At the new Heritage development, the minimum age requirement is 40, compared to 50 at the older Heritage Village in Southbury, Connecticut. Prices run about $8,000 higher at the newer project.

Among moderate and low-income senior citizens, the choices are more basic. 'We used to say that the elderly could only afford the essential trilogy—rent, food and clothing,' said

John Nolon, executive director of Housing Action Council, which studies subsidized housing needs in Westchester. 'Now it seems that anything beyond rent is a luxury.'

Mr. Nolon ran a check of applicants for a new housing project in Peekskill and found that few had more than $1,000 a year left after paying for housing. In Westchester, there are 100,500 persons over 65, and 15 percent of them have incomes below the federal poverty level of $2,364.

The situation is not much better in Nassau County, where there are 128,000 persons over 65. In 1970, approximately 13 percent of them had below-poverty incomes. Fifteen years ago, there were only 80,000 elderly in the county. 'We're faced with a growing population that's getting poorer as it gets older,' said Adelaide Attard, executive director of the Nassau County Department of Senior Citizen Affairs. 'Since 80 percent of them still live in their own homes, they have the usual homeowners' problems, but are less able to cope than young working people.'

Those who opt to remain in their long-time homes complain most bitterly of property taxes. 'That's all they want to talk about at every meeting,' sighed Henry Doliner, president of Senior Forum, an organization of Nassau County senior citizen centers. 'More than Medicaid, it's property taxes.'

Currently, in New York State, elderly persons with annual incomes under $6,500 may be granted real-estate tax exemptions of up to 50 percent. But some are unaware of their eligibility. 'And what if you make $6,501?' noted Abe Seldin, chairman of the Nassau County Board of Assessors. 'I've seen cases where property taxes alone were 40 percent of the gross income.'

'It's a vicious cycle,' said Joseph Tortelli, director of the Westchester Office for the Aging. 'Apartments are so expensive that old people can't afford them. In their homes they can cut back on maintenance to cut costs. But the homes deteriorate and young people don't have the chance to move in.'

'We have a housing imbalance here,' agreed Mr. Nolon of Housing Action Council. 'Old people occupy large space because of high rents. Yet much of our housing stock is overcrowded.'

His agency surveyed thousands of one-bedroom rentals in Westchester and found that most cost between $200 and $300 a month, more than the average Social Security recipient collects each month.

Those who work with the elderly stress the need for many more units of publicly subsidized housing at low and moderate rents. Thousands of units have already been built in New York suburbs under a variety of government programs, but waiting lists of more than three years are common. Affluent suburban towns have not been quick to approve multi-family low-income dwellings, even for aged residents.

In Rockville Centre, a volunteer committee worked for five years to obtain a low-income project of 50 units that will finally open next month. More than 300 old people had applied for the apartments, which were funded under the federal 'Turnkey' program. One third were over the income level for eligibility, according to the committee's chairman, Ruth Ferman, but could not afford private rentals.

'They shouldn't have to uproot themselves in old age and move out of town,' Mrs. Ferman said. With an organization of social service and religious groups, she is exploring a plan for building moderately priced units under Section 8 of the 1974 federal Housing and Community Development Act.

Under Section 8, an elderly person may be eligible for a rent subsidy in existing apartments—if both his income and the apartment rent fall below prescribed levels for his region. Legislators are discussing various other programs of rent subsidy and tax abatement for landlords of elderly tenants.

Meanwhile, Mr. Nolon said, he was hoping for quick action by communities on allowing the sharing of large private homes. 'Old people do not have all the time in the world,' he observed."

1978 FAMILY PROFILE

At 77, Stefano Tornabene is an entrepreneur of the "old school," still actively running the orange juice empire he founded in the 1940s, while fending off lucrative merger offers from Fortune 500 companies. He loves his company, the citrus business and golf.

Annual Income: His salary, including bonus, tops $250,000 a year; his total assets from a stock sale 10 years ago exceed $75 million.

Life at Home

- At 77, and well past retirement age, Stefano is still actively running the Sunshine Orange Juice Company he founded in 1947, playing golf when he wants and living by his own rules.
- Considered an entrepreneur of the old school, he loves his company, his products and his employees, who have no doubts that he is firmly in control.
- He does not hesitate to use his elegant home by the water for company picnics, dinners or negotiating sessions, maintaining three servants year-round to assist in the necessary arrangements.
- He still goes to the office six days a week, working eight to nine hours before going home with additional paperwork.
- On Sundays, after church, he often plays golf—his other all-consuming passion.
- Careful with his money in nearly every other aspect of his life, Stefano cannot resist the urge to buy the latest golf innovations—especially new golf clubs.
- A stickler for detail but a strict manager of time, nevertheless he can spend hours shopping for clubs styled specifically to his personal taste.

Stefano Tornabene is an entrepreneur of the old school.

He often uses his gulf-front home for company events and entertaining.

Golf club sales now equal $185 million annually.

- In the past 30 years, he has owned some 70 sets of clubs, and although he has sold most of his clubs when he traded up, for sentimental reasons, he keeps a set of Hogans custom-made for him a decade ago.
- He believes that the game of golf—like life—is determined by attitude: "If you are comfortable and confident in your clubs, that's always a positive."
- Currently, 15 major and 75 smaller manufacturers battle for a share of the $185 million in U.S. golf club sales.
- Today's modern clubs offer golfers a choice of grip, length, swing weight, flexibility of shaft and angles of loft and lie; "Technology is changing so fast, you have to work hard to keep up," Stefano warns.
- He came to the U.S. from Sicily more than half a century ago and founded Sunshine Orange Juice Company in 1947; a stern, powerfully built six-footer, he still speaks fractured English with a thick accent.
- Although his formal training ended in grade school, he has developed into a superb engineer with an innovative mind that is quick with numbers, and can rapidly spot minor errors on a profitability projection.
- For all his technical skills and head for math, he rarely remembers names, including those of associates with whom he has worked for years.
- None of his three grown children work for the company; two are attorneys and one operates several shrimp boats out of the Gulf of Mexico.

He is constantly enchanted by the shorebirds of Florida.

Life at Work

- As founder and undisputed ruler of his orange juice empire, Stefano recently walked away from a merger with Kellogg, against the wishes of his board of directors.
- Even though the company went public a decade ago, he still controls more than 20 percent of the stock, giving him broad discretion over most decisions.
- He remains chairman and chief executive, but gave up the title of president last year after persistent prodding from the board.
- Currently, more than 40 people report directly to him, including the company's top financial, marketing and production heads, as well as plant managers, maintenance chiefs and even the head painter.
- On Saturdays, he holds an open house to hear the problems of his subordinates who haven't been able to get his ear during the week; sitting in his large corner office on the second floor of the three-story headquarters building, he listens like a bona fide Wizard of Oz, ponders sagely and dispenses solutions.
- When a production executive complained that the bottle machine that picked up and packed orange juice bottles into cardboard cases was causing a bottleneck, Stefano redesigned the production flow; now the cardboard case is lowered over the bottles themselves and then sealed from below—reducing breakage, improving speed and stopping the bottleneck.
- He loves handling the details of the company he created, and is currently preoccupied with the development of a new plastic cap for the orange juice bottles to replace the metal caps purchased from suppliers.

The economic pulse of Bradenton is dictated by oranges.

- He is also the company's official taster, personally sampling the company's beverages each morning while the quality-control team stands by nervously; he prides himself on having keen taste buds and a superb sense of when the product is right.

Oranges, by John McPhee, 1967:

"Just after the Second World War, three scientists working in central Florida surprised themselves with a simple idea that resulted in the development of commercial orange juice concentrate. A couple of dozen enormous factories sprang out of the hammocks, and Florida, which can be counted on in most seasons to produce about a quarter of all the oranges grown in the world, was soon putting most of them through the process that results in small, trim cans, about two inches in diameter and four inches high, containing orange juice that has been boiled to high viscosity in a vacuum, separated into several component parts, reassembled, flavored and then frozen solid. People in the United States used to consume more fresh oranges than all other fresh fruits combined, but in less than 20 years the per capita consumption has gone down 75 percent, as appearances of actual oranges in most of the United States have become steadily less frequent. Fresh, whole, round, orange oranges are hardly extinct, of course, but they have seen better days since they left the garden of Hesperides. Fresh oranges have become, in a way, old-fashioned."

- "This is my baby," he likes to say. "I started it, I run it, I enjoy every minute of it."
- His recent decision to tell the mighty marketing giant Kellogg "no" was the third time he has spurned their advances in the past five years.
- With revenues approaching $1.5 billion—about six times the size of Sunshine Orange Juice—Kellogg appeared to be a good partner, thanks to its $70 million marketing budget.
- By comparison, Sunshine spent $3 million on advertising last year.
- Both sides felt that this merger would allow advertisements not only to feature Kellogg's Special K, for example, but also a glass of orange juice without any increased costs.
- Also, acceptance of the Kellogg offer would have pleased Wall Street analysts concerned about management succession at Sunshine; Kellogg viewed the merger as a way to move into the high-growth area of fruit juices.
- The Sunshine company earnings per share have risen an astounding 1,300 percent in the past decade, compared to slightly more than 200 percent for the larger Kellogg.
- The merger package Stefano eventually turned down was worth $382 million, which is $110 million more than the market value of his company's stock.
- He killed the deal, he says, because of a disagreement over a dividend for stockholders; in actuality, he is simply not ready to relinquish control of the company.
- He also believes many of his best executives who have worked with him in Florida for years will be asked to relocate to accommodate Kellogg, and is unsure whether they will survive the corporate environment of Kellogg.
- In addition, Kellogg made it clear during the negotiations that any significant new capital expenditures would have to be approved by the headquarters staff in Battle Creek, Michigan.

Florida orange groves supply most of the nation's orange juice.

- Instead of selling now, he wants to grow the business even more by pushing its distribution beyond its traditional base on the eastern seaboard to markets in the Midwest and West.
- The company is also experimenting with an expanded product line, including a ground-up citrus-pulp fiber, which would be sold as a bulk additive for baked goods.
- Sunshine has captured 40 percent of the orange juice market by pioneering the mass production of single-strength juice, a bottle of juice that comes ready to use and does not have to be reconstituted with water by the consumer; this "ready to use" approach has developed a large following among consumers willing to pay a few cents extra per quart to avoid adding water.
- Research indicates that the more educated people become, the more orange juice they consume; doctors, dentists, lawyers and corporate executives are the nation's heaviest consumers.
- Since the Second World War, most of the nation's orange juice has been distributed as a concentrate, still an important part of the market.
- Minute Maid is the dominant player in orange juice concentrates; many believe that competing in the future against Minute Maid, now owned by Coca-Cola, will require a merger.
- Thanks to years of high, consistent performance, Sunshine has no debt and little reason to bargain.
- Sunshine Orange Juice has integrated its operations to the point where it makes its own bottles, plastic containers and packing cases, builds its own production machinery, and even owns the 200 railroad cars that carry its products to market.
- The company relies heavily on independent Florida growers for its oranges and grapefruit, and is, therefore, considering whether to buy groves of its own.

> ## "Banker to the Wintering Rich," *Fortune*, February 13, 1978:
>
> " 'We're a one-crop bank, and our crop is the snowbirds from the north,' declared an executive of Florida's First National Bank of Palm Beach 37 years ago. Wealthy snowbirds still migrate in winter to Palm Beach, and the First National Bank is still their bank. This season the bank is supplying highly personalized services to some 15,000 customers—2,000 more than Palm Beach's permanent population.
>
> The bank's officers are ever ready to coddle customers. 'We get them plumbers, secretaries and chauffeurs,' says a sympathetic banker. 'They don't have the staff here that they have at home, but they still want the service.' One bank officer checks up on a yardman's clipping of oleander shrubs, and another inspects a customer's guesthouses to guard against mildew, the Palm Beach curse. That's in addition to providing a fur vault to accommodate 3,000 sables, ermines and minks. Other special vaults and storage areas are set aside for paintings, wines, Oriental rugs, chandeliers and gun collections. There are even dog biscuits for the ubiquitous poodles."

Life in the Community: Bradenton, Florida

- Since the Second World War, when Americans think of Florida, they think of oranges.
- Florida leads the United States in producing more citrus fruit than any other nation, thanks to a warm climate and readily available water.
- In the spring, vast seas of rounded, dark-green trees laden with white blooms produce such an intense fragrance that ships' passengers off the Atlantic and Gulf coasts can smell it several miles out to sea.
- However, the size of the orange groves is shrinking in many areas as land is gobbled up for development.
- For most of the century, the state has been known for its hype and hustle, all designed to attract people to land deals, vacation homes or the next get-rich-quick scheme.
- In 1940, Florida ranked twenty-seventh in population nationwide, boasting only two million people; today, the Sunshine State is ninth and growing, with many communities expanding at a pace of 10 percent or more each year.
- That population growth includes thousands of Vietnamese refugees who came to the state in 1975 after the fall of South Vietnam.
- One of the fastest-growing areas is the southwest coast of Florida, including Bradenton.
- Stefano's business is one of the largest employers in the area; despite increasing tourism, especially in the winter months, he knows nearly everyone in town, and has used the same mechanic and barber for 30 years.
- During most of those years, Bradenton's pulse has been dictated by the nine-month growing season of oranges and the rush to process the delectable fruit into a concentrate for shipping.

HISTORICAL SNAPSHOT
1978

- Harvard University moved toward a more structured undergraduate curriculum and away from the more relevant one adopted in the 1960s
- Television's late-night host, Johnny Carson, made $4 million, while *Happy Days*' Henry Winkler collected $990,000 for his acting talents
- Alex Haley's book *Roots* sparked an interest in genealogy, particularly among African-Americans
- Fifty percent of all shoe sales were for sneakers, topping 200 million pairs
- Airline deregulation eliminated federal controls on fares and routes; eight airlines controlled 81 percent of the domestic market
- The legal retirement age was raised to 70
- Gold sold for $245 per ounce
- Three Gutenberg Bibles were sold within three months of each other, one for $2.2 million
- California voters adopted Proposition 13 to control property taxes
- The tax code permitted 401(k) savings plans for the first time
- Legalized gambling in Atlantic City, New Jersey; microchip technology in washing machines; *Garfield* cartoons; pocket math calculators; and 45-rpm picture disc records all made their first appearance
- Morris, the advertising symbol for Nine Lives cat food, died at the age of 17
- The number of unmarried couples living together more than doubled from 523,000 in 1970 to 1,137,000
- Attracted by jobs and housing, more than 1,000 families were moving to Dallas, Texas, each month
- Pepsico acquired Mexican fast-food chain, Taco Bell
- The cost of a first-class postage stamp rose to $0.15 per ounce
- The USDA warned of the dangers of nitrites in processed and cured meat products, reporting that sodium nitrite may cause cancer
- Edith Bunker, a character on the television show *All in the Family*, said, "With credit, you can buy everything you can't afford"
- The King Tutankhamen show touring America produced $5 million for the Cairo Museum
- Attendance for the North American Soccer League rose 50 percent to 5.3 million fans
- *If Life Is a Bowl of Cherries—What Am I Doing in the Pits?* by Erma Bombeck, *The World According to Garp* by John Irving and *The Complete Book of Running* by James Fixx were all on the bestseller list

1978 ECONOMIC PROFILE

The national consumer expenditures (per capita income) in 1978 were:

Auto Parts	$60.65
Auto Usage	$808.68
Clothing	$359.86
Dentists	$50.77
Food	$1,259.09
Furniture	$80.87
Gas and Oil	$225.08
Health Insurance	$53.46
Housing	$906.17
Intercity Transport	$49.87
Local Transport	$21.56
New Auto Purchase	$217.89
Personal Business	$359.41
Personal Care	$103.33
Physicians	$146.01
Private Education and Research	$119.95
Recreation	$435.79
Religion/Welfare Activities	$132.53
Telephone and Telegraph	$107.37
Tobacco	$82.22
Utilities	$274.95
Per Capita Consumption	$6,384.98

Annual Income, Standard Jobs

Bituminous Coal Mining	$20,160.00
Building Trades	$15,394.00
Domestics	$7,206.00
Farm Labor	$6,438.00
Federal Civilian	$18,905.00
Federal Employees, Executive Departments	$15,068.00
Federal Military	$11,570.00
Finance, Insurance and Real Estate	$13,207.00
Gas and Electricity Workers	$18,277.00
Manufacturing, Durable Goods	$15,841.00
Manufacturing, Nondurable Goods	$13,564.00
Medical/Health Services Workers	$12,179.00
Miscellaneous Manufacturing	$11,494.00
Motion Picture Services	$14,910.00
Nonprofit Organization Workers	$8,933.00
Passenger Transportation Workers, Local and Highway	$11,590.00

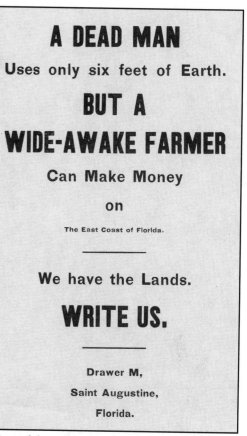
Turn-of-the-century land promotion.

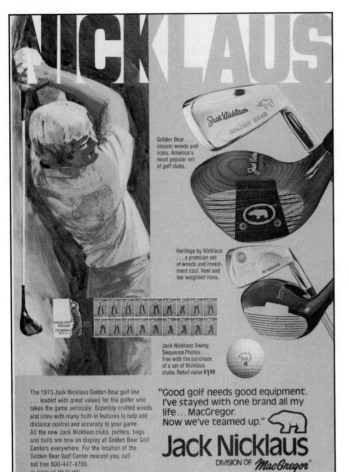

Personal Services $9,048.00
Private Industry, Including
    Farm Labor $13,143.00
Public School Teachers. $13,391.00
Radio Broadcasting and
    Television Workers. $16,879.00
Railroad Workers. $20,605.00
State and Local Government
    Workers $13,022.00
Telephone and Telegraph
    Workers $19,032.00
Wholesale and Retail Trade
    Workers $15,711.00

Selected Prices

Alcohol, Stroh's Beer, Six-Pack $1.49
Baby Walker $10.88
Bandages, Curad $0.69
Bath Scale $17.99
Bean Bag, Vinyl $37.95
Bicycle, 26" $64.99
Bookcase, Antique
    Chippendale $6,600.00
Calculator, Pocket $74.95
CB Radio $39.88
Charcoal Starter, Gulf Lite $0.57
Clothes Dryer $149.00
Hotel Room, New York $31.00
Hummingbird Feeder $13.50
Jumpsuit, Woman's Denim $31.99
Massage Shower Head $26.95
Microwave Oven. $168.00
Sheets, Satin, Twin-Size. $12.00
Tennis Balls, Wilson, Three-Pack $2.29
Tire, Steel-Belted Radial $42.00
Viewer, Viewmaster, 3-D. $17.44

The History of Oranges

- The first mention of oranges in literature appears in the Shu-ching, a Chinese book compiled in the sixth century BC.
- Sanskrit literature of the eighth century BC mentions mandarins, the orange fruit similar to tangerines.
- The earliest citrus fruit known in Europe was the citron, valued for its aromatic rind.
- Before the days of Alexander the Great, Greeks imported citrons from Persia.
- From Greece, citrons spread to Palestine, where one variety became a sacred food to be consumed during the Jewish Feast of Tabernacles.
- In the first century AD Romans ate sweet oranges they called "Indian fruit."

"Leisure: Consumers were willing to pay for entertainment last year if they didn't have to pay too much. And don't look for the big-ticket items to come back this year," *Forbes*, January 9, 1978:

"To talk about the leisure industry is to talk primarily about the consumer's wallet. Last year's consumer was still worried about the economy, energy, taxes and unemployment, so companies that could give him cheap entertainment got him to pull out that wallet more often than those pitching him something for $500 down and three years to pay. This year looks like more of the same.

'In the past, entertainment was expensive in terms of both dollars and energy,' says analyst Anthony Hoffman of Bache Halsey Stuart and Shields. 'One of the best forms of entertainment was just driving around. Now people have turned away from that. You can buy a helluva lot of records for the price of a snowmobile.'

While nobody in the leisure industry did really badly last year, entertainment and publishing companies were the outstanding performers. Total motion-picture box-office receipts were an estimated 15 percent ahead of the $2.1 billion record set in 1975, and paperback books and records were also strong sellers. People entertained themselves or their friends more at home, aided by a Flash Gordon assortment of video games, videotape recorders, pinball machines and home computers, but sales of energy-using boats and recreational vehicles were disappointing. More people ate out: the average family now spends about $20 a week on food eaten away from the home.

Moviemakers had a good year because they were making good movies; and in terms of a big return, nothing beats a hot movie. Twentieth Century-Fox's earnings jumped from $1.34 a share to about $7, largely because of *Star Wars*. Foreign rentals from the movie will continue to flow to Fox this year. Columbia Pictures is counting on its science-fiction entry, *Close Encounters of the Third Kind*, which at $21 million was the most expensive film in the company's history, to work the same magic this year."

- In 1493, on a second voyage to Hispaniola, Columbus brought orange, lemon and citron seeds from the Canary Islands.
- Pedro Menendez de Aviles brought the sweet orange into Florida at St. Augustine in 1565, and by 1579, Menendez reported to Spain that oranges were flourishing in their new home.
- New Yorkers drank no orange juice until Spain ceded Florida to the British in 1763, when enterprising traders began shipping the fruit north.
- William Bartram, the great Philadelphia naturalist, found wild oranges in abundance in 1773.

Stefano is constantly working to keep up with the technology and technique of golf.

- Oranges came into their own in 1821 when Spain ceded Florida to the United States.
- Between 1874 and 1877, the production of oranges in Florida exploded; the eastern United States was annually importing about 200 million oranges with a value of more than $2 million.
- Most oranges were from the Mediterranean, some from the West Indies and some from Florida.
- The crowning touch of Florida's citrus expansion came with the arrival in 1886 of a man named Lue Gim Gong, a Chinese man with tuberculosis, who came to Florida for its healthy climate.
- Lue Gim Gong then spent 39 years hybridizing new varieties of tomatoes, grapefruit and oranges.
- The Lue Gim Gong orange is still a factor in Florida's citrus industry.
- In 1935, the Florida Citrus Commission was established, through which 10 percent of each year's crop value is spent on advertising the health aspects of Florida lemons, grapefruits and oranges.
- In 1960, CBS-TV aired a program about Florida's widespread use of Caribbean migrant workers, whose low pay and poor housing were the norm; the show was entitled, *Harvest of Shame.*
- Today, food-processing plants dominate the 3,000-plus manufacturing establishments in the state, including packing houses, canneries and frozen concentrate plants that draw their raw material from the citrus and vegetable fields of Florida.
- Production this year is expected to exceed 202 million boxes of Florida citrus fruits.

"The Price of Mobility," *Forbes*, **July 24, 1978:**

"Is the practice of shifting executives willy-nilly around the country unraveling the fabric of American society, as some critics charge? The reason is important, if for no other reason, because shifting a family can cost a corporation $15,000 to $20,000 (employers pick up 150,000 to 200,000 relocation tabs a year). That is no small price to pay if it means turned-off employees in the bargain. According to one new survey, the answer looks like 'no.' Chicago's Employee Transfer Corp., which specializes in helping with the real-estate and moving problems of relocated personnel, canvassed 1,000 transferees and, after tabulating the replies of the 346 who answered, found that 84 percent were ready to move again if asked. Traumas there were (69 percent said they considered transfers 'stressful'), but 29 percent said they were 'very willing' to pack up once more, and 51 percent were 'somewhat willing.' The big consideration—money. If such a shift meant a financial burden, 78 percent said they would choose to stay put."

Unlimited Mileage $302-323.*

Fly to as many of 101 Eastern Airlines cities as you can.

Discover the wonders of Mexico, the Caribbean, Walt Disney World, Los Angeles, and much more, all in one trip with Eastern Airlines' Unlimited Mileage Fare (will be available through September 10, 1978).

The fare is just $302-323* per person (children 2-11 only $202-215* each). At least two adult fare coach passengers must travel together for the entire trip, or one adult and two children. You must reserve and purchase tickets at least 14 days in advance, and take a trip of at least seven but not more than 21 days on Eastern.

You must stop over in at least three cities (only once in the same city, except to change planes). Travel to or from Canada is not included.

For more information, call the travel specialist, your travel agent; or write to Eastern's "Unlimited Mileage Fare," P.O. Box 787, Miami, Fla. 33148, for a detailed brochure.

Pick from 101 cities, 11 countries, and one Magic Kingdom.

EASTERN
THE WINGS OF MAN

*Prices quoted are coach fares which will vary depending on the Federal transportation taxes applicable to the particular routing flown. Local airport departure taxes and fuel surcharges, if applicable, are not included. Fare is not available over peak holiday periods and is subject to change. "The Wings of Man" is a registered service mark of Eastern Air Lines, Inc.

The Cricketeers are helping men on their way up get there quicker.

A smart executive knows he has to look smart, too. That's why Cricketeer is suiting so many successful men. All our suits reflect good taste. And good value, too. Take this classic white linen-look suit in a practical blend of Fortrel,® rayon and flax. It has beautiful styling, expensive tailoring, an elegant fabric and a price that makes it a very smart buy. Only about $130.

CRICKETEER® Good taste is our design.

FORTREL FOR SUITS

"Squeezing the Average Family," *Fortune*, February 13, 1978:

"By way of preparing you for this year's great debate on tax cuts, we call your attention to the following proposition: under present tax laws, the average American family is in grave danger of slipping into the 50 percent bracket. That sounds incredible, but it's true—or at least, it's true if you count all Social Security and income taxes.

Let us assume that the family we're talking about is one of those standard models with a husband, wife and two young children. Naturally, they take the standard deduction. They live in California (where state income taxes are about average) and this year will earn around $18,000 (a reasonable guess for the median income of such four-person families). Assume that in the years ahead their income rises in line with the basic inflation rate which, let us assume, will be 6.5 percent—the figure Fortune's Business Roundup is projecting for the next 18 months.

On this unsurprising assumption, our average family reaches the 50 percent bracket in about eight years. By 1986, its income is around $30,000. After taking the standard deduction and four exemptions, it has a taxable income of $24,000, which puts it in the 36 percent bracket for federal taxes (up from the 25 percent bracket it's in now). It will meanwhile be in the 10 percent bracket for state taxes (up from six percent) The Social Security bite will be 7.15 percent (up from 6.05 percent). Total marginal rate for the average family: 53 percent (up from 37 percent)."

1979 FAMILY PROFILE

For seven generations, Blaine Maxwell's family has operated the Maxwell Manufacturing Company, now one of the oldest companies listed on the New York Stock Exchange. Thanks to a plan pioneered by Blaine, the Connecticut-based company is now experiencing rapid growth.

Annual Income: Approximately $1.2 million, including salary, stock dividends and investments.

Life at Home

- Blaine Maxwell's company, community and home are all intertwined; each had its beginnings more than 200 years ago in the small Connecticut village of Windsor Locks.
- Recently, thanks to Blaine's energy and insight, Maxwell Manufacturing—for the first time in its 212-year history—joined the Forbes industry listing of the nation's largest companies.
- Blaine lives in a 199-year-old home built by an ancestor; a family member from every other generation has added a room or an addition to the building—and Blaine is no exception.
- Using lumber from a forest in Pennsylvania, Blaine and his wife Amy have constructed an extensive library off the back to hold her books on architecture, Connecticut history and antiques.
- The entire room was built with traditional tools, and without nails or screws; the cost exceeded $500,000.
- Today, his home and property sprawl over six acres.

Blaine Maxwell's company is now experiencing rapid growth.

Amy serves on a statewide task force to save historic landmarks and buildings.

- Founded in 1767, when the location of Maxwell Manufacturing's headquarters in Windsor Locks, Connecticut, was called Pine Meadow, the company remained largely unchanged from its colonial days—until two decades ago.
- At its origin, the company scoured wool sheared from local flocks and sold cattle feed to farmers.
- After 191 years, it could boast sales of $9.5 million.
- Its transformation began after World War II, when Blaine returned from the war determined to change the family business.
- Today he says, "I saw what the modern world was going to be like and I wanted our company to be part of it."
- With his company now well-positioned for the future, Blaine is spending most of his time working in his community and investing in energy.
- To pay tribute to Windsor Locks and the six generations that came before him, he and Amy have personally paid to have the cemeteries in the community upgraded, cleaned and refurbished.
- He has also established a fund at the public library to acquire books, papers, writings, pictures and etchings from the area.
- Thus far, cost has not been a factor; when an excellent example of local history is found at auction or through a New York book dealer, the Maxwells have donated generously.
- Amy, whose Connecticut roots stretch back five generations, has taken a keen interest in preserving the past, and has authored two local histories which were reviewed well and published by her family trust.

The couple enjoys retreating to their Nantucket Island home.

- Now on a statewide task force to save historic landmarks, bridges and homes, she travels Connecticut, inspecting sites.
- On two occasions she has used her own money to buy dilapidated buildings which were within days of meeting a wrecking ball.
- One building has since been completely renovated and sold—a process that took more than a year; the second is still awaiting word from the architect whether it can be saved at all.
- Through his company, Blaine annually funds scholarships for five students to attend college—provided they go into the sciences.
- Last year, the community did not produce enough high school graduates interested in both going to college and majoring in the sciences to use the generous grants, named after his great-great-great-great-grandfather, who started the company.
- The couple's other great joy is their Nantucket Island home, whose buildings and architecture are little changed in more than 100 years.
- One of its greatest treasures is its isolation; they don't even mind that the Sunday *New York Times* does not arrive there until Monday.
- Once described by Daniel Webster as a "city at sea," Nantucket was home to more than 125 whaling captains in the 1830s.
- Many traditions from the era are preserved; at 9 p.m. the old Lisbon bell at South Tower sounds a curfew, striking 52 times.

Amy has used her own money to save dilapidated buildings from destruction.

- Nantucket has also become the place where the couple's five children gather in the summer with the 11 grandchildren, who have learned to crab, fish and sail on the Island.
- This summer at Nantucket was particularly joyous with the return of their second son from the Peace Corps; he will enter law school in the fall.
- From a personal standpoint, Blaine is now obsessed with being part of the solution to the energy crisis; natural gas, he tells everyone, is the answer.
- This unused resource, which is plentiful in the Western Hemisphere, could be the energy source of the future; he is determined that America should not become dependent on Arab oil, believing it would be the first step in eliminating American freedom.
- He was outraged recently when the Organization of the Petroleum Exporting Countries increased oil prices by 14.5 percent.
- Already *The New York Times* is reporting that residential utility bills will be up an average of as much as $7.50 a month because of the rising price of oil.
- Even Saudi Arabia, a traditional friend of the United States, appears unable to check OPEC's manipulation of oil production to control oil prices.
- To have an impact on America's energy future, he is investing millions of dollars in Canada's Noranda Mines, which sits on one of the continent's richest natural gas deposits.
- Noranda's earnings have doubled in four years, and currently, the cheap Canadian dollar is helping even more; because the company does about a quarter of its business abroad, mainly in the United States, it pays its miners and keeps its books in Canadian dollars while receiving much of its income in foreign currencies.
- The resulting leverage effect on the company's earnings is enormous; for example, where U.S. producers of a product such as copper get $0.72 a pound, Noranda gets $0.85 Canadian.
- In that way, a $0.01 decline in the value of the Canadian dollar means an extra $5 million after taxes to the company; to Blaine, this means Noranda will have the capital to continue exploration for natural gas and the building of pipelines.
- Today, Noranda is the largest landowner in Canada, with 1.2 million of what may be the largest pool of natural gas yet discovered in North America.
- Potentially, the site could contain twice the gas reserves of those in New Mexico's prolific San Juan Basin, and double those in Alaska's Prudhoe Bay.
- So far, more than $140 million has been spent drilling 40 wells, most of them successful, with proven reserves of about one trillion cubic feet.
- As important, Noranda's fields are only 40 miles from an existing pipeline linking the Pacific Gas Transmission system at Kingsgate, British Columbia, with the lucrative markets in the United States.
- The stock of Noranda has doubled in the past year, since Blaine began investing.

Life at Work

- During the past 20 years, Blaine Maxwell has progressively transformed his family-owned company.

- This year, sales will top $350 million and net earnings will be well over $20 million—both double-digit gains over the previous year.
- Thanks to his desire for change, the company makes and sells hundreds of products—ranging from coatings for the inside of beer cans, adhesives for jet planes, cleaning systems for poultry processors and paper for tea bags—manufactured in 100 research and marketing facilities around the world.
- The headquarters are now in a modern concrete and glass building on the site of the company's original office, where from across the way, Blaine can keep an eye on the company's paper and non-woven fabric mill that has been built along the Connecticut River in various stages over the past two centuries.
- Today, the company concentrates on developing new specialty chemicals used by specific manufacturers such as Budweiser, Lear Siegler and Thomas J. Lipton; most of the company's growth has taken place through such innovations.
- One of its first acquisitions, Standard Insulation Company, signaled the company's determination to move away from its dependence on slow-growth, capital-intensive, non-woven production into more research-intensive manufacturing businesses.
- If the company had attempted to grow purely through non-wovens, they would not be in existence today, Blaine believes; to grow, he preaches, the company must be smart and responsive.
- He spends much of his time on the road meeting with customers—and training his staff; an ex-salesman himself, he insists that his more than 700 salesmen be familiar enough with the customers' needs to actually run the machines on which the company's products are used.

The Maxwells love the isolation of the town.

- "When we go into the marketplace, we find out what a customer wants us to invent and then we come back to the lab and invent it," he said recently during a speech at a local Rotary Club meeting.
- Using this concept, the company has developed a high-temperature exterior coating for cookware which will be used to compete with DuPont's Teflon™.
- Recently, to expand its capacity, Maxwell Manufacturing made its first acquisition in five years—an Ohio manufacturer of water-treatment chemicals.
- Thanks to strategic positioning and planning, 22 of the 26 business segments within the company are either first or second in share for their market.

Nantucket has become the place where their 11 grandchildren can learn to swim and fish.

- In addition, Blaine believes his company is less affected by the soaring rate of inflation because of the industries to which he sells; 55 percent of the company's sales are in industries that traditionally resist economic slumps, such as beer, soft drinks and medical supplies.

Life in the Community: Windsor Locks, Connecticut
- The pride of being from Connecticut extends to almost all of the state's three million-plus residents, including those who live in speck-on-the-map villages.
- All of Connecticut could be contained 53 times within the borders of Texas; only two states are smaller—Rhode Island and Delaware.
- Currently, Connecticut's per capita income is the highest in the nation.
- The village of Windsor Locks, and the entire state, have been at the vanguard of preservation efforts; thousands of colonial homes are still actively used, thanks to this dedication.
- Blaine's 199-year-old home is surrounded by dozens of houses of similar age.
- During the American Revolution, the home was used for meetings to determine how cloth, firewood and ammunition would be distributed throughout New England.
- Blaine's ancestors fully realized that if the British won the war, the house would certainly be confiscated or burned.
- For a state known for its urbanization and industry, Connecticut is more than 60 percent wooded, with oak being the most common hardwood in the state.

"Connecticut Journal," *The New York Times*, June 3, 1979:

"The Celebrated Jumping Frog Contest, for 23 years a dependable sign of springtime for youngsters in Hartford, has taken a giant leap into oblivion, prodded by the consciences of natural scientists and the public.

'An undercurrent of disaffection for turtle races, snake races, frog contests and anything involving wild animals has been definite and outspoken,' said Wynn Lee, director of the Mark Twain Memorial at 351 Farmington Ave. The Twain Memorial had been the site of the contest, which was inspired by the Twain short story, 'The Celebrated Jumping Frog of Calaveras County.'

In the last few years, nationwide publicity expanded what had been a brief local activity for children from six to 16 into a daylong sideshow drawing so many adults that 'it was difficult for the children to see,' Mr. Lee explained. 'We had almost 200 frogs last year from several surrounding states. A whole busload came from Vermont.

'In 1976,' he continued, 'the frog that won the weeklong Calaveras contest in California was brought here for the Bicentennial. He won here, too, then went on to Hannibal, Missouri, and lost. He must have been exhausted. Or maybe it was a she.'

Traditionally, members of the staff of the Children's Museum of Hartford, co-sponsor of the event, were present to see that the children were instructed in the care and feeding of frogs, and to protect the frogs from abuse. 'Children would sometimes have to wait for several hours until their frog could compete,' said Mr. Lee. The museum provided frog-sitting services for owners who had to leave the premises temporarily.

'When the people at the museum told us they couldn't participate this year and that this sort of thing basically tells children they can use wild animals as toys, we decided to reevaluate our position,' Mr. Lee said. 'We are not a natural-science facility and have always recognized the need for co-sponsorship by suitable agencies, so we tried some others. We couldn't find anyone else who was interested.'"

- Recently, salmon were restocked in Connecticut waters in hopes that sport and commercial fishing will be possible in the future.
- Like those of their neighbors, the Maxwells' home is furnished with antiques handed down through the family for generations.
- Amy is especially pleased to tell guests that her ancestors built the chairs they are sitting on and were probably the inventors of the roundabout chair.

HISTORICAL SNAPSHOT
1979

- The divorce rate increased 68 percent since 1968; the median duration of marriage was 6.6 years

- The Sony Walkman, a portable cassette player with headphones, was introduced

- U.S. Trust reported that 520,000 Americans—one in every 424—were millionaires

- Numerous brands of hair dryers were recalled because of suspected amounts of asbestos

- The sale of health foods zoomed from $140 million in 1940 to $1.6 billion

- The first Jiffy Lube fast oil-change automotive service center opened

- Inflation was at its worst in 33 years; prices increased more than 13.3 percent

- The Supreme Court ruled that "husbands only" alimony laws were unconstitutional

- Ford Motor Company acquired 25 percent of Japan's Mazda Motor Company

- The near-meltdown of a nuclear power plant at Three Mile Island ignited anti-nuclear fears nationwide

- California became the first state to initiate gas rationing, creating alternate-day purchasing

- Avon Products acquired Tiffany and Company

- The prime lending rate at banks hit 14.5 percent

- Massachusetts became the seventh state to increase the legal drinking age from 18 to 20

- A *New York Times* poll reported that 55 percent of the population saw nothing wrong with premarital sex

- Jane Fonda and Tom Hayden toured 50 cities to speak out against nuclear power

- Electronic blackboards, nitrite-free hot dogs, Cracker Jack ice cream bars and the video digital sound disc all made their first appearance

- The play *Grease* passed *Fiddler on the Roof* as the longest-running Broadway show

- More than 315,000 microcomputers were sold

1979 ECONOMIC PROFILE

The national consumer expenditures (per capita income) in 1979 were:

Auto Parts	$63.98
Auto Usage	$885.12
Clothing	$377.68
Dentists	$54.65
Food	$1,390.33
Furniture	$90.20
Gas and Oil	$294.15
Health Insurance	$55.09
Housing	$1,006.86
Intercity Transport	$58.21
Local Transport	$21.33
New Auto Purchase	$219.06
Personal Business	$397.68
Personal Care	$111.53
Physicians	$163.52
Private Education and Research	$132.41
Recreation	$487.44
Religion/Welfare Activities	$148.85
Telephone and Telegraph	$114.19
Tobacco	$85.31
Utilities	$309.26
Per Capita Consumption	$7,036.95

Annual Income, Standard Jobs

Bituminous Coal Mining	$22,363.00
Building Trades	$16,785.00
Domestics	$7,912.00
Farm Labor	$7,154.00
Federal Civilian	$19,907.00
Federal Employees, Executive Departments	$15,961.00
Federal Military	$12,316.00
Finance, Insurance and Real Estate	$14,326.00
Gas and Electricity Workers	$19,697.00
Manufacturing, Durable Goods	$17,212.00
Manufacturing, Nondurable Goods	$14,738.00
Medical/Health Services Workers	$13,276.00
Miscellaneous Manufacturing	$12,563.00
Motion Picture Services	$16,821.00
Nonprofit Organization Workers	$9,564.00
Passenger Transportation Workers, Local and Highway	$12,266.00

"Roundabout Chair," *New England Furniture*, 1984:

"This simple, inexpensive roundabout is unpretentious. The chair has no splats, and the rear stretchers are unadorned. The one carved foot is so minimally modeled that it seems to suggest a Spanish foot more than to be one. The arms and crest rail are simple versions of those on more stylish roundabouts."

Personal Services $9,723.00
Private Industry, Including
 Farm Labor $14,310.00
Public School Teachers. $14,306.00
Radio Broadcasting and
 Television Workers. $18,329.00
Railroad Workers. $23,021.00
State and Local Government
 Workers $13,879.00
Telephone and Telegraph
 Workers $20,646.00
Wholesale and Retail Trade
 Workers $17,113.00

Selected Prices

Airfare, Los Angeles to Boston $230.00
Alaskan King Crab, Three Pounds $7.50
Baby Holder, Johnny Jump-Up $6.99
Basketball Goal $49.99
Donation, Save the Children
 Federation, per Month $16.00
Espresso Maker. $40.00
Figurine, Steuben Glass. $160.00
Floor Lamp $78.50
Guitar, Student $19.95
Hair Dryer, Presto $3.88
Makeup, Revlon Ultima II $8.50
Maternity Top $9.00
Motor Oil, 10W30 . . . . $0.39
Razor Blades $1.29
Slow Cooker $13.79
Storm Windows, Triple Track. $32.95
Sunglasses $7.99
Touring Cap, Man's L.L.Bean. $7.50
Tricycle $16.99

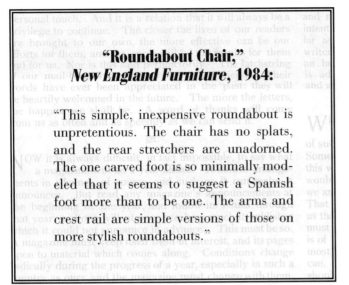

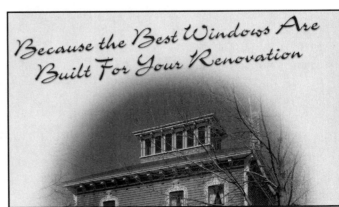

Because the Best Windows Are Built For Your Renovation

"Nepal Is Nepal, New York Is 'Fat City,' " by David Jarmul, *The New York Times*, June 9, 1979:

"People wrote to me before I recently returned home to New York, after two years in the Peace Corps, about all the changes I'd find: disco, roller skating, a new mayor, a decent Rangers team.

But nobody warned me about what's remained the same: how rich and wasteful this city is.

New York's being rich sounds strange, I know. After all, the city was staving off bankruptcy when I left in 1977. And I hear similar sacrificial moans from New Yorkers now about gas prices and inflation.

But today, those cries ring hollow. After I've lived so long in a truly poor country, New York seems like Fat City. People here don't realize how lucky they have it.

My post was in Nepal. My first year was spent in a Himalayan hill bazaar, Ilam, the second in Katmandu, the capital. I taught English and writing, worked with blind students, set up several newspapers and organized a village literacy project.

The Peace Corps paid me $76 monthly, $92 in Katmandu. This was plenty. The per capita income in Nepal is less than $100 a year. Given the skewed distribution of wealth, many Nepalese live on less than $0.15 daily. Most children work. The literacy rate is below 20 percent.

One of my students in Ilam was Mardi Kumar, an untouchable. One week he didn't come to school. I went to his house to see why not. His father told me that Mardi's older brother was dying in the local hospital.

The doctor said Mardi's brother needed insulin. There was none to be had in eastern Nepal. The father pleaded with me. I was a foreigner; didn't I have some insulin? No, I didn't. A few days later his son died.

In Katmandu, I hired a cook, Harka Bahadur. I taught him to read Nepalese and gave him room, board and $1.75 weekly. The neighbors complained this was too much and would drive up local prices. I insisted. Harka supported his mother, wife and baby daughter on his

salary. He had no money for eggs, fruit or medicines. In the winter I had to convince him to take a sweater I'd been given for the holidays.

Now I'm home. My first full day back, my folks took me to see the new shopping atrium at the Citicorp headquarters. I saw imported jams at $10 per bottle, exotic pastries, shiny furniture stores, a giant delicatessen, several chic cafes.

The following morning I had an argument with my father about Mother's Day. My father wanted me to buy my mother an azalea bush. As much as I love her, I couldn't bring myself to spend the money. My mother doesn't need an azalea bush, I told him. 'So why waste money that others need just to survive?'

My father told me that I was cultureshocked. I ought to stop converting New York prices into what they could buy abroad. Nepal was Nepal. This was New York, why take it out on my Mother. . . .

The point is that right now I don't want to get back into a consumptive American life. I don't want to jump on the bottled water bandwagon when I can just as easily drink water out of the faucet like I did before I left and give the $0.70 per bottle to somebody who really needs it.

But, as I've learned quickly, to say these things out loud, even with the excuse of being just out of the Peace Corps, makes one come across like an Asianized Jeremiah. Friends ask me, quite rightly, just what it is that I expect them to do. Give up all of life's small luxuries until there are no more poor people? My instinctive reaction right now is to say yes.

That's idealistic and unworkable, I know, but I remember too vividly my Nepalese friends: Rudra Bahadur, the farmer across the street who thanked me profusely when I gave him my worn-out rugby shirt. Ram Prasad, a fellow teacher who almost burst into tears when I gave him the $7.00 calculator that I'd bought in Times Square. The brahmin village family—I don't even know their names—who shared with

(continued)

"Nepal Is Nepal, New York Is 'Fat City,' . . . *(continued)*

me their dinner of rice, lentils and dried yams when I appeared on their doorstep one evening while hiking.

Intellectually, I recognize that if a friend here spends $20 extra on a pair of blue jeans just to sport a designer label, it isn't going to make any difference in the lives of my Nepalese friends. Not unless the friend chooses to send the $20 to Nepal and just take a pair of Levi's.

But I can't choose for others. And I also know that I must fight off this moralism. I know there

are many poor New Yorkers, poor Americans. Our country can't take upon itself all of the world's suffering. We shouldn't all go through life guilt-ridden. After all, that's Nepal; this is New York.

Still, as I face my new life ahead, I keep wondering: am I really as culture-shocked as people tell me, or is American society as profligate as it now seems to me? Will I be able to hold onto my new convictions about living modestly and helping others? Will I remember?"

"Is Charity Obsolete?" by James Cook, *Forbes*, February 5, 1979:

"Beset by high taxes, controversy and a good bit of dehumanization, the charity business is in trouble. But consider the alternative.

When it comes to charity, Americans are not extravagantly generous these days. Perhaps they feel they are giving more than enough to the needy through the Internal Revenue Service. At any rate, last year they indulged all their philanthropic feelings to the tune of little more than $35 billion, 2.25 percent of their disposable income and about as much as they spent on liquor, cosmetics and movies.

Over 83 percent of that $35 billion comes from individuals, and the rest from bequests (six percent), foundations (5.7 percent) and corporations (4.5 percent). Close to half—a declining half—went to religious organizations, another quarter went to education, culture and the arts. Only 25 percent, or less than three quarters of a cent of the disposable income dollar, went to what most people think of as charity, those health and social welfare agencies that raise funds mainly through community fundraising campaigns.

In a society as superaffluent as ours, you can't, of course, dismiss that fraction of a penny. It added up last year to a resounding $9 billion. That makes charity a very substantial business, employing perhaps five million people and enlisting the volunteer efforts of as many as 45 million more. It is also a business where a great deal is happening these days—not all of it good. 'Many people think charity is a racket and fundraisers are crooks,' confesses one professional fundraiser. And as a result, among those congressmen who feel that government should have a hand in just about everything, there is a growing sentiment for legislation to put charitable organizations under rigid controls. And

that's hardly the worst of it. With the increased use by taxpayers of the standard deduction—75 percent now use it in contrast to 52 percent just eight years ago—charitable contributions have become useless as a tax offset for most Americans. Thus, charitable giving, while rising steadily in dollar terms, has not only failed to keep up with inflation, it has also been dropping steadily as a percentage of disposable income.

According to one estimate, the government itself now provides very nearly as much of the funds used by private charities as private donors do. But for all that, in contrast with Europe, where philanthropy has pretty much become the province of the state, in the U.S. it remains solidly in private hands, a clear sign that Americans are not yet ready to hand over all their responsibilities to Big Brother.

Like any industry with growth problems, philanthropy is experiencing intense competition and a good deal of infighting, some of it quite bitter. The outs—the new activist agencies concerned more with minority rights than with social services—are fighting to get in. The older charities are struggling to maintain or increase their share of the market. What raises the infighting to fever pitch is that between inflation and changing social conditions, the traditional fundraising methods—direct mail and door-to-door solicitation—have become worrisomely costly to ineffective. The result is that more and more agencies have been looking for new approaches—to combined fundraising campaigns and to the payroll deduction plans in particular—as a means of reducing their costs.

This has inevitably brought them into conflict with the United Way of America, the biggest federated campaign organization of them all."

1980–1989

The economic turbulence of the 1970s continued during the early years of the 1980s. Rates for both interest and inflation were at a staggering 18 percent. With the economy at a standstill, unemployment was rising. By 1982, America was in its deepest depression since the Great Depression of the 1930s. One in 10 Americans was out of work. Yet, by the end of the decade, thanks in part to the productivity gains provided by computers and new technology, more and more Americans were entering the ranks of the millionaire and feeling better off than they had in a decade.

Convinced that inflation was the primary enemy of long-term economic growth, the Federal Reserve Board brought the economy to a standstill in the early days of the decade. It was a shock treatment that worked. By 1984, the tight money policies of the government, stabilizing world oil prices, and labor's declining bargaining power brought inflation to four percent, the lowest level since 1967. Despite the pain it caused, the plan to strangle inflation succeeded; Americans not only prospered, but many believed it was their right to be successful. The decade came to be symbolized by self-indulgence.

At the same time, defense and deficit spending roared into high gear, the economy continued to grow, and the stock market rocketed to record levels (the Dow Jones Industrial Average tripled from 1,000 in 1980 to nearly 3,000 a decade later). In the center of recovery was Mr. Optimism, President Ronald Reagan. During his presidential campaign he promised a "morning in America" and during eight years, his good nature helped transform the national mood. The Reagan era, which spanned most of the 1980s, fostered a new conservative agenda of good feeling. During the presidential election against incumbent President Jimmy Carter, Reagan joked, "A recession is when your neighbor loses his job. A depression is when you lose yours. And recovery is when Jimmy Carter loses his."

The economic wave of the 1980s was also driven by globalization, improvements in technology, and willingness of consumers to assume higher and higher levels of personal debt. By the 1980s, the two-career family became the norm. Forty-two percent of all American workers were female, and more than half of all married women and 90 percent of female college graduates worked outside the home. Yet, their median wage was 60 percent of that of men. The rapid rise of women in the labor force, which had been accelerating since the 1960s, brought great social change, affecting married life, child rearing, family income, office culture, and the growth of the national economy.

The rising economy brought greater control of personal lives; homeownership accelerated, choices seemed limitless, debt grew, and divorce became commonplace. The collapse of communism at the end of the 1980s brought an end to the old world order and set the stage for a realignment of power. America was regarded as the strongest nation in the world and the only real superpower, thanks to its economic strength. As democracy swept across eastern Europe, the U.S. economy began to feel the impact of a "peace dividend" generated by a reduced military budget and a desire by corporations to participate in global markets—including Russia and China. Globalization was having another impact. At the end of World War II, the U.S. economy accounted for almost 50 percent of the global economic product; by 1987, the U.S. share was less than 25 percent as American companies moved plants offshore and countries such as Japan emerged as major competitors. This need for a global reach inspired several rounds of corporate mergers as companies searched for efficiency, market share, new products, or emerging technology to survive in the rapidly shifting business environment.

The 1980s were the age of the conservative Yuppie. Business schools, investment banks, and Wall Street firms overflowed with eager baby boomers who placed gourmet cuisine, health clubs, supersneakers, suspenders, wine spritzers, high-performance autos, and sushi high on their agendas. Low-fat and fiber cereals and Jane Fonda workout books symbolized much of the decade. As self-indulgence rose, concerns about the environment, including nuclear waste, acid rain, and the greenhouse effect declined. Homelessness increased and racial tensions fostered a renewed call for a more caring government. During the decade, genetic engineering came of age, including early attempts at transplantation and gene mapping. Personal computers, which were transforming America, were still in their infancy.

The sexual revolution, undaunted by a conservative prescription of chastity, ran head-on into a powerful adversary during the 1980s with the discovery and spread of AIDS, a frequently fatal, sexually transmitted disease. The right of women to have an abortion, confirmed by the Supreme Court in 1973, was hotly contested during the decade as politicians fought over both the actual moment of conception and the right of a woman to control her body. Cocaine also made its reappearance, bringing drug addiction and a rapid increase in violent crime. The Center on Addiction and Substance Abuse at Columbia University found alcohol and drug abuse implicated in three fourths of all murders, rapes, child molestations, and deaths of babies suffering from parental neglect.

For the first time in history, the Naval Academy's graduating class included women, digital clocks and cordless telephones appeared, and 24-hour-a-day news coverage captivated television viewers. Compact disks began replacing records, and Smurf and E.T. paraphernalia were everywhere, New York became the first state to require seat belts, Pillsbury introduced microwave pizza, and Playtex used live lingerie models in its ads for the "Cross Your Heart" bra. The Supreme Court ruled that states may require all-male private clubs to admit women, and 50,000 people gathered at Graceland in Memphis, Tennessee, on the tenth anniversary of Elvis Presley's death.

1982 News Profile

"California's Silicon Valley Is Mass-Producing Millionaires in the Chips," *Life*, March 1982:

"The gold rush of '49 comes to mind. Or maybe the celluloid rush to Hollywood in the 1920s. But in the annals of American fortune building, the boom now rocking the computer industry's California cradle is, like the technology itself, dazzling. This time the migrants flooding into Silicon Valley, 35 miles southeast of San Francisco, are not panhandlers or beauty contest winners but engineers and business administrators with degrees from the nation's top schools. Named for the mineral element basic to the computer microchip, Silicon Valley is a conjunction of human ingenuity and commercial potential that is proving magnetic to venture capital. While the industrial East and Midwest slowly starve for funds, computerland's corporate crapshoot is attracting one out of every four dollars ventured nationwide. Small wonder. Fully half of all new U.S. businesses fail after two years. In Silicon Valley, with two to three new computer-related firms springing up every week, almost every one of them makes it. 'There's too much money available,' cautions ASK Computer Systems head, Sandy Kurtzig. 'Even the turkeys get funded,' agrees Nolan Bushnell, the founder of Atari. Easy money lures carefully trained employees away from the established firms at a time when runaway Pentagon spending is expected only to exacerbate the shortage of civilian engineers. A far more ominous threat is posed by the Japanese, who have stolen the lead in producing large-scale memory chips and threatened to inundate the U.S. market. But for the time being, Silicon Valley is a computer wizard's bonanza that has already spawned upwards to a thousand millionaires. On the following pages, *Life* presents a handful of the most successful.

ASK SANDY: Sandy Kurtzig started a computer programming service in her apartment 10 years ago. She had quit a sales job at GE to raise a family with her husband Arie (a computer research manager), and wanted the extra income. Today, at 35, Kurtzig is the sole female in the

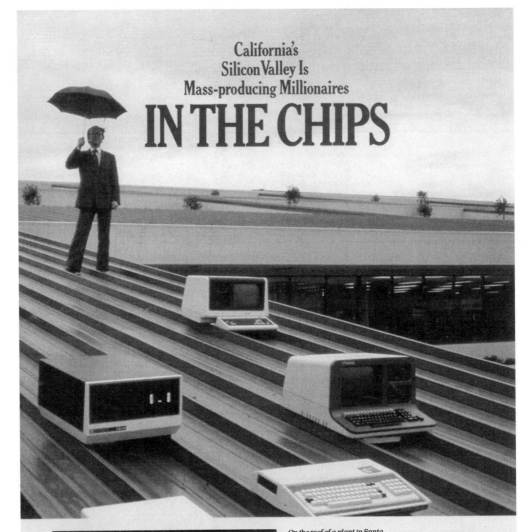

California's Silicon Valley Is Mass-producing Millionaires
IN THE CHIPS

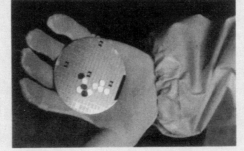

On the roof of a plant in Santa Clara, a phalanx of Silicon Valley executives marches toward an array of the industry's latest desk-top terminals. Armed with umbrellas in anticipation of heavy weather blowing in from Japan, the executives are (left to right): Don Tonn of TeleVideo, Codata's Jim Nakasuji, Harry Garland of Cromemco, Gary Oates of Codata, Bruce MacKay and Chuck Grant of North Star, Exidy's Paul Terrell and Philip Hwang of TeleVideo. At left is a $5,000 wafer of Intel silicon from which 200 computer chips will be made.

youthful ranks of Silicon Valley's founder-presidents. Her ASK Computer Systems are tailored to inventory and accounting, and by mid-decade, annual sales are expected to top $100 million. With 62.6 percent of the stock, Kurtzig can afford to be generous—and not just at the firm's Friday afternoon beer blasts. So far, not a single employee has left ASK for a Silicon Valley rival.

GAMESMAN: With his yachts and passion for racquetball, Nolan Bushnell doesn't mind being called Silicon Valley's Ted Turner. 'It's fun to be crazy,' says the lumbering, six-foot-four 39-year-old who has made $70 million by hypnotizing kids. An ex-Mormon who

GRAND OLD MEN BY 30

TOP APPLE

If Apple Computer is the ultimate success story, Steven Jobs *(right)* is likewise the very model of the brash and brainy whiz-kid chief executive. Still single at 27, Jobs doesn't have to take off his cowboy boots to play chairman of a corporation that has zoomed to annual sales of $600 million in just five years, the fastest growth rate in the history of modern American business. A Reed College dropout who visited a New Delhi guru before glimpsing happiness in Silicon Valley, Jobs was dreaming up video games for Nolan Bushnell when he and Apple co-founder Steve Wozniak raised $1,300 to build their first prototypes. That was six years ago. Today Jobs is one of the company's 100 millionaires, and he believes Apple is on the brink of the next revolution in computer technology—a computer one can learn to use in a half hour.

SOFT SELL

Fresh out of MIT, Dan Fylstra *(below)*, 30, surveyed the home-computer horizon from his vantage as founder of *Byte* magazine, the leading publication in that field. What he recognized was that small businesses were potentially just as juicy a market for household-size computers. Back from Harvard Business School with a master's degree, he began signing up computer programmers and distributing their work like a record company. In three years Fylstra's VisiCorp has topped the business software market. Photographed during a recent move into the $330,000 house he shares with his wife, Hilary, Fylstra has turned a $500 investment into $20 million. ➤

managed amusement park games while at the University of Utah, Bushnell launched the video game craze ($5 billion in 1981) by inventing the first big hit—Pong. His latest obsession is Pizza Time Theatre, a chain of 100 pizza-parlors-cum-video-game arcades, where computerized robot critters delight the youngsters.

IN TANDEM: Even president James Treybig slips a T-shirt over his paunch for workouts in Tandem Computers' cafeteria (adjacent to the pool and corporate basketball court). 'Capitalism and humanism are converging,' maintains Jimmy T., as everyone calls him. 'You can no longer optimize profits and screw people. Tandem's a socialist company.' Maybe so, but profits are staggering at Treybig's debt-free firm. Tandem did $200 million last year in sales

of computers designed with backup systems for banks, hospitals and factories, where break-down is unacceptable. A native of Hebbronville, Texas, Treybig, 41, has designed a house for his wife and three children with a glass dance floor that floats over a garden.

TOP APPLE: If Apple Computer is the ultimate success story, Steven Jobs is likewise the very model of the brash and brainy whiz-kid chief executive. Still single at 27, Jobs doesn't have to take off his cowboy boots to play chairman of a corporation that has zoomed to annual sales of $600 million in just five years, the fastest growth rate in the history of American business. A Reed College dropout who visited a New Delhi guru before glimpsing happiness in Silicon Valley, Jobs was dreaming up video games for Nolan Bushnell when he and Apple co-founder Steve Wozniak raised $1,300 to build their first prototypes. That was six years ago. Today Jobs is one of the company's 100 millionaires, and he believes Apple is on the brink of the next revolution in computer technology—a computer one can learn to use in half an hour."

1986 Profile

German-born Maria Knapp holds the patents for more than a dozen scientific developments derived from a lifetime of molecular research, though the millions she has earned interest her little. At 66, her focus remains her first and only love—science.

Annual Income: More than $150,000, including salary and interest on investments managed by Bank of America.

Life at Home

Maria Knapp is unfailingly gracious—as long as the topic is science.

- At 66, Maria Knapp displays the Old World manners she learned growing up in Germany; unfailingly gracious, she enjoys entertaining guests—as long as the topic is science.
- To stay in shape, she runs every day and continues to do push-ups and calisthenics in the privacy of her bedroom, since she finds public gymnasiums distracting, disorienting and frivolous.
- Although she bought a car last year—an Oldsmobile that is "all American"—she is often driven to work by an associate from the lab.
- Lab assistants also help with her paperwork and chores such as changing the batteries in her hearing aid.
- Her first research paper—published when she was only a 14-year-old child living in Germany—described a series of fruit fly mutations that cast whisker-thin rays of light on the knowledge of embryo development.
- Her parents' home was often populated with eminent scientists from around the world who came to Berlin, the epicenter of brain research in the 1930s.
- She even traveled with her parents to Moscow, where her father was invited to study Lenin's brain, which had been preserved after his death.

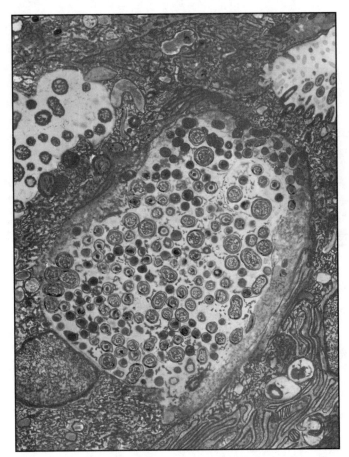

Maria has spent her life studying viruses and telomeres.

- As a university and medical student in Germany, she often skipped classes to putter around the lab, making up the missed lectures by memorizing the textbooks.
- Her work continued throughout the Nazi era, even after her parents were thrown out of a leading institute in Berlin, where her father was director.
- His previous trips to communist Russia, along with the couple's close association with many fellow scientists who were Jewish, made the family untrustworthy; thus, they were banished.
- Thanks to the intervention of a prominent German family who had been her father's patients, Maria's family was not imprisoned.
- Using money provided by their wealthy benefactors, her father established a private institute in the backwoods of Neustadt where their work could continue; there, they were able to offer refuge to many Jewish scientists and their families.
- During this time, Maria avoided every man, refusing to date; "I did not want to end up dating a Nazi, and in Germany at that time, you could never be sure of someone's politics."
- Devoting herself to science, she never married or had children; "Science was my milk," she likes to say.
- Her older sister, a scientist studying the biochemistry of the brain, has also opted against marriage and children.
- Maria wishes to die as her father did—in the laboratory, his last glimpse of life being the view through a microscope.
- She emigrated to Great Britain before the war broke out, becoming prominent in neuroscience, which has earned her election to the Royal Society of London.
- Repelled by her wartime experiences, she jumped at the opportunity to leave Germany in 1950 and come to the United States, even though it meant abandoning fruit fly genetics; "There was no interest in *Drosophila* research, so I had to take up something new," she recalls.
- She then emigrated to the United States when she was 30 years old, going first to the California Institute of Technology, and afterwards accepting a job at the Salk Institute.
- There, she participated in groundbreaking studies of how the polio virus forms distinctive plaques in tissue culture—an essential discovery in the development of the polio vaccine.
- Her intensity for her work has often superseded her own safety; while studying the polio virus, she did much of the work while laboring alongside a pathogen that other biochemists would not touch.
- Her parents were very angry when they learned that she was working with the polio virus.
- When she emigrated to the U.S., the only possession she brought with her was a grand piano, which she still plays regularly, often on Sundays when fellow musician-scientists hold recitals.
- Otherwise, she left Germany behind; when young German scientists come to the lab to meet the famous researcher and chat with her in their native tongue, she replies, often sternly, in English.

- By contrast, when a visiting Sorbonne student recently met with her and spoke in French, Maria's responses were also in French.
- She is known as a soft touch, often lending money from her own pocket to students in need.

Life at Work

- She has spent a lifetime in her own personal toy store—a scientific laboratory.
- Even at 66, she works 10 hours a day, seven days a week; "If I were to stay at home, I'd be bored," she says.

NATIONAL ACADEMY OF SCIENCES

University of South Carolina-Thomas Cooper

1 100 01981643

WHO WILL DO THE SCIENCE OF THE FUTURE?

A Symposium on Careers of Women in Science

Her fellow scientists have lobbied her to donate her money to the education of women scientists.

She has worked with Dr. Barbara McClintock, who won a Nobel Prize in 1983.

- Her credits include groundbreaking studies on the polio virus and how a type of mammalioma virus called the polyoma virus transforms ordinary cells into cancer cells.
- This type of early research has helped lift the study of cancer biology from simply cataloging the gross anatomy of a tumor cell to an exploration of the genetic mutations underlying the disease.
- Two of her colleagues have been awarded the Nobel Prize for research, but she does not like or seek awards, saying, "When you get too famous, you stop being able to work."
- Fellow scientists say she deserves more recognition.
- She has been awarded patents for 16 of her scientific breakthroughs, earning her millions of dollars, most of which are invested in a trust managed by Bank of America.
- Her Last Will and Testament states that her wealth is to be used to promote science.

- Although some of her fellow female scientists have lobbied her to donate her money exclusively to the education of women scientists, she has not responded; money, grants, wills and recipients are not subjects she likes to think about or discuss.

- Her research through the years has ranged from oncogenes, the genes that when mutated result in cancer; immunology; and the behavior of telomeres—the distinctive chromosome tips that serve as molecular timepieces in healthy cells, but play a nefarious role in cancer when they fail to shorten as anticipated.

- She has worked with some of the finest talent in the world, including Dr. Barbara McClintock, the corn geneticist who won a Nobel Prize for her research.

"0.5 Percent of Families Found to Hold 35 Percent of Wealth," Michael Wines, *Los Angeles Times*, July 26, 1986:

"More than a third of the nation's net worth is held by 0.5 percent of America's households, a concentration of economic clout that has snowballed to levels not seen since the Great Depression, Democrats on Congress' Joint Economic Committee concluded in a study released Friday.

Their report, using 1983 figures compiled for the Federal Reserve Board, stated that the 420,000 richest U.S. families controlled $3.7 trillion in assets after debts. That is 35.1 percent of total wealth.

An earlier Fed study using 1962 data concluded that the same 0.5 percent of the population then controlled 25.4 percent of the national wealth. By comparison, the report stated the share of assets held by the poorest 90 percent of Americans dropped during those 21 years from 34.9 percent to 28 percent.

The committee Democrats' report provided the first public comparison of the two studies, both of which were conducted for the Fed by the University of Michigan's prestigious Survey Research Center. The 1983 study was based on projections from a survey of about 4,000 Americans. The sample included 432 members of the country's wealthiest families. . . .

In the report the 1983 data is divided into four classes of households:

- 420,000 'super rich' families with more than a third of the wealth and comprising 0.5 per-

cent of families. None of these families were worth less than $2.5 million; their average wealth after debts was $8.85 million.

- 420,000 'very rich' with 6.7 percent of all net assets and an average wealth of $1.7 million.

- 7.6 million 'rich' with net wealth ranging from $206,000 to $1.4 million and an average net worth of $419,616. The rich, nine percent of all households, owned 29.9 percent of the wealth.

- 'Everyone else,' the 75.5 million households that make up the remaining 90 percent of the population. Their net worth ranged no higher than $206,000 and averaged $39,584.

The wealthy excelled in another crucial statistical measure as well. The net worth of the super rich rose during the 21-year period by 147 percent, adjusted for inflation. The very rich managed only a 64 percent increase and the rich, a 66 percent gain. Everyone else posted a more modest 45 percent increase. . . . .

Nearly half the net assets of the bottom 90 percent were tied up in real estate, most of it in homes. Real estate was among the fastest appreciating assets, more than doubling in value from 1962 to 1983.

The super rich, meanwhile, had less than a fifth of their money in real estate in 1983. But the worth of their property holdings grew sevenfold during the 21 years between surveys."

She loves collecting old postcards featuring her adopted city of San Diego.

Life in the Community: San Diego, California

- Maria loves her adopted city of San Diego; now the second-largest city in California, it is not only picturesque, but has learned how to manage its growth well.
- The seventh-largest city in the United States, San Diego boasts a wonderful climate and a wide range of recreational activities.
- Several years ago, Maria began charting the number of times an executive in the building across the way—who often works the same long hours she does—slips out early in the afternoons for a spin in his sailboat; her chart shows he plays hooky 6.4 times a month.

- On a lark, a dozen years ago, she began collecting postcards of her beloved San Diego; today, she has hundreds.
- She has especially enjoyed watching downtown transform itself from a seedy city center into a vibrant downtown, housing 120 shops, 30 eating establishments, seven movie screens and two performing arts theaters.
- The showcase is Horton Plaza, painted 49 different pastel colors, bordering the historic Gaslamp Quarter, which is now undergoing renovation.
- Today, seven Amtrak connections run from Los Angeles to San Diego daily, taking about two and a half hours, including a stop at Del Mar.
- When scientists come to visit, she always puts them up at the Horton Grand, a 110-room restored Victorian hotel in the downtown section.
- On Sundays, she will sometimes take brunch at the hotel and then rent a horse-drawn carriage for a gentle ride through the city.

HISTORICAL SNAPSHOT
1986

- Harvard University celebrated its 350th birthday
- Consumers who sought professional assistance with home decorating spent an average of $15,584 on the living room
- A New York Stock Exchange seat sold for $1.5 million
- The Dow Jones Industrial Average hit 1,955; the prime rate dropped to seven percent
- The U.S. Supreme Court upheld Affirmative Action hiring quotas
- Federal workers in sensitive jobs were randomly drug-tested after a presidential commission estimated that each month, 20 million Americans smoked marijuana, five million did cocaine and 500,000 used heroin
- Eight airlines controlled 90 percent of the domestic market
- Approximately 35 percent of high school graduates entered college
- The first bio-insecticides, designed to eliminate insects without harming the environment, were introduced
- A supercomputer capable of 1.720 billion computations per second went online
- The average salary of elementary and secondary schoolteachers was $26,700
- Office Depot, one of the first office supply warehouse-type stores, opened in Lauderdale Lakes, Florida
- The national debt passed $2 trillion—twice the level in 1981
- The Supreme Court held that the military may enforce a uniform dress code in a case involving three men who were prohibited from wearing yarmulkes indoors
- The official observance of Martin Luther King, Jr.'s Birthday, the Honda Acura, the one-stick Popsicle and the outdoor testing of genetically engineered plants all made their first appearance
- Estimates of America's homeless included 40,000 in New York City, 38,000 in Los Angeles and 25,000 in Chicago
- Drexel, Burnham, Lambert executive Dennis Levine pled guilty to insider trading, by which he had earned $12.6 million
- The Hands Across America chain, stretching from New York City to Long Beach, California, raised $100 million for the poor and homeless
- Fitness foods high in fiber and low in sodium, fat, cholesterol, calories and caffeine accounted for 10 percent of the $300 billion retail food market

Proof at last that money can buy happiness.

Spend a happy moment with Chateau Ste. Michelle's Cabernet Sauvignon.

Of 59 gold medal cabernets, it was named American Champion by *Wine & Spirits*.

1986 ECONOMIC PROFILE

The national consumer expenditures (per capita income) in 1986 were:

Auto Parts	$76.46
Auto Usage	$1,411.96
Clothing	$576.75
Dentists	$97.65
Food	$1,981.67
Furniture	$130.16
Gas and Oil	$331.18
Health Insurance	$91.83
Housing	$1,752.69
Intercity Transport	$94.32
Local Transport	$32.83
New Auto Purchase	$416.77
Personal Business	$891.31
Personal Care	$180.22
Physicians	$349.46
Private Education and Research	$245.16
Recreation	$846.84
Religion/Welfare Activities	$292.12
Telephone and Telegraph	$187.40
Tobacco	$137.54

"Shopping by TV Becomes New Mania,"
Los Angeles Times, July 21, 1986:

"Jane McElveen had seen bargains on TV before, but this one lit up her life like flares in the night.

Budget Bob from the Home Shopping Network was selling miniature figures by Limoges. Heavens, some of them were only $8.75.

And it was new stuff, too—tiny porcelain shoes and a sewing machine and a grand piano. A feeling came over her a little like madness and a lot like rapture.

She looked over at Duncan, her cockateel. His cage hangs near the display cases where Jane keeps her figurines. 'That's dirt cheap for Limoges,' Jane said out loud.

Then she began dialing Home Shopping's toll-free number, ordering 10, 15, 20 items. Who can remember? It was mania.

To this day, Jane—single and 56—cherishes that one special night. 'It was the best $300 I ever spent.'

Such is the grip of home shopping fever. And what Jane McElveen of Clearwater, Florida, has long known, much of America is finding out. Discount shopping shows—hypnotic as a price tag 50 percent off list— are spreading wholesale across cable TV.

Most often, the shows are run by perky hosts who breathlessly present marked-down goods as if each item had just been excavated from a pharaoh's tomb. First, they give a retail price, then they slash it down to tempting size. Anyone with a credit card or a checkbook can order.

By September, these shows are expected to reach 20 million cable-equipped homes. Some already are broadcast daily, non-stop. The never-ending sales may be the biggest advance in shopping since the mall."

Utilities $487.41
Per Capita Consumption $11,845.00

Annual Income, Standard Jobs

Bituminous Coal Mining $34,837.00
Building Trades $23,590.00
Domestics $10,061.00
Farm Labor $10,216.00
Federal Civilian $27,833.00
Federal Employees, Executive
    Departments $24,273.00
Finance, Insurance and
    Real Estate $25,778.00
Gas, Electricity, and Sanitary
    Workers $33,222.00

Manufacturing, Durable Goods . . . $27,147.00
Manufacturing, Nondurable
    Goods $23,313.00
Medical/Health Services
    Workers $21,652.00
Miscellaneous Manufacturing $20,145.00
Motion Picture Services $28,363.00
Nonprofit Organization
    Workers $14,350.00
Passenger Transportation
    Workers, Local and Highway . . . $16,239.00
Personal Services $13,403.00
Postal Employees $26,362.00
Private Industry, Including
    Farm Labor $21,699.00
Public School Teachers $21,920.00
Radio Broadcasting and
    Television Workers $28,721.00
Railroad Workers $37,673.00
State and Local Government
    Workers $21,949.00
Telephone and Telegraph
    Workers $33,705.00
Wholesale and Retail
    Trade Workers $26,119.00

Selected Prices

Ballet Ticket, *The Nutcracker* $18.00
Bracelet, Sapphire and Diamond $129.00
Bronze Shoes, Baby's First Shoes $5.99
Car Phone $995.00
Compact Disc Player $229.95
Computer, Apple $795.00
Computer Game, Chess $149.00
Easter Lily $4.99
Glue Gun $24.99
Hose, Women's, Three Pairs $8.07
Ice Cream, Dove Bar $1.45
Pen Set, Cross $30.00
Potato Chips, Ruffles 6.5 Ounces $1.19
Radar Detector, FuzzBuster $69.00
Sofa, 82" Leather $599.00
Sweater, Man's Bulk Knit $29.25
Synthesizer, Yamaha $188.88
Television Satellite Dish $1,995.00
Wine, Liebfraumilch $3.99

"High Blood Pressure? It May Be in Your Genes,"
Business Week, April 3, 1985:

"Hypertension has long been the scourge of many active, hard-driving people, and no amount of research has been able to pin down its cause or find a cure for the condition once it has developed.

Now, after 15 years of work in this field, Dr. Lewis K. Dahl, of Brookhaven National Laboratory's medical department, has found a cure that may ultimately reduce the incidence of the disease. Dahl, the man who established a correlation between salt and high blood pressure, has laboratory evidence that heredity plays a role in essential hypertension, the most common form of high blood pressure. Estimates vary, but it's believed that hypertension affects more than 10 percent of the U.S. adult population.

People don't inherit hypertension, Dahl thinks, but may inherit a susceptibility that somehow can be triggered by other factors: kidney infection, emotional stress or, more commonly, too much intake of table salt in the diet.

In his lab, Dahl has bred two strains of rats. Under certain conditions, one strain quickly develops hypertension; under identical conditions, the other strain doesn't.

Dr. Dahl, a senior scientist in Brookhaven's medical research center and chief of medical services for its 48-bed hospital, is among the first to admit this genetic research on rats can't be applied directly to human patients. But it sheds new light on possible predisposition of people to hypertension, and perhaps on how people can avoid triggering the disease."

"One need not go so far as to accept the dictum that money is crystallized freedom. But it is hard to argue that money and freedom have nothing to do with each other. . . . Men will die for freedom but they will not necessarily starve for it. A society that wants to be free must not expose its members to this alternative."
—Economist Henry Wallich

"First Human Vaccine Produced by Genetic Engineering OK'd by FDA," by Marlene Cimons, *Los Angeles Times*, July 24, 1986:

"The Food and Drug Administration on Wednesday announced its approval of the first human vaccine produced by genetic engineering, which will be used to protect against Hepatitis B.

'This vaccine opens up a whole new era of vaccine production,' FDA Commissioner Frank E. Young said in a press conference. 'These techniques should be able to be extended to any virus or parasite to produce other vaccines that normally cannot be propagated in the laboratory.'

Until now vaccines have been made from viruses that have either been killed or weakened.

Young said the recombinant DNA, or gene-splicing, technology could be applied to many diseases for which there are now no preventive vaccines, such as AIDS or malaria. 'The same principles could be tried with an AIDS-related virus, or with the parasite that causes malaria.'

Federal health officials said they expect the new vaccine to be more widely accepted than the existing Hepatitis B vaccine, which uses plasma obtained from infected members of the group also at high risk for AIDS.

Fewer than 30 percent of those at risk for Hepatitis B—including male homosexuals, intravenous drug users, dental and medical workers, immigrants from countries where Hepatitis B is prevalent, and pregnant women in high-risk groups—have been vaccinated using the older vaccine, Young said. . . .

The vaccine, developed by scientists at the University of California, San Francisco, the University of Washington, and Chiron Corporation of Emeryville, California, results from combining brewers' yeast cells with the gene from the outer coat of the Hepatitis B virus.

The yeast cells become 'factories' producing large quantities of the antigen portion of the virus—the part that triggers the human body to manufacture the protective antibodies against future assault by the disease. While the antigen stimulates immunity, it is not itself infectious.

The vaccine, called Recombivax HB, will be manufactured by Merck Sharp & Dohme, which also produces the plasma-derived vaccines.

The vaccine is the fifth major genetically engineered product to be approved for human use, and the third this year."

1987 FAMILY PROFILE

Adam Quigley, the distinguished partner and co-founder of Quigley Ullberg Creswell, a New York-based law firm, is one of the most influential lawyers in America, heading a firm with 650 lawyers in 12 offices across the country. Currently, he is in the middle of a power battle for control of the firm he created. He and his wife Jennifer have six children.

Annual Income: $2.6 million.

Life at Home

- The son and grandson of successful New York lawyers, Adam Quigley has spent the past two decades building one of the nation's most successful and visible law firms.
- A graduate of Yale and Harvard Law School, Adam married Jennifer during his final year of law school, and they immediately began having children; they now have four girls and two boys.
- One of their sons is currently in law school at Harvard, following in his father's footsteps; their oldest daughter has also talked about entering law.
- The fabulous growth of Quigley Ullberg Creswell has allowed Adam and his family the luxury of a Fifth Avenue home as well as a Vermont farm, where Jennifer raises thoroughbred horses.
- The 80-year-old country house, which contains 33 rooms, is situated on 96 acres of pasture and farmland, and features a wide veranda, now used as an outdoor living room, decorated with upholstered wicker furniture to keep the setting informal.
- To care for the house, the couple employs a gardener year-round who grows fields of fresh flowers that decorate every room when they visit from the city.
- Even though many aspects of the home have been updated and modernized, they have returned to the old-fashioned fixtures in the bathroom and kitchen.

Adam Quigley co-founded one of the nation's most influential law firms.

Jennifer often visits the country house to exercise the horses and supervise the birth of new colts and fillies.

- Jennifer visits often to exercise her horses and supervise the birth of new colts and fillies.
- Adam accepts that his wife controls the decorating and furnishings in every room of the sprawling house except one—the traditional gunroom, which he uses as a study.
- A masculine room paneled in walnut at the turn of the century, it has become his hideaway, where he can be messy, disorganized and childlike.
- Dozens of books are stacked up on the floor waiting to be read.
- In one corner, he has the parts of a 1953 Cherokee motorcycle he wishes to restore, along with plans for building a dollhouse-sized haunted house—complete with rotating fireplaces and monsters that fly into rooms when electronically triggered.
- It delights him that his room includes a secret passageway, obviously built during Prohibition, leading to the wine cellar; within the walls of this room, he can read, sip wine and lock out the world—on those rare occasions he is able to slip away from the law firm and into the country.
- Their children have shown a great love for nature and adventure; their youngest daughter spends much of her time rock climbing in the West, while their son loves to backpack on the Appalachian Trail and through the Florida Everglades.

Life at Work

- Quigley Ullberg Creswell was created in 1968, with eight lawyers whose primary expertise was real-estate law.
- By 1982, the firm had either acquired or merged its way into offices in Los Angeles, Miami and Washington.
- Its clients included Occidental Petroleum Corporation and Giant Food, Inc.; today, these relationships have been expanded to include corporations such as Citicorp and Burlington Industries.
- Recently, Citicorp gained worldwide headlines when it decided to write down more than $2 billion in Third-World debt.
- The law firm relishes its involvement with such high-profile cases; its recruiting focus has always been on acquiring the biggest, richest and fastest-growing corporate clients.
- To help them gain the right kind of clients, they have often paid intermediaries such as well-connected politicians and business "rainmakers," including governors, senators and key congressional committee men.
- A decade ago, Adam became active in Republican politics, deciding early to back the presidential aspirations of California Governor Ronald Reagan and personally raising more than $1 million from his friends and clients to fund Reagan's run for the presidency.
- The gamble has paid off handsomely through increased business and unparalleled access to key figures in Washington, including several Cabinet members and education czar William Bennett, who has become Adam's personal friend and confidant.

The law firm's headquarters are in New York City.

Their son loves to backpack, particularly in the Florida Everglades.

Editorial: "Look at an Honest Bank," *The New York Times*, May 21, 1987:

"Any bank that reports a $2.5 billion loss in a single quarter must be in serious trouble, right? Wrong. Citicorp's dramatic decision to set aside enough cash to cover a fifth of its loans to poor countries simply acknowledges facts that have been known for years. The institution remains a major player in global banking, one that deserves credit for injecting a constructive note of reality to negotiations over Third-World debt.

Like most big banks, Citicorp lent billions to countries with ailing economies in the 1970s on the assumption that governments would never permit their loans to default. But the assumption was mistaken. Now, unlike most American banks with big loans outstanding to poor countries, Citicorp has joined European and Japanese lenders in concluding that the stockholders prefer to know the worst.

That gamble appears to have paid off. Market analysts view the one-time hit as a shrewd psychological coup that will distract attention from past errors and reinforce Citicorp's image as a flexible and imaginative competitor. Other benefits are quite tangible: the write-off frees the bank to pursue an aggressive policy of selling dubious debts for less than 100 cents on the dollar. And it preempts debtors tempted to use the threat of formal default to demand more favorable settlements.

The market's positive response makes it more likely that other U.S. banks will follow Citicorp's lead toward honest disclosure of shaky loans. If most take the plunge, the secondary market for their debts will surely boom. Someday soon, private investors and pension funds may be able to add discounted portions of Brazilian and Argentine debt to their portfolio of corporate stocks, Treasury securities and mortgage-backed bonds. That wouldn't reduce the dollar cost of defaults. But it would reduce the adverse impact of such losses on the financial system by spreading the risk to a much larger pool of savers.

There's a more important possible effect. The banks' implicit acknowledgement that impoverished nations will never repay their loans in full could open the way to realistic settlements. Private banks can't be expected to provide the infusions of foreign capital so desperately needed by countries like Mexico and the Philippines. That's a job for multilateral lenders, like the World Bank and International Monetary Fund, which are backed by the credit of the major economic powers.

Nevertheless, formal agreements to write off substantial chunks of the loans, or to accept less-than-market interest rates, would at least staunch the flows of capital from poor lands to rich. Citicorp's show of strength in adversity was intended to serve its stockholders. It also serves the public."

- The firm is headed by a 29-person management committee, which is feuding over how the nationally based firm is being run.
- Many believe that the firm is too much of a one-man show, and are convinced that Adam should no longer be its co-manager, even though it now generates more than $165 million in annual revenues.
- Partners are being asked to take sides concerning the future structure of the firm in a battle that has become so intense, some senior partners are no longer speaking to each other.
- One of the key issues is the lack of communication and relationships among all the offices; despite Adam's best intentions, his sprawling, nationally based legal empire has few connections, resulting in many lawyers being loyal only to their own offices.
- They feel that New York has too much power and provides too little help; one office in a major Florida city issued standing orders not to accept or return telephone calls from any New York partner who "called up shouting."
- Daryl Posner, the lawyer engineering the internal coup, is a New York litigator whom Adam helped recruit to the firm three years ago.
- Posner believes that too much time has been spent in honoring the "finders" of business, and too little in rewarding the "minders"; he wants to lead a law firm based on quality, not on high-profile cases that have the potential to blow up in the media at any moment.

There is something noble in a classic design.

SCHUMACHER

Room designed by Gary Crain Associates, Inc.
Available through fine designers.
F Schumacher & Co. © 1990.

- He also feels that Quigley has sacrificed the integrity of the firm with his deal-making and political connections, and prefers to work for a firm that is respected in New York—not in Washington; a showdown is expected early next year.
- Without question, the firm has been in the news recently because of its ever-expanding client list that includes the flamboyantly ultra rich, such as the Sultan of Brunei, one of the most affluent nations in the world thanks to its oil reserves.
- Recently, the firm has been involved in a spate of acquisitions by the Sultan's brother, who has spent more than $1 billion on hotels in Paris, apartments in New York, racecars and dozens of airplanes.
- As a reward for his work, Adam and his family recently visited Brunei, near Malaysia, where the people enjoy free education and amusement parks, as well as high employment in the oil and gas industry—without paying taxes.
- He and Jennifer were fascinated by the culture and its ability to create a utopian society through the wealth of the monarchy.
- The firm has also represented Cabbage Patch doll inventor Xavier Roberts, whose phenomenal success has allowed him to purchase a 30-bedroom mansion, decorated with three paintings by Picasso and complemented by a waterslide from a second-story window directly into an Olympic-sized swimming pool.
- Through the firm's legal and lobbying efforts, page 219 of the 1986 Tax Reform Act includes an oblique reference to a "taxpayer incorporated on September 7, 1978, who is engaged in the business of manufacturing dolls and accessories," in language that allowed Roberts and his company, The Original Appalachian Artworks, a tax break worth $6 million.

Legal Ads, *Forbes*, June 1, 1987

"Richard Shapero, 44, a Louisville, Kentucky lawyer, has gleefully used television and newspaper advertisements to find clients for his bankruptcy and personal injury practice. Now he's ready to move on to another medium that he thinks will be even better-targeted direct mail solicitation. Trouble is, the Kentucky Bar Association thinks he's gone too far and has prohibited Shapero from sending out any of his targeted mail. 'I'm allowed to take a letter and print it in the newspaper, but I can't send it to one targeted guy,' he complains.

He has challenged the Bar Association, claiming that its action denies his right to free speech. The case is pending before the U.S. Supreme Court. If Shapero wins, the barriers will presumably be lifted for all professionals eager to advertise their services by mail.

Shapero's interest in direct mail is elegantly simple. Court records of bank foreclosures ipso facto provide the names and addresses of people probably in need of a bankruptcy lawyer. What better audience could there be for his legal expertise? And unlike television and newspaper ads, there would be little waste.

But the Kentucky Bar Association is of the opinion that such mailings are akin to the ambulance-chasing that goes on after any mass disaster. 'It's overreaching, intimidating and bad for the public image of lawyers,' says the Association's lawyer, Frank Doheny, Jr. Maybe so. But if the high court continues its record of relaxing the rules on attorney advertising, Shapero's letters will soon be going in the mail."

- In the same section of the Tax Act, the heirs of the late Samuel A. Horvitz, who control a fortune estimated at $400 million, received a special rule worth $1 million.
- Many at Quigley Ullberg Creswell were embarrassed when these personal tax breaks were widely discussed in newspaper and magazine articles across the country.
- Currently, several members of the firm are handling the sale of Burlington Industries, the nation's number one textile producer.
- An investor group headed by Morgan Stanley Group Inc. has offered $2.74 billion as a counter offer made by an alliance of Asher B. Edelman, a New York investor, and Dominion Textile, Inc., Canada's largest textile concern.
- The Morgan Stanley offer includes a group of top Burlington executives who have been fighting the Canadian takeover for months.
- Adam has made numerous trips to Greensboro, North Carolina, where Burlington is headquartered, to structure a deal.
- The Morgan Stanley deal calls for Bankers Trust Company to head a lending syndicate that would provide $2.1 billion of the cost, about $250 million of which would be in bridge loans or temporary financing; the remainder will be provided by Morgan Stanley.
- Adam's firm will earn a fee exceeding $2.5 million for negotiating this deal and structuring the financing.

"Reagan Hails Schools That Educate Poor Children," *The New York Times*, May 20, 1987:

"President Reagan today commended schools that have succeeded in educating poor children, saying, 'They don't use poverty as an excuse for failure and they don't wait around for new federal programs before they start to do their jobs.'

Their message to children, he said, is, 'No matter who you are or where you're from, you can learn.'

The president spoke at a ceremony in which Education Secretary William J. Bennett presented him with a new study by the Department of Education on what measures have proved effective in teaching children in some of the nation's poorest neighborhoods.

Describing the nearly two dozen schools profiled in the study as successful models, Mr. Reagan said: 'They know there are no such things as black values and white values, or poor values or rich values. They know that there are only basic American values. They know that lower standards are double standards, and double standards are wrong.'

But 'too many disadvantaged children are still not getting the education they need,' the president said, adding that 'we can do better' in providing 'universal access to quality education.'

Mr. Bennett said at a news conference that 'education is a child's single best avenue out of poverty,' but that many schools now serving poor children were 'of poor or mediocre quality.'

As he has before, however, the secretary asserted that spending more money on education was not the answer. 'The basic problem with American education is not that it is underfunded, but that it is underaccountable,' he said.

The department's study, entitled 'Schools That Work: Educating Disadvantaged Children,' provides a set of recommendations based on such traditional values as the importance of creating a disciplined school environment, motivating students and enlisting the support of parents.

Schools that are successful, Mr. Bennett said, 'have strong leaders, they emphasize the basics and they teach respect for the right values, including patriotism, community pride and personal responsibility.'"

Life in the Community: New York City

- The children of Margaret Strong de Larrain, heiress to the Rockefeller oil fortune, have gone to court to overturn their mother's will, which disinherits them in favor of her last husband, whom she married when she was 80 and he was 42; at stake is Exxon Corporation stock worth $76 million.

- Jerry Della Femina, chairman of the New York ad agency Della Femina, Travisan and Partners, resigned the Lifestyle condom account after his client was quoted in *Time* magazine as saying "AIDS is a condom marketer's dream."

- New York Governor Mario Cuomo recently announced that he would not make a run for the Democratic presidential nomination, setting off a scramble for a qualified candidate.

- "Butt buckets" have begun showing up throughout the city as thousands of firms move to prohibit employee smoking in buildings, sending thousands of smokers into the streets.

- *The New York Times* is reporting that workers in the city's garment district are often under age, paid less than $3.35 a hour and required to work 11-hour days, six days a week.

The price of collectible artwork is rising rapidly at New York Auction galleries.

- Interstate highway speeds have increased from 55 miles per hour to 65, as New York and the nation bury their fears of another fuel crisis, although government officials continue to predict that the United States will start to run out of gas in as little as three decades.
- Civilian complaints against Transit Authority police officers are up 33 percent over the previous year; the 50 officers against whom the most complaints are lodged will be asked to undergo sensitivity training.
- New York City recently changed the name of 122nd Street to Seminary Row because of the two giant institutions of religious learning located there—Union Theological Seminary on the west side of Broadway, and the Jewish Theological Seminary of America on the east side.
- The City of New York is predicting that within five years, the spreading AIDS epidemic in the city will cost more than $1 billion a year in hospital expenses alone.
- New York City currently accounts for one third of the AIDS cases in the United States.
- Collectors of fishing rods and reels are being lured to an auction in Roscoe, NY, all for the benefit of the Catskill Fly Fishing Center, a nonprofit educational organization devoted to "preserving the heritage and protecting the future of fly fishing in the United States."
- According to a report prepared by the Fund for Renewable Energy and the Environment, New York ranks among the top five states in establishing and enforcing programs to protect the environment.

HISTORICAL SNAPSHOT
1987

- The first open-air use of a genetically engineered bacteria, a frost retardant, was attempted on strawberry plants
- Under a new law, three Americans became the first foreign lawyers permitted to practice in Japan
- The Dow-Jones Industrial Average peaked at 2,722 during August, and then fell 508 points in a single day on October 19; the record drop represented $500 billion in lost equity
- When sports coverage of the U.S. Tennis Open intruded into the traditional news time, journalist Dan Rather stormed off the set; TV screens were blank for six minutes
- The federal budget exceeded $1 trillion for the first time
- *The Last Emperor*, *Fatal Attraction*, *Three Men and a Baby* and *Radio Days* all held their movie premieres
- Fifty thousand people gathered at Graceland in Memphis, Tennessee, on the tenth anniversary of Elvis Presley's death
- Sixty percent of American kitchens had microwave ovens; 40 percent of the food dollar was spent eating out
- Forty states restricted smoking in public buildings, restaurants and schools following the Surgeon General's warnings on the negative impact of secondhand smoke
- Toni Morrison's *Beloved* won the Pulitzer Prize for fiction; David Herbert Donald won the biography prize for *Look Homeward: The Life of Thomas Wolfe*
- The last of the known dusky seaside sparrows died of old age, marking the extinction of the species
- Macintosh II, Kodak Fling, Spuds MacKenzie and Captain Power toys that interacted with the TV show all made their first appearance
- Congress overrode the president's veto of the $20 billion Clean Water Bill
- The phrase "couch potato" came into popular usage
- Allan Bloom's book, *The Closing of the American Mind*, criticized the U.S. educational system and called for a return to "great books" in its attack on cultural relativism
- Fifty-eight-year-old artist Andy Warhol died of a heart attack after routine gallbladder surgery
- Ansell America became the first condom manufacturer to advertise on television
- Professional baseball player Mark McGwire set a rookie record for hitting home runs, smashing 49
- The Supreme Court ruled that states may require all-male private clubs to admit women

1987 ECONOMIC PROFILE

The national consumer expenditures (per capita income)
in 1987 were:

Auto Parts	$77.42
Clothing	$611.98
Dentists	$106.25
Food	$2,062.43
Furniture	$135.90
Gas and Oil	$348.82
Health Insurance	$98.84
Housing	$1,863.52

"Your Taxes at Work," *The New York Times*, May 26, 1987:

"Supplemental appropriation bills are intended to provide government financing for emergency situations that are unforeseen when regular appropriations are enacted. But, like others before it, the supplemental bill now moving through Congress has also become a vehicle for an array of projects, this time ranging from a national weed center to sweeter government subsidies for 20 beekeepers.

Despite pressure to keep spending down and meet deficit-reducing targets, members of Congress have seized the opportunity, as usual, to include numerous favors for particular interests in the $8.5 billion supplemental bill approved last month by the House and in a version the Senate is expected to vote on this week.

If all goes as their sponsors hope, the fishing industry would get federal dollars to advertise the benefits of eating fish. A few universities would get new buildings. Oklahoma would get an industrial park, and Iowa would become the site of a new international agricultural trade center. Beekeepers would no longer be bound by a $250,000 limit on government honey loans. And Abilene, Kansas, where Dwight David Eisenhower grew up, would get $50,000 to help plan a celebration marking the thirty-fourth president's 100th birthday in 1990.

Sea turtles would come up losers under the bill, since the Louisiana delegation arranged to delay a new rule requiring shrimpers to use special devices to prevent the turtles from getting tangled in shrimp nets.

'This is a bill built on pork, sold with baloney, that allows people to bring home the bacon, and no matter how you slice it, it's a budget buster,' Representative Dick Armey, a Texas Republican, complained.

Despite heated exchanges on the House and Senate floors and efforts by a few members to expunge some special favors from the bills, the favors have so far proven impregnable to attack."

Intercity Transport $104.19
Local Transport.................... $32.95
New Auto Purchase............... $385.06
Personal Business $963.68
Personal Care $195.21
Physicians $401.53
Private Education and Research..... $263.98
Recreation....................... $921.26
Religion/Welfare Activities $312.99
Telephone and Telegraph $195.21
Tobacco......................... $144.14
Utilities $495.43
Per Capita Consumption........ $12,569.00

Annual Income, Standard Jobs

Bituminous Coal Mining........ $35,924.00
Building Trades $24,537.00
Domestics..................... $10,289.00
Farm Labor $10,156.00
Federal Civilian $28,828.00
Federal Employees, Executive
　　Departments................ $25,239.00
Finance, Insurance and
　　Real Estate $27,750.00
Gas, Electricity and
　　Sanitary Workers $34,730.00
Manufacturing, Durable
　　Goods...................... $27,899.00
Manufacturing, Nondurable
　　Goods...................... $24,141.00
Medical/Health Services
　　Workers $23,724.00
Miscellaneous Manufacturing..... $20,918.00
Motion Picture Services $32,308.00
Nonprofit Organization Workers .. $15,017.00
Passenger Transportation
　　Workers, Local and Highway ... $16,710.00
Personal Services $13,889.00
Postal Employees............... $27,262.00
Private Industry, Including
　　Farm Labor $22,629.00
Public School Teachers.......... $22,940.00
Radio Broadcasting and
　　Television Workers........... $31,125.00
Railroad Workers............... $39,456.00
State and Local Government
　　Workers $23,075.00
Telephone and Telegraph
　　Workers $35,623.00

Wholesale and Retail Trade
Workers $27,269.00

Selected Prices

Automobile, Mazda RX-7
Roadster $22,000.00
Basketball $19.99
Camcorder $1,799.99
Can Opener, Electric $19.99
Cereal, Kellogg's Corn Flakes $1.59
Clogs, Woman's $19.95
Dressing Table, Baby's $77.99
Hand Lotion, Corn Huskers $1.59
Movie Ticket $2.00
Necklace, 14-Karat Gold 16"
Chain $79.00
Range, 30" Kenmore $559.99
Shirt, Man's Velour $14.92
Shoes, Man's Running $89.95
Software, Lotus Spreadsheet $339.00
Soft Drink, Coke, Two-Liter $1.00
Tape Rule, Six-Inch $8.99
Telescope, Bausch & Lomb
Criterion 400 . . . . $695.00
Television, Sony Watchman $95.00
Water Heater, Kenmore $89.99
Yacht, Hatteras 77 . . . . $1.7 Million

1988 FAMILY PROFILE

When 54-year-old, Egyptian-born Ahmed Waltari realized that cellular telephones represented "the future" four years ago, he transformed his multimillion-dollar business to get a piece of the action. He, his wife Miki and their three children divide their time among Williamstown, Massachusetts; New York City; and Monaco.

Annual Income: More than $5 million a year; his family assets exceed $30 million.

Life at Home

- For more than a dozen years, the Waltari family has lived in Williamstown, Massachusetts, near Williams College.
- They moved there because Miki hated raising children in New York City, and loved the fact that the Williamstown community of 9,000 is dominated by Williams College, known for its art and historic collections.
- Ahmed maintains a 2,000-square-foot apartment a dozen blocks from his office in Manhattan.
- Often spending Monday through Thursday in New York or traveling, and Friday through Sunday in Williamstown, he enjoys hard work, pressure and the freedom and privacy the separate homes provide.
- His New York apartment is decorated with expensive bird prints collected from around the world, including several important Audubon prints and the prized Mark Catsby originals he acquired in England years ago.
- His greatest obsession, however, is the avoidance of alcohol; the son of an alcoholic, he does not allow it to be served in his home or at office parties, but enjoys fine dining.

Egyptian-born Ahmed Waltari is at the forefront of the cellular revolution.

The Waltari family moved to Williamstown, Massachusetts, a dozen years ago to escape New York City.

- His children have been told that drinking is the one sin he will not tolerate.
- The family normally spends six weeks each summer in Monaco, where Miki, the daughter of a diamond merchant, vacationed in her youth.
- The most celebrated gaming tables in the world are in Monte Carlo, part of the 468-acre sovereign principality of Monaco, named after a Ligurian tribe called the Monoikos who occupied the land in the sixth century BC.
- The ruling Grimaldi family seized Monaco from the Genoese in 1297.

"Twins Scott and Stuart Gentling Sell off a High-Priced Audubon and Give Wing to Their Own Bird Book," *People*, June 15, 1988:

"Two records were under siege last week when a standing-room-only crowd converged on Sotheby's auction house in New York. Outside, an early heat wave was threatening to push the mercury over 97 degrees, an all-time high for the date. Inside, brisk bidding closed in on, and soon surpassed, the highest price ever paid for a work by the naturalist painter John James Audubon. When the gavel fell, a New York dealer had paid $253,000 for an 1824 watercolor of two boattailed grackles—known to most people simply as blackbirds.

Just two and a half years ago the same painting had been offered in the mail-order catalog of a Philadelphia print dealer for $18,000—and was snapped up by two Audubon fanatics who recognized it as one of the master's long-missing early works. Not long afterward, the new owners, 44-year-old twins Scott and Stuart Gentling of Fort Worth, decided to use their treasure to help bankroll their own Audubon-inspired masterwork, *Of Birds and Texas*. A massive boxed portfolio of 50 paintings of birds and landscapes, it was 10 years and $550,000 in the making, and might never have seen the light of day without the grackle windfall. 'We literally ran out of money,' says Stuart, like his brother a full-time artist since college, 'and we had to use the grackles as collateral.' Most of the $210,000 profit the brothers expect to clear from the sale will go towards clearing up their grackle-backed debts.

Stuart also hopes the publicity surrounding the auction will produce some national recognition for him and his twin. 'It's so difficult to get people to take us seriously,' he says. 'They don't think that something like Of Birds and Texas could be created in the boondocks.'

They may now, however, since the Gentlings' opus has been getting rave reviews. *The Dallas Morning News* described it as 'destined to become a classic of ornithology and fine printing,' and painter Andrew Wyeth declared it 'overwhelming.' It is certainly that: Two feet long and weighing 46 pounds, it could pass for a coffee table without legs. The price is a Texas-size too: $2,500 for one of a limited edition of 500 books."

- In 1865, the reigning Prince Charles III inaugurated gambling on the island, giving the aristocracy a reason to vacation there.
- The casino was built on a rock and named Monte Carlo, or Mount Charles, in the prince's honor.
- Soon, with the arrival of the railway, the wealthy, noble, famous and infamous came to gamble.
- In 1878, architect Charles Garnier, who built the Paris Opera, constructed a new casino in his signature gilt-edged, belle époque style, complete with a formal tropical garden and terrace.

- Once near bankruptcy, Monaco became rich overnight, and despite the vagaries of history, wars and fashion, it has continued to be the place where the rich have gathered for more than 120 years.
- Today, as predictable as birds flying south, the international moneyed and titled set descends upon the island.
- There they find the Salle Garnier theater, home of the renowned Opéra de Monte Carlo, Monte Carlo Philharmonic Orchestra and one of Europe's most outstanding ballet companies.
- Miki believes that the Princess Grace Classical Dance Academy produces the finest dancers in the world.
- In the opulent casino, Ahmed enjoys European games such as roulette, trente-et-quarante, baccarat and chemin de fer; his 22-year-old son migrates toward American games such as craps, blackjack and one-armed bandits.
- To keep gambling in perspective, Ahmed insists that losses be limited to $10,000 per trip, and so avoids the private gambling tables where millions can change hands in an evening.
- The teenage girls prefer trips to Monaco for the warm waters of the Mediterranean, with its 300 days of sunshine a year and the chance to lie by the pool and watch some of the world's most eligible—and richest—men walk by.
- The family also loves to plan its trips around the automobile rally and Grand Prix each year, where speed, beauty and power are all combined.
- They also love the safety of Monaco, which is a highly monitored state with a vigilant police force.
- When in Monaco, the Waltari family likes to stay at the S.B.M. Hôtel de Paris, which was built around the same time as the casino to support the incoming tourists; with its ideal location, it has long been *the* place to stay.
- Their favorite rooms overlook the sea and are situated across from the casino and the Café de Paris, the central meeting place since 1968 for everyone who has been anyone.
- In addition, the hotel's majestic foyer provides a splendid backdrop for dramatic entrances and exits; the bar serves as an essential point of rendezvous.

Life at Work

- Twenty-eight years ago, Ahmed founded his first U.S. company, Waltari Imports, to import Japanese goods to the United States.
- Thanks to his connections in Egypt and Monaco, he was able to pull together a wide range of deals using only a small portion of his own capital.
- The inheritance he received from his father exceeded seven figures, but he was determined to use the money only as leverage whenever possible and not expose his own capital to the vagaries of business.
- For five years he imported a wide variety of goods from baseball gloves and fishing reels to porcelain dinnerware.
- In 1965, he opened a carton and, finding a car radio, had a revelation—this was the future!

> **"Dining on an Ancient Hilltop,"**
> **_Bon Appetit_, November, 1988:**
>
> "Just outside Monaco there is the ninth-century hilltop village of Eze, perched 1,300 feet almost sheer above the sea on a rocky outcrop. To reach its center, you park and walk narrow alleys. It is worth the trek to visit the Chateau de la Chevre d'Or, an eleventh-century medieval manor house artistically converted into a glorious 10-room hotel and Chateau Eze, a cluster of medieval houses (formerly the summer home of HRH Prince William of Sweden) that has been open to the public as a small luxury hotel since 1983.
>
> At Chateau de la Chevre d'Or, I've enjoyed many of Chef Elie Mazot's delicacies as much as the panorama. At Chateau Eze, the kitchen has recently been handed over to Dominique Le Stanc, and his culinary genius is unmistakable. Highly recommended among his creations are open-face ravioli with sautéed artichokes, asparagus and langoustines; smoked pigeon and lentil salad; and cream of pea soup with asparagus and morel garnish."

- Within months, he phased out the other merchandise, changed the name of his company to Waltari Enterprises and began selling Japanese car radios, and afterwards stereo radios and tape decks, to new car dealers.
- He carved out a market by selling car radios for 30 percent less than Detroit was charging the Ford and General Motors dealers.
- By 1983, his company—still private and owned only by members of his family—achieved sales of more than $100 million; today, it has gone public and is three times larger.
- Unfortunately, while the company is growing, revenues are shrinking because of the huge inventory commitments required by rapid growth.
- In 1984, following his instincts as he had during his entire career, he jumped onto the cellular telephone bandwagon with a vengeance.
- To get a major piece of the action, he set up an exclusive U.S. distribution deal with Toshiba, one of Japan's leading mobile phone manufacturers, whose early phones proved to be exceptionally popular and dependable.
- Then in a stroke of luck in 1985, Waltari Enterprises was able to grab a dominant market share when Panasonic and others were hit with huge, government-imposed antidumping penalties on their phones.
- Today, his company sells 15 to 20 percent of all cellular phones nationwide; of its $277 million in sales, half comes from cellular phones—where the margins are thin.
- Whereas car stereos sold at wholesale for as little as $55 and earned the company gross margins of 30 percent, the cellular phones sell for $1,200 at wholesale and have margins of less than 20 percent; thus, the phones exhaust more capital while producing smaller gross profits.

- To finance the telephone inventory, Ahmed allowed public ownership of his company, raising $33 million on the sale of 2.2 million shares of its nine million shares of stock, and fueling Waltari Enterprises to expand.
- Unfortunately, earlier this year Toshiba came under scrutiny by Congress for selling military gear to the Russians.
- Fearing that the U.S. Government would restrict the import of Toshiba phones, Ahmed dramatically increased his order by more than 30 percent over sales projections, but the feared cutoff never occurred; wholesale prices of cellular phones are now plunging and his warehouse is overstocked.
- Thus, the company is faced with the prospect that it will see a 45-percent increase in the sales of cellular phones, but a 25-percent decline in profits until the inventory glut is dissolved.
- Despite the prospect that Waltari Enterprises' stock price could be cut by half, Ahmed remains optimistic; telecommunications consultants are estimating that the number of cellular subscribers will increase next year from 1.1 million to 1.6 million.
- Ahmed believes that with falling prices, he will double the 127,000 phone sales he made last year.
- His biggest concern today is whether competition will crowd him out in the future.
- As the cellular phone increasingly becomes regarded as a consumer electronic product rather than a specialty product, retailers such as New York's 47th Street Photo or Crazy Eddie could jump into the game, driving down profit margins and cutting sales.
- Some days, he thinks that slowing down might be all right; using his earnings through the years, he has acquired a controlling interest in seven major income-producing office buildings, financed in part with interest-free loans from the company.
- Last year alone, he earned more than $1 million in rent; in addition, his 83-year-old mother earned more than $700,000 on investments that he arranged.

Life in the Community: Williamstown; New York; and Monaco

- Williamstown, Massachusetts, is a small, pretty town of 9,000 people, 2,000 of whom are students.
- Because Ahmed's professional life is centered in New York, Williamstown has been the wrong place to live, but Miki, a lover of art and museums, insists; both New York and Boston are only three hours away.
- The town, originally called West Hoosuc, was reborn as Williamstown in the late eighteenth century in accordance with the terms of the will of Ephraim Williams, who promised to endow a secondary school if the town agreed to perpetuate his name.

"Great Expectations," *Forbes*, April 18, 1988:

"With today's newer portable phones, you can walk down Fifth Avenue in Manhattan while talking to your spouse in Boise, or your partner in Tokyo. Pretty soon the gear will be cheap enough that teenagers can take a phone with them on dates. No more, 'Gee, Mom, I would've called but I didn't have a quarter.' In the U.S., car facsimile machines are just around the corner. So cellular communications is no gadgetry gimmick: it is a service that fills a real need for a society on the go.

But in the real work of business, there's many a slip twixt cup and lip. With little in the way of earnings or cash flow, cellular franchises today sell on the basis of two expectations: 1) the number of potential customers in the area covered by their franchise, and 2) how much each of these customers is likely to spend. The first expectation is the population that lives in the cellular franchisee's area—the so-called pops figure. If a franchise area has a population of, say, two million, and a company owns 60 percent of the franchise (partners accounting for the rest), then the company would have 1.2 million pops.

What's a pop worth? BellSouth is paying some $80 to $85 a pop for Mobile Communications. McCaw, which about 18 months ago was paying only about $20 per pop for franchises, a few months ago paid $80 a pop for The Washington Post Company's Florida cellular business. McCaw itself is being valued in the stock market at $75 to $80 per pop.

These prices are assuming a great deal. They assume that a significant percentage of the pops will sign up for the services and that, once signed, they will use the expensive service on a big scale.

When the Federal Communications Commission started to divvy up the cellular industry in the early 1980s, it awarded two franchises for each market, to make sure there was competition. The 'wireline' franchise went to the local Bell operating company. The independent or 'nonwireline' franchise was at first chosen by the FCC in some markets. Later markets were awarded by lottery.

Let's crunch a few numbers. What 'per pop' amounts to is an assumption that a given independent company will have about half the cellular market, and the local phone company will have the other half. Let's say cellular's penetration will be four percent five years from now. Then the independent franchise's penetration will likely be two percent.

Let's go on with the numbers. If the franchise covers one million pops and ultimately signs two percent of them, it will have 20,000 customers. Paying $80 a pop is the same as paying $4,000 today for tomorrow's projected customer. By contrast, cable TV systems can currently be purchased for around $2,000 per existing subscriber."

Williams College has long been a magnet for fine art and historical artifacts.

- In 1793, the school, in the shadow of three mountains, became Williams College, which has since become a magnet for art and historical artifacts.
- In 1938, the college museum was given the collection of American muralist Edwin Howland Blashfeld.
- This was followed by the Cluett collection of Spanish pre-Goya paintings, plus a substantial part of the Bloedel collection of twentieth-century American art.
- Then came the Robert Sterling Clark collection.
- Clark, one of four grandsons of Edward Clark, the business partner of sewing machine developer Isaac Singer, had no connection to Williams College; nevertheless, in the 1950s, he gave the school a building to house his collection of silver and paintings by notables such as Botticelli, Degas, Manet, Monet, Renoir and Pissaro.
- Then in 1983, an expanded museum opened with shows featuring Indian art, work by Edvard Munch, and displays of Greek art, Roman terra cotta and Renaissance woodwork.
- A few years ago, Williams College bought for $412,500 a recently discovered copy of the Declaration of Independence that had belonged to one of its signers, Joseph Hewes of North Carolina.
- The purchase rounded out Williams' remarkable collection of essential documents of the American Revolution: its copy of the Articles of Confederation of 1777, two early versions of the Bill of Rights and one of the 14 surviving copies of the Committee of Style draft of the Constitution, containing on the reverse the handwritten objections of Virginia constitutionalist George Mason.
- In addition, the school's Chapin Library of rare books contains James Madison's copy of Paine's *Common Sense*, General Greene's written order for boats for the crossing of the Delaware, General Knox's letter thanking Martha Washington for a gift of two hair nets, and the ledger used by the executors of George Washington's will.

HISTORICAL SNAPSHOT
1988

- Black teenager Tawana Brawley gained national publicity when she claimed she was raped by a group of white men; a grand jury found no evidence for the charges and called her advisors, including the Rev. Al Sharpton, "unethical"

- Ninety percent of major corporations reported sexual harassment complaints

- Spending for cultural events topped $3.4 billion, exceeding spectator sports for the first time

- Former chief aid Donald Regan claimed that Nancy Reagan used astrology to plan her husband's activities

- Women accounted for nearly half of all graduating accountants, one third of MBAs and one quarter of lawyers

- American lawyers averaged $914 a week; nurses, $516 and secretaries, $299

- The B-2 Stealth bomber, felony convictions for computer-virus insertions and the Video Walkman all made their first appearance

- Robots were used for picking fruit

- Fundamentalists picketed *The Last Temptation of Christ*; the film was an unexpected financial success

- Professional heavyweight boxer Mike Tyson's fight with Michael Spinks produced a $40 million gate; Spinks was knocked out in one round

- U.S. auto makers produced 13 million cars and trucks

- Harvard scientists obtained the first animal patent for a genetically engineered mouse with immune properties

- *The Eight-Week Cholesterol Cure*, *The Bonfire of the Vanities*, *Trump: The Art of the Deal* and *Swim with the Sharks without Being Eaten Alive* were all bestsellers

- Philip Morris bought Kraft for $12.9 billion

- Scientific experiments on the Shroud of Turin indicated that it dated from the Middle Ages, not from the time of Christ's death

- The Pulitzer Prize for history was awarded to Taylor Branch's *Parting the Waters: America in the King Years 1954-1963*

- The U.S. savings and loan industry lost $13.4 billion

1988 ECONOMIC PROFILE

The national consumer expenditures (per capita income) in 1988 were:

Auto Parts	$84.47
Auto Usage	$1,538.05
Clothing	$648.44
Dentists	$113.85
Food	$2,177.51
Furniture	$138.75
Gas and Oil	$354.62
Health Insurance	$107.73
Housing	$1,975.92
Intercity Transport	$114.26
Local Transport	$33.87
New Auto Purchase	$412.16
Personal Business	$1,040.59
Personal Care	$209.75
Physicians	$451.33
Private Education and Research	$292.18
Recreation	$1,007.14
Religion/Welfare Activities	$350.95
Telephone and Telegraph	$204.86
Tobacco	$147.72
Utilities	$519.48
Per Capita Consumption	$13,450.00

Annual Income, Standard Jobs

Bituminous Coal Mining	$36,660.00
Building Trades	$25,872.00
Domestics	$11,353.00
Farm Labor	$10,472.00
Federal Civilian	$29,957.00
Federal Employees, Executive Departments	$28,725.00
Finance, Insurance and Real Estate	$27,716.00
Gas, Electricity and Sanitary Workers	$35,308.00
Manufacturing, Durable Goods	$29,170.00
Manufacturing, Nondurable Goods	$25,407.00
Medical/Health Services Workers	$25,665.00
Miscellaneous Manufacturing	$20,904.00
Motion Picture Services	$27,716.00

Nonprofit Organization
Workers $15,635.00
Passenger Transportation
Workers, Local and Highway . . . $17,356.00
Personal Services $14,758.00
Postal Employees $28,364.00
Private Industry,
Including Farm Labor $23,794.00
Public School Teachers. $23,992.00
Radio Broadcasting and
Television Workers $30,857.00
Railroad Workers. $40,862.00
State and Local Government
Workers $24,284.00
Telephone and Telegraph
Workers $37,210.00
Wholesale and Retail
Trade Workers. $27,820.00

Selected Prices

Audiotape, Sony, Three-Pack $7.99
Beer, Michelob, per Case. $9.95
Bicycle, Aero Urban Cowboy $600.00
Bicycle Child Carrier. $14.99
Car Radio, Alpine $199.00
Carving Set, Ebony-Handled,
Set of Four. $675.00
Coffee Maker $25.00
Compact Disc $11.99
Computer Printer, Epson. $429.00
Concert Ticket, Carnegie Hall. . . . . $10-$30.00
Corn, Five Ears $1.00
Currency Calculator $32.00
Floppy Disks, Fuji, per Box. $9.95
Grandfather Clock $280.00
Luggage Carrier, X-cargo Rooftop. . . . $169.99
Pillow, Hermes $75.00
Shoes, Naturalizer. $45.00
Silk Spider Plant $54.99
Socks, Child's, Six-Pack $4.99
Sweatshirt, Man's $18.95

The Rise of Cellular

- The cell phone is considered a major breakthrough in telecommunications.
- Experts describe the cellular telephone franchise business as "one of the very few businesses with open-ended growth potential."
- Many believe the big money will arrive when it is possible for Americans to talk by telephone in their cars.

- Recently, BellSouth Enterprises offered $710 million for Mobile Communications of America; the offering price equates to 7.5 times the revenues, 30 times this year's projected cash flow and 100 times the earnings.
- Experts believe that by 1993, five percent of potential customers will own a cell phone.
- That translates into nine million customers nationwide, up from one million customers today.
- New portable cellular phones are now small enough to be carried around in a briefcase or a large pocketbook.

- Typically, the cellular phone price of $4,000 a year and a half ago is expected to drop to around $1,495, and possibly below $500 by 1993.
- The Japanese auto makers are expected to follow BMW's lead and make cellular phones standard equipment in top-of-the-line models.
- Currently, new customers are costly to attract; McCaw Cellular, with franchises covering 47 million potential customers, spent $61 million on marketing and only added 100,000 new customers.
- Older investors are warning that cellular may follow the path of cable television, whereby the considerable capital raised to buy franchises, string cable and sign up customers sent many companies into bankruptcy during the 1973-4 recession, although cable use is now rising rapidly.
- Several investors still brag about buying cable "on the cheap" after many companies failed; some believe the same investment opportunities await cellular telephones.

1990–1999

The 1990s, called the "Era of Possibilities" by *Fortune* magazine, were dominated by an economic expansion that became the longest in the nation's history. Characterized by steady growth, low inflation, low unemployment and dramatic gains in technology-based productivity, the expansion was particularly meaningful to computer companies and the emerging concept known as the Internet. This economy swelled the ranks of the upper class as Americans of all backgrounds invested in the soaring stock market and dreamed of capturing a dot-com fortune.

The decade opened in an economic recession, a ballooning national debt, and the economic hangover of the collapse of much of the savings and loan industry. The automobile industry produced record losses; household names like Bloomingdale's and Pan Am declared bankruptcy. Housing values plummeted and factory orders fell. Media headlines were dominated by issues such as rising drug use, crime in the cities, racial tensions, and the rise of personal bankruptcies. Family values ranked high on the conservative agenda, and despite efforts to limit Democrat Bill Clinton to one term as president, the strength of the economy played a critical role in his re-election in 1996.

Guided by Federal Reserve Chair Alan Greenspan's focus on inflation control and Clinton's early efforts to control the federal budget, the U.S. economy soared, producing its best economic indicators in three decades. By 1999, the stock market produced record returns, job creation was at a 10-year high, and the federal deficit was falling. Businesses nationwide hung "Help Wanted" signs outside their doors and even paid signing bonuses to acquire new workers. Crime rates, especially in urban areas, plummeted to levels unseen in three decades, illegitimacy rates fell, and every year business magazines marvelled at the length of the recovery, asking, "Can it last another year?"

The stock market set a succession of records throughout the period, attracting thousands of investors to stocks for the first time, including the so-called glamour offerings of high-technology companies. From 1990 to the dawn of the twenty-first century, the Dow Jones Industrial Average rose 318 percent. Growth stocks were the rage; of Standard and Poor's 500 tracked stocks, almost 100 did not pay dividends. This market boom eventually spawned unprecedented new wealth, encouraging early retirement to legions of aging baby boomers. The dramatic change in the cultural structure of corporations continued to threaten the job security of American workers, who had to be more willing to learn new skills, try new jobs, and move from project to project. Profit sharing, which allowed workers to benefit from increased productivity, become more common. Retirement programs and pension plans became more flexible and transferable, serving the needs of a highly mobile work force. The emerging gap of the 1990s was not always between the rich and the poor, but the computer literate and the technically deficient. To symbolize the changing role of women in the work force, cartoon character Blondie, wife of Dagwood Bumstead, opened her own catering business which, like so many small businesses in the 1990s, did extremely well. For the first time, a study of family household income concluded that 55 percent of women provided half or more of the household income.

In a media-obsessed decade, the star attraction was the long-running scandal of President Bill Clinton and his affair with a White House intern. At its climax, while American forces were attacking Iraq, the full House of Representatives voted to impeach the president. For only the second time in American history, the Senate conducted an impeachment hearing before voting to acquit the president of perjury and obstruction of justice.

During the decade, America debated limiting abortion, strengthening punishment for criminals, replacing welfare for work, ending Affirmative Action, dissolving bilingual education, elevating educational standards, curtailing the rights of legal immigrants, and imposing warnings on unsuitable material for children on the Internet. Nationwide, an estimated 15 million people, including smokers, cross-dressers, alcoholics, sexual compulsives, and gamblers, attended weekly self-help support groups; dieting became a $33 billion industry as Americans struggled with obesity.

The impact of the GI Bill's focus on education, rooted in the decade following World War II, flowered in the generation that followed. The number of adult Americans with a four-year college education rose from 6.2 percent in 1950 to 24 percent in 1997. Despite this impressive rise, the need for a more educated population, and the rapidly rising expectations of the technology sector, the century ended with a perception that the decline in public education was one of the most pressing problems of the decade. Throughout the decade, school violence escalated, capturing headlines year after year in widely dispersed locations across the nation.

The '90s gave birth to $150 tennis shoes, condom boutiques, pre-ripped jeans, Motorola 7.7-ounce cellular telephones, rollerblading, TV home shopping, the Java computer language, digital cameras, DVD players, and Internet shopping. And in fashion, a revival of the 1960s' style brought back miniskirts, pop art prints, pants suits, and the A-line. Black became a color worn at any time of day and for every purpose. The increasing role of consumer debt in driving the American economy also produced an increase in personal bankruptcy and a reduction in the overall savings rate. At the same time, mortgage interest rates hit 30-year lows during the decade, creating refinancing booms that pumped millions of dollars into the economy, further fueling a decade of consumerism.

1990 News Profile

"Legacy, Heirlooms from Seven Generations of One Southern Family," by Susan Stiles Dowell, *Southern Accents*, July-August, 1990:

"Perhaps nowhere in America is a regional identity more strongly evident than in the South. In literature, lifestyle, historical perspective and even accent, southerners nurture a strong sense of place.

Lest anyone overlook the alchemy of family and homeplace, consider the heirlooms of one southern family. Accumulated over two centuries, during seven generations, and by six branches of the family tree, they are a vivid reminder of place—a link with a past that gives continuity to the present.

The owners represent the eighth and tenth generations of their families in America. Removed by less than a hundred miles from the original seventeenth-century land and manorial grants of their ancestors, they can visit many of their former family seats today. One such house, built in the eighteenth century, still serves as a residence for a branch of the family. And many of the stunning pieces of silver and porcelain in the owners' collection were originally bought for its seventeenth-century predecessor, which stood nearby.

Few American families have memories beyond two or three former generations, never mind this personal link to the past. The husband explains that the generations became closer for having such tangible objects of connection. 'These possessions,' he says, 'knit the generations together. There's an awareness, through the pieces, of being part of a greater whole.'

To illustrate this point, the wife tells a story about the matriarch who was left with her children and servants on the family plantation during the Civil War. Word came from town that Union troops bent on pillage were headed for the house, but the young lady kept her head. She had the family silver buried in the garden and sat on the portico to wait. When the

The owners represent 10 generations in America.

499

Legacy

Heirlooms from Seven Generations of One Southern Family

Photography by Lisa Masson
Text by Susan Stiles Dowell

LEFT: Ceres, Roman goddess of agriculture, bears the family coats of arms on this bread basket intricately wrought with the fruits and implements of the harvest. Among the wealthiest landowners of the South until the Civil War, the owners' ancestors had switched from tobacco to wheat cultivation well before the Revolution. The large silver basket, made in London by John Wirgman, circa 1774, manifests both the source and magnitude of the family's wealth.

Yankees marched up the long drive with an inebriated captain at their head, they were foiled in their attempt to get into the house and its liquor stores. This formidable young matron, so the story goes, was sitting on the keys to the house and would not move. 'She was my great-grandmother who died when I was three. Our generations touched and still do through these heirlooms we have in common.'

Some of the legends about the heirlooms bear repeating. The largest piece of silver in the collection, a massive three-foot ovoid waiter made in London, was used during the twenty-first birthday festivities of an ancestor in 1800. It seems the master was celebrating not only his own birthday with a host of friends around the dining room table, but also the birth of his first son. In honor of both occasions, the baby boy was placed on the great waiter and passed around the table. The event was repeated in this century when another baby boy's advent into the family was celebrated with the same ceremony, around the same dining room table!

The sentiments of both Tories and Patriots cling to many of the pieces, elucidating a tenor of the times undocumented by history books. The pair of miniature portraits on ivory surrounded by seed pearls, painted by celebrated miniaturist Richard Cosway circa 1774, depicts a bright young couple of London society who were collateral ancestors of the owners. On the eve of the Revolution, the gentleman of the pair gave up his position in the British Coldstream Guards to return to the family seat in America. When he subsequently died at home, she returned to England to live out her days. The husband comments, 'I always thought it remarkable that (our ancestors) weren't loyalists during the Revolution because they had so much to lose. There was only one loyalist I can think of, and his son was on George Washington's personal staff.' He speaks with familial experience when he says, 'There seemed to be an understanding of the problem of political loyalty back then and how people, even within the confines of a family, could go either way.'

During the War of 1812 when pirates and Tory sympathizers preyed upon unprotected American estates, some silver was stolen from the family's plantation. Records exist of a claim being made for the pieces, but no dramatic account of the outcome survives. One can always wonder if family member Francis Scott Key's celebrated verses and unbridled patriotism exacted some British retribution.

Perhaps the most stunning part of the family's collection is the tobacco leaf porcelain made in China circa 1860 for the Portuguese market. At least two hundred pieces were ordered by the family through London, and the extant bill of sale indicates that importation to be among the earliest for the pattern in the colonies. Roughly a quarter of the collection belongs to the present owners. The wife laughs when she remembers what she thought of the pattern as a child. 'It was everywhere in my grandmother's house, and I though it was gaudy,' she says. 'Children tend to be conservative in their tastes, and to me this was a weird pattern. Mother told me it had great value, and I don't think we understood why I thought it was hideous.'

Of course, the wife's regard for the tobacco leaf pattern changed as she matured and came to understand its significance to her family. As with most of the pieces, the owners are now of one mind and heart with the predilections of their ancestors and speak of this sentiment in terms of identity. Fortunately for us, that identity sheds a rare light on the too often impersonal documentation of history."

1993 FAMILY PROFILE

Tim Harding is a corporate Mr. Fix-it; when companies don't operate efficiently, he is called in to take them apart and find solutions, often requiring dramatic cuts in spending and layoffs. He is well rewarded financially for his work; he and his wife Louise own three homes, all on the East coast of the United States.

Annual Income: More than $4.5 million a year, including stock options and grants; his assets currently exceed $100 million.

Life at Home

- Tim and Louise enjoy splitting their time among their island home off the coast of South Carolina, their home in Palm Beach and a Manhattan apartment in New York City.
- The South Carolina home is Louise's favorite; it can only be reached by boat, but includes a tennis court, docks and a spectacular view of the ocean.
- Recently, she collected dozens of sand dollars that had been washed ashore during the night by a northeastern storm, and considered it a sign that more good fortune was in store for her family.
- Along the South Carolina coast, she feels free to be herself; currently, she is studying qigong with a mentor in Charleston.
- According to Chinese philosophy, there is qi in everything—in our bodies, our homes, and in the earth itself.
- Acupuncture needles are said to modulate the flow of qi in the body; a feng-shui makeover moves the qi of the home.

When in South Carolina, Tim Harding goes on dove shoots.

Louise's favorite house of the three is along the South Carolina coast.

- When in South Carolina, Tim loves to go on dove shoots, often taking his grandchildren along.
- As he likes to tell friends, "I hunt deer, bear and woodcock, but when it comes to the twisting, turning rocketry of doves, I shoot."
- His favorite home is the house in Palm Beach—the 3.75-square-mile island in Florida, known alternately throughout the world as the most wealthy, glamorous, decadent, extravagant and self-indulgent spot on earth.
- Their first home in Palm Beach was a 3,000-square-foot apartment at the Biltmore, which overlooked both the Atlantic Ocean and the inland waterway.
- About the same time, they bought a $1 million Picasso for their New York home.
- During their visits to Palm Beach, he fell in love with "the season," the social season of the very rich.
- During the week he wrestles with the turnaround of major corporations, often earning the label of "villain" for his propensity to cut costs; then on weekends he can be a hero to the wealthy stockholders of Palm Beach who understand his need to demand layoffs if companies are to produce good financial returns.

- Besides, Palm Beach parties are always done so well with beluga caviar and Dom Perignon champagne.
- While on the island, he dresses like a resident in a blue blazer, open sport shirt and loafers with no socks; it's a look dating back to 1919 and Charles Munn, a descendant of Carrie Louise Gurnee Armour, widow of the meatpacking king.
- Evening wear is often formal; for the season, Louise normally buys a dozen evening gowns, each costing more than $18,000, while Tim pays $2,500 for formal wear, $900 a pair for Ferragamo shoes and $2,500 each for Valentino suits.
- In recent years, using Louise's money, they have purchased a 20,000-square-foot home with 15 bedrooms, 12 bathrooms, two libraries, a media room, sauna and a master bedroom closet that is almost 1,000 square feet.
- Their neighborhood includes a poured cement, art deco home that won the House of the Future Award at the 1939 New York World's Fair and is now owned by the heir of a dog food fortune.
- Tim and Louise have been careful not to mention her Jewish father—the source of their inherited wealth—afraid it will affect their membership in the Everglades Club and the Bath & Tennis Club where she plays tennis many afternoons.
- While living at Palm Beach during the season, she helps organize fundraisers as a way of meeting people; she has

Louise is studying qigong with a mentor.

"Can You Feel the Qi?" *Spirituality & Health*, Summer 1993:

"To Western minds, qi involves magical thinking. But there is the magical thinking of an infant who can't distinguish herself from mom; there is the magical thinking of a mystic who sees everything as connected; and there is the magical thinking of the physicist who knows there are connections between particles that apparently transcend both space and time. While we would like to say that we know which kind(s) of magical thinking we're dealing with here, the simple truth is, we don't. . . .

We're grappling with huge questions: how did the Chinese come to create such radically different maps for the territory of human experience? What happens to our own bodily experience and our faith when we borrow the maps of another culture? Will we be lost? Or healed? What if these Chinese maps of our shared human terrain illuminate a vital connection between all things that Western maps have overlooked? And, if so, are we ready for a world where love is healing and hatred is like secondhand smoke?"

Tim's favorite home is in glamorous Palm Beach, Florida.

helped organize a ball for heart disease, and is now helping to raise money for a social disease called AIDS.

- Tim believes that being part of The Social Index-Directory will help him in business; like most of the families listed in the book, the Hardings' index item includes addresses for additional homes.
- Some families list up to five additional homes in places like Monte Carlo, Paris, London, New York and Newport, Rhode Island, in addition to the names of their planes and yachts.
- Several of the jet set recently purchased expedition yachts, 184-foot boats capable of circumnavigating the globe on a single tank of gas; many come equipped with a 36-foot fishing boat and a personal submarine for times when the boat is in dock and located over an exciting wreck.
- A North Carolina real-estate developer bought an expedition yacht so he could take his family on a voyage to Indonesia, Australia and New Zealand.
- As Charles Dana, commodore of the New York Yacht Club, explains, "A lot of guys have worked too hard all their lives to spend time yoked in with 50 other gin palaces in a marina in St. Tropez. They want to go where no one has ever gone, in a tough boat that can take it."
- Tim recently got together with three other business associates and had a climbing wall constructed for their grandchildren to enjoy when they visit in Florida.
- The 16' x 24' tower is equipped with three different climbing paths, and is made of concrete and crushed granite to look like sandstone cliffs.

Life at Work

- As the current chief executive officer of a 1,300-hotel chain, Tim makes more than $1 million a year.

"Climbing the Walls," *Boys' Life*, **March, 1993:**

"John Omohundro looked like Spiderman climbing a building. His chalk-covered fingers grabbed at dents in the wall. His feet found tiny ledges. He inched his way up.

'Stay with it. Hold,' his friends on the ground shouted. John's buddy, Zack Horwitz, pulled the safety rope taut. With a final burst of energy, John reached the top. 'All right, dude!' yelled Zack.

'It's great when you get to the top,' panted John. 'Climbing gives me a rush.'

John is an 18-year-old mountain climber from Buffalo, Wyoming. But this was not a mountain. John had just scaled an artificial climbing wall—indoors.

Climbing the walls is a popular sport at the Colorado Rocky Mountain School (CRMS) that John attends in Carbondale, Colorado. It's also popular at other schools, health clubs and Boy Scout summer camps across the country.

Artificial wall climbing has certain advantages over mountain climbing. With indoor walls, you don't have to worry about bad weather, ice on the rocks, or darkness at night.

Some climbing walls are set up outdoors. They also have advantages over mountains. Setting up safety ropes is easy, and the walls can be adjusted for different levels of climbing skills.

'Artificial walls are a good way for beginners to learn or for advanced climbers to refine their skills,' John says."

- He was asked to head the company when the merger of two hotel chains ran into trouble, and quickly established himself as the leader, demanding total loyalty.
- During his three years on the job, dozens of key executives have been fired for questioning his leadership style—several were dismissed during a company meeting when they challenged one of his decisions.
- In each of his management roles designed to turn around a company, he has gained a reputation for freely handing out pink slips; he considers himself a head coach who seldom needs or wants assistants, making decisions rapidly and rarely looking back.
- He is currently negotiating to sell the company to a larger, more stable hotel chain; if successful, he will earn a bonus of several million dollars.
- It is a pattern he has worked successfully before; previously, he arrived as head of a major insurance carrier which was nearing bankruptcy and whose stock was falling rapidly.
- He moved decisively—or as his critics claimed, ruthlessly—to save the company; under his direction, the insurance company cut its quarterly dividend from $0.75 per share to a nickel, and the work force of 5,000 was cut in half.
- Within 24 months the company's stock had rebounded and the firm was sold for $2.8 billion; when he left, his exit package totaled $43 million.

Their home in Palm Beach is decorated with art collected from around the world.

- He understands that bankrupt companies have little shareholder value, and that his job is to bring about change—quickly.
- A nameplate-sized sign made of flimsy plastic sits prominently on his desk and summarizes his philosophy of business: "Get the spectators off the field."
- He believes, "There are givers and takers in life. Givers contribute as much as they can. Takers are always trying to hang on to someone else's accomplishments."

Life in the Community: Palm Beach, Florida

- Eighty-seven percent of Palm Beachers are millionaires; megaresidents include John Kluge, worth $10.5 billion from Metromedia; Ronald O. Perelman, worth $4.2 billion from Revlon; Estée Lauder's sons, Ronald and Leonard, (each owning approximately $4 billion from cosmetics), and Diana Stawbridge Wister (owning $900 million from a Campbell Soup inheritance).
- By design, no signs along Interstate Route 95 point to Palm Beach, 65 miles north of Miami; if you have to ask where Palm Beach is, you shouldn't be here, residents like to say.
- The coconut palm trees that dominate the island vegetation are the legacy of a Spanish ship called the *Providencia* which ran aground in 1878; bound for Barcelona from Havana, the ship carried hides, coconuts and wine.
- After the wreck, the crew and local settlers consumed the wine and the captain gave the Americans 20,000 coconuts; palms grew from the coconuts and the party is still going on, local wags enjoy saying.
- In 1892, Henry Morrison Flagler decided to turn Palm Beach into America's Riviera—a playground for the rich and famous.
- To that end, he extended his Florida East Coast railway to the island and built the plush, 1,150-room Royal Poinciana Hotel, at that time, the world's largest hotel; after a few years he built the Palm Beach Inn, later named The Breakers, on the ocean side of the island.

"The Making of the Modern Company," by Richard Tedlow, *Business Week*, August 28, 2000:

"The twentieth century witnessed the rise of the professional business manager. Prior to the growth of the railroads in the late nineteenth century and the huge industrial firms that followed, owners managed and managers owned. But with the railroads, an elaborate hierarchy of individuals was needed to coordinate the fast-growing corporation—setting goals, allocating resources, monitoring performance and awarding compensation. Managerial power grew at the expense of the owners until the 1980s. Large corporations became staggeringly complex, populated not only with laborers, but also by layers of white-collar workers. As ownership became more diffused, it became less possible for a shareholder to have a clear idea of what was going on, never mind influencing policy.

The masters of management became the captains of the corporation. Exhibit A, of course, is Alfred P. Sloan, Jr., CEO of General Motors Corporation. An engineer by training, Sloan's career illustrated how vital it is for an executive to be able to deal with all parts of the job, even those that didn't play to his original strengths. Sloan enabled GM to become the world auto leader, not only because he mastered manufacturing, but also because he made both marketing and management more scientific. Henry Ford's inability to stretch himself in this way made him vulnerable to Sloan's comprehensive approach to the business."

- The hotel's cottages became the winter homes of John D. Rockefeller, John Jacob Astor, Andrew A. Carnegie and J.P. Morgan, who all traveled to the Florida resort in their own railroad cars.
- Flagler was so influential in the state, in 1901 he got the Florida legislature to legalize divorce on grounds of incurable insanity; after his divorce was granted, the law was rescinded.
- As a wedding present to his third wife, Flagler built Whitehall, a 55,000-square-foot marble beaux-arts palace that became the Henry Morrison Flagler Museum.
- Flagler helped establish entertaining as a sacred institution of Palm Beach; for a party in 1898 commemorating George Washington's birthday, the wealthiest men in America were invited to dress as famous women, including wigs, makeup and corsets under sequined gowns, with Flagler himself arriving as Martha Washington.
- However, it was Marjorie Merriweather Post who turned grand parties into a tradition; from her $8 million, 55,000-square-foot "cottage by the sea" built in 1827, Post reigned as the queen of Palm Beach until her death in 1973.
- In more recent times, Sydell L. Miller, worth $1.3 billion from her hair-care company, Matrix Essentials, built a 37,000-square-foot home with 42 rooms and a basement garage for 17 cars.
- Most of the owners of the larger homes occupy them for only a few months during the season, even though the bills continue all year; electric bills are often $5,000 a month, property taxes can exceed $500,000 a year, the bill for landscape maintenance for a five-acre estate is about $140,000, not to mention the cost of retaining a staff of chefs, butlers, maids, chauffeurs and gardeners.

"The Globetrotters," *Art & Antiques,* **Summer 1993:**

"Having the world at your fingertips is easily mastered with a standing library globe. The esteemed Adams Family, a London company which served as scientific instrument makers to George III, crafted these circa-1802 globes. English globes of this period were generally made of 12 engraved gores pasted to a hollow sphere of papier-mâché and plaster. As with most paired globes, one is terrestrial, the other celestial; in this case, the former is current with the political subdivisions of 1805. The pair had been in a private collection for 30 years before showing up for auction in March at Leslie Hindman in Chicago. Fresh to the market, they created quite a stir when they traveled well past their estimates of $5,000 to $7,000 to land at $19,800. Though globe sales hit a peak four years ago, this price may indicate that the globe market is turning again."

- Because of its privacy and tradition of wealth, the famous often pop into Palm Beach knowing they will not be bothered; this season, celebrities have included Elizabeth Taylor, Kim Basinger, Harrison Ford, Mike Wallace, Suzanne Somers and Ann-Margret.
- Worth Avenue is the primary shopping district, where Petrossian beluga caviar can sell for $1,173 a pound and residents, refreshed by an afternoon of tennis, can shop at Ferragamo, Armani, Cartier, Tiffany, Van Cleef & Arpels, Valentino and Saks.
- More exclusive than Rodeo Drive, Worth Avenue is often lined with Rolls-Royces, Jaguars, Ferraris and Bentleys, many driven by chauffeurs.
- At Mary Mahoney, a single cotton pillowcase—300-thread count with hand stitching made by Porthault in France—costs $390.
- Residents frequently shop personally at the only supermarket on the island, Publix, often bringing along a butler to assist with pushing the cart and carrying out the groceries; the grocery store offers free valet parking.
- So customers can safely store their jewels after attending social functions, the local bank offers a special vault where valuables can be deposited after hours.
- City ordinances limit the size of all retail signs, tennis-ball machines may not emit noises above prescribed decibel levels, the use of heavy construction machinery is banned during the season and employees are required to register with the police and submit to fingerprinting and photographing.
- The community of Palm Beach boasts 1,100 swimming pools and 100 tennis courts.
- Currently many people are excited about building environmentally sound homes; one family is currently constructing a 12,000-square-foot compound into a mountain in Colorado for natural cooling and insulation, and heating it with geothermal pumps.
- The home also features a 900-square-foot living room with 21-foot glass windows; to further conserve energy, the couple's five-car garage is equipped with solar panels.

HISTORICAL SNAPSHOT
1993

- Sears ended its mail-order catalog business

- The U.S. began testing of RU-486, the French "morning after" pill

- A bomb blast injured hundreds in New York's World Trade Center; Mohammed A. Salameh was arrested for the bombing when he attempted to reclaim his $400 car rental deposit

- Law enforcement agents raided a religious cult in Waco, Texas, killing many in a fire that ignited a storm of protests

- The U.S. pledged $1.6 billion in aid to assist in Russian reforms

- Chicago Bulls basketball star Michael Jordan retired to play professional baseball

- Thirty-year mortgages dropped to 6.7 percent, the lowest in 25 years

- Cosmologists discovered that stars and other observable matter occupied less than 10 percent of the universe

- Work statistics showed that nearly one out of three American workers had been with their employers for less than a year, and almost two out of three for less than five years

- The brown uniform of the Brownies changed after 66 years to include pastel tops, culotte jumpers, and floral print vests

- President Clinton supported easing a ban on homosexuals in the military

- Civil rights advocate Ruth Bader Ginsburg was named to the U.S. Supreme Court

- IBM, the world's largest computer manufacturer, announced an $8.9 billion restructuring, eliminating 60,000 jobs

- President Bill Clinton promised "universal health coverage" comparable to that of Fortune 500 companies

- The Pentium processor and one-pound personal digital assistants made their first appearance

- Major league baseball owners announced new initiatives on minority hiring

1993 ECONOMIC PROFILE

The national consumer expenditures (per capita income) in 1993 were:

Auto Maintenance	$248.00
Auto Usage	$1,843.00
Clothing	$670.00
Entertainment	$650.00
Food	$2,735.00
Furniture	$126.00
Gas and Oil	$390.00
Health Care	$710.00
Health Insurance	$320.00
Housing	$2,166.00
New Auto Purchase	$486.00
Personal Business	$1,163.00
Personal Care	$154.00
Public Transportation	$125.00
Telephone	$263.00
Tobacco	$107.00
Utilities	$581.00
Per Capita Consumption	$12,276.00

Annual Income, Standard Jobs

Bituminous Coal Mining	$40,493.00
Building Trades	$26,739.00
Domestics	$10,275.00
Farm Labor	$15,019.00
Finance, Insurance and Real Estate	$36,013.00
Gas, Electricity and Sanitary Workers	$36,755.00
Manufacturing, Durable Goods	$26,992.00
Manufacturing, Nondurable Goods	$23,181.00
Medical/Health Services Workers	$20,091.00
Miscellaneous Manufacturing	$20,508.00
Motion Picture Services	$37,541.00
Nonprofit Organization Workers	$14,094.00
Passenger Transportation Workers, Local and Highway	$17,802.00
Postal Employees	$37,609.00
Public School Teachers	$25,816.00
Radio Broadcasting and Television Workers	$30,702.00
Railroad Workers	$40,672.00

State and Local Government
  Workers $27,369.00
Telephone and Telegraph
  Workers $33,871.00
Total Federal Government. $36,940.00
Wholesale and Retail Trade
  Workers $27,820.00

Selected Prices

Ant Poison, Hyponex, Four Pounds	$2.94
Apples, Delicious, One Pound	$0.59
Automobile, Nissan Altima GXE	$14,484.00
Bed, Cherrywood, Full Size	$399.88
Blinds, 35" x 42" Mini	$15.99
Camp, Wilderness, Two Weeks	$515.00
Christmas Tree, Artificial 7'	$124.99
Crackers, Nabisco Ritz Bits	$1.69
Golf Shirt, Man's, Spalding	$14.98
Hibachi Grill	$6.99
Hotel Room, Boston Sheraton, per Night	$104.00
Medicine, Nyquil, 10-Ounce	$4.93
Photocopier, Xerox Personal Copier	$899.99
Refrigerator, Frigidaire 18 Cubic Foot	$396.00
Shoes, Women's, Gitano	$10.87
Smoke Detector	$5.99
Socks, Keds, Four-Pack, Child's	$4.00
Videotape, Walt Disney's *The Jungle Book*	$19.76
Vodka, Absolut, 750 ml	$12.29
Watch, Timex Analog Quartz	$14.99

1997 FAMILY PROFILE

Eighty-year-old Spence Dowling believes that he is worth approximately $400 million, thanks to a machinery business he has run for 50 years. Despite his wealth, he continues to live in a mobile home located behind his factory.

Net Worth: Approximately $400 million.

Life at Home

- Since his divorce 33 years ago, Spence Dowling has been living in a double-wide mobile home located behind the flagship plant for his company.
- The trailer is furnished with hand-me-down furniture from his grandfather's estate, plus chairs and beds bought at Sears and Roebuck.
- The dinnerware was purchased 30 years ago from the Kress' Five and Dime, formerly in downtown Columbia, but closed now for more than a decade.
- He owns one suit for attending funerals and weddings; otherwise, he dresses as he always has—in work clothes.
- His closet is filled with overalls and flannel shirts; his wristwatch—a 1950s gold Longines—typically is looped through a buttonhole.
- He rarely sees his only daughter, whom he accused of stealing money from the company. She has tried to reunite with him, even running advertisements in the newspaper requesting that he contact her. He has declined.
- He has never met three of his six grandchildren, or any of his great-grandchildren.
- His entire life revolves around work; he is fond of saying, "As long as you have work to do, food to eat and a place to sleep, what else do you need?"
- During the past 50 years he has attempted to take only two vacations—and hated it both times; "To work is to breathe," he says.
- He belongs to no social clubs and rarely eats out; he does encourage his employees to support local charities, and he also participates in their fundraising activities.
- In the past decade, he has given away more than $2 million to the local community, on the condition that no one knows that he is the benefactor.

Trinity Cathedral anchors the religious community of the city.

- To protect his privacy, he carries thousands of dollars with him at all times so that he rarely has to write a check or give his name.
- Now that he has turned 80, he is reviewing his will to determine where his money should go; he is considering a major gift to the local YMCA where he does a daily workout.
- Even though the YMCA is in the center of Columbia and requires a commute down the interstate, Spence is a creature of habit and will not shift his loyalty, despite the proliferation of private gyms now close to his home.
- He also plans to create a multimillion-dollar endowment for the school he attended for one year—the University of South Carolina, which now enrolls 25,000 students.
- During his stay there, he planned to major in business; his will, however, directs that his money be used for educating classroom teachers.
- He does not plan to provide any money to his former wife or to his daughter, although he is planning a $250,000 educational fund for his grandchildren, provided they graduate from college in four years.
- He has been told that his IQ tops 160, but puts little stock in tests that don't measure real-life performance.

Life at Work

- Spence's company, Dowling Machinery & Equipment, is a specialized heavy equipment manufacturing firm created by his grandfather in the late 1800s.
- A one-man operation, the company began with his grandfather traveling the countryside in a mule-drawn wagon, visiting textile plants to repair their equipment.
- Eventually, he came to understand which plants needed what equipment and began supplying them with machinery.
- Thanks to his close working relationship with plant owners, Dowling Machinery prospered, even during the Depression when few companies were investing in new equipment.
- Due to a willingness to repair and renovate equipment to keep the plants going during hard times, his company earned the loyalty of many businessmen who became powerful in the years after the Depression and Second World War, when South Carolina began to gain some economic momentum.
- When the woolen and worsted industry migrated to the South from New England after World War II, business exploded.
- After his one year at the University of South Carolina, Spence joined his grandfather in the business, transforming Dowling Machinery into an international conglomerate which now controls 70 percent of the world market for card combing, the teeth that comb fibers to make cloth.
- The company was listed among America's richest in this year's Forbes 500 list of private companies—a fact Spence hates.
- Dowling Machinery has remained privately held, despite the temptation to sell stock and gain instant wealth; Spence doesn't need the money and hates having to discuss his busi-

South Carolina's Governor's Mansion

Columbia, the capital of South Carolina, boasts 450,000 residents.

ness with anyone, even conducting much of his banking in New York so that no one in South Carolina will know about his private affairs.

- Over the years he has purchased more than 40,000 acres across South Carolina, leasing some of the land or selling it to companies like Home Depot or developers of upscale subdivisions.
- Much of the land he owns is near the state's sprawling interstate highways, and has been purchased as sites for giant shopping centers; his holdings also include extensive amounts of timberland.
- For the past decade, he has avoided making sales calls, even to old friends, preferring to stay at the plant and direct operations.
- The company currently employs 1,200 people in plants in South Carolina, Massachusetts, Alabama, Texas, Brazil, Canada, France, Germany, Italy, Portugal, Spain and the United Kingdom.
- He is a hands-on boss who is often on the machine floor at 5 a.m.; it is not unusual for him to put in 12-hour days, even at his age.
- Because he is fair and pays well, many of his employees have worked for him for decades; they understand that there is one way to do the job right—his way.

Life in the Community: Columbia, South Carolina

- Boasting a population of 450,000, Columbia is the capital of South Carolina and is situated in the center of the state.
- Located at the confluence of the Broad and Saluda Rivers, it is nearly halfway between New York City and Miami, Florida.
- The city is bordered by Lake Murray, a manmade, 50,000-acre lake that extends 41 miles upstream.

"Greater Columbia, Diversity Abounds," Columbia Chamber of Commerce Brochure:

"Many great American cities are best known for the towering absolutes: their moss-draped history, their unique ethnic heritage or even the industries that dominate their skylines and economic storehouses. Each image enriches the city, while also binding it—like a badly worn cliché—to a self-perpetuating stereotype of itself.

These images may be one of the reasons that visitors to South Carolina's central city are often surprised to discover that Columbia's greatest strength is its unabashed diversity and overwhelming sense of place. As one longtime Columbia resident explained, 'There is a sense of community here, a chance to get involved and to get to know more people who are involved.' Then with a smile, he adds, 'When people move here, they begin to feel their roots sinking in; ours is a softer dirt with a humus of friendship.'

There is also an overwhelming sense in this sprawling metro community of 410,000 that something is happening, evolving as the natural course of things. It is not simply that the profile of a healthy, viable Main Street is changing to

the tune of the IBMs and Marriotts. Or that on any given weekend as many as four open-air concerts—something for every taste—can be found. It's not even the way spring spreads through the midlands like a slow smile, whetting an artist's palette with its brilliant azalea and dogwood hues.

It's more a feeling that in this city, totally planned 200 years ago and then burned to the ground 80 years later by General Sherman's Union Army, Columbia's third century is going to be an exciting time. Missing here—as you talk to residents—are the smugness and self-satisfaction that emerges when talking to people from so-called 'highbrow' cities. Columbia is a city without a convenient label, despite being the home of the University of South Carolina, the army's Fort Jackson training facility, major centers for banking and insurance, as well as the seat of South Carolina government. This is a community that has been pieced together from widely divergent parts of the country—and thus immensely accepting of others."

- Lake Murray, originally created to supply hydropower to the South, is recognized as one of the nation's top black bass fishing spots and is a popular site for camping, boating and skiing.
- In addition to the University of South Carolina, the capital city has nine other universities and colleges, including the historically black college of Benedict and Columbia College, which focuses on women's higher education.
- Currently, Columbia is focusing enormous energy on bringing back a dying Main Street, offering tax breaks for renovation projects to attract jobs and residents to the core of the city; according the mayor, "Main Street is everyone's neighborhood."
- The city prides itself on businesses like the Capitol Newsstand on Main Street; "The Times Square Newsstand in Manhattan offers a few more newspapers than we do," the owner claims, "but not many more."
- Author, poet and Columbia resident James Dickey held one of his first book signings at the Capitol Newsstand when *Deliverance* was published.

Historical Snapshot
1997

- The Forbes 400 indicated that America's 400 richest families accounted for an estimated 2.6 percent of total personal net worth held by all Americans
- The cost of a 30-year mortgage fell below seven percent
- The nation's largest tobacco companies forged a $368 billion settlement with the states to settle smoking death claims
- The combined stock market value of Microsoft and Intel was $274 billion, more than the combined market value of GM, Ford, Boeing, Eastman Kodak, Sears, J.P. Morgan, Caterpillar and Kellogg
- Scottish researchers announced the first cloning of an adult animal, a sheep named Dolly
- With the spread of cable television, the percentage of the TV viewing audience controlled by the three major networks fell to 49 percent from 75 percent a decade earlier
- Despite a one-day plunge of 554 points, the stock market soared; the Dow was up 20 percent for the third straight year
- The U.S. defense budget, which was at $370 billion in 1987, fell to $260 billion
- President Clinton became the first president to gain line-item veto power over the federal budget
- Affirmative Action programs, designed to aid minorities, came under attack
- A record $920 billion in mergers created corporations of unprecedented size
- Princess Di's death generated more press coverage than any event of the century
- Media magnate Ted Turner donated $1 billion to the United Nations
- Oprah Winfrey's support of reading through her Book Club created dozens of bestsellers as Americans followed her lead
- Flavored vodka, digital cameras, DVD players, voice recognition software and prosthetic knee joints all made their first appearance
- Mattel introduced a new Barbie doll that had a larger waistline, smaller breasts and more modest clothing; she also had a friend in a wheelchair
- Violent crime in New York City was down 38 percent; homicides were the lowest since 1968
- New York ticket scalpers demanded $1,000 per ticket for the play *The Lion King*

Growing up, I got good at taking direction.
"Say your line here." "Hit your mark there." And "Drink your milk."
That's good advice for kids and adults. The calcium in milk helps bones
grow till you're about 35 and helps keep them strong long after.
So I still drink milk. Only now, I'm the one giving direction.

MILK
Where's *your* mustache?™

1997 ECONOMIC PROFILE

Selected Prices

Airline Ticket, Los Angeles to Chicago	$198.00
Armoire	$899.00
Bra, Olga	$20.63
Breadmaker	$129.99
Cat Food, Purina Cat Chow, 20 Pounds	$7.99
Cleanser, Mr. Clean	$2.00
Dental Services, Extraction, per Tooth	$25.00
Electronic Organizer, Palm III	$369.00
Film, Kodak Gold, 24 Exposures	$6.00
Garage Door Opener, Installed	$275.00
Glue, Krazy Glue, .07 Ounces	$1.00
Luggage, Samsonite Hardside Cart	$399.99
Necklace, Cultured Pearls, 18	$425.00
Piano, Yamaha Digital	$997.00
Rollerblades	$34.97
Software, Managing Your Money	$39.99
Suit, Man's Hickey-Freeman	$760.00
Tissue, Kleenex, 150-Count	$0.99
Water, Evian Pure Drinking Water, 1.5 Liter	$0.49

Woolen & Worsted Manufacturing in the Southern Piedmont, by James A. Morris, 1952:

"The expansion of the southern woolen and worsted industry in the last decade has resulted essentially from leading firms building branch plants in the Piedmont [region of South Carolina] instead of in the Northeast. Presuming rational economic behavior and knowledge of comparative resource patterns by manufacturers, empirical evidence is provided that the Piedmont possesses certain locational advantages for wool fabrication over the established center of production, New England. A possible alternative interpretation could be that the market for wool fabrics expanded to such an extent in this region that additional producing facilities were needed to satisfy the demand. While the consumer market in the South is growing, however, the major markets for woolen and worsted products remain in the large cities of the North, and in New York in particular. Furthermore, an analysis of the destination of products turned out by Piedmont firms reveals that a high portion of sales are delivered to northern markets. Since southern plants are producing for a national market, then, new mills are built in this area to obtain savings in costs, or because of pressing non-economic motives."

"Were You Born That Way?" *Life*, April 1998:

"Does the key to who we are lie in our genes or in our family, friends and experiences? In one of the most bitter scientific controversies of the twentieth century—the battle over nature and nurture—a wealth of new research has tipped the scales overwhelmingly toward nature. Studies of twins and advances in molecular biology have uncovered a more significant genetic component to personality than previously known. Far from a piece of putty, say biologists, my daughter is more like a computer's motherboard, her basic personality hardwired into infinitesimal squiggles of DNA. As parents, we would have no more influence on some aspects of her behavior than we had on the color of her hair. And yet new findings are also shedding light on how heredity and environment interact. Psychiatrists are using these findings to help patients overcome their genetic predispositions. Meanwhile, advances in genetic research and reproductive technology are leading us to the brink of some extraordinary—and terrifying—possibilities.

The moment the scales began to tip can be traced to a 1979 meeting between a steelworker named Jim Lewis and a clerical worker named Jim Springer. Identical twins separated five weeks after birth, they were raised by families 80 miles apart in Ohio. Reunited 39 years later, they would have strained the credulity of the editors of *Ripley's Believe It or Not*. Not only did both have dark hair, stand six feet tall and weigh 180 pounds, but they spoke with the same inflections, moved with the same gait and made the same gestures. Both loved stock car racing and hated baseball. Both married women named Linda, divorced them and married women named Betty. Both drove Chevrolets, drank Miller Lite, chain-smoked Salems and vacationed on the same half-mile stretch of Florida beach. Both had elevated blood pressure, severe migraines and had undergone vasectomies. Both bit their nails. Their heart rates, brain waves and IQs were nearly identical. Their scores on personality tests were as close as if one person had taken the same test twice.

Identical twins raised in different families are a built-in research lab for measuring the relative contributions of nature and nurture. The Jims became one of the 7,000 sets of twins studied by the Minnesota Center for Twin and Adoption Research, one of half a dozen such centers in this country. Using psychological and physiological tests to compare the relative similarity of identical and fraternal twins, these centers calculate the 'heritability' of behavioral traits—the degree to which a trait in a given population is attributable to genes rather than to the environment. They have found, for instance, that 'assertiveness' is 60 percent heritable, while 'the ability to be enthralled by an aesthetic experience' is 55 percent heritable.

Studies of twins have produced an impressive list of attributes or behaviors that appear to owe at least as much to heredity as to environment. It includes alienation, extroversion, traditionalism, leadership, career choice, risk aversion, attention deficit disorder, religious conviction and vulnerability to stress. One study even concluded that happiness is 80 percent heritable—it depends little on wealth, achievement or marital status. Another study found that while optimism and pessimism are heavily influenced by genes, environment affects optimism but not pessimism. A third study claimed a genetic influence for the consumption of coffee but not, it seems, of tea. Critics accuse researchers of confusing correlation with causation, yet they admit the data suggests a strong genetic influence on behavior. Far less clear is how it works. Is there a gene for becoming an astronaut? For enjoying symphonies?"

"A Man Who Traded Everything for an Indian Trove," *The New York Times*, May 16, 1997:

"At 15, Frank T. Siebert, Jr., became so frustrated at not finding the books he wanted to read on American Indians and the Western frontier in school or at the public libraries in Philadelphia that he began collecting. His first purchase, a 1904 reprint of John Eliot's *Logick Primer*, from 1672, cost $0.28. Over the next 70 years, he became a pathologist, sold his blood to buy books, got married, then left his wife and children and lived for a while in his car. He sometimes paid dearly for the works he relentlessly tracked.

'Frank Siebert's story bears every mark of the fanatic collector,' said the anthropologist Edmund Carpenter, who first met Siebert in the late 1930s, when both were students at the University of Pennsylvania.

'To buy books, he sacrificed everything, but there was this other side to him: he was one of the major authorities in America on Indian languages, a genius who devoted his life to this study. His eminence in this field is totally unquestioned.'

Siebert focused mainly on the language and legends of various tribes, especially the Catawbas of South Carolina and the Penobscot of Maine. And for the last 30 years of his life, he lived alone in primitive quarters in Old Town, Maine, among the Penobscot, mastering their language and becoming its last speaker. He produced a dictionary of it. He amassed 1,500 books and manuscripts, which filled most of the walls of his cottage.

At his death at 85 from cancer a year ago, Siebert's collection had never been seen by his colleagues in anthropology and linguistics, by the dealers and collectors from whom he bought books or by his two daughters, with whom he reconciled a decade ago. They paid him several visits, exchanged letters with him and spoke to him on the telephone, which he installed toward the end of his life.

'My sister and I ended up caring about him, proud to have a father who was so unusual,' said Stephanie M. Finger, his younger daughter. 'He thought he was indestructible, would live forever and keep the collection forever.'

At Siebert's direction just before he died, Stephanie and her sister Kathleen L. Davis called in Bailey Bishop, the Cambridge, Massachusetts, dealer from whom he had bought most of his books since the mid-sixties.

'He hounded me in his 50-year search for the famous Cherokee Spelling Book from 1819,' Mr. Bishop said. 'It was the first book printed in that language, and only two copies survive.' Mr. Bishop inventoried the collection and sent it to New York.

Now the Siebert library will be auctioned in two parts at Sotheby's, York Avenue at 72nd Street in Manhattan, in a sale estimated to total about $7 million. The first 550 books, which focus on the tribes east of the Mississippi, will go on view today and be offered for sale on Friday; they are expected to bring as much as $3.4 million. The rest of the books, on those tribes of the South and the West, will be auctioned in October.

Among the prizes in the sale is a copy of the first Bible printed in America, a two-volume translation by John Eliot, who was known as 'the apostle to the Indians,' into the Natick-Algonquin language. It was published in the Massachusetts Bay Colony in 1661-1663. Sotheby's expects it will fetch as much as $250,000.

Even among the lesser works that Siebert bought were gems, including a fine 1828 copy of *Sketches of Ancient History in the Six Nations*, by David Cusick, an artist of New York's Tuscarora tribe. Produced to be sold as a souvenir at Niagara Falls, the book has pages that are still uncut, and the images on the distinctive fold-out frontispiece are drawn from Tuscarora legends. One depicts a treelike monster leering through foliage at a woman eating roasted acorns, which he mistakes for burning coals; another shows two giants, covered with sand head to foot, being chased by a god

"A Man Who Traded Everything . . ." *(continued)*

transformed into an even larger giant. Two other images are of an Indian chief and his dog and a war dance. 'In all other copies I've seen, the tail of the dog in one image and the head of the drummer in another are torn off,' Mr. Carpenter said. 'Trust Siebert to get the right one.'

Siebert's curiosity about Indian languages prompted him to buy a letter that George Washington sent to an Indian agent in 1786. In it, Washington relayed a request from Catherine the Great, made through the Marquis de Lafayette, for authentic documents about American Indian vocabularies that she wanted for the dictionary she was working on. (It was never published.) The letter may sell for up to $26,000.

The 1681 Indian deed ceding all the land of what is now Jamaica, Queens, to the British for

15 coats, nine kettles, five guns, two blankets, two pairs of stockings and a pair of shoes may bring up to $15,000.

Several of Siebert's costliest items will be offered at the fall sale. An 1843 travel book of North America by the German Prince Maximilian Alexander Philipp, lavishly illustrated with lithographs of Indians based on Karl Bodmer's drawings, may sell for as much as $200,000. And a rare American edition of George Catlin's most famous work, the 184 portfolios of Indians and hunting scenes, may bring up to $120,000. 'Impressive stuff,' Mr. Carpenter said. 'He put his money where his heart was and was a true scholar. The fact that he didn't take his doctorate in anthropology, forget it. He was ahead of a whole crowd of professionals.' "

"Reeling in the Years, the number of years needed to go from invention to common use," *Newsweek*, April 13, 1997:

Date	Invention	Years Until Mass Use
1873	Electricity	46
1876	Telephone	35
1886	Gas Automobile	55
1906	Radio	22
1926	Television	26
1953	Microwave Oven	30
1975	Personal Computer	16
1983	Mobile Phone	13
1991	Internet	7

Columbia's Riverbanks Zoo attracts thousands of tourists annually.

1999 FAMILY PROFILE

Chinese-born immigrant Liming Shao came to the United States in 1975 when he was 18 years old with just $68 in his pocket. Now in his early forties, he has become a multimillionaire, owning five different companies in New York City. He and his second wife Ping have four children.

Annual Income: $1.25 million, including $250,000 in salary he pays himself and $1 million in stock options.

Life at Home

- His usual uniform is jeans, polo shirt and cowboy boots; his black mane of hair is worn shoulder-length.
- He still shops at the local Chinese open-air markets of New York for fruits native to his Chinese hometown, especially thick-skinned pears.
- When he first arrived in America, he shared a room with 16 other men in a rundown section of the city dominated by prostitutes and drug dealers; the room was a good deal at $12 a month.
- He now drives a Mercedes-Benz and lives in a six-bedroom Victorian home in Greenwich, Connecticut, where the average home costs more than $1 million.
- His five-car garage also holds two Harley-Davidsons—one vintage and one brand-new—plus a pickup truck and a BMW for Ping.
- After founding five companies that will gross more than $40 million this year, he now has a stock portfolio of more than $1 million and real-estate holdings of more than $5 million.
- He enjoys flaunting his wealth and letting everyone know that Chinese immigrants are capable of more than running restaurants or dry-cleaning stores.

Liming Shao loves to take risks and wear beautiful watches.

His five-car garage holds two Harley-Davidsons—one vintage and one brand-new.

- Early on, he fell in love with wristwatches and now owns dozens, many of which cost $10,000 or more to buy; his favorite is a Chase-Durer Combat Command GMT, because of its expensively rugged look, but when he goes to parties, he enjoys slipping on a Cartier Tank American watch.
- As a hobby, he loves to day trade stocks, often taking enormous risks; "I've already taken the greatest risk coming here," he tells friends. "Why should the stock market scare me?"
- Born in a fishing village in the Fujian province of southern China, he was left by his parents when he was four years old so they could find work tapping rubber trees in Indonesia; they sent cash home whenever possible for Liming and his two brothers.
- As a child, he often robbed peach orchards and caught crabs for food.
- At age 13, he took a boat to Hong Kong with no papers and no money; at the border, he dove into the bay and swam to the British colony.
- There he worked odd jobs and saved his money until at age 18 he had accumulated $2,000 for a phony visa and $800 for a plane ticket to America, which he believed was the land of opportunity, and "New York best of all. Best money, best job, best opportunity."
- Upon arrival he worked as a dishwasher and waiter, soon marrying an American cook who also worked at the restaurant; he became a U.S. citizen shortly after and the couple had two children.
- Inspired one day by watching a professional photographer shoot photos, he bought a secondhand Nikon camera for $1,000 and began soliciting for freelance jobs.
- That first year, he made $30,000 shooting pictures, and by the late 1980s, he was earning $300,000 a year.
- In the early 1990s, he realized that no American advertising agency was addressing the growing needs of the Chinese market, so he created his own agency.

Life at Work

- His Manhattan office is painted red for luck and prominently features cutouts of the Chinese character for money.
- The Chinese symbolism is offset by a vintage Coke machine, a row of cowboy boots and a framed picture of a Harley-Davidson motorcycle.
- His advertising agency, which focuses on selling to the affluent Chinese market, now has 75 employees in offices in New York City, Toronto and Los Angeles.
- He also operates a telemarketing company with 300 bilingual workers and a translation agency.
- His two newest companies are designed around the Internet, with one firm designing Asian-language Web sites, and the other serving as a liaison between Asian-owned companies in America and abroad.
- This budding empire is called the New A: New for New Economy, A for Asia.
- He currently has plans to buy an Internet company, a radio station, a newspaper and a magazine, believing that by owning various media outlets he can improve the image of Chinese immigrants.
- "Always I want to change that," he says proudly. "We are not all just sweatshops and laundromats and restaurants. They do dot-com. We do dot-com."

Liming's advertising agency is addressing the growing needs of the Chinese market in America.

"Luxury Index," *Playboy*, August 2000:

$3 million:	Amount *Spawn* creator Todd McFarlane spent at auction to buy Mark McGwire's seventieth home run ball.
$41 million:	Price of a Gulfstream V personal luxury jet.
$70 million:	Amount Henry Ford made in his best year.
$105 million:	Amount Al Capone made in his best year.
$750:	Amount per hour earned by John D. Rockefeller in 1889.
$22,000:	Amount per minute earned by Bill Gates in 1996.
90:	Percentage of American millionaires who have college degrees.
2.9:	The average millionaire's grade point average.
1190:	The average millionaire's SAT score.
28:	Length in years of the average millionaire's marriage.
13:	Number of American billionaires in 1982.
268:	Number of American billionaires in 1999.
4 a.m.:	The hour when Sam Walton liked to start work.

- He is not concerned about failure: "I never think about it. I come here with nothing. What have I got to lose?"
- He is, however, deeply concerned that the accusations of spying against Chinese scientist Wen Ho Lee at the Los Alamos National Laboratory will tarnish the reputation across America of Chinese leaders.
- Currently, more than three million Chinese live in America; approximately 60,000 arrive legally every year, along with another 20,000 illegal immigrants.
- Many are well-educated and highly computer-savvy, often earning more than the average American family within a few years of arriving.
- Eschewing the notion that immigrants must suffer a long period of hard work and poverty before they can succeed, many publicly announce they came to America to become rich immediately.
- The impact of Chinese wealth has not escaped Wall Street; Charles Schwab has a Chinese-language trading site, E-Trade and T.D. Waterhouse are launching sites for Chinese-speaking traders, and Yahoo! now lets Chinese investors track stocks in their own language.
- Brokers report that the Chinese craze for stocks is not confined to affluent professionals; the manager of Schwab's Chinatown branch has seen restaurant workers rush in with their first paycheck to buy stocks.

Life in the Community: New York City

- Many parts of New York City are undergoing massive renovation and change.
- In addition to the remarkable transformation of Grand Central Terminal, work is under way at TriBeCa.
- Once a manufacturing and downtown commercial area, it became a haven for artists in the 1970s; in the 1990s, it began attracting young affluent families looking for comfortable lofts.
- The area features distinguished nineteenth-century architecture—much of it made of marble or cast iron—protected by historic-district designations.
- Today, these former warehousing sites have become a mecca for some of the city's finest restaurants.
- At 48 Wall Street, the former 36-story headquarters of Bank of New York are being transformed into 277 apartments; the renovation of the neo-Georgian landmark is costing $90 million.
- In Chelsea, at the other end of the economic scale, the 33 residents of the McBurney YMCA on West 23rd Street in Manhattan have been evicted; the YMCA of Greater New York, which operates 19 branches in the city and upstate, has decided to sell the 95-year-old structure and build a gym and health club at another location in the neighborhood—this time without residential apartments.
- *The New York Times* is editorializing against "Gridlock City," carping that "Manhattan's hottest piece of real

"The Making of the Modern Company," by Richard S. Tedlow, *Business Week*, August 21, 2000:

" *'I want to congratulate you on being the richest man in the world,'* John Pierpont Morgan to Andrew Carnegie, 1901, after [the former] bought Carnegie Steel and formed U.S. Steel Corporation.

By most accounts, Carnegie and Morgan did not like one another. Carnegie resented high freight rates caused by Morgan's control of the railroads. He disapproved of anything that smacked of 'flesh and the devil,' a colleague observed, and Morgan was a sensual man. For his part Morgan viewed Carnegie as a loose cannon capable of destabilizing steel and railroads, and perhaps the whole economy. For a brief moment in 1901, though Carnegie and Morgan were one high nobility in the kingdom of capital, their joint creation, U.S. Steel Corporation, heralded a new age. The first American corporation with assets worth $1 billion, it owned 149 steelworks.

Yet, by the turn of the century, Yahoo!, run by guitar-playing CEO Timothy Koogle, would boast a greater capitalization than the entire steel industry—even though in 1999 it had a mere 2,000 employees (one percent of U.S. Steel's workforce in 1901) and $58 million in property, plants and equipment."

estate, Times Square, has gotten so crowded lately that pedestrians often have to wait in line to cross the street. The newest arrival, Condé Nast Publications, plans to hold court in its icy tower by mid-August. ABC's *Good Morning, America* will settle nearby in September. The human gridlock can only get worse in November when the World Wrestling Federation hunkers down in the Para-

HOW FAR ARE YOU WILLING TO GO TO MAKE A DIFFERENCE?

mount Building to open a theme restaurant. The real theater this fall will unfold on Broadway, the street."

- The mayor's office recently won a legal fight to keep a Brooklyn artist from assembling 100 naked people in lower Manhattan for a photograph.
- City Hall is currently debating how to improve the health of the city's children by requiring landlords to remove lead paint from apartments.

"Lost in Space, Driving to my college reunion by satellite and mapping software seemed cool—until I got lost," by Anita Hamilton, *Time*, July 19, 1999:

"So I'm sitting on a street corner in New York City at 5:30 in the morning hoping for a sign from above. No, I haven't lost my mind or my way—yet. I'm trying to help the yellow gizmo I've hooked to my notebook computer get a fix on my latitude and longitude using signals from a network of global-positioning satellites. Since the signals can't travel through walls, I'm stuck outside. Finally, a message pops up on-screen: 'No GPS receiver has been detected.' Grrr.

It's the morning before my 10-year college reunion, and I'm already totally stressed—not over the usual stuff (whether my outfit or my job is cool enough to dazzle old flames), but from trying to figure out why, despite fresh batteries and a brand-new adapter, my darned Earthmate GPS isn't talking to the DeLorme AAA Map 'n' Go software that came with it. I'd thought it would be fun and instructive if my friend Karyn and I drove to Dartmouth with no paper maps, only digital ones. I'd picked Map 'n' Go over the competition because it was reasonably priced, created fairly simple-looking routes and gave instructions in a computer-generated voice. Had I made a big mistake?

As often happens with technical glitches, Earthmate mysteriously springs to life a few seconds after I get on the line with tech support. When Karyn pulls up in her blue Saturn, I fake a confident smile: 'This will be really cool.' She looks skeptical as I plug in the car adapter ($120 from Port, based in Norwalk, Connecticut) that will power my Toshiba laptop from her cigarette lighter. But right on cue, a green dot pinpoints our starting location on a detailed map and then morphs into an arrow as we reach the West Side Highway.

Suddenly the computer is barking out directions in a synthesized voice: 'Go north on Henry Hudson Parkway! Go southeast on I-95, East 1A, 2 min. 59 sec. away!' It's at once creepy and reassuring. Karyn steps on the gas. 'I feel I have to keep up,' she complains. But wait! Following the signs south would take us to New Jersey. It's not right. We ignore the computer this one time and head north. After that, we follow the rest of the directions to Hanover, New Hampshire, without incident; even when this one time we wander off course, the green arrow shows where we've gone astray.

Soon we're relaxed enough to think about more important things, like what music to play and where to eat. I click on upcoming exits and find the nearest Boston Market. I scan a list of local radio stations to find some easy listening. For up-to-the-minute status on how far we have to go, I just hit a key. At last, we're having fun!

Disaster strikes on the way home, just before we hit the city. By then we're so comfortable with Map 'n' Go that when a road sign clearly says Manhattan and the computer says something else, we forget to rely on our common sense. All of a sudden we're lost in the slums of the Bronx at 11 p.m. For the next 10 minutes, the little green arrow mockingly charts our circular course.

So I hated it, right? Not at all. I like computers that talk to me, let me zoom in and out of maps, and keep me posted on the nearest Dunkin' Donuts. And as Karyn pointed out, there's security in being lost when you can see where you are on-screen."

HISTORICAL SNAPSHOT
1999

- The United States claimed 274 of the world's 590 billionaires worldwide

- Of the original 30 companies in the 1896 Dow Jones Industrial Index, only General Electric has survived the Great Depression, two world wars and the terms of 20 U.S. presidents

- *Worth* magazine declared Jupiter Island, Florida, the most expensive town in the country; the median home price was $3.9 million

- After 442 years of Portuguese rule, the tiny island of Macao on the southeast coast of China got its first Chinese leader

- The average American woman was 5'4", weighed 142 pounds and was a size 12

- The top one percent of earners in America had an average net worth of $5.5 million

- The annual reunion of Thomas Jefferson's descendents included, for the first time, the descendents of the children who claimed Jefferson as their father and his slave Sally Hemings as their mother

- The United Way of Santa Clara County, California, home of Silicon Valley, collapsed as donations dropped from $32 million in 1990 to $20 million this year

- NATO's mistaken bombing of the Chinese embassy in Belgrade caused further deterioration of U.S. and Chinese relations

- The number of welfare recipients dropped below four percent, the lowest in 25 years; unemployment, interest rates and juvenile arrests all fell to 25-year lows

- A series of fatal shootings at high schools across the country revived the gun-control debate and prompted many to call for mandatory background checks for gun purchases

- AIDS-related deaths fell nearly 50 percent

- The Modern Library's "100 Best Novels of the Century" list included *Ulysses*, *The Great Gatsby*, *A Portrait of the Artist as a Young Man*, *Lolita*, *Brave New World*, *The Sound and the Fury* and *Catch-22*

- Viagra, for male erectile dysfunction, sold at a record rate of $10 a pill

- China announced that it had developed on its own the ability to make neutron bombs and miniature atomic weapons

1999 ECONOMIC PROFILE

Selected Prices

Bathtub Reglazing	$170.00
Beer Mugs, Monogrammed	$40.00
Bulbs, 100 Tulip	$43.00
Cabinet, 54" Utility, Ready to Finish	$44.00
Carpet Deodorizer	$0.99
Fabric Softener, Downy, 20 Ounces	$2.00
Jacket, Man's Polar Fleece	$69.95
Oriental Rug, 9' x 12'	$2,458.00
Pocketbook, Kenneth Cole	$148.50
Roaster Pan, Calphalon	$99.99
Soccer Cleats	$129.95
Shampoo, Vidal Sassoon	$2.50
Shoes, Women's Hush Puppies	$29.99
Tea, Tetley Ice Tea Mix	$0.99
Telephone, Handheld Cellular	$49.99
Television, Zenith 19" Digital Color	$139.00
Tire, Bridgestone	$85.00
Tuna, per Pound	$2.06
Vegetable Slicer	$45.00
Wine, 1994 Chardonnay Reserve	$36.00

"Wealthiest Pay Declining Share of Their Incomes in Taxes," by David Cay Johnson, *The New York Times*, February 26, 2001:

"The richest Americans are paying a declining share of their incomes in taxes, even as their incomes grow more rapidly than everyone else's, according to data that the Internal Revenue Service gave a Republican member of Congress.

The 1998 incomes, after taxes, of the top one percent of taxpayers increased at more than three times the rate of the bottom 90 percent, according to an analysis of this data by the Center on Budget and Policy Priorities, a nonprofit research organization in Washington that seeks to advance the interests of the poor.

Over a long period, from 1989 to 1998, the incomes of the richest one percent, adjusted for inflation, grew about four times as fast. But the share of their income they paid in federal taxes in 1998 was at its lowest level since 1992, the year before Congress added two higher tax brackets that apply only to top earners.

This group, whose 1998 gross income averaged $816,189, paid 27.1 cents of each dollar earned in federal income taxes, down from 27.9 cents in 1997 and 28.9 cents in 1996.

For the other 99 percent of Americans, the share of income going to taxes was nearly unchanged, at 11.5 percent of income in 1998 and 1996 and 11.7 percent in 1997."

"What New Yorkers Make," *The New York Times Magazine*, November 20, 2000:

Kofi Annan, secretary-general, United Nations	$270,206
Gisele Burndchen, supermodel	$8,000 an hour
Kenneth Cole, designer	$1.6 million
Peter Jennings, anchor, *World News Tonight*	$9 million
Katie Couric, co-anchor, *Today Show*	$7 million
Gwyneth Paltrow, actress	$10 million per movie
Jeff Zucker, executive producer, *Today Show*	$1.25 million
Ellen Futter, president, American Museum of Natural History	$441,959
Bruce Weber, photographer	$100,000 per day
Donna Karan, fashion designer	$765,000
Howard Stern, radio personality	$17 million
Arthur Sulzberger, Jr., president, *The New York Times*	$1.4 million
Tommy Hilfiger, fashion designer	$26.9 million
Martha Stewart, CEO, Martha Stewart Living	$1.4 million
Sanford Weill, CEO, Citigroup	$14.5 million
John Welch, chairman, General Electric	$13.3 million
Calvin Klein, designer	$21.5 million
Anna Wintour, editor, *Vogue*	$1 million
Patrick J. Kelly, professor of neurosurgery, New York University	$1 million
Alan Matarasso, plastic surgeon	$6,000 an hour
Maureen Dowd, columnist, New York Times	$350,000
Rupert Murdock, CEO, News Corporation	$6.3 million
Vinny Testaverde, quarterback, New York Jets	$7.5 million
Joseph Volpe, general manager, Metropolitan Opera	$671,000

If you won't help provide beds for homeless children, don't worry, there's always someone else who will.

56% OF HOMELESS CHILDREN HAVE EXCHANGED SEX FOR MONEY, FOOD, DRUGS OR SHELTER.

"Lawyers, Count on Long Hours, Partner," *The New York Times Magazine*, November 20, 2000:

"When you graduate from law school, you're faced with a choice stark enough for a courtroom drama: profits or public service. The current standard for a first-year associate at the city's 25 largest law firms is $125,000, but after the year-end bonus kicks in, total compensation can approach $160,000. Meanwhile, rookies in the city's district attorney office continue to make between $30,500 and $40,000, just as they did before the bull market began. A Legal Aid Society criminal defense attorney starts at $35,000.

Once you get in the door at a firm, your salary rises in lockstep with class year; for instance, an eight-year associate at any of the city's top firms is currently making in the neighborhood of $225,000 plus bonus. The partner track is about eight to nine years. If you haven't made partner by your ninth year, you never will; but as consolation you'll still be bringing down well over $250,000, not counting bonus. If you do make partner, your annual earnings are equal to your share of the firm's operating income—at least $250,000 at a small firm, $600,000 at an average firm, [and

one] like Cravath, Davis, Polk, and Cahill, more than $1 million. At Wachtel, the richest law firm in the city, partners rake in $3.1 million apiece.

The hours are deadly for associates, who are routinely putting in 70 to 100 hours a week. So it's no surprise that after a few punishing years many decide to leave the white-shoe world for a position as an in-house lawyer for a corporation. The advantages of going corporate are that you get to have a life, stock options, and a terrific bonus if your company is still riding the bull market. The disadvantage is a moderate loss of glamour: 'Working as a litigator at a firm, for a variety of clients in a variety of industries, will always be more interesting than working in-house for a single client,' says Penny Windle, a fourth-year associate at Cahill. However, a chief legal counsel at a blue-chip company makes about what a partner at a mid-range law firm would. The median salary for a chief legal officer is $737,000; $360,500 for a general counsel; $293,000 for a chief assistant; $167,000 for a senior counsel; $120,000 for a staff attorney."

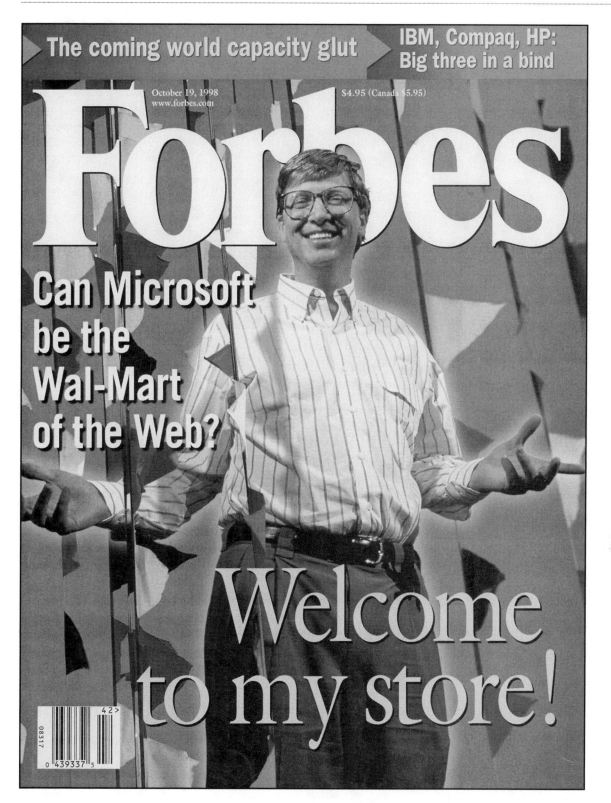

Sources

1880–1899

Edwin S. Grosvenor and Morgan Wesson, *Alexander Graham Bell, The Life and Times of the Man Who Invented the Telephone*, Harry N. Abrams, Inc., New York, 1997

Agnes Rogers, *Women Are Here to Stay, The Durable Sex in Its Infinite Variety Through Half a Century of American Life*, Harper & Brothers Publishers, New York, 1949

Arthur S. Pier, *Forbes: Telephone Pioneer*, Dodd, Mead & Company, New York, 1953

John Brooks, *Telephone, The First Hundred Years: The Wondrous Invention*, Harper & Row, New York, 1975

Harold Evans, *The American Century*, Charles Scribner's Sons, New York, 1955

Arthur Cevil Bining, *The Rise of American Economic Life*, Third Edition, Charles Scribner's Sons, New York, 1955

Jay F. Manning, *Leadville, Lake County and the Gold Belt*, Manning, O'Keefe & DeLashmutt, 1895

Kate Simon, *Fifth Avenue, A Very Social History*, Harcourt Brace Jovanovich, New York, 1978

Edwin G. Burrows and Mike Wallace, *Gotham, A History of New York City to 1898*, Oxford University Press, New York, 1999

Jeff Kisseloff, *You Must Remember This, An Oral History of Manhattan from the 1890s to World War II*, Harcourt Brace Jovanovich, New York, 1989

Harold Evans, *The American Century*, Alfred A. Knopf, New York, 1998

1900–1909

This Fabulous Century, 1900–1910, *Time-Life Books, Inc., 1970*

Grace Shirley, Women's Secrets, or How to be Beautiful, *Street and Smith, New York, 1901*

Mary Murphy, Mining Cultures, Men, Women, and Leisure in Butte, 1814–41, *University of Illinois Press, Urbana, Illinois, 1997*

Clark C. Spence, Montana, a Bicentennial History, *W. W. Norton and Company, Inc., New York, 1978*

David M. Emmons, The Butte Irish, Class and Ethnicity in an American Mining Town, 1875–1925, *University of Illinois Press, Urbana, Illinois, 1989*

Harold Evans, The American Century, *Alfred A. Knopf, New York, 1998*

William Bronson, The Earth Shook, The Sky Burned, *Doubleday and Company, Inc., Garden City, New York, 1959*

Helen Throop Purdy, San Francisco, As It Was. As It Is. And How to See It, *Paul Elder and Company, San Francisco, California, 1912*

Robert Mayer, Editor, San Francisco, A Chronological and Documentary History, *Oceana Publications, Dobbs Ferry, New York, 1974*

William M. Knamer, California: Earthquakes and Jews, *Isaac Nathan Publishing Company, Inc., Los Angeles, 1995*

Cecil Munsey, The Illustrated Guide to the Collectibles of Coca-Cola, *Hawthorn Books, Inc., New York, 1972*

Gilbert E. Govan and James W. Livingood, The Chattanooga County, 1540–1951, *E. P. Dutton and Company, Inc., 1952*

John J. Riley, A History of the American Soft Drink Industry, Bottled Carbonated Beverages, 1807–1957, *Arno Press, New York, 1972*

John J. Riley, Organization in the Soft Drink Industry, A History of the American Bottlers of Carbonated Beverages, *American Bottlers of Carbonated Beverages, Washington, D.C., 1946*

Charles Howard Candler, Asa Griggs Candler, *Emory University, Atlanta, Georgia*, 1950

1910–1919

John Steele Gordon, *Death of a Marque*, American Heritage, April 2001

Peter J. Ling, *America and the Automobile: Technology, Reform and Social Change*, Manchester University Press, New York, 1990

George S. May, *R.E. Olds, Auto Industry Pioneer*, William B. Eerdmans Publishing Company, Grand Rapids, Michigan, 1977

Lois Gordon and Alan Gordon, *American Chronicle, Year by Year through the Twentieth Century*, Yale University Press, New Haven, Connecticut, 1999

John B. Rae, *American Automobile Manufacturers, The First Forty Years*, Chilton Company, Philadelphia, Pennsylvania, 1959

George S. May, Editor, *The Automobile Industry, 1896–1920*, A Bruccoli Clark Layman Book, Facts on File, New York, 1990

Thomas Laurence Munger, *Detroit and World Trade*, The Detroit Board of Commerce, Detroit, Michigan, 1920

Transactions of the Association of the Seaboard Air Line Railway Surgeons, The International Journal of Surgery Company, New York, 1915

Fairfax Harrison, *The Surgeon and the Railroad*, An address before the nineteenth annual meeting of the Association of Surgeons of the Southern Railway Company, June 19, 1914

Lois Gordon and Alan Gordon, *American Chronicle*, Yale University Press, New Haven, Connecticut, 1999

This Fabulous Century, 1910–1920, Time-Life Books, Alexandria, Virginia, 1987

Martha Birney Diary, (Unpublished)

I. Marshall Page, *Old Buckingham by the Sea*, The Westminster Press, Philadelphia, 1936

John Robert Smith, *The Church That Stayed*, The Atlanta Historical Society, 1979

1920–1929

This Fabulous Century, 1910–1920, Time-Life Books, Inc., Morristown, New Jersey, 1987

Jeanine Basinger, *Silent Stars*, Alfred A. Knopf, New York, 2000

Geoffrey Nowell-Smith, *The Oxford History of World Cinema*, Oxford University Press, New York, 1996

Lois Gordon and Alan Gordon, *American Chronicle, Year by Year through the Twentieth Century*, Yale University Press, New Haven, 1999

This Fabulous Century, 1900–1910, Time-Life Books, New York, 1970

Ellen Sue Blakey, Robbie Boman, Jim Downing, Ina Hall, John Hamill, Peggi Ridgeway, *Tulsa Spirit*, Continental Heritage Press, 1979

Angie Debo, *Tulsa: From Creek Town to Oil Capital*, University of Oklahoma Press, Norman, Oklahoma, 1943

Edwin C. McReynolds, *Oklahoma: A History of the Sooner State*, University of Oklahoma Press, Norman, 1954

C. B. Glasscock, *Then Came Oil*, The Bobbs-Merrill Company, Indianapolis, 1938

Glen Romaine Roberson, *City on the Plains, The History of Tulsa, Oklahoma*, University Microfilms International, Ann Arbor, Michigan, 1977

1930–1939

Kate Simon, *Fifth Avenue, A Very Social History*, Harcourt Brace Jovanovich, New York, 1978

John Kenneth Galbraith, *The Great Crash, 1929*, Houghton Mifflin Company Sentry Edition, Boston, 1972

Stephanie Mansfield, *The Richest Girl in the World, The Extravagant Life and Fast Times of Doris Duke*, G.P. Putnam's Sons, New York, 1992

Gavan Daws, *Shoal of Time, A History of the Hawaiian Islands*, University of Hawaii Press, Honolulu, 1974

E. W. Williams, *Frozen Foods, Biography of an Industry*, Cahners Book Division, Boston, Massachusetts, 1970

Edited by Ray Bearse, *Maine, A Guide to the Vacation State*, Houghton Mifflin Company, Boston, Massachusetts, 1969

1940–1949

Joseph A. Pratt and Christopher Castanedo, *Builders, Herman and George Brown*, Texas A&M University Press, College Station, Texas, 1999

1950–1959

Ron Hollander, *All Aboard! The Story of Joshua Lionel Cowen and His Lionel Train Company*, Workman Publishing, New York, 2000

Tom McComas and James Tuohy, *Lionel: A Collector's Guide and History, Volume III*, Chilton Book Company, Radnor, Pennsylvania, 1978

Susan and Al Bagdale, *Collector's Guide to American Toy Trains*, Wallace-Homestead Book Company, Radnor, Pennsylvania, 1990

Hal K. Rothman, *Devil's Bargains: Tourism in the Twentieth-Century American West*, University of Kansas, Lawrence, Kansas, 1998

Ed Reid, *Las Vegas: City Without Clocks*, Prentice-Hall, Inc., Englewood Cliffs, New Jersey, 1961

Richard O. Davies, *The Maverick Spirit: Building the New Nevada*, University of Nevada Press, Reno, Nevada, 1999

George S. Bush, *An American Harvest, The Story of Weil Brothers Cotton*, Prentice-Hall, Inc., Englewood Cliffs, New Jersey, 1982

1960–1969

Philip Goetz, *Britannica Book of the Year*, University of Chicago, Chicago, 1966

Bill C. Malone, *Country Music U.S.A.*, University of Texas Press, Austin, Texas, 1985

1970–1979

John McPhee, *Oranges*, The Noonday Press, Farrar, Straus and Giroux, New York, 1967

Robert Gambee, *Nantucket Island*, Hasting House, New York, 1981

Brock Jobe and Myra Kaye, *New England Furniture, The Colonial Era*, Houghton Mifflin Company, Boston, 1984

1990–1999

Ronald Kessler, *The Season, Inside Palm Beach and America's Richest Society*, HarperCollins, New York, 1999

Walter B. Edgar and Deborah K. Woolley, *Columbia, Portrait of a City*, The Donning Company, Norfolk, Virginia, 1986

James A. Morris, *Woolen and Worsted Manufacturing in the Southern Piedmont*, The University of South Carolina, Columbia, 1952

INDEX